Hermetic Spirituality and the Historical Imagination

In Egypt during the first centuries of the Common Era, men and women would meet discreetly in their homes, in temple sanctuaries, or in solitary places to learn a powerful practice of spiritual liberation. They thought of themselves as followers of Hermes Trismegistus, the legendary master of ancient wisdom. While many of their writings are lost, those that survived have been interpreted primarily as philosophical treatises about theological topics. Wouter J. Hanegraaff challenges this dominant narrative by demonstrating that Hermetic literature was concerned with experiential practices intended for healing the soul from mental delusion. The Way of Hermes involved radical alterations of consciousness in which practitioners claimed to perceive the true nature of reality behind the hallucinatory veil of appearances. Hanegraaff explores how practitioners went through a training regime that involved luminous visions, exorcism, spiritual rebirth, cosmic consciousness, and union with the divine beauty of universal goodness and truth to attain the salvational knowledge known as *gnōsis*.

Wouter J. Hanegraaff is Professor of History of Hermetic Philosophy and Related Currents at the University of Amsterdam. He is the author of six monographs, including *New Age Religion and Western Culture* (1996) and *Esotericism and the Academy* (2012), and editor of eight collective works, including the *Dictionary of Gnosis and Western Esotericism* (2005).

Hermetic Spirituality and the Historical Imagination

Altered States of Knowledge in Late Antiquity

WOUTER J. HANEGRAAFF
University of Amsterdam

CAMBRIDGE
UNIVERSITY PRESS

University Printing House, Cambridge CB2 8BS, United Kingdom

One Liberty Plaza, 20th Floor, New York, NY 10006, USA

477 Williamstown Road, Port Melbourne, VIC 3207, Australia

314–321, 3rd Floor, Plot 3, Splendor Forum, Jasola District Centre, New Delhi – 110025, India

103 Penang Road, #05-06/07, Visioncrest Commercial, Singapore 238467

Cambridge University Press is part of the University of Cambridge.

It furthers the University's mission by disseminating knowledge in the pursuit of education, learning, and research at the highest international levels of excellence.

www.cambridge.org
Information on this title: www.cambridge.org/9781009123068
DOI: 10.1017/9781009127936

© Cambridge University Press 2022

This publication is in copyright. Subject to statutory exception and to the provisions of relevant collective licensing agreements, no reproduction of any part may take place without the written permission of Cambridge University Press.

First published 2022

A catalogue record for this publication is available from the British Library.

Library of Congress Cataloging-in-Publication Data
NAMES: Hanegraaff, Wouter J., author.
TITLE: Hermetic spirituality and the historical imagination : altered states of knowledge in late antiquity / Wouter J. Hanegraaff.
DESCRIPTION: Cambridge, United Kingdom ; New York, NY : Cambridge University Press, 2022. | Includes bibliographical references and index.
IDENTIFIERS: LCCN 2021059216 (print) | LCCN 2021059217 (ebook) | ISBN 9781009123068 (hardback) | ISBN 9781009127936 (ebook)
SUBJECTS: LCSH: Hermetism. | Spirituality – History. | Knowledge, Theory of – History. | Civilization, Ancient. | BISAC: RELIGION / History
CLASSIFICATION: LCC BF1591 .H34 2022 (print) | LCC BF1591 (ebook) | DDC 135/.45–dc23/eng/20220210
LC record available at https://lccn.loc.gov/2021059216
LC ebook record available at https://lccn.loc.gov/2021059217

ISBN 978-1-009-12306-8 Hardback

Cambridge University Press has no responsibility for the persistence or accuracy of URLs for external or third-party internet websites referred to in this publication and does not guarantee that any content on such websites is, or will remain, accurate or appropriate.

For Margôt, ἡ πηγή μου τῆς ζωῆς καὶ τοῦ φωτός

Contents

Acknowledgments		*page* ix
Abbreviations		xiii
Prologue		1
1	Hermetic Spirituality	11
	To Know the Unknowable	12
	Philosophy against Egypt	16
	The Spiritual Turn	19
2	Heart of Darkness	23
	Thessalos in Thebes	26
	The Light of the Godhead	31
	Toward the Light	35
	Private Experiential Practices	42
3	The Presence of Gods	48
	Distant Voices	50
	The Religion of the World	53
	Terrestrial Gods	61
	The Age of Darkness	72
4	Children of Hermes	77
	Getting Together in Private	79
	Matter and the Soul	82
	The Divine Economy	87
	Deep Embodiment	99
	Gods at Work	106
	Innate *Gnōsis* and Powerful Sounds	112

5	Through a Glass Darkly	119
	At the Mercy of Scribes	123
	Hermetica and Hermeneutics	132
	Weirdness at the Center	138
6	Healing the Soul	145
	Ignorance	148
	Enlightenment	156
	The Story of Humanity	167
	The Missionary	179
7	The Path of Reverence	187
	The Beauty of Goodness and Truth	190
	Reverence and Astonishment	194
	Hermetic Psychology	200
	The Third Kind	209
8	Becoming Alive	220
	The Path of Hermes	225
	Spiritual Madness	235
	Born Again	244
	Gratitude	256
9	The Source	264
	The Silent One	266
	Dimensions of Life	271
	Beyond Rebirth	282
	The Sounding Cosmos	288
	Beyond the Stars	297
10	The Conquest of Time	308
	The Drug	311
	The Inscription	318
	Dissemination	327
	Transmission	335
	Thoth's Secret	342

Epilogue — 352

Bibliography — 369
Index of Texts — 411
Index of Persons — 418
Index of Subjects — 428

Acknowledgments

In the spring of 1991, I bought a copy of the *Corpus Hermeticum*, in a brand-new Dutch translation that had just recently been published. There was quite some interest for Hermetic literature in the Netherlands at that time, largely due to the spectacular and widely publicized efforts of the *Bibliotheca Philosophica Hermetica* in Amsterdam. This privately funded research library was in the midst of building up the world's largest collection of original editions and secondary literature about Hermetic philosophy and related currents, and it had made this new publication possible as well. As a young scholar in the early stages of my Ph.D. research at the University of Utrecht, I was fascinated by these developments and eager to learn more about those mysterious Hermetic writings. I happened to be part of a small reading group focused on "gnostic" traditions, and still have a written copy of a presentation I apparently gave in this context, titled "Salvation by Gnosis in the *Corpus Hermeticum*" – my first embryonic attempt at understanding what the Hermetic literature was all about. But as I kept coming back to these texts during the years that followed, I could never shake off the uncomfortable feeling that somehow, *something* remained less than fully convincing about how these texts were being discussed in the scholarly literature or translated into modern languages. What, if anything, was missing? This book is my attempt to answer that question in the only way that such questions can be answered, by going all the way *ad fontes*.

It has been an incredible adventure, for I discovered much more than I had ever imagined. But I would never have had the chance to even embark on such a project at all if it had not been for two people who changed the course of my life during the 1990s, Roelof van den Broek and Rosalie

Basten. It is thanks to them that I have been able to devote my life and my career to studying the Hermetic literature and a wide range of related historical currents from antiquity to the present. The historian of Christianity Roelof van den Broek, one of the two scholars responsible for the 1991 Dutch *Corpus Hermeticum* translation, became my first model of scholarly excellence in these domains. We first met in his office at the University of Utrecht, and ended up collaborating closely on a whole series of projects related to the Hermetic literature. Roelof's sharp and sober judgment as a scholar and his generosity as a human being have been invaluable to me, as have been his perceptive critical comments on earlier versions of this book, not to mention his detailed commentaries on the Hermetica that are available only in the Dutch language.

It so happened that around the same time, Rosalie Basten, a Dutch businesswoman fascinated by the Hermetica, was reading the Dutch *Corpus Hermeticum* as well. It made a big impression, and led her to contact Roelof van den Broek, in order to discuss with him a project she had been pondering for years: to create conditions that would make it possible for future students to study these traditions as an academic subject. Their meeting was a success, and what came out of their collaboration was a unique academic chair and Centre for History of Hermetic Philosophy and Related Currents (HHP), created at the University of Amsterdam in 1999. The *Corpus Hermeticum* was therefore at the very origin of a remarkable chain of events that began in 1991, one outcome of which is this book about the Hermetica published more than thirty years later. It has been the honor and true miracle of my life that I was entrusted with the new academic chair in Amsterdam and was given the chance to devote myself, together with a group of dedicated colleagues and friends, to building up a program in teaching and research that had no parallel anywhere else in the academy worldwide. HHP has been like a pebble thrown in a pond, creating a ripple effect that keeps extending into ever-widening circles, so that today we have a large and vibrant international field of scholarship that is still branching out further into new directions. None of this would have happened without Rosalie's enormous determination and continuous support – not to mention a whole series of further initiatives that, with her uncanny intuition for always choosing "the right time and the right place," she has been taking on behalf of our field over a period of several decades now. I am deeply grateful for her friendship and her incredible generosity.

This is the place to also thank the members of the Foundation for History of Hermetic Philosophy and Related Currents, for all their support throughout

Acknowledgments

the years; all my colleagues who have been affiliated to our Amsterdam Centre from 1999 to the present, for their collegiality and friendship; and all the students who have been passing through our program, for their often infectious enthusiasm and curiosity about things unknown. It has been a pleasure to work with all of them, and their presence has been a continuous source of inspiration. I want to give special thanks here to Marco Pasi, my long-term friend and collaborator in all these endeavors and my successor as HHP's director since 2019. I owe him a big debt of gratitude, for his wisdom and support in times of hardship and adversity as well as of happiness and success. Furthermore, I would like to mention the international organization devoted to our field of study, the European Society for the Study of Western Esotericism (ESSWE), which was founded at Rosalie Basten's residence in 2005. As I sat laboring on this book in the solitude of my study, it was essential for me to feel part of this large and continuously evolving network of scholars, students, and friends who understand and appreciate what our kind of work is all about.

Very special thanks must go to a small group of brilliant younger friends and colleagues, endowed with superior specialist expertise and truly impressive linguistic skills, whose critical feedback, help and advice have been indispensable: Nicholas Banner, Christian Bull, Dylan Burns, and Korshi Dosoo. I owe each one of them a particularly great debt of gratitude for their willingness to read my chapter drafts with so much care and attention to even the tiniest details, for giving me precious advice about a wide range of important issues, for teaching me many things I did not know, and last but not least, for catching mistakes that would otherwise have escaped me. For any errors that might still remain, the responsibility is of course entirely mine. During the final stages of writing this book, it has been a special joy to participate in our small Zoom-fellowship of dedicated *kratērians* (created at Dylan's initiative), reading Hermetic treatises in Greek together while discussing the mysteries of translation and some other secrets as well.

Other colleagues and friends have been helping me out by answering questions and responding to specific requests. In particular, I want to thank Joscelyn Godwin for reassuring me about some musicological issues; Matteo Martelli for his help with translations from ancient Syriac; Matthew Melvin-Koushki for all his support and for sharing materials related to Suhrawardī and Pythagoreanism; Liana Saif for double-checking Arabic transliteration; Gregory Shaw for commenting on my chapters about Iamblichus and theurgy; Christian Wildberg for sharing a few of his unpublished translations and textual editions; and Timothy Williamson for clarifying my thinking about the very nature of knowledge. Furthermore I want to thank my former student Bas Jacobs for his detailed remarks about the entire manuscript; my friend and colleague Jeffrey J. Kripal for his unwavering support and unique perspectives on what the study of religion is all about; and my even older friend and colleague Albert F. de Jong for all his warmth and generous enthusiasm about whatever I am up to at any time.

Finally, I want to thank three people whose importance and influence go far beyond scholarship and academic discussion. Whenever I think about the *pharmakon* of *gnōsis* and the Hermetic *kratēr* filled with *nous*, I see the face of Norberto Jurasek. His unexpected death in March 2020, at the age of just 45, has left a wound that will never be entirely healed. This book owes more to him and the inspiration he has given me than could or should be written down in words. In an entirely different way, the same is true of another extraordinary human being, my mother Leonie Hanegraaff-Lissenberg. She passed away just briefly before Norberto, in February 2020, at the age of 92. Whatever I have been able to do in my life, I owe to her unconditional love and support. And last but certainly not least, this book is dedicated to Margôt, the love of my life. Since you appeared on my horizon early in 2013, nothing has ever been the same. I want to thank you most of all for sharing with me the gifts of love and abundance that this book is ultimately all about – life, health, happiness, and open paths.

Abbreviations

Ascl.	*Asclepius*
CAA I	M. Berthelot and Ch.-Em. Ruelle (eds.), *Collection des anciens alchimistes grecs*, vol. 1, Georges Steinheil: Paris 1887.
CAA II	M. Berthelot and Ch.-Em. Ruelle (eds.), *Collection des anciens alchimistes grecs*, vol. 2, Georges Steinheil: Paris 1888.
CH	*Corpus Hermeticum*
CHD	Carsten Colpe and Jens Holzhausen (eds.), *Das Corpus Hermeticum Deutsch*, vol. 1: Jens Holzhausen (transl. & introd.), *Die griechischen Traktate und der lateinische "Asclepius,"* & vol. 2: Jens Holzhausen (transl. & introd.), *Exzerpte, Nag-Hammadi-Texte, Testimonien*, frommann-holzboog: Stuttgart/Bad Cannstatt 1997.
CMA II	M. Berthelot (ed.), *La chimie au moyen âge*, vol. 2, Imprimerie Nationale: Paris 1893.
Cop	Brian P. Copenhaver (transl. & comm.), *Hermetica: The Greek* Corpus Hermeticum *and the Latin* Asclepius *in a New English Translation with Notes and Introduction*, Cambridge University Press 1992.
GWHT	Dorothee Gall (ed.), *Die göttliche Weisheit des Hermes Trismegistos: Pseudo-Apuleius,* Asclepius, Mohr Siebeck: Tübingen 2021.
HD	*Hermetic Definitions*
HF	Hermetic Fragments (= HT IV "Fragments Divers")
HG	Roelof van den Broek and Gilles Quispel (introd., transl., & comm.), *Hermetische geschriften*, In de Pelikaan: Amsterdam 2016.

HHE I	Jean-Pierre Mahé, *Hermès en Haute-Égypte*, vol. 1: *Les textes Hermétiques de Nag Hammadi et leurs parallèles grecs et latins*, Les Presses de l'Université Laval: Québec 1978.
HHE II	Jean-Pierre Mahé, *Hermès en Haute-Égypte*, vol. 2: *Le fragment du Discours Parfait et les Définitions Hermétiques Arméniennes*, Les Presses de l'Université Laval: Québec 1982.
HO	Hermetica Oxoniensa (Oxford Hermetica)
HT I	*Hermès Trismégiste*, vol. 1: *Corpus Hermeticum I-XII* (A.D. Nock and A.-J. Festugière), Les Belles Lettres: Paris 1991 [1946].
HT II	*Hermès Trismégiste*, vol. 2: *Corpus Hermeticum XIII-XVIII, Asclepius* (A.D. Nock and A.-J. Festugière), Les Belles Lettres: Paris 1992 [1946].
HT III	*Hermès Trismégiste*, vol. 3: *Fragments extraits de Stobée I-XXII* (A.-J. Festugière), Les Belles Lettres: Paris 2002 [1954].
HT IV	*Hermès Trismégiste*, vol. 4: *Fragments extraits de Stobée XXIII-XXIX, Fragments divers* (A.-J. Festugière), Les Belles Lettres: Paris 2002 [1954].
HT V	*Hermès Trismégiste*, vol. 5: *Paralipomènes* (Nag Hammadi VI, 6–8, Clarkianus 11, Hermetic Definitions, Divers Fragments) (J.-P. Mahé), Les Belles Lettres: Paris 2019.
HV	Hermetica Vindobonensia (Vienna Hermetica).
Keizer	Lewis S. Keizer, "The Eighth Reveals the Ninth: Tractate 6 of Nag Hammadi Codex VI," Ph.D. Dissertation, Graduate Theological Union: Berkeley 1973.
KL	Martin Krause and Pahor Labib, *Gnostische und Hermetische Schriften aus Codex II und Codex VI*, J.J. Augustin: Glückstadt 1971.
Meyer	Marvin Meyer (ed.), *The Nag Hammadi Scriptures: The Revised and Updated Translation of Sacred Gnostic Texts*, Harper One: New York 2007.
NH VI	Nag Hammadi Codex VI
NHD	Hans-Martin Schenke, Hans-Gebhard Bethge, and Ursula Ulrike Kaiser, *Nag Hammadi Deutsch*, vol. 2: *NHC V,2-XIII,1, BG 1 und 4*, Walter de Gruyter: Berlin/New York 2003.
NHDS	Ursula Ulrike Kaiser and Hans-Gebhard Bethge (eds.), *Nag Hammadi Deutsch: Studienausgabe*, 3rd revised ed., Walter de Gruyter: Berlin/Boston 2013.

PDM	*Papyri Graecae Magicae*: Demotic Papyri
PGM	*Papyri Graecae Magicae*
RHT I	A.-J. Festugière, *La révélation d'Hermès Trismégiste*, vol. 1: *L'astrologie et les sciences occultes*, Les Belles Lettres: Paris 1942.
RHT II	A.-J. Festugière, *La révélation d'Hermès Trismégiste*, vol. 2: *Le Dieu cosmique*, Les Belles Lettres: Paris 1949.
RHT III	A.-J. Festugière, *La révélation d'Hermès Trismégiste*, vol. 3: *Les doctrines de l'âme*, Les Belles Lettres: Paris 1953.
RHT IV	A.-J. Festugière, *La révélation d'Hermès Trismégiste*, vol. 4: *Le Dieu inconnu et la gnose*, Les Belles Lettres: Paris 1954.
Rob	James M. Robinson (ed.), *The Nag Hammadi Library in English*, E.J. Brill: Leiden/New York/Copenhagen/Cologne 1988.
SA	Clement Salaman, *Asclepius: The Perfect Discourse of Hermes Trismegistus*, Duckworth: London 2007.
Scott I	Walter Scott, *Hermetica: The Ancient Greek and Latin Writings Which Contain Religious or Philosophic Teachings Ascribed to Hermes Trismegistus*, vol. 1: *Texts and Translation*, repr. Shambhala: Boston 1993 [1924].
Scott II	Walter Scott, *Hermetica: The Ancient Greek and Latin Writings Which Contain Religious or Philosophic Teachings Ascribed to Hermes Trismegistus*, vol. 2: *Notes on the* Corpus Hermeticum, repr. Shambhala: Boston 1985 [1925].
Scott III	Walter Scott, *Hermetica: The Ancient Greek and Latin Writings Which Contain Religious or Philosophic Teachings Ascribed to Hermes Trismegistus*, vol. 3: *Notes on the Latin* Asclepius *and the Hermetic Excerpts of Stobaeus*, repr. Shambhala: Boston 1985 [1926].
Scott IV	Walter Scott and A.S. Ferguson, *Hermetica: The Ancient Greek and Latin Writings Which Contain Religious or Philosophic Teachings Ascribed to Hermes Trismegistus*, vol. 4: *Testimonia*, repr. Shambhala: Boston 1985 [1936].
SEC	Alberto Camplani, *Scritti ermetici in copto*, Paideia: Brescia 2000.
SH	*Stobaei Hermetica*
Tröger	Karl-Wolfgang Tröger, "Die sechste und siebte Schrift aus Nag-Hammadi-Codex VI," *Theologische Literaturzeitung* 98:7 (1973), 495–503.

WHCH	Clement Salaman, Dorine van Oyen and William D. Wharton (transl.), *The Way of Hermes: The* Corpus Hermeticum, Duckworth: London 1999.
WHDH	Jean-Pierre Mahé (transl.), *The Definitions of Hermes Trismegistus to Asclepius*, in WHCH, 99–122.
ZMA	Zosimos of Panopolis, *Mémoires authentiques* (Les Alchimistes Grecs IV.1; Michèle Mertens, ed. & transl.), Les Belles Lettres: Paris 1995.

Prologue

> *Sein, das verstanden werden kann, ist Sprache.*
> Hans-Georg Gadamer[1]

This book is about the search for knowledge, the human experience of being in touch with how things really are.[2] I will be analyzing a collection of ancient texts that claim to reveal the true nature of reality and describe a way toward liberation from mental delusion. Their anonymous authors referred to such knowledge as *gnōsis* and described it as ultimately inexpressible in human language. And yet they were using language to make such claims, and in writing a book about them I have been doing the same. Can scholars tell the truth about truths beyond scholarship? Or can truth not be told but only experienced? If what we call knowledge is a function of our state of mind, then could there be other ways of knowing than those of reason and the senses?

---

[1] "Being that can be understood is language." Gadamer, *Hermeneutik I*, 478. On frequent misunderstandings of this famous quotation and their far-reaching implications, see Di Cesare, *Gadamer*, 155–156; Di Cesare, *Utopia of Understanding*, 4–6 (with reference notably to Gadamer, "Idee des Hegelschen Logik," 84; Gadamer, "Dialogischer Rückblick," 286: "But no, I have never thought or said that, that everything is language").

[2] Although "to know" is one of the ten most common verbs in English and belongs to the fewer than one hundred words with precise translations in all 6000+ human languages, interestingly enough "we still do not fully understand what knowledge is" (Nagel, *Knowledge*, 6, 116). Like the Greek *gnōsis*, "knowledge" is ultimately derived from the proto-Indo-European **gno-* ("to know"), but English misses the ability to differentiate between propositional knowledge (e.g. German *wissen*, French *savoir*) and knowledge by immediate acquaintance (e.g. German *kennen*, French *connaître*); see Chapter 4, p. 113 note 147.

I

These are deep philosophical questions that have inspired me in my work, but to which I do not claim to have the answers. I very much doubt whether anybody does or ever will. My objectives in this book are far more modest in comparison, although admittedly still ambitious. On the first and most obvious surface level, you will be reading a study of the Hermetic literature from Roman Egypt in which I deliberately attempt to change the narrative of what these treatises are all about. On a second level immediately below the surface, this book is concerned with the historical imagination and the powerful effects of telling stories.[3] We use words to tell other people about what we have understood or think we have understood, but our language and our way of using it is never just a simple tool of translation and communication – it is always a means of enchantment as well.[4] All writers try to put a spell on their audience. They attempt to catch and hold their readers' attention, gain influence over their consciousness, and induce them to follow their own lead in preference over others. This is true of the anonymous authors who wrote the Hermetic treatises, and it is no less true of the scholars who studied these texts in depth and whose learned publications dominate academic discourse and the academic imagination. Most obviously, of course, it is true of myself as well. I would not have devoted years of my life to studying the Hermetica and the abundant scholarship about them if I did not wish to convince my readers that a better story was possible and that it needed to be told.

But why does it need to be told? Where does the importance lie? This leads me to a third dimension of my project. In our mediatized culture built on speed and instant gratification, the relevance of a book about ancient Hermetic texts may not be immediately obvious. Yet it is precisely in that fact that the relevance lies. Readers who decide to follow my lead through the Hermetic labyrinth will learn about the spell of *phantasmata*, the unruly stream of mental imagery charged with emotion that fills much of our conscious and unconscious life on a daily basis. How can we trust our own thinking or rely on our faculties of knowledge and rational judgment, as scholars or just as human beings, if we are

---

[3] See Hanegraaff, "Religion and the Historical Imagination." For my central concept of "reified imaginative formations," see Hanegraaff, "Reconstructing Religion," 578–581 (here illustrated at the example of "religion").

[4] See below, Epilogue. A *locus classicus* is Plato, *Phaedrus* 230d-e, where Lysias' written speech is described as a *pharmakon* or drug of enchantment strong enough to lure even Socrates out of the city (Derrida, *La dissémination*, 87–88; see discussion in Chapter 10, pp. 311–318).

not in control of our own minds? The subtitle of this book refers to the unquestionable fact that human consciousness is not stable and reliable but fluid and susceptible to alteration,[5] so that what we hold to be "true" must depend very much on how and where we are able (or unable) to direct our attention. Alterations of consciousness result in altered states of knowledge.[6]

Hermetic practitioners believed that the horizon of human consciousness could not just be expanded but could be transcended altogether, resulting in those states of absolute knowledge and direct insight to which they referred as *gnōsis*. As may be inferred from the opening sentences of my Prologue, this conviction would have made them deeply sceptical about a book like this. They would have argued that scholarly or academic knowledge of any kind (empirical, historical, phenomenological, hermeneutic, exegetical, rational, critical, and so on) could never be more than the product of a comparatively low-level, low-quality, altered, narrowed, reduced, and therefore ultimately untrustworthy type of consciousness. Of course, the easiest way for me to respond to such scepticism would be to flip the argument around – as almost all scholars in this field have done – by assuming implicity, or stating explicitly, that not *my* reliance on scholarly methods but *their* belief in *gnōsis* must be an irrational illusion, a pious "mystical" dogma without any true foundation. In making such an argument, I would be dismissing their most basic core

---

[5] E.g. Barušs, *Alterations of Consciousness*, 4–11. In terms of Barušs's four-part typology, when I speak of "consciousness" in general terms I mean his *consciousness₃*. The Hermetic treatises contain descriptions of *subjective consciousness₂* (the stream of events experienced by individual minds) and of *behavioral consciousness₂* (first-person accounts). Hence when I speak of consciousness as fluid and susceptible to alteration, I mean the experiential stream of *subjective consciousness₂* (phenomenal consciousness in terms of Dainton, *Stream of Consciousness*, 2–4). While the processes of *consciousness₁* are always present and active, their neurological modes of functioning are less immediately relevant for research in the humanities.

[6] In this regard I sympathize with Charles T. Tart's radical concept of knowledge as "state-specific": see Tart, "States of Consciousness" (1972; updated versions in Tart, *States of Consciousness*, 206–228 [1983] and "Investigating Altered States" [1998]; see also his response to a few critics in [Diverse authors], "State-Specific Sciences," 1007–1008 and short remarks in "Preface," xvi–xviii). Hermetic spirituality as analyzed in this book may be seen in terms of "state-specific *technologies*, operated in the service of a priori belief systems," whereas state-specific *sciences* (which I take to include scholarly research in the humanities) would be defined by the investigator's commitment "to reexamine constantly his own belief system and to question the 'obvious,' in spite of its intellectual or emotional appeal to him" (*States of Consciousness*, 217–218; "Investigating Altered States," 111). Whether state-specific *sciences* are possible or not, the relevant point for me is that different modalities of consciousness imply different types of knowledge.

conviction, the central assumption on which all their endeavors were built. I would be taking it for granted that only the type of sober consciousness required for scholarly work can be relied on for gaining *true* knowledge, so that the radical altered states of Hermetic practitioners must be some kind of delusion or aberration.

I am not making that assumption. This book as a whole (and here I reach the fourth dimension of my argument) exemplifies a perspective of *radical methodological agnosticism*, which means that I neither affirm nor deny the ultimate truth of Hermetic beliefs.[7] The *gnōsis* that they considered possible I see as beyond either verification or falsification. Agnosticism does not reflect an attitude of intellectual laziness or indifference on my part, as when in common parlance we say "whatever...!" because we do not wish to engage with an argument although we privately think of it as nonsense. On the contrary, it rests on a fundamental conviction about the limits of human knowledge and understanding.[8] The authors of the spiritual Hermetica claimed to have attained perfect knowledge of realities far beyond the scope of what most scholars would consider possible, and I see no reason not to take them seriously. After all, what do I know? I have not been there. The divine *nous* has not appeared to me, my body has not been exorcized, my soul has not been reborn, nor have I ever traveled in my mind to an utterly nondual reality of pure spiritual bliss. As will be seen, Hermetic practitioners claim that they did experience all those things and that it radically changed their lives. I cannot claim to know for sure whether they made it all up, or

---

[7] Hanegraaff, "Empirical Method," 100–108; Hanegraaff, *Esotericism and the Academy*, 357–358; Hanegraaff, "Power of Ideas," 2–5. Methodological agnosticism in my understanding is broadly congenial to the radical empiricism associated with William James (see Lamberth, *William James*, 9–60) and I find myself in sympathy with its recent discussion in Davis, *High Weirdness*, 8–30. I share the latter's "dissatisfaction with the idealism of religious and mystical thinking, on the one hand, and the stinginess of the usual reductionism on the other" and his search for "a middle way, a hybrid path" (ibid., 8). On the history of "agnosticism," see Asprem, *Problem of Disenchantment*, 289–308; regarding *methodological* agnosticism, as my methods and objectives are not explanatory but hermeneutic, the objections formulated in Asprem, ibid., 85 note 118 do not apply.

[8] For critique of the *ignorabimus* thesis, see Asprem, *Problem of Disenchantment*, 304–306. I would respond that the *aporias* of knowledge, the limits of human horizons, and the biological conditioning of human brains make the alternative *cognoscemus* or *cognoverimus* ("we will get to know," "we will have come to know") even far more implausible. In this respect, the classical concept of disenchantment is based not on knowledge but on beliefs, assumptions or presuppositions (Weber, *Wissenschaft als Beruf*; Asprem, *Problem of Disenchantment*, 33–34). In terms of the authors discussed in this book, methodological agnosticism seems remarkably congenial to Iamblichus' perspective of radical embodiment as analyzed in Chapter 4.

were deluding themselves, or whether some of them might actually have been experiencing such things. If I hypothesize that they did, as I am willing to do, still I cannot claim to possess some superior level of insight that would allow me to explain with any certainty what really happened to them. And so I do not.

What I do know is that these authors left us a series of fascinating texts in which they speak about their beliefs, their practices, and their experiences. I consider it my job as a scholar to do what I can to *understand* what they were trying to tell their readers. That brings me back to the beginning, and to my fifth and final core concern in this book, the mysteries of language and translation. What does it mean to put something – anything – in words? What is involved in using language to describe an experience as "unspeakable"? Does it make a difference in this regard whether our words are spoken or written down? Can written sources like the Hermetica ever transmit to us what the authors wanted to say, or do they consist of nothing but empty signifiers at the mercy of our own discourse? Is it possible for linguistic meaning to *not* get lost in translation? If so, what does it mean to practice the art of *hermēneia*, the interpretation of texts? What are its limits and its potentials? By forcing us to ask such questions, the Hermetic discourse of *gnōsis* and *noēsis* (direct "noetic" perception of ultimate reality) confronts us with the unavoidable *aporias* of human understanding.

Summing up, the texture of this book is woven from five different strands. The argument about language and hermeneutics speaks to my broader vision of what *the humanities* are or should be all about, for reasons that I discuss at the end of Chapter 10. A practice of radical empiricism and methodological agnosticism is central to my understanding of *the study of religion* as a neither religionist nor reductionist field of research.[9] My interest in the historical imagination and the effects of narratives and storytelling, to which I will return in the Epilogue, is a further development of my work about *Western esotericism* as the reified imaginal product of discursive dynamics through which dominant academic traditions define their identity by way of contrast with a negative wastebasket category of "rejected knowledge."[10] My focus on consciousness comes from my earlier work on entheogenic esotericism

---

[9] See also Hanegraaff, "Reconstructing 'Religion' from the Bottom Up"; Hanegraaff, "Imagining the Future Study of Religion and Spirituality."
[10] Hanegraaff, *Esotericism and the Academy*. For the notion of "imaginal," see below, Epilogue.

(*sensu lato* and *sensu stricto*) and on alterations of consciousness as a neglected core dimension of religion and spirituality.[11] Finally, the so-called Hermetic tradition has been an object of fascination for me throughout my professional life;[12] but whereas my earlier work was focused on the Renaissance revival of the Hermetica, in this book I travel back all the way to the sources in Roman Egypt.

As regards questions of theory and method, I largely adopt a "show, don't tell" approach. Rather than presenting these five dimensions separately as theoretical perspectives explained in general or abstract terms, I have adopted a deliberately narrative procedure in that I allow them, like the characters of a novel, to unfold and unveil themselves gradually over the course of ten chapters. Such a linear storytelling style of scholarly writing has peculiar advantages and attractions, which I hope my readers will appreciate, but I am aware that it carries risks as well. Rather than revealing all my plots and subplots in advance or giving you the benefit of a bird's-eye view, dear reader, I ask you to step right into the narrative and enjoy the pleasures of discovering or unraveling its secrets step by step, as you make your way forward while staying close to the ground. Unless you are blessed with an extraordinary memory, be warned that by the time you reach the final pages, you may need to go back and read the whole thing again to pull the various strands together. Again, the best analogy is a novel. Readers may not understand why the protagonist acts the way she does in the first chapters, as the author deliberately keeps them in the dark; so only at rereading the story with the benefit of hindsight, what initially seemed puzzling may begin to make sense. Or at least, so one hopes. This is how my book is written and so this is how it wants to be read. Formulated differently, it requires a reading practice of hermeneutic circularity: while the argument as a whole is built up from its component parts, presented one by one in linear succession, to understand those parts you need a synthetic view of the whole.[13]

Specialists of late antiquity will notice quickly that my approach to Hermetic spirituality is somewhat different from the usual one. Most

[11] Hanegraaff, "Teaching Experiential Dimensions"; Hanegraaff, "Entheogenic Esotericism"; Hanegraaff, "Gnosis"; Hanegraaff, "Theosophical Imagination." As regards late antiquity, the present book wholly supersedes my first attempt in this direction, "Altered States of Knowledge." The present work I see as my mature statement on these topics.

[12] Hanegraaff, *Het einde van de hermetische traditie*; Hanegraaff and Bouthoorn, *Lodovico Lazzarelli (1447–1500): The Hermetic Writings and Related Documents*; Hanegraaff, "Better than Magic"; Hanegraaff, "Hermetism"; Hanegraaff, "How Hermetic was Renaissance Hermetism?"; Hanegraaff, "Hermes Trismegistus & Hermetism."

[13] See the quotation by Gadamer at the very end of Chapter 10 (pp. 350–351).

scholarship in this domain is ultimately less concerned with meaning and the understanding of content than with tracing the genealogy of separate elements from a historical and comparative perspective. Thus when the Hermetica use a certain term or describe a certain concept, the first thing that most scholars will ask themselves is "where does this originally come from?" and "where else do we find this in the literature of the period?" This approach has led to voluminous commentaries filled with invaluable information about parallels and origins, and I am deeply indebted to the precious information they contain. However, the methodology carries considerable risks of misinterpretation, as may be illustrated by an example from contemporary culture. Imagine a historian from the remote future who discovers a lost archive of American self-help books. She finds that a certain Deepak Chopra wrote a bestselling book about a mysterious practice called "quantum healing."[14] What does that mean? Our historian dives into the archives and writes a learned commentary to this ancient book. She describes the early twentieth-century origins of this practice in a long-superseded scientific field known as quantum physics and presents a mountain of evidence for textual parallels about quanta in contemporary scientific periodicals. All of that is enormously interesting. But does it help us understand what Chopra meant? Did he actually write about quanta at all? Is it adequate to situate him in the history of quantum physics (and then blame him for so often misunderstanding its concepts)? Shouldn't we rather begin by asking what quantum healing meant *for him*, within *his* discourse, rather than what quanta "really" meant in the twentieth century or what they meant for others?[15]

Few scholars would disagree with the principle that an adequate *historical* approach to Hermetic spirituality, as to any other religious or spiritual phenomenon, must begin with studying the relevant primary sources in their own right and on their own terms. But the implication is that *not* unless we first manage to understand, as well as possible, what they actually mean – what their authors were trying to say *and* what we

---

[14] Chopra, *Quantum Healing*.
[15] This approach is basic to all my work. When my *New Age Religion and Western Culture* was published in 1996, it was virtually the first academic study (for the exception see ibid., 3 note 11) based on actually reading the primary sources of the New Age, focusing on their *contents* and trying to understand what the authors meant to say. Almost all existing scholarship at that time showed far more interest in making the New Age fit already-existing theoretical frameworks that made sense to academics than in finding out what made sense to New Agers.

can tell from the texts themselves[16] – will it even become possible for us to determine the historical trajectories and contexts of comparison in which they must be situated.[17] For instance, a major red thread that runs through my book concerns the Hermetic understanding of *nous* – a term that is perfectly common in ancient Greek philosophical discourse. Instead of assuming that I already know what this word means (something like "mind" or "intellect," as every dictionary will tell us), I want the authors of the Hermetica to tell me *what it meant for them*. As will be seen, their answers are surprising to say the least, and the implications are considerable. If their understanding of *nous* is in fact different from what we commonly take it to mean, can we still be so sure about those standard translations on which we normally rely? Formulated differently, is the Hermetic *nous* a conceptual anomaly, or should it lead us to reconsider our assumptions about what we take to mean "mind" or "intellect" in ancient philosophy?

As I argue at greater length at the end of Chapter 5, scholars are no exception to the rule that humans tend to explain the unfamiliar in terms of the familiar, the unknown in terms of the known. In academic research, this has profoundly conservative effects. It privileges conventional understandings of how things are, while blinding us to whatever is *different* and does not comfortably fit our established paradigms.[18] In this book I take exactly the opposite approach. As my central concern is with

---

[16] I am referring to the core principle of modern hermeneutics that the meaning of texts is not exhausted by an explication of authorial intent (e.g. Simms, *Hans-Georg Gadamer*, 1). For my basic position on textual research and noneclectic historiography, see Hanegraaff, *Esotericism and the Academy*, 364–367, 377–379.

[17] Smith, "In Comparison a Magic Dwells," 34: "Who would disagree? We must describe what we are comparing before we compare." I concur, although with the Gadamerian proviso that any description is already an interpretation, informed by comparison with what falls within the reader's hermeneutic horizon. See also George Steiner's programmatic statement about the historian's task: "The historian must 'get it right.' He must determine not only *what* was said (which may prove exceedingly difficult given the state of documents and the conflicts of testimony), but what was *meant* to be said and at what diverse levels of understanding the saying was to be received" (*After Babel*, 141).

[18] For a fundamental critique of established practice in the study of ancient religions, see the chapter "On Comparison" in Smith, *Drudgery Divine*, 36–53, esp. 47–48 (with reference to a crucial quotation from Smith, *To Take Place*, 14) and see Smith, "In Comparison a Magic Dwells," 21–22: what counts as "comparison" is usually little more than a scholar's spontaneous experience of being reminded of "something like it," followed by the projection of that subjective experience "as an objective connection through some theory of influence, diffusion, borrowing, or the like." In such a "homeopathic magic" of comparison built on erudition, the issue of difference tends to be forgotten (ibid., 21, 35). Among countless examples of this fallacy in scholarship of the

difference, I try to understand the unfamiliar and explore the unknown, allowing it to *defamiliarize* the scholarly knowledge that we tend to take for granted. This leads me back to my opening sentences. If knowledge is the experience of being in touch with how things are, procedures of questioning and destabilizing our certainties in this regard may lead to altered states of knowledge. Only if we *first* understand what we are really dealing with, in these strange Hermetic treatises, can we establish what to compare them with or where to look for their historical origins.

The object of study in this book is neither "the Hermetic tradition" nor "the Hermetic literature" per se. The former I see as a scholarly construct of considerable popular appeal but questionable validity, while the latter refers to a collection of clearly disparate texts that have sometimes little else in common than mere references to Hermes Trismegistus as a figure of authority.[19] The focus is instead on what I call "Hermetic spirituality," for reasons discussed in Chapter 1; and I explain there why this implies a new way of categorizing the relevant materials. Chapter 2 is meant to introduce my readers to Roman Egypt in the first centuries CE and discusses the importance in that context of private spiritual experiences. Having set the scene in these first two chapters, in Chapter 3, I introduce my readers to the basic Hermetic worldview by focusing on the *Logos Teleios* and its Latin and Coptic translations. Chapter 4 is about the only three practitioners of Hermetic spirituality who are still known to us by name: the alchemist Zosimos of Panopolis and his associate Theosebeia, and the Platonic theurgist Iamblichus of Chalcis. To prepare for my in-depth analysis of Hermetic spirituality in the second half of the book, Chapter 5 discusses the problems of textual transmission and my strategies for confronting the task of reconstruction and interpretation.

In the next four chapters, I dive deeply into the texts. Chapter 6 is focused on CH I, the famous "Poimandres," and discusses the basic Hermetic concern with healing the soul from its contamination by the

---

Hermetica, see for instance the obsession with biblical or early Christian "parallels" in Dodd, *Bible and the Greeks* or Grese, *Corpus Hermeticum XIII*; and discussion of the "Fall of Man" projected on CH I, pp. 170–175.

[19] On the problematics of a reified "Hermetic tradition," see e.g. Hanegraaff, *Esotericism and the Academy*, 327–334 (focusing on Frances Yates); van Bladel, *Arabic Hermes*, 17–22 (for the Arabic context). Generally on the construction or invention of tradition, see e.g. Hammer, *Claiming Knowledge*, 85–200; many contributions in Kilcher, *Constructing Tradition* and Lewis and Hammer, *Invention of Sacred Tradition*. On the lack of coherence that results from defining our corpus as "Hermetic" merely because texts mention Hermes Trismegistus, see Hanegraaff, Review of Lucentini-Parri-Perrone Compagni.

negative passions. Chapter 7 discusses the essential Hermetic virtue of reverence (*eusebeia*) in connection with learning to "open one's heart" to divine beauty, and culminates in a discussion of what it meant to "become the *aiōn*" as described in CH XI. Chapter 8 is about the crucial treatise known as CH XIII, the account of rebirth, in which Hermes helps his pupil Tat to get liberated from the powers of darkness that have taken possession of his body. In Chapter 9, we see how Tat after being reborn is led to a supreme hypercosmic experience of the Ogdoad, the dimension of divinized souls, the Ennead of noetic powers, and even the *pēgē*, the supreme Source of all manifestation. In Chapter 10, finally, we return to earth and explore the question of what it means to transmit such experiences through the medium of language. Can the unspeakable be spoken or transmitted through writing? We end up with the art and practice of *hermēneia*, interpretation or understanding, that takes its name from Hermes.

Hermetic spirituality was a joyful path that celebrated life and light. Its purpose was to heal the soul from negativity, free it from such powerful influences as fear and aggression, and open its eyes to the beauty of existence. It was not concerned with domination but with knowledge and understanding – or, more precisely, with knowledge *as* understanding. It is in such a thoroughly positive spirit, inspired by *enthousiasmos*, that I offer this book to my readers for their pleasure and education.

I

Hermetic Spirituality

Qui non intelligit res, non potest ex verbis sensum elicere.
Martin Luther[1]

In Egypt during the first centuries of the Common Era, men and women would meet discreetly in their homes, in temple sanctuaries, or in solitary places to learn a powerful practice of spiritual liberation. They thought of themselves as followers of Hermes Trismegistus, the legendary master of ancient wisdom. Pupils would listen to venerable teachers speaking about the nature of the cosmos – its admirable beauty, its harmonious structure, its mysterious depths, and the subtle dangers it posed to the human soul. They would learn about the supreme universal Source of Life and Light that was ever-present behind the screen of appearances and in the depths of their own minds. They were taught that human beings could open the eyes of the heart, leave delusion behind, connect to the Source, and perceive reality as it really is. And last but not least, they learned how to do it. The teachers claimed to have gone through profound experiences of inner transformation and spiritual rebirth; they had encountered transcendent beings and traveled out of their bodies to places beyond the stars; and so they could offer guidance and advice to pupils who wished to follow in their footsteps. But the Way of Hermes was not an easy path. It required patience and devotion, trust and discipline, diligent study, persistent practice, and a willingness to question conventional wisdom.

---

[1] Luther, *Tischreden*, Bd. 5, 26 [nr. 5246]. "He who does not understand the thing cannot elicit the meaning from the words."

TO KNOW THE UNKNOWABLE

To speak about these practices as "Hermetic spirituality" means breaking with a longstanding tradition in academic research. Scholars have long been used to speaking of Hermetic *philosophy* instead, but we will see that this terminology is misleading.[2] To explain why this is so, and why it matters, I will begin with the term "spirituality." Some modern readers might feel it makes these ancient groups look a bit too much like contemporary New Age practitioners, and trained classicists will be quick to point out that such modern terminology does not correspond exactly to its equivalents in ancient Greek. To address these objections, we may consider some pertinent observations by the French scholar André-Jean Festugière (1898–1982), a classicist and Dominican friar whose work dominated the study of the Hermetica until the 1970s. The passage in question, quoted below, confronts us head-on with a problem that will occupy us throughout this book: the enormous difficulties of translation and understanding across the thresholds of language, time, and culture. Even just rendering Festugière's words from modern French into English is far from easy, but we will see that the problem in this case goes deeper than that of intercultural translation from one language to another. Nothing less is at stake here than the paradox of *translation across the threshold of language itself*. Festugière was discussing a Greek word, *nous*, that happens to be so central to the Hermetica that we absolutely need to get it right.

> [T]he philosophical language of Platonism lacked a specific term for referring to an organ of perception meant *exclusively* for mystical intuition. If one divides all that exists in *noēton* [that which can be thought] and *aisthēton* [that which can be perceived by the senses], then God belongs evidently on the side of the former. But by calling him that, one simply wants to make clear that he does not have a body – one does *not* mean to say that he can actually be known or understood through discursive language and can be named. This ambiguity of the word *noēton* comes from the ambiguity of the Platonic *nous*. Its function is to perceive realities that can be thought. However, when we are dealing with that particular *noēton* referred to as God, then the *nous* is no longer the human "intellect" properly speaking but a pure faculty of intuition or spiritual apprehension.[3]

---

[2] Cf. Van den Kerchove, *La voie*, 1, 92; Kingsley, "An Introduction," 33.
[3] RHT IV, 138–139. My translation slightly modifies the French original in the interest of clarity. Notably, I give the Greek terms in transliteration. Throughout the rest of this volume, I write *nous* in small letters whenever it seems to mean primarily a human capacity or metaphysical reality, but capitalize it as *Nous* if the latter functions as a deity.

We see here that, in discussing the idea of direct transcendental knowledge by means of a human faculty referred to as *nous*, Festugière appears unable to avoid terms that are hardly less ambiguous in French or English, notably "spiritual" and "mystical," not to mention "intuition."[4] The significance of this point emerges from the remainder of the passage:

> As moderns we have at our disposal the word "spirit" and its derivatives "spiritual," "spiritualizing," "spirituality," which have become technical terms in the literature of devotion. But the Greek *pneuma* [breath, spirit] appeared too much tainted with materiality to play that role[5]: no Platonist would have dreamed even for a second to apply it to phenomena that, while beyond human understanding, still implied the entire intellectual ascent towards the prime *noēton*. And so it is that the same word *nous* refers at the same time to the normal instrument for knowing things that can be thought *and* to the instrument of mystical intuition that enters into contact with the *anoēton* [that which can *not* be thought].[6]

For moderns like us, to say that something "cannot be thought" means that our mind cannot grasp it. Our mind, of course, resides in our brain and is concerned with rational thinking. However, according to ancient Egyptian, Semitic, and Greek anthropologies, our intellectual faculties rather resided in the heart.[7] This must very much be kept in mind (or taken to heart) while reading the Hermetica, where we often encounter references to "knowledge of the heart" or perception through the "eyes of the heart."[8] For moderns it can be more natural in such cases to speak of "spiritual knowledge" and think of "the soul" rather than "the mind," although this conflicts in many ways with the original meaning and connotations of such central terms as *pneuma* ("spirit"), *psuchē*

---

[4] The term "mysticism" would deserve separate treatment and is particularly problematic in the work of Roman Catholic authors such as Festugière. General overview in Schmidt, "Making of Modern 'Mysticism'"; for a short discussion of my perspective, see Hanegraaff, "Teaching Experiential Dimensions," 154–158, with critical discussion of Louis Bouyer's classic treatment in "Mysticism."

[5] Cf. Sedley, "Thrice-Greatest Hermes," 8: "... although *pneuma* was latinized as *spiritus*, in a Greek philosophical or scientific context the adjective 'pneumatic' has, if anything, more in common with pneumatic drills than with Christian spirituality."

[6] RHT IV, 139. The same argument about *nous* appears in Festugière, *Personal Religion*, 45; cf. Grese, *Corpus Hermeticum XIII*, 5 note d.

[7] Broze and Van Liefferinge, "L'Hermès commun," 43 with note 38; Kingsley, "Poimandres," 51; Tardieu, *Écrits gnostiques*, 232–233; Onians, *Origins*, 82–83 (Homer).

[8] See discussion below, p. 200 with notes 53–54.

("soul"), *nous* ("mind"), or *kardia* ("heart").[9] The problem is that modern terms seldom if ever map very well, and often do not map at all, on the Greek words (or words in any other ancient languages) that they are trying to translate. Nevertheless – and this is where we encounter the essential dilemma – we still cannot avoid using such terms as mind, spirit, soul, or the heart in our attempts to convey how Hermetic authors thought of the faculties for gaining access to higher salvational "knowledge," often referred to as *gnōsis*. In our efforts to reveal the meaning of ancient words, we have to resort to modern equivalents that in fact conceal their meaning; and yet we have no choice, because only through such acts of concealment can we hope to reveal at least something of the original.[10]

This basic dilemma has been known to translators throughout history and carries implications far more radical than is often realized. The truth is that once you enter the rabbit hole of translation in pursuit of just one single word, you find yourself in a wonderland of meaning where literally nothing is what it seems and there are no stable rules to hold on to.[11] David N. Wigtil has formulated the point with particular clarity:

> [I]n translating, a person in effect rewrites a text entirely. The grammar and vocabulary of the original text are abandoned for an entirely different set of linguistic structures, and the only control over this rewriting process is *the idea or thought* of the source.[12]

How radical the implications really are becomes clear when we realize that, logically, this "idea" or "thought" itself therefore cannot be translated. Somewhere between sender and receiver there appears a strange discontinuous gap or abyss, a liminal space of nothingness that we are routinely crossing all the time, without knowing how we do it. This gap is mysteriously bridged by "something" that cannot itself

---

[9] On the general history of these interrelated concepts, see MacDonald, *History of the Concept of Mind*. Hans-Georg Gadamer remarks that, compared with the complex web of nuances (*das Bedeutungsleben*) of the spoken word, "a *term* is a paralyzed word, and terminological use of a word is an act of violence committed against speech," a point that tends to be underestimated by modern interpreters of ancient texts (*Hermeneutik I*, 419).

[10] See the paradox of hermeneutics frequently emphasized by Elliot R. Wolfson in his interpretations of Jewish "mystical" texts, for instance *Language, Eros, Being*, 229: "... it must be said that the veil conceals the face it reveals by revealing the face it conceals. Language is decidedly inadequate to mark the middle ground wherein concealing and revealing are identical in virtue of being different and different in virtue of being identical."

[11] For the classic treatment of this point, see Steiner, *After Babel* (with some mind-boggling examples on pp. 319–350).

[12] Wigtil, "Incorrect Apocalyptic," 2287 (my emphasis), cf. 2297.

be put into language. Communication is therefore made possible only by "something" that itself cannot be communicated and, by definition, cannot even be understood. In short, translation presupposes the untranslatable.

Such reflections on linguistic relativism and their dazzling implications may be unavoidable to our postmodern minds but were of little or no concern to the authors of the Hermetica. They strongly believed in the metaphysical stability of meaning and the accessibility of truth, while insisting that ultimate meaning and truth could be found only *beyond* the sphere of thought and language.[13] The Hermetica are full of statements to the effect that true knowledge of ultimate realities "that cannot be thought" is not just possible, but *essential* to human salvation and true felicity; and we will see that the pursuit of such "knowledge" is at the very heart of the ancient experiential practices that modern scholars refer to as "the Way of Hermes."[14] The human faculty of direct perception known as *nous* was believed to make such knowledge possible; but because this word was also used for normal thinking, as Festugière pointed out, the unfortunate result is that none of its translations will work in English – or, for that matter, in other modern languages.[15] "Noetic perceptions" as understood in the Hermetica (and, as Festugière reminds us, in Platonism) are not the normal "intellectual" or "mental" activities we commonly have in mind today but are claimed precisely to go *beyond* them. They have absolutely nothing to do with thinking, let alone with sensory perception. So here we have our first major reason why the true concern of the Hermetic writings is *not* with philosophy as commonly understood today.[16] What their authors meant by "knowledge" is something entirely different from the

---

[13] On the radicality of this notion, see Van den Kerchove, "Notion of Truth."

[14] The notion of a "Way of Hermes" already appears in Iamblichus, *Response to Porphyry* VIII 5, and was placed at the center of attention by the two most influential modern scholars of the Hermetica, Jean-Pierre Mahé ("Voie d'immortalité") and Garth Fowden (*Egyptian Hermes*, pt. II). It has now been widely adopted: see e.g. WHCH; Van den Kerchove, *La voie*; Bull, *Tradition*, 187–372; and discussion below, pp. 225–235.

[15] Godel, "Socrate et Diotime," 26 with note 58: "The Νοῦς is not the intellect but a principle of lucidity superior to ordinary reason. This word is strictly untranslatable."

[16] Or, for that matter, as understood in antiquity. Socrates' "love of wisdom," as described by Plato, was likewise focused on an ultimate level of reality – the eternal forms or ideas – that could only be beheld directly in a trans-rational state of *mania*, divine madness (e.g. *Phaedrus* 249d; *Symposium* 210e-211b; cf. Ustinova, *Divine Mania*, 313–328). Philosophers are those who have recognized their own ignorance and desire to become wise: therefore Plato's ideal philosopher, Socrates, is precisely *not* the man of wisdom (*Apology* 21b-e; Burkert, "Platon oder Pythagoras?", 165–166, 172, 175; Hadot, "The Definition

intellectual understanding achieved through mental activity – thinking – that our modern philosophical traditions have taught us to understand by that word.

PHILOSOPHY AGAINST EGYPT

A second reason not to speak of Hermetic "philosophy" has less to do with the exact content of that term than with its polemical *function* in common academic and even in everyday discourse. Specialists have always been aware that the texts they labeled as "philosophical" might as well be described as "religious," "theological," "mystical," or "theosophical."[17] If they still preferred to speak of Hermetic *philosophy*, this was because it helped them draw a normative boundary. For them, the eminently serious and respectable pursuit of intellectual reflection about the nature of reality could have nothing in common with the so obviously disreputable and unserious business of magical or occult practice as reflected in many texts attributed to Hermes Trismegistus or associated with his name. The former type of activity deserved respect in their eyes, while the latter did not, and many scholars found it hard to imagine that one and the same text or author could be involved in both. Philosophers did not practice magic, for magicians were not thinking straight.

On a rather obvious level, this juxtaposition of respectable Hermetic *philosophy* against disreputable Hermetic *practice* seemed perfectly self-evident to academic armchair intellectuals trained to value thinking as a noble pursuit and dismiss "occult" practices as embarrassing nonsense.[18] More specifically, it reflected the strong ideological allegiance of professional classicists to ancient Greece as the idealized home of rational thought, an attitude referred to as philhellenism or hellenophilia and intimately linked to the liberal neo-humanist perspectives of

---

of 'Philosopher'," in: *What is Ancient Philosophy?*, 46–49). By contrast, the ideal Hermetic sage resembles Socrates' teacher Diotima: a priestly visionary who no longer needs to *aspire* to knowledge because she *knows* the truth through direct experience (RHT II, 30–31; cf. RHT IV, 79ff.; Fowden, *Egyptian Hermes*, 72; and below, pp. 187–194). For "philosophy" as a Hermetic self-designation, see Bull, *Tradition*, 380–383.

[17] The first three are ubiquitous in the literature; for the last one, see e.g. Reitzenstein, *Poimandres*, 45; Windisch, "Urchristentum und Hermesmystik," 186; RHT I, 13; RHT II, 32; Bickerman, Review of Festugière (1948), 457; Mahé, "Théorie et pratique," 15; Moreschini, *Dall'Asclepius*, 9, 15 and *passim*; Dieleman, *Priests*, 1; HG, 17.

[18] For the general history of the academic construction of "rejected knowledge," of which this discourse is a part, see Hanegraaff, *Esotericism and the Academy*.

nineteenth-century German *Kulturprotestantismus*.[19] This stance was accompanied by profound feelings of suspicion, hostility, and contempt for anything reminiscent of its traditional competitor, that is to say of Egypt, the symbolic center of pagan idolatry, the primitive heart of irrational darkness. That the Hermetica were *Greek* texts written in *Egypt* was an irritant to the scholarly imagination and made them an ideal arena of ideological contestation. Thus immediately after the German historian of ancient religions Richard Reitzenstein (1861–1931) placed the Hermetica on the agenda of academic research with a fundamental study published in 1904, the Polish classicist Tadeusz Zielinski (1859–1944) responded with great alarm to his suggestion that Greek "philosophical" texts might be rooted in Egyptian culture:

> Reitzenstein's chief error was that he completely obscured *the distinction between higher and lower Hermetism*. The lower type, which combines magic and alchemy and whose literature consists in the magical papyri and recipes of gold-making, has actually drawn from Egyptian sources, and could do so because it could use what was present. But the higher Hermetism ... had no way of doing so. What is referred to as "Egyptian philosophy of religion" had to be incomprehensible to the Greek spirit and educated mind; for as the Hermetic mocker says,[20] it really consists not of words (*logoi*) but of mere sounds (*phōnai*) that cannot even be translated into Greek.[21]

In other words, anything philosophical in the Hermetica must be Greek by definition, for even the very language of the Egyptians prevents them from understanding rational thought. Zielinski's "higher Hermetism" stood for Greek philosophy, while its "lower" counterpart stood for Egyptian magic; the former was worthy of attention, the latter was not.

Reitzenstein's blurring of these boundaries was experienced as a provocation, and classicists responded by claiming the Hermetica for themselves – that is to say, for "Greece." When Walter Scott (1855–1925) published the first volume of his problematic but influential English edition of the Hermetica, in 1924, he felt free to focus on the "religious or philosophic teachings" ascribed to Hermes Trismegistus while formally excising all those "masses of rubbish" concerned with "astrology, magic, alchemy, and kindred forms of pseudo-science."[22] During the first half of the twentieth century, as classicists won the Hermetic turf war, this distinction was widely

---

[19] Marchand, "From Liberalism to Neoromanticism"; see also Pingree, "Hellenophilia"; Burkert, *Orientalizing Revolution*, 1–6. I will return to the general topic below, pp. 360–363.
[20] A reference to CH XVI 2 (see below, p. 116).
[21] Zielinski, "Hermes und die Hermetik II," 27 (emphasis in original).
[22] Scott I, 1.

accepted as normative and self-evident. Festugière, in his four-volume standard work published between 1942 and 1954, spoke of a "popular" Hermetism as opposed to its "learned philosophical" counterpart, devoting one volume to the former and three to the latter. His standard edition of the Hermetica, published in collaboration with Arthur Darby Nock (1902–1963) in 1946 and 1954, was limited to the "philosophical" texts. No comprehensive study or textual edition of the "popular" Hermetica has been published after Festugière's first volume of 1942.[23]

From the 1970s, the pro-Greek/anti-Egyptian ideology was gradually weakened and finally abandoned, due partly to the discovery of new Hermetic manuscripts in Coptic and other ancient languages and partly to a slow decline of philhellenic bias in the study of ancient religions more generally. To both phenomena we will return. For our present concerns, the important point is that these developments did *not* lead scholars to abandon the basic distinction between two types of Hermetica.[24] Only the terminology was adapted somewhat: in the wake of Jean-Pierre Mahé's seminal publications of the 1970s and 1980s, most scholars now refer to the astrological, magical, and alchemical materials ascribed to Hermes as "practical" or "technical" Hermetica.[25] Their counterpart is usually still referred to as "theoretical" or "philosophical" even by scholars who are quick to point out that those adjectives are inadequate.[26]

Why does this matter so much? Because of the power that language exerts over our minds. The terminologies we choose will not just color and influence our interpretations, but often *determine* which other texts, practices, ideas, or traditions will be seen as most relevant for understanding what the Hermetica are all about.[27] If we call them "philosophical" we will try to analyze their philosophy and compare them with other philosophical traditions, and if we call them "theoretical" we will be looking for theories and systematic speculation. In both cases, this will lead us to relativize, minimize, marginalize, or even wholly overlook dimensions that may be important or even central to the texts themselves but are hard to understand in terms of philosophical theories. By and large, as will be seen, this is exactly what happened in the study of the

---

[23] Christian Bull is now working on a study that should fill this gap.
[24] See for instance Fowden, *Egyptian Hermes*, 1–11; Cop, xxxii–xl; Van den Kerchove, *La voie*, 1 and passim; HG, 16–26.
[25] HHE II, 22: "In what follows, to the theoretical or philosophical writings of Trismegistus we will therefore oppose his technical or practical works."
[26] For instance HHE II, 290–291; Van den Kerchove, *La voie*, 1; HG, 16–18.
[27] For this essential point, see Bull, "Ancient Hermetism," 126.

Hermetica. By speaking of "Hermetic spirituality," I hope to highlight precisely those dimensions that philosophers (and, for that matter, theologians[28]) have always found most difficult to handle but which are central to the study of religion: experiences and practices.

THE SPIRITUAL TURN

In a seminal study published in 2012, Anna Van den Kerchove approaches the so-called "philosophical" Hermetica from a perspective inspired by Pierre Hadot,[29] known for his influential thesis that ancient philosophy was not so much a theoretical pursuit as a "way of life" grounded in "spiritual exercises."[30] If we scan the scholarly literature about the Hermetica, from Reitzenstein to the present, we may be surprised to discover how frequently the words spiritual and spirituality have in fact been used, although rarely in a systematic manner.[31] The terminology is even quasi-omnipresent in Garth Fowden's ground-breaking study *The Egyptian Hermes* (1986), which closes with a sentence that could hardly be more explicit: "At heart [Hermetism] was a spiritual way, the way of Hermetic *gnōsis* – a means to an end immune from the scrutiny of philologist, philosopher and historian alike."[32]

Yet Fowden never explained what he meant by Hermetic spirituality – he seemed to take the term for granted. If we wish to define it more

[28] For theological agendas in the study of Hermetism, see below, pp. 80–82, 171–174, 362–363. Marchand summarizes the key conflict with reference to Reitzenstein, whose "principle heresy in the eyes of liberal theologians was that he had given Christianity an irrational, oriental origin, not a rational Greek one, as had Harnack several decades earlier" ("From Liberalism to Neoromanticism," 158).

[29] Van den Kerchove, *La voie*, 1, 129; cf. Van den Kerchove, "Visions et légitimation," 794 note 2.

[30] Hadot, *Exercices spirituels*; Hadot, *What is Ancient Philosophy?*

[31] For instance Bousset, Review of Kroll (*Frömmigkeit*), 700; Grant, Review of Nock/Festugière, 58; RHT IV, 139; van Moorsel, *Mysteries* ("spiritualization"); Podemann Sørensen, "Ancient Egyptian Religious Thought," 41–42; Fowden, "Late Antique Paganism," 181–182; Fowden, *Egyptian Hermes*, passim; Mahé, "Introduction" in: WHDH, 101–106; Kingsley, "Introduction," 24; Fraser, "Baptised in *Gnôsis*," 33–34; Van den Kerchove, *La voie*, passim; Bull, "Notion of Mysteries," 401; Bull, "Wicked Angels," 27; Bull, "No End to Sacrifice," 144–145; Bull, *Tradition*, passim.

[32] Fowden, *Egyptian Hermes*, 215. Scholars of the Hermetica have a way of admitting their limitations at the very end of their books. After 1700 dense pages of analysis, these were Festugière's final remarks about CH XIII: "It is an ecstasy ... How much illusion may be mixed up in it? We do not know. ... It is beyond the domain of reason. ... [I]t is expressed in a language about which there is nothing abstract or theoretical, but which carries the imprint of lived experience. ... Is it mysticism? The historian knows only what he is being told. He does not penetrate the secret of the heart" (RHT IV, 267).

precisely, my previous discussion should have made sufficiently clear that it cannot possibly convey the exact original meaning of ancient terms such as *pneuma*, *nous*, their cognates, or any of their Greek, Coptic, Armenian, Syriac, or Latin equivalents.[33] The Latin term *spiritualitas* seems to have made its first appearance in the fifth century CE, against a background of Christian theological understandings of *spiritus* and *spiritualis* (translating *pneuma* and *pneumatikos* in the letters of Paul, about the "way of the spirit" against "the way of the flesh"). During its somewhat complicated evolution through the middle ages, the term began to appear in French and English vernaculars, but then declined during the eighteenth and nineteenth centuries. It made a strong comeback in apologetic arguments for the superiority of Hinduism over "Western materialism" in an English colonial context as well as in French circles of Roman Catholic theology (very much those of Father Festugière) during the late nineteenth and early twentieth centuries.[34] After World War II, and increasingly since the 1960s and 1970s, this led to a complex and confusing popular discourse in which the term "spirituality" is widely used but almost never defined. As we have just seen, even modern scholars with deep linguistic training such as Fowden, Hadot, and Van den Kerchove feel at liberty to use this modern coinage in discussing traditions of late antiquity where the term did not yet exist. I am taking the extra step of making this terminology explicit and assigning it a central role in interpreting the nature of the Hermetica.

Based on extensive empirical research of what the term "spirituality" actually means in contemporary discourse, the sociologists Heinz Streib and Ralph W. Hood conclude that it can be defined with sufficient precision as "privatized, experience-oriented religion."[35] This means that it can be applied to currents and traditions which (1) are considered *religious*[36] rather than rational or scientific, (2) have a focus on direct *experience*

---

[33] On the limits of translation, see Ashton, "Translating Philosophie," 16–17 (followed by some excellent illustrations, including Kant's *Verstand* or Hegel's term *aufheben*, "the despair of translators"); Steiner, *After Babel*, 255 (with many elaborate illustrations throughout the book).
[34] Principe, "Toward Defining Spirituality," 130–133; Schmidt, *Restless Souls*, 1–23.
[35] Streib and Hood, "'Spirituality'"; Streib and Hood, *Semantics and Psychology of Spirituality*.
[36] Streib and Hood argue at length that "spirituality" should be understood as a subcategory of "religion," not as a separate genus ("'Spirituality'," 448–449). It follows that the latter concept should not, along Durkheimian lines, be limited to social formations alone. For my take on "religion" as a theoretical concept, see Hanegraaff, "Defining Religion" and "Reconstructing 'Religion'."

rather than on doctrine or belief, and (3) are concerned with the cultivation of *private individual practice* rather than with membership of a social organization. With respect to our topic, of course this does not mean that in the Hermetica we encounter no rational or scientific elements, no doctrines and beliefs, and no forms of social organization – far from it. Rather, the argument is that their primary focus is not on those particular dimensions but on practices for the cultivation of private individual experiences. Their purpose, as will be seen, was to heal the soul from its afflictions and restore the human spirit to its original condition of wholeness, divine consciousness, omniscience, even omnipotence.

If Hermetic spirituality was a type of privatized, experience-oriented religion, this has consequences for conventional ways of categorizing the materials. By and large, most of the texts that used to be called "philosophical" remain relevant, but their theoretical discussions about the exact nature of God, humanity, and the cosmos must be considered from the perspective of their *function* in a wider spiritual framework: they do not stand on themselves, as contributions to philosophical debate, but are meant to provide background information that spiritual practitioners need while navigating their journey of healing and salvation. As for the corpus that used to be called "technical," we will see that it contains some texts that are of great importance to Hermetic spirituality, while many other texts concerned with practical astrology, magic, alchemy, or philosophy have little or no relevance to it.

I need to emphasize that my approach does *not* imply a mere reshuffling of the texts according to a somewhat different principle of division, replacing the traditional framework of "philosophical versus technical Hermetica" by one of "spiritual versus non-spiritual Hermetica." I ask my readers to visualize the situation not in terms of two separate blocks at all, but as *one* single field of texts and ideas arranged in a circular manner around a center.[37] The spiritual Way of Hermes forms the heart of this circle (at the very center of which we might wish to imagine a dot, to indicate the nondimensional point of utter transcendence where words fail and only silence remains), while at its outer periphery we find Hermetic materials with little or no relevance to it. The chief criterion for where any specific text must be located might be determined statistically: as we move gradually from the periphery to the center, we will find that certain texts (notably CH I, CH XIII, and NH VI[6]) move increasingly to the forefront of attention because they are quoted ever more frequently,

---

[37] See below, Chapter 5, pp. 140–144.

while others recede into the background because they have little or nothing to say about the spiritual quest. One further important implication of my approach is that on our way toward the center, we will encounter some texts and authors (notably Zosimos of Panopolis and Iamblichus of Chalcis) who are seldom included in the corpus of Hermetic materials but happen to be far more important to Hermetic spirituality than some standard components of that corpus.

After these introductory reflections, it is now time to approach the texts and traditions concerned with Hermetic spirituality. To do so, we need to travel far back in time and venture deep into the heart of darkness itself: the country of Egypt during Roman times.

2

Heart of Darkness

> *But there was in it one river especially, a mighty big river, that you could see on the map, resembling an immense snake uncoiled, with its head in the sea, its body at rest curving afar over a vast country, and its tail lost in the depths of the land.*
> Joseph Conrad[1]

Sailing south from Athens or Rome, then turning east and southwards again, travelers during the Roman Era would reach the delta of the Nile – the largest river of the known world. Arriving in the harbor city of Alexandria, they would easily feel at home in the hustle and bustle of this great cosmopolitan center where Greek was the common language for commerce and intellectual exchange. In fact, native Egyptians formed a minority here, eclipsed by a majority population of Greeks and Jews.[2] The city was known as *Alexandria ad Aegyptum*, "Alexandria near Egypt," for this was not supposed to be an Egyptian city at all, but a Greek one planted on foreign soil.[3] Reaching a total population of about half a million or more,[4] Alexandria was the greatest of the provincial capitals in

---

[1] Conrad, *Heart of Darkness*, 22.
[2] Delia, "Population of Roman Alexandria" (on the large Jewish population until 117 CE, see Harker, "Jews in Roman Egypt"); but note that all non-citizens of the country were classified by the Romans as "Egyptians" regardless of ethnic origin (Jördens, "Status and Citizenship," 254; Vandorpe, "Identity," 263). For the many ethnicities in Alexandria, see Venit, "Alexandria," 104. Among literally thousands of temples and shrines, those devoted to Egyptian deities were mostly relegated to the fringes of the city (ibid., 110–111). Cf. Watts, *Hypatia*, 9: "roughly one temple for every twenty houses."
[3] MacMullen, "Nationalism in Roman Egypt," 187.
[4] Delia, "Population"; cf. Watts, *Hypatia*, 7–19, here 15.

the Roman Empire, and scholars have long seen it as the "crucible" from which Hermetism was born.[5]

But was it? If one of our Greek or Roman travelers would be adventurous enough to sail further south, perhaps with an interest in the cult of Hermes Trismegistus, he might begin to wonder. Traveling from Alexandria southwards along the Nile, he would be moving towards the region that is known as Upper Egypt (to the frequent confusion of modern map-gazers who think that north means up and south means down). Already at his arrival in Memphis, towards the bottom of the Nile delta, he would find himself in a country that breathed a different atmosphere. As a foreigner coming from Alexandria, he might find himself eyed with suspicion if not hostility by native inhabitants who thought of themselves as the "real Egyptians" in opposition to the Hellenized "Alexandrians" who had taken over their land. The capital city and the Egyptian province were practically two separate countries with different civilizations, and Alexandria and Memphis have been described as "culturally antithetical cities."[6] In short, the sense of leaving Hellenic civilization behind would grow ever more strongly on our traveler's mind as he ventured further south.

Next he would pass through the Tomis canal, which the Muslims would later call Bahr Yusuf, "the waterway of Joseph," that connects the Nile Valley to a large oasis known as the Fayyum area today. Its major city was Shedet, referred to as City of Crocodiles by the Greeks. Somewhere around here, a popular movement of devotion to the deified Pharaoh Amenemhet III, known as Poremanres or Porramanres, may well have sown the earliest seeds of the Hermetic tradition.[7] Having traveled further past Oxyrhynchus, our traveler would arrive in Khemenu (Ḥmnw, "City of the Eight"[8]), known to Romans by the name of Hermopolis Magna – "the Great City of Hermes." This was a substantial urban community

---

[5] As recently as 2005, van den Broek could still speak of a "general consensus" on this point ("Hermetism," 567). For a short summary of arguments for the contrary position, adopted in this chapter and this book, see Bull, "Ancient Hermetism and Esotericism," 116–117; Bull, *Tradition*, 454; cf. the more general remarks by Frankfurter, "Religious Practice and Piety," 329–330.

[6] Fowden, *Egyptian Hermes*, 20, referring to MacMullen, "Nationalism," 183–184 and cf. 187–188. In speaking of "cities" to cover both *poleis* and *metropoleis* I follow Tacoma, "Settlement and Population," 124.

[7] Jackson, "New Proposal," 104–105; Bull, *Tradition*, 121–131, 452; see below, pp. 265–266. Amenemhet III reigned during the twelfth dynasty (Middle Kingdom).

[8] Fowden, *Egyptian Hermes*, 174.

Heart of Darkness 25

with a population that may have come close to 50,000.[9] Its name referred to its status as the center of the Egyptian cult of Thoth, the powerful ibis-headed deity associated with Hermes by the Greeks.[10] As late as the early fourth century, priests in the city referred to Thrice-Greatest Hermes as their ancestral god and protector, and a stone-paved processional way towards the temple carried his name.[11]

Traveling further south and venturing ever deeper into Upper Egypt, our traveler would pass by the city of Akhmīm, called Panopolis in Greek. We know it as the birthplace of the alchemist Zosimos, who like his associate and protégée Theosebeia seems to have participated in a milieu of Hermetic devotees – probably in Akhmīm itself and perhaps elsewhere as well.[12] Around the middle of the third century, a votive inscription was set up here for "the great god Hermes Trismegistus."[13] Around this same time, in a bend of the Nile further south from Akhmīm, Christian ascetics had begun clustering together around a place called Chēnoboskion. Many of them were looking for visionary experiences, and it appears that this interest led them to translate some Greek Hermetic manuscripts into Coptic, not so very long after our imaginary traveler came sailing by.[14] Nobody could know that in some unimaginable future, about sixteen centuries later, the place would become famous under its new name Nag Hammadi. When these Coptic

---

[9] Matthews, *Journey of Theophanes*, 14 with note 6; Bagnall, *Egypt in Late Antiquity*, 53.

[10] On Hermopolis, see Matthews, *Journey*, 12–20; Bull, "Hermes between Pagans and Christians," 214–216. On Thoth, see e.g. Fowden, *Egyptian Hermes*, 22–23.

[11] Letter of Anatolios, an inhabitant of Hermopolis who was active in the cult of Thoth and refers to himself as "chief prophet," in a letter addressed to a friend in Alexandria whom he calls "the all-wise Ambrosios … the champion of the wisdom of the Hellenes and one who is pleasing and well-disposed to us" (*P. Herm. Rees* 3, John Rylands Library, Manchester; translation in Matthews, *Journey*, 22). See also Fowden, *Egyptian Hermes*, 175–176, with further reference to two other letters from the same archive and a letter from the Hermopolis city council that invokes "our ancestral god Hermes Trismegistus, who stands by you everywhere"; same material discussed in Bull, "Hermes between Pagans and Christians," 214–215, with references for the stone-paved temple road in note 40 (cf. Bailey, "Classical Architecture," 194). The so-called Strasbourg Cosmogony in which Hermes creates the world (Page, *Select Papyri*, vol. 3, 544–550) seems to have come from Hermopolis, but its Hermes is clearly the Greek one. See also Kingsley, "Poimandres," 56.

[12] Fowden, *Egyptian Hermes*, 125, 173–174, 188; Bull, "Hermes between Pagans and Christians," 218–225; Mertens, "Alchemy, Hermetism and Gnosticism at Panopolis."

[13] Dittenberger, *Orientis Graeci Inscriptiones*, vol. 2, 454–455 (nr. 716); Mertens, "Alchemy, Hermetism and Gnosticism," 172 note 43; Bull, "Hermes between Pagans and Christians," 218.

[14] Bull, "Visionary Experiences," 183–184; Lundhaug and Jenott, *Monastic Origins of the Nag Hammadi Codices*.

Hermetic papyri were discovered in a nearby desert cave in 1945, as part of a much larger collection of heretical Christian texts, they caused a scholarly sensation.[15] Eventually they would revolutionize our understanding of Hermetic spirituality.

Finally, after turning another great bend in the river and heading south again, our traveler would reach Thebes, the extremely ancient Egyptian city Waset, referred to as Diospolis Magna by the Greeks and Romans but known as Luxor today. More than 3,000 years old at that time, the residence of the Pharaohs during the period of the New Kingdom (sixteenth-eleventh centuries BCE) when Egypt was at the peak of its power, this city of the god Amun could be considered the heart of ancient Egypt. It is not surprising that in the centuries after the conquest of Egypt by Alexander, Thebes had emerged as a center of resistance against Greek and Roman rule. Having arrived in Thebes, our traveler could still sail farther south along the Nile, but in a real sense he could not get more distant from Alexandria, the cosmopolitical center of Greek Hellenism. This was the ancient heartland of Egyptian religion,[16] and it is here that we begin our search for the Hermetic tradition.

THESSALOS IN THEBES

At some time probably during the first half of the second century CE, a real traveler is said to have arrived in Thebes. His name was Thessalos and he had come from Asia Minor "with plenty of silver" to study medicine in Alexandria.[17] In the cosmopolitan world of Graeco-Roman antiquity, countless upwardly mobile young men were traveling restlessly – quite like university students in our own globalized world – in search of a good

---

[15] The news was first announced by Jean Doresse: see notably Doresse and Mina, "Nouveaux textes gnostiques coptes" (1948); Puech and Doresse, "Nouveaux écrits gnostiques" (1949).

[16] Fowden, *Egyptian Hermes*, 168–176; Moyer, "Thessalos," 45; Bull, "Hermes between Pagans and Christians," 225–230; Łajtar, "Theban Region."

[17] On the phenomenon of spiritual tourism to Egypt, see Frankfurter, *Religion in Roman Egypt*, 166–167, 217–221; about the standard route, see Dieleman, *Priests*, 252 with note 161. On Thessalos, see Cumont, "Écrits hermétiques II"; Festugière, "L'expérience religieuse"; Festugière, *Hermétisme*, 141–181; RHT I, 56–58; Friedrich, *Thessalos von Tralles*; Smith, "The Temple and the Magician"; Fowden, *Egyptian Hermes*, 162–165; Ritner, "Egyptian Magical Practice," 3356–3358; Moyer, "Thessalos"; Harland, "Journeys"; Moyer, *Egypt and the Limits of Hellenism*, 208–273, 287–292. On the dating of the text (between 75 and 200, probably between 100 and 150 CE), see ibid., 217–219.

education.[18] Thessalos, an ambitious student given to exaggerating his own talents and achievements, was a typical example. Having almost finished his studies in Alexandria and getting ready to return home, one fateful day he came across a book about the medical virtues of stones and plants attributed to Nechepso. This legendary Egyptian king and astrologer had been receiving revelatory epistles from the sage Petosiris and claimed superior knowledge about astrological plant medicine,[19] allegedly due to ecstatic visions and revelations from Hermes and Asclepius.[20] The treatise made such an impression on Thessalos that even before trying out the prescriptions, he was already bragging to his family and fellow students about his incredible medical breakthrough.

But to his enormous distress, the prescriptions proved worthless. This debacle exposed him to scorn and ridicule from his peers, and so humiliating was the experience that he no longer dared return home. So he started wandering around Egypt, "driven by a sting in my soul and seeking to deliver on some aspect of my rash promise."[21] He would rather commit suicide, he was telling himself, than return home as a loser. He clearly needed help.

> My soul always foretold me that I would speak with the gods, and so I kept stretching out my hands to heaven, praying to the gods to grant me some favour through a dream vision or the spirit of a god, so that I could proudly and as a happy person return to Alexandria and to my homeland.[22]

Having arrived in Thebes (Diospolis), Thessalos began hanging out with the elders and priests connected to the temples, hoping for a break. To get a proper view of what happened next, we need to understand how

---

[18] Fowden, *Egyptian Hermes*, 162–163; cf. Smith, "Temple," 175.
[19] On Nechepsos and Petosiris, see Ryholt, "New Light"; Heilen, "Some Metrical Fragments." On their relevance to Thessalos, see Smith, "Temple," 177, 183–185, with reference to Riess, *Nechepsonis et Petosiridis fragmenta magica*, fr 1 and 33; and Moyer, *Egypt*, 228–248.
[20] With reference to Pap. Louvre 2342 bis (Ryholt, "New Light," 71). Hermes and Asclepius can perhaps be identified in this case with Amenhotep son of Hapu and Imouthes son of Hephaistos (Imhotep) (ibid., referring to "Hermes the Theban" and "Asclepius the Memphite" in Clement, *Strom.* I 21 and Cyril, *Contra Julianum* VI 812; Heilen, "Some Metrical Fragments," 30, 52; but see Bull, *Tradition*, 165–167, with reference to Firmicus Maternus, *Matheseos Libri VIII* 3, proem 1-1.1) On the ecstatic experience of the soul "walking in heaven" or "entering the sky" while the body remains on earth, and its relevance to the Hermetica (notably CH I 1, 4; CH X 25) and Egyptian temple rituals, see Heilen ("Some Metrical Fragments," 37–43) and Bull (*Tradition*, 170–174), both with reference to a passage in Vettius Valens.
[21] Thessalos, *De virtute herbarum*, Proem 10 (Friedrich ed., 49–50).
[22] Ibid, 11.

radically life had changed for religious functionaries in Upper Egypt since the beginning of the Roman Empire.

The country had been under foreign control since the conquests of Alexander, who at his death in 323 BCE had been succeeded by his general Ptolemy I Soter.[23] The Ptolemaic dynasty would rule Egypt for almost 300 years, until the death of Cleopatra VII and the Roman conquest under Octavian, the future emperor Augustus, in 30 BCE. During this long period, the Greek intellectual culture emanating from Alexandria had deeply penetrated Egyptian society, especially among the wealthier and more highly educated strata of society. This cultural milieu of Egyptian Hellenism continued under the Roman Empire, but now the country was subjected to a political regime of unprecedented severity, inspired partly by Octavian's personal animosity to all things Egyptian and partly by its economic importance as the "imperial granary" responsible for about one third of Rome's annual grain supply.[24] For members of the priestly class, the results of these changes were dramatic. They had been enjoying great wealth and authority during the Ptolemaic period, when the sacerdotal elites had been actively involved in the economic and political life of the kingdom and its high priests had been ruling almost like medieval popes.[25] But after the Roman conquest, quite suddenly they found themselves deprived of power, prestige, and economic revenue, as eloquently explained by Robert K. Ritner:

> [After 23 BCE] temple matters were subject to the secular authority of the imperial "private account." By the reign of Hadrian (117–138 CE), religious authority was centralized under an appointed civil bureaucrat of equestrian rank ... Priesthoods were reduced in number, temple holdings were decreased, and the civil bureaucracy now monitored the order and tenure of the hierarchy, their duties, dress and personal finances. Higher clergy were forbidden to engage in any financial activities outside their designated religious duties. All priests were required to wear linen (but never wool) and to be circumcised, unblemished and, subject to a 1,000-drachma fine, shaven bald. ... Admission to the priestly caste now required official certification before the provincial administrator ... In return for such social isolation, the temple hierarchy was provided with a government subvention (*syntaxis*), and the upper echelons were exempt from taxation and compulsory public service. From these Roman restrictions derives the later stereotyped

---

[23] For the political history of Egypt under the Ptolemies, see short overview in Chauveau, *Egypt in the Age of Cleopatra*, 6–28.

[24] Ritner, "Egypt under Roman Rule," 1–2, 6; for the Roman annexation of Egypt, see overview in Herklotz, "*Aegypto Capta*."

[25] Ritner, "Egypt under Roman Rule," 4–7.

image of cloistered, ascetic Egyptian priests, devoted to purity and contemplation and "enduring hunger and thirst and paucity of food during their whole life."[26]

So those are the priests that Thessalos would have met in Thebes. They were aged, impoverished, socially isolated men, humiliated and demoralized by the decline of their ancient traditions and undoubtedly resentful of the foreign powers responsible for destroying their ancestral traditions and their way of life. Practicing the ancient rituals in temple complexes that had been falling into disrepair for centuries, their personal power and authority had been reduced entirely to the spiritual realm.

The priests seemed friendly enough to Thessalos, but withdrew in indignation when he inquired about magic.[27] Just one of them did not turn away but mentioned that he knew the procedure for seeing visions in a bowl of water. So Thessalos invited him for a walk. Having found a solitary place, he suddenly threw himself on the ground crying, clinging to the priest's feet and imploring his help. His very soul was in his hands, for he absolutely had to see a god or otherwise would kill himself! Whether impressed or alarmed by this emotional outburst, the priest promised to help him. Having "kept himself pure" for three days, through fasting and abstinence, at dawn after the third day Thessalos was led to a "pure room" – possibly in a known sanctuary at Deir el-Bahri that had dark chambers for incubation rites associated with Imhotep (Asclepius) and Amenhotep son of Hapu (possibly linked to Hermes), or perhaps a

---

[26] Ritner, "Egypt under Roman Rule," 7–8 (I have changed a few sentences from present to past tense in the interest of readability); and similar overviews in Dieleman, *Priests*, 208–211; Moyer, *Egypt*, 270–273; Bagnall, *Egypt*, 261–268; Assmann and Frankfurter, "Egypt," 160–162. The "private account" (*idios logos*) refers to a set of regulations established by the deified Augustus, see Ritner, "Egypt under Roman Rule," 5. The closing quotation is taken from Chaeremon, fragm. 10.7 = Porphyry, *De Abstinentia* IV 6–8 (van der Horst, *Chaeremon*, 21). On these general developments, see also Frankfurter, *Religion in Roman Egypt*, 27–30, 198ff., 219 (with a programmatic emphasis on the priesthood's "persistence and resilience" under adverse circumstances). On the decay of the temples, see for instance Smith, "Temple and the Magician," 178 note 30, with reference to the classic description by Strabo, *Geography* XVII.1.27–29; Matthews, *Journey of Theophanes*, 18–19.

[27] Harland ("Journeys," 125) translates εἴ τι τῆς μαγικῆς ἐνεργείας σῴζεται (Thessalos, *De virtute herbarum*, Proem 10; Friedrich ed., 49–50) as "whether any magical power saves a person from illness"; but since the use of *mageia* for medical purposes was uncontroversial for Egyptian priests, Korshi Dosoo suggests sticking to the earlier standard translation (cf. RHT I, 58; Moyer, *Egypt and the Limits*, 57; Bull, *Tradition*, 409 with note 49) "whether some magical power [or energy] was preserved" (Dosoo personal communication, referring to the almost identical construction εἰ δὲ ὅλως μέρος τι τοῦ ἔργου σῴζεται in Epiphanius' *Panarion* 1.312.15). On the term "magic" in this specific context, see Otto, *Magie*, 376–378, and below, pp. 42–44.

smaller temple at present-day Qasr el-'Aguz, devoted to the same deities.[28] When the priest inquired whether he wanted to see a dead soul or a god, Thessalos answered that he wished to speak with no one less than Asclepius himself – face to face and alone.[29] Although visibly displeased, the priest complied. He told him to sit down opposite the "throne" on which the god would appear, pronounced the ineffable names that would summon the god, then left the room and shut the door.

What followed is known as a ritual of apparition.[30] Asclepius appeared right in front of Thessalos. The god's facial expression and the beauty of his surroundings were so wondrous that he writes he cannot describe them, but felt that the spectacle "released him from body and soul."[31] The god reached out his hand, and after some flattering remarks about Thessalos' greatness and future success, offered to answer any questions he might want to ask. Struggling to gather himself together, Thessalos managed to ask why Nechepso's prescriptions had failed, and Asclepius proceeded to instruct him about the true way of using the powers of plants. The rest of the text is a technical treatise about astrological plant medicine. Having finished his discourse, Asclepius ascended and Thessalos went looking for the priest.[32] According to some of the Latin

---

[28] Here I follow Bull's argument concerning the probable meaning of οἶκος καθαρός (*Tradition*, 427 note 3) and David Klotz's suggestion as for its probable location at Deir el-Bahari (*Caesar in the City of Amun*, 25–28, accepted by Moyer, *Egypt*, 250–251, who also mentions Qasr el-'Aguz, and by Bull, *Tradition*, 427); however, Dosoo tends towards interpreting οἶκος καθαρός in terms of a private dwelling ("Rituals of Apparition," 213, 311, 378–381). Purity was "the essential element of a temple" (Dieleman, *Priests*, 211–213; Sauneron, *Priests*, 35–42). For the identification of Amenhotep son of Hapu as Hermes, see above, note 20.

[29] Here and elsewhere, my reconstruction is based on the only surviving Greek manuscript (Codex Matritensis, Paris BN 4631). Concerning the formulation μόνος πρὸς μόνον, which has no equivalent in the Latin versions: contrary to Smith's suggestion ("Temple," 180–181 with note 40), Peterson rejects the idea of a neoplatonic "theurgic" interpretation and shows that Thessalos simply wanted to be left alone ("Herkunft und Bedeutung," 35–37).

[30] Dosoo, "Rituals of Apparition." Moyer speaks more specifically of an *pḥ-nṯr* or "god's arrival" ritual ("Thessalos," 48–49; *Egypt*, 252; cf. Ritner, "Egyptian Magical Practice," 3346); on this important category in the Theban Magical Library, see Dosoo, ibid., 241–252, who concludes that in the context of the Theban Magical Library the term refers to a dream oracle.

[31] Thessalos, *De virtute herbarum*, Proem 24.

[32] At least according to the Greek version and the Latin manuscript M: see Friedrich, *Thessalos*, 17–18, 21–22; Moyer, *Egypt*, 263 with note 220. Thessalos' claim of "receiving money sufficient for myself" (*recipiens auro mihi sufficiens*) remains mysterious, as it is hard to see why the priest would give Thessalos money, especially since the ritual had been a success (cf. Dosoo, "Rituals," 315 note 1315).

manuscripts, they ended up traveling to Alexandria together, where Thessalos tested the prescriptions "within the space of one year" and finally succeeded in convincing all the sceptics.[33]

Rituals of apparition – in which a god appears to a practitioner to answer his questions, bestow favors, or establish an ongoing relationship – are extremely frequent in the large manuscript collection known as the "Theban Magical Library."[34] Such rituals typically required a period of purification to prepare the practitioner for his encounter with the god, a burnt offering (often just the smoking of incense), and a spoken formula.[35] Many of these materials remain incomprehensible unless we assume that far from being mere "literary fictions," they reflect practices that actually took place in Egyptian temple contexts and could result in spectacular visions. Before zooming in on the specific phenomenon of Hermetic spirituality, we need to look at this wider context of Egyptian ritual and visionary practice during the Roman period and ask ourselves how it may have worked.

THE LIGHT OF THE GODHEAD

The story of Thessalos provides us with an excellent point of entry. Of course we cannot know for sure where his narrative should be placed on a scale between pure fiction and literal autobiography, but we may assume it is somewhere in between. Thessalos was in trouble and must have decided that he had to come up with a new treatise on plant astrology. Still based on the original Nechepso text, the crucial difference was that it would provide exact technical details concerning the astrological times the plants had to be harvested.[36] If he wanted to overwrite the shameful memory of his Alexandrian debacle, this time it really had to work. Since Thessalos' personal reputation was in shatters, he needed to attribute his treatise to an authority high enough to correct Nechepso. Who could be more suitable than the god of healing himself, and what

---

[33] For the relevant passages with English translation, see Moyer, *Egypt*, 263–264 note 222.
[34] Dosoo, "Rituals of Apparition," 221–222; cf. Dieleman, "Coping," esp. 354–356. On the Theban Magical Library and its importance, see Fowden, *Egyptian Hermes*, 168–173; Ritner, "Egyptian Magical Practice," 3335; Dieleman, *Priests*, 11–23; Dosoo, "History"; Dosoo, "Rituals of Apparition." On the high probability that the collection really does come from Thebes, see the careful argumentation in Dosoo, "History," 253–254 with note 11; and for proof focused on the Leiden I 384 and London-Leiden papyri (PGM XII/PDM xii and PGM XIV/PDM xiv), see Dieleman, *Priests*, 21, 40–44.
[35] Dosoo, "Rituals of Apparition," 222.
[36] Moyer, *Egypt*, 229 (hence the "space of one year" that he needed in Alexandria, see above).

better place to meet him than a temple in Thebes? Whether the author of our text ever sat in a closed chamber gazing at an apparition is impossible for us to determine, but it is important to consider all the possibilities. Perhaps he just took his description from the abundant oral and written record of divine epiphanies, because he needed it for his story. Perhaps he did participate in the ritual, but it failed, and so he ended up describing what *should* have happened. But then again, perhaps he did see the god, and the god spoke to him. How can we reasonably account for that possibility?

Consider the situation. Thessalos needed an apparition, and the priest could provide it. Did he expect nothing in return for his services? That is unlikely. By accepting Thessalos' request, he could get into serious trouble with his colleagues, for what happened inside the temples was supposed to be secret, and "Asiatics" – foreigners such as Thessalos – were specifically excluded from the sacred rites and spaces.[37] If he took the risk of transgressing such traditional restrictions to provide a ritual service for a foreigner, we may assume that he expected a handsome payment[38] – and we remember that Thessalos had come to Egypt with "plenty of silver." In short, while using the stereotype of the "wise and powerful magus" to his best advantage,[39] the priest seems to have been commodifying temple rituals to supplement a meager income, and Thessalos was behaving very much like a consumer on a tourist market of exotic rituals and experiences.[40] Traditional restrictions notwithstanding, such transactions had become a rather frequent occurrence during the Roman period, as illustrated by an anonymous author from the third century CE:

What, then, shall I do? This shall I do. I shall proceed to Egypt, and there I shall cultivate the friendship of the hierophants or prophets, who preside at the shrines. Then I shall win over a magician by money, and entreat him, by what

---

[37] Moyer, "Thessalos," 50–52; Moyer, *Egypt*, 261–262.
[38] Moyer, "Thessalos," 52–53, 56; Dosoo, "Rituals of Apparition," 315; Bull, *Tradition*, 449–450. On payment for private priestly services, see e.g. Frankfurter, "Religious Practice and Piety," 326; Tallet, "Oracles," 411–412.
[39] I am referring to Frankfurter's oft-quoted concept of "stereotype appropriation" (*Religion in Roman Egypt*, 225–233; see also Moyer, *Egypt*, 225–226). I am less than convinced by Moyer's argument that Thessalos himself tries to appropriate the stereotype (ibid., 226, 249).
[40] Moyer, "Thessalos," 56. On the Hellenistic romanticization and exoticization of Egyptian priests as purveyors of superior ancient wisdom, who could then appropriate such stereotypes and use them to their own financial advantage, see Frankfurter, *Religion in Roman Egypt*, 217–237; Dieleman, *Priests*, 239–254.

they call the necromantic art, to bring me a soul from the infernal regions, as if I were desirous of consulting it about some business.[41]

Once having paid the fee, Thessalos would expect something serious in return for his investment. Therefore it wouldn't do for the priest to just leave him behind in a closed room, hoping for Asclepius to take care of the rest.[42] Something impressive needed to happen. Now Thessalos was certainly in a receptive state. He must have felt weak and dizzy after fasting for three days, and he tells us how excited he was about the prospect of meeting the god. It is not easy for us moderns to take the required leap of imagination, but we need to understand that he was not playing around. Our postmodern attitudes of ironic reserve would be alien to him – the gods were perfectly real and extremely powerful, and so the prospect of encountering a great deity like Asclepius face to face would be literally awe-inspiring. If we add to this the fact that a burnt offering was standard in Egyptian rituals of apparition,[43] we can see the situation move into focus. Thessalos found himself alone in a dark temple room, sitting in front of an empty throne, dizzy and hungry, hoping for something extraordinary to happen but filled with anxiety, while inhaling the smoke of *kuphi* incense. The ingredients of this famous compound, which was used in temples all over Egypt, have been analyzed in detail. They appear to have had narcotic properties[44] inducing a state of sleep-like reverie and relaxation in which the subject's imagination would be greatly empowered. Plutarch writes about *kuphi* that "the imaginative faculty susceptible to dreams it brightens like a mirror."[45]

Therefore it is safe to assume that Thessalos beheld Asclepius in an altered state of consciousness. What could he have seen? Most probably the apparition took the form of a bright light, a phenomenon that

---

[41] Pseudo-Clement, *Recognitions* 1.5 (cf. Frankfurter, *Religion in Roman Egypt*, 218; Dieleman, *Priests*, 253).
[42] On the "business relationship" between priest and client, which required the former to produce predictable results, cf. Luck, "Psychoactive Substances," 479–480.
[43] Dosoo, "Rituals of Apparition," 222.
[44] See the extraordinarily detailed analysis by Loret, "Le Kyphi." Further discussions can be found in Hopfner, *Griechisch-Ägyptischer Offenbarungszauber* § 544–551 (with many references to classical sources); Derchain, "La recette du Kyphi"; Meslin, "Réalités psychiques," 291–292; Scarborough, "Pharmacology," 157–161; Yébenes, "El kyphi" (with careful distinction between narcotic and hallucinogenic effects, 360); and cf. LiDonnici, "Single-Stemmed Wormwood," esp. 65, 76, 78–79; Aufrère, "Parfums et onguents," esp. 50, 56. Luck lists the ingredients of incenses used in the PGM without mentioning *kuphi* specifically ("Psychoactive Substances," 479–480).
[45] Plutarch, *De Iside et Osiride* 80.

was known as *phōtagōgia* and is mentioned frequently in the Theban Magical Library.[46] The light would announce the arrival of the deity, who would then appear within it (entering it, shining through it, or taking form within it). Given Plutarch's report on how *kuphi* enhances the imaginative faculty, the light would function like a reflective mirror in which a drowsy Thessalos beheld what he expected and hoped for: a luminous shape that was impossible to describe exactly but could not be anything other for him than the body of the god.

All that remains to ask then is where the light came from. We cannot know for sure, but it seems reasonable to assume that the priest disposed of some kind of procedure for making a bright light appear in the darkness above the throne.[47] We have seen that he needed an impressive "event" to make sure that Thessalos would walk out satisfied and properly impressed, rather than just doze off in the darkness and demand his money back afterwards. Contrary to what we might think, such a scenario does not need to imply any conscious fraud (even though in specific cases, like this one, it certainly could). In discussing the nature of the "Egyptian Mysteries," the philosopher Iamblichus is perfectly clear about the fact that luminous effects in which divinities appeared could be produced by technical artifice:

> Sometimes [the Egyptian priests] conduct the light through water ... At other times they cause it to shine on a wall, having expertly prepared in advance a place on the wall for the light with sacred inscriptions of characters [i.e. hieroglyphs], and at the same time fixing the light on a solid place so that it will not be too diffused. There might be many other ways for conducting the light, but all are reduced to one, i.e. the shining of the bright light in whatever way and through whatever instruments it may shine forth.[48]

Again we must beware of jumping to modern conclusions and reading this passage in terms of priestly deception or magical trickery. The key to luminous epiphanies, according to Iamblichus, lies in our faculty of

---

[46] Dosoo, "Rituals of Apparition," 351–355; Dodds, *Greeks and the Irrational*, 298–299; Dieleman, "Coping," 352–353.

[47] On artificial light in antiquity, see Moullou, Doulos and Topalis, "Artificial Light Sources"; and several contributions to Papadopoulos and Moyes, *Oxford Handbook of Light in Archaeology*.

[48] Iamblichus, *Response to Porphyry* III 14 (transl. Clarke et al., *Iamblichus* De Mysteriis, 155–156; but with "magical symbols" replaced by "characters [hieroglyphs]," see Iamblichus, *Réponse*, 100 and 288 note 3). As regards Iamblichus' reference to "conducting the light through water," it remains an open question whether Thessalos' vision had anything to do with lecanomancy ("vessel inquiry"). The priest had claimed that he knew its secret, but it is never mentioned again, and he might have decided on a different procedure.

imagination (*phantasia*). What happens is that the external light has an effect on the luminous vehicle of our soul (*ochēma*),[49] and this allows the gods, acting by their own volition, to "take possession of the imaginative power in us."[50] In other words, the human imagination was considered not as an agent of illusion but as a faculty of *perception* that made it possible to see the gods. The priests were merely facilitating their appearance, by using procedures and techniques of proven effectiveness.

TOWARD THE LIGHT

We can now consider the wider question of how to account for the impressive visionary experiences described in countless ancient texts within the wider milieus of Graeco-Roman antiquity from which the Hermetica emerged. Iamblichus referred to such practices in the context of *theurgy* (*theourgia*), a term that may be translated as god-working, or the activity of the gods (divine acts, *theia erga*, or the workings of the gods, *theōn erga*). The term was meant to make a specific point: although theurgic rites were performed by human beings, it was the gods themselves who directed the work.[51] Rather than seeing such practices as attempts by "magicians" to gain power and control over invisible entities such as gods or demons, it is much more correct to see them as ritual procedures whose goal was *to create suitable conditions for the gods to manifest themselves*. The ritual setting had to be right, you had to follow the right procedures, and you had to be in the right mental state. Fortunately, to create such conditions you did not need to start from scratch or proceed by trial and error on your own, for there were ancient traditions and

---

[49] On the *ochēma-pneuma*, see Kissling, "OXHMA-ΠΝΕΥΜΑ of the Neoplatonists"; Lewy, *Chaldaean Oracles*, 178–184; Finamore, *Iamblichus and the Theory of the Vehicle*; Majercik, *Chaldean Oracles*, 31; Dodds, "Appendix II"; Johnston, "*Fiat Lux*," 11–12; Shaw, *Theurgy and the Soul*, 51–53; Shaw, "Theurgy and the Platonist's Luminous Body."
[50] Iamblichus, *Response to Porphyry* III 14. The *ochēma-pneuma* was regarded as the seat of both sensation and imagination (Majercik, *Chaldean Oracles*, 32; Kissling, "OXHMA-ΠΝΕΥΜΑ," 321, both with reference to a passage in Simplicius, *In libros Aristotelis De Anima commentaria*, 214).
[51] Shaw, "Theurgy," 1 (but cf. Louth, "Pagan Theurgy," 434: Iamblichus used the term as more or less equivalent to *mustagogia, hiera hagisteia, thrēskeia, hieratikē technē, hē theia epistēmē*, and *theosophia*). Shaw's article of 1985 stands at the origin of the modern study of theurgy that has broken with older approaches dominated by an obsession with "rationality and irrationality." On this crucial shift, see Tanaseanu-Döbler, *Theurgy in Late Antiquity*, 9 (with references to the most important titles representative of the new scholarship in note 3).

trained practitioners who could tell you what to do and how to do it. If such ritual procedures resulted in impressive, even spectacular visionary experiences, as claimed by so many texts from Graeco-Roman antiquity, it will not do to dismiss such claims as mere "literary fictions" grounded in "irrational superstition."[52] Such an approach – which, unfortunately, dominated research in these domains until the 1990s – is in fact deeply irrational itself, because it fails to provide any realistic account of what, according to the textual evidence, may actually have happened in theurgic rituals and related practices.

Next to rituals of apparition in which gods appear to human beings, we find descriptions of ritual ascent (*anagōgē*) in which the practitioner himself is carried upwards to heaven and sees spectacular visions. A particularly famous example from the "Theban Magical [or Priestly] Library" is the so-called Mithras Liturgy (PGM IV 475–829).[53] It describes how a practitioner guides his "only child," a woman addressed as his "daughter," upwards to the heavens and into the realm of the immortal gods. In preparation of the ascent, seven days of "purity" are required in which she must "abstain from meat and bath."[54] After a lengthy invocation to the supreme solar deity Helios Mithras, the divine source of light, he instructs her to "draw in breath from the rays three times, drawing in as much as you can,"[55] after which she will see herself lifted upwards until reaching a position in midair. At this point she will find herself surrounded by utter silence, while watching the planetary constellations – not just as physical planets but as deities endowed with agency and intelligence. It is at this point that readers may begin to wonder how such information is to be understood. We find similar procedures of "inhaling" in the foundational collection of theurgical texts, the

---

[52] See the classic discussion by Festugière (RHT I, 309–354), who specifies his approach in these words: "I said *fictions* because for us, moderns, it is evident that the Hellenistic stories of revelation contain absolutely no foundation of truth" (RHT I, 309). Festugière's blind spot is on full display in his statement that "the authors who speak of ecstasy and celestial ascent are perfectly aware that this does not concern a real fact but a psychological phenomenon" (RHT I, 315): apparently he does not consider psychological phenomena to be "real facts" or entertain the possibility that they may provide his materials with a "foundation of truth."
[53] Betz, *Greek Magical Papyri*, 48–54; Dieterich, *Mithrasliturgie*; Betz, *The "Mithras Liturgy"* (discussion of its relation to the Hermetica on 35–38, unfortunately based on Festugière's notion of "literary fictions").
[54] PGM IV 735–736 (transl. Betz, *"Mithras Liturgy"*, 57). This requirement of purity appears in the instructions about how the "daughter" can initiate another person, so we may logically assume that it applies to her as well.
[55] PGM IV 539 (transl. Betz, *"Mithras Liturgy"*, 51).

Chaldaean Oracles,[56] and it seems clear that this "breath from the rays" must mean the divine *pneuma* that is emanating from the supreme source of light. As an effect of inhaling *pneuma*, the vehicle of the soul (the *ochēma*, see above) becomes illuminated, literally "having the appearance of light."[57] The gods have now taken possession of it and lift the soul upwards.[58]

This is what the authors of the "Mithras Liturgy" and the *Chaldaean Oracles* are telling us, but we are still left at the level of pure description. How are we to *understand* what we are reading here? To be more precise: what could have been happening to the practitioner that would convince her that she *was* actually drifting upwards in the air, entered a great silence, and beheld the heavenly bodies as living beings? This question is the elephant in the room of modern scholarship on theurgy – almost without exception, even the most knowledgeable and perceptive specialists ignore or avoid it.[59] This silence is all the more remarkable because at least in the case of the "Mithras Liturgy," it so happens that the keys for a plausible solution are readily available. We have seen that the gods appeared to the theurgist by "taking possession" of his luminous vehicle and activating its imaginative powers. Michael Psellos (who had access to materials that we no longer possess[60]) writes that according to Proclus, the vehicle is "empowered" (*dunamōsomen*) or "purified" (*kathairesthai*) by means of "stones, herbs, and incantations":

The Chaldaean says that we cannot be borne upwards towards god, unless we empower the vehicle of the soul by material sacraments. For he believes that

---

[56] Chal. Or., fragm. 124 and 130 (Majercik, *Chaldean Oracles*, 96–99). Admittedly, the *pneuma* is not mentioned explicitly here; but like Johnston ("Fiat Lux," 13–14; "Rising to the Occasion," 181) and Edmonds ("Did the Mithraists Inhale?," 15–16), I find it plausible that what is being inhaled in fragm. 124 must in fact be the "warm breath" (fragm. 123) or the "flowering flames" (fragm. 130) of the solar *pneuma*. Bull contests this interpretation, while emphasizing the inhalation of *kuphi* incense instead (*Tradition*, 417–424). The two interpretations do not strike me as mutually exclusive: while breathing hard to inhale solar *pneuma*, the practitioner would in fact be filling her lungs with *kuphi* smoke.

[57] Cf. Chal. Or. fragm. 122–123: the soul is "set ablaze with fire" and "rendered light by a warm *pneuma* ... causing a rising up through the anagogic life" (Tanaseanu-Döbler, *Theurgy*, 30).

[58] See Johnston, "Fiat Lux," 11–14; Johnston, "Animating Statues," 459–460; Edmonds, "Did the Mithraists Inhale?"

[59] But see Bergemann, "Inkubation"; Litwa, "'Immortalized'." For theurgy generally, cf. Luck, "Theurgy and Forms of Worship."

[60] Johnston, "Fiax Lux," 7.

the soul is purified by stones, herbs and conjurations and consequently becomes more agile with a view to the ascension.[61]

Such a use of "herbs" is confirmed explicitly by the author of the "Mithras Liturgy": "it is necessary for you, O daughter, to take the juices of herbs and drugs, which will be [made known] to you at the end of my sacred treatise."[62] In sum, there is really no mystery here. Some kind of herbal concoction was required that would enable the pupil to inhale *pneuma* into her soul vehicle so that the gods could empower its imaginative faculties. The actual effect must have been enhanced by the simultaneous practice of inhaling the smoke of *kuphi* incense, a standard ingredient of such practices mentioned explicitly in our text.[63]

We do in fact find a detailed recipe affixed to the "Mithras Liturgy." You need to prepare a cake from honey and the fruit pulp of the lotus, and feed this to a sun scarab. It will kill the scarab, who must then be thrown into a glass vessel with high-quality rose oil; and having placed the vessel on "sacred sand," a consecration must be spoken over it during seven days. Then the scarab must be buried in a piece of linen together with myrrh and Mendesian wine, finally resulting in an ointment that can be used for the ritual of ascent.[64] It is known that Egyptian water lilies (*lōtos*, genus *Nymphaea*) had narcotic and hallucinogenic properties,[65] and myrrh (*bꜥl*) is described in the Demotic Magical Papyri as a component of an eye paint prescribed for visionary applications.[66] Indeed, that is exactly what the author of the "Mithras Liturgy" appears to have in

---

[61] Psellus, *Exposition on the Chaldaean Oracles*, in: Migne, *Patrologia Graeca*, vol. 122, 1131 A (Lewy, *Chaldaean Oracles and Theurgy*, 178; Majercik, *Chaldean Oracles*, 36).

[62] PGM IV 479–491 (transl. Betz, *"Mithras Liturgy"*, 50; on the translation of εἰδῶν as "drugs," see ibid., 97).

[63] PGM IV 512. See Bull, *Tradition*, 417–424 (and above, note 56); and below, Chapter 3, p. 71 with notes 101–103.

[64] PGM IV 752–772 (transl. Betz, *"Mithras Liturgy"*, 57–58); on Mendesian wine, see LiDonnici, "Beans, Fleawort," 363–364.

[65] Emboden, "Transcultural Use of Narcotic Water Lilies"; Emboden, "Sacred Journey in Dynastic Egypt"; Bertol et alii, "*Nymphaea* Cults in Ancient Egypt"; Aufrère, "Parfums et onguents liturgiques," 49, 52: Greek λωτός means "Nile water-lily, Egyptian lotus, Nymphaea Lotus" (Liddell and Scott, *Greek-English Lexicon*, 1070).

[66] PDM XIV 295–308, 805–840, 875–885 (LiDonnici, "Single-Stemmed Wormwood," 67 with note 33; on myrrh more generally, see also Aufrère, "Parfums et onguents," 29 note 1). See also PDM XIV 93–114, where myrrh and *qs-ꜥnh*-stone (identified as "probably hematite") are prescribed for a fumigation that will induce a sleep in which you will see a god. Even the Sun Scarab juice may have had hallucinogenic properties due to dung beetles ingesting psilocybin from mushrooms of the *Psilocybe* genus (on the preference of this genus for feeding on mushrooms, see Frolov, Akhmetova and Scholtz, "Revision," 1483–1484; on *Psilocybe* species growing on cow dung, see Guzmán, *Genus Psilocybe*; Guzmán, "Supplement").

mind: "get the juice of the herb called kentritis, and smear it, along with the rose oil, around the eyes of whomever you wish; and he will see so clearly that you will be amazed (*thaumazein*)."[67] This kentritis plant and several other ingredients have so far resisted identification,[68] but clearly the authors of the Papyri knew them and were able to prepare the ointment. Apart from this substance that was to be rubbed into the eyes, or smeared around it, we are also told about letters (ϊ εε οο ϊαϊ) that must be written on a leaf with an ink made of kentritis, honey, and myrrh, and then licked off. The author claims that he has often done this himself and has been "super-amazed" (*huperethaumasa*) by the effect.[69] These instructions make perfect sense, for the Greek Magical Papyri contain literally dozens of references to myrrh, not only as a psychoactive agent but also as a component of black ink for the writing of ritually important words, characters, or pictures.[70]

Since we cannot decipher all the components of these recipes, the exact psychological effects of combining myrrh, water lilies, and kentritis with other unidentified ingredients, while simultaneously inhaling *kuphi*, must remain a matter of speculation.[71] However, we can be confident that they would have a strong impact on the state of consciousness of theurgical practitioners, making them highly sensitive and receptive to suggestion while inducing powerful visual and possibly auditory hallucinations. To properly understand the theurgic process from such a perspective, it remains important to emphasize the crucial importance of mental expectations and ritual context,[72] for these are largely responsible for what is

---

[67] PGM IV 773–775 (transl. Betz, "*Mithras Liturgy*", 58).
[68] For the most serious attempt at identifying kentritis, see Dieterich, *Mithrasliturgie*, 21–22, based on an analysis made by his friend M. Wellmann; but see also the detailed analysis in Hopfner, *Griechisch-Ägyptischer Offenbarungszauber* § 500.
[69] PGM IV 791–792 (transl. Betz, "*Mithras Liturgy*", 58).
[70] PGM I 1–42, 232–247, II 1–64, III 165–186, IV 850–929, 930–1114, 3209–3254, V 304–369, VII 467–477, 505–528, VIII 64–110, XII 179–181, XIXb 1–3 (LiDonnici, "Single-Stemmed Wormwood," 66–67 with note 23–26).
[71] The problem is compounded by the fact that priests used code-names to conceal the nature of herbs and substances they were using: see the fascinating de-codification list in PGM XII 401–444 (discussion in Scarborough, "Pharmacology of Sacred Plants," 159–160; LiDonnici, "Beans, Fleawort," 366–377; and Dieleman, *Priests*, 189–203).
[72] Johnston assigns a central place to the "Mithras Liturgy" in her reconstruction of theurgic ritual ("Rising to the Occasion," 183) and asks the crucial question "How often did practitioners really manage to see or hear the remarkable things that ancient spells promised them they would see and hear" ("Authority," 51). She answers it in terms of their mental conditioning by the "vivid story-world" of Greek Mythic narratives (ibid.); but although she seems to assume that practitioners were in a "trance state" (ibid., 52), she does not address the question of how it might have been induced

actually seen and heard in any drug-fueled experience.[73] Since our female practitioner in the "Mithras Liturgy" has been told that she is about to see the gods, she is prepared for awe-inspiring experiences of fire and light. She must have expected to be overwhelmed and deeply impressed, and we know that the exact content of her experience will have been determined by how the subjective contents of her own mind (including her belief in the gods, the stories she knows about them, fears about their awesome power, and so on) interact with the objective impact of a specific psychoactive compound. Furthermore, she is being guided through the experience by a ritual leader who gives her precise instructions about what to do and say at any moment.

If we reread the text with this information in mind, we discover that in fact he does *not* begin by asking his daughter to inhale the *pneuma*. Rather, what happens is that he recites the long opening invocation while simultaneously "anointing her face with the mystery"[74] – that is to say, with the hallucinogenic ointment. While it is beginning to take effect, she is instructed to do the inhalations, three times in succession, "drawing in as much as you can."[75] The drugs must be responsible for the ensuing sensation of ascending upwards and floating weightlessly in midair. Having been enveloped by deep silence (another possible drug effect), initially the practitioner feels threatened by the awesome presence of the divine powers, which are glowering at her and seem ready to attack her. To keep them at bay, she must put her right finger on her mouth and say "Silence! Silence! Silence! Symbol of the living imperishable god. Guard

---

and never mentions the textual references to herbs and plants (in "Rising," 182 she mentions the "honey-milk" of PGM I 1-42 and the swallowing of ink in PGM XIII 124-136, but the recipes in the "Mithras Liturgy" itself are passed over in silence). Likewise, Tanaseanu-Döbler discusses theurgy as ritual tradition but does not seem to see this dimension as relevant.

[73] I am referring to the fundamental concept of "set" (personality, preparation, expectation, and intention of the person having the experience) and "setting" (the physical, social, and cultural environment in which the experience takes place); see Hartogsohn, "Constructing Drug Effects," 1 and passim.

[74] *Contra* Edmonds, "Did the Mithraists Inhale?," 13 ("no other mode of ascent [than inhaling *pneuma*] is ever mentioned. The sun's rays are clearly the primary means..."). Cf. above, note 54: again I assume that the procedure for initiating a third person must be identical to how the instructor proceeds with his "daughter."

[75] PGM IV 539 (transl. Betz, *"Mithras Liturgy"*, 51). Depending on a person's individual susceptibility to trance states, certain breathing techniques involving hyperventilation can induce powerful visionary experiences even without the use of hallucinogenic agents (e.g. Grof, *Beyond the Brain*, 387–390); in combination with them, the effect will be further enhanced.

me, Silence! *Nechtheir thanmelou!*"[76] Then she has to hiss at them and make a popping sound, followed by a longer formula of incomprehensible words, all of which will have the effect of restoring them to peace. Likewise, when disturbed by a sound of crashing thunder, she has to repeat these same words, reassuring the gods that she is no alien intruder but an immortal being like themselves: "I am a star, wandering about with you."[77]

Now the sun will start expanding – another fearsome event to which she must respond with the same formulas, the hissing, and the popping sounds. Multiple five-pronged stars will proceed from the sun and fill the air, to which she can respond in like manner. From a perspective informed by modern psychology, all of this makes perfect sense: whenever some new phenomenon threatens to throw her off balance in her fragile state, she can hold on to the formula and the sounds to help her restore a sense of balance and control. Finally, she will see the sun "opening up" in front of her, and notice great doors inside that are tightly shut. Now she has to recite a long prayer, including strings of incomprehensible words, asking for the doors to open. She must repeat it seven times, for each of the seven planetary gods, until finally (with a great noise and shaking, to which she can respond again with the "Silence..." formula) the doors open. Then she will behold the world of the gods inside, and this spectacle will give her great pleasure and joy.

Next she has to invite the gods to come forward through the gate, by inhaling more *pneuma*, keeping her gaze fixed on the sun's inner space, and pronouncing a new formula with many incomprehensible words. The rays of the sun will turn toward her, and while she keeps gazing firmly into the center, a beautiful young god will appear. Greeting him with the proper words, she asks him to announce her presence to his father, the greatest god, pointing out that although born as a mortal human being, today she has been reborn as an immortal one. In other words, again, they should not claim that she has no business being here. Without losing sight of the god, she is instructed to make a strong bellowing sound, exhaling all her breath while squeezing her loins, kissing her phylacteries (protective amulets), and asking for protection. Seven virgins with the faces of asps and carrying golden wands will emerge from the deep within, followed later

---

[76] PGM IV 558–560 (transl. Betz, *"Mithras Liturgy"*, 52). We have no explanation for the Greek words (ibid., 149 with note 349–350). On the complex meanings of σύμβολον, see Struck, *Birth of the Symbol*.
[77] PGM IV 574 (transl. Betz, *"Mithras Liturgy"*, 52).

by seven gods with the faces of black bulls and carrying golden diadems.[78] She has to greet them all with the correct formulas. Finally the great god Helios himself appears, as a youthful golden-haired entity of enormous size, and again the practitioner must respond with bellowing sounds, full exhalation of breath, and kissing of the phylacteries. Having implored the god to "dwell in her soul" and not abandon her, she then asks him for a revelation, to which he will respond immediately by pronouncing an oracle in verses.[79] After this he departs. The practitioner is told that she will be left behind feeling "weak in her soul" and quite beyond herself, speechless and wondering how to comprehend the message. Later on, her father/guide assures her, she will find it all back in her memory.

PRIVATE EXPERIENTIAL PRACTICES

When discussing texts of this kind, many scholars feel compelled to distance themselves from their contents by using disparaging qualifiers such as "murky," "bizarre," "abstruse," or "sub-philosophical"[80] – almost like apotropaic formulae to ward off the suspicions of colleagues who might think they take it all too seriously. A variant of the same reflex mechanism consists in overemphasizing the "magical" nature of such rituals, thereby distancing them from the greater legitimacy that would be implied by adjectives such as "religious" or "priestly."[81] We speak of the Theban *Magical* Library and the Greek *Magical* Papyri, but while those labels were already current early on, it is significant that Karl Preisendanz in his standard German translations of 1928 and 1931 kept arbitrarily adding the prefix "*Zauber-*" and interpreting everything as "magical" by default: hence, any reference to *praxis* and *pragmateia* (act, acting) was turned into a "magical act (*Zauberhandlung*)", *botanai* (plants) automatically became "magical plants," *charaktēras* (signs) became "magical

---

[78] On the identification of these male and female deities, representing the stars in the constellations of Ursa Minor and Major, see Betz, "*Mithras Liturgy*", 175–179; Edmonds, "Did the Mithraists Inhale?," 11.
[79] Cf. discussion of divine possession below, pp. 110–112. It seems reasonable to assume that the invitation to the god to "dwell in her soul" is not intended metaphorically but means that his divine light takes possession of her soul. It would be consistent with a scenario of divine possession in an altered state of consciousness that the god gives his oracle by using the voice of the practitioner herself.
[80] These adjectives, used by John Dillon in a well-known chapter about what he calls "the Underworld of Platonism" (*Middle Platonists*, 384), are repeated for instance by Majercik, *Chaldean Oracles*, 3–4 and Edmonds, "Did the Mithraists Inhale?," 10.
[81] See for instance Ritner, *Mechanics*, 4–13, with some good examples in note 4.

signs," *epaoidais* (songs) became "magical songs," and *onomai* (names) became "magical names."[82] By such translation procedures, scholars have been actively creating "magic" rather than finding it in their materials. In reality, it is clear that the Egyptian authors of the papyri simply did not share the opinion of their Roman occupiers that "magic" (*mageia*) was something negative, nonreligious, or shameful. On the contrary, while they did use the term when writing in Greek, they consistently described it as a "holy" and "divine" pursuit for which they had perfectly positive terms available in their own language, as we do in ours.[83] The conclusion is simple: "Roman notions of 'magic' were alien to Egypt, and Egyptian practices were suspect to Rome."[84] The problem is that our tradition of modern scholarship has taken its cue from Rome, not from Egypt. When we refer to the Mithras Liturgy as containing "murky," "abstruse," or "bizarre" forms of "magic," we are still speaking like Romans, not like Egyptians. It is the language of suspicion and contempt.

A mountain of theoretical scholarship would like to convince us that the problem of "magic versus religion" is enormously complicated and probably impossible to resolve, yet it seems to me that the situation is more simple than it might seem.[85] Essentially we are dealing with the basic translator's dilemma[86] and need to make a choice: do we want to stay as close as possible to the original lexical *terms*, regardless of what these have come to mean for us in our own common discourse, or should we look for words that help us make their *meaning* understood by modern readers? As already demonstrated by my argument concerning the term "spirituality," I am consistently opting for the latter. This means that the "Theban Magical Library" should better be referred to as the "Theban *Priestly* Library," simply because it documents the activities of Egyptian priests. We complicate the task of understanding their

---

[82] Otto, *Magie*, 385; for an illustrative example, see note 48 (translations of Iamblichus, *Response to Porphyry* III 14). The label "Greek Magical Papyri" was current well before Preisendanz; see e.g. Mead, *Thrice-Greatest Hermes*, vol. 1, 82–98.

[83] Otto, *Magie*, 386; Ritner, *Mechanics*, 14–28; Brashear, "Greek Magical Papyri," 3390–3392. For the "paradigm shift" in ancient Athens which had led to a separation between "religion" and "magic" that was inherited by the Romans, the fundamental discussion is Graf, *Gottesnähe*, 31–36 (cf. Dickie, *Magic and Magicians*, 21–21 with note 8, pointing to the limitations of the English translation of Graf's book).

[84] Ritner, "Egyptian Magical Practice," 3355.

[85] For the larger argument, see Hanegraaff, "Magic"; and cf. Hanegraaff, *Esotericism and the Academy*, 164–177. For a decisive analysis of the debate as a whole, see Otto, *Magie*, 37–132 (for English summary, see Hanegraaff, Review of Otto).

[86] Raffel, "Forked Tongue," 49.

practices, while underestimating the power of language over our own and our readers' imagination, if we keep insisting on the pejorative categories of their opponents even where more neutral terminologies are readily available. Referring to these practitioners as "magicians" while pretending to take them seriously is equivalent to insulting them while claiming to be impartial. It is simply not consistent, and has never worked.

Interestingly, a reverse logic seems to govern the virtual taboo on discussing psychoactive agents in such texts as the "Mithras Liturgy." While most classicists keep speaking of "magic" *in spite of* its pejorative connotations, they avoid mentioning "drugs" probably *because* it carries such connotations![87] This fact can be explained from the history of the field. From the 1980s, a new generation of excellent scholars began challenging the old patterns of prejudice against theurgy and finally succeeded in restoring it to academic agendas. But while it is one thing to convince your colleagues that theurgy is governed by "a rationality of its own,"[88] having to tell them that it involved drugs is something else entirely – the latter suggestion might easily lead them to conclude that those old prejudices were perhaps not so wrong after all, and those alternative rationalities might not be so rational. The effect that such information can have on nonspecialists is even harder to control, and very few scholars have been willing to take the risk – especially in the field of ancient religions, where several established academics have seen their reputations ruined by mediatized sensationalism about "religion and drugs."[89] No wonder then that most scholars would like to avoid those "herbs" and their troublesome effects. Nevertheless, the references are there in our sources,

---

[87] A notable exception is Georg Luck, "Theurgy and Forms of Worship"; Luck, "Psychoactive Substances."

[88] Tanaseanu-Döbler, *Theurgy*, 9; and see Emma C. Clarke's well taken reservations about this general approach (*Iamblichus'* De Mysteriis, 1–2, 30, 119–121).

[89] For the classicist Carl A.P. Ruck and academic responses to his thesis of a psychoactive sacrament at the heart of the Eleusinian Mysteries (see Wasson, Hofmann and Ruck, *Road to Eleusis*, published by Ruck in collaboration with two iconic figures of the psychedelic counterculture), see summary overview in Luck, Review of Wasson, Hofmann and Ruck (referring, *inter alia*, to Walter Burkert, *Ancient Mystery Cults*, 108–114: an authoritative but problematic analysis that shows how even a very great scholar can be led astray by popular stereotypes about "drugs"). For the Dead Sea Scrolls specialist John M. Allegro, who ruined his academic reputation with his bestseller *The Sacred Mushroom and the Cross* (1970), see Hanegraaff, "Academic Suicide." For the German historian Will-Erich Peuckert and the media hype that was provoked by a passing reference he made, in a public lecture, about an experiment in his early youth with the medieval witches' ointment as a hallucinogenic agent, see Hanegraaff, "Will-Erich Peuckert," 280 with note 4 (referring to Jacobsen, "Boundary Breaking").

and much more abundantly than is often thought. The information is obviously important for understanding how these rituals may have worked and why practitioners could be so impressed by their efficacy. If our own *hinterland* of cultural biases makes it hard for us to consider this dimension seriously, then the burden is on us to do something about it.[90]

What happens if we *really* stop imagining Roman Egypt as a primitive "heart of darkness"[91] full of murky magic, superstition, and irrational delusions? We then see one of the greatest cultures of the ancient world struggling to survive under foreign domination. Its religious institutions had been the fabric of society for thousands of years, but now the temples are in decay and have lost most of their traditional power and prestige. They have been reduced essentially to private enterprises, and its priests are forced to compete on a pluralistic religious market imposed by external forces that are hostile or simply indifferent to their sacred traditions. In the terms of a famous analytical model, the result during the Roman period was a growing tension between "locative" and "non-locative" ("utopian") modes of religious practice.[92] The former were inherently conservative, as they represented ancient cultic traditions tied to specific places: the temples and sanctuaries where the gods were at home. But in the cosmopolitan culture of the Hellenistic world, characterized by unprecedented degrees of mobility and intercultural exchange, this locative character of traditional religion began to give way to a type of religion that could be practiced "here, there, and anywhere"[93]:

> Certain cult centers remained sites of pilgrimage or sentimental attachment, but the old beliefs in national deities and the inextricable relationship of the deity to particular places was weakened. Rather than a god who dwelt in his temple or would regularly manifest himself in a cult house, the diaspora evolved complicated techniques for achieving visions, epiphanies or heavenly journeys. That is to say, they evolved modes of access to the deity which transcended any particular place.[94]

---

[90] On the *hinterland* concept and its background in "enactment realism," see Law, *After Method*, esp. 140–142; for its relevance to "collective set and setting," see Hartogsohn, "Constructing Drug Effects," 10.

[91] Frankfurter, *Religion in Roman Egypt*, 166.

[92] For a short summary, see Smith, *Map is not Territory*, xi–xvi; cf. Frankfurter, "Religious Practice and Piety," 326. Smith's choice for the term "utopian" is unfortunate because its literal meaning of "no place" has obviously been overwritten in common parlance by the concept of an ideal society.

[93] Smith, "Here, There, and Anywhere."

[94] Smith, *Map is not Territory*, xiv.

What we see here is a truly momentous development that is typical of cosmopolitan situations (including, obviously, what we would call globalization today). Next to religion understood as a social formation, representative of traditional communities and intimately tied up with the very fabric of society, we get other and more fluid types of religion more suitable to mobile individuals because they can be practiced anywhere and are focused on the cultivation of private experiences. Not by any coincidence, this is the very definition of what we call "spirituality" today.[95] Once again, the ingrained tendency of referring to spiritual practitioners as "magicians" is deeply misleading.[96]

The emerging market for spirituality provided Egyptian priests with obvious opportunities. It was easy for foreigners to romanticize and idealize these mysterious, bald, clean-shaven men in their white robes as initiates in superior wisdom, masters of ancient mysteries – and the appropriation of such stereotypes could be very much in the interest of the priests themselves. Forced to redefine their role in society, they discovered the great appeal that they held for a new audience willing to look up to them as spiritual leaders and teachers. The inevitable commodification of ritual services and visionary experiences that resulted from this situation does not need to be interpreted in terms of a cynical commercialism.[97] Priests need to eat too, and it would make sense for their pupils or clients that something was expected from them in return for the privilege of receiving precious spiritual insights, ritual guidance, and initiation into deep mysteries. This is very much how things still work in contemporary spiritual contexts on the global marketplace,[98] and we have no reason to assume they would work in any way differently in Roman Egypt.

---

[95] See above, pp. 19–21. In such a context, "spiritualities" (plural) may be defined in terms of the individual manipulation of symbolic systems basic to "religions" (Hanegraaff, "Defining Religion," 371–373; cf. Hanegraaff, *Western Esotericism*, 138–140).

[96] For instance, see how easily the "spirituality" concept resolves the disagreement between Jonathan Z. Smith and Robert K. Ritner (Ritner, "Egyptian Magical Practice," 3356–3358; Ritner, *Mechanics*, 219–220; summary in Moyer, "Thessalos," 39–41, 49), which is grounded in little else than the fact that both hold on to the idea of "magic" as the practice of private entrepreneurs against "religion" as a social formation. This approach comes ultimately from the French social-scientific school in the study of religions linked to the names of Marcel Mauss and Emile Durkheim, who took their cue from the pejorative understanding of "magic" typical of the Roman Empire. For the circular logic, internal contradictions, and ethnocentric bias that governed their thought on this matter, see Hanegraaff, "Defining Religion," 341–345; cf. Hanegraaff, "Magic," 394–395.

[97] Tallet, "Oracles," 412; Frankfurter, "Voices," 238–239.

[98] For an instructive parallel, see the analysis in Brabec de Mori, "From the Native's Point of View."

If I have called some special attention to the role of psychoactive substances in this context, it is because the relative neglect of that dimension needs to be corrected while the underlying mechanisms of discursive marginalization must be properly understood. The implication is not that psychoactives are in any way central to the spiritual culture under discussion or to the Hermetica more specifically. Rather, they should be seen as part of a much broader, far more diverse and complex repertoire of techniques and procedures that were available to spiritual practitioners in late antiquity. Michel Foucault's famous concept "technologies of the self" defines the topic exactly:

> [T]echnologies of the self ... permit individuals to effect by their own means or with the help of others a certain number of operations on their own bodies and souls, thoughts, conduct, and way of being, so as to transform themselves in order to attain a certain state of happiness, purity, wisdom, perfection, or immortality.[99]

It is hard to think of a better short summary of what Hermetic spirituality was all about. The impact of such technologies on an individual's state of consciousness could range from subtle perceptual changes to powerful altered states. The argument of this book is that such psychological effects are key to some of the most important Hermetic treatises (notably CH I, CH XIII, and NH VI[6]) and are taken for granted even in philosophical or theological discussions with a theoretical rather than practical focus. This is true to such an extent that if we fail to take them seriously, the most important dimensions of the Hermetic literature will remain incomprehensible for us. But before moving to an in-depth analysis of those treatises in which alterations of consciousness and visionary experiences take center stage, we will begin with a broad introduction to the Hermetic worldview as presented in a comparatively nonexperiential treatise. This is the *Logos teleios*, known in Latin as the *Asclepius*.

---

[99] Foucault, "Technologies of the Self," 18.

3

The Presence of Gods

> *Things fall apart; the centre cannot hold;*
> *mere anarchy is loosed upon the world,*
> *the blood-dimmed tide is loosed, and everywhere*
> *the ceremony of innocence is drowned.*
> W.B. Yeats, "The Second Coming."

On March 19, 235 CE, the young Roman Emperor Severus Alexander and his mother were assassinated at the order of a general who had assumed control over the army.[1] This was the beginning of what historians call "the crisis of the third century," a fifty-year period of anarchy and civil war that brought the Roman Empire close to total collapse. No fewer than twenty-four emperors came and went, most of them meeting a violent death. Some committed suicide, many were killed by the Pretorian Guard, while others died on the battlefield. A few of them succumbed to the plague, for in the midst of this period of crisis, the empire was struck by a frightening pandemic. It killed so many people on both sides of the Mediterranean – at one point, the death toll in Rome seems to have been around 5,000 each day – that Cyprian, the Bishop of Carthage, believed the end of the world had arrived.[2] As if all that were not enough, Egypt was invaded in 270 CE by the armies of the Syrian queen Septimia Zenobia. She brought the eastern part of the empire under her control for a few years but was eventually defeated by the Emperor Aurelian.

---

[1] Herodian, *Hist.* VI.8–9.
[2] Cyprian, "De mortalitate," in: Roberts, Donaldson and Coxe, *Ante-Nicene Fathers*, vol. 5, 469–475. For further contemporary perspectives, see Alföldy, "Crisis of the Third Century."

As Roman military control was weakening, Upper Egypt suffered invasions by desert tribes from Libya and Nubia.[3] In the midst of all this violent turmoil and chaos, more and more Egyptians were leaving their ancient religion behind and converted to Christianity, the new religion that seemed to be taking the world by storm.

At some time during this period of crisis, somewhere in Egypt, an anonymous devotee of Hermes Trismegistus composed a text in Greek about the way of true wisdom. Known as the *Logos teleios*, usually translated as "Perfect Discourse," it is the longest and most explicitly Egyptian text among all the spiritual Hermetica that have come down to us.[4] Situated in the inner sanctuary of an Egyptian temple, it describes a divinely inspired speech by Hermes Trismegistus directed at his pupils Asclepius, Tat, and Ammon. Initially, the atmosphere of pious serenity might seem like a contrast with the social and political realities outside the temple precincts, exemplifying an "inward turn" towards spiritual experience as a way of ignoring or trying to escape from the evils of the world. But as we read further, it becomes evident that those evils are very much present, like a rumbling noise in the distance that keeps coming closer. In the older scholarly literature the *Logos teleios* has often been described as an "optimistic" treatise, but something is wrong with that assessment.[5] Hermes is telling his pupils that all true spiritual wisdom is in decline on earth: just a few people are still keeping it alive, but very soon there will be literally none of them left.[6] The gods are abandoning Egypt, and ruthless criminals are taking their place. The future of humanity looks very dark indeed.

---

[3] Lindsay, *Origins of Alchemy*, 339–340.

[4] The most serious contender would be the collection of Isis-Horus discussions known as SH XXIII–XXVII, which I see as marginal to the spiritual Hermetica for reasons explained below, Chapter 5, p. 141. On the Egyptian background of the *Asclepius*, see Sternberg-el Hotabi, "Ägyptische Religion und Hermetismus."

[5] The distinction between "optimistic" (monistic, pantheist, or "Hellenistic") and "pessimistic" (dualistic, "gnostic," or "orientalist") Hermetic treatises was introduced by Zielinski ("Hermes und die Hermetik," 1905) and decisively by Bousset (Review of Kroll, 1914). Festugière (RHT II–IV) adopted it as his basic conceptual framework for understanding the Hermetic literature as a whole. It has been abandoned as a misleading straitjacket by modern scholars in the wake of Mahé (HHE II, 290–291, 438, 459); cf. Mahé, "Le rôle de l'élément astrologique"; Mahé, "Mental Faculties") and Fowden (*Egyptian Hermes*, e.g. 102). Taking inspiration from the comparison with closely related figures, notably Zosimos and Iamblichus (see below, Chapter 4, pp. 82–118), scholars now approach the dynamics of transcendence versus immanence in Hermetic literature from completely different perspectives, to which I will return (e.g. Chlup, "Ritualization"; Fraser, "Baptised"; Shaw, "Taking the Shape"; Bull, *Tradition*, 187–372).

[6] *Ascl.* 12, 14.

DISTANT VOICES

Modern readers encounter this "Perfect Discourse" under the title of its Latin translation, the *Asclepius*. But how reliable are the versions that we have at our disposal? Before trying to make sense of their content, we need to consider what happened to the text between the third century and our own time. To begin with, the original *Logos teleios* is lost to us: of the Greek text, nothing remains but a few short passages quoted by Christian writers plus the closing prayer, preserved in one of the so-called Greek Magical Papyri known as the Papyrus Mimaut.[7] During the following century, some time after 320 CE somewhere in northern Africa (but not in Egypt itself),[8] an unknown individual produced a Latin translation – or rather, something close to a paraphrase or an adapted version "more concerned with solemnity than with precision."[9] This is the origin of the text we know as the *Asclepius*.

It is important to gauge the distance that existed already between this Latin translation and its lost Greek original. The Church had not yet emerged victorious by the middle of the third century, and there is no clear trace of Christian influence in what we know of the *Logos teleios*. But in the first half of the fourth century, when Constantine the Great began profiling himself as the first Christian emperor, the balance shifted decisively in favor of the new religion. During the period when the Latin *Asclepius* must have been written down, only the short reign of the Emperor Julian (from 361 to 363 CE) could still have kindled some hopes for pagan restoration among Hermetic practitioners. It would seem that the Latin translator was a warm supporter of traditional Egyptian worship but not an active participant in the Way of Hermes – if any such practice still existed. We may imagine him as a cultivated man, "an important man, certainly, but not eminent; perhaps one of those gentrified gentlemen from the provinces, proud of their education and belonging to the last defenders of paganism."[10] The explicit sexual passages in the *Logos teleios* embarrassed him, and he tried to

---

[7] Papyrus Mimaut = PGM III, see lines 591–610. For references to the *Logos teleios* in Lactantius, see overviews in CHD, 570–571; Litwa, *Hermetica II*, 183 note 5; testimonia in ibid., 184–192. For Cyril of Alexandria, see testimonia in ibid., 205–214.

[8] Dating and geographical origin: Mahé, "Fragment du *Discours Parfait*," 309–310; HHE II, 55–58; cf. Fowden, *Egyptian Hermes*, 198; Moreschini, *Dall'*Asclepius, 71–72 note 2.

[9] HT II, 276. Cf. Mahé, "Prière," 54; HHE I, 23; HHE II, 36, 51–52; Wigtil, "Incorrect Apocalyptic," 2286; Fowden, *Egyptian Hermes*, 10.

[10] HHE II, 60–61.

play down its emphasis on the immortality of the soul and man's inner divinity.[11] In other words, he seems to have been somewhat detached already from the original Hermetic and Egyptian perspective, approaching it as a sympathizing outsider rather than a convinced adherent.

We can draw these conclusions because, independently but around the same time (arguably between 340 and 370),[12] some lengthy passages from the *Logos teleios* were translated from Greek into Coptic as well. Therefore the Greek text must have been circulating in northern Africa in several copies at least, but we cannot tell how faithful they were to the original. The Coptic translations were discovered in 1945 as part of the Nag Hammadi library; and as it turned out, they included the closing prayer already known in Greek from the Papyrus Mimaut (see above). Close comparison shows that the Coptic version is considerably more precise and reliable than its parallel in the Latin *Asclepius*; and this conclusion is further confirmed by comparing the Greek fragments known from Christian writers with their parallels in the Latin and the Coptic versions.[13] This means that we must be careful not to rely too easily on the Latin *Asclepius* for learning what Hermetic spirituality was originally all about. And there are even more reasons for caution. While the Latin treatise must have been written during the fourth century (in any case prior to Augustine's *City of God*, composed after 410 CE, where it is quoted at length), our earliest surviving manuscripts are much more recent: they date from the eleventh century and are based on a lost "archetype" from the final decades of the ninth.

That is half a millennium after the text was written. Early on during this period, some scribe must have miscategorized the *Asclepius* as a philosophical text by Apuleius (c. 124–170 CE), the Numidian author and Platonic philosopher from Madauros (nowadays M'Daourouch in Algeria) famous for his novel *The Golden Ass*.[14] We should be grateful for this mistake, because otherwise our text – condemned as idolatrous by no one less than St Augustine[15] – would certainly not have survived. As

[11] HHE I, 146–155; HHE II, 60–61.
[12] At least according to Mahé: HHE II, 80.
[13] Mahé, "La prière d'actions de grâces"; HHE I, 157–167 (closing prayer from PGM III, 591–610; *Ascl.* 41; NH VI7); HHE II, 145–207 (parallel passages *Ascl.* 21–29; NH VI8; and Greek fragments inserted on pp. 185–187, 194–197, 206–207); conclusions in HHE I, 137–155; HHE II, 47–67.
[14] Overview of manuscripts in Scott I, 49–51. For a useful narrative discussion (in Dutch) of the history of textual transmission, see Quispel, *Asclepius*, 251–258.
[15] Augustine, *De civitate Dei* VIII; on Hermetism in Augustine's oeuvre and his condemnation of Hermes as an idolater based on the *Asclepius*, see Hanegraaff, "Hermetism" and discussion below, Chapter 10, pp. 131–132.

it is, the *Asclepius* was passed on to posterity as the work of a respected Latin author, but it hardly survived unscathed. The original was written in a very difficult late Latin idiom heavily influenced by Greek grammar, and medieval scribes must have been making a string of "corrections" while copying (see Figure 3.1).[16]

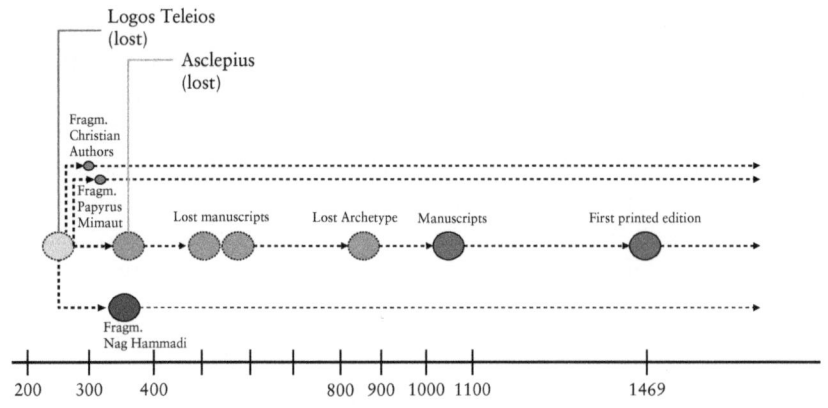

FIGURE 3.1: Manuscript timeline for the *Logos Teleios* and *Asclepius*

As a result, already the ninth-century archetype seems to have been corrupt or mutilated "in a quite exceptional way,"[17] and the process of adaptation and emendation continued through the eleventh-century manuscripts up to the first printed edition of 1469 – and indeed from there to all later editions and translations even up to the very present. In his notoriously problematic version of 1924, Walter Scott went to such extremes of "improving" the text that he ended up transforming "an obscure religious document into a clear philosophical treatise, which it had never been."[18] A quarter of a century later, Scott's work was replaced by the much better edition of Nock and Festugière that has remained the standard reference for the Latin text. Only in 1991 did Claudio Moreschini publish a critical edition of the philosophical works attributed to Apuleius, including the *Asclepius*, in which he meticulously listed all previous attempts at improving or correcting the text.[19]

[16] Quispel, *Asclepius*, 253.
[17] Scott I, 50.
[18] Quispel, *Asclepius*, 255. Scott's editorial procedures have been universally condemned: see reviews by Cumont (1925), Nock (1925, 1927), Puech (1925), Reitzenstein (1925, 1927), Rose (1925, 1926, 1936), Coppens, (1926), Riess (1926, 1927).
[19] HT II; Moreschini, *Apulei Platonici Madaurensis Opera quae supersunt*, vol. 3, 39–86. See discussion by Quispel (*Asclepius*, 257–258), who describes Nock as a theologian

The Presence of Gods

After this long and troubled history of textual transmission, it is perhaps no surprise that the *Asclepius* as it has come down to us is anything but a clearly written and carefully edited treatise. It is quite disorderly and often repetitive,[20] and we have no way of determining how faithful our text is to the original Greek treatise that some Egyptian devotee penned down during the third century. In short, we are hearing echoes of distant voices and often cannot make out for sure what they were trying to say. Given these conditions, all modern translators have been struggling to make sense of the *Asclepius*, with limited success.[21] The only compensation is that an impressive apparatus of critical commentaries has been built up over time, providing a wealth of detailed references, explanations, and contextualizations for almost every single word or sentence. What, if anything, does this allow us to say about the spiritual perspectives of the followers of Hermes?

THE RELIGION OF THE WORLD

Famously, the author of the *Asclepius* describes Egypt as "the Temple of the Whole World."[22] He sees the country of the Nile as a sacred space

---

rather than a philologist, questions his expertise in Late Latin, and argues that "as an editor he was conservative, which made him find recognition among reviewers who were conservative as well."

[20] See e.g. Moreschini, *Dall'*Asclepius, 74–75; Parri, *La via filosofica*, 17–19.

[21] Copenhaver's literalist approach to translation (Cop, 67–92) often results in contorted sentences that make it hard to understand the meaning. Salaman's translation (SA, 53–98) is somewhat more readable but not always reliable in the details. Scott's translation (Scott I, 286–377) is based on his defective edition of the Latin original. Nock and Festugière's French translation (HT II, 296–355) is generally reliable and more easy to read, but one must beware of "Catholicizing" readings. Quispel's Dutch translation is a disaster, as promoting his own personal beliefs and idiosyncrasies overwhelms any attempt at translating the original with a semblance of accuracy (*Asclepius*; but see the new edition, with a limited number of improvements by van den Broek, in HG, 191–227). Only the Italian translation by Moreschini and the German one by Holzhausen (Moreschini, *Dall'* Asclepius, 121–201; CHD, 252–316; but see now also GWHT, 30–91) succeed in striking a good balance between textual precision and readability. Mahé provides the Coptic and Greek parallels to the Latin text in parallel columns, with two successive French translations of the Coptic (HHE I, 160–167; HHE II, 152–207; HT V, 122–132 and 146–191); but note the many and often far-reaching differences between Mahé's two French translations and between these and the English translations by Meyer published in collaboration with Mahé (Meyer, *Nag Hammadi Scriptures*, 422–423, 430–436).

[22] *Ascl.* 24. The metaphor was popular and widely spread (RHT II, 233–238; refuting Cancik and Cancik-Lindemaier, "Tempel der ganzen Welt," 49; cf. Fowden, *Empire to Commonwealth*, 46–47). For its centrality to Egyptian religion generally, see the splendid discussion in Assmann, *Search for God*, 17–52.

designed for divine worship, a marvelous structure of supreme harmony and beauty, filled with countless sanctuaries that are made to accommodate the gods so as to make them feel at home. From a Hermetic treatise preserved by Stobaeus, we learn how literally this was taken:

> [T]he most sacred land of our ancestors lies in the center of the earth, and the center of the human body is the precinct of the single heart, and the heart is the headquarters of the soul ... The central region ... is superior in itself and by virtue of all its inhabitants. In unremitting serenity it generates, adorns, and instructs.[23]

Thus Egypt, the temple of the soul, is located at the heart of the world. It is the home of divine instruction, the jewel of creation from which all good things flow. This "heartland" is of vital importance in the most literal sense, for the world (not just the earth, but the cosmos as a whole) is itself the body of a great living and breathing Being, a "second god" that can be apprehended by the senses and has been created or born from the ultimate divine Source.[24] The divinely appointed task of human beings is to take good care of the world and all living things; and since the Egyptians among all other human beings find themselves living in the most sacred space on earth, they have a special responsibility to act and behave with priestly devotion as servants of divinity. Human beings and the world are designed as "ornaments to one another,"[25] for both are divine, and both have received all blessings from the great universal Source of Beauty and Goodness. Ultimately all human beings should devote themselves to a life of "continuous service."[26] The spiritual keynote of the *Asclepius* is an ethos of loving care for all of creation, in an attitude of gratitude, worship, wonder, and praise for the awesome divine Source of bounty, wisdom, and beauty from which all things have come. Of course it is conventional to refer to this ultimate Source as "God," but in fact he is so far beyond language and human comprehension that no single name can possibly be appropriate:

> He has no name, or rather, he has every name, because he is One and All; so that one would have to call all things by his name, or give him the name of all things. ... Such a being, then, that cannot be perceived by the senses, is unlimited, incomprehensible, and immeasurable. It cannot be captured, nor grasped, nor hunted down. Where it is, whither it is going, whence it has come, or how

---

[23] SH XXIV 13, 15 (Litwa transl.). See discussion in Bull, *Tradition*, 175–178.
[24] *Ascl.* 8, 10.
[25] *Ascl.* 10.
[26] *Ascl.* 9–11.

it is, or what – all that is uncertain. For it moves in sovereign stillness, and this stillness moves in it, be it God, or eternity, or both, or one in the other, or both in both.[27]

The ultimate incomprehensibility and inexpressibility of divine reality, which is wholly beyond language and the senses, is a constant theme in the Hermetica.[28] To minimize the risk of overdetermination by our common religious language, where the word "God" cannot but evoke specifically Christian associations and assumptions, I will give preference whenever possible to terminology that emphasizes the *functional role* of this mysterious divine reality in the Hermetic imagination. Our texts leave no room for ambiguity in that regard: "God" for them means the ultimate creative or generative *Source* of all that is.[29] What it really is, in and of itself, we do not know. How it can be both immobile and moving, eternal but in time, is beyond our comprehension. Its true nature and manner of operation cannot be explained. All we know is that there is this mysterious Source from which comes everything that we take to be real.

Typical for the *Asclepius* (and many other Hermetic texts) is that this generative Source is addressed with deep emotion, marked by attitudes of profound love and gratitude for all the blessings that it bestows. Hermes and his followers are glad to be alive in this beautiful world, grateful for all the opportunities they have been given, eager to participate in the splendid work of creation so as to further enhance its perfection: this

---

[27] *Ascl.* 20 and 31. For the namelessness and ineffability of God, see also CH V 10; SH VI 18; HF 3a; HV 2 (B).

[28] For instance CH I 31, V 8; SH I 1 ("Noeticizing God is difficult; to speak of him is impossible even for a person capable of noeticizing") and 2 ("I noeticize, Tat, I noeticize. That which cannot be expressed, that is God"); HD I 4. On the need for this neologism "noeticizing," see below, Chapter 6 note 119. SH XI 2:1 and 11 imply that the immovable ultimate Source is even beyond "being" (cf. Litwa, *Hermetica II*, 69 note 6); see Chapter 9, p. 278 note 53.

[29] Whether this religious conception is ultimately Egyptian or Greek may be left for specialists to decide, but it is clear that the author of the *Logos teleios* tried to discuss it in Platonic terminology. This is demonstrated by the remarkable fact that although Arthur O. Lovejoy never mentions the Hermetic literature in his classic *The Great Chain of Being*, his discussion of the "two Gods of Platonism" (ch. 2) nevertheless remains the most incisive and perceptive analysis of basic Hermetic theology known to me. The God of the *Asclepius* is the Platonic "generative source" (Lovejoy, *Great Chain of Being*, 45–55), but it is typical for this tradition that the author tries to combine it with its logical opposite, the "self-sufficient absolute" (ibid., 24–45; see *Ascl.* 30, final lines). This fact alone undermines the old idea of a conflict between an "optimistic" and a "pessimistic" strand in the Hermetica: in fact, far from demonstrating the inconsistency or superficiality of Hermetic "philosophy," this conflict is inherent in Platonism itself.

is why they never stop expressing their gratitude to the divine Source of Being to whom they owe all these marvelous gifts. Because the great Source of all life and consciousness[30] must itself be alive and conscious in some sense, it can be addressed in personal and even intimate terms as "Father" or "Lord" – but in an explicit rejoinder, Hermes points out that these are just terms of convenience, concessions to our limited minds. For reasons of mutual understanding, we need to use some kind of name; but in fact, any such spoken word is no more than just "a sound that is produced when our breath strikes the air."[31]

As it turns out, terms such as "Lord" or "Father" are truly misleading, for the great Source cannot be reduced to one gender, as becomes perfectly clear from a remarkable and unique passage about the nature of creative fertility and divine procreation. The divine Source is both male and female:

> He, the only one and all things, infinitely full of the fertility of both sexes and ever pregnant with his own will, always begets whatever he wishes to procreate. ... And if you wish to see the nature of this mystery, consider the marvellous image of sexual intercourse between male and female. For when he [the man] reaches his climax, the semen is ejaculated. At that moment the female receives the strength of the male and the male receives the strength of the female, for that is what the semen does. ... Each of them contributes to procreation.[32]

Human sexual intercourse is described as an admirable image of the never-ending process of procreation by which the divine Source brings forth all of reality. The *Asclepius* says clearly that the internal male/female duality of the Source is mirrored on all levels of the reality to which it gives birth. The same creative polarity of male and female is found in the world as a whole and in each single human being as well: "each of the two sexes is full of generative power, and so is the connection of the two. Or to speak

---

[30] In line with my basic approach to translation, I am using the word "consciousness" not as a direct rendering of a Latin, Greek, or Coptic term but according to our modern understanding of the word. This is important because some modern translations (e.g. Copenhaver) render *nous* as "consciousness." I consider this misleading because all human beings have consciousness, whereas *nous* has a much more specific meaning, on which see above, pp. 12–16.

[31] *Ascl.* 20.

[32] NH VI[8] 65 (cf. the quite different version in *Ascl.* 20–21). That the Hermetic authors were interested in the biological aspects of sexual procreation is clear from SH XII, HO V 2–4, and HD X 1 (female "receptive fluid" versus masculine "seminal fluid"; see HG, 442 and HT V, 270 with 271 note 179: for some reason Mahé prefers the reading "dissolution, corruption").

more truthfully: their union [of love] is something beyond comprehension."[33] "Love" is therefore understood in sexual and erotic terms, as the ultimate mystery of birth or creation: it is not the *agapē* ("charity") of Christian language, and not exactly the Platonic *erōs* either, but the very power of life itself.[34] This makes the spectacle of human intercourse a sacred mystery to those who understand its true nature; but it must be practiced behind closed doors because the ignorant would ridicule it and embarrass the lovers.[35] Likewise, or so we may assume, while we are able to see the world that has come from the ultimate Source, we are barred from direct perception of the creative process itself.[36]

Hermes spends much energy trying to explain the nature of the world in philosophical terminology that would be understandable for an educated audience in the third century. With reference to theoretical concepts derived particularly from Platonism and the Stoa, he addresses such problems as the relation between time and eternity, space and place, spirit and matter, and the various genera and species of living beings.[37] While these aspects have been discussed at great length by classicists and historians of philosophy, they are of somewhat limited importance for understanding the nature of Hermetic spirituality. The *Asclepius* is concerned much more with evoking an imaginal vision of reality, as a beautiful whole in which human beings have a meaningful role to play, than with resolving technical problems of natural philosophy and metaphysics. Judged by strictly philosophical criteria, the text is a mediocre composition and an easy prey for critical deconstruction. It is full of minor contradictions and inconsistencies, some of which may already have been there in the Greek original while

---

[33] *Ascl.* 21.
[34] According to *Ascl.* 1, "divine love" itself is speaking through the mouth of Hermes. Moreschini is right to call this statement "very obscure" (*Dall'*Asclepius, 125 note 3), but it seems that "love" (awkwardly translated as "Cupido") is meant to refer not to the Platonic *erōs* but to the ultimate divine Source of life and creation: it is not the force of desire that impels us to move *toward* the eternal beauty of the forms or ideas but, on the contrary, a force that flows outwards *from* the eternal Source (consistent with a Iamblichean "embodied" perspective: see below, Chapter 4, pp. 106–112). For alternative solutions cf. CHD, 254 note 59.
[35] *Ascl.* 21; NH VI[8] 65.
[36] As will be seen (pp. 300–301 below), such direct perception is in fact granted to the reborn initiate who has attained conscious experience of the Ogdoad and the Ennead.
[37] For detailed analysis of these dimensions, see (apart from the extensive notes to the great standard editions and translations) Parri, "Tempo ed eternità nell'*Asclepius*" and especially Parri, *Via filosofica di Ermete*; for an attempt to turn Hermetic speculation into a consistent "theological philosophy," see Law, "*Das* Corpus Hermeticum," vol. 1 (for a critique, see Hanegraaff, Review of Esteban Law).

others may have been caused by faulty translations and the hazards of textual transmission. Unless a copy of the *Logos teleios* comes to light, these questions will never be resolved.[38] For instance, what does the *Asclepius* mean by "genera"? Are they to be seen as taxonomical families subdivided into species, or as Platonic archetypes, or both?[39] We do not know, but to be honest, it does not really matter all that much. The situation is similar to that of a modern spiritual treatise written for a "New Age" audience. Its author may be using concepts from natural science or psychology to express a spiritual worldview in terms that his readers will understand, but the result will be popularized science at best and will never satisfy true specialists of quantum mechanics or psychoanalysis.[40] Likewise, there is no point to reading Hermes as if he were a professor of philosophy – judged by that yardstick he is certain to fail.[41] Whatever value one may find in the *Asclepius* will have to do with its spiritual message.

That message concerns the nature of human beings and what it is that makes life meaningful. That man is referred to as the "third god" (the Source being the first, and the world the second)[42] is far less significant than it has seemed to countless scholars with Christian-trinitarian concepts in the back of their minds, for in fact it would be hard to find anything in Hermes' universe that is *not* divine! Apart from the divine Source itself, the cosmos, the planets, the earth, and human beings are all referred to as gods at some point or other.[43] Far more important – and rightly famous indeed – is the great emphasis that Hermes places on humanity's *middle status*. Note that the passage in question nicely illustrates the pattern of contradictions and inconsistencies referred to above, for although man has been described as a "third god," first we read that he is merely *connected* to the gods through his *nous*, and can "almost" (but not quite, presumably) attain divinity, whereas elsewhere we are told that precisely his share in mortality makes him even superior to the gods.[44] Irritating as such statements might be from a philosophical or theological perspective, they merely illustrate the futility of reading the *Asclepius* from such perspectives at all.

---

[38] On the disorder, repetitiveness, and lack of coherence of the text, see e.g. Moreschini, *Dall'Asclepius*, 74–75; Parri, *La via filosofica*, 16–17ff.
[39] See remarks in SA, 51–52; cf. Cop, 217.
[40] For many examples, see Hanegraaff, *New Age Religion*.
[41] Cf. Moreschini, *Dall'Asclepius*, 78.
[42] *Ascl.* 10. Cf. CH VIII 2, 5; X 14, 22; SH XI 2:6; HD I 1; VII 5.
[43] See especially *Ascl.* 19, 23, 27 about different types of gods.
[44] *Ascl.* 5; cf. 22 and NH VI[8] 68.

Man is therefore a great miracle, a being to be admired and honoured.[45] He passes into the nature of a god as if he is a god himself. He knows the nature of the daimons inasmuch as he recognizes himself to have come from the same source. He looks down on [*despicit*] the part of him that is human, because he has put his trust in the divinity of the other part. O, how much luckier a mixture human nature is! He is joined to the gods by a kindred divinity while looking down on the part in himself that is no more than terrestrial. All other beings, to whom he knows to be connected by heavenly disposition, he draws close to him in a bond of affection while raising his gaze to heaven. Thus he is placed in the happier state of a middle position: he values [*diligat*] what is below him and is valued by what is above him. He takes care of the earth, quickly mingles with the elements, and plumbs the depths of the sea with the sharpness of his mind. All things are open to him. Heaven does not seem too high, for he measures it as if from nearby with his soul's sagacity. No misty air troubles the directedness of his soul, no dense earth obstructs his work, no depth of water impairs his view. He is everything and everywhere at the same time.[46]

Rather than with theology or philosophy, here we are dealing with a spiritual poetics.[47] It is easy to see why this inspired passage made such an impression on later authors such as the Renaissance philosopher Giovanni Pico della Mirandola (1463–1494), who used it to exalt man as the only creature in the universe who can freely determine his own destiny for better or worse.[48]

In a later chapter we will look more closely at the importance of the faculty of *imagination* to how the spiritual Hermetica consider the relation between the divine Source, the world of appearances, and the

---

[45] See also HD IX 6.
[46] *Ascl.* 6. On man's unique status as an intermediary "double being," see also *Ascl.* 8, 22–23; cf. HD VI 1, VII 1–2, VIII 6 ("you have the power of not wanting to understand, you have the power to lack faith and be misled, so that you understand the contrary of what really is ... Only the human being is a free living entity, only he has the power of good and evil"); cf. HV 1 (A). On the uniqueness of this message in late antiquity and its centrality to the *Asclepius*, see Moreschini, *Dall'*Asclepius, 93. I translate *despicit* as "looks down on" (rather than "despises") and *diligat* as "values" (rather than "loves") to suggest a predominantly spatial rather than moral perspective. For the final sentence, see discussion of CH XI below, pp. 215–219.
[47] On the general importance of poeticity, see Hanegraaff, "Religion and the Historical Imagination." For an important technical analysis, see Sándor, "Poeticity" (where I would opt for the second position outlined on p. 302: poeticity is not "epiphenomenal as far as human cognitive processes are concerned" but represents "a significant aspect of natural language processing in human minds").
[48] Pico della Mirandola, *Oratio* 1–6 (ed. Copenhaver, *Magic and the Dignity of Man*, 459–461; cf. Borghesi, Papio and Riva, *Pico della Mirandola: Oration*, 108–117). For the actual ascetic and otherworldly rather than world-affirming message of Pico's *Oratio* as a whole, see Copenhaver, *Magic and the Dignity of Man*.

human mind.⁴⁹ At this point it is worth emphasizing that if human beings enjoy a uniquely central position in the Hermetic universe, their own center in turn resides in the divinity of their *nous*. As already indicated in Chapter 1, the importance of *nous* to the Hermetica can hardly be overstated, but a proper understanding is frustrated at every turn by the virtual impossibility of translating it into modern languages. As formulated by Nicholas Banner, "modern English lacks a word that even approximates its meaning."⁵⁰ *Nous* is usually rendered as "mind," "intellect," or even "consciousness," but all such translations are strictly incompatible with what the *Asclepius* says about it:

> But the *nous* [*sensus*] – that heavenly gift enjoyed by man alone, and not by all but only by a small number, only those whose consciousness [*mens*] is such as to be capable of receiving such a great gift – this *nous* indeed enlightens human consciousness, like the sun enlightens the world, and even more so – for everything that the sun illuminates is regularly deprived of this light, by the interposition of the earth and the moon at night. But the *nous*, once it is joined with the human soul, becomes a single substance with her through an intimate fusion, so that such souls are nevermore obscured by the delusions of darkness.⁵¹

Clearly this means that *nous* cannot be identical to the common capacity of "mind," "intellect," or "consciousness" that all human beings have in common: for the latter, our passage uses a different word, *mens*.⁵² By

---

⁴⁹ Below, Chapter 7, pp. 214–215.
⁵⁰ Banner, *Philosophic Silence*, 187 (here more specifically about *noēsis*, the activity of *nous*). Banner's subtle analysis of *nous* and *noēsis* in Plotinus (ibid., Chapter 6) is of the greatest relevance here. The founder of Neoplatonism was a native of Egypt born in Lycopolis around 205 (see MacCoull, "Plotinus the Egyptian?"), received his education in Alexandria and was alive during the period when the *Logos teleios* was written. The Hermetic references to *nous* read very much like simplified popular echoes of Plotinus' technical discussions. It is crucial to distinguish between two ways in which *nous* is understood: ontologically as primary being (*ousia*, as distinct from the One above being: Banner, *Philosophic Science*, 183), and epistemologically as the capacity to access or comprehend that being though *noēsis*. However, these conceptual realms of ontology and epistemology "are simply not separate for Plotinus, [who may well have been] the earliest known philosopher fully to equate levels of being with states of consciousness. ... *Nous* is an intelligible world, and also acts as a faculty of *noēsis*; but there is only one *nous*, which is both of these things" (ibid., 196; same point in Van den Kerchove, *La voie*, 29; I find Banner's remarks apply equally to the Hermetica).
⁵¹ *Ascl.* 18.
⁵² Note that the standard Latin translation of *nous* in the *Asclepius* is *sensus* (Moreschini, *Dall'*Asclepius, 87, 107–108). Cf. *Ascl.* 32, where *nous* is distinguished not only from *mens*, but also from *intellectus*.

contrast, *nous* must refer to a higher capacity for *noēsis* that is active or awake in only a small minority of spiritually "enlightened" human beings.[53] For them, it becomes like an interior sun that illuminates their soul so permanently and completely (through an "intimate fusion" that is never interrupted once it is there) that no room is left in it for delusionary shadows.[54] We are not dealing here with a spiritual elitism according to which only a few human beings are privileged to have *nous* and are capable of finding salvation. Rather, the universal divine Source has generously made the gift of *nous* available to all human beings,[55] but the sad reality is that only few of them show any interest. Most people are living lives that make them simply incapable of receiving it: they allow themselves to be "deceived by delusionary images"[56] rather than cultivating their potential for receiving *nous*. It should be noted that even if *nous* illuminates the inner universe of the human soul with divine light, still this does not necessarily imply perfect or absolute knowledge of transcendent reality in its true essence; rather, "human beings can perceive the things that are in heaven as if through a mist, in so far as the condition of the human *nous* permits it."[57] Direct and wholly unobscured knowledge of the absolute requires an extra step towards a unitive experience beyond *logos* and the internal senses, as will be seen.[58]

TERRESTRIAL GODS

By no means should the *Asclepius* be understood as a mere theoretical exposition of how everything in the world is hanging together. Hermes' instruction of Asclepius is marked by evident pedagogical concerns and a strong sense of moral urgency. Whenever he needs to discuss a particularly difficult and sublime topic, he calls for divine assistance and inspiration so that he may find the right words and his pupils may be able to understand them. Even so, he goes out of his way to instruct his audience at crucial spots to concentrate and pay close attention, because the true meaning of what he is about to tell them is so subtle that it can hardly be put into words at all.

---

[53] *Ascl.* 18, 22; NH VI[8] 66.
[54] *Ascl.* 18. On noetic enlightenment, see below, pp. 206–209.
[55] As described paradigmatically in CH IV 4; see discussion below, pp. 149–151, 196–197.
[56] *Ascl.* 7.
[57] *Ascl.* 32.
[58] See Chapter 9, pp. 297–302.

Now be completely present, give me your whole attention, with all the understanding that you are capable of, with all the subtlety you can muster. For the teaching about divinity requires a divine noetic concentration if it is to be understood. It is just like a torrential river, plunging headlong down from the heights so violently that with its rapidity and speed it outstrips the attention not only of whoever is listening but also of whoever is speaking. ... If you pay attention, you will see what I mean. For what I am saying is sublime, and divine beyond the power of human minds and purposes unless you hear and receive with full attention the words that are spoken to you. Otherwise they will just fly or flow past you, or rather, they will flow back in themselves and return to the waters of their own source.[59]

So as readers we had better pay attention too. A particularly difficult moment occurs when Hermes remarks that humans imitate the supreme Creator by making terrestrial gods. Evidently Asclepius's face betrays incredulity or even stupefaction about that statement, for Hermes interrupts his discourse to address him directly: "Does that cause you to wonder,[60] or do you too have doubts, like so many?" Asclepius readily admits to being confused and at a loss about what to say, but declares himself willing to be convinced.[61] Clearly his puzzlement remains, for a similar prickly moment occurs not much further on, when an evidently still incredulous Asclepius blurts out "You aren't talking about statues, are you?," to which Hermes responds with evident irritation: "It is *you* who are talking about statues! Look at your incredulity... You are talking about beings endowed with *nous* and spirit [*pneuma*] and call them 'statues'..."[62]

What is going on here? These passages were written at a time when communities of Jews could be found throughout the Roman Empire

---

[59] *Ascl.* 3 and 19 (translation Kingsley, "An Introduction," 38–39; because *sensus* in the *Asclepius* means *nous*, I prefer "divine noetic concentration" over "divine concentration of consciousness"). For similar expressions of urgency and demands for paying attention, as well as frequent calls on divine assistance, see *Ascl.* 8, 10, 21, 28, 32; CH XI 18. The importance of these elements is noted by Kingsley, "An Introduction," 33–35, 38–39; Moreschini, *Dall'Asclepius*, 81; and Van den Kerchove, *Hermès Trismégiste*, 84.
[60] *Mirari*: see discussion below, pp. 194–195. By writing "are you surprised?" (Cop, 80; cf. CHD, 248: "Wunderst du dich darüber?"), the implied contrast with the doubters is lost. In translating the Coptic parallel (ⲕⲣⲟⲁⲩⲙⲁ), Mahé had originally "t'étonnes-tu" ("are you astonished?" HHE II, 164), later "admires-tu cela?" ("do you admire that?" HT 5, 158). For reasons discussed below, I assume that the original Greek verb must have been θαυμάζειν and Hermes means to ask Asclepius whether he sees the animation of statues as the wondrous or admirable thing that it is.
[61] *Ascl.* 23; cf. slightly different formulation in NH VI⁸ 69.
[62] NH VI⁸ 69, parallel to the first lines of *Ascl.* 24. On the difference between the two versions, see CHD, 286 with note 144; my translation follows HHE II, 168. On Hermes' irritation, cf. HHE II, 64, 98; cf. Van den Kerchove, *La voie*, 188.

The Presence of Gods 63

(although precisely not in Egypt between 117 and the later third century)[63] while Christians were increasing in their numbers with astounding rapidity. At the very heart of their religious identity was a radical rejection of religious image worship, denounced by both traditions as the ultimate sin of "idolatry." What really defined the radical or exclusive monotheism of Jews and Christians, even more than their belief in One God, was an absolute horror of worshiping "graven images" (Exodus 20: 4–5) – this was the sin *par excellence*, the point on which no compromise could ever be possible, "the thick wall that separated the non-pagans from pagans."[64] For Egyptians who adhered to traditional modes of worship, these polemics and attacks must have been profoundly puzzling and disconcerting. After all, their entire religion was grounded in a daily practice of reverent care for the gods who were living in the temple statues.[65] What could possibly be wrong with such acts of piety and devotion? Nevertheless, younger generations of Egyptians must have begun entertaining a somewhat different perspective. Influenced by the mounting critique of image worship as well as philosophical doubts about the spiritual efficacy of material artefacts,[66] they may no longer have been so sure about the value of those ancient rituals kept alive by elderly priests in the decaying temples of Roman Egypt.

Precisely this tension seems to be reflected in our discussion. Hermes speaks like an initiated temple priest familiar with the daily practice of ritual animation,[67] whereas Asclepius sounds like an outsider. The traditional Egyptian practice of making images of the gods is under threat because of the people's ignorance; but when the master refers to it in

---

[63] The Jewish revolt in Cyrenaia and Egypt in the spring of 116 CE led to a devastating campaign of ethnic cleansing under Q. Marcius Turbo in 116–117. Few Jewish individuals or families and no communities remained in the area until the later third century (Kerkeslager, "Jews in Egypt and Cyrenaica"). Therefore Jewish influences on the Hermetica must almost always have been indirect, either based on sources predating the early second century or transmitted through Christians. I am grateful to Dylan Burns for his specifications on this point.

[64] Halbertal and Margalit, *Idolatry*, 237; and see the classic discussion by Assmann, *Moses the Egyptian*, 1–22; cf. Assmann, *Mosaische Unterscheidung*. For a further development, see Hanegraaff, "Trouble with Images"; Hanegraaff, "Idolatry."

[65] Moret, *Rituel du culte divin journalier*; and critical discussion in Lorton, "Theology of Cult Statues," esp. 131–147.

[66] Van den Kerchove, *La voie*, 185–187, 219. For another expression of Hermetic scepticism about image-worship, see HD VIII 3.

[67] Only initiated priests were allowed to approach the statues in their sanctuaries and perform the animation ritual: see inscriptions in the temple of Dendara, transl. in Derchain, "*L'Atelier des Orfèvres*," 234; Van den Kerchove, *La voie*, 198.

tones of praise, he is dismayed to notice that even his own pupil responds with doubt and incredulity – like "so many,"[68] as he bitterly remarks. That Asclepius does not understand the true nature of the gods is confirmed later on, when he refers to them as mere "statues," using Latin and Coptic words that suggest they are really just matter.[69] On the contrary, Hermes exclaims, they are living beings endowed with *nous* and spirit! They deliver oracles and accomplish great wonders – for they *are* in fact gods. A very important point is being made here, but its subtlety has seldom been recognized, so Asclepius should perhaps be excused for missing it too.

The key lies in the embodied condition of human beings, the makers of those gods.[70] We remember that when they were called a "great miracle," that was because of their unique middle status in the universe: the fact that each man or woman is a "lucky mixture" of both spiritual essence and terrestrial matter. Hermes sees this human condition of embodiment *not* as a regrettable fall into materiality but as a divine gift. He makes a point of emphasizing that precisely their participation in mortal existence makes humans more than divine: they are *superior* even to the immortal planetary gods.[71] Since the latter are made of nothing but celestial fire,[72] they are incapable of experiencing the full range of existence, whereas human beings can enjoy the best of both worlds. This makes them quite literally into "terrestrial gods" themselves, incarnated deities whose true vocation is to care for the world through their bodies while their spiritual part stays in communion with the divine source.[73]

---

[68] I am indebted to the sensitive discussions by Van den Kerchove, *La voie*, 185–222. See ibid., 189–190 for the *Logos teleios*' agenda of protecting a threatened practice and the connotations of "so many" (Latin, Coptic, and probable origin in Greek), which surely refers to the uneducated, ignorant, and impious rabble but may also be a semitism adopted by Christians as a self-designation. A further possible dimension to the confrontation between Hermes and Asclepius could be the transition from a traditional "locative" context represented by the former, with animated statues present in specific temple locations (cf. Bull, *Tradition*, 441), toward Hermetic spirituality as a more cosmopolitan, non-locative practice reflected in the perspective of the latter (cf. Chapter 2, pp. 45–46).

[69] For the Coptic ⲧⲟⲩⲱⲧ, see HHE II, 228; for the Latin *statuas*, see Van den Kerchove, *La voie*, 188.

[70] HHE II, 63–64.

[71] *Ascl.* 22; NH VI[8] 68.

[72] On "pure matter" as celestial fire, see HHE II, 219.

[73] Probably the most distinctive characteristic of the Egyptian cult ritual is that it "*was not conceived of as a communication between the human and the divine, but rather as an interaction between deities*" (Assmann, *Search for God*, 49; emphasis in original).

It is because they participate simultaneously in the world of matter *and* in the generative power of divinity that humans have the unique ability to imitate their creator[74] by making, that is, "making alive" or "giving birth to,"[75] gods in their own image. Those gods are really and quite literally "living beings endowed with *nous* and spirit" just like themselves. Thus we understand why Hermes is so irritated with Asclepius: to speak of the temple gods as mere "statues" is to miss the whole point. It is about as careless and ignorant as if he had described human beings as lifeless corpses! We also gauge the depth of the abyss between Hermetic spirituality and exclusive monotheism. That the veneration of images could be construed as an attempt to direct human worship away from God and towards the work of one's own hands is a thought that never seems to occur to Hermes – one imagines that it would have struck him as contrived and perverse, a malicious distortion based on regrettable ignorance. Obviously the divine Source of All That Is need not fear competition from any other god; he is far above such petty feelings as jealousy or anger anyway, and cannot be hurt or offended by our actions; he just generously dispenses Life and Light to all beings no matter what happens, without the slightest reservation. Therefore if humans turn away from those blessings, they are not offending God. They are only hurting themselves by neglecting the very source of universal energy that sustains their own existence. As for the human activity of making gods and caring for them in the temples, this directly mirrors the divine activity of making humans and caring for them in the temple of the whole world. As such, it gives symbolic and ritual expression to the great work of embodying the spiritual on earth while spiritualizing terrestrial bodies.

That the gods were alive in their temples, delivering oracles and accomplishing great wonders such as sending dreams or healing illnesses, was a perfectly common belief in ancient Egypt.[76] It survived well into the Roman period, when reference began to be made to mysterious ritual practices known as "the telestic art,"[77] concerned with animating

---

[74] The parallel is explicit at the end of *Ascl.* 23; NH VI⁸ 69.
[75] Assmann, *Search for God*, 46. A sculptor of divine statues was called a sꜥnḫ, "one who makes alive" (Zandee, "Hermetisme en het oude Egypte," 112).
[76] E.g. Derchain, "L'authenticité," 187; Iversen, *Egyptian and Hermetic Doctrine*, 37–38; Robins, "Cult Statues in Ancient Egypt"; Assmann, *Search for God*, 17–52.
[77] Dodds, *Greeks and the Irrational*, 291–295; Boyancé, "Théurgie et télestique néoplatoniciennes"; Lewy, *Chaldaean Oracles and Theurgy*, 495–496; Majercik, *Chaldean Oracles*, 26–27ff; Van Liefferinge, *La théurgie*, 92–97; Johnston, "Animating Statues";

statues so as to make them come alive.[78] In a well-known passage, the Egyptian philosopher Plotinus[79] referred to such practices in positive terms:

> And it seems to me that the ancient wise men who made temples and statues so that the gods might be present in them, showed insight in the nature of the All. They perceived that since the soul is everywhere easy to attract, it would be secured most easily by constructing some appropriate receptacle capable of receiving some portion of it, something reproducing it or representing it and serving like a mirror to catch an image of it.[80]

In a fragmentary treatise of the *Corpus Hermeticum*, we find the same idea of statues as "mirrors" in which incorporeal entities can be reflected and caught (and whose images are reflected back to the incorporeal world in turn).[81] Reflections in mirrors are transmitted by light, and in fact the animation of statues is described explicitly as a practice of *illumination*. The exact statements to which Asclepius responds with so much incomprehension can be translated most plausibly as follows:

Van den Kerchove, *La voie*, 201–222. Except for one isolated inscription from around 500 BCE, the adjective *telestikos* is not attested before Plato, *Phaedrus* 248e and 265b (Van den Kerchove, *La voie*, 203 note 86); by the second century CE, animators of statues could be referred to as *telestai* (Maximus of Tyrus, *Philosophumena* IV, 5: see Van Liefferinge, *La théurgie*, 94 with note 433); the exact term *hē telestikē technē* for animating statues was introduced by Proclus during the fifth century (Lewy, *Chaldaean Oracles and Theurgy*, 495–496). On the futility of trying to keep Neoplatonic *telestikē* apart from the Hermetic animation of statues (as nevertheless attempted by Van Liefferinge, who calls the parallels "almost perfect" but for some reason finds that fact "very troubling": Van Liefferinge, *La théurgie*, 96–98), see e.g. Johnston, "Animating Statues," 450–451; cf. Shaw, *Theurgy and the Soul*, 47 note 6, with reference to Derchain, "Pseudo-Jamblique."

[78] Johnston insists that no such practices are attested earlier than "very late antiquity" ("Animating Statues," 447; same point in HHE II, 228) because they presuppose a cosmology with "firm boundaries between each of the different ontological realms" (ibid., 459, cf. 446–450). Whether even the Egyptian "opening of the mouth" ritual has as little relevance to theurgy as she believes (ibid., 473–474) may be left for Egyptologists to judge; note that Bull is understandably puzzled by a Greek classicist agenda that seems to minimize Egyptian elements even in such texts as the Mithras Liturgy, "a papyrus found in Egypt, containing Old Coptic script, and referring extensively to Egyptian deities" (Bull, *Tradition*, 424–425 note 120).

[79] Cf. above, note 50 (MacCoull).

[80] Plotinus, *Enn.* IV.3.11.

[81] CH XVII. See discussion in Lévy, "Statues divines"; Van den Kerchove, *La voie*, 199–200. The embodiment of spiritual entities through mirrors and mirroring reflects a long speculative tradition (double pun intended!) with multiple applications in magical practice, from Plato and Aristotle through the Renaissance and early modernity. For a convenient introduction to many relevant sources, see Kodera, "Stuff Dreams are Made Of."

The Presence of Gods

Just as the Lord and Father (or God, as is his highest name) is the maker of the celestial gods, likewise man is the maker of the gods that are content to live close to human beings in the temples; and not only is he illuminated [or: are they illuminated], but he illuminates [or: they illuminate][82] in turn. Not only does [man] advance towards God, but he also makes gods.[83]

This language of illumination was current in discussions of the telestic art. For instance, Proclus writes that "by means of symbols and ineffable *sunthēmata* ("signatures")[84] [it] represents and makes statues suitable for becoming receptacles for the illumination of the gods,"[85] and the empowerment or animation of images could be described as "sparking" or "kindling into flame."[86] But the most important key passages are found in Iamblichus. Such is the power of the superior spiritual entities, he explains, that nothing can prevent them from being present in all things, very much like the rays of the sun. In a similar manner, the transcendent universal light of the gods illuminates the totality of existence while nevertheless remaining fixed in itself.[87]

[Therefore they] illuminate even the lowest levels, and the immaterial [beings] are immaterially present in the material. So nobody should be surprised if we say that

---

[82] Both Nock and Festugière and Moreschini (*Apulei ... opera quae supersunt*, vol. 3, 63) accept Paul Thomas' emendation, based on a scribal correction, of the plural *inluminantur/inluminant* to the singular *inluminatur/inluminat* (cf. Cop, 237). In this they are followed by all modern translators except Mead, who translates "... the gods who, in the temples, suffer man's approach, and who not only have light poured on them, but who send forth [their] light [on all]" (*Thrice Greatest Hermes*, vol. 2, 349). Since the statues are "illuminated" in both scenarios, the question is not crucial to my argument.

[83] *Ascl.* 23 (emphasis added). For the delicate problems of textual reconstruction and translation here, see Van den Kerchove, *La voie*, 208–210. Contra Mahé (HHE II, 164–165, 224) but in line with Festugière (HT II, 325 with note 193), she convincingly argues that behind the Latin *illuminare* must be a Greek word like φωτίζεσθαι. Similar conclusion in CHD, 285. Still, φωτίζεσθαι cannot be at the origin of the Coptic ϥⲧⲁϫⲣⲟ (thanks to Christian Bull, personal communication).

[84] See below, p. 69.

[85] Proclus, *In Cr.* 19.12 (see Johnston, "Animating Statues," 454). For similar statements, see Proclus, *Th. Pl.* 70, 9f (see Lewy, *Chaldean Oracles*, 495).

[86] Ζωπυρέω, ἀναζωπυρέω. See the fascinating *ouphor* ("opening of the mouth") invocation of a miniature cult image in the form of a ring, described in PGM XII 270–350 (Moyer and Dieleman, "Miniaturization", 59–66 with note 55; Ciraolo, "Warmth and Breath of Life," 247–248; cf. Hopfner, *Griechisch-Ägyptischer Offenbarungszauber*, vol. 1, § 808–809).

[87] Iamblichus, *Response to Porphyry* I 9: "the single, indivisible light of the gods ... is one and the same in its entirety everywhere, is indivisibly present to all things that are capable of participating in it, and fills everything with its perfect power," thus illuminating "even precincts of sacred statues" (see below, Chapter 4, pp. 109–110; and cf. Athanassiadi, "Dreams, Theurgy and Freelance Divination," 120).

there is such a thing as pure and divine matter [which] possesses a perfection that makes it suitable to receive the gods. ... Observing this, and discovering in a general manner the various receptacles convenient to each of the gods according to their specific characters, the theurgic art often combines stones, plants, animals, aromatic substances and other such sacred things that are perfect and similar to the gods, so as to compose from all of them a perfect and pure receptacle.[88]

This passage provides us with a close parallel to Hermes' second, longer, and most controversial statement about the animation of statues. Having briefly discussed how ideal incorporeal realities are reflected in their bodily manifestations, towards the end of his discourse he again connects the double nature of human beings with their ability to make gods. This "god-making passage" is of the greatest importance, not only for its intrinsic interest and the light it throws on Hermetic practice, but also because its defense of "idolatry" would very much determine the fate of Hermetic spirituality after the rise of Christianity.[89]

[M]ore admirable than all other wonders is the fact that man has been able to discover the divine nature and make it manifest.[90] As[91] our ancestors were very much confused as to what the gods were all about (for they were unbelieving and inattentive to worship and divine reverence), they invented a procedure for manifesting the gods. They empowered their invention by adding a virtue drawn from the nature of the world, thus bringing both natures together and mixing

---

[88] Iamblichus, *Response to Porphyry* V 23. For additional references to "batons," "pebbles," and "incense," see Shaw, *Theurgy and the Soul*, 167–168.

[89] Hanegraaff, "Hermetism"; see below, Chapter 10, pp. 331–332.

[90] I follow Salaman's translation of *efficere* as "making manifest" (SA, 94; and unlike him, apply it to the following sentence as well), but not his suggestion that the divine nature discovered by man was specifically his own. The standard translation (see e.g. Cop, 90) says that man not only discovered the "divine nature" (*divinam naturam*, i.e. not "the nature of the gods") but learned how to *make* it. This would imply a bizarre worldview reminiscent of Feuerbach but incompatible with everything the *Asclepius* and the rest of the Hermetica have to say about God, and is hard to reconcile with the later statement that humans "could not make souls"; it would, however, be congenial to Christian suspicions about the arrogance of idolaters who seek to reverse the order of creation and place themselves above God.

[91] *Quoniam* presents translators with a major problem of interpretation. Augustine was happy to choose the most direct and literal translation and conclude from it that humans therefore created idols *because* they were unbelievers (*De Civitate Dei* VIII.24). As this is obviously incompatible with Hermes' positive regard for the practice, many modern translators have tried to resolve the contradiction by interpreting *quoniam* as an indication of time: "they were unbelievers [etc.] ... *but then* they discovered..." My translation avoids an argument of direct causality ("unbelief leads to idolatry") while mitigating this suggestion of a sudden revolution; rather, it simply emphasizes that the discovery was beneficial and welcome as a corrective (similar solution in Mead, *Thrice-Greatest Hermes*, vol. 2, 381; CHD, 309; Van den Kerchove, *La voie*, 194; GWHT, 85).

them. As they could not make souls, they evoked the souls of daimons or angels, drawing them into these images through sacred and divine mystery rites, so that these idols could have the power to produce good and evil. ... The terrestrial and material gods are easily angered, because human beings have made and composed them of both natures. ...

[Asclepius:] What is the quality of those gods that are called terrestrial, Trismegistus?

[Hermes:] It consists of herbs, stones and aromatic plants that contain a natural divine power. They are entertained by frequent sacrifices, hymns, praises, and lovely sounds in a mode that reflects the divine harmony, so that the part in them that is celestial, which through constant celestial practice was drawn into the statues, may be content to endure the presence of humanity and remain there for a long period of time. This is how man fashions the gods. ... The gods down here all have their own specific assignments and are helping us out in a spirit of friendly communion, whether by giving specific prophecies through lots and divination, by foreseeing specific things, or assisting us appropriately in our human affairs.[92]

Exactly as in Iamblichus' theurgy, the natural virtue or power that allows statues to be illuminated by the gods resides in a mixture of "herbs, stones and aromatic plants." This, then, was Iamblichus' "perfect and pure receptacle,"[93] so perfect that it could receive and transmit the light of divinity. There is general agreement among specialists that such materials were supposed to work through the universal power of *sympathy*. In theurgical contexts, herbs, stones and aromatic plants were referred to as "material *sunthēmata*" or signatures;[94] they should be seen as being part of great "chains" (*seirai*) of creatures and objects ranging from the highest to the lowest levels of the universe that were all intimately connected, not through links of instrumental causality but because they participated in a common ontological essence that they reflected and could make present each on their own appropriate level.[95] This theory gave philosophical justification to the view that specific organic or inorganic substances could contain a higher divine "virtue" and render it present in a specific location such as a statue in a sanctuary.

---

[92] *Ascl.* 37–38.
[93] Iamblichus, *Response to Porphyry* V 23 (see quotation above).
[94] Shaw, *Theurgy and the Soul*, 162–169.
[95] E.g. Johnston, "Animating Statues," 454–458; cf. Van den Kerchove, *La voie*, 203–207. Johnston points out that *symbola* and *sunthēmata* are virtually synonymous terms in these contexts, and to understand them we need to "forget the connotations of our own word 'symbol'" (ibid., 454; see Struck, *Birth of the Symbol*). To avoid those associations, I follow Shaw (*Theurgy and the Soul*, 162–228) and give preference to the latter terminology. On theoretical distinctions between correspondences and occult causality as distinguishable from instrumental causality, see Hanegraaff, *Western Esotericism*, 124–128.

However, we are not just dealing with theories but primarily with *practice*. How do we explain that priests and philosophers were convinced that they had witnessed temple statues become alive and lighten up with the power of the gods? First of all, in our attempts to understand the animation of images, we are mentally handicapped by what is known as the "museum effect."[96] Our culture predisposes us to see god statues as inanimate "art objects" displayed in artificial environments far removed from their original setting: "standing on pedestals by themselves, unadorned, carefully spotlighted by track lights, against a subdued background."[97] But that is not how they would appear in their original cultic settings, where priests and devotees would typically interact with them in a much more physical and personal manner – touching, anointing, bathing, dressing, adorning, or feeding them, while speaking to them and entertaining them with songs and instrumental music.[98] Furthermore, as known to any cathedral visitor today, even such a familiar statue as the Virgin Mary in a side chapel, placed in a devotional setting of silence and respect enhanced by incense and candles, can dominate its immediate environment in such a powerful and natural manner that even determined unbelievers may find it hard to avoid the sense of some kind of "presence" over there on the altar. We are dealing here with a pre-rational phenomenon of "primary response" that makes it easy for human beings to invest god images with a mysterious power of life and agency, particularly in ritual settings that impinge directly on the senses of sight, hearing, and smell simultaneously.[99]

---

[96] Alpers, "Museum as a Way of Seeing"; Davis, *Lives of Indian Images*, 23.

[97] Davis, *Lives of Indian Images*, 17; and cf. ibid., 23: "Culturally heirs of the Israelite prophets who had disdained the religious idols of neighboring tribes (and of their own past) as false, and Cartesian in their ontological outlook, Western museum goers understood these old images from the past of another culture as fundamentally inanimate objects."

[98] Cf. Assmann, *Search for God*, 47: "the priest awakened, greeted, worshiped, purified, anointed, and dressed the cult statue and provided it three times daily with the huge variety of foods of the daily offerings." Since the logic of human "primary response" to images is similar across cultures, it is instructive to draw analogies with contemporary cases of image worship for instance in Indian contexts: see Davis, *Lives of Indian Images*, 19; or Waghorne and Cutler, *Gods of Flesh, Gods of Stone* (with a particularly striking cover image). The ritual "establishment" (*pratiṣṭhā*) of images as described by Davis (*Lives of Indian Images*, 33–37) is remarkably close to what we know of the "telestic art" of animation. Śrīvaiṣṇavas have a special ontological category for the god's "pure, luminous, immaterial matter" (*śuddhasattva*; cf. Iamblichus' "pure and divine matter") and animation is often thought of in terms of illumination or kindling a fire (ibid., 34).

[99] Hanegraaff, "Trouble with Images," 126–131, with a distinction between "primary" and "secondary" response that can be either positive or negative, resulting in four possible combinations. See also e.g. Freedberg, *Power of Images*, 1.

The Presence of Gods

Still, even this does not seem to be the whole picture, for we are told that sometimes the gods made spectacular appearances right in front of the theurgist. Such theophanies could be awe-inspiring, as explained by Sarah Iles Johnston:

> Iamblichus tells us that when the gods appear directly, they shine with a formless brilliance greater than any earthly light that moves more rapidly than the human intellect, although the god himself remains motionless. ... The brilliance of this light, morever, can be tolerated only briefly by terrestrial eyes – and even when it enters the eyes, such light is actually "seen" only by the soul. Although a brief encounter with divinity in this form could help purify the soul of the theurgist and enhance his long-term health, he was enfeebled and struggled to breathe while experiencing it.[100]

So what was going on here? The most reasonable explanation for such radical experiences leads us back again to the herbs and aromatics that were discussed in Chapter 2 and are mentioned both by Iamblichus and the *Asclepius* explicitly in the context of statue animation. In a characteristically thorough discussion, Friedrich Pfister pointed out that "Occasionally, fumigations also served *to arouse religious hallucinations and ecstatic states of consciousness*" (emphasis in original),[101] and Georg Luck has drawn the logical conclusion: most plausibly, "incense was *nominally* offered to the deities but *effectively* inhaled and experienced by the priests and some of the people."[102] For instance, the medical authority Galen reports that "*Enthusiasm* is a state of ecstasy produced in some people from smoke in the sanctuaries, when they see apparitions, listening to drums or flutes or cymbals."[103] Moreover, Iamblichus mentions not just fumigations inhaled by practitioners, but also unspecified substances that (alongside ritual incantations and rites of conjunction practiced in darkness) should be swallowed or ingested to make the

---

[100] Johnston, "Animating Statues," 461–462 (description based on various passages throughout Bk II of *Response to Porphyry*). Johnston again asks the crucial question "what was really going on?" (ibid., 466; cf above, Chapter 2, note 72) but does not seem to answer it conclusively.

[101] Pfister, "Rauchopfer," 283, with references to twelve classical sources. For abundant further source references to "power plants," fumigations, and their relation to statue animation, see Hopfner, *Griechisch-Ägyptischer Offenbarungszauber*, vol. 1, esp. § 386–387, 395–396, 464–472, 515–516, 530, 539–551 (with exact discussions of specific plants and substances), 808–809. Cf. Aufrère, "Parfums et onguents liturgiques," 30, 53.

[102] Luck, "Psychoactive Substances," 482; cf. Aufrère, "Parfums et onguents liturgiques," 40.

[103] Galen, *On Medical Terminology* 187, XIX, 462 K, as quoted in Luck, "Psychoactive Substances," 484, who discusses the textual corruptions (Hopfner's correction of *epi* to *hupo* seems logical; Rohde's correction of *sumbolon* to *kumbalon* makes sense given the mention of drums and flutes).

divine light manifest.[104] The conclusion, then, is quite straightforward. Rather than suspecting our sources of serious irrationality and insane delusions (assuming that they must have kept imagining things that we know to be impossible) or systematic deception (assuming that they must have made it all up), it is much more reasonable to assume that sometimes they really *did* see statues lighten up and witnessed other awesome luminous phenomena – not because they were deluded or crazy but because they were under the influence of psychoactive agents that we know to be capable of creating such effects.[105] Whether this dimension was also present in the ritual practices alluded to in the *Asclepius* is impossible for us to establish, but we can say with confidence that it was part of the complete scope of what "statue illumination" could mean in the context of the telestic art.

THE AGE OF DARKNESS

Having to dwell in material bodies was never easy for the gods. The impurity of their surroundings made them irritable and quick to anger. To endure such uncomfortable living conditions, to stay where they were and remain willing to assist humanity in caring for the world, they had to be entertained and kept happy "by frequent sacrifices, hymns, praises, and lovely sounds" reminiscent of their celestial origin. This is what we read in *Asclepius* 37–38. The implication is clear. If those sacred practices are ever neglected or abandoned, the gods will surely leave their statues and return to where they came from, leaving nothing behind but empty shells.[106] From a traditional Egyptian perspective as represented

---

[104] Iamblichus, *Response to Porphyry* III 14. Saffrey and Segonds translate καταπόσεις τινῶν as "*certaines drogues*" in both instances (Iamblichus, *Réponse*, 99–100); Clarke, Dillon and Hershbell (Iamblichus, *Iamblichus: De mysteriis*, 153, 155) translate the first instance as "potions" but unfortunately obscure the meaning in the parallel second instance by writing "objects that are akin to the gods who are about to intervene." That the light was "'seen' only by the soul" (Johnston, "Animating Statues," 462) is consistent with Iamblichus' emphasis on the faculty of imagination (το φανταστικόν, φανταστικὴν δύναμιν) "that is woken up ... by the gods to modes of apparition that are totally different from what human beings are accustomed to."

[105] For an excellent phenomenological analysis from a perspective of cognitive psychology, see Shanon, *Antipodes of the Mind*, esp. the chapter "Light" (ibid., 273–283); for the imputation of "irrationality" resp. insanity, see Hanegraaff, "Psychedelica."

[106] Van den Kerchove, *La voie*, 217; Assmann, *Search for God*, 48. Contrary to e.g. Quack ("Der *Asclepius*," 265) I therefore see a clear connection between the discussion of the statues and the famous "apocalyptic" passage that follows.

The Presence of Gods

here by Hermes Trismegistus, such an event would be not just regrettable but simply catastrophic.[107]

To really understand why this is so, we need to make an effort of the imagination. What were the gods all about? What was their essential function? Living deep inside the darkest interior of their temples, enclosed in very small spaces and protected from outside contamination by many protective layers, they have been compared to the pulsating energy at the core of modern nuclear reactors.[108] Their enormous and potentially deadly power had to be carefully contained and managed by trained professionals, the priests, so that it could be safely channeled and distributed towards the outside world. Without this beneficial life-giving energy at its very core, the social organism would fall apart.

According to the unknown author of the *Logos teleios*, that is precisely what he sees happening in his own time. Through the persona of Hermes Trismegistus we find ourselves listening to the voice of a third-century Egyptian who knows that the culture he cares for is dying. With deep sorrow and resignation, he tells his pupils that they are the last generation to be in touch with the truth:

> After us, no one will have that simple love, the love of wisdom, that consists only in knowing the divinity through frequent contemplation and sacred reverence ... The people who will come after us will be deceived by cunning sophistry and estranged from the true, pure, and sacred love of wisdom.[109]

Very soon there will be literally nobody left on earth who still knows how the gods are to be venerated and cared for. When that moment comes, what will happen? It makes perfect sense that immediately

---

[107] Assmann, *Search for God*, 17.
[108] This metaphor comes from Assmann and rests on the very architecture of temples such as that of Horus at Edfu: "From the exterior to the interior, the rooms become ever smaller, while the floor becomes higher and the ceiling lower. Corresponding to the diminution of space is an increasing darkness. The courtyard, which is flooded with light, is followed by the crepuscular Hall of Appearance. The inner rooms lie in deep darkness ..." (see ibid., 31–32). Hence the invisible divine light is contained in the temple's inner darkness, while the visible daylight outside is relatively empty of its presence.
[109] *Ascl.* 12, 14. Van den Broek remarks that "the author seems to have forgotten for a moment that this conversation is supposed to take place in an ancient past" (HG, 518 nt 407). I would turn the argument around, reading the *Asclepius* as reflecting real conversations of the kind that must have taken place between Hermetic teachers and their pupils, but slightly fictionalized so as to enhance their authority and their claim to universal validity ("these are not just my words but those of Hermes himself"). In this context, see also Van den Kerchove's reference to the rhetorical genre of *Progymnasmata* as a possible background to how figures such as Hermes, Tat or Asclepius are presented as models to be imitated (*Hermès Trismégiste*, 69–70).

after introducing the animation of temple images to a still incredulous Asclepius, Hermes continues by describing the terrible consequences that follow when the daily practice of veneration and divine worship is neglected or even abandoned altogether. This is perhaps the most famous passage from the entire Hermetic literature. It has been referred to as an "apocalypse" and a "prophecy," but neither of those labels is entirely right.[110] Technically we are reading a "prediction" of events that still lie in the future, but in fact it is clear that the author speaks from personal experience. What we are reading may be described as the vivid and almost visionary nightmare of a Hermetic devotee who is watching helplessly how his spiritual world is falling apart:

> All that is divine will depart from Egypt and return to heaven, and Egypt will be a widow, abandoned by the gods. Foreigners will enter Egypt and rule it. Egypt, and the Egyptians most of all, will be prohibited from worshipping God, and more than that, whoever will be found honoring and serving God will be severely punished. In those days, this land that is reverent beyond all other lands will become irreverent. It will no longer be filled with temples but with tombs, and no longer with gods but with corpses. O Egypt, Egypt, your divinities will be like fables, and so will be your divine modes of worship. ... Barbarians will surpass you in reverence, o Egyptian, whether they are Scyths, Indians, or others of that kind. ... And you, o river, a day will come when you will be filled with blood more than with water. Corpses will be piled up higher than the banks, and the dead will be mourned less than the living. ... Egypt, the lover of the gods, the home of the gods, the school of divinity, will become the picture of irreverence. That day, the universe will no longer be admired ... but it will risk becoming a burden to all people. So they will hold it in contempt, this magnificent world made by God, this incomparable work ... Shadows will be preferred over light, death will be preferred over life. Nobody will raise his gaze to heaven. The reverent man will be considered crazy, the irreverent man will be honoured like a sage, the coward will be considered strong, and the good man will be punished like a criminal. As for the soul and all that is related to it ... all that will be held laughable and ridiculous. Believe me: to be devoted to the religion of *nous* will even constitute a capital crime. A new legal system will be created, with new laws. ...
>
> And they will leave, the benevolent gods. But the wicked angels will remain with human beings to induce them, miserable wretches, to all kinds of evil excess: wars, looting, deceit, and all that is contrary to the nature of souls. Then neither will the earth be stable, nor will the sea be sailed, nor will heaven and the movements of the stars keep their balance. Every divine voice will be forced to fall silent, the fruits of the earth will rot, the earth will no longer be fertile, and the very air will hang heavy in lifeless torpor.[111]

---

[110] Mahé, HHE II, 68–97; Wigtil, "Incorrect Apocalyptic," esp. 2288–2289.
[111] *Ascl.* 24–25; NH VI[8] 70–73. My concern here is with the basic content of this passage rather than exact textual comparison between the Coptic and Latin versions. I broadly follow the former, but take inspiration from the latter for a few specific sentences.

It is not hard to place this description in the context of real life in Egypt under the impact of the third-century crisis. The country had of course been "flooded by foreigners" for centuries, ever since the conquest by Alexander and the emergence of a cosmopolitan Hellenistic culture radiating from Alexandria. Moreover, the final decades of the third century were marked by rampant violence and bloodshed, with Queen Zenobia's armies entering the country from the east and Upper Egypt suffering a series of invasions by nomadic tribes from Libya in the west and Nubia in the south.[112] Meanwhile the Roman authorities had always been treating Egyptian religion with contempt as mere "magical superstition" and introduced policies and restrictions that caused the priesthood to lose its prestige and social relevance. As the economy declined during the catastrophic third century, temples became dependent on the diminishing finances of local councils. Thus while the empire descended into chaos, the infrastructure of Egyptian religion fell apart.[113] Such developments were obviously traumatic for Egyptians who still tried to hold on to their ancestral traditions.

As for the "new laws" and "prohibitions" that are mentioned twice in the *Asclepius* fragment, they most probably have to do with an imperial decree issued in 199 CE by the Roman prefect of Egypt Q. Aemilius Saturninus. It imposed capital punishment on anybody found guilty of practicing divination, consulting oracles, engaging in public processions of cult images, or claiming higher knowledge based on "written documents supposedly granted in the presence of a deity."[114] The decree was publicly displayed in every Egyptian city or village and must have been deeply intimidating to practitioners of traditional Egyptian religion, temple priests in particular. It is true that this attempt to put an end to Egyptian "superstition" seems not to have been very successful[115]; but whatever its effectiveness, such an imperial decree meant that from the beginning of the third century onwards, not just ritual worship of temple images but even divinely inspired discourses such as we find in the *Asclepius* were officially illegal and punishable by death.

---

[112] Lindsay, *Origins of Alchemy*, 339–340, with many source references on p. 429 note 23.
[113] Assmann and Frankfurter, "Egypt," 161–162; Frankfurter, "Religious Practice and Piety," 321.
[114] Bull, *Tradition*, 447–449. See Parássoglou, "Prefectural Edict"; Rea, "New Version"; Ritner, "Egyptian Magical Practice," 3355–3358; Moyer, "Thessalos," 49–50; Moyer, *Egypt*, 255 note 190.
[115] Lane Fox, *Pagans and Christians*, 213; Frankfurter, *Religion in Roman Egypt*, 153–156.

No wonder then that the author of the *Logos teleios* believed the end was near. Under such terrible conditions, Egypt could no longer fulfil its sacred mission of caring for the gods in their temples, and therefore the gods were abandoning humanity. Seeing that foreign invaders were plunging Egypt into chaos and ruthless criminals could pollute the Nile with the blood of their victims, he must have drawn a perfectly logical conclusion: the dramatic end of Egyptian religion that had long been predicted in visionary prophecies was happening right here and right now.[116] In fact he was not wrong. What had begun under the Romans was about to be finished by the Christians – hence the continuing relevance of the Hermetic prediction to those who would translate it into Latin and Coptic during the fourth century.[117] As the country that once thought of itself as the "temple of the whole world" was turned into a desolate graveyard filled with tombs and corpses, the world was entering an age of utter darkness.[118] Henceforth deprived of any spiritual protection, human beings would be exposed helplessly to the malice of demons or wicked angels bent on poisoning their souls through the passions of the body. What, if anything, could still be done? The way of Hermetic spirituality sought to answer that question.

---

[116] For earlier literary models, some of which were probably known to the author of the *Logos teleios* and may have influenced his imagination, see HHE II, 72–90; Quack, "Der *Asclepius*."

[117] As was to be expected, Christian authors since the fourth century began interpreting Hermes' prediction, with obvious glee and *Schadenfreude*, as prophesying the victory of Christianity over pagan idolatry; and the argument made an impression on non-Christians as well (van den Broek, "Hermetic Apocalypse"). Hermes' prediction makes no reference to Christians and is unrelated to the systematic "holy war on idolatry" that would get underway after Constantine the Great; yet even as recently as 1986, Garth Fowden could still write that this basic fact "has not hitherto penetrated the scholarly mind" (*Egyptian Hermes*, 39).

[118] At the end of that age, God will finally restore the world to its ancient beauty, as briefly announced toward the end of *Ascl.* 26 / NH VI[8] 74.

4

Children of Hermes

> *Senses dimmed in semi-sentience, only wheeling through this plane,*
> *only seeing fragmented images prematurely curtailed by the brain,*
> *but breathing, living, knowing in some measure at least*
> *the soul which roots the matter of both Beauty and the Beast.*
> Van der Graaf Generator[1]

By the end of the third century or the beginning of the fourth, in or around the city of Panopolis (Akhmīm) in the Thebaid region of Upper Egypt, an Egyptian woman named Theosebeia was teaching some kind of secret knowledge to small circles of initiates.[2] She may have been a widow from an aristocratic family who had inherited her husband's or father's metalworking business along with the leadership of an artisanal *collegium* (a professional guild or society) that kept meeting in the workshop at her house.[3] What little information we have about her comes from letters written by a close associate or friend of hers, who was mentoring his "sister" Theosebeia by sending her technical advice along with moral

---

[1] Van der Graaf Generator, "The Sleepwalkers," album *Godbluff* (1975). Lyrics Peter Hammill.
[2] Zosimos, "The Letter heth" (VIII 1), in: CMA II, 239; English translation and preliminary edition of the Syriac original in Martelli, "Alchemical Art of Dyeing," 11–13 and 18–20; cf. Fowden, *Egyptian Hermes*, 125, 173–174, 188.
[3] Grimes, *Becoming Gold*, 102–103 (with reference to van Minnen, "Did Ancient Women..."; van Minnen, "Urban Craftsmen," 51; Venticinque, "Family Affairs," 285–288). For Theosebeia's house as a meeting place, see Mertens in ZMA, 197 note 1 (with reference to *Mémoires authentiques* VIII 1). See also Hallum, "Theosebeia"; and for her possibly aristocratic background, see Hallum, "Zosimus Arabus," 21 note 16.

warnings.[4] This man was an artisan specialized in metalworking – among other things, he knew the secrets of manufacturing temple statues that almost looked as though they were alive.[5] A native of Panopolis named Zosimos, "vigorous, capable of living,"[6] he was to enjoy enormous prestige among later generations as a chief pioneer of the technical practice that today is known as alchemy, the Hermetic art.[7] His letters provide us with some tiny glimpses – but no more than glimpses, unfortunately – of who the Children of Hermes may have been in real life.

While such artisans and alchemists stood laboring in their workshops to discover the secrets of matter, philosophers were pondering mysteries of the soul. It must have been roughly in the same period that two Platonists from Syria engaged in a heated argument about philosophy and religion, intellectual contemplation and ritual practice. Was it possible for the human soul to attain knowledge of its own immortal essence, or did it need to be saved and illuminated by the gods? Did salvation mean escape from one's bodily prison or could the body itself be filled with the light of divinity? Iamblichus of Chalcis believed that it could. In a lengthy letter to Porphyry, the famous pupil of Plotinus, he claimed that philosophy was not sufficient to find spiritual salvation. The human soul must be healed of its afflictions and its bodily vessel empowered by the gods, but none of that was just a matter of intellectual contemplation.

---

[4] Whether "sister" should be taken literally cannot be established with certainty (Mertens in ZMA, xvii–xviii), but I consider it unlikely. See e.g. Zosimos, *Mémoires authentiques* VIII 1 (ZMA, 27–28): it would be odd for her brother to write that he had been staying at her place "because of the attention you give me." Artisanal *collegia* often functioned as virtual families with members addressing one another as "father," "mother," "brother," or "sister" (Arlandson, *Women, Class, and Society*, 86–88; Waltzing, *Étude historique*, vol. 1, 75, 329–330 with note 3). Hence the popular idea of Theosebeia as Zosimos' *soror mystica* seems a later projection (Grimes, *Becoming Gold*, 105–107 with note 152).

[5] Zosimos, "The Letter Waw" (VI 8–9, 31) in: CMA II, 224–225, 228–229. On the importance of statue-making to understanding Zosimos' oeuvre, see Grimes, *Becoming Gold*, 34–41; cf. Fraser, "Baptised in *Gnôsis*," 36.

[6] Mertens in ZMA, xii note 4. That Zosimos wrote so many letters to Theosebeia suggests that they did not live in close vicinity, and he may have spent part of his life in Alexandria (Mertens, "Alchemy, Hermetism and Gnosticism," 165–166; Hallum, "Zosimus Arabus," 20). His account of travels through Asia minor in a letter preserved only in Syriac (French transl. in CMA II, 297–308; cf. Scott II, 113–114; Jackson, *Zosimos*, 4) seems to have been copied from Galen (Fowden, *Egyptian Hermes*, 120 note 15; Berthelot, "Sur les voyages").

[7] General introductions to Zosimos: de Jong, "Zosimus of Panopolis"; Principe, *Secrets of Alchemy*, 15–24; Hallum, "Zōsimos of Panōpolis." Just a tiny part of Zosimos' output has been preserved, which leads Mertens to call him a beautiful or sad example of "a literary shipwreck" ("Alchemy, Hermetism and Gnosticism," 167; Mertens, "Graeco-Egyptian Alchemy," 215).

Salvation required ceremonial *practice*, ritual theurgy or "the work of the gods," as cultivated by Egyptian priests in the tradition of Hermes Trismegistus.

At first sight, Zosimos and Iamblichus might seem worlds apart. The man from Panopolis and his female colleague represent an Egyptian milieu of alchemical practitioners and manufacturers of statues, practical people who made a daily living by working with their hands. By contrast, the philosopher from Syria was born in a wealthy noble family and could afford to spend his days as he liked. But while these people were moving in different social circles, they had important things in common. All three of them were followers of Hermes Trismegistus – in fact, it so happens that they are the only Hermetic practitioners still known to us by name. Moreover, although they came at it from very different perspectives, they shared a fascination with *the embodiment of spirit*. We have already encountered that theme in Chapter 3, where we looked at the strict parallel between temple statues and human beings, both defined as miraculous "double entities" with the unique capacity of participating in spiritual and bodily realities at the same time. Just as gods were embodied in physical statues, human souls were incarnated in physical bodies. As will be seen in this chapter and the rest of the book, this theme of embodiment is of central importance to what Hermetic spirituality was all about.

GETTING TOGETHER IN PRIVATE

Nobody knows who wrote the Hermetic treatises, and we have no direct descriptions by independent observers of Hermetic groups or individual practitioners. Zosimos, Theosebeia, and Iamblichus are as close as we ever get. But our evidence for what they were doing is fragmentary and hard to interpret, and so it is tempting for scholars to fill in the blanks. When Richard Reitzenstein published his foundational study *Poimandres* in 1904, he boldly identified Zosimos as "a member of the Poimandres community,"[8] and this reflected his broader concept of what the Hermetica were all about. He thought of them as the sacred scriptures of a sectarian movement that must have been founded by some

---

[8] Reitzenstein, *Poimandres*, 8 (followed in his own time by e.g. Bousset, "Review of Joseph Kroll," 737–738; and recently by Bull, "Hermes between Pagans and Christians," 224). Fraser calls him "a genuine Hermetic practitioner" ("Baptised in *Gnôsis*," 34; seconded by Bull). Mahé seems to quote him as part of the Hermetic literature e.g. in HT V, clxxv, cxlii.

Egyptian priest during the first century CE and had presumably led to "numerous Hermes communities" spread all over the Roman Empire.[9] But if such a large movement had really existed, one might ask, then why had no contemporary observer noticed it? When Festugière published the first volume of his *Révélation d'Hermès Trismégiste* in 1942, he sharply dismissed the whole idea as a fantasy: "j'avoue que tout cela me paraît du roman" – "frankly, all of that seems like a novel to me."[10] To him the Hermetica were just "reading mysteries" and "literary fictions," not the "gospel" of some actual social movement with communal practices.[11]

But if we take a closer look at Festugière's arguments, they quickly begin to crumble.[12] The problem is that his polemics left no room for anything else than *either* a church-like sectarian movement *or* a purely literary phenomenon. This narrow perspective can be explained in terms of a commonly overlooked pitfall of textual hermeneutics: if we look closely at how they present their arguments, we can see that most participants in this debate succumbed to the power of the anachronistic imagination and its vulnerability to suggestive language.[13] Reitzenstein had spoken of a *Poimandresgemeinde*; and the word *Gemeinde* is used in Protestant Germany for a Christian community that gathers on Sundays for the weekly service. Father Festugière, for his part, had Roman Catholic models in the back of his mind: he disagreed with Reitzenstein because he assumed that *if* any Hermetic groups had existed, we should have evidence of "a clergy, a church, and sacraments."[14] Since he found nothing reminiscent

---

[9] Reitzenstein, *Poimandres*, 248.
[10] RHT I, 82.
[11] Reitzenstein, *Poimandres*, 8: "... the history of the community whose Gospel [*Evangelium*] we have in front of us here."
[12] Festugière's four objections as presented in RHT I, 81–87, are surprisingly weak. (1) Hermes' literary authority does not make it "absurd" to assume the existence of communities focused on cultivating a spiritual Way of Hermes; (2) that discussions of natural philosophy were often combined with devotional passages carries no evidential force; (3) for the supposed absence of ceremonial, sacramental, hierarchical, or initiatory elements in the Hermetica, see my discussion on pp. 225–235; (4) the idea of a doctrinal conflict between "optimistic" and "pessimistic" treatises is little more than an obsession of modern scholars (see Chapter 3 note 5, and the present chapter), we need look no further than the history of early Christianity to know that "doctrinal antinomies" do not need to "fundamentally ruin any possibility" for a religious community to exist (as claimed in RHT I, 84), and the idea that communities require "doctrines" to exist is yet another example of Christian-theological prejudice.
[13] See also the Epilogue. What I refer to as the anachronistic imagination could be understood in terms of Gadamer's concepts of prejudice (see Chapter 5, pp. 132–138) but also in terms of prototype theory (see e.g. Hanegraaff, *Western Esotericism*, 3–5).
[14] RHT I, 83.

of "the sacraments of the gnostic sects: no baptism, no communion, no confession of sins, no laying-on of hands to consecrate the ministers of the cult,"[15] it followed for him that there had been no Hermetic communities, period. Among later scholars who *did* believe in their existence, we still see the same basic pattern: those with Protestant backgrounds would imagine them as akin to Calvinist "conventicles," while others with modern esoteric sympathies would even dream of Masonic "lodges."[16]

None of that makes any historical sense. In fact, it seems as though Festugière was arguing against his own deeper intuitions about the probable social setting of the Hermetica. He begins his influential chapter about "the Hermetic 'logos' of instruction" by evoking the image of the alchemist from Panopolis in an intimate spiritual circle:

> At first encountering the writings of Zosimos, one has the feeling of having entered a chapel, of having access to an esoteric religion full of passwords, fantastic beliefs, and strange rites. ... The tone is that of confidentiality, of an intimate colloquium between master and disciple, of the instruction that a father gives to his spiritual sons in private. ... Even though in most cases nothing specifies the location of the encounter, the atmosphere is that of a closed chamber, or even (as seen in the *Asclepius*) of a solitary chapel, a Holy of Holies.[17]

This time the chief background model ("an esoteric religion full of passwords, fantastic beliefs, and strange rites") is not that of Roman Catholic rituals but rather of *fin-de-siècle* French occultism, a type of esoteric practice that flourished in Paris and received much attention in contemporary literature and the popular press.[18]

---

[15] RHT I, 83.

[16] Interestingly, many of these ideas seem to have been born in the Netherlands. Van Moorsel's dissertation (1955) is an extreme example of how good observations and intuitions can get distorted by Calvinist theology as a general interpretive framework. The crypto-Pietist perspectives evident in van Moorsel's "Hermetic conventicles" and "Hermetism as a singing community" (*Mysteries*, 128-131) were further developed by the much more famous Gilles Quispel, who introduced the fantasy (rightly dismissed by Bull, "Ancient Hermetism," 116-117) of a "Hermetic lodge" and even "a sort of *Bnē Berith* lodge, for liberal Jews only" in Alexandria (Quispel, "The *Asclepius*"; Quispel, "Hermes Trismegistus"; Quispel, "Reincarnation and Magic," 170, 177, 186, 207). For Quispel's esoteric leanings, see the biographical overview in Köhlenberg, *Gnosis als wereldreligie*, 23-58; cf. Hanegraaff, "Third Kind."

[17] The passages about Zosimos in RHT I, 260 (first line of quotation) and RHT II, 29 (beginning of the "Hermetic 'Logos' of Instruction" chapter) are so close that I have combined them here to show the similarity.

[18] More specifically I am thinking of (neo)Martinism in the tradition of Papus, "the pope of occultism" (see Introvigne, "Martinism: Second Period"; André and Beaufils, *Papus biographie*). For the general milieu of *fin-de-siècle* French occultism, see e.g. Webb, *Occult Underground*; Churton, *Occult Paris*.

In this short review of the scholarly debate about Hermetic communities, we have already encountered Protestant church services, Gnostic sacraments, Pietist conventicles, Roman Catholic Masses, Masonic ceremonies, and Occultist ritual. All of these have been casually imposed on the Hermetica as hermeneutical prototypes or interpretive models of what might have been going on. But if we consult the sources themselves, we encounter something much more simple. These texts are all about teachers and pupils meeting in intimate, private, confidential settings. There is nothing to indicate large numbers of participants, and this makes it easy to see how Hermetic gatherings could escape the attention of external observers. The case of Theosebeia suggests that devotees could be either male or female and might get together simply in somebody's home.[19] In short, Hermetic spirituality seems to have been a very low-key affair.

Contrary to the notion of an organized "cult," such private settings are easily compatible with what we find in the sources. Due to the dominance of Festugière's "literary fictions" perspective, the social milieus of Hermetism were neglected for decades, until the spell was finally broken by Garth Fowden with his seminal study *The Egyptian Hermes* (1986). Specialists now began looking more seriously at the real-life contexts in which Hermetic spirituality must have been at home, not just in Alexandria but in Middle and Upper Egypt as well.[20] To Fowden's further credit, he clearly saw the relevance of those few historical personalities who had not just been physically around in Roman Egypt during the period when the Hermetica were written, but had spoken highly about them as well – the alchemist from Panopolis and the philosopher from Chalcis.[21]

MATTER AND THE SOUL

Zosimos and Theosebeia were no stereotypical armchair philosophers but practical people, crafts(wo)men used to laboring with their hands in smoky workshops.[22] For obvious professional reasons, it was very

---

[19] It is striking how many practitioners and authorities of early Graeco-Roman alchemy, whether fictional or historical, are depicted as female: Zosimos speaks with the greatest respect about Mary the Jewess and has Theosebeia as his chief pupil; other female practitioners appear under such names as Cleopatra or Isis; and among the pupils of Zosimos' rival Neilos was "the virgin Taphnoutiē" (see Martelli, "Alchemy, Medicine and Religion," 211).

[20] Fowden, *Egyptian Hermes*, Pt. III; but see also Fowden's earlier publications on these topics, notably "Late Antique Paganism" and "Pagan Holy Man."

[21] Fowden, *Egyptian Hermes*, esp. 120–141.

[22] For what we know and do not know about such workshops, see Martelli, "Greek Alchemists at Work."

important for such practitioners to keep improving their apparatus and technical procedures for refining and transmuting natural substances. But as they stood sweating above their furnaces, the chemical processes they were observing could not fail to make them wonder about the nature of material bodies – including their own – and the relation between corporeal realities and their spiritual counterparts – including human souls.

An anonymous *Dialogue of the Philosophers and Cleopatra* (probably from the same period, second half of the third century CE) illustrates how natural it was to think of the alchemical vessel as both a *tomb* of dissolution and death and a *womb* of life and rebirth.[23] We are told in vivid language about the sad fate of unspecified material bodies that are lying "imprisoned and powerless" in Hades, the dark realm of death. They are unable to move because their souls and spirits are in chains, "afflicted in darkness and gloom." But then salvation comes: they are brought back to life under the impact of a "medicine of life" (*pharmakon tēs zōēs*) that penetrates their dark prison from above. The "blessed waters" of this medicine awaken the bodies from their torpor, drive out the darkness that had invaded them, and fill them with the light of divinity instead. Having been restored to health, they are now able to reunite with their souls and spirits in a state of perfect unity and love.[24] While these passages are badly preserved and difficult to interpret, they can help us understand a famous sequence of hallucinatory dreams that Zosimos has left us.[25] The Cleopatra fragment and Zosimos' dreams both speak of metals and other material substances in strikingly anthropomorphic language. Zosimos for his part dreamt of people being boiled alive in altar-shaped vessels, and of priests subjected to "intolerable violence" as their bodies were mutilated and killed in sacrificial rites – all of this so that they might be reborn as spiritual beings.

---

[23] Fraser, "Baptised in *Gnôsis*," 41–42, 49.
[24] Greek text in Ideler, *Physici et Medici Graeci*, vol. 2; CAA II, 289–299, with French translation on pp. 278–287; thoroughly revised and improved Greek edition in Reitzenstein, "Zur Geschichte der Alchemie," 14–20, 23–25. English translation based on Ideler in Browne, "Rhetoric and Religious Aspects," 22–24; different translation based on Berthelot in Luck, *Arcana Mundi*, 373–378 (2006 ed.: 448–454). Charron failed to consult Reitzenstein ("*Apocryphon*," 443 note 19), and her reconstruction of the passages under discussion on pp. 444–445 must be used with caution, as it is based on fourteen short textual fragments cherry-picked from different parts of Berthelot's edition and placed in a different order under rubrics of Charron's own invention.
[25] Zosimos, *Mémoires authentiques* X (ZMA, 35–42); with discussion on pp. 207–225. English translations in Lindsay, *Origins of Alchemy*, 343–357; and Sherwood Taylor, "Visions of Zosimos."

It is a common mistake to assume that such descriptions by the earliest alchemists must *either* be just fanciful allegories of strictly chemical processes (as we understand them today) *or* refer to purely spiritual processes that are just being "projected" onto chemical materials. Zosimos and his contemporaries lived far before the rise of Cartesian dualism and had never heard of a "war between religion and science." They would have seen absolutely no reason to place chemical and spiritual processes neatly in separate categories, one for the body and one for the spirit. On the contrary, they were trying to understand how body, soul, and spirit could be manifestations of *one* single dynamic reality.[26] What makes the Cleopatra fragment important for our concerns is that salvation is described there *not* as a liberation of spiritual essence from the gross material body but the exact opposite: as a process of healing that *restores* the lost harmony of body, soul, and spirit. The bodies lying in Hades are not really dead – it is just that their spirits and souls have been overwhelmed so utterly by "darkness and gloom" that they have lost the power to keep their bodies conscious and alert. The "medicine of life" awakens them from the state of mortal lethargy and torpor into which they have sunk, by filling them with divine light that drives out the darkness. Having been cleaned of heaviness and impurity, they can find their way back to a healthy state of natural harmony and unity with their spirits and souls. In short, they are restored to an integrated *bodily* state of life, health, and happiness that sets them free to move out into the world.

So what had happened to those bodies in the first place? What caused them to descend into this semi- or unconscious lethargic state? How and why had they lost their freedom and agency? For people living in the third and fourth centuries CE, the answer would be perfectly obvious. As our souls are born into this material world, all human beings come under the dominating influence of the *heimarmenē*, the cosmic astral machinery of necessity or "fate." We fall under the spell of powerful forces, those of space and time, that limit our freedom by binding our souls and spirits to the passions of the body. As formulated by Garth Fowden, this is nothing less than "the grand theme of late Greek

---

[26] See the pertinent remarks by Principe, *Secrets of Alchemy*, 21–22. For a longer discussion, see Hanegraaff, *Esotericism and the Academy*, 196–197, with historical application on 197–207. For the problematics of Jung's "projection" theory, see ibid. 289–295; and cf. Mertens in ZMA, 208–211. I find it unfortunate that in her recent discussion of Zosimos, Grimes (*Becoming Gold*, 127ff) still continues the "literary fiction" tradition by speaking of "allegories styled as a series of dreams."

philosophy: the ensnarement of the soul in the bonds of fate, its liberation, and its return to its creator."[27]

But there it comes. *What exactly did it mean for the soul to "return"?* It would be hard to think of a question more central to Hermetic spirituality, for the manner in which practitioners answered it very much *defines* what "salvation" meant to them. To understand their answers correctly, we must come to terms with a notorious problem that has dominated much of the scholarly debate about the Hermetica: that of "dualism versus monism."[28] Does the soul need to *escape* from the material body, so as to return to its divine source and unite with it in a purely spiritual reality? Or could the soul return to unity in an *embodied* state? This second "monistic" option is what the Cleopatra fragment seems to suggest, but readers are bound to find it puzzling, counterintuitive, or simply insufficient. Since we know that the body will die, how could embodiment possibly save the soul?

Before turning to that question, we will look at the first, "dualistic" option. Because it might initially seem closer to what we find in Zosimos, he has often been framed as a "gnostic."[29] But what is gnosticism? Until just a few decades ago, scholars used to imagine it as a "dualistic" religion of "anticosmic world-rejection" which teaches that the spark of divinity trapped in the human body can only find salvation by escaping from the prison of this material world to find its way back to an alien reality of pure spiritual bliss.[30] But this understanding of "gnosticism" has been thoroughly dismantled since the 1990s and is now widely seen as "a dubious category" invented by Christian theologians.[31] The all-important point is that while such extremist worldviews of radical dualism were entertained in some milieus during the period of late antiquity, most religious or spiritual traditions that have come to be categorized

---

[27] Fowden, *Egyptian Hermes*, 88.
[28] Cf. Chapter 3 note 5.
[29] Stolzenberg, "Unpropitious Tinctures," 4, 17–29; Fraser, "Zosimos," 131, 137, 139; Mertens, "Alchemy, Hermetism and Gnosticism," 170–175.
[30] The classic statement is Jonas, *Gnosis und spätantiker Geist*; and see his influential volume *The Gnostic Religion* (discussion below, Epilogue, pp. 353–354). For the context of Jonas' thinking in the German theological/philosophical culture of the interbellum, see Lazier, *God Interrupted*, 27–72. For the remarkable mnemohistorical impact of this "gnostic imaginary" during later periods from antiquity to the present, see many contributions to Trompf, *Gnostic World*.
[31] The game-changing publications have been Williams, *Rethinking "Gnosticism"* (1996) and King, *What Is Gnosticism* (2003). For general overviews of the debate, see e.g. Brakke, *Gnostics*, 19–28; Burns, "Gnosticism, Gnostics, and Gnosis."

as "gnostic" do *not* fit the description – and this definitely includes the Hermetic writings. A further complication comes from the fact that "gnosticism" as a term is built from the word *gnōsis*, higher or superior salvational knowledge.[32] This has made it hard for scholars to resist the temptation of convenient but rather sloppy shorthand terminology: thus individuals who value *gnōsis* are routinely referred to as "gnostics," whether or not their worldview fits the frame of "anticosmic dualism."

The result of all this is a vague and expansive terminology that works well in popular books for the general market, but is concocted of two different concepts that have little or no real connection: that of a supposedly universal religious experience independent of history or culture on the one hand (*die Gnosis* in German, *la gnose* in French),[33] and that of a dualistic theology of world-rejection on the other. For all these reasons, it is preferable to avoid the "gnosticism" category altogether, as many scholars have begun to do since the 1990s, or otherwise use it in a more limited and precise sense, as referring strictly to beliefs in an evil or incompetent world-creator.[34] Whatever choices one wishes to make in this matter, in any case they should have little or no bearing on Zosimos, for his worldview fits none of the older or newer definitions of "gnosticism." He was undoubtedly a Hermetic practitioner in search of *gnōsis*, but that does not make him a gnostic.

---

[32] Hanegraaff, "Gnosis."
[33] In an otherwise solid and informative overview, Dylan Burns seems to impute a similar perspective to me as well, although my concern is not with *die Gnosis/la gnose* as a quasi-historical category but with the original meaning of γνῶσις as a special kind of "knowledge" (Hanegraaff, "Gnosis," 386–387; Hanegraaff, *Esotericism and the Academy*, 335–337). As a result, my work is seen as indebted to the tradition of Eranos religionism that inspired Gilles Quispel and his American pupil April DeConick (Burns, "Gnosticism, Gnostics, and Gnosis," 17–21; similar assumptions in Robertson, "Gnostic History of Religions"). My actual perspective is very different, as can be seen at many places in my work, from "Empirical Method" (1995) to the Eranos chapters in *Esotericism and the Academy* (2012), 277–314 and beyond. Burns and Robertson must have been led astray by my interest in the "reason–faith–gnosis" typology, which does have its origin in an obscure Dutch volume edited by Quispel that I read in my twenties (*Gnosis: De derde component*; see Hanegraaff, "Third Kind") but then developed along entirely different methodological lines (Hanegraaff, "Reason, Faith, and Gnosis," esp. 138–141; *Western Esotericism*, 87–93).
[34] For this third way between the discredited typological approach to "gnosticism" and a complete rejection of the category, see e.g. Bentley Layton, "Prolegomena"; Brakke, *Gnostics*, 27 and passim; Burns, "Gnosticism, Gnostics, and Gnosis," 12–13. As conveniently summarized by Burns, this third way defines the "'Gnostic' school of thought" in terms of "a distinction between God and an evil or incompetent creator-deity, and ... the kinship of humanity with the truly divine, as opposed to the creator or creation" ("μίξεώς τινι τέχνῃ κρείττονι," 82 note 1).

THE DIVINE ECONOMY

If the "gnosticism" frame is to be avoided, then what *can* we say about Zosimos' worldview? The most relevant texts here are two epistles addressed to Theosebeia known as *On the Letter Omega* and *The Final Account*.[35] They show that our two alchemists were involved in a rather heated dispute with other practitioners about the nature and correct use of *tinctures*. Tinctures are chemical agents capable of "transmuting" metals (that is, not just outwardly transforming them but inwardly changing their very nature), and a process of transmutation was signaled visually by the metals changing color. In the lower part of the distillation apparatus, specific transmuting reagents (*pharmaka*, a term that could mean "medicines" but also "poisons") such as sulfur, mercury or arsenic were exposed to heat. This would result in vapors ascending to the upper part, where a chemical reaction with "impure" metals such as lead or copper would produce a new volatile substance that would condensate and drain back to the lower part as "divine water" or "sulfur water" (playing on the morphological identity of *to theion*, "sulfur" and the adjective *theion*, "divine"), and react with its contents again.[36] In a "hermetically closed" vessel, the result was a continuous cycle of vaporization and condensation, finally resulting in a blackened mass or liquid that could then be subjected to further processes of tincturing or purification, which alchemists hoped would ultimately result in silver or gold.

The technical vocabulary speaks of tinctures (*baphai*) as "dyes" because they caused the metals to change color, and of *deep* tinctures (*katabaphai*) to emphasize that such procedures resulted in thorough and permanent change or transmutation.[37] These words for tinctures are etymologically related to the verb *baptō* (to dip or dye), which is the root of *baptizō*, to baptize. In other words, metals were being baptized,[38] exposed to vapors

---

[35] *On the Letter Omega*: see standard critical edition of the Greek with French translation by Michèle Mertens: ZMA, 1–10. See also the older translation by Festugière, RHT I, 263–273; and Greek edition with English translation in Jackson, *Zosimos*. For *The Final Account*, unfortunately we still have to use the unreliable Greek edition by Berthelot, CAA II, 239–246. See French translation by Festugière, RHT I, 275–281; and English translations in the old study by Lindsay, *Origins*, 334–340.

[36] On these chemical procedures and apparatus, see Mertens in ZMA, cxiii–clxix. For the basic procedure summarized here, see e.g. Fraser, "Baptised in *Gnôsis*," 40–41; Burns, "μίξεως τινι τέχνῃ κρείττονι," 86–88. On "divine water," see Martelli, "'Divine Water'."

[37] Stolzenberg, "Unpropitious Tinctures," 5 note 4.

[38] Charron, "*Apocryphon*," 442; Fraser, "Zosimos," 128; Fraser, "Baptised in *Gnôsis*," 39.

or dipped into liquids that were meant to purify and permanently change them – very much like the human figures in Zosimos' dreams. It is crucial to see that within the general "divine economy" (*oikonomia*)[39] of these processes, tincturing/dyeing was strictly equivalent to *spiritualization*. As explained by Lawrence Principe,

> [I]t is clear that [Zosimos] viewed the metals as composed of two parts: a non-volatile part that he calls the "body" (*sōma*) and a volatile part that he calls the "spirit" (*pneuma*). The spirit seems to carry the color and the other particular properties of the metal. The body seems to be the same substance in all metals ... Thus, the identity of the metal is dependent on its spirit, not its body. Accordingly, Zosimos uses fire – in distillation, sublimation, volatilization, and so on – to separate the spirits from the bodies. Joining separated spirits to other bodies would then bring about transmutation into a new metal.[40]

This is what Zosimos was teaching Theosebeia. However, it seems that other practitioners were trying to instruct her as well – to his considerable worry and distress. A group of competitors under the leadership of a priest named Neilos was promoting a different approach that, in Zosimos' firm conviction, was misguided and pernicious – a danger to the soul. They were working with *kairikai katabaphai*, "propitious" deep tinctures whose effectivity depended on the observance of astrologically opportune times.[41] Zosimos rejected these practices. He insisted that the true and authentic tinctures worked all by themselves, in a manner that was wholly "natural" yet independent of astral powers.

This controversy involved much more than just a technical disagreement. It concerned Zosimos' most basic beliefs about the origins and true nature of alchemy, and we will see that it can teach us something crucial about the goal of Hermetic spirituality. He was warning Theosebeia that

> [T]here is a race of daimons who avail themselves of women. Hermes also mentioned this in his *Physika*, and nearly every book, esoteric and exoteric, makes mention of this. So the ancient and divine scriptures said this, that certain angels lusted after women, and having descended taught them all the works of nature. And since they stumbled thanks to these women, he says, they remained outside

---

[39] Charron, "*Apocryphon*," 450 (referring to οἰκονομία in the Cleopatra fragment and its equivalent in NHC II 30: 26–27 as "plan of salvation").
[40] Principe, *Secrets of Alchemy*, 16. Cf. Janowitz, *Icons*, 114; Grimes, *Becoming Gold*, 51–52.
[41] Stolzenberg, "Unpropitious Tinctures," 4–9 (correcting the interpretation of Jackson, *Zosimos*, 1) and passim; Fraser, "Zosimos," esp. 137–142; Martelli, "Alchemy, Medicine, and Religion," esp. 210–211. On Neilos, see Hallum, "Neilos."

heaven, because they taught the humans everything wicked and nothing benefiting the soul. The same scriptures say that from them the giants were born.[42]

So we are told that human beings learned "all the works of nature" from daimons or angels, and this included the art of *chēmeia*. This belief was evidently based on a Jewish apocryphal Book of Enoch, *The Book of the Watchers*, where we read how the angel Asael "taught men to make swords of iron and weapons and shields and breastplates and every instrument of war. He showed them metals of the earth and how they should work gold to fashion it suitably ... And he showed them concerning antimony and eye paint and all manner of precious stones and dyes [tinctures]."[43] Yet other angels were teaching men astrological knowledge. The angels lusting after women had taught such arts to human beings in exchange for sexual favors, as the texts make perfectly clear, and because of these transgressions they were expelled from heaven.

All this might initially seem puzzling, because it is evident that Zosimos thought very highly of the art of *chēmeia* and by no means considered it wicked and without benefit for the soul. An explanation can be inferred from what follows after the passage just quoted: "The first transmission from them regarding these arts is [by?] Chemeu [*hē prōtē paradosis Chēmeu*]. He [Hermes] called [*ekalese*] this the *Book of Chemeu*, whence also the art is called *chēmeia*, and so forth."[44] As has been carefully argued by Christian Bull, Zosimos must be referring here to an *earlier* transmission of chemical knowledge written down by a certain Chemeu (Agathos Daimōn) in a book that carried his name. It is plausible to assume that he took this reference from the lost *Physika* of Hermes mentioned earlier in the same passage, which must have contained this mysterious "Book

---

[42] Zosimos as quoted in Syncellus, *Ecl. Chron.* 24 (Mosshammer, 14; cf. Adler and Tuffin, *Chronography of George Synkellos*, 18–19), transl. Bull, "Wicked Angels," 7, and see Martelli, "Alchemical Art of Dyeing," 10–15. In a fascinating *Letter from Isis to Horus*, a female practitioner describes how two angels wished to have intercourse with her and in return she made them reveal to her the mysteries of preparing gold and silver (Mertens, *Traité gréco-égyptien*; Mertens, "Scène d'initiation alchimique"; Mertens, "Sur la trace des anges rebelles"; cf. Fraser, "Zosimos," 132–137; Martelli, "Alchemical Art of Dyeing," 8–9; Bull, "Wicked Angels," 18–21).

[43] *1 Enoch* 8:1 (transl. Nickelsburg and VanderKam, 25). The biblical reference is Gen. 6. See discussion in Fraser, "Zosimos," 127.

[44] Zosimos as quoted in Syncellus, *Ecl. Chron.* 24 (Mosshammer, 14), transl. Bull, "Wicked Angels," 7; cf. different reconstruction in Martelli and Rumor, "Near Eastern Origins," 38 with note 9, following Mertens, *Traité greco-égyptien*, 67–68. For Hermes as the subject of ἐκάλεσε ("he called"), see Bull, "Wicked Angels," 8; and for Bull's identification of Chemeu as Agathos Daimōn (Kmēph), see ibid., 10–12, 23–24.

of Chemeu."⁴⁵ It probably consisted of twenty-four books, also including a *Book of Imouth* (derived from Imouthes, the Greek transliteration of Imhotep, that is Asclepius).⁴⁶ Zosimos seems to have believed that the true art of *chēmeia* taught by Chemeu – not to be confused with its false surrogate taught by the fallen angels – had been available since the creation of the world. It was reserved for those who were devoted to purifying their divine soul (*theian psuchēn*) chained to the world of the elements, and to liberating the divine spirit (*theion pneuma*) confounded with the flesh.⁴⁷ Even a philosopher as great as Aristotle himself did not know its secrets, because his knowledge too came from the angels and was limited to what they knew.⁴⁸

Zosimos therefore believed that the "propitious tinctures" used by his opponents stood under the influence of dubious entities, daimons or fallen angels, who used them to keep the human soul and spirit under their dominion. A passage in CH XVI explains with particular clarity how this was supposed to work:

[The daimons] try to reshape our souls after themselves and arouse them, lying in ambush in our muscle and marrow, in our veins and arteries, in the brain itself, reaching to our very guts. For as each one of us is born and receives a soul, the daimons arrayed under each of the stars who are on duty at that exact moment take possession of him. For they change places from moment to moment, not staying in position but moving by rotation. Those that enter through the body into the two parts of the soul twist the soul about, each towards its own energy. But the rational [*logikon*] part of the soul stands free of the tyranny of these daimons and remains fit to receive God.⁴⁹

This passage is a major key for understanding what spiritual liberation meant to the followers of Hermes. It says that from the moment they come into this world, humans are literally invaded by daimonic beings, ministers of the precise astral constellations that preside over their moment of birth. Having entered our bodies and taken full possession of them, these

---

[45] Bull, "Wicked Angels," 5–8.
[46] Bull, "Wicked Angels," 9 with note 28, based on additional information provided in the parallel Syriac passage (cf. note 2), see Martelli, "Alchemical Art of Dyeing," 11–12.
[47] Zosimos, "True Book of Sophe the Egyptian," (XLII 1), in: CAA II, 213; see Bull, "Wicked Angels," 10 and note 31 on the authenticity of this text (with reference to Mertens in ZMA, lxvii–lxix).
[48] Zosimos, "Book on Electrum" (Syriac, see French transl. in: CMA II, 264; cf. Scott IV, 114 note 1): Aristotle knew little about invisible things or spiritual substances because he did not know how to make himself worthy of being raised to the celestial realms.
[49] CH XVI 14–15; cf. SH IV 8 about how energies become active in the body from the moment a person is born.

entities are constantly influencing us from within, secretly and without our conscious awareness, by arousing our passions and shaping our souls in accordance with their own astral energies. In short, we may think we are in charge of ourselves, but in truth we are possessed by invisible forces that limit our freedom and control us from within. Zosimos was convinced that the "propitious tinctures," linked as they were to astrologically opportune moments, were used by the fallen angels and their priestly helpers as a snare to keep humans in this state of enslavement. Only the *natural* tinctures that had been revealed by Chemeu since the beginning of the world were free of such astral determination. They could be used safely because they would not interfere with the practice of spiritual liberation.

It is of the greatest importance to see clearly how this perspective differs from the stereotypical "gnostic" frame of "anticosmic world-rejection." The point is *not* that matter is evil and the world a prison from which the spirit must escape[50]: in modern terminology, we might say that the problem is not physical but psychological – it is not about the properties of matter or who made it, but about the soul's vulnerability. The world is a dangerous place full of powerful forces that seek to enslave our souls and make us forget our true divinity. As newborns we simply cannot resist the powerful daimonic invasion of our bodies and souls that takes place at our moment of birth; but what we *can* do is free ourselves from their dominion later on in our lives. Difficult as this may be (whence the small number of practitioners), we can learn to first recognize and then resist the powerful forces of daimonic temptation that try to keep us enslaved. We can practice techniques of liberation that weaken and may finally break their dominion over our souls. This possibility, I will be arguing, is utterly central to what the path of Hermetic spirituality was all about.

In *Letter Omega*, Zosimos is telling Theosebeia that according to Hermes himself, those who have not been liberated from dominion by the astral powers are like sleepwalkers, marching along like mindless zombies in a procession ruled by astral fate, with no conception of anything incorporeal.[51] By contrast, those who truly love wisdom can rise above the dominion of fate. If they succeed, they are no longer enslaved

---

[50] Pace "gnosticizing" interpretations as in Stolzenberg, "Unpropitious Tinctures," 29.
[51] Zosimos, *Letter Omega* 4 (ZMA, 2–3; RHT I, 265; Jackson, *Zosimos*, 20–21). We do indeed find a very similar description by Hermes in CH IV 4–5, 7 (Fowden, *Egyptian Hermes*, 123).

to bodily pleasure and do not care about the favors of worldly fortune or the ill chances it may bring, because they lead an inner life "at home with themselves."[52] While Zoroaster recommended magic as a means to vanquish fate, Hermes rejected such methods. The true spiritual human, the one who has come to know himself (*pneumatikon anthrōpon ton epignonta eauton*), has no need to waste his time on such practices or bother with the workings of fate:

> He should proceed on his path, devoted only to the search for self-understanding, and when he has come to know God he must hold fast to the ineffable Triad and leave fate to do what she will with the residue that belongs to her, that is, the body. And with this attitude of mind and this way of regulating one's life, he says, you will see the son of God become everything ... See him become everything: a god, an angel, a suffering human being. For being capable of everything, he becomes everything he wishes [and obeys the father] by pervading every body. He fills everyone's mind with light and pushes it up to the realm of bliss, where it already was before it assumed a body, following after him, filling him with desire, and guiding him into that light.[53]

Further on in *Letter Omega*, the human *nous* itself confirms once more that "the son of God" is "capable of everything and becoming everything, when he wills and as he wills."[54] For obvious reasons, given our Christian default associations, there has been much discussion about what Zosimos may have meant by this expression "son of God." I assume that here it means simply a human being who has gone through the experience of spiritual rebirth that (as will be seen) is at the very heart of Hermetic spirituality.[55] Perhaps "children of God" would be better, for we have good reason to assume that women too could be reborn, as "daughters of God." The rest of *Letter Omega* contains a rather confused mythical account about the external man of flesh and the internal spiritual "man of

---

[52] Zosimos, *Letter Omega* 5 (ZMA, 3 with pp. 69–70 note 28 about the meaning of ἐναύλιος and an important parallel in Arnobius; cf. RHT I, 266; Jackson, *Zosimos*, 22–23 with note 20; Stolzenberg, "Unpropitious Tinctures," 20).

[53] Zosimos, *Letter Omega* 7 (ZMA, 4 with extensive commentaries on pp. 74–82 note 36–44; cf. RHT I, 266–268; Jackson, *Zosimos*, 24–25). I follow Jackson's assumption that the person of wisdom must "hold fast to the ineffable Triad" rather than "dominate it" (the latter seems incompatible with the general meaning: he may dominate fate, but not the ultimate divine triad). Jackson's "this way of thinking and of regulating one's life" seems close to what is intended, except that (as noted by Mertens in ZMA, 78 note 37) νοέω certainly means more here than just "thinking" as we understand it today. As for ἄνθρωπον παθητόν: Jackson has "passible man," but I follow Mertens' "homme sujet à la souffrance." On πηλός as "residue," see note 82.

[54] Zosimos, *Letter Omega* 12.

[55] On the expression "son of God," see discussion by Mertens in ZMA, 79–80 note 37.

light." It is mainly because of these passages that Zosimos has been considered "a gnostic," for they refer clearly to such texts as the *Apocryphon of John* and twice mention the visionary Nikotheos, who belonged in the same contexts.[56] The connections between Graeco-Egyptian alchemy and these "archontic" traditions require deeper study[57]; but in the context of *Letter Omega*, I see these mythical frameworks as merely secondary attempts on Zosimos' part to find some kind of narrative frame for the practice of spiritual liberation that was central to his message.[58]

In *Final Account*, Zosimos returns to the two kinds of tincture, but now in a context that is framed as historical rather than mythical. He writes that the genuine and natural tinctures taught by Hermes were captured by the daimons, who kept them secret from the people and replaced them with their own "propitious" tinctures linked to the cosmic machinery of fate. It is here that the narrative takes a highly dramatic turn, as Zosimos tries to open Theosebeia's eyes about a dark conspiracy of planetary deities (*ephoroi*: "guardians," or "overseers"[59]), who are collaborating with the temple priests to keep humanity enslaved.[60] They are using their false tinctures in the context of sinister sacrificial rites.

Look what they did. They concealed the natural tincture and introduced their own non-natural tincture in its place, and they gave it to their priests. And when the village folk neglected the sacrifices, they prevented them from succeeding

---

[56] On Nikotheos, see Jackson, "Seer Nikotheos"; ZMA, 55–57 note 4; Fraser, "Baptised in *Gnôsis*," 47–49.

[57] Burns, "μίξεώς τινι τέχνη κρείττονι," 89, 103. As persuasively argued by Thomas Cowan, "archontism" should not be seen as identical to "gnosticism" but as referring to a more specific "transhistorical, theoretical pattern of spiritual thought" exemplified in Sethianism but also for instance in a literary author such as William Burroughs. It can be defined as "a sort of 'negative epistemology' as Marco Pasi calls it, that sees human existence as controlled by 'archons,' or agentified barriers built into the natural world in order to block the paths to psychic transcendence" ("Sidelined," 43–46; with reference to Pasi, "Arthur Machen's Panic Fears," 68).

[58] Methodologically, I am arguing against the effects of a "gnostic confirmation bias" that risks overestimating the importance of "gnostic" materials to any text that merely refers to them. Given Zosimos' concern with the evil machinations of daimonic powers, it is no surprise that such "Sethian" ideas would interest him; but he was clearly a voracious reader, and I see no good reason to assign a pivotal importance to these particular myths for understanding his worldview as a whole.

[59] See discussion of ἔφοροι, and its parallels in Proclus and Cosmas of Jerusalem, in Stolzenberg, "Unpropitious Tinctures," 22–26. More specifically, the deities are described as κατὰ τόπον, "guardians with respect to place" (ibid., 24), that is, they are not universally present but tied to specific places.

[60] On priests in Panopolis as astrological specialists, see Geens, "Panopolis," 324–325.

even in the non-natural tincture. All those then who learned the false doctrine <of the daimons> of the time produced waters [*hudrogennēsanto*] and their sacrifices multiplied through custom, law and fear. Still, the daimons did not fulfil even the false promises they had made. But then when a complete upheaval of the region had taken place and the region was torn apart by war and the human race had disappeared from it, when the temples of the daimons were no more than a desert and their sacrifices were neglected, they began to flatter those humans that remained, persuading them through dreams, because of their falsity, and through numerous predictions, to apply themselves to sacrifice. And as they renewed their false promises of non-natural tinctures, all those unfortunate people rejoiced, friends of pleasure and ignorant as they were. So dear lady, that is what they want to do to you as well, by means of their pseudo-prophet. These local <deities> flatter you, for they hunger not just for sacrifices but also for your soul.[61]

It is very likely that this terrible "upheaval of the region" refers to the events that took place in Egypt during the "crisis of the third century" and are echoed in the famous lament of the *Logos teleios*.[62] But whereas Hermes Trismegistus saw them as deeply tragical, lamenting the end of all true divine worship as the temples fell into decline and the gods departed from Egypt, Zosimos had a very different interpretation.

To understand his perspective, it is important to remember that he was an artisan specialized in manufacturing temple statues. This means that his clients must have been the local priests who, for obvious professional reasons, were trying to keep control over the metallurgical knowledge needed for such work.[63] Zosimos must have known them well and appears to have developed a low opinion of their characters and motivations. They were teaching the common people that statues became alive with the presence of the gods, but Zosimos' technical expertise must have made him sceptical about any such claims. In a fascinating letter to Theosebeia that survives only in Syriac, he gives

---

[61] Zosimos, *Final Account* 7 (Greek in RHT I, 366–367; French transl. in RHT I, 279–280; cf. English transl. in Lindsay, *Origins*, 338).

[62] As persuasively argued by Bull, who assumes that the "prophecy" too must have been contained in Zosimos' primary source, the lost *Physica* of Hermes ("Wicked Angels," 13–14); furthermore see the fascinating parallels with *Korē Kosmou* (ibid., 25–26), where we read how through the destructive passions, the dominion of fate blinds human souls to the divine spirit that surrounds them and leads the stronger to practice violence against those who are weaker (SH XXIII 48, 53).

[63] Martelli, "Zosime gréco-syriaque," 9, 12; Martelli, "Alchemy, Medicine and Religion," 206. It is possible that as an expert in manufacturing temple statues, Zosimos himself held priestly rank (Grimes, *Becoming Gold*, 17, 33, 74–75, 230 note 121; referring to Quack, "Religious Personnel," 290), but we do not have direct evidence (Bull, "Hermes," 219–220, 223–224). The question is not crucial to the present argument.

her expert advice about how to create the illusion of animation, for instance to give a statue the brilliant texture of a woman's skin.[64] He cannot help admiring the brilliance of his own art: "how moving it is to admire the invention of these arts, how beautiful is the sight!"[65] No wonder that people are taken in by these effects and frightened by the images, which seem so evidently alive that they do not even dare look at them straight.[66]

As Zosimos learned more about the priests and their motivations, he seems to have developed serious moral qualms about his own role in helping them deceive the common people. He speaks in tones of disgust about their envy, vanity, foolishness, malice, and poverty of spirit, and declares that he has finally turned his back on them and their writings, "but without jealousy on my part, for that is a product of passion."[67] Still, that doesn't keep him from being deeply upset about their abuses: "I condemn Neilos' disciples, who are astonished [about] and admire things that do not deserve admiration. In fact they are ignorant, and to them one must apply the saying 'know yourself!'."[68] So here again we have the basic opposition of those who seek dominion over others and those who wish only to gain control over themselves – the search for power against the search for self-knowledge.

We have seen that when Hermes Trismegistus praised the practice of animating statues in the *Logos teleios*, his pupil Asclepius responded with puzzlement and incomprehension. I suggested that we may see here the echo of a generational conflict in third-century Egypt: Hermes seems to represent the traditional perspective of an Egyptian priest, familiar with the daily temple practice and horrified about its decline, whereas Asclepius responds like a sceptical outsider. He seems to have the attitude of a younger generation that has been losing faith in the worship of statues and no longer expects salvation from local temple worship – for him, it can come only from a universally accessible path of spiritual liberation. In other words,

---

[64] Zosimos, "The Letter Waw" VI 9 in: CMA II, 225; Hunter, "Beautiful Black Bronzes," 657, 659; Martelli, "Zosime gréco-syriaque," 8.
[65] Zosimos, "The Letter Waw" VI 30, 228. Here and in the rest of the alinea I am grateful to Matteo Martelli for checking these translations from the Syriac.
[66] Zosimos, "The Letter Waw" VI 31, 228; Syriac with new translation in Martelli, "Alchemy, Medicine and Religion," 214. See color images of statues in Grimes, *Becoming Gold*, 37, 39–40, 43.
[67] Zosimos, "The Letter Waw" VI 4, 224. On jealousy or envy as a Hermetic vice, see Chapter 6 note 22; for envy as the eighth "tormentor" in CH XIII 7, see Chapter 8, pp. 245–250.
[68] Zosimos, "The Letter Waw" VI 31, 228; see Syriac with new translation in Martelli, "Alchemy, Medicine and Religion," 214.

we see the emphasis shifting here from a traditional "locative" to a new "nonlocative" cosmopolitan perspective focused on the individual.[69]

Zosimos would no doubt have shared Asclepius' scepticism, but for additional reasons of his own that reflect his belief in a sinister conspiracy of daimons and priests. The Hermes who speaks in the *Logos teleios* may be sincere in his praise of statue animation, but his pious convictions are clearly old-fashioned and quite naïve. He still believes that statues can come alive and the true gods inhabit them as long as the sacred practice of daily sacrifice continues; but in fact he is being duped by ruthless priests of Neilos' ilk. He does not realize that the entire machinery of temple worship no longer serves divinity but has fallen under the control of the enemy – those very same "wicked angels" that (in his own words) are teaching "unnatural things"[70] to human beings and try to poison their souls through the passions of the body. That statues come alive is an illusion produced by technical artifice, as Zosimos knows all too well. However, the daily sacrificial practice of statue animation *does* have the effect of attracting daimons, because such entities are nourished and replenished by the incense and smoke.[71] In other words, although the statues are empty of any divine power, the temples are in fact full of sinister daimons!

Zosimos is representative of a broader movement not from "optimism" to "pessimism" or from "monism" to "dualism" (let alone "gnosticism"), but from confidence in traditional cultic and communal worship controlled by the priesthood to a universal path of "inner liberation" centered on the individual. The children of Hermes believed that the world was going to hell, and they had reason enough to think so. Most people seemed spiritually blind to them, behaving like sleepwalkers or zombies, dominated by powerful passions that they could not control, manipulated by daimons and priests like puppets on a string. Once having seen through the illusion, what else could one do but take care of one's own soul first, work hard on cleaning it from impurities and breaking the control of the bodily passions, while doing one's best to convince at least some others to pursue the same path? That is exactly what Zosimos is doing at the end of his *Final Account* (again, note the many references to *space* and *place*):

---

[69] See Chapters 2 and 3, pp. 45–46, 64 note 68. On the individual nature of instruction, cf. Van den Kerchove, *La voie*, 55–56.
[70] Bull points out that the Coptic terminology in NH VI^8 73, 5–12 is a close match to Zosimos' "unnatural tinctures" ("Hermes," 222–223 with note 71).
[71] Fraser, "Zosimos," 141–142.

So do not allow yourself to be pulled back and forth like a woman ... Do not roam about searching for God, but sit calmly at home, and God (who is everywhere, and not confined in the smallest place, like the daimons) will come to you. And while being calm in your body, calm also your passions of desire and pleasure and anger and grief and the twelve portions of death [*moirai tou thanatou*]. In this way, taking control of yourself, call on the divine to come to you, and truly it will come, that which is everywhere and nowhere.

And without being told, offer sacrifices to the daimons: not such that entice them, not such that nourish and comfort them, but such that drive them away and make them disappear ... In doing so, you will obtain the true and natural tinctures. Do so until your soul has been healed. And then when you realize that you have reached completion, and having found the natural [tinctures], spit on matter, hasten towards Poimenandres, and having been baptized in the mixing-bowl, hurry up to your own people.[72]

Hermetic spirituality as taught by Zosimos was a meditative path.[73] Theosebeia needs no local priests or sanctuaries to find her way to salvation, for wherever she may find herself, the force of divinity will freely come to her if she sincerely asks for it. Daimons are tied to the "smallest place" of a physical statue deep in the interior of some temple somewhere,[74] but the true divine Source of being is free from local constraints and can be encountered "here, there, and anywhere."[75] Theosebeia must calm her passions, realizing that they have nothing to do with the true essence of who she really is but come from the

---

[72] Zosimos, *Final Account* 8. The "perfection" of the soul has slightly unfortunate connotations for us, due to the influence of Christian assumptions about "perfection," implying "sinlessness," implying hubris. Such a perspective is alien to Zosimos. What he means is that the soul is cleaned of its astral imperfections and regains a state of perfect spiritual health (see pp. 148-155, 244-253), so I have taken the liberty to translate τελειωθῆς as "healed" but τελειωθεῖσαν as having been completed or "reached completion" (see Fraser, "Baptised in *Gnôsis*," 43-44 for the initiatory connotations of those Greek words). As for γένος τὸ σόν: this has often been translated as "your own race" but really seems to mean "your own people," "those among whom you belong," or metaphorically "your own [spiritual] family." Cf. *Letter Omega* 5 about τὸ φιλοσόφων γένος: "our people" are all those devoted to the love of wisdom. Cf. Athanassiadi about the later Platonists' belief of belonging to a "sacred race" (*Lutte*, 24-26). Nowadays people might speak metaphorically of their "tribe."

[73] Cf. Zosimos, "The Letter heth" (VIII 1), in CMA II, 239: "the word of wisdom says that meditation is all. Isidore too says that meditation accomplishes the work"; and Zosimos, "The Letter kaf" (XI 21), in CMA II, 259: "So never stop meditating and working, and you will understand." The Syriac *hergō* comes from the verb *hrag*: "to muse upon," "to apply the mind" (Payne Smith dict.) or "to meditate" (Sokoloff dict.)(Martelli, personal communication).

[74] See Chapter 3 note 108: the statue stood literally in the "smallest place" inside the temple. Cf. above, note 59 about the ἔφοροι as κατὰ τόπον.

[75] Smith, "Here, There, and Anywhere"; and discussion in Chapter 2, pp. 45-46.

astral powers residing in her body and working through her soul. The daimons she can drive away by offering sacrifices, undoubtedly some kind of purifying incense or smoke.[76] Then when she feels that her soul is truly cleaned of all imperfections – that is, when she has been baptized in the "mixing-bowl" of purification – she can afford to spit on matter (not her body, *sōma*, but *hulē*: pure matter[77]), and join with her true spiritual family, her brothers and sisters, in the universal light of Poimandres, the divine *Nous*.[78] As we will see, this short passage contains references to no less than three Hermetic treatises: Poimandres as the divine *Nous* will appear in CH I, the "mixing bowl" in CH IV, and the "twelve portions of death" in CH XIII. We will return to all three of them in the following chapters.

How did the story end? Did Theosebeia heed Zosimos' advice or did she end up listening to Neilos and his companions? We do not know, but there are clear signs of anxiety on Zosimos' part about the circle of initiates in secret knowledge that she had gathered around her.[79] Did they include Neilos or the virgin Taphnoutiē? Zosimos seems to have been wary of secret practices: for him, all true knowledge relied on natural procedures that should be open and accessible, not kept hidden behind passwords and controlled by a power elite.[80] In the end, there was only

---

[76] Zosimos recommends a recipe associated with Membres and Solomon. See his longer discussion in one of the treatises transmitted in Syriac (CMA II, 264–266; cf. Scott IV, 140–141) about Solomonic "bottles" that presumably contained some kind of daimon repellent. See also Fraser, "Zosimos," 143–145.

[77] This admittedly drastic expression is usually seen to confirm a "gnostic" rejection of matter and the body. See also references to the divine soul "ensnared in the elements" and the divine spirit "mixed into the dough of the flesh" (Zosimos, "True Book of Sophe the Egyptian," [III.XLII 1], in: CAA II, 213; cf. Fraser, "Baptised in *Gnôsis*," 40). Again, in reading such expressions we must try to avoid a gnostic confirmation bias (see note 58), while not confusing references to "the body" with references to "matter." The "ensnarement" of the soul I would read psychologically, and the "dough" analogy merely observes that spirit and flesh are "mixed." I find it unlikely that an alchemist so deeply fascinated by natural substances and chemical processes would be contemptuous of bodies; but the attainment of spiritual liberation and deep relief as described at the end of *Final Account* could well inspire a momentary impulse of triumph over the utterly nonpsychical/nonspiritual stuff known as pure inert matter (ὕλη).

[78] While the entheogenic hypothesis should not be pushed farther than the evidence allows, note that here we have another practitioner inhaling the smoke of incense or suffumigations (somehow linked to or even identical with those mysterious "natural tinctures") and then making her meditative "ascent" to the spiritual realm.

[79] Zosimos, "The Letter heth" (VIII 1), in CMA II, 239 (see p. 77 with note 2); Bull, "Wicked Angels," 10.

[80] Fowden, *Egyptian Hermes*, 125; Fraser, "Baptised in *Gnôsis*," 37–38; Martelli, "Alchemical Art of Dyeing," 12; Bull, "Wicked Angels," 10.

one kind of knowledge that really counted. Neglected by the many, it could not be kept secret from those who sincerely searched it, because it was the knowledge of one's own true self.

DEEP EMBODIMENT

We have seen how the true son or daughter of God, this "spiritual human being who has come to know himself/herself" (*pneumatikon anthrōpon ton epignonta eauton*), must follow the path of self-understanding until (s)he attains "the ineffable triad" and is liberated from the daimonic powers of astral fate.[81] Those details in the text that have been read as an "anti-cosmic" rejection of the body I believe should be understood in a slightly different manner. They mean that whatever the astral powers may henceforth wish to do with "the residue [*pēlos*] that belongs to [fate], that is, the body"[82] is no longer of any concern to the practitioner because his or her spirit is not under their dominion anymore. The reason, as will be seen below, is that it has literally been born again in a *new* body that is invisible and not made of matter (*hulē*). It is still living in this world, to be sure, but no longer as a separate material entity whose range of perception and activity is constrained by the constellations that governed the birth of the *material* body. The radical liberty of the spirit's new body comes from the fact that it is beyond the restrictions of *any* particular time and place, so that no astral power linked to any specific moment and location can possibly affect it. This is why, in Zosimos' formulation, being reborn as a son of God means "becoming everything," "pervading every body," and "filling everyone's mind."[83] In other words, one's consciousness will be literally "everywhere," exactly

---

[81] See the quotation above, p. 92 (*Letter Omega* 7; ZMA, 4; Jackson, *Zosimos*, 24–25).

[82] In her long footnote 36 (ZMA, 74–78), Mertens notes that Zosimos seems to reduce the triad of spirit (*pneuma*), soul (*psuchē*) and matter (*hulē*) to just the first and the third (ibid., 75–76). This actually makes sense because the astral daimons influence both body and soul. In this passage, all that really matters (excuse the pun) is the liberation of the spirit from the compound of a body animated by a living soul; once this liberty is achieved, the incarnational bond is broken and all that remains is pure spirit and dead matter (i.e. the ὕλη on which Theosebeia can afford to spit, see note 77). The hulic body is an empty shell, very much like a corpse that astral daimons may play with as they will since the spirit is now beyond their grasp. I realize that the standard translation of Πηλός is "clay," but would like to suggest that in line with Zosimos' chemical practice, he may well have been thinking here of the residue, dregs, deposit or sediment left after an operation (Liddell and Scott, *Greek-English Lexicon*, 1401: "thick or muddy wine, lees").

[83] *Letter Omega* 7 (ZMA, 4; Jackson, *Zosimos*, 24–25).

like God himself who is "everywhere and nowhere," not pinned down to any particular space or place.[84] We will come back to this at length.[85]

Immediately after making these statements, Zosimos asks Theosebeia to consider "the tablet that Bitos wrote, and Plato the thrice-great [*trismegas*] and Hermes the infinitely great [*muriomegas*]."[86] This close association between Plato, Hermes and Bitos is confirmed by a Byzantine manuscript where the name is spelled Bitus.[87] Now it so happens that the only other ancient writer who mentions Bitos is Iamblichus of Chalcis – and what is more, he does so in the very sentence where he coins the concept of a "way" or "path" [*hodon*] of Hermes.[88] Having sketched how the Egyptians conceptualized nature, soul, and *nous*, he emphasizes that, for them,

> [T]his is not just a matter of theorizing, but they recommend that by means of hieratic theurgy we elevate ourselves towards what is higher, more universal, and superior to fate, towards God the creator, without using anything material and without concerning ourselves with anything else than just observing the critical moment. Hermes was teaching this path, but it is the prophet Bitus who explained it to king Ammon, having found it inscribed in hieroglyphic characters in a sanctuary in Saïs in Egypt.[89]

Further on in his treatise, Iamblichus confirms that Bitus translated these works by Hermes from Egyptian to Greek.[90] We can only wonder what it might mean that the *only* two authors still known to us by name who wrote about Hermetic spiritual practice are also the only two who mention this mysterious authority. Be that as it may, we have every reason to

---

[84] *Final Account* 8 (see quotation above, p. 97).
[85] Discussion of the *aiōn* in Chapters 7 and 8, pp. 213–219, 252–253.
[86] *Letter Omega* 8 (ZMA, 4; Jackson, *Zosimos*, 26–27). On these delightful references to Plato Trismegistus and the even infinitely greater Hermes, see Mertens in ZMA, 85–86 note 47–48.
[87] Whittaker, "Harpocration," 60 with note 15; see Fowden, *Egyptian Hermes*, 152–153; Mertens in ZMA, 84 note 46, who points out that this spelling confirms the common scholarly assumption that Zosimos' Βίτος must be the same as Iamblichus' Βίτυς (see text).
[88] As emphasized by Fowden, *Egyptian Hermes*, 140–141, 150–153. The same notion appears also in a passage from Porphyry, where he confesses his ignorance about the existence of a "universal way" (*universalem viam*) for the liberation of the soul taught also by the Indians and Chaldaeans (preserved only in Augustine, *Civ. Dei* X.32; see Fowden, *Egyptian Hermes*, 132; Clarke, *Iamblichus'* De Mysteriis, 13 note 10).
[89] Iamblichus, *Response to Porphyry* VIII 4–5. Iamblichus seems to differ from Zosimos' more radical perspective in suggesting that although we are elevated above the realm of fate, the ascent must still be timed for the right astrological moment.
[90] Iamblichus, *Response to Porphyry* X 7; on such translations, see also VIII 4 (without explicit reference to Bitus).

assume that it was largely thanks to these texts that Iamblichus attributed his praxis of theurgy to "the Egyptians."[91]

Iamblichus (a transcription from the Syriac *ya-mliku*, "he is king" or "may he rule") was born between 240 and 250 CE in a very wealthy and politically influential noble family from Chalcis (nowadays Qinnasrin), a town located southwest of Aleppo in northern (Coele-)Syria.[92] He left his native country to study philosophy but eventually returned to Syria, where he founded some kind of philosophical school or spiritual community in Apamea and died in 325 or 326 CE. While these meager biographical data are uncontroversial, almost everything else is a matter of conjecture. Standard accounts in the history of philosophy used to present Iamblichus as a pupil of Porphyry, suggesting a straight linear descent from Plotinus through Porphyry to Iamblichus. The barely hidden subtext was that this descent must be read as a decline, from the original philosophical genius that was Plotinus to his diligent and eloquent disciple Porphyry to the superstitious fantasies of Iamblichus and his weird theurgical rites.[93] However, although the two philosophers must have met at some point somewhere in Italy, most probably in Rome, there is no evidence that Iamblichus ever saw Porphyry as his master or Porphyry thought of Iamblichus as his pupil.[94] Nor do we have any certainty about Iamblichus' movements between his departure from Syria and his return.

This includes the question of his sojourn in Egypt. In his short sketch of Iamblichus' life, Eunapius writes that the Syrian philosopher became the disciple of a certain Anatolius, described as "second in rank to Porphyry."

---

[91] Fowden, *Egyptian Hermes*, 151, 153.

[92] For Iamblichus' biography, see Dillon, "Iamblichus of Chalcis"; Iamblichus, *Iamblichus: De Mysteriis* (ed. Clarke, Dillon, and Hershbell), xviii–xxvi; Athanassiadi, *Lutte*, 153–155, 160–162; Iamblichus, *Réponse* (Saffrey and Segonds), xxxiii–xlvi. The scant data we have about Iamblichus come from Eunapius' "Life of Iamblichus" in his *Lives of the Philosophers and Sophists* V 1–4 (see Wright, *Philostratus and Eunapius*; and French translation in Iamblichus, *Réponse*, xxxiv–xl).

[93] The palpable contempt for Iamblichus' theurgy among scholars even during the late 1980s is evident for instance in Armstrong, "Iamblichus and Egypt" (in fact about "Iamblichus and No Egypt") or Dillon, "Iamblichus" (where he is blamed for a trend with "mischievous results" that would continue "until the Athenian School recalled Platonism to some sort of sanity," ibid., 875).

[94] For this crucial point, see Smith, *Porphyry's Place*, xvii with note 18; Athanassiadi, "Oecumenism of Iamblichus," 244–245; [Porphyry], *Porphyre* (Saffrey and Segonds), xxv–xxvi, cf. xlii. Eunapius writes only that after studying with a certain Anatolius (on whom, see text), Iamblichus "attached himself to Porphyry," without further information about time and place (cf. Iamblichus, *Iamblichus: De Mysteriis*, xi (Clarke, Dillon, and Hershbell): "Our direct evidence of their association is not overwhelming").

This must be the Anatolius to whom Porphyry had dedicated one of his early works, a native of Egypt who was teaching peripatetic philosophy in Alexandria and later became Bishop of Laodicea in Syria.[95] Most likely it was Anatolius who introduced his pupil to the Pythagorean perspective for which Alexandria was renowned and that would remain a constant in Iamblichus' later work.[96] Additional clues can be gleaned from Eunapius' account of Iamblichus' friendship with Alypius, a philosopher of very tiny stature who was born in Alexandria and died there at an advanced age. Apparently the two met in public one day, each of them surrounded by a large crowd of his own pupils. Iamblichus was annoyed by the question Alypius asked him at such a public occasion, because he seemed to be insinuating that a wealthy man like himself could not be virtuous and just. However, he later changed his mind and came to appreciate the question. Eunapius writes that he ended up having "many meetings" with Alypius in private and even wrote his biography. Putting the pieces together, the most likely scenario then is that Iamblichus first studied in Alexandria with Anatolius; then went to Italy to continue his studies in the circle of Plotinus' pupils, where he met Porphyry; then moved back to Alexandria where he made his name as a teacher; and finally decided to return to Syria where he continued his teaching activities (even more successfully) in Apamea.[97] There is no mystery then about Iamblichus'

---

[95] See Goulet, "Anatolius." Porphyry's *Homeric Questions on the Iliad*, dedicated to Anatolius, were probably written before he joined the school of Plotinus (MacPhail, *Porphyry's* Homeric Questions, 2). Clarke, Dillon and Hershbell deny that Eunapius meant Anatolius of Alexandria; however, their argument rests entirely on the conjecture that his expression μετὰ Πορφύριον τὰ δεύτερα φερόμενος must mean "was deputy to Porphyry" (*Iamblichus*: De Mysteriis, xxi). In line with his concern to keep Iamblichus out of Egypt at all costs (see below, note 97), Dillon has him study with Anatolius in Caesarea ("Iamblichus," 867).

[96] Athanassiadi, "Oecumenism of Iamblichus," 246. For Iamblichus' Pythagoreanism, see for example Shaw, "Pythagorean Approach"; Shaw, *Theurgy and the Soul*.

[97] For the relevance of the Alypius episode and various other aspects of this scenario, see Athanassiadi, "Oecumenism of Iamblichus," 246; Athanassiadi, *Lutte*, 163. Although Dillon calls it "not improbable" that Iamblichus studied for some time in Alexandria, he still claims that "there is no evidence for it, either in Eunapius or elsewhere" ("Iamblichus," 867 note 15). On the contrary: Eunapius writes that Alypius was a native of Alexandria who died there too, and describes how at a time when the fame of both philosophers was in the ascendant, their paths just happened to cross one day, "like the course of two planets." What then could be more natural than placing this encounter and the "many meetings" they later had in Alypius' own city, Alexandria, at a time when Iamblichus was no longer a student but making his name as a teacher? Dillon can avoid such a conclusion only by moving Alypius together with all his students from Alexandria to Apamea or its environs, so that Iamblichus can come to "visit" him there ("Iamblichus," 873) – a scenario for which we truly have no evidence.

concern with Egyptian religion and his familiarity with the Hermetic literature.[98] Keeping in mind that he was a very wealthy man (undoubtedly with slaves at his disposal) who could afford to travel wherever he wished, I confess I find it hard to imagine that he wouldn't have used the opportunity to take a boat up the Nile and explore upper Egypt as well.

After Iamblichus' return from Italy to Alexandria, Porphyry must have been left with many unanswered questions about how his brilliant compatriot (Porphyry himself was a Phoenician from Tyrus in southern Syria) saw the exact relation between philosophy and theurgy, the ritual praxis that Iamblichus was advocating as superior to philosophy. Therefore he wrote him a letter with a series of questions. Although clearly meant for Iamblichus, it was addressed to one of his pupils, an otherwise unknown priest named "Anebo the Egyptian." Iamblichus responded on behalf of Anebo while presenting himself as another priest, "Master Abamon."[99] The original manuscript did not in fact mention Iamblichus as the author at all, but presented the text as "Master Abamon's response to Porphyry's letter to Anebo, and Solutions to the Questions it Contains."[100] It has been known as *De mysteriis* since 1497, when Marsilio Ficino published his translation under a new title of his own invention: *On the Mysteries of the Egyptians, Chaldaeans, and Assyrians*. Following the most recent critical edition, I will refer to it as Iamblichus' *Response to Porphyry*.[101]

What was at stake in this discussion? A separate letter from Porphyry to Iamblichus that has reached us only in fragments shows that among their topics of debate was the meaning of the famous Delphic saying

---

[98] For further support see the pertinent discussion by Quack, who reveals a pattern of anti-Egyptian prejudice among most scholars of Iamblichus and argues that while the influence of the *Chaldaean Oracles* has been overemphasized, that of Hermetic and other Egyptian materials has been played down ("(H)abamon's Stimme?," 150–156)

[99] I see no reason to doubt Iamblichus' identification of Anebo as a priest and as his pupil (*Response to Porphyry* I 1). Saffrey and Segonds follow Festugière's concept of "literary fictions" in speaking about a "game of Egyptian masks" based on common tropes of "barbarian wisdom" ([Porphyry], *Porphyre*, xxx–xxxvi, with an analysis by the Egyptologist Elsa Oréal on pp. xxxii–xxxvi; titled "La fiction égyptienne," the chapter refers explicitly to Festugière's "Les prophètes de l'orient," RHT I, 19–44). Quack rejects their argument on linguistic grounds and shows that "Anebo" and "Abamon" are both attested as genuine Egyptian names ("(H)abamons Stimme?," 149 note 1, 160–167). If Iamblichus received Porphyry's letter when he was actually in Egypt, and given his great enthusiasm for their religious rites, there is nothing strange about the presence of priests among his entourage of students.

[100] Sicherl, *Handschriften*, 166. The archetype with this title dates from between 1200 and 1450.

[101] Iamblichus, *Réponse à Porphyre* (Saffrey and Segonds).

"know yourself," which we encountered as central to Zosimos' perspective too.[102] Referring to Plato's *Charmides* and *Philebus* and probably alluding to Hermetic views of *gnōsis*,[103] Porphyry writes that knowledge of our immortal essence can lead us beyond the realm of mere speculation to direct contemplation of "the beings that really are" (*tōn ontōs ontōn*), the only source of true wisdom and felicity. A beautiful passage in Porphyry's letter to his wife Marcella shows how he personally conceived of such knowledge:

> What was it then that we learned from those men who possess the clearest knowledge to be found among mortals? Was it not this – that I am in reality not this person who can be touched or perceived by the senses, but that which is farthest removed from the body, the colourless and formless essence which can by no means be touched by the hands, but is grasped by the mind alone?[104]

Porphyry told Iamblichus that those who prefer their mortal terrestrial body over their immortal essence should be regarded with "pity and ridicule in the tragicomedy of this mindless life," and if we confuse our true essence with something as base as the body we are bound to become "miserable and unjust."[105]

It seems that Porphyry was in fact "ashamed of being in the body,"[106] and this is what must have made Plotinus' philosophy so attractive to him: it held the promise of direct experiential knowledge of our true spiritual essence that could lift us beyond our embodied condition. The theoretical justification for such aspirations lay in Plotinus' doctrine that the soul does not *fully* descend into matter but some part of it stays in the noetic world.[107] Embodiment causes our soul to lose its original state of crystal clear consciousness as it descends into a sleeplike state of reduced

---

[102] Of course this interest was shared by countless other authors as well (see Wilkins, "*Know Thyself*"); the relevant question here is how this saying was understood in the context of Hermetic spirituality.

[103] Porphyry fr. 273–275 (ed. Smith, 308–314). Porphyry, "Treatise on the Precept 'Know Yourself'"; French translation by Bouillet in Plotinus, *Ennéades*, vol. 2, 615–618; discussion by Saffrey and Segonds in [Porphyry], *Porphyre*, xxvi–xxviii.

[104] Porphyry, *To his Wife Marcella* 8. See Porphyry, *Vie de Pythagore / Lettre à Marcella* (Des Places, ed.), 110–111; transl. *Porphyry ... the Philosopher to his Wife Marcella* (Zimmern, transl.), 60.

[105] Porphyry fr. 275 (ed. Smith, 313).

[106] The famous opening sentence of Porphyry's *Life of Plotinus* seems to reflect his own perspective rather than that of Plotinus: see Song, "Ashamed of Being in the Body."

[107] Plotinus, *Enn.* IV.8.4 & 8. See the fundamental discussion in Steel, *Changing Self*, 34–38, who emphasizes the centrality of this notion to Porphyry's doctrine of the soul (cf. Smith, *Porphyry's Place*, 34: "it is clear that Porphyry stakes all on this means of freedom"; and see ibid., 38–39).

awareness and confusion; but because the soul's connection is never lost completely, we may sometimes wake up from the dream and see reality as it really is. Plotinus claimed that this had happened to him many times, as described in a famous passage:

> Often I have woken up out of the body to my self and have entered into myself, going out from all other things. I have seen a beauty wonderfully great and felt assurance that then, most of all, I belonged to the better part. I have actually lived the best life and come to identity with the divine, and set firm in it I have come to that supreme energy [*energeian*], setting myself above all else in the noetic [*noēton*]. Then after that rest in the divine, when I have come down from the *nous* [*ek nou*] to discursive reasoning [*logismon*], I am puzzled how I ever came down, and how my soul has come to be in the body when it is what it has shown itself to be by itself, even when it is in the body.[108]

The final sentence is particularly significant for our concerns, as Plotinus writes here that even while being in the body, still his soul retained the capacity of revealing to him its true essential nature ("what it is by itself"). It was about this precise point that Iamblichus disagreed with Porphyry, and the difference lies at the heart of their entire discussion about philosophy and theurgy. Iamblichus believed that the soul descends *completely*, so that no part of it stays in the noetic realm.[109] Embodiment means full immersion in matter. The entire soul plunges into a state of reduced consciousness and utterly loses its connection to the divine – a bit like bungee jumping without a rope. For Iamblichus this meant that we could not find liberation by means of philosophy alone: whatever Plotinus might have been experiencing in his moments of ecstasy, then, it could not possibly mean that his soul had woken up from the body and regained consciousness of its true essence up there in the noumenal realm.

For Porphyry, this must have been a shocking thought. If Iamblichus was right, did this mean that Plotinus had been deluding himself and his pupils about the liberating potential of philosophy? Iamblichus' completely descended soul looked to him like a spiritual entity hopelessly lost in matter, cut off, utterly unable to save itself by finding the way back to its origin. For a thinker like Porphyry, who was prone to severe depression and deeply pessimistic about "the tragicomedy of this mindless life," embracing Iamblichus' doctrine would be tantamount to concluding that even philosophy itself was an ultimately pointless pursuit. If the liberating

---

[108] Plotinus, *Enn.* IV.8.1 (transl. Armstrong, in Plotinus: *Ennead IV*, 397; with minor changes of punctuation, *nous/noēton* instead of "intellect," and "energy" instead of "actuality").

[109] Fundamental discussion again in Steel, *Changing Self*, 52–69.

knowledge to which it aspired was unattainable for human beings, because our soul cannot connect with the divine, then no hope was left in this life.

GODS AT WORK

Paradoxical as it might seem at first sight though, Iamblichus' doctrine of the fully descended soul was not an argument for existential despair. On the contrary, he clearly considered it a highly positive, constructive, world-affirming response to Porphyry's otherworldly pessimism. As such, we will see, his perspective was perfectly congenial to Hermes Trismegistus' "religion of the world" as outlined in the *Logos teleios*, where precisely the embodied condition of human beings makes them a "great miracle" uniquely capable of imitating their creator and giving birth to other gods.[110]

The essential point is that Iamblichus did not read Plato from a dualist perspective.[111] In the famous terms of Arthur O. Lovejoy, he did not think of divinity as the "self-sufficient absolute" residing in an alien otherworld of pure spirit (the object of a possible "flight of the alone to the alone"),[112] but as the "generative source" of manifestation that works from within.[113] This all-important difference between Porphyry and Iamblichus can be illustrated by Socrates' discussion with Diotima as told in Plato's *Symposium*:

> "You see, Socrates," she said, "love is not exactly the desire for beauty, as you think."
> "Well, what is it then?"
> "It is begetting and giving birth in beauty."
> "I suppose you're right," I said.
> "Of course I'm right," she said.[114]

---

[110] See above, pp. 59, 64. Of course this perspective sets him apart not only from Porphyry, but also from Plotinus' "black sheep" (Athanassiadi, *Lutte*, 121–144), the "heretical Christians" among his students who are usually described as "gnostics" (see e.g. Burns, *Apocalypse*, 8–47).

[111] On common interpretations of Plato as a dualist, and Iamblichus' non-dualist reading, see Shaw, "*Chôra*"; Shaw, "Theurgy and the Platonist's Luminous Body," 537–540; Shaw, "Taking the Shape," 150.

[112] Plotinus, *Enn.* VI.9.11. My concern here is less with how Plotinus himself might actually have meant these words (see Corrigan, "'Solitary' Mysticism") than with their mnemohistorical impact.

[113] See Chapter 3, note 29.

[114] Plato, *Symp.* 206e (the crucial words are Τῆς γεννήσεως καὶ τοῦ τόκου ἐν τῷ καλῷ); and cf. 206b, "ἔστι γὰρ τοῦτο τόκος ἐν καλῷ καὶ κατὰ τὸ σῶμα καὶ κατὰ τὴν ψυχήν", "it is giving birth in beauty, both in body and in soul"); cf. Shaw, "*Chôra*," 124; Shaw, "Theurgy and the Platonist's Luminous Body," 539.

Beauty here stands for the "great ocean" of ultimate reality that the lover of wisdom may finally behold after climbing all the stairs of Diotima's ladder, from the indirect or reflected beauty of physical bodies up to the ultimate beauty that is the source of everything good and true.[115] But Iamblichus was correcting Porphyry the way Diotima had been correcting Socrates. The point is *not* to escape from the cave of embodiment to a bodiless state of pure spiritual bliss, but quite the contrary: our task is to bring beauty *into* the world. Throughout her discourse, Diotima uses the language of conception, pregnancy and giving birth: her way toward wisdom through love is not about the infinite desire for some unattainable beauty that can exist only in an utterly transcendent realm beyond the senses, but about participating in creation and making an active contribution to our world. It is about using our divine superpowers to imitate the creator (the demiurge from Plato's *Timaeus*) and make the world better, more beautiful, and more true.[116]

How was that supposed to work? Because our soul does not itself have the means to reascend, Iamblichus argued, *it needs divine assistance*. The descent into embodiment is painful and difficult for the soul. It changes us not just externally but in our very substance.[117] As the body encloses our soul from all sides, our consciousness gets darkened as by the walls of a prison cell.[118] Our vehicle (*ochēma*) suffers serious trauma and damage while entering the dominion of astral fate, where it gets exposed to constricting daimonic energies and powerful irrational passions.[119] Perhaps

---

[115] Plato, *Symp.* 210d–211c. See Chapter 7, pp. 190–194.

[116] For the crucial explanation, see Plato, *Symp.*, 206c–e. The relevant Greek terminology is gender-inclusive in a way that makes it hard to translate into English, but means that both men *and* women can "impregnate," "engender," "beget," and "give birth" (Evans, "Diotima and Demeter," 13–16; cf. Dover, *Plato: Symposium*, 146–147). Diotima explains to Socrates that *all* humans "are pregnant" in body and soul, meaning that once having come of age, they naturally wish to "bring forth" (κυοῦσι, τίκτειν). Whether it leads to things of the soul or of the body, this process of bringing forth is *always* "beautiful," "divine," "immortal" and "harmonious" (*Symp.* 206c–d). Hence the true nature of the Goddess who presides over it, Moira or Eilithuia, is Beauty (*Symp.* 206d).

[117] This point is essential: see Steel, *Changing Self*, 52, 61 and passim. The notion was too radical even for Iamblichus' exegete Proclus, who to some extent returned to Plotinus' position (ibid., 73).

[118] Iamblichus, *Response to Porphyry* III 20. All this is based on Plato, *Tim.* 43a–44b; cf. de Vogel, "*Sōma-Sēma* Formula," 86–87.

[119] The standard analysis is Finamore, *Iamblichus and the Theory of the Vehicle of the Soul*. See Shaw's definition of daimones as "the blind, contractive, and individualizing energies that separate one thing from another," with reference to Iamblichus, *Response to Porphyry* I 5 (Shaw, "Theurgy and the Platonist's Luminous Body," 544, cf. 546; cf. Shaw, *Theurgy and the Soul*, 40).

most important of all, we lose our very connection with the realm of divinity. Therefore the gods, who are supremely powerful, need to come to our aid – and that is what theurgy was all about: the healing work or activity of the gods on earth.[120] For Iamblichus this work is not about lifting the soul beyond the realm of suffering but about alleviating suffering itself, by working creatively on improving – and ultimately perfecting – the world. One might say that Iamblichus is telling Porphyry to toughen up. Difficult and painful as embodiment may be, there simply is no other way for goodness, beauty and truth to become manifest in reality – literally, to get incarnated in this world.[121] Human beings should not seek to evade their responsibility by dreaming of escape but must accept the burden of suffering, working diligently in the body while serving the divine – the exact ideal described by Hermes in the *Logos teleios*.[122] Only by being creative in the world, by healing its afflictions and helping all beings move toward perfection can they find healing and fulfillment for themselves as well.[123]

For Iamblichus, then, the world was not a spiritual desert deprived of divinity[124] but a splendid theophany. As formulated by Gregory Shaw, "gods were everywhere: in plants, in rocks, in animals, in temples *and in us*."[125] But their presence had to be revealed, their voices made audible. That is what theurgy did, by means of ritual practices in which the gods appeared to human beings. Iamblichus spends much energy correcting Porphyry's misconception that theurgists are therefore trying to evoke,

---

[120] See Chapter 2, p. 35 (θεουργία, θεῖα ἔργα, θεῶν ἔργα) with note 51 for equivalent terms.
[121] Cf. Shaw, Review of Clarke, 493: "theurgy allows the soul to enter the supernatural through nature, for *there is no other way to enter it*." Cf. Shaw, *Theurgy and the Soul*, 42; and Shaw, "Theurgy," 12: embodiment as "an opportunity to cooperate in manifesting the divine."
[122] See the famous "mediation" passage of *Ascl*. 5–6 (discussion above, pp. 59, 64).
[123] Shaw, *Theurgy and the Soul*, 144; Shaw, "Theurgy," 15. Note that a very small number of "noetic" souls with extraordinary powers descend voluntarily for the sake of "the salvation, purification, and perfection of things in this world," specializing in purely "noetic rites" (Shaw, *Theurgy and the Soul*, 151, 199–215; Shaw, "Pythagorean Approach," 55–60).
[124] Iamblichus, *Response to Porphyry* I 8.
[125] Shaw, "Theurgy and the Platonists's Luminous Body," 538; Shaw, "Taking the Shape," 150, 154. See e.g. Iamblichus, *Response to Porphyry* I 6, I 9, III 12. In this regard, see Shaw's important correction of Emma C. Clarke, who in an otherwise excellent analysis interpreted Iamblichus' *Response to Porphyry* as a supernaturalist "manifesto of the miraculous." Shaw points out that "by *opposing* the supernatural to nature Clarke reinforces the rationalist paradigm she means to refute" (Review of Clarke, 493).

Children of Hermes

command, or otherwise exert power over the gods. On the contrary, he insists, the gods are wholly superior and infinitely more powerful than we are; they appear to us wholly by their own free volition; and in fact it is only *they* who are accomplishing the work.[126] A "magical" interpretation of theurgy would be similarly mistaken as Plotinus' "mystical" interpretation of philosophy, insofar as both give human beings some kind of control over divinity whereas in fact they have none. In theurgic ritual, the gods themselves are giving dazzling demonstrations of their power and will, making their presence known through luminous epiphanies and other spectacular phenomena. The practitioner is facilitating their appearance and needs to make himself receptive, but does so blindly: his mind "neither understands nor directs epiphanies, it is merely a passive witness to the divine appearances (*phasmata*)."[127]

So what was really happening in those rituals of theurgy that Iamblichus insists are the *only* way for the soul to find peace and happiness?[128] Unfortunately for us, he stuck quite closely to Porphyry's questions and did not go into much specific detail. It is nevertheless clear that in one way or another, theurgical practice involved visible manifestations or revelations of divine *Light*.[129] Incorporeal Light is the all-encompassing reality of the gods. It surrounds and envelops the realm of Being or nature, which in turn surrounds and envelops our bodies and souls.[130] Referring to the commonplace saying that "all is full of gods,"[131] this is how Iamblichus explains the greater divine reality of universal Light:

> So even as sunlight envelops what it illuminates, likewise the power of the gods embraces from outside all that participates in it. And just as light is present in the air without blending with it ... likewise the light of the gods not only illuminates while staying by itself, but while firmly established in itself it proceeds through the totality of existence. ... In the same manner then the entire world, spatially divided as it is, brings about a division throughout itself of the single, indivisible

---

[126] Iamblichus, *Response to Porphyry* I 12, I 14, II 11, III 17–19, IV 1, V 25. For discussion, see for instance Clarke, *Iamblichus' De Mysteriis*, 47–50; Shaw, Review of Clarke, 491.

[127] Shaw, Review of Clarke, 492. On actions and symbols used blindly, without understanding their rationale, see the famous passage about "unspeakable acts" and "inexpressible symbols that are understood only by the gods" in Iamblichus, *Response to Porphyry* II 11; cf. Shaw, "Theurgy," 18–20.

[128] Iamblichus, *Response to Porphyry* X 1, 4, 6.

[129] Clarke, *Iamblichus' De Mysteriis*, 25. For a general overview of light in theurgy, see Johnston, "*Fiat Lux*"; and see my discussion on pp. 66–67, 71–72, 83–84, 109–111.

[130] Iamblichus, *Response to Porphyry* I 8.

[131] Iamblichus, *Response to Porphyry* I 9 (see Iamblichus, *Réponse* [Saffrey and Segonds], 245 note 5 for the sources of this *lieu commun*).

light of the gods. This light is one and the same in its entirety everywhere, is indivisibly present to all things that are capable of participating in it, and fills everything with its perfect power ...[132]

It appears that by whatever techniques they may have been using, theurgical ritual could induce powerful alterations of consciousness that allowed participants to be possessed by the gods (the literal meaning of "enthusiasm," *enthousiasmos*). Depending on the kinds of gods that were present – for Iamblichus insists that they are multiple and cannot be reduced to one single essence[133] –, such divine possession could take different outward forms: practitioners' bodies would start making involuntary movements, they might find themselves dancing to the harmony of inspirational music, sometimes they would be singing, but they could also be shouting.[134] However, the principal sign of divine possession was that both the director of the procedure and the person about to be possessed, but sometimes even outside spectators too, would be able to see the god's fiery spirit (*pneuma*) come down as a luminous form and enter the practitioner's body.[135]

In a fascinating passage, Iamblichus explains how we are able to observe such phenomena in a conscious although altered state. It is because the divine Light leaves our soul's faculties of attention (*prosochē*) and thinking (*dianoia*) unaffected, but our faculty of imagination (*to phantastikon*) is "woken up ... by the gods to modes of apparition that are totally different from what human beings are accustomed to."[136] Remembering Plutarch's remarks about the effects of *kuphi* incense on the imaginative faculty,[137] one would like to know more about the "drugs" or "potions" mentioned twice in this same passage,[138] but Iamblichus does not spill any entheogenic secrets. What he does make clear is that, like ritual

---

[132] Iamblichus, *Response to Porphyry* I 9; cf. II 8.
[133] Iamblichus, *Response to Porphyry* I 4; II 10 (cf. Steel, *Changing Self*, 28).
[134] Iamblichus, *Response to Porphyry* III 5 and 9 (music). Such effects (including invulnerability to pain or fire, cf. Clarke, *Iamblichus' De Mysteriis*, 76–78) are well known from the phenomenology of possession trance in contemporary contexts (e.g. Oesterreich, *Possession*; Obeyesekere, *Medusa's Hair*).
[135] Iamblichus, *Response to Porphyry* III 6. See the discussion of luminous epiphanies in Clarke, *Iamblichus' De Mysteriis*, 100–118 (including a discussion of how they change according to the entity's position in the spiritual hierarchy, from the "consummate brilliance" of the true gods through daimonic manifestations as "fire rather than light," up to "a smoking or turbid fire, which is blurred and obscure," ibid. 107–110).
[136] Iamblichus, *Response to Porphyry* III 14. See discussion in Clarke, *Iamblichus' De Mysteriis*, 83–86.
[137] See Chapter 2, p. 33 with note 45.
[138] See Chapter 3, p. 72 note 104.

possession trance in many other periods and cultural contexts, the essential purpose of theurgy was *healing*. We have seen that the descent into a body was understood by Platonists as a deeply traumatic event that damaged the soul and even transformed its very substance. During theurgic rituals, the gods themselves would therefore enter practitioners' bodies to fill them with divine Light and restore them to harmony.[139] Moreover, they even allowed their souls to do what they could not do by themselves:

> [T]he gods, in their benevolence and graciousness, generously shed their light upon the theurgists, call their souls towards themselves and allow them to unite with themselves; and they accustom their souls to leave the body even while still being incarnated, and turn towards their eternal noetic principle. That what we are presently talking about is salutary for the soul is shown by the facts themselves. In fact, when the soul contemplates those felicitous visions, it exchanges its life for another one and begins another kind of activity. It then thinks it is no longer human, and rightly so. For often, having abandoned its own life, it has received in exchange the infinitely blessed activity of the gods.[140]

Theurgy aimed at healing the practitioners' souls and bodies. As regards the former, this passage claims that the gods could do what Plotinus' and Porphyry's philosophy could not: during the ritual, they made it possible for the soul to leave its body at least for a while, so that it could turn toward its noetic origin and unite with the life of the gods. Returning from such a spiritual vacation trip refreshed and energized, the soul would then find its vehicle purified by the divine light that had been filling it; and theurgists could do their part to keep it pure, by observing dietary rules combined with physical exercises, visualizations, and prayers.[141] Moreover, during rituals the theurgists themselves would be working with gods or good daimons on healing the physical body, "when we clean it of old impurities, or free it from diseases and fill it with health, or remove from it what is heavy and sluggish while giving it lightness and energy."[142] Finally, theurgy was clearly therapeutic in a psychological

---

[139] Shaw, "Theurgy and the Platonist's Luminous Body," 549–551. Note that in the alchemical Cleopatra fragment discussed above (pp. 83–85) we seem to find something very similar.
[140] Iamblichus, *Response to Porphyry* I 12.
[141] Shaw, "Theurgy and the Platonist's Luminous Body," 546–549 (with reference to Iamblichus, *Response to Porphyry* V 26 and Hierocles, *In carmen aureum* 26). Note the paradox: Iamblichus' embodied Platonism (based on the fully descended soul) made it necessary for the soul to actually leave the body, whereas Plotinus' partially descended soul implied that it could wake up to its noetic side while remaining *in* the body.
[142] Iamblichus, *Response to Porphyry* V 16.

sense, providing emotional relief through controlled catharsis. In response to Porphyry's puzzled questions, Iamblichus explains why sacred rituals could even involve such vulgar elements as the shouting of obscenities, in terms that make him sound like a modern psychologist:

> If the powers of human affect that are in us remain completely contained, they become more violent. But if they are pushed towards a brief action and up to a certain measured degree, they find their pleasure and satisfaction within measure; and once they are purified profoundly, they are brought to peace through persuasion and without violence. ... in the sacred rites, it is by ugly spectacles and sounds that we are delivered from the damage that results from practicing those ugly things. These rites are therefore practiced in view of healing our soul, to moderate the evils that have become attached to it because of the fact of generation, to liberate it and relieve it from its chains.[143]

In sum, theurgy was an integral practice of healing both body and soul. It worked through the ritual induction of altered states that made it possible for the gods to enter practitioners' bodies and purify their souls, so that they might be as effective as possible in the task of channeling spiritual energies into the material world. The function of philosophy was to provide theoretical justification for this practice.

INNATE *GNŌSIS* AND POWERFUL SOUNDS

As the gods were healing the souls and bodies of theurgists from within, simultaneously they were *making themselves known* to them. What kind of "knowledge" was that? We will see that this question is of central importance, not just for understanding Iamblichus' perspective but for that of the Hermetica as well. Iamblichus begins the systematic part of his treatise by objecting to Porphyry's statement that he "concedes the existence of the gods."[144] This very formulation is totally wrong, he points out, because it makes the existence of the gods a matter of philosophical dialectics, something we can acquire by reason, a matter for agreement or disagreement. *Gnōsis*, however, is of a wholly different kind:

> The innate knowledge [*emphutos gnōsis*] concerning the gods coexists with our very being. It is superior to all judgment and voluntary decision, prior to reasoning and demonstration. From the beginning it is one with its own cause and goes together with the soul's essential striving for the Good. To tell the truth, the

---

[143] Iamblichus, *Response to Porphyry* I 11. See discussion of "aversion therapy" in Clarke, *Iamblichus' De Mysteriis*, 78; cf. [Porphyry], *Porphyre*, 8–10 (frg. 13–13a).
[144] Iamblichus, *Response to Porphyry* I 3.

contact we have with the divine is not even really knowledge [*oude gnōsis estin*]. Knowledge, after all, is separated from its object by some degree of otherness. But beyond the kind of knowledge that knows its object as different from itself, there exists a unitary connection with the gods that is natural [and indivisible]. Therefore we should not claim that this is something to which we can concede or not concede, or consider it as something open to question ..., nor is it correct to discuss it as though it were in our power to accept or reject it; for it is rather the case that we are enveloped by it, we are filled with it, and in fact it is only by virtue of knowing that the gods exist that we grasp what *we* are.[145]

This is a subtle and extremely important passage. In the same section, Iamblichus insists that *gnōsis* has nothing to do with human conjecture, reasoning, or opinions because such common understandings of what "knowledge" means are all subject to the restrictions of *temporality*: we acquire it at a certain moment, when we "get to know" something we did not know before. By contrast, *gnōsis* is not something we ever need to learn or acquire, because it is the superior understanding inherent to our soul that we have *received* from the gods since all eternity.[146] As such, it is not cognition but *recognition* in the most literal sense of the word: when the gods make themselves known in theurgical ritual, the practitioners *recognize* them. They realize that they have always known them but had just forgotten what they looked or felt like. Now that they are present right here in the room, their existence cannot possibly be doubted.

Therefore, Iamblichus' "innate *gnōsis*" (*emphutos gnōsis*) might be defined as knowledge by personal (re)acquaintance with the gods. It is a matter of common human experience and language convention that "to know somebody" is not the same thing as just knowing *about* that person "by name" – as a theoretical entity whose real existence we may be willing to "concede" as plausible even though we have never met.[147] This distinction between knowing just by name and knowing by personal acquaintance seems critical for understanding the basic difference

---

[145] Iamblichus, *Response to Porphyry* I 3.
[146] Iamblichus, *Response to Porphyry* I 3. Cf. Shaw, *Theurgy and the Soul*, 119–121; Shaw, "*Chôra*," 118–119; Shaw, "Taking the Shape," 142, 164; Clarke, *Iamblichus' De Mysteriis*, 12, 19, 25, 29.
[147] Elaine Pagels points out that English is unusual in having just a single verb ("to know") for expressing both general intellectual knowledge and the more intimate kind of knowledge suggestive of personal relationships: see e.g. *savoir* and *connaître* in French, *wissen* and *kennen* in German, *saber* and *conocer* in Spanish, *sapere* and *conoscere* in Italian, or *weten* and *kennen* in Dutch. *Gnōsis* is derived from *gignōsko*, referring to the second type (*Origin of Satan*, 167). For *gnōsis* as "acquaintance with God," see also Layton, *Gnostic Scriptures*, xv.

between Porphyry's philosophy and Iamblichus' theurgy, and leads us to one more key concern that Iamblichus shares with the Hermetica. Porphyry does not know what to make of the frequent use, in theurgic ritual, of "names without signification," the so-called *nomina barbara*. Why are theurgists using words that they know have no meaning? First of all, Iamblichus denies the very premise. It is true that these names are unknowable for us, but they do in fact have meanings that are known to the gods.[148] Moreover, these meanings are not based on human convention: they are "natural" in the sense of participating directly in the very *being* of whatever they express.[149] What this really means is that such words need no translation, and in fact cannot be translated. They can only be spoken.

In a world without telephones or sound recordings, this meant that *one had to be physically present* to hear them and experience their effect. It is very difficult for us to appreciate what was meant by the power of the spoken word during late antiquity, a period halfway between traditional local cultures grounded in direct oral transmission and the translocal culture of communication through writing that we take for granted today (finally culminating in the codification of canonical texts that make it possible to define orthodoxy, and hence make heterodoxy possible). As formulated by Polymnia Athanassiadi, "the divine word spoken by a mouth (whether prophetical or philosophical) [was] converted into writing by the Greeks," but we must realize that originally, "the divine revelation, far from being understood as a unique phenomenon, [was] neither codified nor integrated into a closed system."[150] The process of scriptural codification and canonization had not yet advanced to its final stages during the first centuries CE.

---

[148] Iamblichus, *Response to Porphyry* VII 4. Cf. Shaw, *Theurgy and the Soul*, 179.
[149] Iamblichus, *Response to Porphyry* VII 4. As pointed out by Shaw, *Theurgy and the Soul*, 182–183, this was not an argument for some special sacrality of the Egyptian language; rather, the Egyptians just happened to be there first.
[150] Athanassiadi, *Lutte*, 35–36. Athanassiadi's work is all about the "creation of orthodoxy" in the Platonic tradition through this very development from orality to canonicity. Note the strong resonance of my argument with Gadamer's discussion of linguistic philosophy in the wake of Plato's *Cratylus* (*Hermeutik I*, 409–442): "wherever the word assumes a purely semiotic function, the original connection between speaking and thinking ... is changed into an instrumental relation. This transformed relation between word and sign lies at the basis of scientific theorizing as a whole and has become so self-evident for us that we must be artificially reminded that, next to the scientific ideal of uniform signification, the life of language itself just continues as it always did" (ibid., 437).

I believe it would be hard to overstate the importance of this point. We tend to think that by writing something down we are securing it for posterity; but over half a millennium earlier, Plato's Socrates was emphasizing the other side of the coin. He explained to Phaedrus that in contrast to the written word, "the living and ensouled word of him who sees"[151] is far less vulnerable to misinterpretation. He gave a whole series of reasons that would still have made perfect sense to philosophers such as Iamblichus during the first centuries CE. Oral communication allows meaning to be transmitted not indirectly but straight to the mind of the listener; verbal expression is fluid and flexible, as opposed to the rigidity of one single written formulation that cannot be changed once it is written down; if the speaker notices that his pupils do not understand, he can act immediately to protect his true meaning from misinterpretations; and finally, he can make sure he speaks only to those he thinks are worthy to receive his knowledge and capable of understanding it in the first place.[152] Today we are easily seduced into thinking of ancient philosophers as *writers*, because we cannot hear them talk and have to make do with their written works. But Socrates and Plotinus were first of all oral teachers, whose words are known to us thanks to Plato's writings and Porphyry's editorial work. As for Iamblichus, although he was a writer, we constantly see him stressing the immediacy of personal contact and immediate experience over the indirect and impersonal transmission of knowledge through the written word. If we know the gods only "by name," without ever meeting them, then we do not really know them at all. We need to get personally acquainted to know who and what they actually are. This is why in the end, neither Iamblichus' written works nor even his own oral teaching, but only the direct personal experience that theurgy provided could convey *gnōsis* of the gods.

The *nomina barbara* should not be seen as human attempts to communicate with the gods, as if those wholly superior beings would not understand us otherwise. Rather, because our souls already contain a "secret and unspeakable image" of the gods, merely pronouncing those names that carry all the tremendous energy of their true essence causes our souls spontaneously to take flight and unite with that energy.[153] Again, it is all

---

[151] For my translation, see Chapter 10, p. 312 with note 17.
[152] Plato, *Phaedrus* 275d–276a (cf. Van den Kerchove, *La voie*, 128). Of course this is the basic Pythagorean premise of esotericism in the sense of secret teachings for a chosen elite: the teacher addresses only those whom he thinks will be able to understand, and can correct them immediately if he notices they do not get it.
[153] Iamblichus, *Response to Porphyry* VII 4; cf. Shaw, *Theurgy and the Soul*, 110–111, 179–188.

about practice, not verbal communication. The very act of writing or even speaking about theurgy already distances us from the lived experience and causes most of what it's all about to get lost in translation – but it gets even much worse, Iamblichus insists, if one is forced to use Greek! Because the divine names are *not* conventional linguistic signifiers suitable for written communication but powerful energies activated by oral speech, "once they are translated, [they] do not preserve the same meaning ... and even if it were possible to translate the names, they would not maintain the same power."[154] Here we encounter a final reason for Iamblichus' evident frustration about Porphyry's misunderstandings. As has often been noted, his argument is a close match with that of Asclepius to King Ammon in the sixteenth treatise of the *Corpus Hermeticum*. Having pointed out that his writings might seem clear at first sight but in fact contain many hidden meanings, Asclepius advises the king against having them translated:

> Expressed in the language of our fathers, the discourse preserves the clear spirit of the words. For the very quality of the sound [*to tès phōnes poion*] and the <?> of the Egyptian names [*onomatōn*] carry in themselves the energy of what is being said. So my king, as far as it is in your power (which is unlimited), please keep this text from being translated, lest such great mysteries reach the Greeks – lest the arrogant, flaccid and (as it were) dandified Greek speech extinguish the majesty and strength and energy of our own spoken names [*onomatōn phrasin*]. For the Greeks, o King, use empty words suitable only for [dialectical] demonstration, because really that is the philosophy of the Greeks: just a noise of words. We, by contrast, do not use mere words but sounds [*phōnais*] full of power.[155]

Of course, the great irony is that this text has reached us in Greek! Once again, it is crucial to see that Asclepius refers to the power of *spoken* language: the Egyptian *names* are described as *sounds* that carry divine energy, presumably in a ritual context. Greek words are empty of such power even when spoken. When written down, they are weakened even more. At best they can give us mere echoes of the ritual experience; they are incapable of transmitting or communicating what really happens when the gods are present in the room.

This superiority of Egyptian religious practice over Greek philosophy was basic to Iamblichus' worldview. In a famous passage of the *Timaeus*, an Egyptian priest described the Greeks to the Athenian sage Solon as "eternal children" obsessed with novelty but ignorant about the ancient

---

[154] Iamblichus, *Response to Porphyry* VII 5. As a result, Iamblichus points out, the ancient prayers too are losing their efficacy.
[155] CH XVI 2. Cf. Van den Kerchove, *La voie*, 109.

wisdom.[156] Evidently this was Iamblichus' conviction too, and so he begins his *Response to Porphyry* by exalting not Plato but Hermes as the ultimate source of all true knowledge concerning the gods.[157] Porphyry was quite right to address his questions to Anebo, he points out, for the Egyptian priests are indeed the guardians of the most ancient wisdom. Speaking on their behalf and even claiming priestly status for himself, Iamblichus will answer Porphyry by referring to the same "ancient steles of Hermes" that were already consulted by Pythagoras and Plato themselves – who ended up building their entire philosophy on them.[158] We have seen that the otherwise unknown Bitus is credited with discovering these treasures of Hermetic wisdom engraved in hieroglyphic characters in a sanctuary in Saïs (where Solon met the priest according to Plato's *Timaeus*),[159] then explaining their meaning to King Ammon (Asclepius' addressee in CH XVI), and finally translating them into Greek (presumably ignoring Asclepius' advice!). This at least is how Iamblichus must have seen the situation.[160]

It is therefore clear that the Hermetic writings carried enormous traditional authority for Iamblichus. While his theurgy is greatly indebted to another collection of inspired writings, the *Chaldaean Oracles*, these were not an ancient tradition but a recent revelation from the late second century CE.[161] Like the writings of Pythagoras and Plato, they were seen as confirming the one universal tradition of true wisdom that could be traced back to primordial times and had been known to all the "peoples of high renown,"[162] such as the Indians, the Jews, the Persians, and of course the Egyptians. It seems that this "Platonic Orientalist"[163] belief in a perennial tradition of primordial wisdom originated in the second century CE with the philosopher Numenius, a major influence on Plotinus, who came precisely from the city of Apamea in Syria.[164] Whether or not

---

[156] Plato, *Tim.* 22b.
[157] Iamblichus, *Response to Porphyry* I 1.
[158] Iamblichus, *Response to Porphyry* I 1-2.
[159] Fowden, *Egyptian Hermes*, 30.
[160] Cf. Iamblichus, *Response to Porphyry* VIII 4. Iamblichus notes that the books attributed to Hermes really do contain his doctrines, but often use Greek philosophical language because they were translated into Greek "by men not unversed in philosophy."
[161] On the reception of these oracles by Julian the Chaldaean and his son, Julian the Theurgist, see Majercik, *Chaldean Oracles*, 1-2; Athanassiadi, *Lutte*, 31-70, esp. 50-51.
[162] Numenius, Περὶ τἀγαθοῦ, Bk. I, frg. I a (des Places ed., 42).
[163] Hanegraaff, *Esotericism and the Academy*, 12-17. The terminology was introduced by Walbridge, *Wisdom of the Mystic East*, x, 2-3, 8-12 (cf. Hanegraaff, *Esotericism and the Academy*, 15 with note 31) and is unrelated to the better-known work of Edward Said.
[164] Athanassiadi, *Lutte*, 71-107; Frede, "Numenius."

the *Chaldaean Oracles* were received in Apamea itself and kept there in the famous temple of Bel,[165] they show striking parallels with what is left of Numenius' writings, suggesting at least that they come from the same milieu; Plotinus' pupil Amelius, who knew Numenius by heart, was a native from Tuscany but chose to settle in Apamea and stay there for the rest of his life[166]; and of course it is here too that Iamblichus established his school and community somewhat later. For the followers of this Numenian lineage of Platonic Orientalist wisdom,[167] Apamea in Syria therefore became the practical center of activity, whereas Egypt was seen by them as the original source of its spiritual tradition.[168]

Iamblichus begins his *Letter to Porphyry* with Hermes, returns to his "Egyptian theology" in book VII, and keeps referring to it until the very end of the treatise. He is evidently familiar with much of the Hermetic literature and considers it foundational for theurgy. This theurgical "Way of Hermes," as he understands it, is the only reliable way by which human beings can find happiness. Therefore if we accept Iamblichus as a contemporary authority who must have known firsthand what Hermetic spirituality was all about, then it cannot have been just a *Lesemysterium* (a "reading mystery"), an intellectual exercise for philosophers without practical application. Quite the contrary – the Way of Hermes was all about experiential practice.

---

[165] For this attractive hypothesis, see the reconstruction of a Numenian tradition of "perennial philosophy" centered on Apamea as proposed by Athanassiadi, *Lutte*, 31–107; cf. shorter summaries in Athanassiadi, "Creation of Orthodoxy."
[166] Athanassiadi, *Lutte*, 89–90; Brisson, "Amélius."
[167] Athanassiadi, "Creation of Orthodoxy," 273; Athanassiadi, *Lutte*, 90.
[168] On the intimacy of this community (with master and pupils living together, discussing philosophy informally and during evening *symposia* with plenty of wine, communal prayer, long walks to holy sites and so on), see Athanassiadi, "Creation of Orthodoxy," 277, 283–284.

5

Through a Glass Darkly

Ein Zweifler bin ich, wie ich hier sitze, nicht weil ich nichts glaubte, sondern weil ich alles für möglich halte.
Thomas Mann[1]

Whenever we hope to catch a glimpse of the Hermetists, they always just seem to have turned a corner and vanished out of our sight. We may reasonably assume that some of Iamblichus' Egyptian students were Hermetic practitioners, but he tells us nothing more than the name of one otherwise unidentified priest and never quotes any Hermetic treatise.[2] Zosimos does mention several texts; but he advises Theosebeia to pursue her spiritual practice in the privacy of her home, and we simply do not know what she and her pupils were doing in their restricted meetings. We have seen that if Hermetism was more than a strictly literary phenomenon, its adherents must have been small in number and highly discreet in their activities. In sum, the people we are trying to catch sight of seem to have been flying below the radar and managed to remain invisible to the public eye. They left no evidence by which they could be identified; and except for a few vague references to temples

---

[1] Thomas Mann, *Joseph und seine Brüder*, vol. 2 ("Zum Herrn"): "A doubter I am, as I sit here – not because I believed in nothing but because I consider anything possible."
[2] The same is true for Iamblichus' dependence on the *Chaldaean Oracles*. Van den Kerchove points out that absence of evidence is no evidence of absence here: "It is possible that Iamblichus was so strongly impregnated by the traditions of the Chaldaeans and the Egyptians that they were completely integrated in his thought, manifesting themselves in a more subtle and profound manner than through explicit citations" (*Hermès Trismégiste*, 24).

or deserts, they do not tell us where they met or what their meetings were like.³

The conclusion is unavoidable: in our efforts to reconstruct Hermetic spirituality as a lived practice, we have to depend almost entirely on evidence internal to the texts themselves. We read there how authoritative teachers, respectfully addressed as "father," are offering their spiritual "children"[4] two things: theoretical instruction about the true nature of reality *and* practical guidance about how to move beyond mere theory and actually reach a state of divinely enlightened consciousness. We learn from these texts that the theoretical part of the Way of Hermes is necessary as a preparation but not sufficient to reach the goal: actually getting to know the divine Source is something quite different from just knowing *about* it.[5] To really know what it's all about, one must encounter the true reality of the divine *directly*, in a personal experience that is not verbal but noetic and requires the use of interior senses.

In tracing the ideal pupil's development from spiritual ignorance to perfectly enlightened consciousness, as described in the Hermetica, we can *not* assume that the anonymous authors saw themselves as passive transmitters of ancient teachings that had been handed down to them. They certainly believed that the true way of wisdom had been known and proclaimed by the earliest sages and teachers of humanity, so it was natural for them to put their message into the mouth of such great authorities as Hermes Trismegistus, Asclepius, or even the divine *Nous* itself. But of course the authors knew perfectly well that it was *they* themselves who were writing these teachings down, right then and there. So where did they get them from? Not, as far as we can tell, from any earlier written "master source" that they were just copying or using as their basis.[6]

---

[3] Van den Kerchove, *Hermès Trismégiste*, 62, 71–72; Van den Kerchove, *La voie*, 6. For ὄρος as desert, see Chapter 8, p. 236 note 59.

[4] On the spiritual terminology of "father" and "child" in Greek and Coptic, see Van den Kerchove, *La voie*, 56–61.

[5] See above, Prologue, p. 1 note 2; Chapter 4, p. 113 note 147 (*connaître* vs. *savoir* etc.).

[6] While the authors of the Hermetica were obviously using elements from a great variety of previous traditions (Egyptian, Greek, or Jewish) as their building materials, out of them they created something new and distinctive. My emphasis on the creative novelty of Hermetic spirituality stands in complete and deliberate opposition to Festugière's endlessly repeated refrain (rightly criticized e.g. by Kingsley, "Poimandres," 68–69) of how utterly unoriginal and "banal" the contents of the Hermetica are. In this regard, his work exemplifies a methodological pitfall of great scholarly erudition: by focusing just on the building blocks and where they came from, we risk overlooking the building, as though recycled materials could not be used to build something new.

Through a Glass Darkly 121

The perfectly reasonable alternative then is to assume that these were actually their *own* teachings. In other words, the authors were trying to write down what they themselves had learned from their spiritual masters and were teaching their pupils in turn,[7] hoping that in this manner their knowledge might not get lost. Hence whenever we read about Hermes Trismegistus teaching Tat or Asclepius, it is not very helpful to keep emphasizing (as modern scholars have been doing just a bit too much) that "this is all supposed to be happening in ancient pre-Roman times."[8] On the contrary, the Hermetica give us a chance to learn what second- or third-century practitioners were doing.

So what *were* they doing? In an extremely influential chapter, Festugière evokes the image of a Hermetic school curriculum: "We are therefore dealing with a *course*, and hence we may imagine that the teacher writes down in advance what he wants to say, that he has his course book in front of him, and the pupil is taking notes."[9] Along somewhat similar lines, Jean-Pierre Mahé has argued that the Hermetica have their origin in gnomologies consisting of short aphoristic statements, "definitions" or *sententiae*, that students had to copy down and learn by heart.[10] So is that really what the Hermetists were doing? The problem with this perspective does not lie in its constituent elements – it is plausible enough that pupils took notes and tried to remember what they had learned, or that our dialogues originate from attempts to capture the contents of oral teachings. Much more important is a set of unexamined background assumptions that have the unfortunate effect of trivializing the textual contents while subtly manipulating the reader's imagination. Specifically, the contents of the Hermetica are reduced to mere theoretical information of the kind that can be learned by heart and written down in a notebook. Festugière's formulations lead us to imagine Hermetic pupils as though they were children at school, licking their pencils and rehearsing their lessons by rote learning, ready to stand up and rattle off sentences when the schoolmaster calls on them in class.

---

[7] This chain of transmission, in which pupils becomes masters, is central to the argument of Van den Kerchove, *La voie*.
[8] See above, Chapter 3, note 109.
[9] RHT II, 40 (emphasis in original). Finally, the pupil is supposed to make a clean copy ("mis au net et édité," RHT II, 42). Adopted without question by Law, *Das Corpus Hermeticum*, vol. 1, 66–67; see also Van den Kerchove, *La voie*, 134, 137.
[10] HHE II, 276–278 (quoting Festugière's chapter in note 12), 408–410; HT V, cvii–cxiii.

That such a perspective "lacks historical realism"[11] is to put it mildly – in fact, I consider it incompatible with the central Hermetic message. Students in a school do not get to experience what the Hermetica promise them: they do not get to see visions of divine entities, they are not reborn into new invisible bodies, they do not get exorcized and cleaned of demonic entities, they do not traverse the world with the speed of their imagination, they do not experience heavenly realities or listen to angelic hymns, and they do not get united with the divine Source. Adopting the school analogy means reducing all such elements to secondary or marginal status. Our textual sources are saying exactly the reverse: radical experiences like these were *central* to the path of spiritual transformation and the acquisition of salvational knowledge. Theoretical knowledge, oral instruction and book learning were important but ultimately just propaedeutic. To be a follower of Hermes did not mean sitting in some kind of school, memorizing the teacher's statements about God and the cosmos. It meant practicing a way of spiritual transformation to find true knowledge, peace of mind, ultimate salvation, and perfect enlightenment.

It seems most likely that the Way of Hermes was practiced in very small gatherings, probably not much larger than what we find in the texts themselves: one teacher and one to three pupils – hardly more. Some teachers may well have been priests who could receive their pupils in a temple sanctuary,[12] but other scenarios are possible too, for instance meetings at private homes or in remote places outdoors. That these discreet practitioners took the trouble to compose extensive and well-edited treatises suggests to me that at least a few of such circles must have been active in different Egyptian cities, for if you cannot meet regularly in one and the same place, you need the written word to stay in contact and preserve some degree of unity in teaching and practice. Rather than writing under their own names and giving literal descriptions of what had happened at this-or-that meeting or location, Hermetic practitioners were exchanging inspirational texts describing the ideal teacher, the ideal student, the ideal discussion, the ideal message, the ideal proceedings, the ideal rewards. In other words, our sources do not try to tell us what happened exactly at some moment somewhere in ancient or Roman Egypt, as if they were the written minutes of a meeting. Rather, they tell us what devotees of Hermes were supposed to learn and what they should expect to happen if they managed to get it all right.

---

[11] The formulation comes from Fowden, *Egyptian Hermes*, 72.
[12] Bull, *Tradition*, 427–455.

AT THE MERCY OF SCRIBES

But can we trust our sources to provide reliable information at all? The earliest manuscripts of what modern scholars since Reitzenstein call the "Corpus Hermeticum"[13] date from as late as the fourteenth century – that is more than a millennium after the originals were written down! They all consist of seventeen treatises, except for the most influential of them all (Laurentianus 71.33) that was used by Marsilio Ficino (1433–1499) for his famous Latin translation published in 1471 and contains only CH I–XIV. A series of further manuscripts, some more complete than others, date from the fifteenth and sixteenth centuries.[14] One of the complete versions was used by Ficino's contemporary, the poet Lodovico Lazzarelli (1447–1500), for his Latin translation of the remaining treatises, CH XVI–XVIII.[15] However, all these different manuscripts on which our *Corpus Hermeticum* is based are derived from just *one* textual original, or archetype, which is no longer extant and must already have been in a very bad condition at the time it was copied.[16] Reitzenstein's sobering remarks are worth quoting:

We owe the preservation of the Hermetic corpus to one single manuscript, rediscovered in a sad state during the eleventh century. Entire quires and pages were

---

[13] Reitzenstein, *Poimandres*, 319ff ("das Hermetische Corpus") and 380 ("*Corpus Hermeticum*").

[14] Overview in HT I, xi–xii. We should add the manuscript *Clarkianus* 11 discovered in Oxford (Bodleian library) by Mahé and Paramelle and published by them in 1991 (Paramelle and Mahé, "Extraits hermétiques"). Dated perhaps somewhat earlier than the other manuscripts (thirteenth or fourteenth century), it contains fragments of CH XI (final passage) to XIV, then some of the *Definitions* previously known only in Armenian, followed by CH XVI and finally some additional Hermetic passages that had not been known before. Because they sometimes give a better version than the standard edition published by Nock and Festugière, they cannot come from the lost archetype on which the other CH manuscripts are based but must depend on a different, parallel source that kept the same order of succession at least as far as CH XI–XVI are concerned (Van den Kerchove, *La voie*, 149).

[15] Hanegraaff and Bouthoorn, *Lodovico Lazzarelli*. Note that Adrien Turnèbe composed a "CH XV" from some excerpts of Stobaeus in the first edition of the Greek text; but while later editors kept his numbering, this fifteenth treatise was thrown out again (see e.g. van den Broek, "Hermetic Literature I," 489). Lazzarelli's translation was published posthumously by Symphorien Champier (1507) and consists not just of CH XVI (as assumed by Van den Kerchove, *La voie*, 148; Van den Kerchove, *Hermès Trismégiste*, 18; Moreschini, "Rezeption," 295) but of all three treatises presented as one continuous text titled "Diffinitiones Asclepii" (Champier, "Commentarium," 251–259: CH XVI = pp. 251–255 l. 10, CH XVII = 255 l. 10–23, XVIII = 255 l. 23–259 l. 10).

[16] For the realities of textual transmission, including the common practice of discarding originals after a copy had been made in minuscule script, see the excellent discussion by Reynolds and Wilson, *Scribes and Scholars*, 44–79, here 60.

missing, both at the beginning (after ch. I) and at the end (after XVI); and on the pages that were preserved, parts of the text, especially in the final third, had become unreadable.[17]

Most scholars assume that this original Corpus can be dated to the eleventh century and must have been available to the great Byzantine philosopher Michael Psellos. The chief argument is that two of the fourteenth-century manuscripts (Parisinus Gr. 1220 and Vaticanus Gr. 951) contain some highly polemical comments that are attributed to him.[18] They refer to CH I 18 and basically accuse Hermes, "this sorcerer" (*goēs*), of plagiarizing Moses. Technically this is no proof that Psellos knew our *Corpus Hermeticum* as a compositional unity, for these remarks are attributed to him indirectly about three centuries after his death and refer only to the first treatise.[19] Whatever may be the truth of Psellos' involvement, and at whatever moment between late antiquity and the fourteenth century our Corpus may have been put together in more or less its present shape, three facts are undeniable. First, there is no proof that these seventeen treatises were originally part of one "Hermetic corpus"; it is only with Ficino's Latin translation (1471) that the collection was presented as if it were a book with seventeen (still unnumbered) chapters. Second, we have no reason to attribute a special significance to the sequential order in which the treatises happened to be copied in the lost archetype;[20] they might as well be put in any different order, and a few show hardly any Hermetic content at all. Third, and most seriously, for many passages it is completely impossible to reconstruct the exact original formulation with any degree of certainty.

It would be hard to overstate the importance of this last point. As formulated by Christian Wildberg, "our most important evidence, the collection of Hermetic texts in the *Corpus Hermeticum*, is in ruins, or at

---

[17] Reitzenstein, *Poimandres*, 319; cf. Scott I, 17–30; HHE II, 19–20.
[18] Greek text in Scott IV, 244–245. The scholion is written in the margin of Parisinus Gr. 1220, attributed there to Psellos in a different hand; in Vaticanus Gr. 951 it has been inserted in the main text, without the attribution (Scott IV, 244 note 9; cf. Fowden, *Egyptian Hermes*, 9). English translation in Moreschini, *Hermes Christianus*, 128–129. Generally on the importance of such scholia in Byzantine manuscripts, see Dickey, "Classical Scholarship," 67–68, 71–72.
[19] Scott I, 25–28; Mahé, HHE II, 19–20; Van den Kerchove, *La voie*, 148 with note 255. Nock and Festugière's list of further references to Hermetica in Psellos' oeuvre (HT I, xlix–li) demonstrates his familiarity with these texts, and may make it plausible but does not prove that he thought of the CH as a compositional unity.
[20] *Pace* Van den Kerchove, *La voie*, 147–148. As she clearly demonstrates the absence of any clear didactic or paedagogical order from CH II to XII, it is not clear to me why she still speaks of a "logical and coherent general organization."

least partially so ... the texts are in a much poorer literary condition than nearly any other classical, Hellenistic or late antique text."[21] The sobering but unavoidable truth is that often we do *not* know the exact words that were written down by the original authors of the *Corpus Hermeticum*. This uncertainty is caused partly by the dependence of all our manuscripts on that single damaged and long vanished archetype; but in addition, there is the absolutely crucial question of how reliable were the scribes to whom we owe our manuscripts in the first place. Jean-Pierre Mahé has pointed out that while the sheer length of the *Corpus Hermeticum* makes it our most important reference, yet among all our Hermetic sources it also "offers the most mediocre guarantees of sincerity."[22] It is important to realize that in the modern standard edition of the Corpus, Arthur Darby Nock was concerned to play down the implications of tampering by Byzantine scribes, because he preferred to think of the collection as an "esoteric book" composed by some "devotee" already during the Roman period.[23] But later scholars have not been so sure. Commenting on Walter Scott's ill-fated attempt to reconstruct (or rather, create) a "reasonable" version of the original Hermetica, an early reviewer noted that "the obscurity of the subject matter must have puzzled the scribes considerably" and surely "offered much inducement to the interpolation of Christian thoughts and expressions."[24] The effect of such interpolations may have been underestimated or played down, whether consciously or unconsciously, by Nock and Festugière in their standard edition.

To illustrate the seriousness of this situation, let us consider the case of CH I 6 (a passage of great importance, as will be seen). A divine entity who calls himself Poimandres has appeared to the anonymous author in a vision and identifies himself as the divine light, "the *nous*, your God." He continues by stating that "the luminous *logos* that came from the *nous* is the son of God [*huios theou*]" – a formulation that would be obviously congenial to Christian beliefs in Christ as the divine *Logos*. The passage continues by stating that the visionary's internal faculty of seeing and hearing is "the Lord's *logos* [*logos Kuriou*]" and points out that "*nous* is God the Father

---

[21] Wildberg, "*Corpus Hermeticum*, Tractate III," 128. See also HT V, 361–362: "The manuscript tradition of the *Corpus Hermeticum* is so bad that the establishment of the text still remains hypothetical."
[22] Mahé, HHE II, 40. In HHE I, 22, Mahé states quite bluntly that "the Byzantine excerptor has not faithfully reproduced the original text of our treatises."
[23] HT I, xlvii–xlviii, and cf. xiii, xliv; Cherniss, Review of Festugière (1950), 205 note 1; HHE I, 22.
[24] Riess, Review of Scott (*Hermetica*, vols. 1–2), 193.

[*ho de nous patēr theos*]." The result is a rather neat picture, congenial to Christian-theological sentiments, of *nous* as God the Father and the *logos* as God the Son. But should we trust this version? One reviewer's suspicion was evoked by a grammatical error: *logos kuriou* without the article is a "barbarism" known only from the Septuagint and otherwise not attested in pagan Greek literature. He concluded that "the son of God," "the Lord's," and "*nous* is God the Father" must all be interpolations by a Byzantine scribe.[25] If we eliminate them, we get a different text. Poimandres now seems to be saying "I am that light ... the *nous*, your God ... the luminous *logos* that came from the *nous*" (that is, he now identifies himself with both *nous* and *logos* at the same time) and continues by stating that "that entity in you which sees and hears is the *logos*." According to the sentence that follows, "they are not separate from one another, for their union is life," meaning presumably that light, life, *nous* and *logos* are ultimately all one (or, if one prefers, that life = the unity of light, *nous* and *logos*). On the other hand, if we want to see no Christian interpolations here, it seems as though the Hermetic author is making a neat profession of Christian orthodoxy again: Father and Son (God and his *Logos*) are not separate from one another because their unity is life.

Specialists have discussed the dilemmas of this case in erudite texts and long footnotes, but this has led to no conclusive outcome.[26] As for how modern scholars have dealt with those elements in the Hermetica that seem suggestive of Christian theology, no strategy has been more popular than to explain them as depending on Philo and Alexandrian Judaism.[27] The effect has been twofold. Firstly and most obviously, by highlighting

---

[25] Bickerman, Review of Nock and Festugière, 458; see also Dodd, *Bible and the Greeks*, 117–119.

[26] The long discussion in Scott II, 23–26, nicely illustrates the ease with which he rewrites the manuscripts to solve any problem that bothers him. The passage ὁ δὲ ἐκ νοὸς φωτεινὸς λόγος υἱὸς θεοῦ is bracketed by him as follows: ὁ δὲ ἐκ [νοὸς] φωτ[εἰν]ὸς λόγος υἱὸς θεοῦ, because "[i]f we write ὁ δὲ ἐκ φωτὸς λόγος, all difficulties are removed" (ibid., 24). Scott keeps the υἱὸς θεοῦ, however, and explains it in terms of hypothetical influences from "Jewish speculations similar to those of Philo," that is, from Alexandrian Judaism (same strategy in Dodd, *Bible and the Greeks*, 117–121; followed also e.g. in Cop, 102 and HG, 458 note 8; see discussion in text). That those difficulties might be removed at least as easily by interpreting υἱὸς θεοῦ as a Christian interpolation is never seriously considered.

[27] Here as in so many other cases, Festugière's influence has been decisive. As many critics have noted, his second volume (the largest of the four) in fact discusses the Hermetica only in the introduction (pp. 1–71), while the remainder of its 610 pages are devoted to other traditions, culminating in the volume's fifth and final part (66 pages) devoted entirely to Philo (RHT II, 521–585). By contrast, see Mahé's discussion of "Hermes and Philo: Superficial similarities and fundamental differences" (HHE II, 316–320).

Philo as a mediating factor, this approach confirmed the dominant apologetic tradition (at least since Lactantius and in spite of Augustine[28]) of reading the Hermetica as broadly compatible with Christian theology and its Jewish origins. Secondly, it meant that the Hermetica had to be products of Alexandria, so that the rest of Hellenistic Egypt along with Egyptian religion could drift to the margins of scholarly attention. But how convincing is this strategy? In his landmark study *Hellenism in Byzantium*, Anthony Kaldellis makes the following observations:

> For over a thousand years the fate of the Greek tradition was in the hands of those who saw themselves as its opponents in a fundamental sense, albeit in a sense that was always negotiable. This basic continuity also shaped the reception of Hellenistic Judaism, and continues to do so even today. We have the writings of Philon, Josephos, and others only because Byzantines like Eusebios of Kaisareia (ca. AD 300) were also struggling to define the relationship between Scripture and Greek *paideia*, between the history of the Jewish nation and that of the rest of the ancient world. Otherwise, these writings seem to have had little impact on the development of Greek or Jewish culture in antiquity, a fact that usually goes unnoticed. "Philon and Josephos," wrote the Byzantine statesman and essayist Theodoros Metochites in the early fourteenth century, "became more famous than any other Jews from time immemorial for having acquired Greek wisdom in addition to their ancestral beliefs" – famous, we should add, only among Greek-speaking Christians.[29]

Not, in other words, among the Hellenized Egyptians who wrote the Hermetica! In the mnemohistorical imagination[30] of historians of Christianity and other scholars with Christian backgrounds or commitments, Philo looms very large as a dominating presence in Alexandria at the time of Jesus. But how much relevance, if any, would he have had for those small circles of Hermetic devotees pursuing their "pagan" Egyptian-hellenistic path of spiritual salvation? In light of Kaldellis' observations, it seems plausible that passages such as CH I 6 are exactly what they seem to be: not echoes from Alexandrian Judaism but pious "improvements" made by Christian scribes. Given the political realities of Byzantine society, such tacit revisions are exactly what we should expect. Byzantium was not an intellectually free society; it did not encourage such rarefied ideals as "disinterested" philological scholarship; and its authorities would be

---

[28] See below, pp. 330–332.
[29] Kaldellis, *Hellenism in Byzantium*, 30 (the reference is to Theodoros Metochites, *Moral Maxims* 16.1.9).
[30] On the concepts of mnemohistory and the mnemohistorical imagination, see e.g. Assmann, *Moses the Egyptian*, 1–22; Hanegraaff, *Esotericism and the Academy*, 375–376; Hanegraaff, "Religion and the Historical Imagination," 136–139.

distrustful of the notion that "pagan superstitions" should be transmitted to posterity with scrupulous care and respect. On the contrary, the powerful institutions of imperial state and Church sought to control the circulation of ideas by any means available, and this included an agenda of "domesticating" pagan texts. With the partial exception of Judaism, no deviation from orthodoxy was permitted, and it was extremely dangerous for anyone to be suspected of heretical ideas or pagan sympathies.[31]

As they were faced with a wealth of original sources, scribes did not have the luxury of copying them all. They had to make decisions about what to select and what to ignore, and it was perfectly common for ancient manuscripts to be "significantly rewritten by Byzantine writers who abridged, expanded, and combined material from different sources."[32] As formulated by Mahé, the anonymous clerk responsible for compiling the archetype of our *Corpus Hermeticum* must have been motivated first and foremost by edifying and moralizing intentions: "Why be surprised then if, from among the enormous and probably extremely varied mass of Hermetic writings, he deliberately chose the most philosophical and devout ones, while omitting texts that were mythological and filled with too many exotic elements?"[33] There would simply be no incentive for him to spend much time copying stuff that would strike his readers as clearly idolatrous and offensive to Christian tastes.

Rather similar remarks must be made about a second crucial collection of Hermetic materials. During the early fifth century CE, an otherwise unknown Macedonian named Johannes compiled an enormous collection of philosophical excerpts for the education of his son Septimius. He is known as Johannes Stobaeus after the town where he lived, Stobi (still a chief archaeological site in Macedonia today). While the name Johannes suggests he was a Christian, his collection is focused entirely on Hellenic philosophy and contains no Christian materials or references. Among the more than five hundred entries were forty Hermetic fragments: ten from our *Corpus Hermeticum* (CH II, IV, X), one from the *Logos Teleios*, and twenty-nine that are unattested elsewhere and now known as the "Stobaean Hermetica." Their length varies from one single sentence to a complete treatise. Sometime during the ninth century, a manuscript of Stobaeus' "Excerpts, Sayings and Precepts" (nowadays referred to as the *Anthologion*) came into the hands of the Byzantine scholar and Patriarch

---

[31] For all these elements, see Kaldellis and Siniossoglou, "Introduction," 19.
[32] Dickey, "Classical Scholarship," 64.
[33] HHE II, 40.

Photios, who described it in his *Bibliotheca*. He confirmed that Johannes' introduction (now mostly lost) contained a praise of philosophy and an overview of the various philosophical schools. Photios' manuscript is no longer extant. Some time around the year 1000 CE, his own copy or a similar archetype was separated into two parts that were henceforth copied independently from one another. The standard edition by Curth Wachsmuth and Otto Hense (in three volumes, 1884–1912) is based on manuscripts from the fourteenth and fifteenth centuries.[34]

Stobaeus was interested in Hermes as a philosopher and placed him next to such great authorities as Plato and Pythagoras. This makes it likely that materials with a more practical and experiental focus would not have made it into his collection to begin with. Moreover, as pointed out by David Litwa, Stobaeus "probably edited his Hermetic material to increase its intelligibility and to fit the scope of his (mainly philosophical) project. He may also have split up or combined Hermetic excerpts from different treatises."[35] Christian Wildberg goes even further:

> There is a certain amount of evidence ... (which would require a great deal of philological discussion to lay out) that the Macedonian polymath John of Stobi (early fifth century CE) was already dealing with a severely impaired text. The main reason why the Hermetic fragments preserved in his writings read so much clearer than our manuscripts is not that he had access to an unspoiled tradition, but rather that he doctored, corrected, and emended for the benefit of his own readers, not at all unlike what modern editors have done. If this is true, we may infer that already before Stobaeus' time, in the centuries in which most Hermetists were supposedly active (second to fourth centuries), the treatises now in our collection had already undergone quite dramatic changes. Moreover ... such alterations likely occurred when annotated working copies owned by "Hermetic scholars" were copied out by rather irresponsible scribes whose charge it was to produce clean and legible copies. Either on account of their lack of training or an overly developed reverence for every single written word, they incorporated the marginal notes into a new continuous text without regard for sense and syntax, by a process best described as mechanical interpolation.[36]

Wildberg has called attention to the profoundly distorting effects of such "mechanical interpolation" not only in the Stobaean fragments but in the *Corpus Hermeticum* as well.[37] In a fascinating analysis, he demonstrates

---

[34] For introductions to the Stobaean Hermetica and the manuscript transmission, see Scott I, 82–86; HT III, i–ccxxviii; Litwa, *Hermetica II*, 19–25 (followed on pp. 27–159 by what should now be considered the standard English translation).
[35] Litwa, *Hermetica II*, 20.
[36] Wildberg, "*Corpus Hermeticum*, Tractate III," 134–135.
[37] Wildberg, "*Corpus Hermeticum*, Tractate III," 129–135.

that although the short treatise known as CH III consists of just 326 words, it contains no fewer than *nine* substantial marginal notes that did not belong in the original version at all but were inserted into the main text by incompetent or irresponsible scribes, possibly at a very early stage even prior to the Byzantine period. What seemed to be an incomprehensible text full of grammatical errors becomes perfectly clear once these additions are restored to their original place in the margins of the text.[38] The implications are far-reaching. Ever since the universal condemnation of Walter Scott's editorial practices,[39] the new edition by Nock and Festugière that took its place has been considered the gold standard that could be safely used as a basis for new translations and interpretations. But if Wildberg is right, we need an entirely new edition, and it is likely to change our understanding of the Hermetica in many fundamental respects.[40] Almost uniquely among scholars of the Hermetica, he does not hesitate to critique what he calls the "questionable editorial practice, generally adopted by Nock and Festugière and other editors and translators, to prefer the (intelligible) readings in Stobaeus to the more difficult readings in the codices."[41] In other words, if Stobaeus provides us with a "better text" of parallel passages in CH II, IV, X and the *Asclepius*, this does not prove that his version is closer to the original. More likely he was cleaning up already corrupted passages and turning them into readable prose.

Finally,[42] we have a collection of forty-nine short *Definitions of Hermes Trismegistus to Asclepius*, most of which have reached us only in Armenian.[43] The historical background is that at the second council of

---

[38] Wildberg, "*Corpus Hermeticum*, Tractate III," 135–147. See the new cleaned-up translation on pp. 146–147. One may add that while G.R.S. Mead's edition and translation (1906) was universally ignored by scholars because of the author's Theosophical commitments (see Hanegraaff, "Out of Egypt"), he sometimes saw more clearly than his learned despisers: see Wildberg, "*Corpus Hermeticum*, Tractate III," 147 note 46 quoting Mead, *Thrice-Greatest Hermes*, vol. 2, 82.

[39] See above, p. 52 note 18.

[40] Such a project is announced in Wildberg, "*Corpus Hermeticum*, Tractate III," 149 note 50; Wildberg, "*General Discourses*," 140 note 17.

[41] Wildberg, "Astral Discourse in the *Corpus Hermeticum*," 8 note 12.

[42] On the so-called "Testimonia" and the Christian reception history, see below, pp. 327–332.

[43] Critical annotated edition with French translation in HT V, 193–279 (including Greek parallels from the manuscript Clarkianus Graecus 11, Oxford). The first critical edition (with Russian translation) was published in 1956 by the Armenian scholar H. Manandyan ("Ermeay Eṙameci aṙ Asklepios Sahmankʻ"), and noted only by Dörrie, Review of *Banber Matenadarani* vol. 3 (1957). Two parallel but independent French translations were published in 1976 (Durand, "Un traité hermétique"; Mahé, "'Les définitions'"), followed by the fundamental discussion with critical edition and French translation in HHE II, 273–406; English translation in WHCH, 99–122; new edition in CH V, 210–279.

Dvin in 555 CE, the Armenian Apostolic Church separated from the Greek Church because of conflicts over the Christological doctrine adopted at the Council of Chalcedon (451 CE). The Armenian position was rejected as monophysite heresy by the Greek Eastern Orthodox Church but described as "miaphysitism" by its adherents. The break of 555 CE led to a wave of new translations into Armenian to support the creation of a national educational curriculum that should replace dependence on Greek.[44] As part of these efforts, it appears that a series of short Hermetic statements were translated into Armenian. Because neither the Greek original nor the translator's own manuscript still exist, all we have is a series of later transcripts dating from between the thirteenth and the eighteenth centuries.[45] This means that again we must count with significant alterations by Byzantine scribes, as already noted by the first modern editor:

> In particular it must be emphasized that this small work, attributed to Hermes Trismegistus because of its pagan contents that were disparate and unfamiliar and unintelligible to scribes with a Christian view of the world, has been sensibly altered by them. For this reason, reading and correctly establishing the text was very difficult and required a great deal of effort and work for me.[46]

Like the Byzantine scribes who copied the treatises of our *Corpus Hermeticum* and the Stobaean fragments, the clerk who put these *Definitions* into Armenian was inspired not by scholarly concerns but by pious educational agendas that would leave little room for copying stuff that might offend Christian tastes. It is therefore no surprise that they read like smooth statements of philosophical theology without overt references to religious cultic practice or religious experience.

The overall conclusion should be clear. Apart from a very limited number of original papyri,[47] for most of our information about Hermetic spirituality we are at the mercy of scribes. All these materials went through a narrow bottleneck of Byzantine transmission that functioned very much like a black box: we know what came out of it at our end, but we hardly know what went in. Most of all, we can only speculate about what could

---

[44] HHE II, 327–328. For these historical backgrounds, see Inglisian, "Chalkedon und die armenische Kirche"; and for the movement of translation, see Tirian, "Hellenizing School."

[45] Overview of the manuscript tradition in HHE II, 320–327; HT V, 200–208. For some passages we have Greek parallels from other sources, as indicated in Mahé's standard edition.

[46] Manandyan, "Ermeay Eṙameci aṙ Asklepios Sahmankʿ," 297; my English is based on Mahé's French translation of the passage in HHE II, 275–276 note 6.

[47] Convenient short overview in Van den Kerchove, *Hermès Trismégiste*, 15–17.

have gone in but just didn't make it or was deliberately suppressed. It is perfectly clear that much has been lost that will never be recovered; and there is no doubt that most of what *was* recovered has been severely damaged in the process of transmission. It only reached us in severely diluted and doctored versions that may easily distort the original picture, possibly beyond recognition. If such are the facts, then can we hope to reconstruct Hermetic spirituality at all?

HERMETICA AND HERMENEUTICS

To address this crucial question, let us step back for a moment and consider *what it means* to reconstruct a lost practice by interpreting textual sources. We tend to take for granted that in such an undertaking, our superior technical skills and philological sophistication give us an advantage over medieval and early modern scribes and intellectuals. They were blinded by theological prejudice but our eyes are open; therefore our task consists in cleaning away their false interpretations to the best of our ability so as to recover the original meaning. While I share that ambition in principle (otherwise there would be no point to writing this book), our confidence should be tempered not only by the obvious limitations of what our sources still allow us to recover, but also by acknowledging the limits imposed by our own intellectual horizon. We will have ample occasion to see that in modern scholarship of the Hermetica, powerful patterns of intellectual prejudice have distorted the evidence at least as seriously as happened in the work of our medieval and early modern predecessors.

To understand why this is the case *and* how we can handle such a situation, much can be learned from the great German theoretician of hermeneutics Hans-Georg Gadamer (1900–2002). His central insight was that there is no such thing as understanding without prejudice. Why this is so can be explained in German a bit easier than in English: the direct translation of prejudice, *Vorurteil*, means literally "prior judgment," and Gadamer uses it as equivalent to such terms as *Vormeinung*, "prior opinion" or *Vorverständnis*, "prior understanding." The following remarks are applicable to *all* readers of the Hermetica without exception, whether they are medieval scribes or modern scholars. Obviously that includes the author of these lines.

He who wants to understand a text always practices some kind of projection. As soon as some initial meaning shows itself in the text, right away he projects a meaning of the whole. But that initial meaning shows itself only because one is already reading the text with certain expectations suggestive of some specific meaning. The process of understanding what has been written consists in the further development of such an initial projection, which, however, is revised continuously because of what emerges as one delves deeper into the meaning.[48]

This is the famous "hermeneutic circle."[49] In the publications produced by more than a century of scholarship about the Hermetica, we encounter strong examples on almost every page. Because the entire history of reception, selection, and transmission (from Church fathers and Byzantine scribes to Humanist translators of the Renaissance period and beyond) was already built on the projection of Christian theological notions on Hermetic texts, it is no wonder that in their attempts to make sense of the Hermetica, twentieth-century scholars have constantly been tempted to continue that basic process.[50] This happened all the more easily because until the most recent decades, "history of religions" was considered a theological subdiscipline and most of its practitioners had gone through years of training in Christian-theological faculties. As for classicists, most of them were working in an intellectual framework known as philhellenism, built on a nineteenth-century liberal humanist culture in which not just Western civilization but even the very phenomenon of civilization as such was seen in terms of Greek science and rationality combined with Christian morality.[51] Even early critics of philhellenism such as Reitzenstein participated in a cultural discourse where Christian theology determined the basic rules of engagement; and hence it was widely taken for granted (although not always acknowledged explicitly) that the ultimate relevance of studying the "pagan" religions of late antiquity lay less in their intrinsic interest than in the contribution such research could make to understanding "the rise of Christianity." Under the influence of grand narratives on broadly Hegelian foundations, most scholars saw this rise not as a historical contingency that might as well have happened differently or not at all, but as

---

[48] Gadamer, *Hermeneutik I*, 271. Again, the meaning of the word "projection" is clearer in German than in English: "Wer einen Text verstehen will, vollzieht immer ein *Entwerfen*. Er *wirft* sich einen Sinn des Ganzen *voraus*... Im ausarbeiten eines solchen *Vorentwurfs* ..." (my emphasis). The German verb *werfen* suggests the physical act of throwing an object through space.
[49] Gadamer, *Hermeneutik I*, 194, 202, 221, 270–281; Gadamer, "Vom Zirkel des Verstehens"; Di Cesare, *Gadamer*, 84–86.
[50] For examples, see below pp. 80–82, 125–127, 171–174, 194, 362–363.
[51] See the impressive overview article by Marchand, "From Liberalism to Neoromanticism"; and for the larger story of philhellenism, see her monograph *Down From Olympus*. For the relation to the study of the Hermetica, see Hanegraaff, "Out of Egypt," and below pp. 360–363.

a momentous evolutionary shift towards a new and higher level of human consciousness and human civilization as a whole. This very will to believe in the necessity of cultural progress through history led to a simultaneous obsession with the specter of "decline."[52]

All these heavy ideological assumptions, agendas, commitments, frames, and narratives created a systemic pattern of intellectual prejudice that automatically privileged Christian theology, rational science and philosophy, and "civilized values" as understood by modern intellectuals, while discrediting everything that had traditionally been perceived as their radical counterpart. Egypt was a prime example in the scholarly imagination.[53] It was from the darkness of Egypt that the people of Israel had once been liberated; this country's religion epitomized the pagan idolatry that was rejected with horror by Jews and Christians alike; it stood symbolically for all those perverse temptations and delusions typical of "the Orient" and its irrational cults; in short, with its obscure hieroglyphs and weird animal-headed deities, it was widely imagined as a sinister "occult" threat and dark counterpart to the light of science and reason that was shining from Greece.[54] Even its very attraction relied on such negative perceptions.[55] All these patterns of prejudice were running

---

[52] The well-known fascination with decadence and decline in the decades around 1900 found its classic formulation in Oswald Spengler's bestseller *Der Untergang des Abendlandes* (*The Decline of the West*, 1918/1922). Festugière's *Révélation d'Hermès Trismégiste* is built entirely on the notion of a "decline of rationalism" under the influence of "the prophets of the Orient" (RHT I, 1–44). If science and reason had fallen into decline during late antiquity, this could conceivably happen again, as suggested by Spengler's cyclical historiography. If so, the Hegelian grand narrative of progress and evolution could turn out to be an illusion: the age of modern science and Enlightenment might be just another cycle that had already passed its zenith. This fear that we might be entering a new "age of darkness" explains much of the frantic obsession, among turn-of-the-century philhellenists, with defending rationality against the rise of "irrational cults." These concerns reached fever pitch when European civilization descended into destructive war after 1914, an event that seemed to confirm their worst fears.

[53] On historical narratives as imaginal constructs, see Hanegraaff, "Religion and the Historical Imagination"; and below, Epilogue, pp. 352–368. On the "memory of Egypt" in the collective imagination of Western culture, see the indispensable oeuvre of Jan Assmann, notably his *Moses the Egyptian: The Memory of Egypt in Western Monotheism*. For the general story of how mainstream Western culture has been defining its own identity against paganism as "rejected knowledge," see Hanegraaff, *Esotericism and the Academy*.

[54] For the anti-pagan/anti-idolatry discourse, next to Assmann see notably Halbertal and Margalit, *Idolatry*. Concerning Egypt as emblematic of "the Orient" in the study of the Hermetica, Festugière's *Révélation d'Hermès Trismégiste* remains the ultimate example.

[55] On the dialectics of explicit rejection and secret desire in such constructs of identity and alterity, see the brilliant typology in Baumann, "Grammars of Identity and Alterity."

like a background script in the minds and imaginations of scholars as they were reading the Hermetica in search of frameworks of interpretation. Greece versus Egypt, philosophy versus religion, reason versus superstition: ultimately these were codes for "good" versus "bad," and scholars felt that they had to choose sides.

Now Gadamer's point is that without any *Vorurteil* there can be no hermeneutics, no interpretation, no understanding. But this does not imply a relativist perspective in which "anything goes" and scholars are free to impose their own subjective readings on ancient texts; on the contrary, hermeneutics is all about trying to *understand* those texts as adequately as possible, by *listening* to what they have to tell us. Far from legitimizing a passive attitude of "objective" detachment, this requires an active *encounter* of subjectivities, a true conversation between reader and text.[56] In an important passage, Gadamer explains why such an encounter can be conducted *neither* in the scholar's "etic" language *nor* in the "emic" language of the text[57] but requires a subtle art of mediation between both languages at the same time:

[T]he legitimate requirement that historical consciousness should understand a historical period in terms of its own concepts [is] essentially a relational requirement that makes sense only with reference to one's own concepts. Historical consciousness misunderstands its own nature when in order to understand, it would like to exclude that which alone makes understanding possible. *To think historically* in fact means *managing the transposition that the concepts of the past undergo* when we try to think in them. Thinking historically always involves some mediation between those concepts and one's own thinking. Wishing to avoid one's own concepts in the act of interpretation is not just impossible but an evident absurdity. Interpreting means precisely bringing in one's own prior concepts, so that the text may truly be allowed to express its meaning.[58]

My general approach to translation as outlined in the first chapter is based on the same hermeneutic principle.[59] So what are the implications for my project of reconstructing Hermetic spirituality on the basis of sources that

---

[56] E.g. Gadamer, *Hermeneutik I*, 309–310. Gadamer speaks of *Horizontverschmelzung* ("merging of horizons").

[57] The emic/etic terminology is not used by Gadamer but may be helpful to connect his argument to relevant methodological discussions in the study of religion. On the dialectical relation between "emic" and "etic" language, see Hanegraaff, *Esotericism and the Academy*, 157–158 note 12 (and note that the common tendency of pitting "the emic approach" against "the etic approach" reflects a fundamental misunderstanding of that dialectics).

[58] Gadamer, *Hermeneutik I*, 400–401 (emphasis in original).

[59] See above, pp. 12–16.

are so heavily infected by misreadings, interpolations, and rewritings of Christian scribes? We need to make subtle distinctions here. We already saw that the positive function of *Vorurteil* in textual hermeneutics does *not* give us a license to just impose our own concepts on the texts we are reading, so that they will comfortably echo our own obsessions back to us. On the contrary, hermeneutics is all about leaving our intellectual comfort zone and "placing *ourselves* there."[60] As we enter a strange world of meaning where we do not know the way, we cannot avoid bringing all our prior assumptions and prejudiced opinions with us; but the all-important point is that *we put them to the test* and allow them to be challenged by the new environment into which they have been projected. If we just keep speaking our own language and do not listen, we learn nothing. But if we think we can somehow remove ourselves from the situation, together with our patterns of prejudice, we fall into the contrary delusion of false objectivity and will learn nothing either. In both cases we avoid the opportunity of an encounter. The conclusion is that we must neither talk to the text nor sit back and wait for the text to talk to us; rather, the art of hermeneutics involves talking *with* the text and allowing it to talk with us. Texts, like their readers, have agency in the practice of conversation.[61]

It follows that our core problem lies not in the unavoidable presence of *Vorurteil* in any act of interpretation, but in a lack of full engagement with the *otherness* of the Hermetica. We tend to use interpretation so as to make these texts fit our own agendas rather than allowing those agendas to be challenged by the texts. A particularly sneaky variant of this temptation lies in the naïve assumption that prejudice can be corrected by "letting the sources speak for themselves" and just "sticking to the facts alone"; that is, in refraining from interpretation altogether. The first perspective ("talking to the text") is evident in countless publications informed by more or less explicit theological or philosophical frameworks or background assumptions. The second one ("just let the text talk") reflects a quasi-positivist descriptivism that allows scholars to repeat, translate, paraphrase or summarize the exact statements of their sources while dismissing any interpretive move as "mere speculation."[62] Both perspectives are hermeneutically deficient.

---

[60] Gadamer, *Hermeneutik I*, 310 (literally "*Sichversetzen*").
[61] Gadamer, *Hermeneutik I*, 273, 304, 367, 375, 465. Note that while the verb *Verstehen* means "understanding," the almost untranslatable noun *Verständigung* is closer to "agreement," as *sich verständigen* might be translated roughly as "having an understanding" (cf. Zenk, "*Verständigung*"). Also: Felski, *Limits of Critique*, 84.
[62] Hanegraaff, "Altered States of Knowledge," 131–132.

How then can we deal with our problem of a heavily corrupt transmission of Hermetic materials? It seems to me that the answer follows from the preceding discussion. Understanding requires an encounter of subjectivities in which as readers we move out of our comfort zones to confront the *otherness* of a world that challenges and violates our own assumptions and patterns of prejudice. This means that precisely those elements in the Hermetica that strike us as familiar (those that make us feel comfortably "at home" in our own mental world, surrounded by concepts and ideas that we readily know and understand) are most likely to lead us astray. This was precisely the methodological error at the heart of Festugière's *Révélation d'Hermès Trismégiste*: by searching only for what the Hermetica had in common with the Greek ideas and traditions that he knew so well, while marginalizing or discrediting anything with which he did not feel comfortable, he ended up seeing little else in them than secondhand "collections of philosophical banalities ... self-contradictory clichés puffed up by feeble minds."[63] On the contrary, the challenge is to look precisely for what is unfamiliar, strange, baffling, and obscure – in short: for what we do *not* understand. Furthermore, and at least as important, we must be alert to the risk that what strikes us as familiar and readily recognizable may not actually be what it seems to us – that without realizing it, we may already have placed it in a frame that makes sense to us but is not what the original authors had in mind. We will encounter strong examples on the pages that follow.

But the hermeneutical challenge goes deeper than removing inadequate frameworks and replacing them by better ones. To perceive what *is* actually there, we must put ourselves on the line and allow for the possibility that as scholars we may simply not know yet *what it would even mean to "understand" these things*.[64] We think of "understanding" as a mental process that reduces strangeness to familiarity, so that what used to be obscure will finally become clear: "first we did not know what to make of it, but now it all makes sense." However, the authors of the Hermetica were searching for something that is unknown to us, something for which *qua* scholars we have no room in our mental universe: a supra-rational *gnōsis* that can be accessed only by an enigmatic faculty called *nous*. This cannot be the

---

[63] As well formulated by Kingsley, "An Introduction," 20.
[64] Here I have taken inspiration from the anthropologist Matthijs van de Port in his study of Brazilian candomblé, notably his reflections on the nature of what the adherents of the cult refer to as "deep knowledge" (van de Port, *Ecstatic Encounters*, 11–15 and passim).

"knowledge" familiar to us from our common intellectual culture – it must be something else. Taking this seriously means coming back once more to the dialectical nature of hermeneutics as analyzed by Gadamer: "managing the transposition" that Hermetic concepts undergo "when we try to think in them"[65] includes managing the transposition that our *own* concepts must undergo at the same time. As we have seen already in the discussion of Iamblichus' concept of "innate knowledge" (*emphutos gnōsis*), this means that grasping the meaning of *gnōsis* may very well require questioning our most basic concepts of what "knowledge" is all about.[66]

WEIRDNESS AT THE CENTER

In Chapter 1, I asked my readers to imagine the Hermetic texts and their ideas as arranged in a circular manner around a center, with the spiritual Way of Hermes at the heart of the circle. Prime candidates for a position close to this center are (1) the only Hermetic treatise known to us exclusively from a papyrus manuscript in Coptic, and usually referred to as "The Ogdoad and the Ennead" (NH VI⁶); (2) the crucial treatise on rebirth known as CH XIII; and (3) the revelatory account in CH I, known as the Poimandres. What they all have in common is a strong emphasis on experience and praxis as opposed to mere theoretical reflection. The first two texts in particular are our strongest available testimonies of *Hermetic otherness*, that is to say, of information that would have struck Christian scribes as unfamiliar, strange, baffling, and obscure. This simple fact speaks for their authenticity and for comparatively low probabilities of scribal tampering. Having been discovered as late as 1945, "The Ogdoad and the Ennead" did *not* survive the process of scribal selection and transmission, and we can only speculate as to how many similar treatises may be lost to us forever.[67] As for CH XIII, we are lucky to have it at all; if its contents raised any scribal eyebrows, all one can say is that apparently it was given a pass, most probably because the copyist failed to understand what he was reading. As for CH I, I would see it as a prime example of the phenomenon, mentioned towards the end of the previous section, of a text getting misframed as something different from what it really was. Reassured by

---

[65] Gadamer, *Hermeneutik I*, 401 (see quotation above, p. 135); see also the dialectics of imagination briefly discussed below, Epilogue, pp. 364–368.
[66] I will return to this point in Chapter 10, pp. 310–319.
[67] On the scribe who copied the Nag Hammadi Hermetica and claimed to have "a very great number" of other treatises by Hermes in his possession (HT V, 146–147), see below, p. 282.

apparent similarities with the Genesis account and probably adapting it further to fit Christian tastes, scribes and scholars miscategorized as a creation myth what was in fact the account of a visionary revelation.

From this center of Hermetic weirdness[68] focused on experiential praxis, we may envision the remainder of our treatises – or selected parts of them – as fanning out further towards the periphery the more strongly they concentrate on pure theoretical reflection. The more a text or fragment would be concerned with conventional questions of philosophy and theology (the nature of the world, of the human being, and of God), the greater would be its chance to get copied at all, and the more vulnerable would it be to editorial tampering during the long process of transmission. In sum, statistically the chances both of survival *and* of corruption increase as we move further away from the center. Additionally, a few of our treatises and fragments have little or no relevance to Hermetic spirituality at all and may therefore be placed even beyond the periphery altogether.

In taking this approach, I do not mean to suggest that theoretical reflection was unimportant to Hermetic spirituality. Still, *how* important it really was remains a matter of speculation. In a textual "survival of the fittest" over long periods of time and under rough dogmatic conditions, theological and philosophical reflections along broadly Platonic lines enjoyed a strong advantage, especially if they could be seen as compatible with Christian doctrine. By comparison, descriptions of overtly pagan practices and strange experiential phenomena had just a slim chance to make it through. Therefore the much larger quantity of purely theoretical passages among the surviving Hermetica tells us pretty little about the original situation. They certainly do not allow us to recreate a "systematic theology" of Hermes.[69]

Let us now take a closer look at those Hermetic texts that came to us through the bottleneck of Byzantine transmission. Because the

---

[68] On *weirdness* as a category in the study of religion and culture, see the stimulating discussions in Davis, *High Weirdness*, 1–41. I see remarkable resonances with van de Port's anthropological analysis of *bafflement* as central to Candomblé (*Ecstatic Encounters*, Chapter 6); see especially the story of an informant named Walmir (ibid., 194–196) in relation to Davis' material, as well as Jeff Kripal's very similar notion of *the impossible* (Kripal, *Authors of the Impossible*); finally, see van de Port's emphasis on bafflement and the experience of "impossibly" weird events as crucial to Candomblé's insistence that "deep knowledge" is incommunicable because it requires physical *immediacy* here and now (*Ecstatic Encounters*, 203, 207; cf. my discussion of Iamblichus' "innate *gnōsis*" [ἔμφυτος γνῶσις] in Chapter 4, pp. 112–118).

[69] For a major recent example, see Law, *Das Corpus Hermeticum*; and see Hanegraaff, Review of Law.

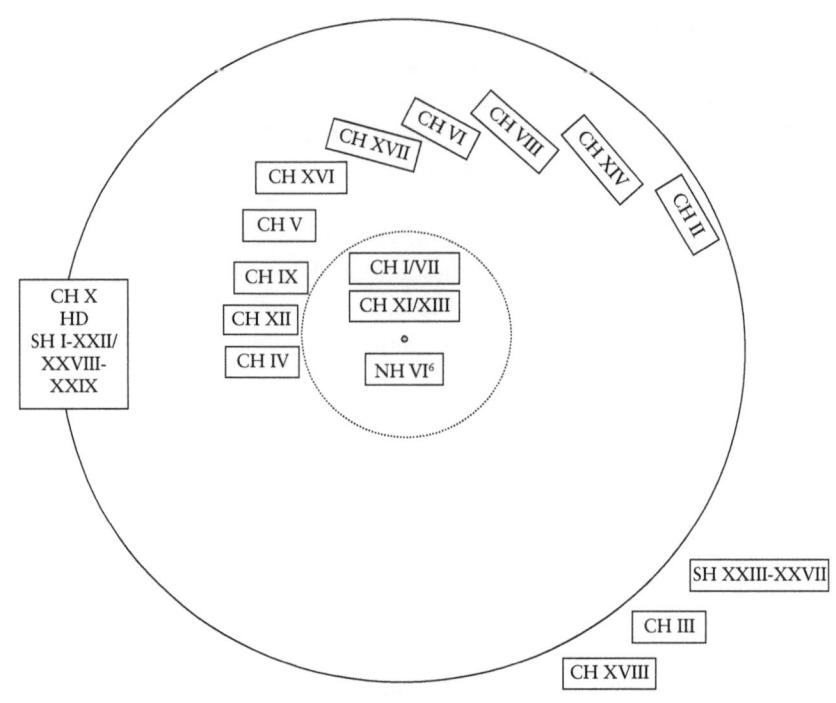

FIGURE 5.1: Circular ordering of the Spiritual Hermetica

conventional order of the treatises (CH I–XIV, XVI–XVIII; SH I–XXIX; HD I–X) tells us nothing about their original sequence, if there was any, my first step consists of an attempt at reshuffling the materials in a circular arrangement on the basis of their contents (see Figure 5.1).

As already indicated, two treatises are not actually Hermetic and are therefore placed just beyond the periphery, while a further series has no relevance to Hermetic spirituality:

- *CH III*. Only the title, "A Sacred Discourse of Hermes," is Hermetic. This fragmentary account of creation shows influence from the Stoa and the Septuagint rather than Platonic speculation. Its relevance to Hermetic spirituality is limited to some vague similarities with the account of creation in CH I.
- *CH XVIII*. A piece of rhetorical praise of God and Kings, without any clear connection to the Hermetica. Hermes or his pupils are never mentioned.[70]

---

[70] On the non-Hermetic nature of CH XVIII, see Scott II, 461; HT II, 244 (but see note 3); cf. Cop, 209–210 and Van den Kerchove, *La voie*, 148 with note 253.

- SH XXIII–XXVII. Contrary to common usage, I do not include these treatises under the spiritual Hermetica because they are sharply different from the rest of our treatises in terms of their alleged authors, contents, worldview, and literary style. Hermes does not appear either as a teacher or as a pupil; instead, we read conversations between Isis and Horus in which "all-knowing Hermes" is presented as their remote divine ancestor. The mythological narrative describes God as an anthropomorphic and authoritarian Craftsman who punishes the souls he has created for transgressing his commands. The great beauty of the higher world does not inspire love and admiration but fear; and when the souls are disobedient, they are punished for their sins by imprisonment in the "dishonorable and lowly tents" or "shells" of material bodies. Throughout, the emphasis is on God's despotic power and his creatures' fear of him. Because I see all of this as incompatible with what we find in the rest of our corpus, I assume that these Isis-Horus treatises represent a separate tradition.[71]

Ten treatises are more or less exclusively theoretical in nature. I place them provisorily in a sequential order (CH II – XIV – VIII – VI – XVII – V – XVI – IX – XII – IV) that roughly approximates the increasing relevance of their contents to the central practice of spiritual salvation. The first six treatises in this series are mostly concerned with God and how his perfect goodness gets obscured by the bodily passions; the final four treatises are placed closer to the center because they are much more strongly concerned with the divine *nous*, the faculty of spiritual salvation.

- CH II. Theory of movement, space, and emptiness. Only the generative source of all that is, referred to as God, can really be considered good.
- CH XIV. The whole of creation has been made by God who is wholly good. He is not responsible for what is bad.

---

[71] On SH XXIII–XXVII, see Scott III, 471–628; HT III, cxxvi–ccxxviii. The different "setting" and "intellectual climate" of these texts was already highlighted by Dodd, Review of Nock and Festugière (1956), 303–304; cf. Fowden, *Egyptian Hermes*, 28–29, 33. Bull, on the other hand, does not treat the series as separate (*Tradition*, 101–121). Specifically about SH XXIII (*Korē Kosmou*), see Festugière, "La création des âmes"; RHT III, 37–41, 83–89; Betz, "Schöpfung und Erlösung"; Jackson, "Κόρη Κόσμου"; Carozzi, "Gnose et sotériologie"; CHD, 400–420; HG, 340–349; Litwa, *Hermetica II*, 100–106.

- *CH VIII*. Theory of God, the cosmos, and the human being. Death does not exist, for all change is transformation.
- *CH VI*. Similar to CH II, the point is that only God can be considered good. The universal reality of the divine gets obscured by the bodily passions, which must therefore be overcome.
- *CH XVI*. God as the ultimate source, here with the Sun as the creator of the cosmos. We are dominated by cosmic fate through the agency of daimons, but can be saved by divine light through mediation of the Sun.
- *CH XVII*. [fragm.] The incorporeal can be reflected in corporeal images.[72]
- *CH V*. Theology of God as the invisible true reality that can, however, be perceived through our *nous*. Theoretical justification for the praxis of salvational *gnōsis*.
- *CH IX*. Theory of perception, resulting in what might be called a treatise on Hermetic psychology. Perception through the bodily senses is unreliable because they get infected by daimons; but our *nous* allows a higher perception of divine realities, *noēsis*.
- *CH XII*. A more specific focus on *nous* and *logos*, with attention to the extent to which they are subject to fate; followed by an account of God's universal presence in the universe and the nonexistence of death.
- *CH IV*. God has sent a mixing-bowl with *nous* down to earth as a prize to be won by human beings. Salvation through *nous* requires liberation from the bodily passions because the object of divine knowledge is purely incorporeal.

CH X and the Armenian "Hermetic Definitions" can be given a special status insofar as they present summaries of the Hermetic worldview as a whole. To them I attach most of the Stobaean fragments as well; of course the selection comes from Johannes of Stobi, but his collection as a whole amounts to something like an encyclopedic overview of Hermetic topics insofar as they could interest philosophers.

---

[72] The placement of this short fragment, of which we do not know the original context, is admittedly questionable. Because its point is that incorporeal essences can be reflected in corporeal images, I provisorily place it between CH XVI and V, which both focus on the relation between the invisible incorporeal God and the visible corporeal world; but of course one might also want to connect it to the discussion of temple images in the *Asclepius*.

- *CH X*. Titled "The Key," this is our most comprehensive overview of Hermetic theory. Discussions of God/the Good, the cosmos, reincarnation and the punishment of the soul, the effect of bodily passions, Hermetic psychology (*nous, logos, psuchē, pneuma*), salvation through noetic vision, and deification.
- *HD*. The Hermetic Definitions too could be seen as a summary of Hermetic theory, now in the form of short statements.
- *SH I–XXII/XXVIII–XXIX*. Considered as a whole, these Stobaean Hermetica consist of fragments on a variety of theoretical topics, notably God, creation, the world, the demiurge, the decans, justice, providence, necessity, fate, free will, time, being, life, the soul, reincarnation, energies, matter, the body, procreation, secrecy, *nous, logos*, and reverence.

Finally, at the center of the circle we find first of all the divine revelation of CH I, to which I attach the visionary's sermon based on that revelation (CH VII).

- *CH I* (Poimandres). Revelation by the divine *nous* in a visionary state, including an account of the loss and regaining of knowledge, after which the visionary embarks on a mission to spread the word.
- *CH VII*. A Hermetic sermon based on the revelation of CH I.

Next we have the account of rebirth known as CH XIII. I will be arguing that it must be read in tandem with the theoretical account of the *aiōn* and noetic vision in CH XI.

- *CH XI*. As in CH I, we hear the divine *nous* himself addressing Hermes. He discusses the nature of the *aiōn* and the perception of the cosmos through noetic vision following rebirth.
- *CH XIII*. The process of Hermetic rebirth by which such vision is activated.

And finally there is the unique description of Hermetic ascent in NH VI[6], where the reborn pupil joins his brethren in the eighth and the ninth sphere.

- *NH VI[6]*. Hermes leads Tat into the Ogdoad and the Ennead.

It goes without saying that this procedure of reshuffling in a circular arrangement must be seen as a heuristic device, and my sequential order of the theoretical treatises can never be more than a rough approximation. The intention is to facilitate access to the materials while insisting that there is a hierarchy of greater or lesser importance in relation to the central concerns of Hermetic spirituality. I have no doubt that theoretical discussions as in CH II or V, for instance, were studied very seriously by aspiring pupils; still, they cannot have been as important to them as the impressive account of how a visionary met Poimandres face to face, or how Tat achieved spiritual rebirth and his spiritual eyes were opened, not to mention the dazzling description of how he finally ascended to the noumenal realms under the guidance of Hermes. *This* was the real thing. *This* is what the path was really all about.

6

Healing the Soul

> *So that with much ado I was corrupted, and made to learn the dirty devices of this world. Which now I unlearn, and become, as it were, a little child again that I may enter into the Kingdom of God.*
> Thomas Traherne[1]

In the most peaceful and prosperous years of the Roman Empire, the philosopher Plutarch (*c.* 46–119 CE) retired to his small country home in Boeotia to devote himself to writing. Born into a wealthy and educated family from Chaeronea, as a young man he had studied philosophy in Athens and later served his country as Greek deputy to the Roman governor. He had traveled to Asia Minor and Egypt, and spent years as a teacher of philosophy in Rome. He knew many of the powerful men who dominated the politics of the day and had been closely observing their characters and behavior. Back home now in Boeotia, where he served as a priest in the nearby sanctuary of Apollo at Delphi, he settled down to reflect deeply on what he had learned about human nature. In a long series of writings collected under the title *Moralia*, he analyzed the psychological mechanisms behind good and bad behavior; and in a series of biographical studies known as the *Parallel Lives*, he compared the characters of famous Greek and Roman politicians or military men.[2] The focus of Plutarch's interest was on personal self-improvement, for through the examples of these powerful figures one could study the battle between inborn virtue and the temptations of vice. Each biography could

---

[1] Traherne, *Centuries of Meditation* III.3 (*Selected Poems and Prose*, 227).
[2] For the scant biographical data we have, see [Plutarch], *Lives*, vol. 1, xi–xiv ("Introduction"); for the *Parallel Lives*, see Stadter, "General Introduction."

serve as a useful mirror for the soul, an occasion for readers to examine their own moral condition so that they might change it for the better.[3]

What did self-improvement mean? Together with Marcus Aurelius and Seneca, Plutarch is among the very few classical authors who have left us writings about the practice of *meditation*.[4] Its Greek equivalent, *meletaō*, referred to careful and attentive mental praxis, a way of training the mind. As its concern was not with the communication of theoretical content but with the cultivation of mental discipline, techniques of meditation were a matter of direct oral transmission from master to disciple. Hence the relative scarcity of written manuals or descriptions, which should however not lead us to underestimate the importance of spiritual practice in the lives of philosophers. As the French scholar Pierre Hadot has famously pointed out, it was nothing less than *central* to what ancient philosophy was all about:

In antiquity, true philosophy ... means spiritual exercise. Philosophical theories are either put explicitly at the service of spiritual practice, as in stoicism and epicureanism, or they are taken as objects of intellectual exercises, that is to say, of a practice of the contemplative life that itself comes down to nothing else than a spiritual exercise. It is therefore impossible to understand the philosophical theories of antiquity without taking into account this concrete perspective that gives them their true significance. ... Originally philosophy emerged not as a theoretical construction but as a method of formation that aimed at a new way of living and seeing the world, as an attempt to transform the human being.[5]

Meditation was not limited to techniques for disciplining one's thinking alone. The practice was relevant to all dimensions of the soul, including an individual's inner sensations, imaginations, and affects or emotions.[6] The central type of exercise consisted in training the mind's faculty of *attention* (*prosochē*), its ability to stay in the present moment without allowing its inner peace to be disturbed by bodily sensations, interior images, or emotional states.[7]

---

[3] For Plutarch's description of these historical personalities as "guests" invited to share his daily life for a while, so that he can use "history as a mirror" for self-examination, see Plutarch, *Timoleon* 1 (*Lives*, vol. 6, 261–262; cf. Stadter, "General Introduction," xiii). Regarding self-improvement, see Wardman, *Plutarch's Lives*, 18–19; about Plutarch's intended minority audience of "those who know," see ibid., 43, 47.
[4] Rabbow, *Seelenführung*, 20–25.
[5] Hadot, "Exercices spirituels," 65, 71. Cf. Hadot, *What Is Ancient Philosophy?*
[6] Hadot, "Exercices spirituels," 20–21, 28–29.
[7] Hadot, "Exercices spirituels," 26–27. Spiritual exercises in antiquity seem closely equivalent that what is known as "mindfulness" today, which covers a spectrum between "focused attention" on one particular object, thereby minimizing or even excluding disturbance by other objects of attention, and its counterpart, "open awareness," which accepts all salient stimuli as they occur, without pursuing them (van Vugt, "Cognitive Benefits").

Described sometimes as "soul medicine," this meditative practice of philosophers consisted first and foremost in a *therapy of the passions*.[8] It was concerned with healing the sicknesses of the soul that were caused by powerful destructive forces such as insatiability (*aplēstia*), greed (*pleonexia*), wrath (*orgē, thumos*), grief (*lupē*), lust for wealth (*philochrēmatia, philoploutia*), craving for glory and honours (*philotimia, philodoxia*), or the drive to excel and dominate others (*to philoprōton, to philonikon*).[9] As Plutarch pointed out, these were not the *natural* passions, which have a useful and necessary role to play because without them, humans would simply lack the drive for any ethical, social or political activity. The problem lay in the unnecessary and harmful passions that caused a corruption or perversion (*diastrophē*) of the soul. Philosophers like Plutarch pointed out that in our daily lives as embodied human beings, we are constantly exposed to the seductive power of mental representations or fantasies (*phantasiai*), and if our mind lacks the strength to stand firm against their influence, we fall prey to false judgments and delusions of all kinds. Worse than that, as our soul itself gets diseased by those infections, it begins misperceiving its own condition so that it believes itself to be healthy while it is actually sick.[10] Gradually, through daily habit, we get used to our corrupt state of being and come to experience it as natural. This is how we end up living our lives in profound confusion and spiritual ignorance, believing we are in control of ourselves where in fact we are enslaved by harmful passions.

Plutarch's writings were widely disseminated and his influence on later generations was profound. The basic doctrine of the harmful passions was

---

[8] Hadot, "Exercices spirituels," 23, 26. For philosophy as "soul medicine," see Cicero, *Tuscul.* III. 6 (*Est profecto animi medicina philosophia*). Origen reports that Chrysippus had composed a *Therapy of the Passions* (see Arnim, *Stoicorum veterum fragmenta*, III. § 474). See Hadot, "Exercices spirituels," 23 note 5.

[9] See Becchi, "Doctrine of the Passions," 51–52. For Plutarch's contributions, see notably "On the Control of Anger" (Περὶ ἀοργησίας), "On Envy and Hate" (Περὶ φθόνου καὶ μίσους), "On Love of Wealth" (Περὶ φιλοπλουτίας), "Concerning Talkativeness" (Περὶ ἀδολεσχίας), "On Curiosity" (Περὶ πολυπραγμοσύνης), "On Praising Oneself Inoffensively" (Περὶ τοῦ ἑαυτὸν ἐπαινεῖν ἀνεπιφθόνως). All in: [Plutarch], *Moralia*, vols. 6–7. The relevant Greek words, πάθος and παθητός, are difficult to translate (HT I, 76 note 8; CHD, 68 note 169; Cop, 143; cf. Peters, *Terms*, 151–155) because modern readers tend to think positively about "having passions" or "being passionate," although older usage that emphasized suffering still survives in such expressions as "the passion of Christ." As for the word "affect," it has lost most of its poignancy for us and hardly survives as a noun at all.

[10] Plutarch, "Whether the Affections of the Soul are Worse than those of the Body" 500E ([Plutarch], *Moralia*, vol. 6, 381–384); Becchi, "Doctrine of the Passions," 48.

very well known in late antiquity and taken for granted by the authors of the Hermetica, as will be seen. I will be arguing that to a much greater extent than has been recognized, spiritual practices of liberation from the destructive passions – techniques for healing the soul of its afflictions – were central to what the Way of Hermes was all about. However, it is important to see that what the Hermetists were doing went considerably beyond the profound but still relatively gentle meditative exercises practiced widely by philosophers trained in the standard traditions of Stoicism, Epicureanism, or Platonism. The children of Hermes were building upon those foundations, but it appears that they had developed additional techniques as well. Pierre Hadot is at pains to draw a sharp distinction between those types of spiritual exercise that were central to standard philosophical training and those that resulted in more extreme alterations of consciousness, insisting that the former "has absolutely nothing to do with a state of trance or catalepsy in which the body would lose consciousness and thanks to which the soul would find itself in a supernatural visionary state."[11] In this he is certainly correct. However, the Way of Hermes *did* involve such states. Like Iamblichus and his students in Egypt and Syria, Hermetic practitioners believed that to really break our condition of enslavement to the harmful passions, more was needed than calming the mind and cultivating states of serene equilibrium and equanimity. They were after total liberation, radical enlightenment, perfect *gnōsis*.[12] To understand what those ideals meant to them, we will begin by investigating their negative counterpart, the condition that had to be cured. What exactly was meant by mental enslavement, spiritual darkness, blindness to the truth?

IGNORANCE

"As soon as it has entered a body," we read in CH XII, "every soul gets corrupted by pain and pleasure." This happens because the body is a composite, full of pains and pleasures that are "seething in it like

---

[11] Hadot, "Exercices spirituels," 49, and cf. 38–39 note 4; cf. Hadot, *What Is Ancient Philosophy*, 182–188; but see Dubois, "Préface," xix. Hadot's discussion is understandably dominated by the controversial thesis of an "ancient Greek shamanism," which I believe has created more confusion than clarity. As pointed out by Ustinova, "Tagging Greek thinkers as 'shamans' or 'mystics' is a simple way to call attention to their engagement with alterations of consciousness," so the latter terminology is much to be preferred (Ustinova, *Divine* Mania, 339; cf. Hanegraaff, "Platonic Frenzies," 553).

[12] HD VIII 6: "you have the power to liberate yourself, since you have been given everything."

juices," and into which the soul is "dipped and fully immersed."[13] One might say that it enters a poisonous environment where it cannot help but get infected by overpowering destructive passions.[14] The text is explicit: having been plunged into this bubbling cauldron that is the body, our soul fully *drowns* in it.[15] If we remember the discussion between Porphyry and Iamblichus, we see the importance of this image, which means that the soul descends not just partially but completely. The implication, as we have seen, is that philosophy is not enough. The soul has to be healed and rescued by the gods: lost in the body, it cannot save itself but is in need of divine intervention. Therefore it makes perfect sense that we read in CH IV how God decided to send down the means of salvation:

> He filled a large mixing-bowl [with *nous*] and sent it down. And he also sent a herald, ordering him to make this announcement to the human hearts: "If you are able to, then immerse yourselves in this bowl, you who believe that you will rise up towards Him who sent this bowl down to earth, you who know for which purpose you were born."[16]

So here too we have the image of dipping and full immersion (conveyed by the Greek terms for "baptizing" and "baptism," otherwise rare in the

---

[13] CH XII 2; similar combination of pain and pleasure in SH IV 21–22; XI 2:13 (where the combination of pleasure and pain is specific for embodied entities; by contrast, "*nous* cannot suffer" [SH XI 2:15]); cf. HD IX 4. Cf. CH VI 2 "all things that are born are filled with painful emotions – birth itself is already painful" (for my interpretation of πάθος and παθητός here, see above, note 9); and SH XXV 8.

[14] CH III 3 "Here below it is impossible for the good to stay wholly free from what is bad – whatever is good gets corrupted here"; CH VI 6 "[Humans] are overwhelmed from the outset by all that is bad, they believe to be good what is actually bad"; CH X 12 "As a mortal being [the human being] is in fact corrupt"; CH X 15 "[the soul] gets corrupted, and that happens by necessity ... It is the forgetting that corrupts her"; see also SH III 7, XI 5. In translating words like κακία or κακός and their cognates, which are extremely frequent in the Hermetica, I try to avoid "evil" insofar as it carries Christian connotations of moral sin (Van den Kerchove points out that in the Hermetica, we are dealing "not with sin but with passions": *La voie*, 308). In most cases, terms like "bad" or "corrupt(ed)" are to be preferred, as they can be *descriptive* without being condemnatory, somewhat similar to the observations of a physician who can tell his patient "you have a bad heart" or "your lungs are diseased by smoking" without implying sin or evil. See for instance SH XI 2:18–20 and 48: the point is not that humanity is "evil" but that human beings inevitably get corrupted. Nevertheless, we remain capable of choosing the good and can be blamed for not resisting what is bad (SH XI 2:29).

[15] HT I, 175 ("se noie"); Cop, 43 ("drowns"); WHCH, 59 ("is drowned"); CHD, 147 ("völlig eintaucht"). For the rather common image of the body as a "vessel" filled with passions, and various other terms in that context, see Lewy, *Chaldaean Oracles*, 277 note 72.

[16] CH IV 4.

Hermetica[17]) into some kind of bowl or vessel, as in the alchemical procedures practiced by Zosimos.[18] While the vessel of the body contains an unhealthy mixture of pain and pleasure, the divine vessel is filled with the healing medicine or remedy: *nous*.[19] The former causes ignorance, the latter leads to *gnōsis*. To be cured of its afflictions, not just the soul but the heart[20] more specifically is invited to immerse itself in *nous* – if, indeed, it is able to.[21] In a spirit of universal benevolence and boundless generosity, qualities that are essential to what the divine Source is all about,[22] the medicine of the soul is offered to all human beings who are suffering in the body. However, it is up to them to actually take the plunge and profit from its curative powers. Those who choose to make the attempt will need to prepare themselves, by sustained spiritual practice on a firm foundation of knowledge and faith.

Our text holds out the promise that all those who choose to follow the Way of Hermes and persist to its very end will be able to immerse themselves wholly in the vessel of *nous*, thereby achieving *gnōsis* and human perfection.[23] By logical contrast, all those who fail to pursue that path remain in a deplorable state of ignorance and imperfection. Worse than that, the negative passions are bound to pervert their souls and may well end up destroying them altogether:

---

[17] Van den Kerchove, *La voie*, 301: apart from CH IV 4 and XII 2, we find βαπτίζω only in SH XXV 8, where being "dipped" or "plunged" in the body is described as "punishment" (see Litwa, *Hermetica II*, with note 12 about Orphic and Pythagorean backgrounds).

[18] Fraser, "Baptised in *Gnôsis*"; see above, pp. 97–98.

[19] On the *nous* as a medicine for curing the sickness of the soul, see CH XII 3 and discussion below, pp. 179–180, 196.

[20] Nilsson, "Krater," 57–58; Van den Kerchove, *La voie*, 295–297, 301; Bull, *Tradition*, 213–214.

[21] Next to CH IV 4, see also CH VII 2 ("those of you who can").

[22] CH IV 3: God knows only universal generosity, for envy (φθόνος) is one of the major destructive passions "born only here below in the souls of human beings who do not have *nous*." On envy or jealousy as a vice *par excellence* in the context of Hermetic spirituality, see Van den Kerchove, *La voie*, 61, 292; and cf. HD X 6.

[23] CH IV 4. Several scholars have wondered whether this passage about "baptism" in a *kratēr* or mixing-bowl might reflect some kind of Hermetic baptismal rite or the sharing of a ceremonial drink. For the most detailed attempt at such an interpretation, see Van den Kerchove, *La voie*, 279–322, esp. 301–316. While highly ingenious, the hypothesis leaves me unconvinced, and Van den Kerchove admits herself that it rests on minimal foundations (ibid., 312). While discussing Zosimos' reference to the mixing bowl (ibid., 314–315), she does not mention a possibility that would seem slightly more plausible to me, although it remains speculative: in Hermetic circles we could be dealing with a metaphorical interpretation of the alchemical vessel understood as an instrument of purification and healing, not unlike what we saw in the anonymous *Dialogue of the Philosophers and Cleopatra* (see above, pp. 83–85).

Healing the Soul　　　　　151

[I]f a human being makes the inferior choice, it ruins that person ... just as you might see processions of people marching through the crowd, achieving nothing themselves but hindering the others, likewise these people are just parading through the cosmos carried along by their corporeal lusts. ... The sensations those people have are quite close to those of unreasoning animals, and as they are dominated by passion and anger, they have no awe for things worthy of admiration. They are focused on bodily pleasures and appetites, believing that human beings are born for that purpose.[24]

In many other Hermetic treatises we find similar references to the ignorance of the multitudes. Most people spend their lives wandering in darkness, deluded by the senses; many of them are evil, wicked, full of envy, greedy, murderous, without any awe or respect; their state of ignorance resembles drunkenness and sleep; without knowing it, they are the slaves of their own insatiable passions, helpless victims of their fears and desires; like wild animals, they blindly follow their lusts and violent impulses.[25]

Why such deplorable behavior? The reason seems perfectly clear. Having been "dipped and fully immersed" in the seething cauldron of the body, the souls of these people are poisoned and thoroughly corrupted by destructive passions. It is no surprise then that when Tat expresses his ardent wish to be immersed in the other vessel, that of *nous*, Hermes points out that he cannot have it both ways. Only if he first "hates his body" will he be able to "love himself" and embark on the path of true knowledge,[26] for only what is incorporeal and divine deserves his love – not this corporeal vessel filled with painful lusts and desires. In this particular case, I suspect that the rather drastic expression "to hate" (*miseō*) may be inspired by the author's wish to establish a clear contrast, in the same sentence, with having "love" (*phileō*) for one's true self and true knowledge. However, there is no doubt that the strong contrast between corporeality and incorporeality (*sōmatos/asōmatos*) was capable of inspiring true feelings of hatred and disgust of the human body, as is clear from an extreme statement in CH VII that requires our careful attention:

---

[24] CH IV 7 & 5 (I have changed the order for clarity). On anger and recklessness, see HO IV 1.
[25] CH I 19, 22–23, 27; IV 5; VI 2–4, 6; VII 1–2; IX 3–4; X 8–9, 20–21; XII 2–4. As for enslavement, cf. SH XI 2:26. HO III 1–3 emphasizes their ignorance of the principle of true justice: they hate and mutually accuse one another, based on laws that are merely human inventions, instead of cultivating mutual affection and love of humanity (φιλανθρωπία versus μισανθρωπία).
[26] CH IV 6. It is not clear to me why Van den Kerchove finds the reference to loving oneself "étonnante" ("astonishing"; *La voie*, 315). On the contrary, to me it seems to reflect an acute psychological understanding: a person's addiction (enslavements) to the corporeal passions may inspire feelings of self-loathing, whereas his or her true spiritual essence inspires love.

> [F]irst you must tear off that garment you're wearing – this web of ignorance, this foundation of badness, this chain of corruption, this dark cage, this living death, this sentient corpse, this portable tomb, this criminal who lives in your own house, who shows his hatred for you by what he loves and by what he hates shows what he begrudges you. Such is the hostile garment that you have put on and that drags you down to itself, so that you will not look up and see the beauty of truth and the goodness that lies in it, that you will not hate its evil because of having perceived the trap it has laid for you. Your organs of spiritual perception (which do not seem to be what they really are, so that their nature gets misunderstood) it makes insensitive, by obstructing them with matter and filling them with disgusting lusts, so that you may have no ears for what you should hear nor eyes for what you should see.[27]

Here the ruling metaphor is not that of a polluted vessel in which the soul is drowned, but of a heavy garment (*chitōn*) that the soul put on as it entered the cosmic domain. It now envelops the soul from all around, like the walls of a portable prison that is weighing it down while shutting out the light. However, it is important to note that the image of the garment is intermingled here with yet another one, that of possession by a sinister demonic entity operating from within. In their embodied condition, human beings carry some kind of malevolent "criminal" with them that is secretly poisoning their consciousness while filling them with lusts.

Therefore we encounter no less than three images for the human condition and its state of ignorance: the soul is drowned in a poisonous vessel, trapped in a material garment, and possessed by a demonic entity. The first two are clearly metaphors but the third should be understood quite literally, as will be seen. The metaphor of the body as a burden that the soul has to carry around also occurs in CH X 8, where the basic point is made with particular clarity:

> Ignorance is the sickness of the soul. For when the soul perceives none of the things that really are, nor their nature, nor the Good, it is blindly shaken by the bodily passions; and this poor wretch that does not know itself becomes a slave to disgusting and monstrous bodies, bearing its body like a burden, not ruling it but being ruled by it. This is the sickness of the soul.[28]

---

[27] CH VII 2–3. "The hostile garment" can also be translated as "the enemy that you have put on as a garment" (cf. HT I, 82; CHD, 75).

[28] CH X 8 (cf. HD VII 5; HD IX 5). In κακία δὲ ψυχῆς ἀγνωσία I interpret κακία as "sickness" for the reasons explained above, note 14: the passage means to say that the soul has "gone bad" or "has been corrupted." In CH XII 3, "the great sickness of the soul is denial of divinity" (νόσος δὲ μεγάλη ψυχῆς ἀθεότης). Generally on the body as a "garment," see HT I, 82 note 9; Cop, 147.

A crucial point should be emphasized here. As far as I can tell, it has been neglected by all previous commentators but has far-reaching implications for our general understanding of what the Hermetica are all about. Strictly speaking, *the efficient cause of this sickness is not the body as such but the destructive passions that are active in it.*[29] Formulated differently, the problem is not the material vessel but its poisonous contents. If we read the passage closely, we see that the person who *does* know himself and is able to "perceive the things that really are, their nature, and the Good" will no longer be dominated by the passions and should be able to rule the body instead of being ruled by it. Likewise, the "resident thief" or "criminal who lives in your house" (*ton enoikon lēistēn*) cannot actually be the body but must be some hostile entity that is secretly active *in* the body.[30]

Admittedly this distinction is rather subtle, and so it may not have been fully evident even to some of the Hermetic authors themselves. The passage from CH VII about "tearing off the garment" is unique not only for the extreme abuse it heaps upon the body, but also as our sole sample of a "Hermetic sermon" addressed *not* to a pupil but to the ignorant crowd. My suggestion is that its unusually drastic language must be read in that context and may well betray the alarmist sense of high urgency typical of recent converts. Should we read the passage literally and assume that this zealous preacher meant to tell his audience they should begin ("first") by actually getting rid of their bodies, even though he himself had obviously not yet "torn it off" either? Of course not. He began his sermon by exhorting them in similarly extreme language to "vomit out the teachings of ignorance," wake up from their stupor, come to their senses, and look up with the eyes of the heart.[31] If we assume that any of his listeners heeded these words, they would still have a long way to go before "tearing off their garments" would bring them any spiritual benefit at all. Of course the point was not to kill the body but to recognize its pernicious power over the soul, so as to gain the motivation to begin resisting and ultimately breaking that power.[32] Actually doing so would require persistent practice.

---

[29] The point was noted in passing by Haenchen, "Aufbau," 151.
[30] *Contra* CHD, 84 note 12: "the body loves carnal pleasures, it hates the beauty of Being" (with reference to Ferguson) and "that through which your body (seemingly) loves you, (actually) it hates you ... (etc.)" (Zielinksi). "Resident thief": Cop, 24.
[31] CH VII 1.
[32] Of course, this is what Christian practices of "mortification" were all about. When the Christian desert father Heraclides writes about his body "I am killing it because it is killing me" (Heraclides, *Paradeisos* 1, as quoted by Dodds, *Pagan and Christian*, 30), again he is referring to extreme ascetic austerity, not suicide.

What the vessel and garment metaphors have in common is a strong suggestion of entrapment and vulnerability, a sensation of no escape. Both signify that the soul *cannot get out*. It finds itself helplessly exposed to overpowering corrupting influences. Its organs of spiritual perception are blunted and rendered insensitive to reality as it really is. They are overruled by the input of the bodily senses, which keep feeding the soul with "phantom images (*eidōla*) and illusions (*skiagraphiai*)."[33] What the authors of the Hermetica are really telling us is that our faculty of imagination is being invaded on a daily basis by a barrage of information that severely constricts our consciousness – our inner world gets cluttered with meaningless junk or trash. Because our passions and desires end up dominating our consciousness, they latch onto these false images, and so we end up becoming their slaves. We lose sight of the beauty and goodness of true reality that is truly worthy of our desire; instead, we are now driven blindly by irrational forces such as greed, craving, lust, anger, fear, and grief. Our craving for pleasure makes us suffer. Our lust for power makes us slaves. And as the soul's true objectives have vanished from our awareness, even our desire for knowledge turns into greed and makes us blind.

In modern terminology, what we are really seeing here is a Hermetic *psychology of addiction*, in the sense of strong mental dependency or enslavement to what is harmful to the soul.[34] Hence when the soul is liberated and finds its way back to the realm of truth, the "garments" that it sheds in the process are described precisely as those harmful passions and their negative results: malice, desire, the arrogance of power, recklessness, brutality, craving for wealth, and falsehood.[35] Living in a state of ignorance means being dominated by these passions, daimonic energies that are binding us to the body while blinding us to what really is; and so it follows that loosening and discarding those bonds must be essential to the attainment of *gnōsis*. But the potent image of spiritual ascent (one pictures the soul releasing its garments one by one while rising upwards through the cosmic spheres) should not lead us to conclude too hastily, along with countless modern scholars, that it is therefore the body that must be left behind. On the contrary, we will see that Hermetic

---

[33] CH VI 4.
[34] The Dutch translation of addiction is *verslaving*, which literally means enslavement; in French one speaks of *dépendance*, dependency. Unfortunately these meanings are lost in standard English as well as German (*Sucht*).
[35] The list appears in CH I 25. See discussion below, pp. 183–184.

practitioners believed it possible for the soul's condition of ignorance to be healed already *during* life here on earth. This, I will be arguing, is what Hermetic spiritual practice was ultimately all about: not discarding the body but healing the soul.

It would be difficult to overstate the importance of this point. If the body as such causes the sickness of the soul, then that condition can obviously not be cured in a state of embodiment, and therefore salvation can happen only after death. By contrast, if the efficient cause lies in the destructive passions that are active as daimonic energies *in* the body, then it should not be impossible to drive them out and purify the vessel, presumably leaving it open to be filled with divine light. We already encountered such practices in Iamblichus' theurgy,[36] and we will find them to be central to Hermetic spiritual practice as well. Moreover, if we think back to that other Hermetic devotee still known to us by name, Zosimos' advice to Theosebeia now appears in its true light. She has to calm "[her] passions of desire and pleasure and anger and grief and the twelve portions of death,"[37] driving away any demonic entities until her soul is healed from its afflictions and has reached completion. Having thus been baptized in the mixing-bowl of *nous*, she can afford to "spit on matter" and hasten up to her own spiritual "tribe" – the community of souls that are already united with Poimandres. We will see how much of the Way of Hermes is encoded in these few lines of text.

Summing up, the condition of human "ignorance" as understood by the Hermetica may be defined as a state of severe addiction or enslavement to the harmful passions. Because this sickness of the soul is an unavoidable effect of embodiment as such, all human beings without exception suffer from its afflictions. In modern terms, what we consider to be normal human consciousness is in fact an altered state of knowledge: a delusionary condition of mental alienation and profound confusion that makes it very hard for us to see reality as it actually is. To put it very bluntly, the Hermetica are telling us that as embodied human beings, we are living our lives in a dreamlike state of hallucination. Some of us may experience fleeting moments of enlightenment, when the mental fog is momentarily lifted and we see glimpses of the real; but ultimately the spell is much too powerful for any of us to truly break it by ourselves. What we need is a revelation.

---

[36] See above, pp. 109–112.
[37] Zosimos, *Final Account* 8 (above, p. 97).

ENLIGHTENMENT

The Greek word for a revelation is *apokalupsis*, "apocalypse."[38] Its most evident example for us is the first treatise of the *Corpus Hermeticum*,[39] where a divine being named Poimandres appears to Hermes Trismegistus[40] and promises to answer his questions.

One day when I had come to reflect on the things that truly are, and my mind was soaring high while my senses were restrained (as happens to someone overwhelmed by sleep from too much food or from physical exhaustion), an enormous being of immeasurable dimensions seemed to appear to me and call my name. He said to me: "What do you want to hear and see, and learn to understand by your *nous*?"[41]

These famous opening words are dense with signification. Surprising as the vision may be in its sudden splendor and magnificence, it comes to a recipient who has been preparing himself well for the eventuality of such an event. Turning away from the deceptive illusions of external reality, Hermes has been focusing his mind on *ta onta*: the things that truly are. This makes perfect sense because for the authors of the Hermetica, the bodily senses perceive no more than *phenomena*,

---

[38] The popular association of "apocalypticism" with end-of-time scenarios is a secondary result of the fact that some Jewish and Christian revelations (with the New Testament Book of Revelations as obviously the most famous example) are dominated by such eschatological visions. Attempts to synthesize these two different meanings of apocalypse as a genre of "revelations" and as "end-of-time visions" have led to an unstable and highly confusing discourse in modern scholarship: see discussion below, pp. 159–160 with note 50.

[39] Previous analyses of CH I: Reitzenstein, *Poimandres*, 36–59; Dodd, *Bible and the Greeks* (1935), 99–209 (with an extreme over-emphasis on biblical parallels or influences); Haenchen, "Aufbau und Theologie des Poimandres" (1956; thorough and perceptive but marred by a biblical "Fall of Man" narrative projected onto the text); Jansen, "Frage nach Tendenz" (1977; argues that the author must have been a Jew); Pearson, "Jewish Elements in *Corpus Hermeticum* I" (1981; argues that an individual closely associated with a Jewish community had formed a new group devoted to Hermes-Thoth); Mahé, "La création," 36–43 (1986; largely following Dodd's emphasis on parallels with Genesis); Büchli, *Der Poimandres* (1987; sees CH I as a pagan response to the Christian gospels); Mahé, "Générations antédiluviennes" (1988; again emphasizing parallels with Genesis); Holzhausen, "*Mythos vom Menschen*", 7–79 (1993); Bull, *Tradition*, 121–131, 136–154 (the only scholarly analysis free from theological models and agendas).

[40] That the anonymous visionary in CH I should be identified as Hermes Trismegistus is suggested by CH XIII 15. See discussion in Van den Kerchove, *La voie*, 26–28. I will adopt this identification here, while acknowledging the distinct possibility that CH I is the reflection of a proto-Hermetic cult of Porramanres (Amenemhet III), in which case CH XIII 15 reflects a later interpretation of the visionary as Hermes (Jackson, "New Proposal," 105–106).

[41] CH I 1. On the bracketed sentence, see Haenchen, "Aufbau," 151–152.

appearances; to behold noetic realities (*noumena* in terms of later Kantian terminology), one needs to use internal senses whose very existence is unknown to the great majority of people.[42] The multitude's state of blind ignorance consists in that very fact: because all they ever know is what comes to them through their bodily senses, their souls are utterly dominated by mere physical sensations, emotional states and interior images that keep feeding their passions with useless desires, thus leading them to run ceaselessly after goals and ambitions that are empty of true meaning.

In reflecting on *ta onta*, Hermes has certainly been doing more than just thinking. Like other lovers of wisdom, he must have been practicing meditational techniques (*meletaō*) to discipline the mind and body. He knows that the soul needs active care,[43] that measures must be taken for protecting it against those powerful corrupting influences to which it is exposed on a daily basis; and so he has been training his faculty of attention (*prosochē*), its ability to not get caught up in the meaningless flux of impermanence and change but stay in the moment and remain focused on what is really real. That his senses are restrained while his mind is soaring high indicates that he has reached a rather advanced level of such practice, usually referred to as *ekstasis*, ecstasy, literally "standing outside."[44] Alterations of consciousness that fall under this heading result from a drastic reduction of sensory stimulation combined with heightened mental concentration and occur most easily under conditions of silence, solitude, physical immobility, and darkness. In sufficiently susceptible subjects, they can give rise to intense visions or hallucinations that are typically described as more "real" than normal waking experience and are retained in the subject's memory after the event.[45] This overwhelming

---

[42] *Ascl* 7; CH I 19, 22–23, 30; IV 9, 11; V 2; VI 4; VII 1–3; X 4–5, 9; XI 6; XII 3; XIII 1, 3, 7, 11, 14, 17; HD IX 2.

[43] Plato, *Apol.* 30a–b.

[44] For the extensive referential corpus regarding ecstasy in antiquity and its many modifications (e.g. ἔκστασις, ἀλλοίωσις, κίνησις, ἔνθεος, ἐνθουσιασμός, δαιμονισμός, θειασμός, ἔκπληξις, μανία) see the extraordinarily detailed overview article by Pfister, "Ekstase" (with discussion of the Hermetic materials on pp. 980–981); and see now the comprehensive modern overview and discussion by Ustinova, *Divine Mania*.

[45] Here I follow Rouget, *Music and Trance*, 3–12, while noting that his typological distinction between ecstasy and trance allows for a spectrum of intermediary states (Hanegraaff, "Trance," 512; with reference to Wulff, *Psychology of Religion*, 69–89; cf. Ludwig, "Altered States," 12–15). For the neurological mechanisms, see Shantz, *Paul in Ecstasy*, 81–87; d'Aquili and Newberg, *Mystical Mind*. To Rouget's elements of silence, solitude and physical immobility I have added darkness as a possible contributing factor, in view of Ustinova's discussions in *Caves and the Ancient Greek Mind*.

sense of reality, of having the veil of appearances torn away and perceiving what is true, is crucial to understanding the life-changing impact that such visions can have on those who experience them. As formulated by Yulia Ustinova,

> A major characteristic of these states is suppression of "objective relativistic framework" that allows an experience to be evaluated as real or unreal. Disconnection from "consensus reality" generates the feeling that the alternative reality created inside one's mind truly exists. ... The noetic quality of these experiences manifests itself in feelings of illumination and ultimate salience, and they may change the person's attitude towards life. ... For the individual who has experienced alterations of consciousness, the truth attained in hallucinations is purer than mundane knowledge and immutable. During these states, people often feel that they are in contact with supreme reality, and everything in the world becomes salient and deeply meaningful. These experiences are much more valid for them than percepts, feelings or thoughts when in the alert state.[46]

It is clear that Poimandres appears while Hermes is in such a state. Here it must be noted that while the term "hallucination" may be suggestive of psychopathology in the minds of many readers, that assumption is not supported by the medical and statistical record. Visual or auditory hallucinations are remarkably common among healthy individuals,[47] although typically underreported in modern society due to fears of social stigma; and this makes it simplistic to interpret such experiences as straightforward diagnostic markers of psychosis. It is not the nature of hallucinatory experiences per se that determines whether people become psychotic, but the manner in which individuals react to their experiences.[48] Thus when the author of CH I claims to have talked with Poimandres, this tells us nothing about his state of sanity. All it means is that his consciousness must have been altered temporarily, probably through spiritual practices that are known to be capable of such effects.

---

[46] Ustinova, *Divine Mania*, 27.
[47] Ustinova, *Divine Mania*, 21: "Between 10% and 25% of the non-clinical population in the West report having had at least one hallucinatory experience." For the impressive statistical evidence, see Bentall, "Hallucinatory Experiences," 93-96.
[48] Bentall, "Hallucinatory Experiences," 96. For depathologizing discussions of the concept of "hallucination" in the wake of Brierre de Boismont's pioneering *Des hallucinations* (1845), see e.g. Sarbin and Juhasz, "Historical Background"; Sacks, *Hallucinations*; Godderis, *Bestaan dingen alleen als men ze ziet?*; Luhrmann, "Hallucinations and Sensory Overrides."

The revelation by Poimandres appears in a narrative frame reminiscent of the so-called apocalyptic literature in ancient Jewish and Christian milieus.[49] This important although ill-defined genre of writings[50] deals with spiritual entities who appear to prophets and other human recipients, revealing the mysteries of what is above and what is below as well as past events and the future to come.[51] The frequent and explicit references in this genre to visionary and dream experiences, auditions, possessions, and their attendant altered states have been a source of acute embarrassment for countless scholars who would prefer to think of prophets as "relatively rational."[52] The chief strategy for keeping these troubling dimensions at arm's length has been to reduce the texts by default to mere "literary fictions," invented stories that need not reflect any actual lived experiences but just follow the conventional requirements of an established genre. In a seminal chapter by Michael E. Stone, a major specialist in the field, this line of reasoning has been tested at the example of *Fourth Ezra* and cogently put to rest.[53] This obviously does not mean that no genre exists at all, that literary conventions are irrelevant, or that any description of a divine revelation is to be taken literally and treated as a direct first-hand report. All it means is that when these textual traditions claim to reflect real experiences and

---

[49] See e.g. Pearson, "Jewish Elements in *Corpus Hermeticum* I," 339–340 (comparison with 2 Enoch); van den Broek, "Spiritual Transformation"; van den Broek in HG, 457 note 1 (comparison with the "Revelation of Enos" and the "Revelation of Sem" referred to in the *Cologne Mani Codex*). Cf. Van den Kerchove, *La voie*, 90, 318.

[50] Collins's influential "morphology of a genre" suffers from an attempt to combine ἀποκάλυψις in its general sense of "revelation" with an overemphasis on the eschatological content congenial to biblical scholars and theologians ("Introduction"; see critique in Rowland, *Open Heaven*, 1–2, 23–24, 28, 37, 47–48, 193; Collins, "Apocalypse Now," 450). Another problem is the relative neglect of materials beyond the spheres of Judaism and Christianity (see Collins, "Introduction," 2; Rowland, *Open Heaven*, 10; Collins, "Apocalypse Now," 456).

[51] Here I rely on the standard work by Rowland, who emphasizes the centrality of revealing the mysteries of "what is above, what is below, what had happened previously, and what is to come" (*Open Heaven*, 73–189). In spite of its slant towards eschatology, the same basic elements recur in the definition provided by Collins ("Introduction," 9; *Apocalyptic Imagination*, 5).

[52] Wilson, "Prophecy and Ecstasy," 321.

[53] Stone, *Ancient Judaism*, 90–121 (and an earlier version, "Reconsideration"); see 93–94 for his observations about the "discomfort" and "embarrassment" felt by many colleagues who still refuse to see the relevance. See also the earlier, very detailed discussion in Rowland, *Open Heaven*, 214–247. For these conventional patterns of resistance against straightforward textual evidence, see for instance the peculiar combination of erudition and prejudice evinced in Alden, "Ecstasy and the Prophets."

practices, that claim must be taken seriously.[54] Hence when I write that "Hermes met Poimandres while in an ecstatic state of consciousness," this implies no statement on my part about the personal experiences of the person who wrote CH I (let alone, of course, about any real existence of Hermes or Poimandres). It simply means that the text refers to ecstatic visions and auditions of a type that must have been known, experienced, and deeply appreciated in Hermetic milieus.

If a visionary revelation is reduced to just a "literary fiction," this has far-reaching effects on how we are led to perceive and interpret the text as a whole. In their standard edition of the *Corpus Hermeticum*, Nock and Festugière suggest that CH I begins with a short Introduction whose function is to frame the text as a conventional revelation narrative (1–3: appearance of Poimandres and request for revelation). The central text itself (4–26) is said to consist of a cosmogony (4–11), an anthropology (12–23) and an eschatology (24–26), after which it concludes with a short description of the prophet's apostolic mission (27–29) and a final prayer (30–31).[55] In this manner, the opening and closing sections are effectively reduced to a status of marginal importance while the "cosmogony, anthropology, and eschatology" is placed at center stage, a move that gets strengthened and further supported by an extraordinarily detailed structural analysis of only that section (see Table 6.1).

This manner of presentation and subdivision has the effect of reducing our text to a conventional philosophical treatise based on a mythical narrative, while suppressing its emphasis on noetic perception and the pursuit of *gnōsis*. While Nock and Festugière's subdivision has been almost universally adopted, I consider it to be fundamentally misleading. If we

[54] Examples of the default reduction of CH I to narrative fiction are legio. As *pars pro toto*, see the influential analysis by Haenchen, "Aufbau und Theologie," who correctly critiques Dodd for imagining the author of CH I as "sitting with the LXX open in front of him" (ibid., 169) but likewise seems to imagine that author as some kind of armchair novelist putting a fictional composition together from literary building blocks. For instance see his pages 150 ("dieser Kunstgriff des Verfassers"), 158 with note 2 ("seine der Stoa entlehnte Lehre"), 160 ("hat der Autor auch hier eine Lesefrucht verwertet..."), 162 ("Vielleicht hat die Wendung ... dem Verfasser den Gedanken eingegeben, den Erzähler 'in' dem Gott Nus die Urwirklichkeit schauen zu lassen"), 169 ("Aber der Verfasser weiß Rat"), 184 ("ein schriftstellerisches Problem ... dieser kurze Abschied des Poimandres war ein sehr schlechter Buchschluß. Darum hat der Autor es gewagt, das 'Evangelium' des Poimandres durch eine Art 'Apostelgeschichte' zu erweitern ..."); 189 ("Für die Darstellung des Urwerdens hat er eine iranisch-gnostische Tradition gewählt ... Die Entstehung und Ordnung der Elemente hat er mit Hilfe der stoischen Logoslehre beschrieben ... " etc.).
[55] HT I, 2–6.

TABLE 6.1: *Nock and Festugière's Analysis of CH I*

1–3 Intro	Cosmogony	4–26 Anthropology	Eschatology	27–29 Mission	30–32 Prayer
	1 Father (nous1)	1 Archetypal human	1 Dissolution		
	Phase 1	Origin and nature	a Body		
	a Light	a Archetypal human	b Visible form		
	b Darkness	b Demiurgic activity	c Morality		
	c Logos	c Governors' welcome	d Bodily senses		
	Phase 2	Fall	e Anger/lust		
	a Organization	a Appearance to nature	2 Return		
	b Separation	b Nature's response	3 Divinization		
	2 Demiurge (nous 2)	c Reflection in nature	a Ogdoad		
	Celestial bodies	d Unification	b Ennead		
	Birth of nous 2	2 First 7 humans	c Unity with God		
	7 governors	Birth of 7 humans			
	Animal Life	Birth of 7 humans			
	Logos vs earth	Their double nature			
	7 circles of fire	They remain like this			
	Generation of animals	3 Current humanity			
		Origin			
		Male/female division			
		Holy word			
		Doubling			
		Multiplication			
		Self-knowledge			
		Ignorance			
		Divine grace			

approach CH I as an *apokalupsis*, the account of a visionary revelation, this leads to an entirely different emphasis:

1. The opening of vision (1–3)
2. Two questions answered by two visionary episodes (4–7)
3. Poimandres' account of the story of humanity (8–26)
4. The visionary's transformation and missionary activity (27–30)
5. Final prayer (31–32)

That the third part (CH I 8–26) is by far the longest follows simply from the nature of text and discourse: verbal descriptions and explanations take time to pronounce and space to write down. However, we will see again and again that according to the Hermetica, what is truly important cannot be adequately expressed through words at all, but only perceived directly through the internal noetic senses.

This point emerges immediately in the opening passage that we are still considering. To describe his initial practice of mental reflection on "the things that truly are," Hermes uses fairly conventional terms for thinking or intellectual reflection, *ennoia* and *dianoia*; but when Poimandres appears, he asks Hermes what he would like to *hear* and *see* and understand by his *nous*. The words that he uses here, *noēsas* and *gnōnai*, are impossible to translate adequately because (as we saw at the beginning of Chapter 1) the English language has no words for the specific kind of noetic activity that transcends normal thinking.[56] Hence we are forced to use conventional verbs such as "knowing" or "understanding" although the ultimate object of this so-called "knowledge" (for which we can and will use the noun *gnōsis*[57]) is precisely the *anoēton*, that which our thinking can *not* comprehend and can only be perceived by the *nous*.

Since Poimandres has skipped the niceties of a formal introduction to get right to the point ("what do you want to hear and see?"), one understands that Hermes first blurts out in amazement "but who are you?" Poimandres responds by giving his name[58] and revealing his true

---

[56] See above, pp. 12–14 with reference to RHT IV, 138–139; and pp. 60–61 with reference to Banner, *Philosophic Silence*, 187; cf. Cop, 95–96. Here my interpretation diverges from that of Van den Kerchove, who does not differentiate between the highly specific Hermetic understanding of *nous* and common understandings of "intellect" (*La voie*, 319).

[57] On Mahé's belief in a hierarchical development leading from *gnōsis* via *logos* to *nous*, see below, p. 234 note 52.

[58] For the fascinating debate about the background and etymology of the name Poimandres, see (in chronological order) Granger, "Poemander" (1904); Griffith in Scott II, 16 (1925); Marcus, "The Name Poimandrēs" (1949); Kingsley, "Poimandres" (1993; 2000);

Healing the Soul 163

identity: he is no one less than the *nous* of the sovereign power or divine source itself.[59] Here we must remember a peculiar and important fact that was already mentioned in passing: *nous* is to be understood simultaneously on *two* different levels that may strike us as incommensurable or even contradictory but are considered to be one. *Ontologically* it is an ultimate reality, while *epistemologically* it is the capacity to access or comprehend that very same reality[60] – or in other words, *nous* is the capacity to understand itself. As helpfully noted by Nicholas Banner, this seems to imply that in modern terms, levels of being are equated with states of consciousness.[61] Taking up Poimandres' offer, Hermes now says that he wishes to truly understand *ta onta* (that is, not just intellectually but noetically: *noēsai*) and have *gnōsis* of the divine (*gnōnai ton theon*). He exclaims how deep is his desire to hear the answers, and Poimandres promises to teach him, telling Hermes to "hold" these two questions in his own *nous*.[62]

Then Hermes is granted two successive visions-within-the-vision, the first of which includes audition. Poimandres changes his appearance and "everything is opened" to Hermes' gaze in a single instant. First he sees only a limitless expanse of "clear and friendly" light for which he spontaneously experiences feelings of love. But then the drama begins. A darkness appears, a frightening and depressing presence, twisting and twirling like a snake. It transforms itself into some kind of bubbling moist substance that gives off smoke like a fire while making an unspeakable mournful sound. Then it emits an inarticulate cry that seems to

---

Jackson, "New Proposal" (1999); Van den Kerchove, "Poimandrès" (2014); Bull, *Tradition*, 121–131. For our concerns, the most important conclusion is that the name has Egyptian rather than Greek origins.

[59] CH I 2. *Contra* Haenchen ("Aufbau," 153), Poimandres is therefore *not* identical with the supreme "sovereign power" or divine source: he represents the level of the Ennead, as will be seen. Typical of his trademark editorial distortions, Scott (Scott I, 116; Scott II, 23; cf. Haenchen, "Aufbau," 159 with note 2) "corrects" ὁ σὸς θεός ("your god") to ὁ πρῶτος θεός ("the first god")!

[60] See above, pp. 60–61. For Plotinus, see Banner, *Philosophic Silence*, 196; for the Hermetica, see Van den Kerchove, *La voie*, 29.

[61] Banner suggests that Plotinus may have pioneered this idea (*Philosophic Silence*, 196), but I will be arguing that we find it in the Hermetica as well. Again it seems relevant that Plotinus is contemporary with the Hermetica and shares their Egyptian background.

[62] CH I 3. Re: Van den Kerchove, *La voie*, 133, I see this expression as suggesting more than just memorization. Poimandres is not telling Hermes "don't forget your questions"; rather, he is instructing him to concentrate all his mental powers on his search for understanding "the things that really are" and the nature of the divine, so that the answers will appear as clearly as possible in the inner world of his *nous*.

Hermes "like a voice of light,"[63] to which the universal light responds by sending down "a holy *logos*."[64] Now a pure fire leaps up from the dark substance, "nimble and piercing and active at the same time," resulting in a separation between air and fire above and earth and water below.[65] Hermes sees and even hears how the pneumatic *logos* is passing over the dark moist substance, keeping it in motion.[66] At this point, Poimandres intervenes to give a short explanation, focusing entirely on the nature of the light:

> I am that light ... the *nous*, your God, which existed prior to the moist substance that appeared out of the darkness. The luminous *logos* that came from the *nous* [is the son of God]. ... Know this: that in you which sees and hears is the [Lord's] *logos*, and [your] *nous* is God [the father]. They are not separate, for their union is life.[67]

After Hermes has expressed his gratitude for this explanation, Poimandres tells him: "know the light then and get acquainted with it!"[68] Having uttered those words, Poimandres gazes into his eyes for such a long time that Hermes trembles at the sight. When finally the spell is broken, he

---

[63] Mahé points out that the manuscripts have φονῇ φωτός, but editors in the wake of Reitzenstein replaced φωτός (light) by πυρός (fire). We may assume that the light emits a cry of distress as its finds itself in this unfamiliar environment of moist darkness, and so the *nous* sends its *logos* down to help (HT V, 367). Note the monistic instead of dualistic implication: the dark moist substance is not a wholly independent entity but some kind of emanation from the *nous*.

[64] See parallel in CH III 1 (and reconstruction in Wildberg, "*Corpus Hermeticum*, Tractate III," 146–147). I find it plausible to identify the "voice of light" as the "subtle, intelligent *pneuma*" (πνεῦμα λεπτὸν νοερόν) mentioned here, and the "holy *logos*" as the "holy light" (φῶς ἅγιον).

[65] See similar process of separation in CH III 2.

[66] CH I 4–5 (cf. CH III 2). Detailed references with commentary on the various elements in Cop, 97–101.

[67] CH I 6. As we have seen (above, pp. 125–126), there is good cause for suspicion with regard to "son of God," "the Lord's" and "God the father," which may well be Christian interpolations (as also conceded by Scott II, 26; Dodd, *Bible*, 119; Haenchen, "Aufbau," 160, with note 2 for Scott's and Dodd's textual manipulations; as for how Scott also gets rid of "your god," see above, note 59). Because the question does not crucially affect my argument here, I leave the matter open while bracketing these contested words.

[68] Ἀλλὰ δὴ νόει τὸ φῶς καὶ γνώριζε τοῦτο. Cf. WHCH, 18 "perceive" and "know"; Cop, 2 "understand" and "recognize." HT I, 9 has "Eh bien donc, fixe ton esprit sur la lumière et apprends à connaître ceci" ("Well then, fix your spirit on the light and learn to know it"); CHD, 12 has "Aber konzentriere dich auf das Licht und erkenne folgendes" ("But concentrate on the light and understand the following"). Instead of "get to know it" I write "get acquainted with it" in the second instance, primarily to avoid repetition of the word "know"; but this choice also owes something to the discussion in Chapter 4 of Iamblichus' concept of ἔμφυτος γνῶσις (see above, pp. 112–115).

sees in his own *nous* that the light consists of innumerable powers and has become an immeasurable cosmos. The fire is now securely kept in place by "a mighty force."

What has been happening here? First of all, it is important to see that Poimandres has already answered *both* questions that Hermes had asked him, about the nature of "the things that truly are" and the true nature of the divine. He did this *not* by any verbal explanation or rational analysis but, exactly as promised at the outset, by giving Hermes what he wished to *hear*, *see*, and *understand noetically*. To help him understand what he has just seen and heard, Poimandres explains the nature of the faculties that made this mode of perception possible. The limitless expanse of light that Hermes beheld and loved is the universal reality of divine *nous* that has been existing in all eternity prior to the emergence of the world in time and space. The specific capacity of immediate vision and audition inherent in the *nous* is referred to as its *logos*;[69] and while the latter might seem to detach itself from the former in responding to the "voice of light," the two remain inseparable in their true essence because the very life of divinity consists in their unity. We might say that the *logos* is like the visual and auditory capacities of the divine organism called *nous* – the point being that the *nous* exists eternally in and for itself regardless of whether it is being perceived, or rather, whether or not it opens its noetic senses to perceive itself.

But that is not all. Since Hermes is perceiving all of this in his own *nous*, it must be his own *logos* too that enables him to see and hear. The divine *nous* and *logos* appear as realities that are being perceived by Hermes and therefore seem external to himself. But are they really? It is at this point that Poimandres takes one further and truly radical step: he makes it clear to Hermes that in truth there is no distinction between the universal divine *nous* and *logos* that he is watching and the *nous* and *logos* that are watching them! This is the message conveyed by the long silent moment when Hermes follows Poimandres' request to "know the light and get acquainted with it." The Greek text uses two different verbs

---

[69] Like HT I, 18 note 16, I read the words τὸ ἐν σοὶ βλέπον καὶ ἀκοῦον as a description of the author's specific understanding of *logos*. In sharp contrast, Scott thinks that "that in you which sees and hears" renders the text "meaningless" (Scott I, 16; Scott II, 25–26), while Dodd finds it "irrelevant" and "inconsistent with the general doctrine of the *Hermetica*" (*Bible*, 118). As a result, both change the Greek text so as to make it say what they think it should have said. On the contrary, this definition of *logos* is of considerable importance for understanding the internal consistency of the text as a whole, as will be seen.

here that suggest noetic understanding and direct knowledge, but those meanings are lost in English translation. We remember that Poimandres has already twice identified himself as the divine *nous*,[70] which can only mean that when he "changed his appearance" in front of Hermes, he was revealing himself as the limitless expanse of lovable divine light that is the true essence of manifested reality. Now having shape-shifted back to the persona of an "enormous being" named Poimandres, he tells Hermes to look straight into his eyes. As Hermes does so, the penny drops: as there is no difference between the light of his own *nous* and the noetic light of divinity, he finds himself looking into his own eyes. He himself is "the *nous* of the sovereign power" and its *logos* as well; or in modern terminology, the very distinction between a subject that observes and an object that is being observed turns out to be an illusion, a trick of the mind. Hermes and Poimandres do not truly exist as separate entities but are literally one.

This then is Hermes' moment of illumination in the most radical sense of the word: he understands himself to be divine light gazing at divine light.[71] The long silent moment of "fear and trembling," or so I want to suggest, is an ultimate example in Hermetic literature of what is meant by *direct noetic perception*, the inherently paradoxical *gnōsis* of the *anoēton*.[72] Because the perceiver is identical with that which is being perceived *and* even with the very capacity of noetic perception, this is the true actualization of *nous* in its ability to "understand itself": *gnōsis* as unmediated knowledge of one's own divine nature.[73] It transcends even the level of noetic perception mediated through *logos*, so it has to be silent and non-visual. Only *after* Poimandres turns his gaze away and breaks the spell[74] does Hermes return to his previous capacity of vision and audition, so that he can see the light as consisting of "innumerable

---

[70] CH I 2, 6.
[71] The same conclusion is given formulaic shape in HD IX 2: "Where there is *Nous*, there is Light; and where there is Light, there is *Nous*. Since the *Nous* is Light and the Light is *Nous*, the person who has *Nous* is enlightened and the person who does not have *Nous* is deprived of enlightenment."
[72] As pointed out by Festugière (see above, pp. 12–13), the paradox is that *nous* as the capacity of direct spiritual perception provides access to what is *anoēton* from the more restricted perspective of *nous* as "mind" or "intellect" engaged in "thinking."
[73] Again, this requires understanding *nous* as ontological and epistemological at the same time: see above, Chapter 3, p. 60 with note 50; Chapter 6, p. 163; and cf. Iamblichus' *emphutos gnōsis*, Chapter 4, pp. 112–115. The theme of nonduality will be explored at greater length below, pp. 168, 232, 269, 278 with note 53, 318–321, 359–360.
[74] Not Hermes but Poimandres plays the active role here. I see no reason to follow Scott (Scott I, 116) and Haenchen ("Aufbau," 161 with note 1) in changing the Greek so as to make Hermes turn his gaze away.

Healing the Soul

powers" that have given birth to an "immeasurable cosmos" and hear what Poimandres is telling him. As he is still quite beyond himself about this awe-inspiring moment of gazing silently into the light, while understanding his own divinity as identical to that which does the gazing, Poimandres confirms that what he just "saw" in his *nous* was "the archetypal form [*to archetupon eidos*] that is *prior* to that which has neither beginning nor end [*to proarchon tēs aperantou*]."[75] This latter formulation must refer to the *heimarmenē*, the realm of fate that revolves "from an indeterminate beginning to an infinite end."[76] The "archetypal form" or image (*eidos*) that Hermes perceived was the noetic realm of Poimandres' true essence, which in turn comes from the ultimate divine source or origin (*archē*). Thus while the divine mystery at the heart of all manifestation reveals itself as a reality of universal light to the noetic light that it is itself, and through which it is being perceived, still the two are not strictly identical. We will return to these ultimate levels in Chapter 9.

THE STORY OF HUMANITY

When Hermes returns from his moment of ultimate *gnōsis*, his noetic senses reopen so that his *logos* ("that in you which sees and hears") is able again to perceive the world of his *nous* by something resembling bodily vision and hearing. In Chapter 7 we will return at length to the nature of this "inner world." For now, it is important to emphasize that no further visions-within-the-vision are reported. In the long middle section of CH I 8–26, Poimandres is *telling* Hermes what happened after the initial separation of the four elements (earth, water, air, fire) and the stabilization of an "immeasurable cosmos" born from the light. The two questions that Hermes had asked have been answered noetically, through direct vision and audition. What remains is a verbal account, with Poimandres in the role of the teacher and Hermes in that of the pupil.

Hermes first wants to know where those elements of nature have come from, and Poimandres explains. The dark and moist substance of nature received the luminous *logos* in her womb, and this act of insemination allowed her to imitate the beauty of the noetic world by using "her own elements and her own offspring, the souls" and transform them into an

---

[75] CH I 8 (emphasis added). As far as I can tell, among all modern scholars only Reitzenstein saw the significance of the passage, identifying it correctly as a "second vision" in which Hermes noetically perceives τὸ ἀρχέτυπον εἶδος (*Poimandres*, 38).
[76] CH I 11.

ordered cosmos.⁷⁷ In other words, the original chaos in the maternal womb of nature is being born as a beautiful organic cosmos that mirrors the structure of the original light-world. This vision is entirely in line with standard Aristotelian understandings of sexual generation, which required the female menstrual blood (vehicle of the nutritive soul) as the passive *material cause* to be inseminated by the male seed (vehicle of the sentient soul) as the active *efficient cause*. Just as in animal reproduction, the mother's body contains all the material necessary for creating offspring, but the father's semen is required to put the process in motion.⁷⁸ In addition, note the common belief that the imprint of external realities on the mother's imagination during pregnancy gets transmitted to her offspring.⁷⁹

To understand what happens next, we must emphasize once more that only *one* ultimate reality is said to truly exist. This is the universal boundless light of divine *nous* that Hermes has recognized as identical with his own true essence. The moist darkness of nature does not have the same metaphysical status – it is not the *noumenon* but just a *phenomenon*, an appearance. Therefore literally everything that follows in the rest of Poimandres' account may seem very real from the perspective of human entities like Hermes and like ourselves who are caught up in the world of the cosmos, but is ultimately illusory from the divine perspective of *nous*. Hence it would be a serious mistake to think that the cosmos is born from the sexual union of two preexisting gendered realities (light versus darkness, *nous* versus matter, God versus nature, and so on), for this polarization happens *not* on the primary level of essential being but only on the secondary level of phenomenal manifestation. The Hermetic worldview is not dualistic but radically monistic, or rather nondualistic.

---

77 CH I 8. Here I follow CHD, 13 with note 30; idem van den Broek, in HG, 98 with 458–459 note 10 (*contra* Scott I, 117; HT I, 9; Cop, 2; WHCH 18). Because strictly speaking the noetic light world is not a "cosmos," I find it reasonable for Nock and Festugière to translate τὸν καλὸν κόσμον as "le beau monde archétype" ("the beautiful archetypal world"; cf. CH I 7, where they translate the "immeasurable cosmos" as "un monde sans limites"). The author wants to say that the limitless light of *nous* that Hermes saw appears to be a "light-world" consisting of innumerable powers or luminous entities. In modern terms we might imagine this world of divine "life and light" as a kind of infinite living organism made up of countless luminous cells.
78 Aristotle, *De Generatione Animalium* I.1–2; and see discussion in Aristotle, *Generation of Animals*, xxxviii, lxvi–lxvii (A.L. Peck).
79 See Huet, *Monstrous Imagination* (focused on the Renaissance); Doniger and Spinner, "Misconceptions." The belief has its origin in a statement attributed to Empedocles (Aetius 5.12.2, in: Diels, *Doxographi Graeci*, 423; transl. in Inwood, *Poem of Empedocles*, 193).

Only on this basis can we understand the next point made by Poimandres: the living light of the divine *nous* itself is both male and female (*arrenothēlus*: androgynous[80]). Having already given birth to the dark moist substance of nature that became the cosmos (after which it was inseminated by the *logos*, as we have seen), it is therefore perfectly capable of producing new offspring independent of previous births. And that is what it does: out of itself, the *nous* now brings forth a secondary *nous*, a "god of fire and spirit" who acts as a demiurge, a cosmic architect or craftsman. He proceeds to fashion the "seven governors," the planets that are circling the earth. Their governance is called *heimarmenē*, the cosmic machinery of fate that rules everything in the world of the senses. This installation of the planetary system has an immediate effect on the *logos* that still finds itself down there in the womb of nature: having done its duty, it leaps upwards to this "pure craftwork" of the planets and unites itself with the demiurgic *nous*, thus abandoning the "downward-moving divine elements of nature." Presumably this happens because like attracts like: the *logos* and the demiurge, after all, share the same noetic substance.[81] Having been united with the *logos*, the demiurgic *nous* then puts everything into motion: the cosmic planetary machinery begins its circular movement, and will henceforth keep revolving "from an indeterminate beginning to an infinite end, for it begins where it ends."[82] As everything is moving now, the elements begin to produce unreasoning animals, first of all winged creatures from the air and swimming creatures from the water, and after the demiurge has separated earth from water, animals on the land as well.[83]

---

[80] I translate ἀρρενόθηλυς as "androgynous" rather than "bisexual" (which in common language refers rather to biological males or females who are sexually attracted to both sexes); I prefer "androgynous" over "hermaphrodite" because the text does not use the term ἑρμαφρόδιτος. For the divine as both male and female, cf. my discussion of *Ascl.* 20–21 and NH VI⁸ 65 (above, pp. 56–57).

[81] CH I 10. Almost all editors and translators follow Tiedemann in deleting τοῦ θεοῦ, probably on the assumption that the "lower elements of nature" cannot be "of God" (CHD, 13 note 31; Cop, 106); but this intervention has subtle dualistic implications, whereas in fact *everything* in this Hermetic account is ultimately divine. The downward-moving elements are water and earth, as opposed to the demiurgic "god of fire" (CH I 5); but presumably they also include air (which, after all, is not just up in the heavens but down below as well; cf. CH I 11).

[82] CH I 11; cf. 8. That the *heimarmenē* "begins where it ends" is conveyed very nicely by the famous image of the snake swallowing its own tail.

[83] Wildberg sees the parallel passage in CH III 3 as a scribal gloss ("*Corpus Hermeticum*, Tractate III," 143, 146), but it seems possible also to interpret it as referring to CH I 11. Do we assume that both passages reflect a biblical influence or do we consider both to be glosses?

Having already brought forth the cosmos and the demiurge, the *nous* now gives birth to yet a new offspring, a supremely beautiful Human very similar to itself. At this point we are faced with some difficulties concerning gendered language. We have seen that *nous* is polarized internally as a male-female entity that is continually impregnating itself and giving birth at the same time.[84] Therefore it makes sense that the Human (*Anthrōpos*),[85] fashioned in its image, is described explicitly as "an androgynous being from an androgynous father."[86] But of course, this combination begs the question. One could argue that by definition, a truly androgynous deity must be both father *and* mother; but it seems more likely that whether deliberately or not, the Hermetic perspective ultimately prioritizes masculinity as the active principle of generation, the generative source. Hence the author imagines the *nous* as somehow like a "heavenly father" endowed with female reproductive capacities as well. This fits with the fact that Poimandres himself is clearly gendered male too, both grammatically and in terms of how he appears to Hermes. Likewise, although the Human is technically androgynous, he presents himself as gendered male; and we will see that this is how he behaves towards Nature, gendered female.

Again, it is only on this basis that we can understand what happens next. We are told that immediately after having given birth to the Human, the divine *nous* is enchanted by the beauty of his own offspring and experiences deep love for his latest child. Therefore he wants to put him in charge of all that exists. For his part, the Human is impressed by what the demiurgic *nous* ("his brother") has fashioned and now wants to make something too. Having received permission from his "father," he enters the demiurgic sphere to observe his brother at work. The seven governors (the planets) are full of love for him too, so he receives a happy welcome and is allowed to learn their essence and participate in their nature. To explore the rest of the cosmos, he then bends down and breaks through the circumference of the spheres to look at the world of Nature below. And Nature, too, is happy to see him arrive. His shape is divinely beautiful and he comes endowed with all the powerful energies of the planetary spheres as well. As she sees his image reflected in her waters while his shadow falls upon her earth, she smiles up to him with love. For his part, the Human sees in the waters that her shape is similar to his own, and he

---

[84] For even stronger statements in the *Asclepius*, see Chapter 3, pp. 56–57.
[85] Not Ἀνήρ; see Cop, 107.
[86] CH I 15: ἀρρενόθηλυς δὲ ὤν, ἐξ ἀρρενοθήλεος ὤν πατρός.

Healing the Soul 171

is overcome with love and desire to dwell there below.[87] So that is what happens: without a moment of hesitation, they join in a deep embrace and begin to make love.[88]

We will see in a moment that this account is challenged by an influential tradition of scholarship; but before addressing objections, let me summarize my interpretation. What we are reading here is a love story, a happy fairy-tale of mutual love at first sight followed by blissful union between the noetic Human and material Nature. Nowhere do we find even the slightest suggestion of evil, transgression, or sin. Everything happens in perfect harmony with the divine will, and with its explicit permission. As everybody loves the beautiful Human, he receives a warm welcome wherever he shows himself. The "generative source" of boundless creativity can only be happy and satisfied to see how its children embrace in mutual love and will continue to carry on the great work of creative manifestation. All this seems perfectly evident. And yet, countless scholars have wanted to see these passages as something very different: a mythical account of "the Fall of Man," the tragic descent of humanity into sin, a "catastrophe"[89] of cosmic proportions. Here we encounter what I do not hesitate to qualify as a spectacular, indeed shocking pattern of systematic misinterpretation found throughout the body of scholarship on the Hermetica.[90] The matter is so important that before continuing our analysis of CH I, it needs to be addressed.

Already Reitzenstein makes the demiurge into a demonic opponent of the Human, introducing an element of fraternal strife that resonates with biblical models but has no support in our text.[91] What I called a love story, he turns into a sinister tale of seduction and entrapment by a demonic feminine, very much in line with the imaginaries of *fin-de-siècle* "decadent" art and literature: "he has hardly descended when the

---

[87] In line with his belief that the Human falls in love with his own image (see discussion in text, p. 173 with note 103), Scott notes that "The word ἐφίλησε does not signify the passionate desire expressed by ἔρωτι ἀκορέστῳ; it is not until Anthropos has actually descended into the lower world that he is said to be overcome by ἔρως" (Scott II, 43).
[88] CH I 14.
[89] Haenchen, "Aufbau," 167–168, 175.
[90] While Bull's argument follows a different route from mine, he reaches broadly similar conclusions on this point (*Tradition*, 149–154, 211, 215). However, I do not believe that neophytes "would be encouraged to interpret the embodiment of the primal Human as a great disaster" (ibid., 211) even at the early stages of the Way of Hermes.
[91] As correctly noted by Haenchen, "Aufbau," 166, 173 note 1 (as for his remarks on p. 166 with reference to CH I 15 and 25, see discussion below); see Reitzenstein, *Poimandres*, 49 with note 2.

phūsis already embraces him in lustful love" (... *kaum ist er niedergestiegen, so umschlingt ihn die φύσις in brünstiger Liebe*)."[92] His critic Zielinski describes the account of CH I as "*die Lehre vom Sündenfall des Menschen*" (The doctrine of the human fall into sin)[93] and proceeds to utterly misrepresent the content. For instance, he claims that instead of "giving permission," the Father has *forbidden* the Human to transgress the boundary of the heavenly spheres, after which "the Human breaks the commandment, in the illusion that he may thus gain higher power."[94] These are complete fantasies on Zielinski's part. In a singular feat of contorted reasoning,[95] Festugière begins by admitting that CH I does not ever say that the Human's wish "to create something" is bad – but only to argue next that nevertheless it *must* be bad. Festugière has already decided that these are "gnostic speculations"; for him it is axiomatic that such speculations see matter as bad; *ergo* the desire to create can only be "a kind of original sin."[96] Likewise, that bending down through the planetary spheres implies the "Fall of Man" is considered "evident"[97] because of the same axiom. Matter is bad. Don't look down!

So what about the love story? When Festugière remarks that "Man's sin is to love something *material*,"[98] we do not know whether we are listening to a classicist analyzing a pagan hellenistic text or a celibate priest pondering the human condition. For him, if the Human descends into matter while passing through all the seven planetary spheres, this means that he gets afflicted with the seven "capital sins" (Zielinski had already spoken of "the seven mortal sins").[99] Why then has God given his "permission"? Festugière responds with the Roman-Catholic concept of *felix culpa*, the

---

[92] Reitzenstein, *Poimandres*, 50. The German has nuances that are difficult to capture in translation: *umschlingen* rather than *umarmen* carries the suggestion of capturing and binding, while *brünstig* has strong connotations of animal lust. Festugière uses almost the same language in discussing the "seven governors": "Having hardly descended, Man already comes into contact with evil. For the governors of the circles fall in love with him" (RHT III, 89). In short: love is a trap. However, nothing indicates that either the demiurge or the governors are evil (as admitted, against his own agenda, by Haenchen, "Aufbau," 172).

[93] Zielinski, "Hermes und die Hermetik I," 325ff.; idem in Dodd, *Bible*, 145-169.

[94] Zielinski, "Hermes und die Hermetik I," 326. Zielinski seems to impose the biblical prohibition of eating from the tree of knowledge on to CH I and to impute Christian notions of *hubris* to the Human. None of this is even remotely suggested by the text.

[95] RHT III, 83-96: "Sin before the Fall" and "Sin consisting in the Fall" (in reality, as argued in the text, we find neither sin nor a Fall).

[96] RHT III, 88, cf. 90.

[97] RHT III, 89.

[98] RHT III, 92 (emphasis in original).

[99] RHT III, 90; Zielinski, "Hermes und die Hermetik I," 365.

fortunate Fall: "this sin is in some way necessary."[100] Throughout the entire analysis, the hermeneutical web of Christian-theological *Vorurteil* is palpable and omnipresent; this is what allows Festugière to make sense to himself of what he is reading, but at a very heavy price. Ernst Haenchen, too, imposes a "gnostic" framework by default while interpreting the love scene as a sinister seduction; but he adds a remarkable twist by claiming that the Human *resists* the attempt. He does not fall in love with Nature at all, only with his own image mirrored in the waters – he had not even *noticed* the smile of the temptress! But innocent as he may be, it makes no difference: he falls into the trap of matter anyway.[101]

This entire line of interpretation is made possible by the fact that precisely those passages most central to the idea of a Hermetic "Fall of Man" are in a serious state of corruption and disarray, and the relevant sentences in CH I 14 are ambiguous at best.[102] Depending on how one prefers to resolve the textual dilemmas, in the end one is forced to choose between two different scenarios. One makes the Human into a narcissist who falls in love with the reflection of his own image and thus becomes the innocent victim of matter.[103] As soon as he has got close enough, he is caught like a fly in the spider's web of Nature. The other scenario makes him fall in love with Nature herself. In this case the blame cannot be put on her seductive charms alone, resulting in serious theological difficulties: if the Human is such a perfect image of divinity and has not yet fallen, then why is he afflicted with this fatal flaw of erotic desire? Be that as it may, in the imagination of many older scholars, the end result was still very much the same: like Hylus seduced by the Naiads in a pre-Raphaelite painting, he is captured and drawn down into the dark waters. I want to insist on the relevance of these comparisons. The *fin-de-siècle* imaginary of demonic femininity and the occult dangers of sexual attraction, combined with fears of cultural decline and degradation, was very much part of the daily culture of scholars like Reitzenstein

---

[100] RHT III, 95.
[101] Haenchen, "Aufbau," 173–174.
[102] See for instance Van den Kerchove, *La voie*, 368 note 162, who compares her choices with those of Reitzenstein and Salaman. Illustrative of the problem are the heavy textual manipulations by Scott (Scott I, 120–123; see his characteristic remark with reference to the previous paragraph: "I have rewritten it freely, by way of an attempt to make it express what the author presumably meant"). For the solution most congenial to my perspective, see CHD, 15 with note 33.
[103] Thus e.g. Scott II, 43: "Narcissus-like, he loves it"; Haenchen, "Aufbau," 171, 174, where this "love of a Narcissus" allows Hermes to let the Human off the hook. See also Jonas, *The Gnostic Religion*, 161–165 ("The Narcissus Motif").

or Festugière.[104] When they see CH I 13–14 as an account of "The Fall of Man" into matter and sin, this can in no way be seen as "dispassionate" scholarly analysis. We are dealing with heavily sexualized and misogynic imaginaries of Adam's temptation by Eve projected onto the Hermetic text.[105]

What does the text really say? Nature sees the Human and smiles with love. His likeness is reflected in her waters and his shadow is seen on her earth. Dodd suggests quite nicely that by reflecting his own image back to him in the mirror of her own body, she seems to be trying to catch his attention.[106] If so, the flirt is successful. He looks at her and perceives a shape like his own down there.[107] One may argue forever whether the Hermetic author meant to say *her* shape or the reflection of *his* own shape in *her* body, but what matters is the outcome. He experiences love for that shape and wants to dwell there. The rest we know: they become lovers. She is making love to him and he is loving her back.

So again, does CH I give us any reason to assume that matter and embodiment are the problem for practitioners of Hermetic spirituality? Not at all. It is true that Nature with whom the Human is making love is described as an "unreasoning form" (*alogon morphēn*); but that was only to be expected, since we already saw that after having inseminated the material elements, the noetic *logos* had withdrawn himself from Nature. Well, he is back now! He returns in the person of this beautiful child of the divine *nous*, obviously in the possession of *logos* as well. We can now continue with the passage that follows immediately, and where the point of the entire story is explained to Hermes:

So this is why the human alone, among all living beings on earth, is twofold: mortal through his body, immortal through his essential humanity. For though

---

[104] On the "decadent" imaginery of demonic femininity, see Dijkstra, *Idols of Perversity*; Faxneld, *Satanic Feminism*.

[105] Such interpretations were of course facilitated by a veritable obsession with biblical influences among most earlier scholars of CH I (see above, note 39). The most extreme example is Dodd, *The Bible and the Greeks* (criticized by Haenchen, "Aufbau", 150–151, 158, 166; Pearson, "Jewish Elements," 337–338; Grese, "Hermetica and New Testament Research," 48–49).

[106] Dodd, *Bible*, 157.

[107] Holzhausen sees the words ἐν τῷ ὕδατι as a gloss that means to explain ἐν αὐτῇ ("in her") but then overlooks the earthly part (CHD, 15 note 33), so that as a result, the Human "saw in Nature the shape that was similar to his own." Thus whether that shape is that of Nature or his own is still left open by them, as by Dodd (*Bible*, 158). Only van den Broek writes clearly that it is her shape that resembles his own (HG, 99). Salaman writes that he sees a shape like his own "in himself" and then "fell in love with her" (presumably Nature, WHCH, 20).

he is immortal and has authority over all things, he suffers the fate of mortals who are subject to the *heimarmenē*. Even though he is above the spheres, he has become their slave. An androgynous being from an androgynous father, sleepless as he has come from the one without sleep, still he is ruled by love and sleep.[108]

This is exactly what we found already in the *Asclepius*. It is precisely their embodied condition that makes human beings into such a "happy mixture" of noetic essence and terrestrial matter. Embodiment is not to be seen as a regrettable fall into materiality, let alone a sin, but as a divine gift.[109] However – and this is the crux of the matter, as will be seen – *the gift comes at a price*. Pure noetic beings will have to make do without the joys and pleasures that come with embodied existence and the life of the senses; on the other hand, embodiment means coming under the dominion of the planetary spheres, the *heimarmenē*, while losing the crystal-clear consciousness of pure noetic Life and Light. We remember that *logos* was defined as "that in you which sees and hears," so it has to join with the "unreasoning form" of the body in order to come up with a fully functional Human. Exactly this is what happened when the Human and Nature made love.

That we have been reading a love story, not a horrible account of some catastrophic "Fall of Man" into sin, is confirmed immediately by Hermes' enthusiastic reaction: "What next, my *nous*? For I love this story!"[110] Further confirmation comes from Poimandres' response. Out of the union of Nature and the Human comes not some kind of monster or regrettable miscarriage but nothing less than a "most wondrous wonder" or "most miraculous miracle" (*thauma thaumasiōtaton*), something truly admirable: the birth of seven humans, androgynous and sublime like the seven planetary governors.[111] They are made from the elements of maternal Nature combined with the paternal gifts of noetic Life and

---

[108] CH I 15. "Love and sleep" is a conjecture by Reitzenstein (HT I, 22–23 note 45; Cop, 110); it is defended by Mahé against Colpe and Holzhausen, 15 note 34 (HT V, 369).
[109] See above, pp. 64–65.
[110] CH I 16. A suggestion recently made by Mahé (HT V, 370; referring to RHT III, 111 with note 1) would strengthen the point even more, as it makes Hermes say that he himself is "in love" like the lovers in CH I 14. I do not see why πῶς ἀκοῦσαι βούλομαι from CH I 3 should be inserted here in this sentence, as suggested by Mahé. Note that in the same section, Hermes gets so impatient to hear more that he interrupts Poimandres' story to spur him on, and gets severely reprimanded: "silence! I had not finished yet!"
[111] *Contra* Haenchen, "Aufbau," 175, who completely flies off the rails here. Obsessed with the idea of a catastrophic "Fall of Man," he sees in Poimandres' words a "lament" about the sorrow and misery of humanity ("Lebensnot," "Jammer"), seems blind to the incongruence with Hermes' enthusiasm about it, and for no discernable reason claims that because "the Physis [Nature] cannot stand this Being made of Fire and Pneuma," she has to "expel" it from her own body like some alien substance.

Light: the human principle of Life is known as "the soul," while the Light of *nous* in a human being is what in modern terms we might call the inner spiritual principle or spark of divinity.[112] Note that the *nous* is not yet described as a gift that needs to be "sent down" or a "prize that must be won," as in CH IV, but is inherent in the very constitution of these seven humans. In sum, once more, nothing suggests that the union of the Human with Nature and the birth of material bodies is regrettable or bad, let alone evil; on the contrary, it is a stupendous wonder, a splendid manifestation of divinity.

Only after these seven original androgynous humans have completed an entire cycle of life, the situation of blissful harmony between body and *nous* comes to an end. This happens *not* through any human fall or transgression, but by the will of God (*ek boulēs theou*),[113] which also explains why the event is never described as "evil." God decides to break the universal bond of connection between all things that are, by splitting the androgynous humans into males and females and ordering them to procreate:

> Grow and keep growing, multiply and keep multiplying, all you who have been fashioned and made! And may he who has *nous* recognize that he is immortal [*kai anagnōrisatō <ho> ennous heauton onta athanaton*] and that *erōs* is the cause of death, and may he know all that is.[114]

In response to this commandment, the cosmic machinery now begins causing males and females to engage in sexual intercourse and produce offspring. Presumably it does this by stimulating their bodily desires. This is how from an original set of fourteen original humans (seven male, seven female) and their descendants, humanity begins to multiply through countless generations. However, human bodies born in this manner are not immortal. They are subject to temporal cycles of growth and decline, for that is how matter works. Because bodies are composites, they are not eternal: sooner or later they are dissolved into their constituent elements, which can then be recycled as material to be used for fashioning new bodies.[115]

The lapidary statement "*erōs* is the cause of death" (*ton aition tou thanatou erōta*) has been hugely over-interpreted, again under the influence of biblical notions of sexual sin and transgression that are alien

---

[112] For my approach to translation here, see above, pp. 13–14.
[113] CH I 18.
[114] CH I 18.
[115] See also *Ascl.* 3, 6; CH VIII 4; CH XI 14–15; CH XII 16.

to the Hermetic worldview. In fact the text is just making a perfectly straightforward observation: not only are all material bodies mortal composites, but all such bodies are born from sexual desire. That everything mortal comes from sex does not mean that everything has become mortal *because of* sex: the former is elementary biology, the latter is Christian theology. Here and elsewhere it is clear that the Hermetic divinity, the generative Source of all that is, has no objection to sex at all; on the contrary, it is he who introduces this remarkable innovation and orders human beings to try it out![116] Once we have absorbed this basic point, everything else falls into place. Only knowledge of what is truly eternal, the *nous*, enables human beings to cultivate their immortal potential; and only by understanding that no other reality truly exists will they realize that in gaining knowledge of themselves, they gain knowledge of all that is.[117] However, this *gnōsis* is a prize that must be won. As the seven original humans still possessed it by default, they had no freedom to either choose it, neglect it, or reject it altogether. Human beings have been given that freedom. They have been granted a unique ability to seed the world with the divine light of goodness, beauty and truth, so that matter may become a mirror of noetic perfection that will give birth to ever new forms of life in splendid abundance – this is the essence of the love story between the Human and Nature. But all children from that marriage do have the option of using the gift poorly and making an utter mess of it. If they lose their balance by getting obsessed with the experience of embodiment while forgetting their noetic potential, they will "keep wandering in darkness, deluded by the senses and subject to death."[118]

When Poimandres makes that statement, Hermes cries out in shock: "But the ignorant...! What terrible fault have they committed that they should be deprived of immortality?" – yet another confirmation that nothing up to this point had suggested some "fall into sin." The outburst earns him a stern reprimand from Poimandres: "it seems you did not pay much attention to what you just heard. Didn't I tell you to use your *nous* (*ouk*

---

[116] See also *Ascl.* 21 (see discussion in Chapter 3, pp. 56–57); CH II 17 (for people of wisdom, procreation of children is life's greatest and most sacred task); CH XI 14 (the divine *Nous* explains that if Hermes is sexually aroused, this is similar to God's wish to create).

[117] That noetic recognition of one's immortality (CH I 18) is identical to self-knowledge (CH I 19) follows logically from what we have already seen: the human *nous* is no separate entity but identical with the universal *nous*.

[118] CH I 19.

ephēn soi noein, "to noeticize")?"[119] Hermes does so, and immediately sees his mistake (*Noō kai mimnēskomai*: "I use my *nous* [I noeticize] and now I remember"), but Poimandres puts him through a small catechism to check whether he has really understood. "Why do those who are in death (*hoi en tōi thanatōi ontes*) deserve to die?" Hermes now gives the correct answer. It is because an individual's body, as it is shaped in the world of the senses, is made from the dark and depressing substance that he had seen in his first noetic vision-within-the vision. Death is nourished by this substance.[120] What does this answer mean? Not any moral sin or transgression, but a tragical failure of noetic understanding: humans are not being punished for committing some "terrible fault," but will experience that there are consequences to an exclusive focus on bodies at the expense of *nous*. Those who choose to remain ignorant of what is immortal see only that which is mortal. Their own bodies are subject to death and decay, like all composites made from the elements of dark nature; and the five senses with which they are endowed can perceive nothing but other composite bodies, all mortal too. If this is your entire reality, so the message goes, it means that you are wandering in darkness – you are literally living your life "in death" because everything you hold to be real is only finite and mortal.

The dark and moist substance cannot be evil or bad, for it was born from eternal Light and Life like everything else.[121] Yet, it is a finite phenomenal reality subject to limitations of space and time, which means that it has come into being at a certain moment; and its darkly chaotic nature had to be tamed and brought to order by the luminous *logos* that came from the *nous*. Now that is exactly what human beings need to do

---

[119] CH I 20. Again, the absence of an appropriate verb in English and the equation of *nous* with "mind" or "intellect" causes enormous problems for all translators: "Did I not bid you mark my words" (Scott I, 125), "Ne t'avais-je pas dit d'être attentif?" ("Didn't I tell you to pay attention?" HT I, 13; idem in Dutch, HG, 100 "Heb ik je niet gezegd op te letten?"), "Did I not tell you to think?" (Cop, 4), "Did I not tell you to keep these things in mind" (WHCH, 21), "Habe ich dich nicht gesagt, du sollst mitdenken?" ("Did I not tell you to think along with me?" CHD, 17). Note that the verb is deliberately repeated twice: Νῶ in Hermes' response, Εἰ ἐνόησας, εἰπέ μοι… in the following question by Poimandres. I proposed to introduce the verb "noeticizing" as a standard term in our discussions of the Hermetica, and suggest that it might be useful in various other Platonizing contexts as well.

[120] On ἀρδεύεται ("watered" like a plant) see HT I, 23 note 51; van den Broek, in HG, 461 note 25.

[121] Στυγνός I therefore understand not as hateful, hostile, or horrible (as in e.g. WHCH, 17 "loathsome"; CHD, 11 "schrecklich") but rather as gloomy, sullen, or somber (in line with HT I, 6; Cop, 1; HG, 97). I assume that this meant to establish a clear contrast with the lovely "clear and friendly" light of *nous* mentioned just before.

too, if they want to use their potential and achieve the perfect felicity that is possible for them. Having been plunged into this bodily vessel, our souls are overwhelmed by dark and fiery passions that latch on to nothing but mortal things. However, we can be healed from these afflictions if we break the powerful spell of enchantment that tempts the soul to forget its true origin and keeps it running after empty pursuits and illusory goals.[122] The goal is spiritual knowledge, *gnōsis* – literally *re*-cognition or *re*-membering of one's true self as identical with the divine Light and Life, as Poimandres points out to Hermes once again.[123] From the perspective of the Hermetica, this knowledge is the key to living our lives to the fullest potential, experiencing and enjoying the spell of the senses without allowing our passions to drag us down beneath the surface of noetic awareness. In its boundless generosity, the divine source of Light and Life has opened up this perspective especially for human beings; but it is up to us to not squander such a great gift but grab the opportunity and make it happen. And that, it has to be said, is not an easy thing to do.

THE MISSIONARY

So what is the medicine by which healing can be achieved, Hermes asks Poimandres: "How then shall I find my way to life, my *nous*?"[124] The very formulation confirms his understanding that even though he has seen his true identity while looking into Poimandres' eyes, that was just a momentary glimpse. He is still living "in death," not in the true life. Hermes has seen the light and received the gift of *nous*, but as I will argue in the next chapters, he has not yet been reborn into a permanent state of enlightened consciousness. So how can he move from his present life in a world of the mortal senses towards one in which he will perceive the whole of reality as it really is? Perhaps the medicine is readily available, Hermes is thinking: "all people have *nous*, do they not?"[125]

---

[122] See above, discussion of CH IV on pp. 149–152, with the quotation from CH X 8.
[123] CH I 21.
[124] CH I 21: πῶς εἰς ζωὴν χωρήσω ἐγώ. Many translators (Scott I, 127; WHCH, 21; CHD, 18; van den Broek, in HG, 101) speak of a "return" to life, which to me suggests a circular motion of exile and return congenial to "gnostic-dualistic" interpretations or the notion of a "Fall of Man." Nock and Festugière write simply "go" (HT I, 14: "comment irai-je…?"), while Copenhaver writes "how shall I advance…?" (Cop, 5). It seems to me that in some sense we are dealing with a "way back" from human ignorance to an original state of noetic perfection; but ultimately the way leads "towards" a possible state of embodied perfection that is yet to be achieved for Hermes personally.
[125] CH I 22.

But no, it is not that simple! Poimandres tell him to watch his language: *nous* is not just a natural human endowment, so that presumably humans could simply use it to find liberation regardless of their actions or way of life. No – as stated explicitly in CH IV, the divine Source did not just share his *nous* with everybody but offered it to human souls "as a prize to be won."[126] The same point is being made here: the *nous* is a gift, and human beings should make sure that they are worthy to receive it:

> I myself, *nous*, come to those who are blessed and good and pure and merciful, to those who have reverence, and my presence brings them help. Then suddenly they know all things, and by their lives of love they please the Father, and they thank him with songs of praise and hymns that they lovingly sing for him in good order. Before giving up the body to its own death, they [have come to] despise their senses, because they know how they operate – or rather, I, the *nous*, will not allow those bodily impulses to do their harmful work on them. As a gatekeeper I will refuse entry to these bad and shameful impulses by cutting short the imaginations that are built on them.[127]

This passage is of considerable interest from a psychological point of view. The plural *energēmata* is used three times in succession, and clearly refers to obscure emotional impulses and sensations that arise more or less autonomously below the threshold of consciousness, influencing a person's moods and behavior by disturbing his equanimity and clarity of mind. Like Nock and Festugière, I translate *enthumēseis* (emotions, passions, or drives) as "imaginations" because these disturbances are not a matter of ratiocination but of the subtle life of internal images and fantasies that are continuously at work in everybody's mind. We have seen that ancient practices of meditation (*meletaō*) sought to regulate this stream of "irrational" emotions and bodily sensations by training a person's faculty of attention (*prosochē*). Again, the problem was not the body as such, but the bodily passions and their negative effects. Poimandres is saying that this gift of *nous* is like an antidote against the negative passions and their effects, because it blocks them from contaminating the human imagination.

It was natural enough for Hermes to make the mistake of thinking that all humans are naturally endowed with *nous*: he built this assumption on the fact that both the original Human and the seven humans born from his marriage with Nature had retained their noetic consciousness. Poimandres' explanation implies that this natural noetic connection

---

[126] CH IV 3.
[127] CH I 22. On "knowing all things," cf. CH I 18 and HD IX 4; and for the acquisition of a "cosmic consciousness" of all things, see discussion below, Chapter 8, pp. 253–255.

was broken only when God split the humans into male and female and ordered them to procreate. And that makes sense. Only now did they begin to experience sexual desire for other mortal bodies; and no longer did they wish only to bring forth pure noetic entities out of themselves, but they now desired to give birth to new mortal bodies. Sure enough, that is exactly what God commanded them to do. Again we see that the error lies not in procreation and embodiment as such, but in a failure to resist the passionate desires that come with it.

Embodiment is a good thing, then, but very risky. It is easy to lose consciousness of one's inner noetic divinity, be overwhelmed by the spell of the senses, get poisoned by harmful passions, and end up losing oneself in a world of nothing but mortal bodies. If this happens to an individual, Poimandres refuses to let him play the victim or allow him to blame others for his misery or his bad behavior (whether those others are human beings or the divinity itself); on the contrary, he insists that human beings are fully responsible for their own actions and must reap the consequences of their choices. Virtue is its own reward – even in a purely mortal world, one can still choose to be a good person and resist the seductions of vice. Those who refuse to strive for goodness simply do not deserve to be enlightened, and they are making it impossible for themselves to receive the gift of *nous*:

But as for those without *nous* [*tois de anoētois*] who are bad and envious and greedy and murderous and without reverence – I stay away from them, giving room to the avenging daimōn. He attacks such a person with his fiery arrow, assails him through the senses, and makes him ready for even worse acts of lawlessness so that the punishment will be even harsher. Such a person does not cease longing after insatiable appetites, struggling in the darkness without ever reaching satisfaction. It is this that tortures him and keeps augmenting the fire that burns him.[128]

Note that the Greek does not imply any causal connection between the absence of *nous* and bad behavior: it is not the case that those who lack it are necessarily evil.[129] Rather, the meaning is that among the ones without

---

[128] CH I 23.
[129] τοῖς δὲ ἀνοήτοις καὶ κακοῖς καὶ πονηροῖς etcetera. *Contra* WHCH, 22 ("As for those without Nous, the evil, the worthless [etc.]"). All standard translations obscure the centrality of *nous*, again by tacitly reducing it to standard cognitive faculties such as sense (HT I, 14: "Les insensés"; idem Van den Kerchove, *Hermès Trismégiste*, 156), thinking (Cop, 5: "the thoughtless"), *Vernunft* (CHD, 18: "Den Unvernünftigen"), or reasonable judgment (van den Broek in HG, 101: "onverstandig"). Interestingly, only Mead seems to see the point, writing "the Mind-less ones" (*Thrice-Greatest Hermes*, vol. 2, 14), but like Salaman, he too equates lack of mind with wickedness, depravity and so on.

nous, Poimandres will stay away from those who behave badly but will come to those who practice virtue. That is of course a very important point. Again, we are not dealing with an arrogant spiritual elitism that condemns the great majority of people for not having *nous*; rather, the text simply condemns bad behavior. Being exposed to seduction by the bodily passions is a serious challenge but not an excuse, for either with or without *nous*, humans should know better. They are capable of resisting these temptations.

What happens after death to all those who keep "wandering in darkness, deluded by the senses and subject to death"? From other Hermetic treatises we learn that they are reincarnated into new bodies – or worse than that, into those of unreasoning animals "that are unworthy to hold a human's sacred soul."[130] Poimandres does not dwell on this point but concentrates on the afterlife destiny of those who make the right choice. They will ascend through the seven cosmic levels to the eighth and the ninth, the Ogdoad and the Ennead. About those, we will have much more to say in Chapter 9; but here we must take note of the implications with respect to embodiment. Although humans were ordered to procreate and multiply, life on earth is not their ultimate and permanent destiny. I have described it as a divine gift that comes at a heavy price. On the one hand, embodiment enables souls to make active contributions to the divine work of creative manifestation, bringing noetic goodness, beauty and truth into the world so that matter may be transformed into a mirror of divine perfection. But on the other hand, this work has to be done under very heavy conditions of toil and suffering, because the body just happens to be a dark vessel, seething with a chaos of poisonous passions that seek to corrupt the soul and undermine all its efforts. Those who have diligently done their work in the service of divinity, resisting these temptations to the best of their ability while choosing virtue over vice,[131] will be rewarded with the opportunity of transcending the realm of suffering and unite with the ultimate noetic reality of Light and Life. As will be seen, a small elite of the truly dedicated may be rewarded for their efforts, not by an opportunity to escape from the "prison of the body" but by a rebirth of the soul into a *different* kind of body that has transcended suffering and the constraints of cosmic fate.

---

[130] *Ascl.* 12. On reincarnation, see Chapter 9, pp. 275–276 with note 47.
[131] For the soul's battle with its state of addiction to the harmful passions, see e.g. SH IIB 6–7 and cf. SH III. SH XVII 2 describes how the *nous* can turn θυμός into courage and ἐπιθυμία into self-control.

But for now, that is still beyond the scope of Poimandres' message to Hermes. He limits himself to a short summary of what happens in the ascent. At death, the material body is dissolved so that its elements can be recycled. Therefore humans lose their physical shapes as their bodily senses return to the sources from which their energies had come; and they surrender their earthly personalities as their passions and desires return to unreasoning nature. This process is described as a gradual ascent through stages that correspond with the seven planetary spheres according to the standard Ptolemaic system.[132] Although most translators see "the human being" (or "man") ascending upwards, in fact we are not told exactly what it is that makes the ascent; nor is there any reference to bodily "garments" or "envelopes." It seems most economic to speak of the soul and its progressive liberation from harmful passions. To see what is happening in this passage, it may be helpful to not just list these negative psychological traits along with their associated planets, but also to place them in parallel with the positive outcome that should result from their disappearance (Table 6.2):

TABLE 6.2: *The seven planetary spheres with virtues and vices (CH I 25)*

7	Lying and deception	Saturn	Truthfulness
6	Desire for wealth	Jupiter	Freedom from greed
5	Brutal and reckless presumption	Mars	Peace
4	The arrogance of power	Sun	Freedom from addiction to power
3	Deceptive desire	Venus	Freedom from sexual addiction
2	Corruption	Mercury	Goodness
1	Growth and decline	Moon	Stability

As the soul transcends the dominion of the lunar sphere, it is no longer afflicted by restless change but moves into a state of peaceful stability. As it transcends the dominion of Mercury, the "machinery of corruption" (*tēn mēchanēn tōn kakōn*)[133] loses its power so that goodness can take its place. As the soul ceases to be influenced by Venus, it can no longer be led astray by sexual desires. Leaving the sphere of the Sun behind, its addiction to power vanishes too. The reckless brutality of violence that comes from

---

[132] See overview of sources and backgrounds in Cop, 105–106, 116–117. Van den Broek (in HG, 462–463 note 32) refers to the overview of planetary qualities in Vettius Valens, *Anthologiae* I.1, which admittedly lists many other qualities as well, both positive and negative (cf. Haenchen, "Aufbau," 181–182).

[133] On my choice of "corruption" for words like κακία or κακός or their cognates, see above, note 14.

Mars gives way to the energy of peace. Leaving Jupiter's dominion, the soul is no longer addicted to material possessions either. And as it finally leaves Saturn behind too, it turns its back on deceit and embraces truth.

In terms of a Hermetic psychology of addiction,[134] we see here how the soul is being healed and liberated from its enslavement to the negative passions. It regains a state of consciousness that is appropriate to the divine: one of pure truthfulness, goodness, peace, stability, and freedom (from its former addiction to sex,[135] power, and possessions). This enables it to enter the Ogdoad, where it is joyfully welcomed by the other ascended souls. As they are singing hymns of gratitude to the Father, they hear "certain powers" *above* the Ogdoad singing praises to the divine as well. Therefore they make a further ascent together and attain that even higher level, the Ennead, where they abandon themselves to its powers, become powers themselves and thus enter into God. "And that," Poimandres concludes, "is the happy end for those who have received *gnōsis*: to become divine."[136] We will return to these highest levels of divine reality in Chapter 9.

Now that his mind has been illuminated by *nous* and he has learned what *gnōsis* is all about, Hermes is sent on a mission: "So what are you waiting for? Having learned all this, shouldn't you become a guide to those who are worthy, so that through you the human race might be saved by God?"[137] Having spoken those words, Poimandres joins with the powers of the Ennead. Filled with gratitude and praise, Hermes returns to his senses, knowing what he has to do. His consciousness has changed:

> I recorded Poimandres' blessing in myself, and was filled with happiness because my wishes had been fulfilled. For the sleep of my body became sobriety of soul, the closing of my eyes became true vision, my silence became pregnant with good, while the uttering of words gave birth to good things. All this happened to me because I listened to my *nous* – that is to say, to Poimandres, the word of sovereignty.[138]

---

[134] See above, pp. 154–155.
[135] Again, and contrary to common assumptions, the problem for the Hermetic authors lies not in sex as such but in the soul's enslavement to sexual desire (that is, not in the body but in the passions); see e.g. HO IV 2–4.
[136] CH I 26.
[137] CH I 26. Like Van den Kerchove (*La voie*, 34–39), I am unconvinced by the attempts of modern scholars to draw parallels with the apostle Paul's missionary activities.
[138] CH I 30. For this activity of "recording" or "engraving," see Chapter 10, pp. 326–327. Note that Poimandres is described here not as the *nous* but more specifically as the *logos* of sovereignty, presumably because they had communicated through "that in you [Hermes] which sees and hears."

What does this really mean? Does Hermes want to tell us that whenever he closes his eyes and falls asleep now, his soul is seeing the true noetic light rather than the deceptive images of normal dreams? This would be consistent with the theme of liberation from the bodily passions and their disorderly effects on the imagination. But at the same time – and I do not think these two interpretations need to be mutually exclusive – we could be dealing with a broader reversal of common dualities. On such a reading, Hermes has woken up from the sleep of bodily consciousness to the true reality of the *nous*; his inner vision has taken precedence over external vision; his silence is now more expressive than normal language could ever be; and when he does open his mouth, what comes out are "sounds full of power" (XVI 2) – not conventional signifiers but noetic energies or forces that affect their recipients directly.[139]

This does not mean that he is now uttering *nomina barbara* but simply that his discourse is full of noetic power – or at least, that is what it sounds like to himself. Hermes becomes a preacher in the streets, telling his listeners to wake up from their ignorance and see the light. CH I 27–28 contain a few sentences that are so close in content to CH VII 1 that they may safely be considered together. As suggested above, this Hermetic sermon with its extreme formulations has a tone of strident urgency typical of fresh converts who have just recently seen the light. So impressed is Hermes by the extreme splendor of noetic light that anything which falls short of its perfection is perceived in the darkest light imaginable. The people he addresses are living in a horrible condition of spiritual sleep, irrational slumber, drunkenness and stupor[140]; they have surrendered themselves to death and its "shadowy light"[141]; they have "swallowed the undiluted teachings of ignorance" that is "flooding the earth and corrupts the soul that is enclosed in the body."[142]

So don't let yourself be carried along with that powerful current, those of you who can, but use a counter-current to enter the haven of salvation. Drop your anchor there and find a guide who can show you the way to the gates of knowledge [*gnōsis*]. There shines the bright light that is free of darkness. There nobody is drunk but all are sober and their hearts are looking up towards the One who wants to be seen. You cannot hear him and words cannot describe him – you cannot see him with your eyes but only with your *nous* and your heart.[143]

---

[139] CH XVI 2; see discussion above, pp. 115–116; and Chapter 10, pp. 321–327.
[140] CH I 27; VII 1.
[141] CH I 28.
[142] CH VII 1.
[143] CH VII 2 (followed by the notorious passage about having to "tear off the garment" of the body first).

Hermes reports that some listeners responded to his words with mockery and left, thus abandoning themselves to the way of death, while others begged him to teach them. And so he became their guide and brought them the message of salvation: "I sowed the words of wisdom in them and they were nourished by ambrosial water."[144] As will be seen in Chapter 10, he is not just giving them verbal information here; rather, the claim is that he transmits real power to them by means of his spoken *logos*. The text ends with a hymn of praise to the supreme divinity – he who wants to be known and is in fact known by those who are his, whose supreme essence is beyond verbal expression and can be named only in silence, and who is actually even above all praise.[145] Hermes asks for the strength not to fail in his *gnōsis* of the divine essence, promising to join in the work of sanctification and enlightenment of all those ("my brothers, your sons") who are still living in the death and darkness of ignorance. Hermes, for his part, embraces the counter-current: "Thus I believe and bear witness: I go towards Life and Light!"[146]

Throughout this chapter, we have seen that those stark oppositions do not reflect any "dualist" worldview, as countless scholars have imagined under the influence of Christian-theological morality and "gnostic" mythology. We have encountered no "Fall into Sin," no "divine spark trapped in matter," no "bad or evil demiurge," and no "rejection of the body." All those elements that have been read in terms of theology or mythology are much more easily understood in terms of human psychology, as suggested by the very themes that these texts never cease to emphasize. Human ignorance or a lack of adequate understanding is the key to suffering and evil; but this condition can be healed when we gain knowledge (*gnōsis*) of what truly is. The efficient causes of ignorance are not matter or the body, but the harmful passions to which the soul is vulnerable. Therefore the recipe for healing does not consist in ascetic rejection of embodied existence, but in a process of internal illumination that requires a profound alteration of human consciousness.

---

[144] CH I 29.
[145] CH I 31. On God being above praise, cf. V 10–11 (discussion in Chapter 8, pp. 231–232).
[146] CH I 32.

7

The Path of Reverence

> .... *a sense sublime*
> *of something far more deeply interfused,*
> *whose dwelling is the light of setting suns,*
> *and the round ocean and the living air,*
> *and the blue sky, and in the mind of man:*
> *a motion and a spirit, that impels*
> *all thinking things, all objects of all thought,*
> *and rolls through all things.*
> William Wordsworth[1]

We are told that around 440 BCE, a priestess from the city of Mantineia in Arcadia came to Athens. Public sacrifices were performed under her direction or at her suggestion, and there were those who came to think that thanks to her intervention, the gods had postponed the terrible plague that would hit the city ten years later. During her stay in Athens, she is said to have engaged in conversation with a young man who wanted to learn from her about the nature of love. Her name was Diotima and her conversation partner, of course, was Socrates.[2] In Plato's *Symposium*, this priestess speaks

---

[1] Wordsworth, "Lines Composed a Few Miles above Tintern Abbey, On Revisiting the Banks of the Wye during a Tour. July 13, 1798" (*Collected Poems*, 243).
[2] Plato, *Symp.* 201c–212b. We have no independent proof of Diotima's historicity but no particular reason to doubt it either. Plato often uses historical figures as his protagonists and his account is at least consistent with the historical dates: the great plague hit Athens in 430 BCE, so Diotima and Socrates would have met around 440 BCE when the latter was circa thirty years old. The *Symposium* took place in 416 BCE, with Socrates in his mid-fifties (Lamb, "Introduction," 78; Castrucci, "Cither of Mantinea," 470). Of course the degree of historicity in Plato's account is a separate matter; in this respect, all we know is what Plato tells us.

with considerable authority while young Socrates is cast in the role of a respectful pupil, aware of his ignorance and eager for instruction. Whatever may have been his reasons for asking a priestess of Mantineia to explain the mysteries of love to him, he certainly received more than he could ever have expected. We are told that in his mid-fifties, almost twenty-five years later, Socrates was telling his friends that it had been Diotima who taught him the true nature of erotics [*ta erōtika*] and put him firmly on the path.[3]

What kind of path? Diotima was not a philosopher – not in our modern sense of the word and not even in the original sense of a person driven by desire for wisdom.[4] She came from a city known for the predominance of women in its religious practices; and with strong connections to Pythagorean tradition, Mantineia was one of the last bastions of the ancient musical tradition favored by Plato.[5] Last but not least, the very name of the city seemed to refer to its *mantes*, "visionaries" or "prophets."[6] The Greek word *mantis* derives from an Indo-European root that means "one who is in a special mental state" or "one who speaks from an altered state," and this is what it meant for Plato too.[7] So Plato's Diotima

---

[3] Plato, *Symp.* 201d ("it was she who taught me erotics"), 212b ("I was persuaded").

[4] See Chapter 1, note 16. Cf. Evans, "Diotima and Demeter," 12.

[5] Castrucci, "Cither of Mantineia," 459–467. Plato opposed the "new music" (νέα μουσική) that had emerged between the fifth and fourth centuries BCE, characterized by "an exponential growth in harmonies and a race to experiment across-the-board with musical virtuosity" (ibid., 459–460; typified by the "dionysian frenzy" induced by the double flute, expelled by Socrates and his friends in *Symp.* 176e; cf. Plato, *Rep.* 3.398ff). See Visconti, *Aristosseno*; Gibson, *Aristoxenus*; short overview in Bod, *New History of the Humanities*, 40–41. The two kinds of music are visualized on the so-called "Base of Mantineia": see Fougères, "Bas-reliefs de Mantinée," plate between pp. 106–107.

[6] On the city and its history, see Hodkinson and Hodkinson, "Mantineia." For its female practitioners, see Fougères, *Mantinée*, 324–330, esp. 325–326 (with a list of names: Nikippa, Phaënna, Theodora, Julia Eudia, Epigone, Polycrateia, Memmia, and Diotima); Godel, "Socrate et Diotime," 15–16; Castrucci, "Cither of Mantinea," 467–470. On the musical tradition, see Fougères, *Mantinée*, 347–352; Higgins and Winnington-Ingram, "Lute-Players," 68 with note 49; Castrucci, "Cither of Mantinea," 462–467. For the intriguing possibility that the sculpture of a "woman with liver" excavated in Mantineia (Fougères, "Stèle de Mantinée," image on page 376) might be Diotima, see Fougères, *Mantinée*, 329. Note that two women from Mantineia, Axiothea and Lasthenia, are recorded as pupils of Plato (Castrucci, "Cither of Mantinea," 457–459).

[7] Flower, *Seer in Ancient Greece*, 23; Maurizio, "Anthropology," 70; both referring to Nagy, "Ancient Greek Poetry," 60: "it is clear that the *mantis*, 'seer,' is being recognized as one who speaks from an altered mental state ... The philosophical connection being made [in Plato, *Tim.* 71e–72b] between *mantis*, 'seer,' and *mania*, 'madness, dementia,' is in fact etymologically correct: the etymology of *mantis* is 'one who is in a special [that is, marked or differentiated] mental state' (from the root *men-, as in Latin *mens*, *mentis*), while that of *mania* is 'a special [that is, marked, differentiated] mental state' (again, from root *men-)." For extensive etymological analyses, see Chantraine, *Dictionnaire étymologique*, 665; Casevitz, "Mantis: Le vrai sens."

The Path of Reverence 189

is a priestess from the city of inspired visionaries, and in the *Symposium* she is presented not as a seeker of wisdom like Socrates but as one who has *found* it: she looks at the path that must be traveled from the vantage point of its destination. Speaking as an initiate who knows the ultimate mystery of which her pupil is still ignorant, she encourages him in his quest while telling him honestly that it might prove beyond his reach.[8]

As for what Diotima is trying to tell Socrates, one point is absolutely essential to our concerns: she makes clear to him that *neither she nor anybody else will ever be able to "tell him the truth"* about ultimate reality, because it is not the kind of thing that can be told. The best she can do is tell him *about* it.[9] She assures him that there *is* something to strive for; that there *is* indeed an answer to the question of what is good and what isn't; that it *is* possible to know how one should live and how one shouldn't. She makes use of careful argumentation to correct some of his mistakes, pointing out errors of reasoning and false assumptions, very much the way Socrates would be doing with his own pupils later. But all such communication still relies on *dianoia*, the kind of "articulated thinking or reasoning" that lends itself to verbal expression. While it allows us to *talk about* the reality of ultimate Goodness and true Being (*ta onta*, "the things that really are"), to actually *know* them we need *noēsis*, immediate noetic apprehension or what I have called "knowledge by acqaintance."[10]

---

[8] Plato, *Symp.* 201–212. On why the term "mystery" is appropriate here for philosophical reasons, see Hyland, *Finitude and Transcendence*, 193–194; for the Eleusinian mysteries in relation to the *Symposium*, see Evans, "Diotima and Demeter"; Castrucci, "Cither of Mantinea," 456, 470.

[9] Neither Socrates nor any other character in Plato's dialogues ever presents a "theory" of morality, of forms or ideas, of knowledge, or of metaphysics; only Platonism scholars do so. See Hyland, *Finitude and Transcendence*, 13–33, 165–195 (and more specifically 7, 32, 168–170, 172–173); Sallis, *Being and Logos*, 1: "it is highly questionable whether there is any such thing as the philosophy of Plato"; Rosen, "Is Metaphysics Possible?," 242: "As to the 'theory of Ideas,' it is an invention of nineteenth-century scholarship"; Griswold, "Plato's Metaphilosophy," 148: "Plato just *assumes* or *asserts* that the Ideas exist, and *then* explains what 'knowledge' is. ... We do not seem to get an account of how we know these ontological assumptions to be true."

[10] See above, pp. 113–114. For the essential argument, see Hyland, *Finitude and Transcendence*, 178–182, 185–188, 192–193. "We do not 'know' the ideas or even know *that* there are ideas in any strict or comprehensive sense of knowledge" (i.e. in the sense of *epistēmē*), for "what actually happens is that we *begin with* the ideas, and from that beginning their great value is developed" (ibid., 178). For this "other sort of knowledge that is not *epistēmē*," Plato uses *to gignōskein* (ibid., 180), related of course to *noēsis* and *gnōsis*. The conclusion is that in Plato's dialogues, "every philosophic speech is bounded at its beginning and its end by a noetic vision," while *dianoia* (relevant to *epistēmē*) is an attempt to bridge the gap between these two (ibid., 182). As concluded by Evans ("Diotima and Demeter," 8) "human knowledge is indirect, dependent, and always mediated."

THE BEAUTY OF GOODNESS AND TRUTH

Supposing then that the lover of wisdom is granted this supreme knowledge, how will the Good and the True manifest itself to his *nous*? The answer might perhaps seem surprising at first, but is made perfectly clear: it will be experienced as *Beauty*. Suddenly (*exaiphnēs*), Diotima explains, the seeker will perceive something astonishing (*thaumaston*) that is beautiful in its very nature; and this, she points out, "is the purpose of all the earlier effort."[11] She continues by describing what it is *not*. That which is being perceived is unlike anything known from our sensory world of impermanence and change; its beauty is everlasting [*aei on*], complete, self-contained, not relative to anything else; it has nothing to do with visual appearances and nothing with *logos* or *epistēmē* either.[12] So what *is* it then? Diotima does not tell, for reasons that should be evident by now. She *cannot* tell because this knowledge is not discursive but noetic.[13] It cannot be mediated by language or discourse but reveals itself only in immediate experience.

As the conversation between Diotima and Socrates is one of the central foundation texts of Platonic philosophy, its content must have been very well known in Hermetic milieus. Its emphasis on direct noetic apprehension should be compared with what Socrates says about it in his other great dialogue on love, the *Phaedrus*: as the true lover of wisdom stands aside from the busy doings of mankind while "being born into" or "emerging into" the place of divinity (*pros tōi theiōi gignomenos*), the multitudes think he is out of his mind because they do not realize that he is full of divinity (*enthousiazōn*).[14] In such a "mantic" altered state,[15] he becomes conscious of a place above the heavens that is beyond the power of any poet to express: the supreme reality of true beauty, wisdom, and goodness that can only be perceived by the *nous*, "the pilot of the soul."[16] We have every reason to assume that Plato's Socrates is referring to such

---

[11] Plato, *Symp.* 210e.
[12] Plato, *Symp.* 211a–b.
[13] Hyland, *Plato and the Question of Beauty*, 56–58.
[14] Plato, *Phaedrus* 249d. Because English resists translations such as "being born towards" divinity, γιγνόμενος is usually translated here as "drawing nigh to." I prefer to be more literal in view of the evident parallel with *Symp.* 206e (see above, pp. 106–107). The suggestion is of an "opening up" and "emergence" from restricted consciousness into the "open sea" of beauty, similar to the experience of physical birth from the restricted environment of the womb into the light and open space of the external world.
[15] On *mantis* and *manía* in Plato, see above, note 7.
[16] Plato, *Phaedr.* 247c–d.

experiences when he states, elsewhere, that the love of wisdom begins with wonder or astonishment (*thaumazein*).[17]

How do we interpret these famous passages? For modern readers it is very hard not to be led astray here by eighteenth- and nineteenth century constructs of "mysticism" and all their connotations, either of obscurantism and irrationality or of a trans-religious universality.[18] Our default assumption is that Diotima refers to a "mystical experience" – whatever we think that might be. However, if we bracket those associations, it appears that something different is being said. She is actually making a perfectly straightforward observation that should be familiar to any reader who has ever been moved or struck by something beautiful. We know it is possible to talk about what is true and what is good; but it is doubtful (to say the least) whether anybody has ever had a direct experience of "truth" or "goodness" as such. By contrast, countless people *have* had direct experiences of beauty; but it is doubtful (to say the least) whether anybody has ever been able to put them into words. As already indicated, Diotima does not do so either – she just refers to the experience. In addition, she talks *about* it. If we unpack her observations, we find that beauty is given a unique metaphysical status because it is the *only* direct experience of ultimate reality that anybody ever has or ever will have.

The implications are remarkable. It means nothing less than that, far from being merely "aesthetic" or "erotic" in our restricted modern senses (and hence marginal to the search for truth), our human experiences of beauty are completely *central* to the human search for knowledge and meaning. The presence of this ultimate reality cannot be perceived directly by our senses and its true nature cannot be comprehended by our intellect. However, Diotima is teaching Socrates that whenever we experience "beauty" – for instance while listening to great music or poetry[19] or watching an exquisite human body – what we are *actually* experiencing is the powerful impact of the only true and ultimate reality touching our bodies and our souls. Because nothing else than this reality

---

[17] Plato, *Theaet.* 155d.
[18] For an excellent historical overview that shows the eighteenth- and nineteenth-century foundations of the concept, see Schmidt, "Making of Modern 'Mysticism'"; for a shorter and more recent overview, see Huss, *Mystifying Kabbalah*, 19–24.
[19] Of course, in Plato's *Phaedrus* (245a) poetry is given a privileged status as one of the four chief ways of inducing an alteration of consciousness that makes it possible for human beings to experience ultimate reality (comprehensive discussion in Ustinova, *Divine Mania*, 265–292). For the closely related dimension of music, see above, p. 188 note 5.

is perfectly good and true (or even more strongly, because nothing else has true *being*), whatever we say about "goodness" and "truth" will be meaningful *only* in reference to this mysterious "open sea"[20] which we conventionally refer to as "beauty."

This is the central truth of which Diotima's erotics had persuaded Socrates. In the *Phaedrus*, he explains that when our soul experiences that powerful pull of beauty, it is very easily led astray by the "bad horse" of bodily desire (*epithumia*), the source of destructive passions that take us away from the source of beauty in a pointless pursuit of limited and deceptive images, mere simulacra of reality. But if we can manage to resist those distractions, the "good horse" will lead us upwards to the unlimited primal reality of beauty itself. Only when we have "nearly" (*schedon*) reached the end of that journey, our *nous* (taking control of our soul) will be able to actually perceive it directly.[21] However, it would be a mistake to assume that this will be the end of the journey. At least according to Diotima's teaching in the *Symposium*, we are not expected to withdraw from the world, for in fact it is only now that our soul is properly connected to the source that we can truly begin "giving birth in beauty, both in body and soul."[22]

What does that mean? Giving birth to bodies through sexual generation is a "divine work" (*theion to pragma*), because this is how something immortal is allowed to enter into what is mortal.[23] On the level of the soul, Diotima mentions divinely inspired poems and laws that are of a higher order and outlast the timespan of material bodies.[24] To this we may certainly add divinely inspired music. The point is that a person in

---

[20] Plato, *Symp.* 210d.
[21] For the great importance of σχεδόν in this context, see Hyland, *Plato and the Question of Beauty*, 57–59. That this ultimate vision of beauty would be at the center of the Eleusinian mysteries is not essential to my argument here, but can be readily assumed. As pointed out by Evans ("Diotima and Demeter," 18), "Plato's fourth-century audience would have immediately made the connection between Diotima's rites of love (*erōtika*) and Demeter's rites of initiation (*mustika*) when they heard Diotima mention her higher grades of initiation (*epoptika*) and their rituals of sight. *Epoptika*, derived from the verb that means 'look upon,' has *no other meaning* in classical Greek outside of the meanings uniquely attached to the Eleusinian mysteries" (my emphasis).
[22] Plato, *Symp.* 206b. For the progressive movement from one body to many or all bodies and from there on to souls, see *Symp.* 210a–d.
[23] Plato, *Symp.* 206c.
[24] Plato, *Symp.* 209d–e. See the important discussion in Hyland, *Plato and the Question of Beauty*, 49–60. Contrary to common assumptions, "lower" stages in the ascent are not supposed to be "left behind" but to get integrated in a progressively more expansive world-affirming perspective that embraces beauty in all its manifestations. Hence it is not optional but in fact *necessary* (δεῖ) to begin with turning towards beautiful bodies (ibid., 53–55).

love with beauty will give birth to beautiful offspring in *everything* he or she does, producing beautiful bodies, beautiful poetry, beautiful music, beautiful institutions, beautiful laws, and so on. Having "given birth in beauty" while moving through all these levels, he or she may finally gain the open sea of beauty itself and will be able to channel its energies of pure goodness directly into the world.

> Once you have seen it, you will never be seduced again by the charm of gold, or clothes, or handsome boys or youths; you will care nothing for those beauties that now take your breath away and kindle such a longing in you and many others like you... What do you think it would be like if someone should happen to see the beautiful itself, pure, clear, unmixed, not contaminated with human flesh and colour and a lot of other mortal silliness, but rather if he were able to look upon the divine, the uniform, the beautiful itself? Do you think it would be a worthwhile life for a human being to look at that, to study it in the required way, to be together with it? Aren't you aware that only there with it, when a person sees the beautiful in the only way it can be seen, will he ever be able to give birth, not to *images* of virtue (since he would not be reaching out toward an image) but to true virtue, because he would be taking hold of what is true? By giving birth to true virtue and nourishing it, he would be able to become a friend of divinity; and if ever a human being could become immortal, he could.[25]

The great relevance to Hermetic spirituality should be clear. Festugière was right to mention Diotima as a model of the ideal Hermetic teacher,[26] for she appears not as a "philosopher" in search of wisdom but as a *mantis* whose *nous* has perceived the source and essence of beauty itself – very much like Hermes' vision of the limitless expanse of a lovable clear and friendly light.[27] Her advice to Socrates is to break the spell of *epithumia* through which we get enslaved to sex, wealth, power, or prestige – very much like the Hermetic diagnosis of human suffering as caused by the passions and seductive delusions. If he finds the source of true beauty, he will also have found the key of happiness and will discover that it consists not in escaping from "the prison of the body" but in contributing to the work of divine creation by channeling goodness and truth *into* the world.[28] For at the end of the day, that

---

[25] Plato, *Symp.* 211d–212a (for ease of reading I have removed three instances of "she said").
[26] RHT II, 30 (cf. II, 550; IV, 79–81).
[27] On Plato's understanding of light in this context, see Plato, *Rep.* 6.507d–508d, with the valuable commentary in Hyland, *Finitude*, 190–192.
[28] Evans ("Diotima and Demeter," 18) points out that even the word *theory* did not have our abstracted and disembodied meaning but meant very concretely "to travel as a pilgrim to a religious site to see (*theaomai*) things related to the gods and to the sacred realm."

is what the teaching is all about: the concern is not with how to find salvation in the afterlife but with how one should live one's life under conditions of embodiment.

REVERENCE AND ASTONISHMENT

Throughout the Hermetic literature, we find a strong contrast between the small minority of those who are on the path and the great majority of those who have sadly lost their way. The latter are usually referred to as "unbelievers," but our background assumptions derived from Christian theology make it difficult not to misconstrue what it actually meant. With primary reference to the *Asclepius*, Anna Van den Kerchove points out that the concern is not with matters of doctrine or "correct belief":

> The translators ... have used a term that is constructed with a privative or negative particular: *dif-fido* in latin, ⲁⲧ-ⲛⲁϩⲧⲉ in Coptic, with perhaps ἀπιστεῖν [*apistein*] in the original Greek version. Each verb is opposed to another one that signifies "being astonished" and "to admire" (*miror* in Latin and ⲣ̄ϣⲡⲏⲣⲉ in Coptic, constructed after the Greek θαυμάζειν [*thaumazein*]). The astonishment that leads to admiration plays an important role in philosophy: it is at the origin of knowledge [Plato, *Theaet* 155d] and is a motor of contemplation. That being astonished is placed in opposition to lacking faith signifies that astonishment and admiration lead to faith. It appears that the latter has little to do with the classical sense of πίστις [*pistis*]. Linked rather to astonishment and admiration, it would allow the spirit to elevate itself to another reality that is hidden from what appears to the eye.[29]

It is here that we see the true relevance of the preceding discussion. The Hermetica never stop praising the astonishing beauty of creation[30] while lamenting the "irreverence" (*asebeia*) of those who seem to have lost their sense of wonder and admiration. The primary virtue here is *eusebeia*: an attitude of profoundly felt respect or awe that may be captured, along an ascending scale of intensity, by such terms as reverence,

---

[29] Van den Kerchove, *La voie*, 191–192 (with literature references for πίστις in note 34).
[30] The most explicit passages are Ascl. 11 (*pulchritudinem, speciem*), 13 (*dulcissimum*), 34 (*bonus, decens*); CH I 8, 12, 14 (καλόν, περικαλλής, καλλίστης); V 6 (καλὴν), 7 (περικαλλῆ); VI 1 (nothing is more beautiful than God: οὔτε κάλλιον), 4–6 (see text); VII 3 (see text); IX 4 (καλά); X 4–6 (κάλλος, καλλίστης etc.); X 10 (καλὸς), 15 (the beauty of a child, καλήν, καλοῦ); XI 3 (Τὸ ἀγαθὸν καὶ τὸ καλὸν καὶ εὐδαιμονία ...), 6–7 (the beauty of the cosmos), 13 (see text), 21 (καλῶν καὶ ἀγαθῶν); XII 21 (πάντων ἀγαθῶν καὶ καλῶν); XIII (ποιεῖν τὰ καλά).

admiration, and veneration.³¹ From a psychological perspective these are modalities of love: we are dealing not with attitudes of fearful submission to divine power or authority (for as one of the *Hermetic Definitions* puts it, "the person who knows God does not fear God, the person who does not know God fears God"³²), but with a spontaneous positive response to what is beautiful, good, and true.³³ Hermetic spirituality is not really so much concerned with doctrinal assertions, but focuses on opening a person's eyes to the reality of the divine; and while this reality is held to be both good and true, it is *experienced* as beauty. For those who had previously been blind or confused, the initial response to such experiences is captured most clearly by the verb *thaumazein* and its cognates, referring to noetic experiences of astonishment and wonder.³⁴

The virtue of *eusebeia* is absolutely central to Hermetic spirituality.³⁵ As Hermes puts it in the *Asclepius*, "The standard for this double entity – the human being – is first of all reverence, followed by goodness."³⁶ In CH XVI, Asclepius explains the point with particular clarity:

---

³¹ *Ascl.* 5 (εὐσέβειᾶ = religio), 6 (*adorandum et honorandum*), 8 (*mirari atque adorare*), 9 (*admirationibus, adorationibus, laudibus*), 12 (*pie, religio*), 13 (*miretur, adoret, conlaudet*), 22 (*religiosi*), 23 (*pia, miraris, miraculo dignus est*; cf. above, Chapter 3, p. 62 note 60), 24 (*pia, pietas, religio*), 26 (*adorandus, mirandus*), 29 (*religione, pietate*), 37 (*miranda, mirabilium, admirationem*); CH I 22 (εὐσεβοῦσι), 27 (τὸ τῆς εὐσεβείας καὶ γνώσεως κάλλος); IV 7 (εὐσεβείαν); VI 5 (reverence combined with *gnōsis*: ἡ μετὰ γνώσεως εὐσέβεια), 6 ("the way of reverence": τῆς εὐσεβείας ὁδόν); IX 4 (reverence is divine *gnōsis*: εὐσέβεια δε ἐστι θεοῦ γνῶσις), 10 (this beautiful faith: τῇ καλῇ πίστει); X 9 (ἀγαθὸς καὶ εὐσεβής), 19 (ψυχὴ δὲ ἀνθρωπίνη, οὐ πᾶσα μέν, ἡ δὲ εὐσεβής); XI 15 (here δεισιδαίμων could mean either an attitude of awed respect equivalent to veneration or fear about death and dissolution; on the ambiguity of the term, see Hanegraaff, *Esotericism and the Academy*, 156–164).
³² HD IX 3. In Chapter 5, p. 141, I excluded SH XXIII–XXVII from the corpus of spiritual Hermetica *inter alia* because the beauty of the divine world inspires fear instead of love and admiration.
³³ The triad of the so-called transcendentals ("goodness-beauty-truth") and their essential unity is taken for granted in the Hermetic literature. See for instance CH VII 3 ("the beauty of truth and the goodness that is in it," τὸ κάλλος τῆς ἀληθείας και τὸ ἐγκείμενον ἀγαθόν); CH XI 13 ("that is beauty, that is goodness, that is God," τοῦτο δε ἐστι τὸ καλόν, τοῦτο δε ἐστι τὸ ἀγαθόν, τοῦτό ἐστιν ὁ θεός).
³⁴ NH VI⁸ 69,3 (ⲁⲅⲱ ⲁ[ⲉ]ⲓⲣ̅[ⲱ]ⲡⲏⲣⲉ) and 8–9 (ⲣ̅ⲑⲁⲩⲙⲁⲍⲉ); CH I 16 (θαῦμα θαυμασιώτατον); IV 2 (ἐθαύμασε), 5 (people who are like senseless animals do not have the capacity of wonder: οὐ θαυμάζοντες); X 25 (the greatest wonder of all: τὸ πάντων μεῖζον); XI 17 (καὶ μὴ θαυμάσῃς); XIV 4 (see text).
³⁵ Fowden, *Egyptian Hermes*, 107 with note 60; Cop, 114; Van den Kerchove, *La voie*, 81.
³⁶ *Ascl.* 11; cf. 13: "the pure love of wisdom depends only on reverence for God."

[Irreverence] is humanity's greatest offense against the gods. For the duty of the gods is to do good, that of humans is to show reverence, that of the daimons is to help. Whatever else humans may be up to, out of error, recklessness, compulsion (which they call *heimarmenē*), or ignorance – all that the gods can overlook. Only irreverence comes under their judgment.[37]

In other words, it is a human being's basic attitude that counts. The gods are generous – they can forgive human weakness because they know how hard it is to stay on the path while being under the continuous influence of the bodily passions. But no matter how often humans may stumble, they can at least show reverence to the limitless Source of Beauty and Goodness to which they owe their very life.

Those whose lives are governed by an attitude of reverence will naturally be inspired to emulate the essential virtues of goodness and truthfulness, and only such people are able to receive noetic illumination.[38] By contrast, *asebeia* (irreverence) is its own punishment, because it causes the soul to be tormented by the bodily passions and leads it along a downward spiral ultimately to "murder, outrage, blasphemy, and all the kinds of violence through which human beings do wrong."[39] Interestingly, such an irreverent soul is tormented ultimately by its own *nous*, presumably because it cannot endure its purity.[40] The negative bodily passions resist the medicine that is trying to heal them, struggling violently against "the good physician" who "must inflict the pains of burning or cutting on a body that is in the grip of disease."[41]

But why is it then that some people are more reverent than others, more receptive to beauty and hence to goodness and truth, even if they never had a direct experience of noetic illumination? Behind this question lies a chicken-or-egg problem: must one have *eusebeia* in order to receive *nous*, or is *nous* the condition for *eusebeia*? This dilemma is never addressed directly or answered conclusively. While the authors seem to be skirting around the issue, they share a consistent assumption that although not all humans will receive enlightenment, they all have the capacity to live virtuous lives. Admittedly, we have seen that *nous* is not a natural endowment

---

[37] CH XVI 11.
[38] See CH I 22–23, and discussion above, p. 180.
[39] CH X 20–21.
[40] CH X 21; cf. IX 5. It is tempting to assume that what torments the soul is the purity of the "fiery robe" that the *nous* has taken on, but this would be inconsistent with CH X 18, which states that "earth cannot endure such fire: even a tiny spark of it will destroy everything."
[41] CH XII 3.

but a "prize to be won," and Poimandres comes only to "those who are blessed and good and pure and merciful, to those who have reverence."[42] This suggests that *eusebeia* comes first: only those who deserve it can receive the gift. Nevertheless – and this is consistent with the constant emphasis on God's universal benevolence – at least some kind of latent or dormant noetic capacity must be present in *all* human beings, allowing them to experience the impact of noetic realities at all.[43] Only this explains that the *nous* may enter even an irreverent soul and torment it by its purity, as we have seen, although it may also choose to abandon such a soul altogether.[44] The general implication seems clear: as noetic humans we are responsible for our own fate, because deep down we know better than to act the way we often do.[45] No matter how easy it may be to give in to negative impulses and destructive desires, they can never be an excuse. We are literally surrounded by beauty and endowed with a noetic capacity to perceive it, so we can always make the effort to stop and listen.

So what does it mean to listen? It appears that the first step is to open our hearts and make ourselves receptive to the impact of divine

---

[42] CH I 22. Hence statements such as "if you are able to" (CH IV 4) or "this is how it is – for the one who can see it" (CH X 4) do not imply a spiritual elitism where only a noetic minority has the capacity to gain enlightenment, but mean that reverence is a condition for receiving *nous*. See also HD VII 4: the *nous* does not reside in the soul by necessity but due to a choice or judgment (cf. HG, 620 note 1024); HD VIII 4 states very clearly that not every soul has a *nous*, and this is confirmed in HD IX 5 and X 3. For historical backgrounds to the idea that only few people possess *nous*, see von Fritz, "Νοῦς and νοεῖν, and their Derivates, Pt. I," 230–234.

[43] Cf. Luck, "Doctrine of Salvation," 34–35; cf. SH XX 4; HD IV 1. That God would arbitrarily begrudge the means of salvation to part of humanity would be wholly incompatible with everything we are told about his utter goodness and freedom from envy. See also CH XII 2: "there is *nous* wherever there is soul." The point is that not the bodily obsessions (see HT I, 181–182 note 6; here I follow Quispel, HG, 149) but the *nous* should be in the driver's seat governing the soul.

[44] Again, in CH X 22 Hermes tells Tat to pray that God may give him "a beautiful *nous*." All modern translations write "a *good nous*," perhaps in view of CH X 23, where Hermes seems to distinguish between a "good *nous*" and another one that torments the soul as a servant of justice (see text above, p. 196, with reference to CH X 21). But of course this cannot mean that the latter is "bad" or "evil," only that its presence is experienced as painful by an irreverent soul. If the *nous* abandons a soul, what it leaves behind is an empty shell that does not even deserve to be called "human" anymore (CH X 24).

[45] See CH IV 8. In CH XII 5–9, Tat presses Hermes about the conflict between free will and astral determinism. Hermes answers that although humans whose souls are governed by *nous* are subject to astral fate like everybody else, yet they are capable of resisting bad temptations. Because *nous* ("God's soul") is above the *heimarmenē*, it must have governance over all things. The rather confused discussion of *ousia*, *logos*, *noēma*, *dianoia*, *doxa* and *aisthēsis* in SH XVIII reaches the same conclusion.

beauty. For instance, Hermes asks Tat to consider the beauty of an innocent newborn whose soul has not yet been corrupted by the effects of embodiment:

> Look at the soul of a baby, my child, when it is not yet divided from itself, while its body is still small and not fully developed. It is so beautiful in every respect, not yet sullied by the bodily passions and almost still hanging from the soul of the cosmos! But when the body has grown large and has dragged the soul down into its heaviness, then the soul is separated from herself and gives birth to forgetfulness. Then she no longer shares in what is beautiful and good. It is the forgetting that corrupts her.[46]

This seems an excellent example of what Hermes means elsewhere, when he explains to Asclepius how one can move from contemplating the beauty of something visible towards ultimate *gnōsis* of the invisible divinity: "this is how you must contemplate [*noēsai*]; and having contemplated, admire [*thaumasai*]; and having admired, consider yourself blessed [*makarisai*] to have gained knowledge [*gnōrisanta*] of the father."[47] We have an extremely good example here of how hard it can be to translate Hermetic statements adequately into English. Since Hermes is discussing visible beauty, it makes no sense to translate *noēsai* in terms of "thinking" or "understanding,"[48] and a verb like "noeticizing" is not current in our language. Even "contemplating" is far from adequate, as it suggests something more solemn than what I believe is intended here. If we take the baby as an example of divine beauty made visible, *noēsai* here means something like *watching with the eyes of wonder*. We see babies all the time, but it seldom happens that we allow ourselves to be struck by the full realization of how miraculous they really are, or deeply feel the beauty of their innocence. But that is exactly what the author means to convey here, as confirmed by the rest of the sentence. He says that watching in this manner leads to a sense of admiration or astonishment (*thaumasai*), and this is how our spirit gains knowledge of divinity – by being elevated to "another reality that is hidden from what appears to the eye."[49]

---

[46] CH X 15. On the formation of the human body as an "appearance and image of the ideal form" (φάσμα καὶ εἴδωλον του εἴδους), see HO V 1–9.

[47] CH XIV 4.

[48] See HT II, 223 ("Voilà comment il faut penser": "This is how one must think"); Cop, 5 and WHCH, 72 ("understand"); HG, 165 ("Het is goed daarop te letten": "It is good to pay attention to that"); CHD, 194 ("Zu dieser Erkenntnis soll man gelangen": "This is the understanding that one should attain").

[49] Van den Kerchove, *La voie*, 192 (quoted above, 194).

The Path of Reverence

It will be objected that some Hermetic treatises seem to defend a radical "dualistic" perspective that *denies* the presence of beauty in our material world and presumably leaves no room for "reverence" or "astonishment" about visible things. The author of CH VI in particular seems determined to hammer that point home:

> For the cosmos is the totality of all that is bad, whereas God is the totality of what is good, or if you will, the Good is the totality of God. For the most excellent Beauty is found in being itself, but those splendors that are the essence of God's Being are even purer and more perfect. One must dare to say it, Asclepius, that God's being (if he has one) is Beauty; but neither the Beautiful nor the Good are to be found in anything that exists in the cosmos. For whatever can be seen by our visual sight consists of nothing but phantom images and illusions. Only what can *not* be seen, notably the [essence] of the Beautiful and the Good [is real]. And just as the eye cannot see God, neither can it see the Beautiful and the Good. Both are integral parts of God, they are peculiar to him and cannot be separated from him, and are eminently lovable. ... If you can perceive God noetically, then you will perceive the Beautiful and the Good, that which illuminates everything and is illuminated by God alone. For that Beauty is beyond compare, that Goodness is inimitable, like God himself. So as you perceive God noetically, likewise you perceive that which is beautiful and good. As these are inseparable from God, they have nothing in common with the properties of living beings. If you are searching for God, you are searching for the Beautiful. For there is only one way that leads from here to the Beautiful: that of reverence combined with *gnōsis*.[50]

This treatise seems to be written by an author with a radical streak and a theological mindset (not to mention a tendency to keep repeating himself). His great concern is to prevent readers from thinking that anything in the physical world might possess some principle of goodness or beauty in and by itself, *separate* from the divine source; hence his "dualism" is in fact an attempt to refute dualism![51] Our sensory organs show us only phantom images and illusions, whereas the *nous* shows us the only true reality of divine Beauty and Goodness. All of this is perfectly compatible with the explicitly world-affirming perspective of other Hermetic treatises: none of them ever claims that beauty and goodness come from any

---

[50] CH VI 4–5. See also e.g. SH I 2 (God as "the beautiful"); VI 18; XI 2:18 ("There is no good upon earth, there is no corruption [nothing bad] in heaven").

[51] The dramatic formulation ὁ γὰρ κόσμος πλήρωμά ἐστι τῆς κακίας has often been interpreted as close to a stereotypical "dualistic gnosticism" (e.g. HT I, 77 note 17 "absolument mauvais"; Cop, 22 "plenitude of vice"; WHCH, 38 "sum total of evil"; HG, 180–481 note 137); but this is based on translating κακίας as "evil" or malice rather than just a tendency towards going bad or getting corrupted (see above, Chapter 6, p. 149 note 14). I see this as yet another example of "gnostic confirmation bias."

other source than the divine, and none of them ever claim that sensory imagery is "real" in the ultimate sense pertaining only to God.[52] So what is the difference? Merely a radical wish to prevent readers from ever getting confused by worldly beauty, so that they might start paying reverence to the world as separate from or opposed to God. If the author were presented with our previous example, he would probably have responded "yes, but whatever beauty you see in that baby is really the beauty of God reflected in a bodily vessel!" Fair enough – to this the author of CH X would readily agree. Differences like these are easily explained in terms of individual intellectual temperament and do not provide proof of deep disagreement.

HERMETIC PSYCHOLOGY

It is clear then that without reverence there will be no *gnōsis*, no noetic illumination, no liberation from our enslavement to bodily passions and sensory delusions. Those who entered on the path of Hermes were taught first of all to open their hearts so as to look at the world *not* with the gaze of narrow selfish desires but with the eyes of wonder and admiration. This is Hermes' message when he goes out into the street to tell the people to wake up: he tells them to "look up with the eyes of the heart" because the true light of divinity can be seen "only with your *nous* and your heart."[53] Such formulations make perfect sense, as the heart was the seat of the faculty of understanding and intelligence for the Egyptians, just as the Greeks considered it to be the seat of *nous*.[54]

So how did noetic perception work? We have seen that our condition of embodiment is considered unique and admirable because it enables

---

[52] For instance, CH X 10 says that the cosmos is beautiful but not good, and this makes sense. Since matter is mutable and easily affected, it cannot be called good in any absolute sense; yet that does not prevent it from being beautiful and from functioning like a mirror reflecting beauty (or truth: HD VIII 5).

[53] CH VII 1–2. The expression "eyes of the heart" occurs also in CH IV 11; for "eyes of the *nous*," see CH V 2, X 5. "Opening the heart" is therefore not some modern romanticizing interpretation but expresses precisely what candidates must learn.

[54] Kingsley, "Poimandres," 51; Sørensen, "cooyṉ," 143; Van den Kerchove, "Visions et légitimation," 796; Van den Kerchove, "L'image de Dieu," 80; HHE II, 297 (but Mahé's quotation about "opening the heart" attributed to Morenz, *Religion*, 97 seems incorrect). On the two Egyptian words for "heart," see Assmann, *Death and Salvation*, 29–30: the relevant term, ḥꜣ.tj, "designates metonymically mental phenomena, such as consciousness and recollection" and "is connected with concepts of individuality, consciousness, and personal identity that can be held liable, the 'moral self'."

human souls to participate in matter and *nous* simultaneously. What this means is that the living human soul receives noetic and material input simultaneously.[55] One text tells us that the flood of purely material (*hulic*) input, impressive and disturbing as it may be to our consciousness, cannot be properly considered "knowledge" because the external senses simply do not give us access to reality as it really is. By sharp contrast, knowledge in the true and proper sense of the word is incorporeal and uses *nous* as its organ of perception. Therefore all true knowledge in the strict sense consists of *noēsis* and finds its fulfilment in *gnōsis* – in short, the divine gift of *gnōsis* is the only true *epistēmē*.[56] This is how the situation is explained in CH X, by an author who clearly sees all perception through the corporeal senses as wholly unreliable and deceptive. Note that again we are dealing here with an argument written in the radical mode: while the author of CH VI wanted to emphasize that nothing except God is strictly "good" and "beautiful," the author of CH X now wants to make clear that nothing except God is strictly "true" or "real" either.[57]

However, in CH IX we find a slightly different theory of perception (*peri aisthēseōs logon*),[58] by an author who seems less concerned with metaphysical absolutes than with a psychological understanding of phenomenal experience. He begins by distinguishing three cognitive faculties: sense perception, *logos*, and *noēsis*. But while these are analytically distinct, he continues, in reality they are inseparable: "there is no *logos* without *noēsis* and no *noēsis* without *logos*," and "neither is *noēsis* possible without sense perception, nor sense perception without *noēsis*."[59] Now what does that mean? The term *logos* is notoriously difficult to translate, but we should keep in mind that CH I described it as "that in you which sees and hears."[60] As for the even greater difficulty of translating *nous*, it has been a central concern throughout our discussions. Unfortunately, all modern translators without exception reduce these

---

[55] CH X 10: ἀμφότερα οὖν χωρεῖ εἰς σῶμα, τά τε νοητὰ καὶ τὰ ὑλικά.
[56] CH X 9–10.
[57] Likewise in SH IIA. Litwa (*Hermetica II*, 30 note 1) points out that ἀλήθεια means not just "truth" but has the additional sense of "reality"; it seems to me that the meaning of SH IIA in fact comes out much more clearly if one consistently chooses the latter translation.
[58] CH XI 1.
[59] CH IX 1–2. The author seems to find it difficult to make up his mind about perception in non-human animals, as in CH IX 8 he seems to attribute sense perception and *noēsis* to "all living beings."
[60] CH I 6.

two sentences to trivial platitudes,[61] for a simple reason. They ignore the fundamental fact that *nous* in the Hermetica does *not* mean what we today mean by "thinking, intellectual knowledge, or understanding" but is the name for the ultimate reality of divine Light and Life as well as the faculty for perceiving it. In a similar manner, the term *logos* too gets narrowed down to definitions congenial to rational discourse, at the price of obscuring a much more subtle and complex field of meanings and connotations. One does not have to follow Martin Heidegger's philosophical argument as a whole to agree with his basic observations about what happened to *logos* and *nous* in the course of Western intellectual history:

Thinking becomes the *legein* [saying] of the *logos* in the sense of uttering a proposition. At the same time, thinking becomes *noein* in the sense of apprehension by reason [*die Vernunft*]. The two definitions are coupled together, and thus determine what is henceforth called thinking in the Western-European tradition. The coupling of *legein* and *noein* as proposition and reason are distilled in what the Romans call *ratio*. Thinking now appears as what is rational. ... *Ratio* becomes reason [*Vernunft*], the domain of logic. But the original nature of *legein* and *noein* disappears in *ratio*. As *ratio* assumes the dominant position, all relations are turned upside down; for medieval and early modern philosophy now explain the *Greek* essence of *legein* and *noein*, *logos* and *nous*, in terms of *their* own concept of *ratio*. But that explanation no longer illuminates – it obfuscates.[62]

---

[61] No speech without thought; no thought without speech; no thinking without perceiving; no perceiving without thinking (Scott I, 179). No intelligizing without discourse; no discourse without intelligizing; no intellectual knowledge without sense perception; no sense perception without intelligizing (HT I, 96). No reasoned speech without understanding; no understanding without reasoned speech; no understanding without sensation; no sensation without understanding (Cop, 27). No Word without understanding; no understanding without the Word; no understanding without sense; no sense without understanding (WHCH, 42). No words without thinking; no thinking without words; no thinking without perception, no perception without thinking (CHD, 85). No words without understanding; no understanding without words; no reasonable thinking without perception; no perception without reason (HG, 129).

[62] Heidegger, *Was heisst Denken?*, 213–214 (my translation, with transliteration of the Greek terms; cf. Heidegger, *What is called Thinking?*, 210–211). Heidegger's argument is based on his analysis of a famous formulation by Parmenides, χρὴ τὸ λέγειν τε νοεῖν τ'ἐὸν ἔμμεναι (Mansfeld and Primavesi, *Die Vorsokratiker*, 322, frg. 9). Note that according to Heidegger, thinking never gets farther from its original meaning than "when it gets the idea that thinking must begin with doubting" (Heidegger, *What is Called Thinking?*, 214). This remark is of course directed at Descartes and suggests what we find in the Hermetica too: knowledge consists rather in a revelation or disclosure of true being. Heidegger's point is confirmed by von Fritz: "Hellenistic philosophy replaced the contrast between νοῦς and αἴσθησις, which is characteristic of the latest stage of pre-Socratic philosophy, by the contrast of λόγος and αἴσθησις" ("Νοῦς and νοεῖν, and their Derivates," Pt. II," 32).

The Path of Reverence

Given the unquestionable centrality of these terms to what "thinking" is supposed to mean in Western intellectual history, this is no small matter.[63] If we are willing to accept that *logos* and *noēsis* in the Hermetica do *not* mean what we moderns have come to understand by these terms, we discover that the discussion in CH IX is much more subtle and interesting than one would gather from the standard translations. So let us return to the text.

Noēsis gives us direct access to the ultimate divine reality (*nous*) that is beyond sense perception and is inseparable from *logos*. *Logos* appears in CH I as the faculty, or reality, that can mediate between *nous* and the cosmos.[64] Hence the work of *logos* is to express ineffable noetic realities in language or speak about what ultimately cannot be spoken. However, if we consider the situation more closely, we realize that ineffability characterizes not only the noetic world of divinity but the material world as well! We easily forget that while we experience the latter through our five senses, the world does not *speak* to us directly either, except through mediation of whatever it causes our consciousness to see and hear. I want to suggest that this is the most likely background to why *logos* in CH I 6 was defined as "that in you which sees and hears": it means that the world of the senses can connect with our consciousness only thanks to our *logos*, which then allows us to actually speak about what we see and hear, to "make sense" of it.[65] Still, just as in the case of *noēsis*, our spoken language can never be more than just a secondary reflection: it does not tell us the truth but only tells us *about* the truth. In sum, *logos* seems to be understood as that which mediates between human consciousness and the two most fundamental polar opposites in Hermetic metaphysics, matter and *nous*, neither of which can ever be truly *known* otherwise than in immediate personal experience.

---

[63] Heidegger notes correctly that investigating the meaning of *logos* and *nous* means questioning the very foundations of Western thought. See e.g. *Was heisst Denken?*, 182–183, 199, 207–208 (against those who think such questions to be eccentric or useless, he points out that without λέγειν and λόγος and what these words signify, we would have had no Christian trinitarian speculation, no modern technology, no Age of Enlightenment, no dialectical materialism, and so on: "the world would look different without the λόγος of logic").

[64] Likewise in SH XVII 4–6, where *nous* appears as the διανοητικὲ οὐσία and *logos* as the περινοητικὸς λόγος. Thus calculative rationality is no more than a dim imitation of true reason: to unreasoning (*alogos*) nature it appears like the echo of a voice or sunlight reflected by the moon.

[65] I owe this idea of *logos* as "that which makes sense" to Christian Bull (personal communication).

Once again, we must be sensitive to the fact that by definition, such immediate experiential knowledge (whether through the bodily senses or through the *nous*) never occurs otherwise than at some specific point in time and space and always does so only through the consciousness of one specific individual then and there. By contrast, the mediate knowledge enabled by *logos* has this unique property that it can be retained, transmitted, and discussed by different individuals in the absence of direct experience. We can now see why it makes sense what Hermes tells his pupil at the end of the treatise under discussion: "*Logos* does not get to the truth, but *nous* is powerful, and when it has been guided by *logos* up to a point, it has the means to get [as far as] the truth."[66] *Logos* can act as the mediator that retains and transmits knowledge;[67] but truth appears only in *im*mediate experience and resides exclusively in *nous*. Thus we see the essential dilemma at the heart of Hermetic *gnōsis*: the ultimate truth cannot be communicated, and whatever *can* be communicated is not ultimately true. We will return to this in Chapter 10.

But what then about the bodily senses? What do we make of the claim that all *noēsis* involves sense perception and all sense perception requires *noēsis*? Part of the answer follows from what we saw above: *noēsis* is intimately linked with *logos*, and only through *logos* can sensory input be translated from something experienced directly to information that lends itself to communication and discussion. More specifically, however, it seems that the background reference is to a famous passage in Aristotle. In *De anima*, he observes that internal images (*phantasmata*) appear to the noeticizing soul as objects of perception, which it then avoids if they seem

---

[66] CH IX 10 (cf. HD V 1). Like Nock and Festugière I am convinced by Zielinski's emendation οὐ ("not"; see "Hermes und die Hermetik" I [1905], 338 with note 1), but not by his interpretation of CH XVI 16 as a "blasphemic insertion." That *logos* is both the victim and the cause of perversion I actually find quite perceptive. Holzhausen's emendation (τούτων instead of οὐκ, see CHD, 212 with note 592) seems quite attractive: "their *logos* is desire."

[67] The other occurrences of *logos* in the Hermetica are unproblematic. NH VI⁷ 64,8 and the parallel in *Ascl.* 41 discuss *nous* and *logos* together with *gnōsis*; *logos* and *nous* also go together in CH IV 2–4 and XII 12, 14; CH XII 13 seems to use the word in a commonsense meaning. To the *logos* in CH XIII 8, 18, 21 I will return below (pp. 250–251). The differences between CH X 13 and XII 13 are of little significance (perhaps the former thinks of *nous* as the deeper essence of *logos* while the latter might see *logos* as a specialized function of the *nous*; both see the two as being contained by the soul; the soul in turn is contained in the body, which is animated by *pneuma*). The stand-alone statement that God made everything "through his *logos*" (CH IV 1) occurs in a corrupt and contested passage and is most plausibly interpreted as a Christian interpolation (as suggested by Scott II, 136).

bad and pursues when they seem good. Thus it is, he notes, that "the soul never noeticizes without a phantasm" (*oudepote noei aneu phantasmatos hē psuchē*).[68] Seen against this background, all of a sudden our Hermetic statement makes perfect sense. As the noeticizing soul is focusing its attention on the world of the senses, what it actually perceives is *phantasmata*, phantasms or mental images that appear as attractive or repellent objects of perception (*aisthēmata*) on the screen of the imagination.

While Aristotle's theory of imagination is notoriously obscure, it appears in one of the most popular of all his texts (*De anima*, On the Soul) and its basic insights were very widely known.[69] Imagination (*phantasia*) is distinct both from sense perception (*aisthēsis*) and noetic perception (*noēsis*). What characterizes it first of all is its ability to store and manipulate images in human consciousness,[70] and this storage capacity links it closely to the faculty of memory.[71] Thus imagination and *logos* both make it possible to transcend the immediacy of experiential knowledge restricted to a specific time and place[72] – the difference being that the former remains enclosed in an individual's own consciousness while the latter makes communication possible. A crucial further point is that once *phantasmata* appear to our consciousness, they easily become objects of either avoidance or desire: hence we may be afraid of things that are not actually present, or go in pursuit of things that we do not have but that seem desirable in our imagination.[73]

---

[68] Aristotle, *De anima* III.7.431a.

[69] Aristotle, *De anima* III.3. For the scholarly debate, see e.g. Brann, *World of the Imagination*, 40–46; Schofield, "Aristotle on the Imagination"; Frede, "Cognitive Role of Phantasia"; Wedin, *Mind and Imagination in Aristotle*; Watson, *Phantasia in Classical Thought*; Modrak, "Φαντᾶσία reconsidered"; Rees, "Aristotle's Treatment of Φαντᾶσία." A particularly incisive analysis with far-reaching implications is Castoriadis, "Discovery of Imagination"; see also Bottici, *Imaginal Politics*, 15–31 (discussion below, Epilogue, pp. 364–368). For the medieval and early modern reception history, see e.g. Fattori and Bianchi, *Phantasia-Imaginatio*; Karnes, *Imagination*; Hughes, *Texture*.

[70] Shields, *Aristotle:* De anima, 274–275, 389. The common formulation "*mental* images" begs the question here, as it comes from *mens*, i.e. νοῦς, so I prefer to use the term consciousness. Note that in *De anima*, Aristotle uses νοῦς mostly as a faculty of the human soul, but sometimes as "a cognitive state in which a faculty or a person may be" (ibid., 285, 303, and 292 for how νοῦς is "pressed into service in a variety of ways in the Greek of Aristotle's time, sometimes indicating a faculty and sometimes indicating a state of a faculty, sometimes referring to a kind of cosmic principle or entity").

[71] Aristotle, *De memoria* 1.450a; cf. Yurdin, "Aristotelian Imagination," 78–79.

[72] For the centrality of this point to Aristotle's theory of imagination, see Yurdin, "Aristotelian Imagination," 79–80.

[73] In fact, for Aristotle "desire is possible only through the imagination" (Brann, *World of the Imagination*, 45); cf. Yurdin, "Aristotelian Imagination," 82 (focusing on desire rather than avoidance); cf. Karnes, *Imagination*, 33 (imagination as a catalyst of desire).

The relevance to our concerns should be clear now. From the perspective of Hermetic spirituality, this is exactly how our consciousness gets obsessed with worldly objects or conditions that aren't there but that we would like to possess: our passionate desires latch on to our *phantasmata* and we end up becoming their slaves. For instance, we read in CH VI that "whatever can be seen by our visual sight consists of nothing but phantom images and illusions."[74] In the *Asclepius*, we read how easily human beings are "deceived by a delusionary image that infects their minds with malice, and transforms the best of all living beings into wild beasts that behave like savage monsters."[75] And we already saw how Poimandres promised to protect the good and reverent from such infection: by "cutting short the imaginations" [*enthumēseis*] built on bad and shameful impulses.[76]

But what about the positive counterpart to such harmful imaginations? If the soul "never noeticizes without a phantasm," one has to assume that a *true* noetic image of the divine should be possible. What could that be like? In CH IV we read the following:

> Visible appearances [*phainomena*] delight us, but we doubt what we cannot see. Bad things are actually all too apparent, whereas the Good is invisible to the external eye, as it has no shape or form. Thus it resembles only itself but is unlike everything else, for it is impossible for something incorporeal to appear to the body. ... Now since the Monas is the origin and root of all things, it is present in all things as their root and origin. ... And whatever can grow, grows thanks to the Monas, but it collapses from its own weakness when it can no longer contain the Monas. So that is God's image [*eikōn*], Tat, as best I have been able to sketch it for you. Trust me, child: if you consider it closely and seek to understand [*noēseis*] it with the eyes of your heart, you will find the way that leads to above – or rather, the image [*eikōn*] itself will show you the way. For this vision has a peculiar virtue: it takes possession of those who have once seen it, and attracts it towards itself the way a magnet attracts iron, so they say.[77]

What we read here is that the ultimate act of noeticizing must be focused not on images that belong to the world of multiplicity and

---

[74] CH VI 4 (εἴδωλά, σκιαγραφίαι). On phenomenal reality as a display of illusionary phantom images, see also e.g. SH I 1; IIA 3–12, 17; XI 2:16 (ἀληθές, i.e. "real," cf. above, note 57), 27 (see Litwa, *Hermetica II*, 71 note 17).
[75] Ascl. 7.
[76] CH I 22. See quotation above, p. 180. On the translation "imaginations," see HT I, 24 note 56.
[77] CH IV 9–11. For present purposes I cut out the standard arithmosophical explanations about the One (*monas*) as the root of all numbers, and the latter as the basis of divisibility, change, and imperfection. First two sentences: see parallel in HD X 1.

impermanence but on the supreme unchangeable image of the divine Monas, the unity of the *Nous*.[78] This image has a unique power of taking possession of those who have perceived it and then drawing them up towards itself.[79]

But shouldn't the noetic Monas be beyond imagination or visibility altogether? As modern readers we easily get confused here, because images for us must be somehow visible by definition. An invisible image is no image. However, the Hermetic author does not share that assumption. Visible images of corporeal things reach our consciousness by way of the external eyes; but the internal noetic "eye of the heart" can receive input from an utterly incorporeal reality that has "no shape or form." That such an image is possible – that something imperceptible to our normal senses can still be "seen" or "perceived" with the eye of our *nous* – is exactly the point that Diotima had been making in the famous *Symposium* passage discussed above,[80] and we find it confirmed elsewhere in the Hermetica as well. In CH X, Hermes says that God is the unique source or essence of all that is and concludes that this truth will be evident for "the one who can see."[81] He adds that God is not indifferent to such a vision, because he wishes his supreme beauty and goodness to be perceived by human consciousness. When Tat responds by exclaiming that God has indeed filled them both with this good and beautiful vision, Hermes points out that the divine radiance is superior to physical light

---

[78] Contrary to e.g. Festugière (HT I, 57 note 29) and Van den Kerchove ("L'image de Dieu," 79) I do not believe that the "image" (εἰκών) refers to the text itself, our CH IV, understood as an "écrit iconique." A text is not an image. Even if we were to assume for the sake of argument that perhaps Hermes means his *oral* teaching (so that the "peculiar virtue" of taking possession and drawing upwards might mean the power of the spoken word according to CH XVI 2, see above, pp. 115–116), still words are not images and a spoken discourse is not an image either. In Greek terminology, words or discourse would pertain not to images but to *logos*. Nor can the hypothesis be saved by assuming that the author might mean the "virtue" of spoken *Egyptian* words: this would still imply some kind of direct "energy" transmitted by verbal sounds, not an "image" with energetic power.

[79] For the imagery of magnetism, see the valuable discussion in Van den Kerchove, "L'image de Dieu," 82–85.

[80] That the One is "figurable/imaginable/representable, the unthinkable condition of all thought, which is given only as figuring figure" was known already to Plato and confirmed by Aristotle's doctrine of the "first imagination," as explained by Castoriadis: "Yes, the one is 'visible,' but 'within,' *in* the soul – by means of a phantasm, with a phantasm, or *like* a phantasm. *Is* the *one* phantasm? Perhaps" ("Discovery of the Imagination, 239).

[81] CH X 3–4. For different solutions to the final sentence of CH X 3, see e.g. HT I, 114 with note 12; CHD, 102 note 279.

in that it penetrates more deeply and is wholly beneficial.[82] As it turns out, Tat's exclamation was somewhat premature, for whatever he was seeing or feeling might perhaps be a first step towards the vision but still remains within the order of normal consciousness. Hermes points out that the actual vision involves a properly ecstatic out-of-body experience:

> Those who are able to drink somewhat more deeply of this vision often lose their waking consciousness and move out of their body towards a most beautiful vision, as happened to our ancestors Ouranos and Kronos.
> [Tat:] If only that could happen to us, father...!
> Yes indeed, my son. But we are still too weak now for this vision, we are not yet strong enough to open the eyes of our *nous* and look on the imperishable, incomprehensible beauty of that Good. Only then will you see it, when you no longer have anything to say about it – for the *gnōsis* of this is divine silence and suppression of all the senses. He who has once come to this knowledge [*noēsai*] can know nothing else, he who has seen it can see nothing else, he cannot hear of anything else, nor can he move his body at all. He is immobile, all bodily perceptions and movements forgotten. Having illuminated his entire *nous*, this beauty illuminates his entire soul too and draws it up from the body, transforming the complete human being and making it one with what truly is. For it is impossible, my child, for the soul to see the beauty of the Good and be deified while still being in a human body.[83]

Note the repeated emphasis on beauty. Because the noetic "vision" is entirely independent of perception by the normal external senses, it is perfectly consistent that the bodily faculties must be switched off for the

---

[82] CH X 4. There are several ways of translating the passage. If one follows the manuscripts in reading ἐσεβάσθη, this means that Tat is "feeling dread," interpreted by Festugière in terms of "reverential fear" or awe (HT I, 120 note 16; WHCH, 46; HG, 134; cf. *deisidaimonia*); Hermes then responds in an affirmative manner, pointing out that the noetic vision of light does not dazzle the eye like normal sunlight does. For this interpretation, see HT I, 114: "sans doute, car..."; WHCH, 46; HG, 134 (Quispel): "That could very well be the case, for..."). An alternative reading has ἐσβέσθη (Scott IV, 571, emendation Ferguson): in this case, Tat feels that his eye is "almost blinded" by the vision (Scott I, 189; Cop, 31; CHD, 103), so that Hermes' response amounts to a correction (Scott: "Nay"; Cop: "Yes, but"; CHD: "Nein"). As a third option, Bull chooses to adopt Nock's emendation to ἐπετάσθη (Review of Scott [1927], 281; HT I, 114) and translates "my mind's eye was almost hallowed by such a vision" (*Tradition*, 236-238).
[83] CH X 5-6. For the image of "drinking" *nous* and its parallel with the *kratēr* filled with *nous* (CH IV 4, see above, pp. 149-150), see Festugière, "Hermetica," 6-7 and HT I, 21, where Festugière notes that he should have quoted this passage from CH X 5 in that earlier article. I take the liberty to translate κατακοιμίζονται as "losing their waking consciousness" because the author clearly does not mean just normal sleep. On possible backgrounds for the reference to Ouranos and Kronos, see Waszink, "Dreaming Kronos"; Bos, "'Dreaming Kronos'." That the body is specified as "human" may be significant, as will be seen (Chapter 8, pp. 240-241, 244-255).

duration of the experience, like a computer on standby. The faculty of *logos* is temporarily inactive as well: no speech, no language, nothing that "sees and hears." Exactly as described in the passage from CH IV 10 quoted above (using the same verb, *anelkei*) the soul is drawn out of the body as by the force of a powerful magnet. The active force of attraction is nothing else than the ultimate noetic reality of true beauty and goodness, the Monas radiating from the One. Difficult though we may find this to reconcile with our common notions of imagery and visuality, the soul in this altered state of knowledge is anything but blind. On the contrary – the point is that its noetic organ *perceives* the only reality that truly is,[84] whereas normal visual imagery consists ultimately of nothing but illusions.

But is this the sum conclusion of Hermetic psychology? So far, we have seen that with our eyes wide open we are blind to reality; our normal consciousness keeps us unconscious of what truly is; and while we think we are awake in the material world, in fact we are spiritually asleep. To attain *gnōsis* then means reversing this situation, waking up from the spell of the senses, opening our consciousness, seeing reality as it really is. But does this mean then that we end up with a thoroughly world-denying perspective that teaches us to leave all bodily sense experience behind to find spiritual rescue in a unitary reality beyond all manifestation? That conclusion might seem hard to avoid from the dualistic perspective of our normal consciousness; nevertheless, I will argue, it would be wholly incorrect.

THE THIRD KIND

We are now approaching a crucial point in our analysis. While the history of research has been haunted by the idea of a conflict between dualistic and monistic perspectives in the Hermetic literature,[85] recent scholarship

---

[84] For this important point, see the excellent discussion in Wolfson, *Speculum*, 58–67. In terms of his typology, Hermetic spirituality is not "introvertive" but "cognitive," although for this latter category I would prefer the term "noetic" (since this type of cognition is concerned not with *epistēmē* but with *gnōsis*, technically it could be called "gnostic," but that term is no longer available due to its dominant association with anticosmic "dualism" and so on: see above, Chapter 4, pp. 85–86). For reasons explained above (pp. 13 note 4, 191), I avoid the term "mysticism."
[85] See above, Chapter 3, p. 49 note 5. Bousset (Review of Kroll, 749–750) saw CH III, V, VIII, XI, XIV and the *Asclepius* as optimistic, monistic or world-affirming; CH I, IV, VI, VII, XIII as pessimistic, gnostic, oriental, dualistic, or world-denying; CH IX, X, XII and XVI as mixtures. How questionable this categorization was can be seen already from the different listing in e.g. Bräuninger, *Untersuchungen*, 40. Cf. HHE II, 15–16; Mahé, "Hermes Trismegistos," 3940.

has seen an increasing trend towards non-dualistic readings.[86] An older generation of scholars, from Festugière to Fowden, saw the soul of the Hermetic devotee progressing from a world-affirming "religion of the world" towards a purely spiritual salvation beyond the body and materiality[87]; but contemporary specialists reverse that narrative and see the occasional expression of hostility towards the body as evidence for a merely "pedagogical dualism" limited to an early stage of the Way of Hermes.[88] It seems to me that one must go even one step further and recognize that the very distinction between dualism and monism is *itself* a reflection of dualistic thinking. From the perspective of divinity to which practitioners aspired, such oppositions would be meaningless – little more than evidence of our limited consciousness.[89]

Such an emphasis puts scholars of the Hermetica in a very peculiar position. As our publications are in the domain of *logos*, we must communicate by means of verbal language that relies on dualistic thinking to make itself understood. Hence we normally analyze the Hermetic worldview in terms of the "two basic kinds" (*eidē*), "being and becoming," as technically formulated in Plato's *Timaeus*:

> [T]he following must first be distinguished: what is that which always is [*to on aei*] and has no coming-to-be, and what is always coming to be [*to gignomenon aei*] and never is? The former is to be noeticized with the help of *logos* [*noēsei meta logou*], being always the same, but the latter is to be opined by opinion [*doxēi*] with the help of unreasoning sense perception [*aisthēseōs alogou*], coming to be and passing away but never really being.[90]

Thus the timeless noetic reality of "what really is" stands against our perceptual space-time reality of impermanence and multiplicity, sense perception and mere opinion. This opposition pervades the entire Hermetic literature, resulting in the unavoidable impression of a dualist worldview.

---

[86] Mahé, "Symboles sexuels," 142–145; HHE I, 52–54; Petersen, "Hermetic Dualism?"; Shaw, "Taking the Shape"; Bull, *Tradition*, 151, 188, 209–215; Pleše, "Dualism in the Hermetic Writings."

[87] The very structure of Festugière's RHT vols. 2–4 of course reflects this movement from the world-affirming "religion of the world" (vol. 2) to "the unknown God" (vol. 4). For Fowden's reconstruction of the *paideia* of the Hermetic *religio mentis*, see his *Egyptian Hermes*, 95–115 and summary in Cop, xxxix. See discussion in Shaw, "Taking the Shape," 151–152.

[88] As formulated by Bull, *Tradition*, 210, 315, 457. Similar approaches in Shaw, "Taking the Shape"; Pleše, "Dualism".

[89] My argument resonates strongly with that of Chlup, "Ritualization of Language," 150–153.

[90] Plato, *Tim.* 27d5–28a4; cf. Miller, *Third Kind*, 41–42.

The Path of Reverence

Notoriously, however, Plato was preparing the way here for his introduction of a "third kind," something utterly mysterious referred to as the *chōra*. While the passage in question may seem obscure or enigmatic at first sight, in fact that impression results from the extreme precision of its formulations. It therefore deserves to be read with the utmost care:

[T]here is a third kind, the everlasting *chōra* [*triton de au genos on to tēs chōras aei*] which does not receive destruction, which provides an abode [*hedran*] for everything that comes to be, but is itself apprehended without sense experience [*met' anaisthēsias*] by a kind of bastard reasoning [*logismōi tini nothōi*], hardly trustworthy; which we see as in a dream, and affirm that it is necessary for all that is to be somewhere in some place and occupy some *chōra*; and that that which is neither on the earth nor in heaven is nothing.[91]

Regardless of how we interpret the exact nature of this *chōra* (if indeed it can be interpreted at all), it is generally agreed that by introducing this "third kind," Plato utterly deconstructs the dualism of eternal Being versus ever-changing Becoming.[92] While the *chōra* is everlasting like Being, yet it functions like a necessary, indispensable substrate or receptacle of everything pertaining to the domain of Becoming; it is imperceptible to the senses and cannot be grasped by proper or legitimate reason; and since it neither *is* nor *becomes*, one can only refer to it as "nothing." Therefore is it or is it not? Somehow it must be neither or both. While the *chōra* lacks any formal qualities, it both receives and reveals them; while it never appears itself, yet it makes everything apparent.[93]

While we cannot presume to know for certain what Plato meant by *chōra*, I suggest that it would be natural for readers during the first centuries CE to be reminded here of Aristotle's concept of *phantasia*, the imagination. This elusive faculty never appears directly but only through what it does; it is "different from either sense perception or discursive thinking (*dianoia*), although it is never found without sense perception"[94]; and it enables human consciousness to store images and remember them. Commenting on Plato's statement that the *chōra* escapes our proper faculty of reasoning and is seen only "as in a dream," John Sallis notes that

---

[91] Plato, *Tim.* 52a–b (with very slight adaptations in the interest of readability; cf. translations in Sallis, *Chorology*, 118, and Hyland, *Questioning Platonism*, 116–117).
[92] Hyland, *Questioning Platonism*, 109–122 (here 114), with a very important critique of Derrida's influential analysis in *On the Name*, 89–127 (as summarized by Shaw, "*Chôra*," 108, "Derrida deconstructs a house that was never built, at least not by Plato or his Neoplatonic successors"); Sallis, *Chorology*, 91–124; Miller, *Third Kind*.
[93] Shaw, "*Chôra*," 111.
[94] Aristotle, *De anima* 427b.

what we see in our dreams is always "an image that goes unrecognized as an image, an image that in the dream is simply taken as the original" – one must be awake to distinguish between the two.[95] And of course, that is exactly what Hermetic spirituality was all about: waking up from the dreamlike spell of delusionary images to the truth of what really is.

What are the implications? If we approach the Hermetica from the dualistic perspective that comes to us so naturally, we must conclude that "waking up" can only imply what is promised in the passage from CH X discussed above: having left the body and the spell of the senses behind, our pure noetic vision will perceive nothing but the undivided ineffable image of the Monas. However, profoundly liberating as it may be, note that this would still be a limited "view from somewhere": it is what the individual soul can be expected to perceive when it gets out of its bodily cave and looks out with astonishment at the unlimited expanse of ultimate reality opening up before its gaze. It is very tempting to assume that this vision is the soul's final destination, as it is so obviously a perfect opposite of where it came from: the person who perceives it has moved from the darkness of illusion into the light of true knowledge, and now all is well. However, it is far from insignificant that Hermes's initial vision of *nous* as an unlimited "clear and friendly light" stands at the very beginning of his experience as described in CH I, *not* at its conclusion. As we have seen, the light gets transformed into a stream of *images* intermediary between the pure noetic reality of "what really is" and daily events in the fluctuating world of waking experience – the realm of "becoming" that vanishes from Hermes's consciousness while his senses are "restrained."

What is this intermediary imaginal world, and what role did it have to play in the context of Hermetic spirituality? Apart from CH I, we have just one single Hermetic treatise, CH XI, where no one less than the divine *Nous* itself speaks in the first person as teacher of Hermes. Therefore it must have carried special authority for Hermetic practitioners. It so

---

[95] Sallis, *Chorology*, 121. At the expense of its radical nonduality, *chōra* was identified with matter (*hulē*) by the time of the Middle Platonists, and Plotinus concluded that matter itself was incorporeal, "a sort of fleeting frivolity ... nothing but phantoms" (*Enn.* III.6.7; see Sallis, *Chorology*, 151). As pointed out by Sallis, Kant's concept of the transcendental imagination in the first edition of his *Kritik der reinen Vernunft* is in fact "a reinscription of the chorology" (ibid., 155). For the very important story of how Kant withdrew from his conclusion in the second edition, highlighting reason at the expense of imagination, see Heidegger, *Kant und das Problem*, 126–132; Böhme & Böhme, *Das Andere der Vernunft*, 231–250; Warnock, *Imagination*, 13–71; Kneller, *Kant and the Power of Imagination*, chs. 1 and 5.

happens that in this text, the *Nous* calls Hermes' attention precisely to a "third kind" of reality intermediary between God and the Cosmos but not reducible to either of those two. Therefore it undercuts the dualism of Being and Becoming just like the *chōra* does in Plato's *Timaeus*. This third kind is referred to as the *aiōn*. As a first introduction, Hermes is presented with a systematic overview of how the whole of reality is structured. There is a hierarchy of five levels, each one of which is the source of the one below it: from God comes the *aiōn*, from the *aiōn* comes the Cosmos, from the Cosmos comes Time, and from Time comes Becoming. Each level has an essence (*ousia*) and two energies (*energeiai*) (see Table 7.1).[96]

TABLE 7.1: *Five levels of reality with their essences and energies (CH XI 2)*

[Name]	[essence]	[energies]
GOD	wisdom	*nous* & soul
AIŌN	remaining identical	permanence & immortality
COSMOS	order	recurrence & counter-recurrence
TIME	change	increase & decrease
BECOMING	life & death	quality & quantity

That the cosmos with its circular movement of the planetary spheres brings forth time is of course unproblematic, as is the statement that becoming depends on time: clearly the three lower levels belong together as the cosmic domain of time and change. Therefore it is easy to simplify this five-part division by reducing it to a more basic triple division: God – Aiōn – The World (= Cosmos/Time/Becoming). The result is a familiar standard structure of Being (God) pitted against Becoming (the world) – but with the *aiōn* added in between, as a surprising "third kind" that apparently neither *is* nor *becomes*. The treatise continues by explaining that while God is the ultimate source (*pēgē*) of all things, the *aiōn* is their true being (*ousia*); more specifically, it is the divine power or soul that allows the cosmos to function and move. As it always remains identical, it is imperishable, indestructible, immortal, and wholly envelops the cosmos.[97]

---

[96] CH XI 2. Following Nock and Festugière (HT I, 147), I see τὸ ἀγαθόν, τὸ καλόν, ἡ εὐδαιμονία as a scribal error. Whereas in CH XI 2 these words have no clear function and are stylistically out of place, they appear in CH XI 3 as a clear response to Hermes' question about the nature of wisdom; therefore I assume that "wisdom" is meant to be the primary term (contrary to Scott I, 206, who leaves out ἡ σοφία instead of τὸ ἀγαθόν). Scott's addition of ποσότης (quantity) seems perfectly reasonable and has been universally adopted.

[97] CH XI 3.

Before the teaching returns to the *aiōn*, Hermes is now invited to look at the cosmos through the eyes of the *nous* itself (*theasai de di' emou...*). As in our earlier case of the newborn baby, what this means is that he must look with the eyes of wonder and love: "behold the cosmos as it extends before your gaze, and carefully contemplate (*katanoēson*) its beauty: a flawless body, while older than anything else, yet always in bloom, young and flourishing in ever more abundance."[98] All is filled with divine Light and Love, everything is full of soul and in never-ending harmonious movement,[99] and the whole is forever held together by the universal goodness of God alone: "one single soul, one single life, one single matter."[100] As the central power of creative abundance, the generative Source in its boundless generosity never stops giving birth to all that is. "And that, dear friend, is life. That is beauty. That is goodness. That is God."[101]

So here we have Hermes looking at the cosmos with "the eye of the heart," the internal gaze of wonder and love, marveling at the beauty of it all. It is at this point that his teacher makes one of those characteristic Hermetic requests for extra concentration:[102] *some of my words require special attention, so please try to understand* [*noēson*] *what I'm about to say now!*[103] And what follows is important indeed. As Hermes is looking at the cosmos, what is he *really* looking at? This is what the *nous* explains to him:

All beings are in God – not as though they were in some place ... but in a different manner: they rest in his incorporeal imagination [*en asōmatōi phantasiāi*]. ... You must conceive of God as having all *noēmata* in himself: those of the cosmos, himself, the all. Therefore unless you make yourself equal to God, you cannot understand [*noēsai*] God. Like is understood only by like. Allow yourself to grow larger until you are equal to him who is immeasurable, outleap all that is corporeal, transcend all time, and become the *aiōn* – then you will understand [*noēseis*] God.[104]

---

[98] CH XI 6.
[99] CH XI 7–8. Several commentaries (HT I, 159 note 23; CHD, 127 note 355) are painfully blind to the obvious meaning of divine "light" and "love" (conjunction of opposites and contraries) in this passage. For the explicit distinction between light and fire, cf. HD II 6 (and note that the light appears wholly "as it is in itself": it is not a phenomenal appearance but a noumenal reality).
[100] CH XI 11. This direct equivalence of divine light with soul, life, and even matter (ὕλη) is a particularly strong confirmation of the nondualistic perspective of CH XI.
[101] CH XI 13. Since God is only life and abundance, what we call death and dissolution is really just change and transformation (CH XI 14–15); see below, Chapter 9, pp. 271–274.
[102] See above, Chapter 3, p. 62 with note 59.
[103] CH XI 18.
[104] CH XI 18 and 20.

The Path of Reverence

Regretfully, one has to conclude that modern scholars have not heeded the request for special attention. On the contrary, the secondary literature shows a singular lack of interest in precisely this key passage about the incorporeal imagination.[105] We find lengthy and erudite discussions of what *aiōn* could mean in late antiquity, but no recognition or discussion of what our text so clearly says: that this term refers to God's incorporeal imagination filled with the *noēmata* of all that is.[106] And yet, precisely that statement is of key importance, not only for CH XI as a whole but also (as will be seen in Chapter 8) for CH XIII, the pivotal treatise on Hermetic rebirth. Let us take a closer look.

We have seen that normal human consciousness gets deluded by the "phantom images" of the imagination, as opposed to the supreme image of the Monas that is capable of drawing the soul up from the body. But in CH XI we are presented with a *third kind* of imaginal awareness. Unlike the other two, this is not an inherently limited perspective "from somewhere" (for even the image of the Monas described above will still be perceived by one single human consciousness as it freshly emerges from the cave of impermanence and multiplicity) but the eternal divine perspective *from everywhere*. In other words, this is not the image of God as it appears to human consciousness, but the All as it is perceived in God's *own* consciousness. Whereas isolated images that appear in human consciousness attract our selfish desires so that we pursue them and end up getting enslaved in matter, God perceives *all* images simultaneously. He feels no need to pursue any of them, because he already possesses them all and privileges none over the other; therefore this universal divine perspective alone is perfectly free from the limiting temptations of desire. The truly remarkable statement made by CH XI is that

---

[105] See the close parallel with CH V 1, discussed below (Chapter 8, p. 231). Scott I, 218–219 puts φαντασίᾳ within brackets and distorts the original so completely that his translation does not even remotely reflect the original; HT I, 154 ("représentation," without footnote); no commentary in Cop, 172; CHD, 133 ("Vorstellungskraft," no footnote); HG, 146 ("het zuivere denken van God": "the pure thinking [!] of God," no footnote).

[106] Festugière's sixty-page discussion of CH XI and the *aiōn* manages to overlook almost everything of importance. As will be seen, the opposition between CH XI as "extravert" and CH XIII as "introvert" is false (RHT IV, 143 and *passim*); from pp. 146 on, Festugière vanishes down a rabbit hole of extreme erudition in pursuit of the word αἰών, distinguishing seven possible meanings of which the first two are considered relevant, but at the expense of what CH XI itself says about it; his discussion of "the psychological conditions of the problem" (RHT IV, 149–151) provides nothing of the sort; and his analysis on pp. 159–175 imposes a dualistic "static/dynamic" straitjacket on the Hermetica that obscures precisely the intermediary nature of *aiōn* as a "third kind."

human consciousness is not separate from this divine consciousness but is capable of full participation in its universal mode of imaginal perception.

> Behold [*noēson*] him who contains all that is, and behold [*noēson*] that there are no boundaries to the incorporeal, that nothing is quicker or more powerful. ... You can see [*noēson*] this for yourself. Tell your soul to travel to India, and it will be there faster than your command. Tell it to go to the ocean, and again it will be there quite as quickly – not as though it were moving from one place to another but as though it was always already there. Then tell it to fly to heaven, and you will find that it needs no wings. Nothing can stop it, neither the fire of the sun, nor the ether, nor the cycles of the stars, nor the other heavenly bodies. Cutting through all spaces, its flight will carry it all the way up to the ultimate corporeal thing. And if you wish to break through the outer rim of the cosmos to see what is beyond it (if anything beyond the cosmos can be said to be),[107] you can do even that. See what power you have, what quickness! ... Having perceived that nothing is impossible for you, consider yourself immortal and capable of understanding [*noēsai*] everything – all arts, all learning, the nature of all living beings. Rise higher than every height and descend lower than every depth; gather all sensations inside you of all that is made – fire, water, dry and humid. Be everywhere at once: on earth, in the sea, in heaven, before you were born, in the womb, young, old, dead, in the hereafter. If your *nous* can behold all these things simultaneously [*noēsas*] – times, places, actions, qualities, quantities – then you can know [*noēsai*] God.[108]

Again and again we see the difficulty of translating the Greek word for "noeticizing." The passage makes clear that the activity of *nous* is perceptual and not just conceptual, imaginal rather than just intellectual in our narrow post-cartesian sense of that term.[109] In Aristotelean terms, God himself "never noeticizes without a phantasm"; but in Hermetic terms, he never does so without *all* phantasms! If indeed the human soul could participate in this universal consciousness, it would evidently be freed from its enslavement to the bodily senses, which limit and constrict our field of perception by forcing our consciousness to concentrate always on just one particular time and one particular place to the exclusion of all others.

---

[107] Since we cannot assume that the text means to say there is nothing beyond the cosmos, not even God or his *nous*, I interpret this as a question about the nature of "being" along the lines of what we find for instance in Iamblichus, *Response to Porphyry* I 8 (the realm of the gods cannot be enveloped by being; it must be the other way around).
[108] CH XI 18–20. Cf. HD V 1: "the *nous* sees everything" whereas the eyes see only corporeal things. It is not that the eyes allow the *nous* to see, but rather that the *nous* allows the eyes to see reality as it truly is; hence this is not about rejecting the senses but about using them noetically.
[109] The ability "to make far off things present" through the imagination was an important aspect of *nous* since as far back as Homer (see von Fritz, "Νοῦς and νοεῖν," 91; "Νοῦς and νοεῖν, and their Derivates, Pt. I," 224 with note 10, 225, 239).

Hence the significance of the final sentences: this is not about some kind of Superman ability to travel through the universe with the speed of light, but about the possibility of being consciously present at all times and in all places simultaneously (*homou*). This universal consciousness is described as God's "incorporeal imagination" and referred to as the *aiōn*.

It is therefore misleading to translate *aiōn* simply as "eternity," as in most modern translations.[110] From Homer through the Hellenistic period and into the Christian era, the word could be interpreted as long or even infinite duration or as timeless eternity, but could also mean the human life force or source of vitality. In the central tradition of Parmenides and Plato, *aiōn* was understood as a *monas* in which temporal distinctions were all present together, and Plato seems to have thought of it as a living being.[111] Keeping in mind that time was described as a *phantasma* by Democritus and probably Epicurus as well,[112] an interpretation of *aiōn* as God's incorporeal imagination (*phantasia*) makes perfect sense. Exactly like the *chōra* in Plato's *Timaeus*, in CH XI it functions as a "third kind" that cannot be reduced to either Being or Becoming but mediates between the divine noetic world and the material world of the senses. As such, it transcended the limits not just of time but those of space as well. In terms of modern philosophy it is remarkably similar to the crucial Kantian concept of the transcendental imagination (*transzendentale Einbildungskraft*) that allows *noumena* to be perceived as *phenomena* (appearances) in human consciousness.[113]

It is significant that on no fewer than three different occasions, the Hermetica explain human perception by the analogy of a painting,

---

[110] Scott I, 21 ("become eternal"); Cop, 41 ("become eternity"); WHCH, 57 (idem); HG, 146 ("word een eeuwig wezen": "become an eternal being"). Only HT I, 155 has "deviens Aiôn" (but see ibid., 164 note 58: "Ou: deviens éternité," followed by references to the PGM that I consider irrelevant to the meaning of *aiōn* in CH XI); and CHD, 134 has "werde zum Aion."

[111] Von Leyden, "Time, Number, and Eternity," 36–37 (with reference to Simplicius).

[112] Von Leyden, "Time, Number, and Eternity," 37–38.

[113] Castoriadis, "Discovery of the Imagination," 244. See also above, note 95, and consider the remarkable statement in HD VI 1: "humanity's creation is the world; if there were nobody to see [the world], neither would he truly exist, nor that which is seen" (cf. HD VIII 6 "Everything came into being for you"; IX 2 "external things would not exist if there were no internal ones"). Whereas Mahé and van den Broek here choose to translate the Armenian *stac 'uac* as "possession" [κτῆσις] instead of "creation" [κτίσις], I suggest that this latter option results in a much more logical statement (see HT V, 234 note 80; WHDH, 119 note 69; HG, 618 note 1010). From the same perspective it is tempting to speculate about the possible relevance of SH X, about the nature of time (see the very useful footnotes with source references in Litwa, *Hermetica II*, 67 note 2–3).

pointing out that although we actually look at a flat surface we see images that give the illusion of three-dimensionality. Thus the *nous* explains to Hermes in CH XI 17, again with that characteristic request for special attention ("*try to understand noetically [ennoēson] what I've been telling you...*"), that the notion of an incorporeal idea, a word that comes from *idein* ("seeing"), is not so astonishing as he might think: "on paintings you may see mountain ridges rise up in sharp relief although the painted surface is actually smooth and even."[114] Likewise, Hermes says in the *Asclepius* that we think the world is visible "because of the forms of species that seem to be imprinted on her as images .... similar to a painting."[115] But in fact, he insists, the world is not visible. Finally, the same point is made in one of the Stobaean fragments.[116] All these passages reach the same conclusion: what makes vision possible must itself be invisible, that which allows things to appear must forever dis-appear. Today the Hermetic authors might have said that our daily perception of phenomenal reality is similar to watching a movie: one needs a projection screen *and* one needs to be unaware of its presence.

In CH XI, the *Nous* tells Hermes explicitly that learning to participate in God's own imaginal consciousness is the indispensable key to *gnōsis*. Such knowledge is impossible in our normal state of restricted consciousness, because

[I]f you shut your soul up in your body and humiliate it, saying "I can know nothing [*ouden noō*], I can do nothing, I fear that celestial ocean,[117] I cannot rise to heaven, I do not know what I have been, I do not know what I will be,"[118] then what do you have to do with God? Then you are powerless to know [*noēsai*] anything beautiful or good, in love with the body and bad as you are. For

---

[114] CH XI 17.
[115] *Ascl.* 17.
[116] SH IIA 3-4.
[117] I see this as an obvious reference to the "open sea" of ultimate beauty in Plato, *Symp.* 210d. Reitzenstein saw it as referring to *der Himmelsozean* in Mandaean and "gnostic" texts (Review of Scott [1927], 282 note 3); Festugière qualified this as "décidément fausse" (RHT IV, 141 note 3) but provided no plausible alternative. To me it makes no sense to suggest that the author means just the normal sea (as in HT I, 156; Cop, 42; WHCH, 58; CHD, 135; HG, 147). Note that Mahé draws close connections between the *aiōn* and the Egyptian *Noun*, described as "the original ocean" of being ("La création," 23-24, cf. 29; referring to Morenz, *La religion égyptienne*, e.g. 222).
[118] Quispel imposes a reincarnational reading on the text (HG, 147); Holzhausen sees a parallel to the well-known "gnostic" passage from Clement, *Exc. ex. Theod.* 78 (CHD, 135 note 383). I see neither of those interpretation as obvious, since the statement refers to the soul's transcendence of temporality ("before you were born, in the womb, young, old, dead, in the hereafter").

The Path of Reverence

ignorance of the divine is the worst defect there is. But to be capable of knowing him [*gnōnai*], to wish it and hope for it, is the straight and easy path that leads directly to the good. On that road he will meet you everywhere, you will see him everywhere, at places and times where you least expect it, while waking or sleeping, on sea or on earth, at night or in daytime, while you speak or as you're silent – for there is nothing that he is not.

So will you say "God is invisible"? Don't speak like that. Who is more visible than he is? He has made everything so that you might see him through all that is. That is God's goodness, therein lies his excellence: to make himself apparent through all that is. For nothing is invisible, not even among the incorporeals. *Nous* shows itself in the act of *noēsis*, God in the act of creating.[119]

Again there is no conflict between the strongly world-affirming perspective of CH XI as a whole and the message that divine knowledge will escape those who are "in love with the body." As we have seen, the problem lies not in the body as such, but in a limited consciousness that "shuts the soul up in the body" and allows it to be dominated by the negative passions. The soul must be liberated from enslavement by opening its eyes to the beauty and goodness of divinity that literally surrounds it on all sides.

All this can only mean that to have seen the luminous "image of the Monas" (CH IV 11) in an out-of-body state of dazzling ecstasy may be perfectly wonderful and a life-changing experience, but is simply not enough. True salvational *gnōsis* must mean something more and different. Most of all, it must be more permanent. As the soul returns to the body, the luminous vision will fade, and its place will be taken by the usual play of mental imagery with all its seductive potential. Thus having returned from a state of "astonishment" to normal consciousness, practitioners would still be faced with the daily challenge of living a life of reverence, of "giving birth in beauty, both in body and soul" instead of getting sucked back into limited awareness and negative patterns all the time. Was it at all possible, they must have asked themselves and their teachers, to really and permanently change one's consciousness – to actually become the *aiōn*? To this question the answer was "yes, that is possible – but you need to be reborn."

---

[119] CH XI 21.

8

Becoming Alive

> But while all are deceived, yet usually those are less deceived who at some time, as happens occasionally during sleep, become suspicious and say to themselves: "Perhaps those things are not true which now appear to us; perhaps we are now dreaming."
>
> Marsilio Ficino[1]

We are born, we live, we die. Nothing seems more obvious. However, what can it possibly mean to "become alive" at birth if the soul is considered immortal to begin with? In an important text by Cicero, we read how the Roman general Scipio Aemilianus (185–129 BCE) has a dream vision of his famous grandfather by adoption, Scipio Africanus (236/5–183 BCE), who tells him that humans got it all backward. Speaking about the deceased, he observes that "those who have flown from the bonds of the body as from a prison are living, of course. That life of yours, as you call it, is actually death."[2] Cicero's account became the object of a lengthy commentary written after 430 CE by Macrobius Ambrosius Theodosius, a praetorian prefect of Italy and an enthusiastic neoplatonist (as reflected in the middle name he gave to his son, Macrobius Plotinus Eusthatius).[3] This *Commentary on the Dream of Scipio* would enjoy enormous popularity during the Middle Ages and contains some passages that deserve our

---

[1] Ficino, *Theologia Platonica* 14.7.7 (*Platonic Theology*, vol. 4, 276–279).
[2] Cicero, *De re publica* VI 18 (Powell ed., 138).
[3] For these identifications, see the impressive argument in Cameron, *Last Pagans of Rome*, 231–239. Macrobius describes himself as "born under another sky" (*Saturnalia*, Praef. 11: *nos sub alio ortos caelo*), which probably means he came from Northern Africa (Cameron, *Last Pagans of Rome*, 232, 237).

special attention. Macrobius describes what happens when souls travel downwards into the realm of matter. Originally each soul is shaped like a perfect sphere, "the only divine form"[4]; but as it descends from its home in the Milky Way that circles the zodiac and passes through the "portal of the sun" in the sign of Cancer, this spherical form is protracted into a cone. This must be understood in terms of basic Pythagorean arithmology. While the original monas is not itself a number, it is the beginning of numbers; hence the dimensionality that makes physical manifestation possible begins when the monas becomes a dyad, similar to how the nondimensional point can be protracted into a line. Now as soon as this happens to the soul, its dimensionality renders it vulnerable to material influences:

> [I]t begins to experience a tumultuous influx of *hulē* [matter] rushing upon it. This is what Plato alludes to when he speaks in the *Phaedo* of a soul suddenly staggering as if drunk as it is being drawn into the body; he wishes to imply the new draught of onrushing matter by which the soul, defiled and weighed down, is pressed down. Another clue to this secret is the location of the constellation of the Crater of Bacchus in the region between Cancer and Leo, indicating that there for the first time intoxication overtakes descending souls with the influx of matter; whence the companion of intoxication, oblivion, also begins quietly to steal upon souls at that point.[5]

Here the soul's descent that culminates in physical birth is described in terms of progressively more serious states of drunkenness or intoxication [*ebrietas*]. In other words, incarnation implies a profound alteration of consciousness that causes the soul to lose its original clarity of perception and forget where it even came from. It falls under the spell of delusionary images or hallucinations and comes to accept them as real. So how could that possibly be the true life? Macrobius points out that according to the followers of Pythagoras and Plato, we must distinguish between the death of the living organism [*animal*] and the death of the soul [*anima*]: "the organism dies when the soul leaves the body, but … the soul itself dies when it leaves the single and indivisible source of its true nature and is dispersed in a mortal frame."[6] Therefore being born is like dying, for

---

[4] Macrobius, *Commentarii in Somnium Scipionis* 1.11.5 (Willis ed., 48).
[5] Macrobius, *Commentarii* 1.12.7–8 (Willis ed., 49). Translation Stahl: Macrobius, *Commentary*, 135 (with minimal changes). The reference is to Plato, *Phaedo* 79c.
[6] Macrobius, *Commentarii* 1.11.1; cf. translation Stahl: Macrobius, *Commentary*, 130. I prefer to translate *animal* as "organism"; instead of "individual" I write "indivisible," because it is closer to the actual meaning and modern notions of individualism are not at issue here; Stahl translates *fonte naturae* as "the source of its origin," but I prefer to keep the term "nature" while specifying that it clearly means the soul's true nature; and for the final words I prefer the literal translation according to Stahl's footnote 1.

it means that the soul is "thrust from the radiance of its immortal state into the shades of death, as it were."[7] In order for an organism to exist at all, the body must "bind" the soul, so that it loses the freedom of its true spiritual life and gets confined by materiality as in a tomb.[8]

All of this happens as souls come under the influence of the astral machinery of fate, referred to as *heimarmenē*.[9] As they are born in a three-dimensional body at a specific spot on earth, humans become subject to the conditions of space; and as they are born at a specific moment as well, they simultaneously fall under the dominion of time. As Macrobius puts it, not only do souls assume dimensionality as their spherical shape becomes conical, but they also become "subject to the numbering of days and to time."[10] Reminiscent almost of modern satellite surveillance technology, what happens is that at the exact moment we are born, we appear on the radar of space-time reality: our presence is captured in a kind of universal cosmic grid or coordinate system over which we have no control and from which there is no escape. This was the foundation of the classical birth horoscope. By calculating the exact constellation of stars and planets at the moment of birth, astrologers sought to determine the unique spatiotemporal *quality* of an individual's "nativity" and what it could mean for his or her individual possibilities and potentials.[11]

Thus "being born" in late antiquity meant much more than just "becoming alive" – if indeed it meant that at all. Macrobius at least suggests that it was rather like *losing* one's true life, losing one's clarity of consciousness, losing one's spiritual freedom, losing oneself in a maze of illusions. Such drastic formulations may not have been to everyone's taste; but it was broadly understood that being born on earth came at a heavy price, as it meant being forced to accept the limitations of time and space while

---

[7] Macrobius, *Commentarii* 1.11.2.
[8] Macrobius, *Commentarii* 1.11.3: "hence the Greek words for body are δέμας, that is a 'bond,' and σῶμα, a σῆμα, as it were, being a 'tomb' of the soul." For the backgrounds of this famous *sōma-sēma* equation, see de Vogel, "*Sōma-Sēma* Formula."
[9] For the history of the concept, see Lewis, *Cosmology and Fate*, 86–92; summary focused on the Hermetic context in Mahé, "Le rôle de l'élément astrologique," 164. Discussions specifically of *heimarmenē*, often in relation to providence and necessity, in SH VIII, XII–XIV, XXIX.
[10] Macrobius, *Commentarii*, 1.11.6.
[11] While determining the place of birth was unproblematic, determining the exact time of birth was by no means easy in antiquity, especially during daytime: see e.g. Jones, "Precision of Time Observation." On this qualitative dimension of astrology, see the discussion of *Zeitqualität* in von Stuckrad, *Das Ringen um die Astrologie*, 76, 86–87.

coming under the influence of powerful cosmic forces.[12] We can never be present in more places than one at a time, or live at any other moment than the present. A person's movements through life – traveling from one place to another and from one moment to the next – were seen as heavily conditioned, if not fully determined, by continuously changing patterns or constellations of invisible astral influences beyond one's personal control.

Moreover, as we have already seen, embodiment as such made it difficult for the soul to stay focused on true reality, as it got exposed to powerful harmful passions that seduced it into running after meaningless and spiritually destructive objects of desire. In the Middle Platonic type of speculation from which the Hermetica took many of their ideas, the cosmic *heimarmenē* was described often as not just an impersonal system operating by natural law, but as actively administered by intermediary spiritual entities, *daimones*.[13] We already encountered this concept in the discussion of Zosimos, with reference to an important passage in CH XVI. When we are born, "the daimons arrayed under each of the stars who are on duty at that exact moment"[14] take possession of us, entering through our body into the two parts of our soul (the higher one focused on *nous* and the lower one focused on matter). Henceforth and until the very end of our lives, they are always "lying in ambush in our muscle and marrow, in our veins and arteries, in the brain itself, reaching to our very guts," always trying to shape our souls in accordance with their own peculiar astral energies – "for the essence of a daimon is its energy."[15]

Now taking all this into consideration, the conclusion might seem natural that embodiment must be simply a curse and therefore death means

---

[12] Cf. HD VII 4: the soul has no quality or quantity, but as it is born it acquires them by necessity as accidents of matter.
[13] Dillon, *Middle Platonists*, 46–47; Smith, "Toward Interpreting Demonic Power"; Lewis, *Cosmology and Fate*, 87 with note 5, 112–113 (with reference to Plutarch, "On Tranquillity of Mind" 575B; *Moralia*, vol. VI, 220–221: μοῖραι καὶ δαίμονες).
[14] CH XVI 15. See Chapter 4, pp. 90–91.
[15] CH XVI 13–14, and same point in SH VI 10. SH III 7, IV 8 and VII 3 all confirm the same point that we carry such harmful energies (referred to as θυμος and ἐπιθυμία) with us from the moment of birth. SH IV 6–16 provides a long discussion of energies that "dwell in bodies and work through them" as "all things are full of energies" (cf. the famous statement "all things are full of gods" attributed to Thales fr. 32; see Litwa, *Hermetica II*, 46 note 13 with reference to SH IV 16). On daimons as astral energies, see the useful short discussions in Fowden, *Egyptian Hermes*, 78; Mahé, "Le rôle de l'élément astrologique," 164. See also the long discussion of energies in SH IV; specifically for the daimonic energies of the thirty-six decans, see SH VI 7–11. The word "energies" occurs more frequently than one might conclude from modern translations, see for instance SH V, "the magnificent energy of sleep" (usually translated as "effect," "activity" etc.).

liberation. After having been told that birth is a kind of death and the dead are truly alive, Scipio Aemilianus asked his father (who had joined them in his dream) why then he should linger on earth at all. Shouldn't one seek death as quickly as possible? No, he was told, that would be a serious mistake.

> Until the God who rules the whole of this temple that you currently see has liberated you from the custodians of your body, you cannot gain admission here. Humans were generated with the understanding that they were to take care of that sphere called earth which you see in the middle of the temple. … Like all dutiful humans, you too must keep your soul in the custody of your body, and must not leave this human life without the command of him who gave it to you, that you may not appear to have deserted the human task that God assigned to you. Like your grandfather here and like me, who generated you, devote yourself to justice and pious duty. … This kind of life is your path towards heaven and to being united with those who have finished their lives on earth, and who after having released their bodies inhabit the place at which you are now looking.[16]

Note how strongly this message resonates with the famous passage in *Asclepius* 24 where Egypt is described as "the temple of the whole world," and its almost priestly ethics of service grounded in deep reverence for the divinity of creation. According to both texts, human beings are supposed to take care of the world. In terms of Plato's *Symposium* as well as Iamblichean theurgy, difficult as it may be for the soul to do its work under conditions of embodiment, that is what we are asked to do: our task is "to give birth in beauty" by channeling divine truth and goodness into the world. For politicians or military men like Scipio this meant promoting justice while diligently working to serve the commonwealth (the "beauty of institutions" in terms of Plato's *Symposium*). People with different occupations or social positions could of course find their own ways of serving humanity and be a force for goodness in the world.

The essential point is to resist a dualistic hermeneutics. When we read that birth really means death for the soul, we assume automatically that therefore it should not happen, that being born means a tragical fall or degradation that should be prevented. Life is good while death is bad, so if embodiment means death then we should try to avoid it. But the Hermetica are explicit in rejecting that logic.[17] They never stop

---

[16] Cicero, *De re publica* VI 19–20 (Powell ed., 138–139). See the strong condemnation of suicide in Macrobius, *Commentarii* 1.13.

[17] For polemics against stereotypical types of "gnostic" anti-cosmism, see notably CH IX 4, 9 (corruption does exist on earth, but it is blasphemy to think that the cosmos is bad or that God lacks sense perception), CH XIV 8 (against those who think it is reverential to *not* credit God with creating all things, i.e. by assuming a lower demiurge).

praising God as the *generative* source of all that is, the infinite fountain of fertility from which everything is born into existence. Out of pure goodness and generosity, God unceasingly brings forth the world in all its splendid diversity, as a bodily temple that should be filled with his own Life and Light. As human souls participate in the power of divinity, they are uniquely qualified to help channeling or infusing that Life and Light into matter and the body. Being born is certainly difficult, and our bodies resist the influx of divinity; matter is heavy while divinity strives upwards; bodies exist in space and time while the spiritual influx is infinite and eternal; and so it is hard to keep the balance and maintain harmony between those polarities. Still, that is the task of the soul: to enter the darkness of matter so as to bring it to life and fill it with Light. Giving birth is what Life is all about.

THE PATH OF HERMES

From this perspective, the fact that so many human souls fall short of fulfilling their task, or never even get close to fulfilling it, can be explained by what happens to them at incarnation. We have seen that the body overwhelms the soul with its passions; the newborn gets invaded by powerful daimonic energies; and as its consciousness gets clouded and intoxicated, the imagination starts running like crazy after *phantasmata*, hallucinatory images. For most souls this is simply too much to handle. Therefore the central goal of Hermetic spirituality was to clear up human consciousness and get the soul back on track.

How did they go about it? After Garth Fowden introduced the concept of a "Way of Hermes" in 1986,[18] many scholars have tried to distill from the Hermetica something resembling a "coherent course"[19] or systematic training program. Fowden spoke of "different levels of enlightenment" and different "steps" (*bathmoi*) along the Hermetic *paideia*, suggesting that "Hermetic initiates were expected to proceed

---

[18] Fowden, *Egyptian Hermes*, 95–115. Fowden noted quite correctly that while "such insensitive theories as that of the so-called *Lesemysterien* have proved depressingly popular ... this sort of desk-bound religion has little connection with the way of Hermes" (ibid., 149).

[19] HHE I, 132; Van den Kerchove, *La voie*, 71. Both refer to Reitzenstein, *Hellenistischen Mysterienreligionen*, 47; but an earlier and even clearer example is already found in Reitzenstein, "Zum *Asclepius* des Pseudo-Apuleius," 404, where the Mysteries of Isis, the "prophetic initiation" of CH XIII and the *Asclepius* are seen as "three stages of a uniform developmental process."

systematically from elementary to more sophisticated texts."[20] A few years later, Jean-Pierre Mahé provided a synthesis outlining "the different stages of the Hermetic 'way of immortality'," described as "a method of spiritual guidance" including "meditational exercises and mystery initiations."[21] In her more recent analysis, Anna Van den Kerchove states that "the existence of a course appears certain," although it may be hard for us to reconstruct; and she proceeds to describe "a progression with several stages" involving didactic instructions from masters to pupils combined with "a sequence of concrete ritual practices."[22] While Christian Bull dismisses Quispel's fantasy of a quasi-masonic Hermetic "lodge" in Alexandria,[23] still he writes that "there seems to have been outer and inner grades of initiation, corresponding to the level of insight gained"; and so his reconstruction of the Way of Hermes involves a "first stage: Knowing Oneself," a "second stage: Becoming a Stranger to the World," followed by "The Ritual of Rebirth" (CH XIII) and finally "The Heavenly Ascent" (NHC VI[6])."[24]

But how much evidence do we have for a systematic training method, or a formal sequence of ritual initiations through which candidates had to progress in correct and orderly fashion from one stage to the next? It is certainly true that some Hermetic practitioners were seen as farther advanced along the path than others and were endowed with spiritual charisma that gave them authority to act as guides and teachers. Presumably they knew the teachings better, understood them more deeply, and left their pupils convinced that they themselves spoke from personal experience – that they *knew*. They must have been able to lead by example because they embodied or at least projected an ideal image of what an enlightened teacher should be like. We are told that a person with *gnōsis* is supposed to be "good and reverent and already godlike." Rather than wasting his time "fighting shadows," getting lost in "empty discussions and the latest opinions," he speaks only if he has something meaningful to say;[25] and because "his noetic world is divine" and "all things are good for such a person," he stays serene in the face of adversity or even persecution.[26]

---

[20] Fowden, *Egyptian Hermes*, 97, 99.
[21] Mahé, "Voie d'immortalité," 348–349.
[22] Van den Kerchove, *La voie*, 71, 374.
[23] Bull, "Ancient Hermetism," 116–117; Bull, *Tradition*, 454.
[24] Bull, *Tradition*, 372 and chapter headings 4.5, 4.6, 5 and 6.
[25] CH X 9.
[26] CH IX 4. Cf. HD IX 3: the person who has true knowledge loses all fear.

Becoming Alive 227

Such passages seem suggestive less of a formal initiatory system or method than of a community that valued the cultivation of wisdom and was convinced it could come only from an interior process of spiritual awakening. There is a tendency in scholarship to conflate the "spiritual exercises" highlighted by Pierre Hadot with concepts of "ritual" or ritual performance, so that the Way of Hermes comes to be imagined as a sequence of formal ceremonial acts.[27] However, we should be sensitive to the differences. As formulated by the authoritative voice of Catherine Bell, ritual performance consists of "ceremonial actions characterized by a self-conscious formality and traditionalism,"[28] but my point is that spiritual exercises do not need to be formalized as performative ceremonies enacted in a social setting and authorized by a fixed tradition. An important aspect of ritual performance is its *symbolic* character: hence, having successfully gone through a process of "ritual death and rebirth," the candidate is considered to be reborn, regardless of whether anything happened to his interior constitution. He is now considered "a new person" by default, and so it does not matter if in fact he feels or behaves exactly as he did before. By sharp contrast, the notion of spiritual exercises reflects the idea of interior *training* that is supposed to result in demonstrable and lasting personal transformation. Just as a physical athlete will be rewarded for his daily regime of exercise by developing powerful muscles and an excellent physical condition, a spiritual athlete should begin to notice interior changes in his or her consciousness, and these should be reflected in this person's external patterns of behavior observable for others. In short, he or she must *really* become a different person. As formulated in one of the Stobaean fragments, already here on earth one must exercise (*progumnazein*) one's soul, so that it will not "slip from the path" by the time it has arrived at the superior level where immediate vision becomes possible.[29]

---

[27] For instance, Van den Kerchove's monograph has "ritual practices" in the subtitle but contains no discussion of ritual theory; CH I is interpreted as a "ritual of investiture that turns the disciple into a master" and Hermes as "the equivalent of a ritual leader" (*La voie*, 79, 165). While Bull's chapter about CH XIII is titled "The Ritual of Rebirth," he admits that it should rather be seen as "an idealized representation of a ritual" that contains "a marked lack of ritual action" (*Tradition*, 244) but can nevertheless be analyzed in terms of van Gennep's and Turner's classic tripartite "separation-liminality-incorporation" structure (ibid., 244-315).
[28] Bell, "Performance," 205. For useful discussions of ritual as a field of research, with attention to the history of the term and its different conceptualizations, see e.g. Boudewijnse, "Conceptualization of Ritual"; Asad, "Toward a Genealogy"; Bogdan, *Western Esotericism and Rituals of Initiation*, 27-30.
[29] SH VI 18.

We will see that the information we have about Hermetic practice, scanty as it may be, contains elements of formal ritual or ceremonial acts in the precise sense of the word. They had an important and perhaps even crucial role to play in the candidate's progress from ignorance to spiritual rebirth and deification. Nevertheless, I will argue that the Way of Hermes *as a whole* is more easily understood in terms of spiritual training than in those of a formal ritual system or method. In other words, while the dimension of spiritual praxis and transformation was absolutely central to the Way of Hermes, we need not assume that it took the shape of a prescribed "coherent course" in which the candidate was expected to go through an orderly series of initiatory steps. Rather, it was understood that if a candidate was *ready*, he or she might be granted an intense transformative experience resulting in the opening up of a new, previously inaccessible level of consciousness.

One such experience we have already encountered in the visionary episode of CH I; in this chapter and Chapter 9 we will discuss the two other chief cases, described in CH XIII and NH VI[6]. I find it important to emphasize that with the possible exception of the final case, most of these experiential events are described as beginning unexpectedly and as though spontaneously. They are not deliberately induced by a ritual technique but are described as occurring because the candidate has reached a point in his or her training and internal development where such an experience becomes possible. Then once the process has started, the spiritual master knows what to do and may fall back on formulas and ritual acts that are prescribed for such cases. Yet when the procedure is crowned with success, this is understood to be a divine *gift* to which pupil and master respond with profuse expressions of gratitude and joy. Hence we should be very precise in our formulations: the candidate neither receives this spiritual blessing by a pure sovereign act of divine grace, nor does he obtain it as a result of his actions.[30] Rather, we are told about practitioners who have been doing all that was necessary to make it possible for them to receive such a gift at all; but then when they *do* receive it, this is because God in his boundless generosity responds by indeed giving it to them. The nuance of gratitude is

---

[30] I am referring to the distortive effect of stereotypical "magic versus religion" distinctions and their connotation of "either manipulative *or* purely receptive" (Hanegraaff, "Entheogenic Esotericism," 393-394).

important. Think of the difference between ordering a beautiful book and paying for it, as opposed to hoping you might receive it as a birthday present – and then receiving it.[31]

The chief elements of communal practice suggested by the sources are prayers or hymns, and it seems that meetings were followed by a vegetarian meal. As practitioners got together, they probably opened their sessions with a prayer for divine inspiration or a moment of meditative silence. Hence at the beginning of the *Asclepius*, we are told that the room falls silent while the four men feel the divine presence taking possession of the space,[32] and the experiential part of NH VI⁶ begins with a prayer.[33] What happened next? I assume that a large part of the actual practice would be done at home, in the form of meditative exercises focused on calming the bodily passions, achieving a state of equanimity and learning to concentrate on true reality. Hence it would make sense that during communal meetings, practitioners would seek advice from the elders about how to deal with problems or obstacles they were encountering in their daily practice, how to meditate more effectively, or how to respond to changes in consciousness or unexpected phenomena that might occur. It seems likely that part of the meetings would be devoted to some form of group meditation under guidance of the leader.

Then, of course, teachers would be giving lectures and engage in discussions of the kind that we find in the Hermetic treatises. Here we encounter the notorious question of the "general discourses" (*genikoi logoi*) that are mentioned somewhat regularly in the Hermetic treatises.[34] I am convinced by Christian Wildberg's argument that this expression was never meant to refer to "some sort of mysteriously lost

---

[31] Van den Kerchove points out correctly that Hermetic practitioners do not try to influence the deity or petition him for material gifts, but do express hopes for salvation and knowledge (*La voie*, 238–239).

[32] *Ascl.* 1.

[33] NH VI⁶ 55, 23–57, 25.

[34] CH X 1; X 7; XIII 1; SH III 1; NH VI⁶ 63, 1–4, plus three indirect references in Manetho fr. 5c (Wildberg, "*General Discourses*," 141–142 with note 21). Wildberg helpfully points out that next to these γενικοί λόγοι and διεξοδικοί λόγοι (the correct interpretation of the Coptic ⲉϫⲱⲇⲓⲁⲕⲟⲥ mentioned in NH VI⁶ 63,3: see HT V, cxv), we also hear of ἐξωτικοί λόγοι, and ζῳδιακοί λόγοι (another interpretation of ⲉϫⲱⲇⲓⲁⲕⲟⲥ) next to the Λόγος τέλειος ("perfect discourse," *Asclepius*), a Λόγος ἀπόκρυφος ("secret discourse," CH XIII), and a ἱερός λόγος ("holy discourse," CH III) (Wildberg, "*General Discourses*," 138–139).

collection of introductory Hermetic *treatises*," as most scholars have assumed, but simply to oral instructions and conversations.[35] Intimate encounters between teachers and pupils must have been at the heart of Hermetic practice, and I would like to remind the reader of my discussion of oral instruction and immediacy.[36] As already suggested, in a society without quick and efficient public transport, it is unlikely that the members of very small spiritual communities would be able to meet on a very regular basis. Whenever they could make it happen, this would be an important event for them, a precious occasion for pupils to meet their teachers face to face; and so we may well assume that pupils would be making notes so as not to forget the key elements of these precious exchanges. However, unless they mastered shorthand, it would be impossible for them to produce complete and accurate transcripts in real time; and even if they could, this would cause them to be occupied with note-taking at the expense of paying attention to the content and interacting with their teachers.

So that is not how it could have worked. To stay in contact between meetings and ensure some degree of unity in teaching, it would make perfect sense for session leaders to circulate edited treatises with idealized descriptions of what devotees were supposed to learn and what could happen to them if they stayed on the path. Hence we arrive at a combination of oral instruction (the "general discourses") and written materials (the Hermetic treatises). It goes without saying that given the paucity of hard data, this reconstruction must necessarily be speculative to some extent; but unless better scenarios are forthcoming, it seems the most economical way of explaining why our Hermetic literature was produced and how it may have functioned in these communities and networks. My further suggestion is that the size of these communities may have stood in reverse proportion to the abundance of written treatises that seem to have circulated. The need for written circulars would be somewhat less urgent for communities that were large enough to have frequent local meetings, such as the Christians. Precisely if Hermetic communities were

---

[35] Wildberg, "*General Discourses*," 144 (emphasis in original). Contrary to Wildberg, I believe the references must not be seen as a literary device "in the fictional world of extant *Hermetica*" but as referring to actual oral instructions. For earlier discussions of γενικοὶ λόγοι and διεξοδικοὶ λόγοι, see notably Fowden, *Egyptian Hermes*, 97–100; van den Broek, "Hermetic Literature I," 496–497; Van den Kerchove, "Redécouverte," 172–173; Van den Kerchove, *La voie*, 71–72, 144–145. Mahé in HT V, cxiii–cxviii, cxlviii seems to have overlooked Wildberg's article.

[36] See above, Chapter 4, p. 115; and below, pp. 251, 336 with note 125, 342.

Becoming Alive 231

tiny, with participants scattered over large areas, they would need written treatises to stay in contact at all.

In all likelihood, meetings would be concluded by a prayer of thanksgiving or praise, possibly in the form of a hymn.[37] Of this we have two examples: the *Logos Teleios* and CH V.[38] The latter prayer comes at the end of a lecture about seeing the omnipresent but invisible God of CH XI, who himself has no image but contains all things in his incorporeal imagination, the *aiōn* or "third kind":

> He makes all things appear but does not appear himself. He generates but himself is not generated. He is not in the imagination but imagines all things (*en phantasiāi de <ouk esti> panta phantasiōn*). For there is imagination only of generated things. To be generated means to appear in the imagination.[39]

Note how radical this is: literally everything that gets born is in fact imagined by God. Again, to understand such statements we need to unlearn our habitual assumption that something imagined is not real: on the contrary, here we read that God makes reality appear precisely by imagining it. Therefore when God "imagines all things," this has nothing to do with our idea of "fantasizing" or daydreaming but means his active generation (production, creation, engendering, bringing-forth) of images.

The hymn[40] itself is concerned with what is involved in praising such a deity. *How* is he to be praised, since it seems doubtful (to say the

---

[37] Generally on prayers/hymns in the Hermetica, see Zuntz, "On the Hymns"; Van den Kerchove, *La voie*, 235–272; Chlup, "Ritualization of Language," 135–137. Van den Kerchove notes that the closing prayers are more developed than the introductory prayers (*La voie*, 236) and draws attention to subtle gradations between "gratitude" and "praise" (ibid., 251–259, esp. 255). I will return to the musical aspect in discussing NH VI[6].

[38] At the end of CH I, Hermes thanks God for the illumination he has just received; at the end of CH XIII we find a prayer of gratitude for the experience of rebirth (see discussion later on in this chapter). Hence these two instances do not come after regular sessions but after sudden and unique transformative experiences that could occur "spontaneously" outside a community setting. The special case of NH VI[6] will be discussed in the next chapter.

[39] CH V 1 (and see the close parallel in CH XI 18 and 20, discussed above, Chapter 7, pp. 214–215). The three key words here are φανερόω (revealing or "causing to appear," as in *phenomena* as opposed to *noumena*), γεννάω (generating, bringing forth), and φαντασία (imagination, mentioned here three times in immediate succession). Furthermore the verb φαντάζω is used in an *active* sense, i.e. not as "appearing" or "becoming visible" but as "imagining" in the literal sense of *forming* an image.

[40] CH V 10–11 is presented as prose in Scott I, 164–165; HT I, 64; Cop, 20; WHCH, 36–37. I agree with Holzhausen and van den Broek (CHD, 62–63 and HG, 120, supported by Zuntz, "On the Hymns," 68), who bring out the hymnic structure by printing it as such.

least) whether one can even speak about him at all, or address him adequately?[41] *Where* should one's gaze be directed while praising a divinity who is not in space – upward, downward, outward, inward? *When* should it be done, since he is not in time either? For *what* should he be praised – for that which he has made or that which he hasn't made, for what is manifested or what is concealed? And finally *why* should one do it? The divine source "gives everything and receives nothing,"[42] because it is exclusively *from* him that everything flows forth and is brought to manifestation. This can only mean that he is not in need even of receiving praise. In fact, since God alone really *is*, does that not mean that the person praising him is ultimately praising himself? "For you are everything I am, everything I do, everything I say."[43] Paradoxically, then, the divine source is being praised here for the fact that it neither can nor needs to be praised! We see here how the radical nonduality of Hermetic spirituality could be seen as undermining the very possibility for humans to actually "interact" with God, whether ceremonially or otherwise. The dualistic illusion of alterity required for such interaction is precisely what needs to be overcome. Reminiscent again of Iamblichus, the suggestion is rather that absolutely no one except God himself is *ever* truly active at all.

The other example of a communal closing prayer comes at the end of the *Asclepius*, preceded by some rare and therefore precious details referring to actual ritual practice. As Hermes, Asclepius, Tat and Ammon leave the sanctuary, they start praying with their faces turned south. This seems puzzling because the text explains "if somebody wants to address God at sunset, he should turn his gaze in that direction, and likewise at sunrise in the direction of the east."[44] Therefore should they not be facing West? The confusion seems to come from a background in traditional Egyptian culture: the earth was imagined in the shape of a man lying on his back, with his head in the south looking up at the heavens, and we

---

[41] Like Holzhausen and Salaman c.s. (CHD, 62 with note 156; WHCH, 36) I follow the manuscript version τί (instead of Scott's emendation τίς: Scott I, 164; HT I, 64; Cop, 20; HG, 120). Rather than asking *who* can praise God, the following questions *where* and *when* are intended to specify the initial *how* question.

[42] CH V 10; cf. II 16.

[43] CH V 11. This is of course the same point made in CH I 7 (see above, pp. 164–167); see also HD III 1.

[44] *Ascl.* 41; similar direction in CH XIII 16 (discussed below, p. 259). The discrepancy leads Holzhausen to translate the Latin *austrum* as "West" (CHD, 313), without further discussion.

have seen that Egypt itself was seen as the "heartland" situated at the world's center.[45] Therefore it would make sense for Egyptians to direct their gaze south, toward Upper Egypt, as the Nile came flowing from that direction as well.[46] Still, as the sun was the most obvious visible reflection of the divine source of Life and Light, for devotees of Hermes it would also make sense to face east during morning prayers and west while praying at sunset. How exactly they resolved this dilemma is not entirely clear.[47]

And then there is another detail with ceremonial implications. We saw that Asclepius already clashed with Hermes over the question of statues, and right before the finish he makes another embarrassing slip. While Hermes and Ammon are already praying, he starts whispering to Tat: "shouldn't we suggest to your father to add some frankincense and perfumes to our prayers?"[48] Hermes overhears him, interrupts the prayer, and reprimands him severely. Burned offerings may be fine for the gods who are confined in their temples, but it is a sacrilege to use them while praying to the divine Source itself, which lacks nothing because it already *is* everything and contains all that is. So again we encounter the same motif as in the prayer of CH V 10–11. By wanting to offer something material to the Source, Asclepius is missing the point entirely: he considers addressing it as though it were just another local deity craving for sacrifices in his temple. The best "incense" human beings can offer the Source is simple gratitude of the heart for the universal presence of Life and Light. Coming from Hermes, who has just been defending the practice of statue animation (which always involved *kuphi* incense and other kinds of ritual offerings), this correction suggests that Hermetic practitioners may not have been wholly averse to standard sacrificial practices as long as it was well understood that only words of sincere reverence should be

---

[45] See above, pp. 53–54; and SH XXIV 11–15.
[46] Derchain, "L'authenticité," 182; Bull, *Tradition*, 175–177.
[47] But see Bull's reconstruction of a ritual prayer in PGM XIII 824–841, with a diagram suggesting a counter-clockwise movement from east to south (*Tradition*, 344–345; cf. Cox Miller, "In Praise of Nonsense," 498–499). See the intriguing parallel in al-Masʿūdī, *Kitāb at-Tanbīh wa-l-išrāf*, about the Ḥarrānian pagans: the common non-philosophical Hellenes supposedly pray towards the east, while "the Egyptian Ṣābians whose remainder is at this time the Ṣābians of the Ḥarrānians, their orientation in their prayer toward the south, which is [their] *qibla* [prayer direction], with their backs turning toward the north, and their abstention from many of the foods that the Greek Ṣābians would eat such as pork, chicken, garlic, fava beans, and other foods" (transl. van Bladel, *Arabic Hermes*, 96 note 144).
[48] Ascl. 41.

offered to the Source itself. It seems that the Hermetists referred to such prayers offered to God as *logikē thusia*, "verbal offerings."⁴⁹

The prayer itself has attracted scholarly attention mostly because parallel versions have been preserved in the Greek "magical" papyri and the Nag Hammadi collection.⁵⁰ The radical nonduality of CH V 10–11 is not in evidence here, and it begins with some fairly conventional expressions of gratitude. Then the divinity is thanked more in particular for the three gifts of *nous*, *logos*, and *gnōsis*: "*nous* that we may understand you (or "noeticize": *noēsōmen*, ⲉⲛⲁⲣⲛⲟⲉⲓ), *logos* that we may make ourselves your interpreters, and finally *gnōsis* that we may get to know you."⁵¹ All this makes perfect sense: the attainment of *gnōsis* is what the path is all about, we can receive it only thanks to our noetic capacity, and thanks to *logos* we can communicate with others to speak on divinity's behalf.⁵² The prayer continues by thanking God for actually deifying the practitioners, not after death but already during their present state of embodiment,⁵³ so that they were able to receive *gnōsis*:

---

⁴⁹ The more literal translation "logical offering" would obviously not do for us moderns, and again confirms the problem of translation discussed above with reference to Heidegger (p. 202). On sacrifice and prayer (or rather, prayer as sacrifice) in the Hermetica, see the exhaustive discussions by Van den Kerchove, "La voie"; and Van den Kerchove, *La voie*, 223–274. Wherever convenient, I prefer "offering" over "sacrifice" because Hermetic practitioners are typically just offering something to God (mostly a prayer or hymn) as a token of gratitude, without the connotations of "sacrificing" something that will be missed: an attitude of *do ut des* seems alien to their mindset.

⁵⁰ Reitzenstein, "Zum *Asclepius* des Pseudo-Apuleius" (the first comparison between *Ascl.* 41 and PGM III 591–610, as well as with the closing prayers of CH XIII); Mahé, "La prière"; HHE I, 137–167 (with the Coptic, Greek, and Latin in parallel with French translation on pp. 160–167); Fowden, *Egyptian Hermes*, 84–87; Philonenko, "O vitae vera vita"; Mahé, "Voie d'immortalité," esp. 350–351; Mahé, "Théorie et pratique," 9–11; Zago, "Pneuma éloquent"; HT V, 113–131 (with Coptic, Greek, and new French translation in parallel on pp. 122–131).

⁵¹ NH VI⁷ 64, 9–14; PGM III 596–598 (HHE I, 162–163; HT V, 124–135). The parallel in *Ascl.* 41 loses most of the nuances: "sensu, ratione, intellegentia: sensu, ut te cognoverimus; ratione, ut te suspicionibus indagemus; cognitione, ut te cognoscentes."

⁵² Mahé invests much energy in arguing that the three terms refer to successive stages, while insisting that the order must be reversed (HT V, lxxxv–xcviii; polemicizing in note 103 against Van den Kerchove). His chief argument is that in CH IX 10, we find *nous* placed after *logos* (see above, Chapter 7, p. 204), so that *gnōsis* must necessarily move to the beginning ("Voie d'immortalité," 351; "Mental Faculties," 77–78). However, this argument is based on the preconceived notion of a "coherent course" consisting of a prescribed series of steps or stages; in fact, nothing in the prayer indicates that the three terms were meant to be placed in a definite order of succession at all (cf. Bull, *Tradition*, 243).

⁵³ NH VI⁷ 64, 18–19; PGM III 599–600 (HHE I, 162–163; HT V, 124–125). The Greek πλάσμα comes from the editor of PGM III (Papyrus Mimaut) and should undoubtedly be replaced by σῶμα (HT V, 124; Reitzenstein, *Hellenistischen Mysterienreligionen*, 286 note 9).

We have known you, o noetic Light! O Life of life, we have known you! O Womb of all generation, we have known you! O Womb inseminated by the Father's nature, we have known you! O eternal nature of the generating Father, see how we venerate your goodness! This alone do we ask you: we do not want to lose your *gnōsis*. We wish for just this one assurance: that we will not fail in this way of life.[54]

Therefore the practitioners just had an experience of direct *gnōsis* of the eternally fertile source of Life and Light that sustains their very existence.[55] But while still feeling full of its power, they already seem a bit afraid they might lose the intensity of the experience once they return to their normal lives and get exposed again to the everyday spell of the senses. How do you ensure that your *gnōsis* will not be transitory but lasting and permanent? We may assume that this was an important topic of discussion for practitioners after they had finishing their prayer, embraced one another, and sat down together for a pure vegetarian meal.[56] They seem to have reached agreement about the solution: to enjoy *gnōsis* on a permanent basis, one would have to be reborn.

SPIRITUAL MADNESS

The initial revelation (*apokalupsis*) as described in CH I happened to a practitioner who had been preparing himself for the eventuality of such an event by training his mind to focus on *ta onta*, the things that truly are. In another unique treatise, known as CH XIII, again we meet a pupil who has been practicing diligently to liberate his mind from deceptive

---

[54] NH VI⁷ 64, 22–27; PGM III 601–605 (HHE I, 164–165; HT V, 126–127; "we do not want to lose...": more literally "we want to be maintained..."). "Nature" seems an obvious phallic euphemism here (cf. van den Broek in HG, 635 note 1107).

[55] The past tense indicates that this is not knowledge in the sense of information that is absorbed and then stays in the mind (*wissen*, *savoir* etc.), but an immediate experience of gaining knowledge in the sense of getting acquainted with that which is known (*kennen*, *connaître* etc.): see above, Prologue, p. 1 note 2, and Chapter 4, p. 113 note 147.

[56] *Ascl.* 41/NH VI⁷ 65, 3–7 (the embrace is mentioned only in the Coptic version). There has been some speculation about this communal vegetarian meal as part of Hermetic ritual practice (van den Broek, "Religious Practices," 87–88; Van den Kerchove, *La voie*, 268–269); but since a single reference is all we have, the suggestion relies on parallels such as meals after Christian baptism, mystery initiations, and indirect reports about the Therapeutae or Essenians (see references in van den Broek and Van den Kerchove). These parallels lose some of their substance in the absence of proof for a formal system of Hermetic initiation. I assume that a communal meal was probably customary, and the vegetarianism is suggestive of Pythagorean backgrounds, but I doubt whether much more can be said about it (see, however, the intriguing food restrictions mentioned for the Harrānian pagans: above, note 47).

imaginations and is rewarded by an impressive experience described as rebirth (*palingenesia*). All specialists agree about the special importance of this treatise, which has even been the focus of several book-length analyses.[57] I will be arguing that the Hermetic rebirth as described here was not a formal ceremony or ritual performance but a dramatic alteration of consciousness that could happen to practitioners as a desirable outcome of their spiritual training regime, a reward for their efforts at opening their internal senses to perceive reality as it really is.

CH XIII describes an encounter between Hermes Trismegistus and his pupil Tat. In the title (which may have been a later addition) their conversation is described as *apokruphos*, secret or hidden: clearly what happens is private, just between the two of them, although evidently shared now with readers of the treatise.[58] Where does the encounter take place? Not in a sanctuary but out of doors in the Egyptian desert.[59] As Tat refers to a previous conversation when the two of them were on their way back from the desert, the suggestion is that such retreats from urban civilization into the solitude of nature may not have been uncommon among Hermetic practitioners. It appears that Hermes had been speaking about

---

[57] Discussions focused on CH XIII (in chronological order): Reitzenstein, *Poimandres*, 214–250 (1904); Denier van der Gon, "Driewerf-grootste Hermes" (1918); Jonas, *Gnosis und spätantiker Geist*, vol. 1, 200–203 (orig. 1934); Dey, ΠΑΛΙΓΓΕΝΕΣΙΑ, 117–125 (1937); Festugière, "Corpus Hermeticum 13.12" (1953); RHT IV, 200–257 (1954); van Moorsel, *Mysteries*, 105–116; Zuntz, "On the Hymns in *Corpus Hermeticum* XIII" (1955); Zuntz, "Notes on the *Corpus Hermeticum*," 75–78 (1956); Tröger, *Mysterienglaube und Gnosis* (1971); Grese, *Corpus Hermeticum XIII* (1979); Fowden, *Egyptian Hermes*, 107–109 and passim (1986); Kingsley, "Introduction to the Hermetica," 27–29 (2000); Van den Kerchove, *La voie*, 324–371 (2012); Bull, *Tradition*, 244–315 (2018).

[58] While Tat critiques Hermes repeatedly for being too ἀπόκρυφος in the sense of "obscure, recondite, hard to understand" (see Bull, *Tradition*, 247), presumably that is not how the author of CH XIII means to qualify his own text.

[59] The treatise title speaks of a conversation ἐν ὄρει, and in CH XIII 1 Tat refers to his request to Hermes ἐπὶ τῆς τοῦ ὄρους μεταβάσεως. Because Reitzenstein understood ὄρος to mean "mountain," he changed the verb to καταβάσεως, resulting in the translation "as we came down from the mountain" (followed by Nock and Festugière in HT II, 20; Cop, 49; Grese, *Corpus Hermeticum XIII*, 2, 63; HG, 156; Bull, *Tradition*, 246–247). However, Fowden points out that "[i]n Egypt, ὄρος/*mons* meant both 'mountain' and 'desert,' the abrupt edge of the desert plateau to either side of the Nile being the only 'mountain' visible to the Egyptian eye." Hence there is no ground for Reitzenstein's emendation and we end up with the much more plausible reading "as we were leaving the desert" (see Fowden, *Egyptian Hermes*, 40 note 156, 98; CHD, 174 with note 492; WHCH, 65). Note that the idea of mountains in Egypt seems to reflect the "literary fiction" assumption, whereas a historical-contextual approach must look for types of physical location that would be actually available for Egyptians.

divinity in his *general discourses*, presumably during an oral teaching session, but Tat found his statements enigmatic and obscure. When he pressed his teacher to be more explicit at that time, the answer was that for anybody to be saved, he or she would need to be reborn. But when Tat pressed Hermes to explain this rebirth to him, he was told that he first needed "to become a stranger to the cosmos" (*kosmou apallotriousthai*). So that is what Tat claims to have done now. Having firmly set his mind "against the delusion of the cosmos" (*apo tēs tou kosmou apatēs*), he declares himself ready for rebirth.

In a classic study that has had a momentous impact on scholars of the Hermetica, Hans Jonas highlighted precisely this passage to explain his famous concept of the gnostic as a "stranger" trapped in a hostile material world and aspiring to be released from its bondage:

> Thus ensnared within himself, the human being stands helplessly in a hostile world that utterly entangles and penetrates him. To get free from it and from oneself, from the terror of the world and the terror of one's own "psychic" ego, to come back to oneself – that becomes the era's deep desire. The solution is therefore *kosmou apallotriousthai* ("to become a stranger to the cosmos," Corp. Herm. XIII 1), but also: *eauton diexerchesthai* ("to pass out of oneself," ibid. 4), and the more this gnostic principle is transformed into practical mysticism, the more the two fall together, both conceptually and in terms of praxis.[60]

Jonas' work is largely responsible for the widespread assumption that Hermetic spirituality rests on a "sharp dualism" (*schroffer Dualismus*).[61] On such a reading, Hermetic *palingenesia* ("rebirth") would somehow have to imply a reversal of physical birth, a kind of salvational counter-birth into the true disembodied life that humans in their ignorance call death. Since birth means embodiment, rebirth would in some sense have

---

[60] Jonas, *Gnosis und spätantiker Geist*, vol. 1, 199, cf. 200–201 (referred to by Festugière in his footnote to this passage in CH XIII 1: HT II, 205 note 8; with further reference to Jonas's pages 122–126 ["the stranger"] and 199–200 ["salvation"]). Compare my previous discussion of "entrapment" by Nature imagined as a demonic feminine (above, pp. 171–172): Jonas, too, depicts humans as helplessly ensnared (*verstrickt*), entangled (*verschlungen*), and thoroughly penetrated (*ganz durchdrungen*) by the demonic powers of the world. Jonas was a pupil of Heidegger, and his perspective reflects the dark existentialism that came to dominate the worldview of intellectuals between World War I and II (see e.g. Lazier, *God Interrupted*; and below, Epilogue, pp. 353–355).

[61] Jonas, *Gnosis und spätantiker Geist*, vol. 1, 5 and *passim*. Cf. Bousset, *Kyrios Christos*, 222ff (*schroffer Dualismus*); Dey, ΠΑΛΙΓΓΕΝΕΣΙΑ, 119 ("The doctrine of rebirth rests on the Hermetic core dogma of dualism"), 117–128; Tröger, *Mysterienglaube und Gnosis*, 82–97 and *passim* (convincingly critiqued in Grese, *Corpus Hermeticum XIII*, 50–55).

to mean *dis*embodiment, an escape from the body. However, this cannot be what the author of CH XIII has in mind. The infinite creative fecundity of the androgynous divine Source, which never stops generating, bringing forth, creating, giving birth, is one of the most constantly repeated themes throughout the Hermetic literature and appears in CH XIII as well.[62] Being born in a body cannot be an event that needs to be corrected or undone, as if it were an error or a fall, a tragic digression that should never have happened. On the contrary, sexuality, procreation, and giving birth in the Hermetic universe are always good by definition, because this is how the divine activity of Life and Light manifests itself in the world (and *as* the world). Therefore *re*birth cannot be its reversal or correction but must mean some kind of *new* and even better birth – birth taken to the next level of manifestation.[63]

If so, what does it mean to "become a stranger to the cosmos"? It cannot mean turning one's back on the world that God has created. Rather, the key lies in a profound alteration of consciousness. Although being born in a body is never a tragedy or fall, it is certainly true that incarnation comes at a heavy price, as we have seen in the introduction to this chapter: as the soul enters the cosmos, it loses its clarity of perception and falls under the sway of powerful forces beyond its control. By the very fact of assuming dimensionality as a body-soul organism, it becomes subject to the limitations of time and space. Again, there is nothing "bad" about this process in any moral or metaphysical sense – on the contrary, it is good and necessary. But it is certainly very difficult, limiting, and confusing for the soul. As long as a person's consciousness is still dominated by the spell of the senses that took control of it at birth, a new birth is simply not possible. This is why Tat was told by Hermes that he first needed to train his consciousness in the art of resisting the tricks that the cosmos and its powers unceasingly play on our mind and imaginations. Undoubtedly this is what those famous

---

[62] E.g. *Ascl.* 14, 16, 21, 27, 41 (and Coptic parallels); CH IV 10–11; V 1; VI 1–2; VIII 2; X 3; XI 14, 17; XIII 21; XVI 7. In a splendid discussion, Mahé points out that the Hermetica draw no clear distinctions between "making," "creating" or "fabricating" and "generating," "bringing forth" or "giving birth to," while insisting that their perspective is primarily Egyptian and quite distinct from that of the LXX and Alexandrian Judaism ("La création dans les Hermetica," 8–23). As pointed out by Evans ("Diotima and Demeter," 14–15), as none of the relevant Greek terms (κυέω, τίκτω, γεννάω) is gender-specific, they could all be used with either male or female subjects – or indeed with a divine androgynous subject as in the Hermetica.

[63] In spite of his belief in Hermetic dualism, Dey draws the same conclusion in his study of rebirth (*ΠΑΛΙΓΓΕΝΕΣΙΑ*, 122–123).

"spiritual exercises" were all about: meditational techniques for taking back control over one's own internal world instead of remaining a slave to the passions (literally: remaining *passive*, as opposed to becoming an active agent in the world). So that is what Tat has been doing. Like an athlete who has been exercising for months and is now in excellent shape, he has been training his consciousness and feels ready for the challenge of taking the next step. That step must consist of nothing less than transcending the default conditions of human incarnation in space and time, by getting reborn as a new creature in full command of his inherent divine potential.

So Tat begins querying Hermes about the meaning of rebirth. Surely it must require a different kind of womb and a different kind of semen than those of his biological parents. So what could they be?[64] Hermes responds that the womb of rebirth consists of "noetic wisdom in silence" (*sophia noera en sigēi*) while its semen is "the true good" emitted by "the will of God."[65] But that is all much too vague for Tat. He does not understand what kind of child will be born from such a union, or what this newborn could possibly have in common with his own body and mind.[66] Hermes confirms that the nature of the newborn entity will indeed be different entirely from that of a normal human being: "the one who is generated by God is different, a god, a son, the All in All, consisting wholly of powers [or: composed of all the powers]."[67] This description is significant and remarkably precise, as will be seen; but for the present its meaning is still completely lost on Tat, who responds with evident frustration. Why does Hermes keep speaking in riddles? Can he

---

[64] CH XIII 1.
[65] CH XIII 2. With his usual confidence, Scott (II, 376) dismissed νοερά as a corruption of μήτρα. All later translators have interpreted the passages as referring to noetic wisdom, so it seems pointless to me to write "noeric."
[66] Reitzenstein (*Poimandres*, 340) bracketed the words καὶ τῆς νοητῆς ("and with my *nous*"), and has been followed in this by many later scholars (HT II, 201; Grese, *Corpus Hermeticum XIII*, 6 note 1; Cop, 49, 184). I strongly agree with Holzhausen (CHD, 175 with note 499; see also Jonas, *Gnosis and spätantiker Geist*, vol. 1, 201; WHCH, 65), who rejects this deletion as "unfounded." Οὐσία and νοητός here stand for Tat's material constitution and his mind; but he has not yet understood the full extent of how *nous* as a supreme divine reality as well as the faculty that can grasp the *anoēton* differs from commonplace understandings of *nous* as just the thinking "mind" or "intellect." This solution seems more economic to me than Bull's interpretation in terms of "a binary nous, one divine and one human" (Bull, *Tradition*, 252, 260; cf. Van den Kerchove, *La voie*, 335 note 32).
[67] CH XIII 2 (for the alternative translation, see CHD, 175 note 500). For different translation options, see Grese, *Corpus Hermeticum XIII*, 7 note a.

not talk to him straight, as father to son? But Hermes defends himself. It is not that he deliberately tries to be vague, but that what the rebirth is all about simply cannot be taught.[68] Only God can make this knowledge appear in a person's mind.[69]

So Hermes' answer is clear: "Sorry, I can tell you nothing." Now Tat gets really furious. He has been practicing so hard to make himself ready for rebirth, but Hermes seems unwilling to keep his promise. His statements strike Tat as impossible and contrived, as though he tries to avoid his responsibility and is reluctant to share his knowledge. Is Hermes treating him like a stranger to the lineage of his father? "No," he tells him, "I am a legitimate son! Show me clearly the way of rebirth!"[70] At this outburst, one imagines Hermes heaving a deep sigh and throwing up his hands:

What can I say, my child? I have nothing to say but this: I see in myself an immaterial vision that came to me by the mercy of God, I went out of myself into an immortal body, and now I am not what I was before, but I have been born in *nous*. This thing [*pragma*] cannot be taught, nor can it be perceived by this fabricated element that allows us to see [i.e. one's bodily eyes]. Therefore I no longer care about this composite form [*eidos*] that used to be mine. Colour, touch, or size I no longer have – I am a stranger to them. You see me with your eyes now,

---

[68] I interpret γένος as referring to the phenomenon of the new birth under discussion, similar to Holzhausen's "Dieses Geschehen der (Wieder-)Geburt," "this event of (re)birth" (CHD, 176). Cf. Scott I, 241 "this sort of thing"; followed by HT II, 201 "cette sorte de chose"; WHCH, 65 "this kind of knowledge"; Cop, 49 "such a lineage"; HG, 157 "een geheimenis als dit," i.e. "a mystery like this." Grese (*Corpus Hermeticum XIII*, 7) follows Scott even while referring to Tröger's translation as *Geburt* (*Mysterienglaube*, 112) and Festugière's explicit self-correction in RHT IV, 201 with note 1: "cette divine descendance" or "cette descendance raciale." Van den Kerchove seems to hesitate about the meaning of "ce genre" (*La voie*, 334–335 with notes 29–31); Bull's translation "offspring" translates γένος as referring to the person who is reborn rather than the phenomenon of the rebirth (*Tradition*, 252).

[69] More literally: "when he wishes, it will be recalled to memory by God" (transl. Grese, *Corpus Hermeticum XIII*, 9 note c; presumably a reference to the Platonic concept of innate knowledge, ἀνάμνησις (*anamnēsis*).

[70] CH XIII 3. Like Holzhausen (CHD, 176 note 501) I am sceptical of Festugière's idea (HT II, 210 note 20; accepted *inter alii* by Tröger, *Mysterienglaube*, 24; Grese, *Corpus Hermeticum XIII*, 85–86; Bull, *Tradition*, 353–355) that the sentence ἀλλότριος υἱὸς πέφυκα τοῦ πατρικοῦ γένους is meant as some kind of ritual password. On different interpretations and translation options see Bull, *Tradition*, 253–254 with notes 49–50. Like Scott I, 241 and Holzhausen, ibid., I am inclined to interpret the sentence as a question: "am I born a son foreign to the paternal lineage?" Note that it remains unclear whether the "father" is meant to be Hermes (Tat's "spiritual father"), the grand Human, or God as the ultimate generator of all that is.

my child, but by gazing with bodily sight you do not understand [*katanoeis*] what I am. I am not seen with such eyes now, my child.[71]

We have reached a crucial point in the dialogue. Note that everything in Hermes' statement runs against the idea of a ceremonial event or formal ritual practice. Something radical happened to Hermes, not by his own agency but "by the mercy of God," and it cannot be taught to others. Having gone out of himself, he was born in an immortal noetic body. While this new body is perfectly evident to his own consciousness and internal senses, it is wholly imperceptible to outsiders who have to depend on just their external senses in a normal bodily state of consciousness. As for Hermes' physical body, it is still there and he still inhabits it. But it is no longer the seat of his soul.

Now this statement by Hermes appears to have a very strong impact on Tat. He finally understands why Hermes could not answer his questions and realizes that the rebirth happens on a level of perception to which his senses have no access. His bodily sight is useless, his sense of touch is useless too. And the implication is that even the sense of hearing through which he is listening to Hermes' words cannot possibly transmit their actual meaning. Surely this is what was meant by the statement in CH IX that *logos* cannot get to the truth. Its function is to guide our *nous* up to the point from where, by its own power and with God's help, it can make the final step of reaching the truth.[72] As the meaning of Hermes' statement is sinking in, Tat begins to feel very strange. The words by which he chooses to describe his state of mind are of the greatest importance, as will be seen: "Father – you have thrown me into no small state of *mania* and frenetic frenzy. I do not see myself now" (*Eis manian me ouk oligēn kai oistrēsin phrenōn eneseisas, ō pater. emauton gar nun ouch horō*).[73] As the Greek terminology makes clear, Tat is experiencing a dramatic alteration of consciousness, traditionally referred to as a state of

---

[71] CH XIII 3. "I see": here I follow Holzhausen's conjecture ὁρῶν τε (CHD, 176 with note 502) because it seems evident that Hermes speaks not of a vision that lies in the past but of his present state of perception, that of a person who through rebirth has "become *aiōn*" (see below). If we retain the manuscript reading, we could assume with Bull (*Tradition*, 256) that it was due to the vision that Hermes went out of his body, following the scenario of CH IV 11 (discussed above, pp. 206–207). For alternatives to "immaterial" (ἄπλαστον), see Cop, 185. "Fabricated element": here I follow not Copenhaver's translation "elementary fabrication" but the alternative in his notes (Cop, 185). In "this composite form that used to be mine" I follow Festugière (CH II, 201, admitted as a possibility by Copenhaver: Cop, ibid.).
[72] CH IX 10 (see above, p. 204).
[73] CH XIII 4.

mania ("divine madness") and being driven out of one's mind as by the gadfly's sting.[74]

Tat's statement that he "does not see himself" must reflect his realization that the physical person he perceives by his senses cannot actually be his true self.[75] Hermes, for his part, takes Tat's exclamation as a hopeful sign that what happened to himself may now be happening to Tat as well: "My child, would that you, too, had passed out of yourself, as happens to those who are dreaming in sleep, but then in full consciousness."[76] Again, the element of uncertainty in Hermes' reaction works against the idea that we are reading about an initiatory ritual or ceremony. The process is set in motion not by any human act, Hermes explains in response to Tat's question, but by the agency of no one less than the great Human that we encountered in CH I, the beautiful beloved son of God who united with Nature.[77] I will return to the significance of that point.

Tat repeats that he is no longer in his normal mind, using terms that confirm his condition of altered or frenzied consciousness,[78] while admitting (perhaps with a wink) that Hermes has finally "brought him to

---

[74] The classic reference for the four types of μανία is of course Plato's *Phaedrus* 244–245c, 249d. The standard treatment of alterations of consciousness in ancient Greece is now Ustinova, *Divine Mania*. As for οἴστρησιν φρενῶν, see ibid., 239 note 159, 295 (οἶστρος) in connection with "losing one's mind" (φρήν) (ibid., 3, 7, 9–10, 298). The connection to "ecstasy" (but not divine *mania*) was mentioned in passing by van Moorsel, *Mysteries*, 107 and Tröger, *Mysterienglaube*, 20, but without further development. Salaman c.s. clearly have no idea what to make of the sentence: "you have cut me to the quick, and destroyed my faculties" (WHCH, 66). Grese's belief that the sentence is "Tat's attempt at a little humor" (*Corpus Hermeticum XIII*, 95) is utterly bizarre and has dramatic consequences for the rest of his analysis. Claiming that the passage cannot describe Tat's ecstasy because "Tat has not yet gone out of himself ... and has not yet been regenerated" (ibid., 95 note 199), he misses the entire mental process that in fact leads up to the rebirth. Bull interprets *mania* as "an introverted, sleeplike state" (*Tradition*, 257).

[75] Most commentators seem to think that he is blinded to his own physical appearance, but that interpretation would make little sense. Evidently Hermes' powers of perception have not been lessened but *expanded* due to this altered state, as he remains quite capable of seeing Tat's physical body. Nothing suggests that the expanded perception of rebirth would be preceded by an intermediary period of blindness.

[76] CH XIII 4. Obviously, dreaming "without sleeping" means dreaming in full consciousness (cf. Quispel in HG, 158).

[77] CH XIII 2; see discussion below, pp. 250–251. This remark in CH XIII 4 seems to interrupt the description of Tat's state of *mania* (see Grese, *Corpus Hermeticum XIII*, 96–97). A version of CH XIII 1–2 and 4 preserved in a Syriac manuscript suggests that the line may be misplaced here (see Brock, "Syriac Collection," 231 [Syr-A 21]; cf. Brock, "Some Syriac Excerpts").

[78] CH XIII 5: τῶν πρὶν ἀπολειφθεὶς φρενῶν; cf. the previous formulation οἴστρησιν φρενῶν ἐνέσεισας, and note 74 with reference to Ustinova for the connotations of losing one's φρήν.

speechlessness."[79] But since he has now gained a different kind of perception, shouldn't that enable him to see Hermes' regenerated body? He is clearly disappointed to note that this is not the case: "I see that your size and features are the same."[80] Hermes responds by reminding him that any such impression of physical stability is an optical delusion in any case, because a human's mortal body is subject to continuous change and transformation. It is ultimately a deception (*pseudos*). But if that is so, Tat asks, then what is true? To this Hermes can only answer indirectly, largely in standard apophatic terms: true reality is "unsullied ... boundless, without color, formless, unchangeable, naked, brilliant, self-comprehended, the unalterable good, the incorporeal."[81] Well, that is still not what Tat is seeing! Therefore it seems that even in his newly acquired state of modified consciousness he remains blind to true reality. At this point one imagines him sinking his head in despair: "I am really deranged then, father... I thought that through you I had become wise. But my perceptions of this noetic reality [*noēmatos*] are blocked."[82]

Tat has now reached his lowest point of disappointment and disillusionment. It seems that all his efforts have been in vain! Hermes responds by reminding him once more of the difference between normal sense perception (the default condition of human beings born on earth) and true noetic perception (the condition of human beings who have been *re*born on earth). The former gives us access to the world of the elements. The latter enables us to perceive true reality, which is "neither rigid nor fluid and neither constricted nor volatile," as he puts it.[83] It can be known only in terms of its own essential force and energy [*to monon dunamei kai energeia nooumenon*], and only by a person who is capable of understanding [*noein*] the generation in God. "Am I then incapable of it, father?," Tat asks. "May that not be so," Hermes answers. One imagines Tat raising his head at those word – could there still be hope for him?

---

[79] Van den Kerchove takes ἀφασία rather literally and thinks that Tat has trouble expressing himself coherently (*La voie*, 337–338), but in fact he explains his speechlessness quite eloquently. Transposed to modern English, he would seem to be saying something like "Well, Hermes, you finally managed to shut me up, didn't you...?" This makes sense because, as Van den Kerchove indicates herself (ibid., 326), Tat had been doing most of the talking, while Hermes was not saying much.

[80] CH XIII 5.

[81] CH XIII 6.

[82] CH XIII 6. ἐνεφράχθησαν αἱ αἰσθήσεις τούτου μου τοῦ νοήματος. For translation dilemmas see e.g. Grese, *Corpus Hermeticum XIII*, 11 with note g; CHD, 178 with note 508.

[83] CH XIII 6.

BORN AGAIN

Up to this point, Hermes' role has been strictly passive. He responded to Tat's questions, watched him struggle and shift into an altered state of frenzy or *mania*, but did not take any initiative. Now, however, he becomes active and begins giving Tat instructions. His very first statement is hard to interpret with certainty because the words *epispasai eis heauton* can have two different meanings: either "withdraw into yourself" or "draw it towards you" (or "into yourself").[84] If we assume the former, Tat is asked to enter a state of meditative concentration in which he focuses on his inner world; and this is consistent with Hermes' additional advice to "suspend the perceptions of the body." In case of the latter, Tat is asked to actively draw the divine "force and energy" towards himself while fervently wishing for it to come.[85] And Hermes promises that indeed it will come. Whereas the initial shift into a state of *mania* happened to Tat just like that, presumably by God's will, it is now up to Tat to continue the process by allowing the divine energies entry into his body and soul.

As it turns out, this spiritual exercise has a very specific objective. Quite similar to what we saw in the case of Iamblichus' theurgy, the energies of Life and Light will enter the practitioner's body for the purpose of healing, to clean it of the negative energies that have taken possession of it. We have already seen how that had happened: these daimonic forces invade an infant at the very moment of birth, thereby binding the soul to the astral energies specific to its time and place and taking permanent residence in all parts of a person's body.[86] Surely this is what the author of CH VII 2–3 meant by "the criminal who lives in your house" who keeps secretly poisoning our consciousness from within.[87] It is crucial to see the simple underlying logic at work here: if being born means getting possessed by these negative energies, then being *re*born on a higher level requires expelling or exorcizing them from one's body and soul.

---

[84] For the former option, see Mead, *Thrice-Greatest Hermes*, vol. 2, 223; Grese, *Corpus Hermeticum XIII*, 13; WHCH, 66. For the latter option see Tröger, *Mysterienglaube*, 10; CH II, 203 (but cf. RHT III, 169); Cop, 50; CHD, 179. Quispel has "concentreer je op jezelf" ("concentrate on yourself," HG, 158). See also Bull, *Tradition*, 260–261.

[85] CH XIII 7. All these elements are mentioned in the passage: κατάργησον τοῦ σώματος τὰς αἰσθήσεις and θέλησον, καὶ γίνεται. For the "force and energy," see end of previous section. Cf. HD VIII 7: "[you have to] want, noeticize, have faith, have love, and you will have become it [i.e. a divine being]." Love here is not ἔρως but ἀγάπη.

[86] CH XVI 13–14.

[87] See above, pp. 152–153.

Thus while Tat is allowing entrance to the healing energies, Hermes tells him what this exercise is really all about: "Cleanse yourself of the *alogon timōriōn* of matter."[88] I give the crucial words here in transcription because they are almost impossible to translate adequately into modern English. *Alogos* is usually translated as "irrational," "reasonless," or "unreasoning," but in our post-Enlightenment culture those terms carry an enormous amount of additional baggage that obscures the original meaning. The point about brute matter is simply that it has no *logos* – it cannot speak, it can only act. Hence it affects us mutely: it just does what it does, and we cannot engage it in conversation or persuade it to act differently. This is also true for the negative daimonic entities in question, who are first referred to as *timōriōn*, "torments," and personalized immediately afterwards as *timōrous*, "tormentors."[89] So these are negative daimonic energies that are tormenting us from within and cannot be reasoned with.

Tat is an advanced student who should presumably know about daimons, but still he seems surprised that they are present in his body. Hermes confirms that "they are dreadful, and there are many of them." Tat admits that he didn't know that, which gives Hermes his cue for explaining what they are:

That very ignorance, my child, is the first torment. The second is grief. The third is intemperance. The fourth is lust. The fifth is injustice. The sixth is greed. The seventh is deceit. The eighth is envy. The ninth is treachery. The tenth is anger. The eleventh is recklessness. The twelfth is corruption. These are twelve in number; but under them, child, others more numerous use the prison of the body to torment [lit. force to suffer] the inner person through his sense perceptions. But they depart, one after the other, from the one to whom God has shown mercy – and that is the manner and the meaning of rebirth.[90]

We will return in a moment to the exact nature of these twelve torments. The important thing to note is that the rebirth is said to consist precisely in the progressive expulsion or exorcism of these negative energies. Again, note the underlying logic: these tormentors enter our body when we are born and leave them when we are reborn. Being born means falling under their dominion; being reborn means being freed from their troubling

---

[88] CH XIII 7.
[89] While the usual standard translation of τιμωρία is "retribution" or "vengeance" (Liddell and Scott, *Greek-English Lexicon*, 1795), it is also used more broadly as referring to acts of violence or cruelty, hence "torment" (Lampe, *Patristic Greek Lexikon*, 1394b; with thanks to Dylan Burns). Scott (II, 384) observes correctly that the common translation of τιμωρίαι as "punishments" (cf. "avengers," in Bull, *Tradition*, 260 and further) is not appropriate here because "the writer of CH XIII does not speak of them as punishments of previous sin."
[90] CH XIII 7.

presence. So this is the meaning (*logos*) of rebirth,[91] and this is the manner (*tropos*) in which it is done: it involves a purging of negative energies by means of the systematic invocation of positive energies. These noetic forces of Life and Light enter the candidate's body, drive out the resident forces of death and darkness, and take their place. As suggested by the very term rebirth, the result of this spiritual house-cleaning process is assumed to be permanent: as the candidate is filled wholly with divine energies, he or she will never be the same again.

While Tat is in a meditative state, mentally inviting these powers to come and do their work, Hermes now tells him to remain completely silent so as not to interrupt the process of God's mercy or compassionate care. The adverbial *loipon* indicates that this silence is kept for quite some time.[92] As noted by Anna Van den Kerchove, Hermes "modifies the atmosphere" as the two practitioners enter a deep reverent silence pregnant with expectation of what is about to happen.[93] I use that formulation deliberately, for as she further points out with reference to CH XIII 2, Tat must make himself into a receptive womb of "noetic wisdom in silence" so that it can be inseminated by "the true good" emitted through "the will of God."[94] He is about to discover now what was meant by those formulations from CH XIII 2. After an unspecified period of time has passed, Hermes breaks the silence to hail the arrival of the generative or life-carrying healing forces, veritable *logoi spermatikoi*. They are ten in number, and while coming from the Father, they are all of them feminine:[95]

Rejoice now, child! The divine powers are thoroughly cleansing you so that the *Logos* may take shape in you.

- The *gnōsis* of God [*gnōsis theou*] has come to us. And with its coming, ignorance was driven out, my child.
- The *joy* of *gnōsis* [*gnōseōs chara*][96] has come to us. At its arrival, my child, grief must fly off towards those who have room for it.

---

[91] I follow Grese (*Corpus Hermeticum XIII*, 15 note c), who finds λόγος somewhat hard to translate here but agrees with Festugière's suggestion (HT II, 203: "le sens").
[92] Bull, *Tradition*, 264 (and see entire section on "receptive silence," 265–271).
[93] Van den Kerchove, *La voie*, 343; Bull, *Tradition*, 264.
[94] Van den Kerchove, *La voie*, 343; Bull, *Tradition*, 264; see discussion of CH XIII 2 above.
[95] Mahé, "Générations antédiluviennes," 168 note 20. The gender polarities are fascinating: the father emits feminine seeds, while Tat becomes the womb from which he himself will be reborn.
[96] Lit: "*gnōsis* of joy." Here I follow Holzhausen (CHD, 180; cf. Grese, *Corpus Hermeticum XIII*, 123 note 362), who assumes that the author must have meant γνώσεως χαρά rather than γνῶσις χαρᾶς. I suspect that there is an attempt here to connect the first three powers: first there is *gnōsis*, then joy (of *gnōsis*), then self-control is described as joyful.

- The power I summon after joy is *self-control* [*tēn enkrateian*]. O joyful power, let us gladly welcome her too. See how, right away, it has driven out intemperance!
- Fourth now I summon *perseverance* [*karterian*], the power against lust.
- The next step, o child, is the seat of *justice* [*dikaiosunēs*], for see how without trial it has driven out injustice. With injustice gone, child, we have been made just.
- I call towards us the sixth power, *generous sharing* [*koinōnian*], the one opposed to greed.
- Greed having left, I further summon *truth* [*tēn alētheian*]. Deceit flees, truth arrives.
- See how *the good* [*to agathon*] finds its fulfilment, my child, at the arrival of truth. For envy has withdrawn from us. So after truth followed the good, together with *life* [*zōē*] and *light* [*phōs*].

No torment attacks from the darkness anymore. Vanquished, they have winged away with a rushing sound.[97]

What are we witnessing here? Tat has been making himself as receptive as possible, silently asking for the powers to come, and then the first two powers (*gnōsis* and joy) arrived. Only from that moment on do we read about Hermes "summoning" or "calling upon" the next five. Hermes' words do not have the shape of a fixed ritual formula but essentially just describe what is happening: the successive arrival of ten noetic energies that drive out the twelve tormenting energies.[98]

So what is it that causes the process to happen? At this point it seems to be largely automatic, meaning from the practitioners' point of view that the work of healing is done by the forces themselves and the insemination process is initiated by the Father.[99] We can only speculate about what exactly Tat and Hermes are *doing* to facilitate the process and allow it to run smoothly. Comparison with practices of spiritual healing by means of exorcism in other cultural contexts suggests the likelihood of some form of physical manipulation, notably laying on of hands, possibly combined with controlled breathing; but if so, we are not informed about it. It is somewhat unclear whether a deliberate distinction is implied between the first two

---

[97] CH XIII 8–9. Most modern translators interpret ῥοίζῳ as suggesting winged creatures: Scott I, 247 ("with rushing wings"); CH II, 204 ("avec un grand bruit d'ailes," i.e. "with a great noise of wings"); Cop, 51 ("with a flapping of wings"); WHCH, 13 ("with a rush of wings"); HG, 159 ("met luid gedruis van hun wiekslag," i.e. "with the beating of their wings making a loud noise"). But see Grese, *Corpus Hermeticum XIII*, 17 ("with a rustling sound") and CHD, 180 ("mit Getöse," i.e. "noisily").

[98] Unlike Van den Kerchove (*La voie*, 342), I see no indications of a ritual formula or of "passwords" for opening a pathway through the zodiac.

[99] Cf. Van den Kerchove, *La voie*, 343, 345.

powers that arrive unsummoned and then five further ones that require a verbal call to make their appearance. The fact that no verbal summoning is mentioned for the fifth power suggests that the author is simply not very strict and precise about what probably seems obvious to him, while confirming that we are not reading a fixed traditional formula that carries sacred ceremonial power. It seems more likely that the entire process, with the pupil making himself receptive and the master summoning the powers, is *neither* verbal *nor* ritual in a strict sense but procedural: Tat is being cleansed of his *timōriōn* by a procedure of spiritual healing under divine direction. When a surgeon removes the cancer from a patient's body, he is not performing a ritual or ceremony but is following a technical procedure. When he says "I now insert the scalpel," there is no implication that the patient is being cured by those words – the surgeon merely describes what he is doing.[100]

The description of what happens is based on the confrontation between *ten* divine energies and *twelve* tormentors linked to the zodiac (see Table 8.1 on the next page; but keep in mind that these are just the most important ones, as "others more numerous" are ranged under each one of them).[101]

The first seven pairs are easy to understand, of course: if you have *gnōsis* you are no longer ignorant, joy takes the place of grief or sadness, you have control over the intemperate passions and permanent power over lust (nos. 3 and 4 are very close), all your actions are ruled by justice, your attitude is one of generous sharing instead of selfish greed, and you always let truth prevail. All these seven powers or energies are to be understood as attributes of the divine state of consciousness:[102] God

---

[100] My interpretation therefore differs from that of Bull, who (while drawing interesting parallels with the PGM, Hekhalot literature, and Egyptian temple rituals) refers to the work of J.L. Austin and John R. Searle to analyze the invocation of divine powers as ritual "speech-acts" carrying illocutionary or perlocutionary force (*Tradition*, 271–281).

[101] On those "others," see Van den Kerchove, *La voie*, 341. Contrary to e.g. Scott (II, 385) and Grese (*Corpus Hermeticum XIII*, 121, 127–128), I attach importance to the specificities of the list. Scott's visceral contempt for astrology even leads him to print the list of twelve torments and ten positive energies in small type because he thinks they are a later addition; these are just "silly" passages lacking in "good sense and taste," and "when these excrescences have been removed, *Corp.* XIII is less unworthy to take its place among the other *Hermetica* ... "(I, 242–245; II, 385). Tröger sets up a list of seventeen (!) oppositions to strengthen his programmatic argument for "Hermetic dualism" (*Mysterienglaube*, 91–92).

[102] *Contra* Festugière in RHT III, 155–156 (who also misses the point that from a nondualistic perspective, γνῶσις θεοῦ implies that if a human being's noetic essence is identical with the divine *nous*, this means that his knowledge of God is an instance of God knowing himself).

TABLE 8.1: *The twelve torment(or)s and the ten divine energies (CH XIII 8–9)*

Ignorance	ἄγνοια	1	γνῶσις θεοῦ	Gnōsis of divinity
Grief (sadness, sorrow)	λύπη	2	γνώσεως χαρά	Joy of gnōsis
Intemperance	ἀκρασία	3	ἐγκράτεια	Self-control
Lust	ἐπιθυμία	4	καρτερία	Perseverance
Injustice	ἀδικία	5	δικαιοσύνη	Justice
Greed	πλεονεξία	6	κοινωνία	Generous sharing
Deceit	ἀπάτη	7	ἀλήθεια	Truth
Envy	φθόνος	8	ζωή	Life
Treachery	δόλος	9		
Anger	ὀργή	10	φῶς	Light
Recklessness	προπέτεια	11	τὸ ἀγαθόν	The Good
Corruption (badness)	κακία	12		

is all-knowing, the source of all joy, he is in full and permanent control of all that is, perfectly just, wholly generous, and utterly truthful. Since in God there is no place for anything that is not good, presumably their opposites (the torments) do not have true existence in *his* consciousness as separate or autonomous powers.

The septenary of energies ranging from *gnōsis* to truth could be seen as an autonomous series. However, its negative counterpart gets expanded into a dodecad by the addition of five further torments (envy, treachery, anger, recklessness, and corruption or badness) that stand opposed to a triad of three supreme powers.[103] The formulation seems to suggest that once the septenary of virtues has been completed with the arrival of Truth, this means that Goodness finds its fulfilment together with Life and Light. I assume that the author means to say that once Truth has been attained, Goodness is there immediately; and because it is one with Life and Light, those two are there as well. This means that we are looking first at a septenary built up in successive order, followed next by *one* final triad that arrives all at once and pretty much blows away its remaining fivefold opposition in one final

---

[103] Like Festugière (RHT III, 155–156), Grese notes that while the first seven are virtues, the three final ones are not (*Corpus Hermeticum XIII*, 128). This is correct only up to a point, for the twelve "torments" should not be understood just as moral vices but as actual energetic powers that are active in the cosmos and negatively affect the human soul and body. Likewise, all their ten positive counterparts are potent divine energies, not just conventional names for moral virtues. Generally on lists of this kind, see Mussies, "Catalogues of Sins and Virtues Personified."

burst of energy. The dodecad of tormenting energies that reflect the twelve signs of the zodiac, manifesting themselves as harmful passions, is thus expelled by the overwhelming force of two clusters of healing energies that act in perfect unison and are ultimately one: a septenary of positive energies linked to seven chief virtues, and a supreme divine triad.[104] Again, I find it important to point out that from the dualistic perspective of human consciousness, the dodecad and the decad appear as contraries, but this very opposition can only be a delusion from the non-dualistic perspective of divinity because ultimately all reality exists only in *Nous*.

As the torments are leaving Tat's body, his soul is literally reborn in a new body constituted entirely of the divine energies. Because his strictly material (*hulic*) body is now thoroughly cleansed of everything bad, it is able to contain this good energetic body of spiritual Life and Light.[105] Interestingly, we have seen that as Hermes announced the beginning of the process in CH XIII 8, he referred to the new body of rebirth as the *Logos*. This might seem puzzling at first sight – should it not rather be a noetic body, a body of *Nous*?[106] I suggest that the passage must be read against the background of CH XIII 4, where Tat asks Hermes who it is that effectuates the rebirth (*tis esti genesiourgos tēs palingenesias?*) and is told that it is "the son of God, the Human" (*ho tou theou paīs, anthrōpos heis*). This must refer to the beautiful

---

[104] Hermes explains all this to Tat in CH XIII 12. In view of our discussions, this account contains almost nothing new or surprising anymore; but see discussion in Grese, *Corpus Hermeticum XIII*, 137–144; Bull, *Tradition*, 184–291. While I will return to the arithmological dimensions of the Decad in the next chapter (pp. 277–282), note that it is described here as the "soul-producer" (ψυχογόνος).

[105] There is no evidence for Mahé's belief that "the visible body dematerializes" (HT V, cxcviii). As for Christian Bull's argument about an out-of-body experience during the rebirth process (*Tradition*, 266–267), I am not convinced. He helpfully points out that the verb ἐξέρχομαι was sometimes used for offspring issuing from the womb; but the relevant passages in CH XIII 3 and 4 (viz. ἐξελήλυθα, διεξελήλυθας) both speak of issuing *from oneself* (ἐμαυτόν, σεαυτόν), not from the body. The main argument in favor of an out-of-body experience comes from comparison with two other treatises, CH IV 11 and X 6 (quoted by Bull, ibid., 266 with note 103), as well as SH VI 18, but it is not evident that these are speaking of the rebirth. Admittedly CH X 6 says that the soul cannot be deified while still in a human body, whereas CH XIII says that it can; but if we insist that there must be strict consistency between CH X and XIII, which in itself is not obvious, this could still mean that it can be deified only in the energetic body of rebirth and not in the physical human body, the zodiacal *skēnos* polluted by daimonic passions (see below, pp. 252–253 with note 113).

[106] As assumed by Grese, *Corpus Hermeticum XIII*, 15 note h.

Human who, by making love to Nature according to CH I,[107] initiated the process of embodiment that would be continued later through sexual procreation. As the most immediate father of incarnated human beings, it makes sense that this supreme divine entity presides over their rebirths as well. We have seen that when the Human unites with Nature, he is already reunited with the *logos*; and whatever else that word may mean in other contexts, it gets defined explicitly as "that in you which sees and hears." Therefore the Human who unites with the *alogon morphēn* of Nature is endowed with *logos*, resulting in the birth of entities that have sense perception (like other animals) and can speak as well. Most important of all, we have seen that what characterizes *logos* is its unique capacity of acting as an intermediary between matter and *nous*: it can retain and transmit knowledge over time.[108] This results in the following model. First, because both *noēsis* and *aisthēsis* (sense experience) exist only in pure immediacy, the knowledge they provide, while infallible, is ineffable and untransmissible. Second, *phantasia* can transcend immediacy by storing images in consciousness, an imperfect but indispensable faculty known to us as memory. However, and this is the third aspect, only *logos* makes it possible for one soul to communicate with another, thus enabling human beings to function in societies.

Therefore it must be the *logos*, fully endowed with *noēsis* and *phantāsia* but henceforth unhindered by any bodily passions or daimonic energies, that is assembled into bodily shape during the rebirth. After the new embryo has been woven together by the ten inseminating powers in "the womb of noetic wisdom in silence," it gets born into the world of matter. Hence it now inhabits Tat's physical body, and will stay there until the latter dissolves at death. Beaming no doubt with the joy of satisfaction and accomplishment, Hermes tells Tat that his wish has come true! He is now reborn as "a god, a son, the All in All, composed of all the powers":[109]

---

[107] Bull draws the same conclusion (*Tradition*, 258–259), but then argues that the *genesiourgos* must be Hermes himself, since he has already become one with the Human. However, I see no evidence that being reborn as a "son of God" means "becoming one with the Human" (except in the very general sense that on an ultimate level *everything* is one with the divine *nous*). Rather, I assume that the Human is still present and active as a metaphysical entity, and is the director of rebirth.

[108] See my exegesis of CH IX 1–2 above, pp. 201–205.

[109] CH XIII 2.

Now you know the manner of rebirth, my child. With the arrival of the Ten, child, the noetic birth has been completed and the Twelve were expelled and through this birth we were deified. Whoever through God's mercy has attained the deifying birth has left bodily perception behind. He knows himself to be composed of these [powers] and is filled with joy.[110]

Once more I find it important to emphasize that the physical body does not get left behind in the rebirth; it is just normal bodily *perception* (*tēn sōmatikēn aisthēsin*) that gets expanded and transformed. This is confirmed immediately by Tat's response. He describes his new state of expanded perceptual consciousness in terms that refer explicitly to CH XI and make clear that he has now "become the *aiōn*."

Thanks to God I have found rest, Father, and I am visualizing [*phantazomai*] – not by visual eyesight but through the noetic energy that comes from the powers. I am in heaven, on earth, in water, in the air; I am in animals, in plants; in the womb, before the womb, after the womb; everywhere. .... Father, I see the All, and I see myself in the *nous*![111]

Hermes confirms that this, indeed, is exactly what the rebirth is all about: "to no longer visualize in terms of the body in three dimensions" (*to mēketi phantazesthai eis to sōma to trichēi diastaton*).[112] The essential rationale of rebirth might thus be illustrated in terms of the metaphor of radar surveillance technology I used earlier in this chapter. When the soul is born in a physical body, it appears as a blip on the spatiotemporal grid, and so the daimons notice its presence and capture it. The bodily vessel is constituted of the zodiac, and therefore it serves the *heimarmenē* as an instrument of control, technically referred to as

---

[110] CH XIII 10. I suggest that SH IIA 13 may be read as an allusion to the rebirth: although everything physically born is impermanent and hence not truly real (on ἀλήθεια see above, Chapter 7, p. 201 note 57), those who are born from the Forefather are made of "real matter." SH IIB 3 states that the *embodied* soul can be liberated from heaviness and will never slip back; in other words, its condition has become permanent. As in Plato's *Symposium*, this process is said to be driven by "erotics."

[111] CH XIII 11 and 13. I see no reason to assume that ἀκλινὴς γενόμενος refers to such formulas as "the immovable race" in several Nag Hammadi treatises (as assumed by Quispel in HG, 499 note 289 and 506 note 349) but see it as indicating simply that Tat has found rest: he is no longer subject to the cosmos of change and instability but is reborn in the eternal stability of *nous*. For "I am visualizing," cf. RHT IV, 243 note 1 ("pris absolument = 'avoir des visions'"); Grese, *Corpus Hermeticum XIII*, 17 ("I visualize"); HG, 159 ("ik stel me de dingen voor").

[112] CH XIII 13. On translation options, see Grese (*Corpus Hermeticum XIII*, 19–21, note I). Clearly φαντάζεσθαι must be understood here in an active sense (cf. previous footnote); see e.g. Festugière's interpretation "ne plus former ses représentations sous la figure du corps à trois dimensions" (HT II, 206).

to *skēnos*.[113] But now this initial body has been cleaned of daimonic infection and has become the vessel of the *Logos*, a new energetic body of eternal Life and Light. *This* body is made of noetic energies that are inherently beyond space and time, hence it is free from the constraints of *heimarmenē*, invulnerable to daimonic contamination, and serves as the vehicle for a universal conscious soul whose range of perception is literally unlimited. Deification therefore means full participation in God's own incorporeal imagination (*phantasia*), filled with the *noēmata* of all that is.[114]

Before moving on to the final part of CH XIII, we might ask how this new state of consciousness is to be understood. In the scholarly literature about the Hermetica this question is never asked, let alone answered; but if we assume that the authors were intelligent human beings like ourselves, their understanding of "becoming the *aiōn*" must correspond to some kind of state that we can identify and recognize in our own terminology. Some critics will object that the state of rebirth was never more than just a theoretical desideratum for Hermetic practitioners; since they conceived of God as containing all *noēmata* in his incorporeal imagination and considered it possible for the human soul to participate in divine consciousness, it followed from those premises that deification would have to involve this condition of unbounded perception. On such a reading, we do not need to assume that any altered state was ever experienced by any Hermetic practitioner: rather, authors and readers were merely aspiring to something that they thought was possible on theoretical grounds, although actually it is not. This seems to be the tacit assumption among most scholars.

However, it is actually not so difficult to assume that some Hermetic devotees did experience alterations of consciousness consistent with the description given in CH XI. It is not sufficiently recognized that some people possess a much stronger natural talent for seeing internal imagery

---

[113] CH XIII 12, 15. See Cop, 190–191: whereas σκηνή means "tent," τό σκῆνος is used figuratively for the body in the sense of a tent-like lodging-place for the soul (strictly an animated corpse, as it is only alive as long as the soul stays in it). It appears that in the Hermetic context of CH XIII 12, τό σκῆνος is understood specifically as the zodiacal body that keeps the soul chained to the daimonic energies of the *heimarmenē*. When Hermes refers to "the *skēnos* from which we have now been released [*diexelēluthamen*]" (ibid.), therefore I do not read this as meaning that the soul has left the body, but that it is now free from the burden of daimonic energies. This interpretation is confirmed by CH XIII 15 (see below, p. 257): Tat seems eager to leave the *skēnos* behind, which implies that he had not yet done so.

[114] CH XI 18 and 20 (see discussion above, Chapter 7, pp. 214–215).

than others, so that they find it easy to "travel in their mind" to what is experienced subjectively as other times and places. Even in less naturally talented subjects this capacity can be cultivated and trained, so that a person who initially has trouble even just visualizing for instance a simple red cube can learn over time to see complicated moving imagery in full color and three dimensions.[115] Techniques for increasing the vividness and clarity of internal imagery typically involve induction of altered states of consciousness; and to the extent that subjects believe in the *veracity* of their visions, they come to think of their experiences as instances of clairvoyance (literally "seeing clearly").[116] Thus while we may not share Tat's personal conviction that he actually participates in God's consciousness and can *really* be immediately present at any time and place in the cosmos, yet we may readily assume that Hermetic practitioners had powerful subjective experiences of "cosmic consciousness" which convinced them that they did and could.

The term "cosmic consciousness" seems appropriate for two reasons. Firstly, it indicates a point that has received little attention from specialists: while Tat believes that he now participates in God's own consciousness, his perception remains focused entirely and exclusively on *the cosmos*. He does not actually perceive God, nor does he experience divine self-consciousness or self-knowledge; rather, what happens is that he shares in the mode of imaginal perception by which God perceives the world. He never leaves the cosmos to see what is beyond it. The full significance of this point will emerge in Chapter 9. Secondly, the term leads us to a modern parallel that is actually quite instructive. The term "cosmic consciousness" was made famous by the Canadian psychiatrist Richard Maurice Bucke (1837–1902), in a book of the same title published a year before his death.[117] At the age of

---

[115] For the debate on mental imagery, see e.g. Holt, "Imagery"; Sarbin and Juhasz, "Historical Background to the Concept of Hallucination"; Noll, "Mental Imagery Cultivation"; George, "Mental Imagery Enhancement Training"; Luhrmann, *Persuasions*, 191–202; Jackson, "Imagination and Psychological Healing"; Kosslyn, "Mental Images"; Kosslyn, Thompson and Ganis, *Case of Mental Imagery*.

[116] For strong examples, see the phenomenon of nineteenth-century somnambulic "information machines" discussed in Hanegraaff, "Magnetic Gnosis"; and for a parallel that did not require alterations of consciousness, see the modern practice known as "psychometry" (a term introduced by Josef Rodes Buchanan in 1849 and popularized by William and Elizabeth Denton since 1863), illustrated at the example of H.P. Blavatsky and modern Theosophy in Hanegraaff, "Theosophical Imagination."

[117] Bucke had borrowed the term from Carpenter, *From Adam's Peak*, 156–161; see Ryan, *Different Dimension*, 20–29 (with thanks to Jeffrey J. Kripal for the reference).

thirty-six (hence in 1874), after an evening of reading Romantic poetry with his friends, all of a sudden he found himself overwhelmed by "an intellectual illumination quite impossible to describe" but accompanied by sensations of internal fire and immense joy. It left him convinced that the cosmos was not dead matter but a living presence, that the human soul was immortal, that the universe was working towards the universal good, that its foundation was love, and "the happiness of every one is in the long run absolutely certain." Bucke claims that while the experience lasted just a few moments, "its effects proved ineffaceable" for the rest of his life.[118] While Bucke never mentions Hermes or the Hermetica, his description of cosmic consciousness is remarkably similar to "becoming the *aiōn*":

> The prime characteristic of cosmic consciousness is, as its name implies, a consciousness of the cosmos, that is, of the life and order of the universe. ... Along with the consciousness of the cosmos there occurs an intellectual enlightenment or illumination which alone would place the individual on a new plane of existence – would make him almost a member of a new species. To this is added a state of moral exaltation, an indescribable feeling of elevation, elation, and joyousness, and a quickening of the moral sense ... With these come, what may be called, a sense of immortality, a consciousness of eternal life, not a conviction that he shall have this, but the consciousness that he has it already.[119]

This comparison is not meant to imply any quasi-perennialist claim about ancient Hermetic practitioners and modern transcendentalists dipping into "the same universal mystical experience," an assumption for which we have no data. It indicates simply that descriptions as found in CH XI and XIII do not need to be dismissed as "narrative fictions" based on nothing but theory. We know that people can have intense visionary experiences; we know that these can involve a vivid sensation of boundless perception unrestricted by time and space; we know that these experiences can be strongly enhanced by alterations of consciousness; and we know that this can happen either spontaneously or be induced artificially by specific spiritual techniques. Therefore we have every reason to assume that the rebirth described in CH XIII corresponds to experiences that occurred to at least some Hermetic devotees as part of their spiritual practice.

---

[118] Bucke, *Cosmic Consciousness*, 8; cf. James, *Varieties*, 385.
[119] Bucke, *Cosmic Consciousness*, 2; cf. James, *Varieties*, 384. Neither *Cosmic Consciousness* nor *Man's Moral Nature* (written as an attempt to "embody the teaching of the illumination," see *Cosmic Consciousness*, 8) mentions Hermes or the Hermetica.

GRATITUDE

Having been reborn after an act of divine insemination, Tat is now literally a "son of God." That he has been deified in this manner does not mean he is *identical* with God, but that his consciousness is filled with noetic power so that he can share in modes of perception unavailable to unregenerate human beings. It should be noted that he keeps referring to Hermes as "father" while Hermes keeps addressing him as "my child" and continues to teach him new things while correcting his mistakes. Tat may be able to perceive all things in the cosmos now and may no longer be hindered by passions and torments; but that clearly does not make him omniscient, infallible, equal to God, or even equal to his teacher. He has been born on a new level but still has much to learn. This becomes immediately clear when he asks whether his new body is susceptible to dissolution. It earns him a rather stern reprimand from Hermes:

> Watch your language and do not give voice to what is impossible! Otherwise you will go astray and the eye of your *nous* will get clouded. The natural body perceptible to the senses is far removed from the birth of true being: the one is subject to dissolution while the other is indissoluble, the one is mortal while the other is immortal. Do you not understand that, like me, you have been born as a divine entity and a child of the one?[120]

As Tat is reassured about that point, it seems he now wants to explore the extent of his new perceptual powers. So far we have been told about *visual* perception through the imaginal eye of the *nous*. But next to this incorporeal imagination (*phantasia*), surely there must be an internal *hearing* sense as well. As will be seen, there lies a deep but hitherto unnoticed significance in the fact that even after his rebirth, Tat's internal ears have still not been opened. That this is so becomes clear from

---

[120] CH XIII 14. An important parallel seems to have been overlooked by previous scholars: HD VI 3 states that if the soul leaves the body without having attained perfection (the text in fact compares this situation with that of a newborn child unfit for survival!), "it is imperfect and lacks a body," whereas "the perfection of the soul is *gnōsis* of the things that really are [*ta onta*]." Contrary to Holzhausen, who is even tempted to delete καὶ ἀσώματος (Armenian *anmarmin*; CHD, 494 with note 42; cf. HT V, 238 note 91), I consider this a clear indication that while normal physical death is a defective incorporeal birth of the soul into immateriality, only rebirth in a superior spiritual *body* allows the soul to attain *gnōsis* of true reality. I read HD VII 1–3 along the same lines: the "ideal form" (VII 1; HG, 619 note 1019 with reference to 614 note 984) of the human being is its body of rebirth, which is simultaneously "in heaven and in the air, on earth and in water" (VII 2) and can perceive all things there simultaneously with the eye of the *nous* (VII 3). I take this to be the state of "cosmic consciousness" described in CH XI 20 and XIII 11 (as also suggested by van den Broek: HG, 619 note 1021).

his next request to Hermes: "Father, I have long wanted to hear the hymnal praise of the powers that you said I would hear at arrival in the Ogdoad."[121] Apparently he does not yet hear their voices. Hermes' response confirms that while Tat's new body is endowed with God's own faculty of imaginal perception, this still does not allow him to hear those powers; to gain that ability, his consciousness would have to leave his physical body and gain access to the Ogdoad, the eighth sphere beyond the planetary cosmos.

As Poimandres spoke with foresight about the Ogdoad, my child, I understand your haste to be released from the *skēnos*.[122] For you have been purified. Poimandres, the *nous* of the sovereign power, told me no more than what has been written down; for he knew that by myself, I would be able to understand [*noein*] all things, to hear what I would want and see all things. And so he left it to me to make things of beauty. Indeed the powers in me are now singing in all things.[123]

It is significant that Hermes interprets Tat's request to hear the hymn as a wish to leave his physical body and enter the Ogdoad. Firstly, that the ability to hear those voices means being in the Ogdoad is apparently taken for granted between the two of them, as a point that is not in need of discussion. Secondly, it means that while Tat has been reborn, still his consciousness is in the cosmos and not in the Ogdoad.[124] Although

---

[121] CH XIII 15. I follow Holzhausen's reconstruction in CHD, 182. It is important to reject Reitzenstein's and Nock's emendation of μου to σου (HT II, 206; followed by Quispel in HG, 160; Grese, *Corpus Hermeticum XIII*, 23): the manuscripts do *not* say that Hermes once heard those hymns, but that Tat would like to hear them (remember that in CH I 16, Poimandres tells Hermes what the ascended soul *will* hear in the Ogdoad, but Hermes does not hear anything at that point). Festugière restores the μου in RHT IV, 206; he is followed by Cop, 52 and CHD, 182; Salaman leaves the matter ambiguous (WHCH, 68).

[122] See above, pp. 252–253 with note 113. While the *skēnos* is strictly no longer an instrument of daimonic control at this point, it is still there as a physical vessel containing Tat's new noetic body in which his soul now resides.

[123] CH XIII 15. Like Nock and Festugière, Holzhausen, Quispel and Salaman c.s. (HT II, 206; CHD, 183; WHCH, 69; HG, 160; but unlike RHT IV, 206; Grese, *Corpus Hermeticum XIII*, 23; Cop, 52) I assume that the first line must be spoken by Hermes. As for ποιεῖν τὰ καλά, there are various options: "faire ce qui est beau" ("do what is beautiful," CH II, 207), "do the beautiful things" (Grese, *Corpus Hermeticum XIII*, 25), "make something beautiful of it" (Cop, 52), "create works of beauty" (WHCH, 69), "to do what is good" ("het goede te doen" HG, 160; "das Gute zu tun" CHD, 183). The word "beauty" occurs in the Hermetic writings much more frequently than one might infer from most translations, which far too often interpret it in terms of "goodness." See e.g. SH IIB 2 and 4 (about how to live one's life "beautifully") and several instances in NH VI[6] (see below, Chapter 9).

[124] As also concluded, although with slightly more hesitation, by Bull, *Tradition*, 295–296.

liberated in principle from astral constraints, for the moment he still resides in his physical body. So should he use his new freedom to abandon it, temporarily or permanently? Hermes leaves it up to him to make up his mind about that question – he says that he understands Tat's desire (after all, even though the bodily vessel has been cleansed of darkness, it still remains heavy and earthbound) but leaves the rest for him to figure out.[125] The point is that Tat needs no further instruction, because like Hermes he has the power now to find his own way of "making things of beauty" – a remote echo of Diotima's teaching about what embodied existence should be all about. Immediately following this reference to beauty, Hermes remarks that the Ogdoadic powers in himself are now singing "in all things," that is, not just in the Ogdoad above the *heimarmenē* but everywhere in the cosmos all around them. Since Tat for his part hears nothing, it is hard to interpret this otherwise than as a rather teasing remark, and so the response is predictable: "Father, I want to hear and I want to know them [*noēsai*]!"[126]

Here we have Tat's second urgent request to Hermes. First he wanted to be reborn so that he might see and understand; and now that his noetic eyes are open, he wants to hear as well. As in the first instance, Hermes tells him to be silent; however, this time what follows is not a healing procedure but a ceremonial prayer described as "the hymn of rebirth."[127] Hermes remarks that he had not planned to reveal it so readily, which probably means that Tat's successful rebirth has taken him by surprise. He could not have revealed it to Tat in his unregenerate state, because like the rebirth itself, the hymn is "not taught, but hidden in silence."[128]

---

[125] An obscure passage in CH XII 7 seems to suggest that even if a person is governed wholly by the *nous* (presumably because s/he has experienced rebirth), his or her *physical* body still remains subject to astral fate. While I am not convinced by George Luck's hypothesis that this passage reflects a psychotherapeutic exercise of "voluntary suffering" ("Doctrine of Salvation," 35–37), it is possible that Hermes means to leave it up to Tat to decide whether he will just escape from the body or choose to share humanity's burden of suffering as long as his physical body remains alive. In this regard, cf. the Iamblichean concept of perfect souls descending into bodies voluntarily for the salvation of others, like theurgical *bodhisattvas* (Dillon, *Iamblichi Chalcidensis*, 243–244; Shaw, *Theurgy and the Soul*, 144 with note 1, 151).

[126] CH XIII 16.

[127] For other analyses (often mostly concerned with parallels and influences, which are interesting but not my chief concern here), see RHT IV, 243–251; Zuntz, "On the Hymns"; Grese, *Corpus Hermeticum XIII*, 171–188; Mahé, "Hymne hermétique"; Philonenko, "L'hymnodie secrète"; Whitehouse, "Hymns of the *Corpus Hermeticum*"; Podemann Sørensen, "Secret Hymn," 480–482; Bull, *Tradition*, 297–312.

[128] CH XIII 16.

Tat now receives ritual instructions about how the hymn is to be sung. One must stand up under the open sky, face south at the time of sunset, and then kneel down; at sunrise one must do the same while facing east. Therefore we see the same peculiar combination of south- and eastward directions as at the end of the *Logos teleios*.[129] Interestingly, Hermes is not just telling Tat what he should do right now; rather, he explains the general procedure to be followed, depending on whether the hymn is sung at sunset or at sunrise. Having received these instructions, Tat is told again to be silent.

I consider it of great importance to emphasize that what Tat gets to hear now is *not* "the song of the powers" that he has been asking for twice. He certainly hears a hymn, but it is sung or intoned by Hermes.[130] We will see that the experience has a strong impact on his inner noetic world; but it is clearly implied that whereas Hermes can hear the powers because he has already made his ascent to the Ogdoad, at least temporarily, Tat has not yet made that ascent and therefore still cannot hear them directly. To understand what is happening as the hymn unfolds, notice first that it involves a new invocation of the ten powers. They respond to Hermes' call, this time not by cleansing Tat of his torments but by hymning the divine Source of all that is. It may be helpful to break the hymn up in four sections, as follows: (1) a call for openness and silence; (2) an announcement of the song of the powers; (3) an invitation to those powers to start singing; (4) Hermes describing the hymn of the powers. The first section thus runs as follows:

> May all that exists in the cosmos listen to this hymn.
> Earth, open yourself!
> May all channels of rain open themselves to me!
> Trees, be still...
> I am about to sing to the Lord of Creation, the All and One.
> Heavens, open yourselves!
> Winds, be still...
> May the immortal circle of Divinity receive my words.[131]

This is a generic call for silent receptivity, reminiscent of the "womb of wisdom in silence" that made Tat's rebirth possible. Silence is needed so

---

[129] See above, pp. 232–233; cf. RHT IV, 244–245.
[130] I was therefore mistaken in my initial and much shorter analysis: Hanegraaff, "Altered States of Knowledge," 149–151. The point was noted already by Festugière: "Tat wants to hear the hymn of the Ogdoad ... Hermes does not have it, but composes a hymn of the powers himself" (RHT IV, 243).
[131] CH XIII 17.

that the hymn may be heard; and the cosmos must open itself to receiving its message. We may assume that these lines are followed by a short intermission that allows the silence to deepen.[132] Now that all things in the cosmos are ready to pay attention, Hermes announces what he wishes to do:

> I want to sing to the one who made all that is,
> the one who fixed the earth and stretched out the heaven above,
> who made sure that apart from the ocean,
> sweet water would be available for the habitable and inhabitable land,
> for the sustenance and use[133] of all humans;
> the one who ordered fire to appear
> for both gods and humans to make use of it.
> Let us all together praise him who is high above the heavens,
> the creator of all that is.
> He is the eye of the *nous*,
> may he accept the praise of my powers.[134]

As so often in the Hermetica, the divine Source is praised for creating the cosmos and making it a good place for humans to live in. There is no way for this hymn to be interpreted in terms of ascetic world-denial, and we should assume that Tat gets the message. He may have to leave his physical body to actually hear the Ogdoadic hymn; but his new energetic body of rebirth already provides him limitless access to all the beauty and creative plenitude that is visually manifest in the cosmos. Having invited "everybody" to join him in the hymn, Hermes now addresses the powers specifically, inviting them to sing:

> You powers that are in me, sing to the One and All!
> Sing along with my will, all you powers in me!
> Sacred *gnōsis*: illuminated by you,
> it is through you that I praise the noetic Light
> and delight in the *joy* of *nous*.
> All you powers, sing with me!
> You too, *self-control*, sing with me!

---

[132] Cf. Mahé, "L'hymne hermétique," 279–280.
[133] See HT II, 207 and CHD, 184 note 528: while most of the manuscripts have κτίσιν ("creation"), the textual content makes it reasonable to prefer the rare variants κτῆσιν ("possession") or χρῆσιν ("use"). I follow Zuntz ("Hymns," 89) in choosing the latter. Water is useful to human beings but does not create them; presumably the idea is that water is necessary in order for creation to be sustained.
[134] CH XIII 17. Note how this hymn emphasizes the two forces of Life and Light that dominated a country like Egypt: the water of the Nile and the energy of the Sun, with above them the ultimate Source here referred to as the eye of the *nous*. We will return to this ultimate triad below, Chapter 9, pp. 278–282.

> My *justice*, sing through me to what is just!
> *Generosity*, praise the All through me!
> *Truth*, sing praise to the Truth!
> *Goodness*, sing praise to the Good!
> *Life* and *Light*: from you comes this praise and to you it returns.[135]
> I thank you, Father, energy of the powers!
> I thank you, God, power of my energies!
> Through me your *logos* praises you.
> Through me accept all of it in speech, a verbal offering.[136]

Hermes mentions nine of the ten powers by name – poor *perseverance* is forgotten or, more likely, got overlooked by a scribe. But it does not matter much, for the noetic energies respond to the invocation and begin to sing. Not just that: they are positively shouting! Rather than sing along with them now, Hermes tells Tat what he is hearing:

> This is what the powers in me are shouting: they praise the All.
> They fulfill your will, for your will comes from you and returns to you, the All.
> Accept from all a verbal offering.
> *Life*: preserve the All that is in us!
> *Light* that is spirit and God: illuminate it!
> For the *nous* guides your *logos*,
> you who carries the spirit and who are the maker of the world.
> It is you who are God, and your Human is shouting
> through fire, through air, through earth, through water,
> through the spirit, through your creatures!
> From you I have learned to praise the *aiōn*
> and by your will I have found the rest I sought.
> As you willed it, I have seen.[137]

Again we see confirmation that the grand Human who united with Nature (CH I 14) is the generating agent active behind the scenes; he caused these divine energies to be born in Hermes and Tat, as a noetic *logos* that drove away the torments and assumed their place. His divine voice is shouting through all the elements, the *pneuma*, and all living creatures. As always,

---

[135] Similar to the hymn of CH V 10–11 (see discussion above, pp. 231–232), see the explicit point of nonduality that is being made here: Hermes is praising the noetic world of Life and Light, but in fact this means that those powers are praising themselves.
[136] CH XIII 18 (italics added for emphasis on the "powers").
[137] CH XIII 19–20. My translation of lines 4–5 is more interpretative than literal; cf. Bull, *Tradition*, 307 with note 289. Like Festugière, Grese, Copenhaver and Holzhausen (RHT IV, 164; *Corpus Hermeticum XIII*, 30; Cop, 53; CHD, 187), but unlike Nock, Salaman c.s. and Quispel (HT II, 208–209; WHCH, 70; HG, 162) I assume that the words τὴν εὐλογίαν ταύτην λεγομένην belong not to the hymn but to the following remark by Tat.

the message is one of reverence and astonished wonder at the miracle of creation, filled with gratitude for all the blessings of Life and Light that come from the universal Source.

The hymn is followed by an intriguing exchange. Tat says that he, too (presumably like Hermes himself), has recorded [*tetheika*] it "in his cosmos." But Hermes corrects his formulation: he should say "in the noetic." This can only be a reference to the inner world of the incorporeal imagination to which Tat gained access when he became the *aiōn*. The remark makes sense because, as we have seen, the imagination is defined by its capacity to store images so that it functions as a kind of cosmic memory[138]; however, the implication is that it can record speech as well. Tat accepts the correction and says that "he can do it now," "he has the power" [*dunamai*] because "from your hymn and your praise, my *nous* has been fully illuminated."[139] There is no further mention of his desire to hear the powers sing.

Inspired by Hermes' hymn, Tat now wants to express a hymn of his own. Hermes warns him to be cautious (*mē askopōs*), another reminder that terminological precision is of the essence. But Tat is full of confidence now: "Father, I say what I perceive in my *nous*."[140] The prayer that follows is actually very short:

> To you, God, first originator of generation,
> I, Tat, send verbal offerings.
> God, you are Father, you are Lord, you are *Nous*.
> Accept from me verbal [offerings] as you want,
> for all is done as you wish it.[141]

These lines have remarkably little content, and are probably just a proem to an actual prayer that got left out of the manuscripts.[142] This is suggested by the fact that Hermes responds by telling Tat to send God an acceptable offering (presumably because he yet has to begin), while

---

[138] Bull draws an interesting comparison here with the discussion of cosmic memory in *Ascl.* 32 (*Tradition*, 309–310).

[139] CH XIII 21. Contrary to commentators such as Scott (II, 405–406; see Bull, *Tradition*, 310–311), I see nothing puzzling in this remark. To argue that Tat has already been enlightened and therefore cannot get enlightened even further reflects a far too rigid way of thinking; on the contrary, as indicated above, Tat's education is far from completed after the rebirth.

[140] CH XIII 21.

[141] CH XIII 21. This translation (largely modeled after Bull, *Tradition*, 311) is an approximation. For the textual problems, see notably Zuntz, "On the Hymns," 69–71; for various solutions, compare the standard modern translations.

[142] Zuntz, "On the Hymns," 70.

specifying that he should add "through the *Logos*." Keeping in mind that burnt offerings such as frankincense or perfumes are not appropriate for the divine Source,[143] this confirms that the offering must be verbal – but not purely noetic, for Tat has as yet no personal experience with "hymns sung in silence." The following sentence is corrupt, but indicates that Tat thanks Hermes for his advice concerning the prayer.[144] Thus it is logical to assume that the lost original contained a full prayer that a scribe did not bother to copy.

And thus we reach the end of the treatise. Hermes expresses his delight at how the truth has given birth in Tat to something immortal, reminding him to preserve silence so as not to betray the palingenetic secret.[145] They have been working well together, he remarks, Hermes by speaking and Tat by listening.[146] It is through the process of rebirth that Tat has finally received *gnōsis*: "you have come to know yourself and our Father noetically" [*noerōs egnōs seauton kai ton patera ton hēmeteron*].[147] The daimonic powers of the cosmos have no control over him anymore, the passions no longer cloud his consciousness, and he is capable now of perceiving all things in God's incorporeal imagination. Tat has truly become alive now. Nevertheless, as we have seen, he has not yet reached the end of the path of Hermes. His consciousness is still in the cosmos. Far though he may have advanced, he has not yet experienced the Ogdoad, let alone the Ennead. Unlike Hermes, he yet has to hear the hymn of the powers.

---

[143] *Ascl.* 42; see discussion above, pp. 233–234.
[144] For various attempts to resolve the corrupt sentence, see Grese, *Corpus Hermeticum XIII*, 32 note 6.
[145] Similar exhortations in CH XIII 13. On the significance of the word διάβολος in both instances, see the subtle discussion in Van den Kerchove, *La voie*, 100–106.
[146] Festugière thinks that ἐπιμελεῖσθαι "leads us back to the classroom" where teacher and pupil work together on "a school exercise or a declamation" (RHT IV, 209–210). In a context such as this I consider that utter nonsense.
[147] CH XIII 22.

9

The Source

Nur in der Wortlosigkeit ist die Seele frei.
Hermann Kurzke[1]

The small town of Narmouthis in the Fayyum area of Middle Egypt is known today as Medinet Mari, "City of the Past." During the twelfth dynasty (1991–1783 BCE), a temple was built here for Renenutet, a goddess of harvest, birth and good fortune later known as Hermouthis in Greek.[2] She shared it with her consort Sobek, the crocodile god associated with fertility and the Nile who was known as Sokonōpis or Souchos during the Ptolemaic period. A shrine dedicated to the goddess Isis was added around this time, a so-called "contra-temple" meant to accommodate lay visitors who were not allowed to enter the inner sanctuary. Now the local goddess Hermouthis merged with the universal Hellenistic goddess Isis, as demonstrated by four hymns in Greek that were composed by a certain Isidorus and inscribed at the outer gates of the temple complex early in the first century BCE.[3] The first hymn shows how Hermouthis-Isis could be associated with a wide range of powerful goddesses worshipped by the Syrians, Lycians, Thracians, and Greeks, who knew her as the Mother of the Gods, Agathē Tuchē, Deo, Astarte, Artemis, Nanaia, Leto, Hera, Aphrodite, Hestia, Rheia, or Demeter. However, "the Egyptians call you Thiouis, since you alone are all the

---

[1] "Only in wordlessness is the soul free." Hermann Kurzke, "Immer auf dem Balkon?," 419; Kurzke in Mann, *Betrachtungen*, 29.
[2] Beinlich-Seeber, "Renenutet."
[3] Moyer, "Isidorus," 210–215. The hymns (in Greek original, with English translations and copious annotations) can be found in Vanderlip, *Four Greek Hymns of Isidorus*, 17–74.

other goddesses invoked by the nations."[4] This name is a Greek transliteration of the Egyptian tȝ wʿ.t: "the one," "the sole," "the unique."

Perhaps most striking about Isidorus' hymns is the exuberance with which they embrace and celebrate life, health, and the pursuit of happiness. First of all, the goddess is thanked for her gift of abundant harvests and fertility, made possible by the two great powers of Light and Life on which the whole of Egypt depended: the radiance of the Sun and the waters of the Nile. She alone saves humans from the threats of war and comes to their aid when they are "bound fast in prison, in the power of death ... in pain through long, anguished, sleepless nights ... bound in mortal illnesses in the grip of death."[5] The second hymn expands the scope of praise to include Hermouthis' consort Sobek, named "agathos daimōn, mighty Sokonōpis," and their son Anchoēs, "who inhabits the height of heaven."[6] Couples who want to have children should pray to them. Again the Nile is praised as the source of abundant fertility throughout the cycle of the seasons, and Hermouthis as the bountiful giver of good things to all those who are reverent (*eusebēs*): happiness and material abundance, "the blessings of children,"[7] a blissful life, soundness of mind, and opportunities to pass all these blessings on from one generation to the next.[8] To be alive in this world is a wonderful thing.

The fourth hymn turns its attention to the person who originally built this temple for the three deities Hermouthis-Isis, agathos daimōn Sokonōpis, and their son Anchoēs. This was the great pharaoh Amenemhet III, who lived in the ninth century BCE and whose projects of irrigation and land reclamation had made him very popular in the Fayyum area.[9] He was more than just a mortal man, Isidorus tells us, for he was born from the "great, great, and most great" agathos daimōn Sokonōpis (Sobek, Souchos) himself.[10] When the Egyptians translate the

---

[4] Transl. Moyer, "Isidorus," 219.
[5] Hymn I, lines 29–30 (Vanderlip, *Four Greek Hymns*, 17–19); Hymn II, line 7 (ibid., 34–36).
[6] Hymn II, line 9, 13 (Vanderlip, *Four Greek Hymns*, 45–36); Hymn III, line 33 (ibid., 50–51).
[7] Hymn II, line 30.
[8] Hymn III, esp. 4–11 (Vanderlip, *Four Greek Hymns*, 49–51).
[9] Bull, *Tradition*, 124–125.
[10] "For he was not a mortal man, nor was he born of a mortal lord / but he was the offspring of a great, eternal god: / of Souchos, the all powerful, the great, great, and most great; / he appeared as king and the son of Agathos Daimon" (Hymn IV, lines 22–25 [Vanderlip, *Four Greek Hymns*, 63–64]; Jackson, "New Proposal," 102; Moyer, "Isidorus," 235; Bull, *Tradition*, 126).

name of this "great immortal" pharaoh, they call him by his "throne name" Porramanres. Possibly this is where the name Poimandres comes from,[11] and the Hermetic community may have originated ultimately from cultic worship of Porramanres in the Fayyum area.[12] The merits of that hypothesis I leave for others to evaluate, but it would fit what we have been seeing throughout the previous chapters: very far from the gloomy dualism and pessimistic otherworldliness imagined by modern scholars obsessed by narratives of fall and decline, Hermetic spirituality was grounded in a strongly world-affirming perspective that fully embraced the positive values of life, fertility, and the pursuit of happiness. Against popular stereotypes of Egyptian religion, Jan Assmann points out that "the Egyptians hated death and loved life," as reflected already in one of the earliest wisdom texts that remained popular during the Roman era: "Heed: death counts little for us; heed: life counts much for us."[13] To a much larger extent than has been realized, this may have been true of Hermetic spirituality as well, for it is remarkable how little our texts have to say about the afterlife. We will see in this chapter that even the treatise about the soul's ascent from the realms of matter and the body towards those of "the Ogdoad and the Ennead" beyond the stars is not really about postmortem existence.

THE SILENT ONE

That Fayyum may have been the original center of Hermetic spirituality gains further support from Isidorus' references to agathos daimōn, "the good daimōn" who appears prominently as the male consort of Agathē Tuchē, "good fortune."[14] Isidorus' grandiloquent "great, great, and most great" prefigures the epitheton *trismegistos*, famously applied later to

---

[11] For this discussion, see Jackson, "New Proposal"; Van den Kerchove, "Poimandrès"; Bull, *Tradition*, 121–124. Moyer explains that while Amenemhet III was the name given to this pharaoh at his birth, Porramanres is a transcription of his "throne name" Ny-$M3^c$ (t)-R^c ("Isidorus," 236–237).

[12] Bull, *Tradition*, 121–131, 452.

[13] Assmann, *Death and Salvation*, 13, 17. For the general argument, see ibid., 1–20: the Egyptians perceived an unbroken continuity rather than a sharp boundary between life and death, and rather than suppressing death, they sought to "handle" the fact of bodily mortality by creating powerful "counter-images" of survival.

[14] Here my concern is with Agathos Daimōn's relevance to the spiritual Hermetica; but note that the name goes back to ancient Greece and appears in various other contexts in Hellenistic Egypt as well: see e.g. van den Broek, "Hermes Trismegistus I," 478; Ganschinietz, "Agathodaimon"; Cop, 164–165; Litwa, *Hermetica II*, 210 note 26.

"thrice-greatest" Hermes,[15] – who in fact seems to speak of Agathos Daimōn as his own spiritual master in CH XII. The description may be more significant than has been previously realized: "he alone ... as a first-born God [*hōs prōtogonos theos*] truly beheld the All and spoke divine words [*to panta katidōn theious logous ephthegxato*]."[16] Agathos Daimōn often spoke about the noetic unity of the all, but to Hermes' deep regret he never put his words down in writing. Thus the anonymous author of this treatise presents him as a human being whom he used to know, whose words carried very great authority, but who presumably is no longer alive. In view of our discussion in Chapter 8, the precise formulation "first-born God" suggests that he thought of Agathos Daimōn as the very first human being to ever be reborn divine and "become the *aiōn*," thereby gaining the ability to see all things as they appear in God's own incorporeal imagination (that is, to "truly behold the All"). This would make him the predecessor of both Hermes and Tat, an ideal model of spiritual accomplishment.[17] Thus behind the literary narrative, possibly we catch a glimpse of a powerful charismatic figure who may once have been active in the Fayyum area and would be an excellent candidate for the original founder of the Hermetic community.

The same mysterious wisdom teacher appears in several other Hermetic fragments that are preserved with minimal variants in two Christian treatises: a discussion of the Trinity attributed (rightly or wrongly) to the Alexandrian exegete Didymus the Blind, and Cyril of Alexandria's polemic against the emperor Julian.[18] We are told here that in three

---

[15] Moyer, "Isidorus," 235; Bull, *Tradition*, 127 (who points out that Agathos Daimōn is addressed as Trismegistus literally in a fragment preserved by Cyril of Alexandria, *C. Jul.* 2.30; see Litwa, *Hermetica* II, 212). For the debate on the name "Trismegistus," see Parlebas, "L'origine égyptienne"; Derchain, "Noch einmal 'Hermes Trismegistos'"; HHE I, 1–3, 14; Daumas, "Fonds égyptien"; van den Broek, "Hermes Trismegistus I," 475–476; Bull, "Hermes Between Pagans and Christians," 214.

[16] CH XII 8.

[17] Further support for this conjecture comes from a passage in al-Mubaššir ibn Fātik's eleventh-century collection of wise sayings, *Muḫtār al-ḥikam wa-maḥāsin al-kalim*: "In the beginning of his career [Hermes] was a student of Agathodaimon the Egyptian. Agathodaimon was one of the prophets of the Greeks and the Egyptians; he is for them the second Ūrānī, and Idrīs is the third Ūrānī, upon him be peace. The explanation of the name Agathodaimon is 'he of happy fortune'" (transl. van Bladel, *Arabic Hermes*, 186). See also above, Chapter 4, pp. 89-90, about the first transmission of true chemical knowledge attributed by Zosimos to Chemeu, identified by Christian Bull as Agathos Daimōn/Kmēph; and see CAA II 208 for an intriguing reference to "the adepts of Agathos Daimōn" (οἱ Ἀγαθοδαιμονῖται).

[18] Based on the fullest comparative analysis to date, Crawford argues against a common source and concludes that Cyril must have been dependent on the author of *De Trinitate*

otherwise unknown discourses to Asclepius, Hermes relates how somebody (possibly "one of the ministers of the sanctuary in Egypt"[19]) once posed Agathos Daimōn a question, in response to which he spoke about the universal Spirit (*Pneumatos*) on which the universe depends. While this Spirit carries all things, keeps them alive and provides them with nourishment, still it is not the ultimate reality. In its turn, it depends upon "the holy fountain [*tēs hagias pēgēs*], eternally existing as a helper to spirits and a source of life for all [*zōēs apasin aei huparchon*], while yet being one."[20] The Christian author who made the excerpt went on to praise the nobility of this teaching about "the self-sufficient Triad which is undefiled, immeasurable, unspeakable, and forever the same." So great is its majesty that "no human is high-minded and lofty enough to behold something proper to it."[21] He then picks up the direct quotation again:

[I]t is not possible to deliver such mysteries to the uninitiated. Just listen with your *nous*: there existed one single noetic light prior to the noetic light, and it is forever the *nous* of the luminous *nous*, and it was nothing else than its unity. Although existing eternally in it, it eternally contains everything by its own *nous* and light and *pneuma*. ... Outside of this one there is no God, no angel, no daimon, nor anything else [*ouk ousia tis allē*]. For he is Lord of all, and Father, and God, and source [*pēgē*], and life, and power, and light, and *nous*, and *Pneuma*, and everything is in him and under him.[22]

Given the way the fragment is presented, I assume that these words were attributed not to Hermes but to Agathos Daimōn. The special importance of this passage lies in the fact that it focuses *not* on the divine *nous* that

---

rather than the reverse. He also argues that the heavily contested question of authorship of *De Trinitate* is still by no means settled and seems to lean cautiously towards the traditional attribution to Didymus ("Reconsidering the Relationship," 251 with note 35). Therefore I assume that the original sequence of the fragments was probably that of the (ps.-)Didymus version (see table of comparison in ibid., 245–248). Agathos Daimōn also appears in several other fragments preserved by Cyril: see Litwa, *Hermetica II*, 210–212.

[19] Litwa, *Hermetica II*, 210 (HF 29) as well as 211–212 (HF 31, 32a–b): it could also be "one of the gods of the sanctuary," presumably Osiris.

[20] Migne, *Patr.Gr.* 39, 757; Scott IV, 172; HT IV, 128–129; CHD, 593; van den Broek, *Hermes Trismegistus*, 206; HG, 424; Litwa, *Hermetica II*, 207 (and 219 for parallel from the Tübingen Theosophy); Crawford, "Reconsidering the Relationship," 246–248.

[21] Migne, *Patr.Gr.* 39, 757; Scott IV, 173; van den Broek, *Hermes Trismegistus*, 206–207; HG, 611 note 959.

[22] Migne, *Patr.Gr.* 39, 757, 759; Scott IV, 173–174; HT IV, 126–127; CHD, 592; van den Broek, *Hermes Trismegistus*, 207; HG, 423–424; Litwa, *Hermetica II*, 206 (and 217 for parallels from the Tübingen Theosophy); Bull, "Hermes between Pagans and Christians," 235–236; Crawford, "Reconsidering the Relationship," 247.

dominates almost all of the literature in which Hermes plays the central role, but on a level that is even *beyond* it. The *nous* itself comes from an ultimate "fountain" or "source" that is described, no fewer than three times, in deliberately paradoxical terms: it is the unique "noetic light prior to the noetic light," "the *nous* of the luminous *nous*," and it "contains everything by its own *nous* and light and *pneuma*." In short, there is a *nous* beyond the *nous*; we might perhaps say that it is that which appears as "noetic" to the *nous* itself, similar to how the *nous* is noetic for us. Although technically this makes it "hypernoetic," the text does not bother to make such a distinction. Agathos Daimōn says that in an ultimate sense, absolutely nothing *truly* exists except this single (hyper) noetic source alone – "no God, no angel, no daimon, nor anything else." This obviously includes all those so-called realities that appear to human consciousness and take up the bulk of discussion in the Hermetic literature, notably "life," "power," "light," "*pneuma*," and even the "*nous*" itself. In our human efforts at making sense of reality, we cannot do without such concepts and distinctions; but from the radically nondual perspective of the ultimate Source itself, they do not truly exist – as far as the Source is concerned, even the *nous* would paradoxically not be a *noumenon* but ultimately just a *phenomenon*, an appearance.

Therefore all the mental constructs that follow from our dualistic consciousness are insufficient when it comes to capturing the one and unique Generative Source from which everything is eternally born – or rather, *seems* to be born, from our limited human perspective! For can we make any assumptions at all about how reality appears to the Source itself? We have seen that the author of the *Asclepius* professes his utter agnosticism about this nameless One to whom all names are equally appropriate:

> It cannot be captured, nor grasped, nor hunted down. Where it is, whither it is going, whence it has come, or how it is, or what – all that is uncertain. For it moves in sovereign stillness, and this stillness moves in it, be it God, or eternity, or both, or one in the other, or both in both.[23]

The utter incomprehensibility of the Source means that what strikes *us* as a logical contradiction between ultimate reality as *either* the "generative source" of being *or* the "self-sufficient absolute" beyond being must

---

[23] *Ascl.* 31; see pp. 54–55 for the connection with *Ascl.* 20. Like Holzhausen (CHD, 299 note 178), I assume that *sensibilis* in the first sentence of *Ascl.* 31 must be understood in terms of this text's convention of translating νοῦς by the Latin *sensus*: therefore not the world of the senses but the noetic world was "created as an image of God, an imitator of eternity."

itself be a dualistic illusion.[24] Only those who were initiated into the true Hermetic mystery and could "listen with their *nous*" would noetically understand the paradox that the generative source indeed "moves in sovereign stillness," very much as we read in a famous fragment by Numenius:

[T]o have communion with the Good, one on one, you must remove yourself quite far from the senses, to where there is nothing human, nothing living, no body either large or small, only a marvellous, wholly unspeakable and indescribable solitude – the home of the Good, its self-sufficiency and splendor, and the Good itself: peaceful, benevolent, who is tranquil, who is sovereign, and smilingly floats above Being.

But if somebody still attached to the senses imagines seeing the Good coming towards him, and then flatters himself to have encountered the Good, he is totally mistaken. For to approach it, you need a method that is anything but easy and more than human.[25]

The authors of the Hermetica claimed to have discovered such a method. A large part of the difficulty that Numenius mentions came from the fact that one had to be reborn as an entity that was more than human: divine (*theias*). We have seen that this rebirth resulted in a permanent state of cosmic consciousness, referred to as *aiōn*, that was no longer constrained by the harmful passions and daimonic energies linked to place and time. Only the very few who managed to come this far would be able to take the next step and establish perfect conscious communion with the *Nous* – an ultimate state of spiritual attainment that would open them up to immediate perception of the ultimate Good itself. Importantly, as seen in the Numenius fragment, this would *not* involve an experience of the Good "coming towards" the practitioner by revealing its presence to his consciousness. Why? Because it was always already doing so! This point is essential to grasp: from a Hermetic perspective, the entire cosmos is a temple filled with Life and Light, and thus the inexhaustible beauty and splendor of all things in it is nothing else than the continuous and infinitely generous self-manifestation of divinity in its own sacred space. Moreover,

---

[24] I am referring again to the famous distinction by Lovejoy between the "two gods of Platonism": see above, Chapter 3, p. 55 note 29. As indicated earlier, the distinction is of great importance to my general argument because, in line with Festugière, the "generative source" would suggest the "optimistic" and "world-affirming" perspective of *la religion du monde* (RHT II) as opposed to the "self-sufficient absolute" that became a "gnostic" *dieu inconnu* (RHT IV).

[25] Numenius, fr. 2. I have taken inspiration from the translations by des Places ([Numenius], *Numénius: Fragments*, 43–44) and Festugière (RHT IV, 129–130). Because translating διατριβαί and ἀγλαΐαι as "pastimes and festivities" makes little sense in this context, I translate the former as "self-sufficiency" to convey the sense of the Good being entirely by and with itself (spending time with itself, so to speak), and the latter as "splendour" (in line with common meanings of the word in Greek mythology). I am grateful to Nicholas Banner for stimulating noetic discussions that directed me towards the Numenius fragment.

no other space exists! Rather than waiting for some special vision, as if all of these gifts were not enough, human beings therefore need to "open their heart" and see what is *already* there all around them. This is what was meant by wonder and astonishment (*thaumazein*), the foundations of reverence (*eusebeia*) and gratitude – the supreme Hermetic virtues.

We have seen that Hermetic rebirth meant salvation from incarnational constraints. By liberating the soul from *kakia* (anything bad or harmful), it enabled human beings to use their condition of embodiment effectively as servants of the Source. Like ideal priests in the temple of the whole world, their job was to help channeling divine beauty, goodness and truth *into* the world of the senses rather than continuing to inflict harm on others and themselves. But while those who had become *aiōn* enjoyed a superior cosmic consciousness, this still did not mean that they had been joined in communion with the other souls in the Ogdoad *beyond* the cosmos, had achieved perfect union with the *Nous* in the Ennead, or had perceived the ultimate Source itself. If Agathos Daimōn was considered to be the first one to have achieved rebirth, it makes sense that he was also the first to have received this vision so that he could speak with authority about the One. As will be seen in this chapter, Hermes Trismegistus was believed to have followed in his footsteps, after which he opened up the door for his pupil Tat as well.

DIMENSIONS OF LIFE

To properly understand this vision of the Source, as described in a unique Coptic treatise known as *The Ogdoad and the Ennead*, we first need to clarify the basic Hermetic perspective on death. The basic point is very simple: *it does not exist*! Hermes makes this very clear for instance in CH XII:

> This entire cosmos (this great God, image of the even greater one, united with God and preserving with him the order and will of the Father) is the fullness [*plērōma*] of life. And through the eternal duration of the cyclical recurrence that comes from the Father, there is nothing either in the whole of it or in its parts that is not alive. There has never been anything dead in the cosmos, nor is there or will there be any such thing.[26]

---

[26] CH XII 15; see also CH VIII 1 (the word "death" refers to some kind of destruction, but in fact nothing in the cosmos ever gets destroyed); XI 14 ("all is alive"); *Ascl.* 29 ("if the world is a living being that lives forever, in the past, present, and future, then nothing in the world is mortal. Since each part of it ... is always alive and finds itself in a world that is itself a single living thing that lives forever, there is no place for mortality in the world"); SH XI 2:9 (I follow Festugière's translation "in its totality, substance [οὐσία] is immortal; in its totality substance is changeable" [HT IV, 54], cf. Litwa, *Hermetica II*, 69; by adding the negation

The Source brings forth only life, never death. What human beings refer to as "death" is therefore an empty word with no reference to anything real.[27] No actual destruction of life ever occurs, only a natural process of *bodily* dissolution followed by transformation: when the body gets old and is worn out by continuous use, it can no longer sustain life, therefore it falls apart and its elements are recycled by nature so that new bodies can be formed from it.[28] That is all, Hermes tells his pupils in the *Asclepius*, "nothing to worry about"[29] – although, admittedly, once upon a time he himself had needed some reassurance from the *Nous*:

> As for death, it is not the destruction of what has been assembled but just the dissolution of their union. … this change is called "death" because the body dissolves while life vanishes into the invisible. Since you are listening to this with fear and trembling,[30] dear Hermes: everything that is said to be dissolved, including even the cosmos itself, I tell you that they merely change because some part of them becomes invisible every day, but does not really dissolve. That is what happens with the cosmos: cycles and processes of dissolution. But those cycles are just returns, and those dissolutions mean renewal.[31]

"not," Holzhausen and van den Broek change the meaning into its opposite [CHD, 369 and HG, 320]; SH XI 2:10, "in its totality, being is double" I see as specifying the previous statement); HD VIII 3 "Humanity has the capacity of killing, God of giving life" (but apparently not of giving death); HD VIII 7 "You do not have the power of becoming immortal, neither does the immortal have the power of dying" (since the human essence is divine Life, it can neither die nor go through a process from mortality towards immortality).

[27] CH VIII 1 (κενόν); the speaker even suggests that the actual meaning of the word "mortal" may be "immortal" – it's just that the first syllable got lost. HD X 6: "death, correctly understood, is immortality; if not understood, it is death" (the statement has interesting parallels in other Armenian sources, see HT V, 277). Similarly, Hermes in CH XII 16–18 repeats twice how easily we get confused by the terminology (προσηγορία) of "death."

[28] SH IIA 16: "Without decay [φθορᾶς] there can be no birth. Every birth is followed by decay so that new beings may be born." Likewise in SH III 3, XI 2: 4–5, 35; HD II 3. In both instances the author seems to deliberately avoid the term "death," instead calling it "the movement of perishable bodies." Not all authors are so attentive, so they sometimes slip into common parlance, for instance HD I 5, II 3.

[29] *Ascl.* 27; NH VI[8] 76, 10–19 (here 17). See also CH I 20, 22, 24 (ἀλλοίωσις); VIII 1, 3–4; XI 2; XII 16–18 ("dissolution is not death, it is just the falling apart of a mixture. [Living beings] are dissolved, not to be destroyed, but to be remade"); XIII 14; XVI 9.

[30] My translation of δεισιδαίμων ὡς ἀκούεις is a matter of interpretation (see discussion in Cop, 171). On the fascinating term δεισιδαιμονία, see Hanegraaff, *Esotericism and the Academy*, 159–164. Holzhausen speaks of *religiöser Ängstlichkeit* (CHD, 132); somewhat similarly, I assume that the text means to refer not just to a "devout" or "reverent" attitude, for which the author would probably have preferred the standard term *eusebeia*. This indication of fear on Hermes' part in a discussion about "death" would seem reminiscent of a strange isolated statement in HD VI 3: "Get a hold of yourself, Trismegistus!" If there is a connection, the intended speaker could be inferred to be the *Nous*.

[31] CH XI 14–15. About the processes of generation/birth and dissolution, see also SH III 6; IV 10–11; XI 2:31–35.

Being born means becoming visible, similar to how the world appears to our vision at the break of dawn; and just as the world disappears for us after sunset, life is not destroyed but just becomes invisible to our conscious awareness when the body dissolves. The process of dissolution and of "life vanishing into the invisible" is described in CH X: the life-giving spirit (*pneuma*) withdraws from the body into the soul, while the blood coagulates so that it can no longer flow through the arteries. Thus deprived of the *pneuma's* circulation, the body stops moving and begins to fall apart.[32]

During incarnation, the *nous* had been safely enveloped all around by its *logos*, this *logos* in turn by the soul, and finally the soul by the *pneuma*.[33] These protective layers were necessary because the physical body cannot endure direct contact with the superior energy of the *nous*, whereas the *nous* cannot tolerate direct contact with the impure bodily passions either.[34] Now that the body dissolves, the *nous* can shed its envelopes. It replaces them by a fiery robe of its own, which it could not wear during incarnation because even a tiny spark of it would have destroyed the physical body.[35] Making use of this shining vehicle, the *nous* is now free from all constraints: "it moves around everywhere while leaving the soul to the judgment and justice it deserves."[36] What we find then is that the difference between embodiment and disembodiment (what we confusingly refer to as "life" and "death") is really a difference in conscious awareness. Being born in the body means becoming aware of the world of the senses while forgetting the greater life of the soul. Through the reverse

---

[32] CH X 13; HD VI 1; IX 5; but see the contradiction between CH X 13 and 16, discussed in HT I, 131 note 56. Holzhausen seems to have found the most convincing solution (CHD, 108 note 299): Hermes means to say that *during incarnation* the soul is in the *pneuma* that circulates through the body by means of the blood, whereas disincarnation means that the *pneuma* withdraws into the soul because the coagulated blood can no longer contain it. For the process of dissolution, cf. CH I 24. For the life-giving *pneuma*, cf. SH XIX 5–6 (whereas the *logos* can look upward to contemplate Beauty, the αἰσθητικὸν πνεῦμα, "sensate pneuma," is distributed through the five senses so that it can judge phenomenal realities; hence sensory perception stops when the *pneuma* can no longer circulate, but the soul is still able to perceive bodiless *phantasmata*). This *pneuma* would seem to be closely equivalent to or identical with the ἀτμός mentioned in SH XXVI 13 (cf. the Armenian šunč in HD I 4, II 1, II 6, with discussion in HT V, 214 note 11, 217 note 24, and HG, 615 note 987).

[33] CH X 13. I would tend to read SH XI 2:37 from such a perspective: one might as well say that the *nous* is in the body, enveloped by these layers, as that the body is enveloped by them.

[34] CH X 17.

[35] CH X 18.

[36] CH X 16.

process falsely called "death," we regain our soul's awareness while forgetting the life of the senses.[37] Only the *rebirth* allows us to enjoy the best of both conditions, as we have seen: enjoying an immortal body that will never be dissolved,[38] while yet being able to use superior noetic senses that provide unlimited access not just to our immediate environment but to the whole of the cosmos. This is the ideal condition of "the human as double" who participates simultaneously in body and *nous*.[39]

While death had no true *reality* in the Hermetic worldview, it did have a *meaning*. As in Egyptian culture more generally, a person could be "more or less alive and also more or less dead or subject to death."[40] Allowing one's life to be dominated by the destructive passions that worked through the body meant falling under the sway of death. Because this condition of "living in darkness" was an almost inevitable side effect of embodiment, as we have seen, such a severely diminished way of living (a kind of dim or shadowy half-life) was the default human condition from which Hermetic practitioners were trying to heal themselves and others. That most people "keep wandering in darkness, deluded by the senses and subject to death" therefore does not refer to their physical mortality but to their failure to live life as it should be lived.[41] Likewise, when Hermes laments a future time when Egypt will be a spiritual desert "filled completely with tombs and corpses" because "shadows will be preferred over light" and "death will be considered more meaningful than life,"[42] he refers to a degenerate culture in which people are physically alive but spiritually dead. In sharp contrast, the

---

[37] CH X 15: as the soul is dragged down by the heaviness of the body, it "gives birth to forgetfulness" (λήθη), and "it is the forgetting that corrupts her." Conversely, those who leave the body experience "the same thing" (CH X 16), i.e. forgetfulness: the sensory world sinks into oblivion. This reading is confirmed by CH XII 18: being born means becoming aware of the sensory world, while what we call death means forgetfulness of that world. The same point is made in HD VI 2, which draws an exact parallel between physical birth and the soul's birth in the nonmaterial that we think of as death (HT V, 236 with note 85 referring to van den Broek's convincing emendation of ἐκτός to ἐντός, see HG, 618 note 1013); similar point in HD IX 5.

[38] CH XIII 14. SH XI 2:17 perhaps alludes to this point.

[39] See also HD VI 1. For concepts of "the human as double" in antiquity (Platonism, Manichaeism, early Christianity), see Stang, *Our Divine Double*; on some modern conceptualizations, see Kripal, *Authors of the Impossible*, 58–66.

[40] Assmann, *Death and Salvation*, 12.

[41] CH I 19. Likewise for CH I 28–29 ("surrendering oneself to death" or "choosing the way of death") and the extreme reference to the body as "this living death" (CH VII 2; cf. the "sluggish soul" that is "held down by the body," CH X 24). See also HD VII 3: the soul is born from Light into the darkness of the body.

[42] *Ascl.* 24–25.

treatise about *aiōn* says that true life means using all one's senses to the fullest, like God himself:

> [Y]ou see and you speak and you hear and you smell and you taste and you walk and you think [*noeis*] and you breathe – and it is not one person who sees, someone else who hears, someone else who speaks, yet another who tastes, another who smells, another who walks, and another who thinks [*noōn*], and yet another who breathes. It is one single person who does all these things. None of those activities would be possible without God. If you don't do them anymore, then you're dead. Likewise if God would not do them – but it isn't right to even say this – then he would not be God.[43]

We have seen that as the *nous* abandons the scene to go roaming the cosmos in its fiery vehicle, it leaves the soul to "the judgment and justice it deserves." Yet the Hermetica tell us remarkably little about the soul's afterlife, and even less about its pre-incarnational existence.[44] Putting the scant pieces of evidence together, it appears that the critical condition required for salvation was *not* whether a person had achieved rebirth or attained perfect *gnōsis* but whether he or she had "passed the test of reverence." This formulation appears in CH X and is defined there as "knowing the divine and harming no other human being."[45] I have been emphasizing the central importance of *eusebeia* to Hermetic spirituality and want to stress it once again: we are not dealing with an arrogant elitism that reserves salvation for only the few, but with a spiritual perspective that placed the emphasis on an ethical life and would like to see the best for all human beings.[46] While the path of rebirth and perfect *gnōsis* was certainly steep and demanding, every human being could live a life of reverence grounded in gratitude and respect for the beauty of the cosmos and concern for the well-being of others.

About the fate of those who fail the test of reverence, we are given somewhat conflicting information. In line with the concept of continual

---

[43] CH XI 12. The speaker stops just short of the sacrilegious statement that "God would be dead" (as if the Source of life itself could ever die).
[44] We find some general statements such as that all souls "whirling around in the cosmos" have originated from the single soul of the All (CH X 7), and cf. SH XXVI.
[45] CH X 19. See also *Ascl.* 11 ("the standard [or measure: *mensura*] for this double entity – the human being – is first of all reverence [*religio*], followed by goodness"); CH XVI 11 (the gods can overlook everything except irreverence, see above, p. 196). SH IIB is entirely about *eusebeia*: the answer to Tat's question about how one should live one's life is "be reverent, my child!"
[46] Unlike Van den Kerchove (*La voie*, 48, 105), I see no evidence for attitudes of "distrust" or "suspicion" (*méfiance*) towards the unenlightened multitudes, but rather of regret and sadness about their blindness and ignorance.

transformation of all things in the cosmos, most of our treatises speak in general terms about reincarnation in human or animal bodies.[47] However, one unique passage in the Coptic version of the *Logos teleios* (and its shorter parallel in the *Asclepius*) suggests a somewhat different scenario. It says that the test is administered by a powerful divinity (*daimōn*)[48] who resides halfway between earth and heaven and whose job is to examine a person's previous behavior. No soul that leaves the body can avoid meeting him. Confusingly, this passage makes no reference to reincarnation: on the contrary, the soul of a person who has spent his life doing evil "has no place either on earth or in heaven." It will find itself thrown violently into all directions throughout the cosmos forever, tormented endlessly by the elements of air, fire and ice. Worst of all, because death does not exist, this condition will never end.[49] Nevertheless, Hermes seems to suggest in another passage that such torments are not even necessary, because irreverence is its own punishment:

> What fire produces greater flames than irreverence? What savage animal mutilates the body as much as the irreverent soul mutilates itself? Do you not see the tortures suffered by the irreverent soul when it cries out for help and shrieks "I am on fire, I am burning, what should I say or do, I do not know! I am being consumed, poor wretch, by the evils that possess me, I cannot see or hear anymore!" Are these not the cries of a soul that is being punished?[50]

It would seem then that not all Hermetic practitioners had exactly the same ideas about what would happen to those who failed the test of reverence. More important than the exact nature of the consequences was the

---

[47] Ascl. 12; CH II 17; IV 8; CH X 7-8, 19-22; SH XXIII 39-42; XXV-XXVI. See discussion in Bull, *Tradition*, 154-158. Bull proposes a solution to what would seem to be a contradiction in CH X about whether souls do or do not reincarnate into animal bodies. Still, his distinction between "three kinds of people" seems to play down the status of *nous* as a divine gift, a "prize to be won" that is theoretically available to all human beings (since the divine Source knows no envy and wishes to share its blessings with all, cf. CH IV 3; HD VIII 6) but can be given only to those whose virtuous life makes them capable of receiving it (see my discussion in Chapter 7, pp. 196-197). Note that the Hermetic affirmation of life has extremely severe consequences in CH II 17: the souls of those who remain childless are "condemned to enter a body that is neither male nor female, the kind that is cursed under the sun."

[48] See notably Bull, "Great Demon." Christian commentators of course identified this entity as a "demon," and Lactantius spoke of the *demoniarchēs* (ruler of demons, *Div. Inst.* II.14.6); but clearly this judge or overseer is a divinity in charge of punishing evildoers and not to be confused with the astral daimons (HG, 540 note 476; HT V, 182).

[49] NH VI[8] 76, 22-77, 37 / Ascl. 28; cf. SH VII 1-2 about a great female daimon or goddess who administers justice (*dikē*).

[50] CH X 20; similar in I 23.

ethical yardstick itself, on which they certainly agreed: *eusebeia*, respect and profound gratitude for the blessings of life. Those who fell short in this regard were tormenting themselves most of all, by cutting their connection with the only Source of true happiness; and as an inevitable result of this deficiency, they were inflicting harm on other living beings as well, from their fellow humans to the world as a whole. The gods could overlook almost every human weakness, as we already saw, with just this one exception: "only irreverence comes under their judgment."[51]

An attitude of reverence, not rebirth or *gnōsis*, was therefore the principle of separation between the good and the bad. The former are described in CH I as blessed, good, pure, merciful, and living lives of love; it is they who receive help from Poimandres so that "suddenly they know all things"; and so it is they who are able to let go of the harmful passions when their souls rise up through the cosmic spheres after the body's dissolution. Having abandoned all that used to diminish the presence of Life and Light, they are free to enter the Ogdoad and ultimately join the powers of the Ennead as well. Having received *gnōsis*, they become divine.[52] Therefore this "happy end" is *not* restricted to just a spiritual elite of Hermetic virtuosos. It is available for all humans who live their lives the way they should be lived. Reverence is sufficient to receive the gift of *gnōsis*.

Admittedly though, the reverent would not receive it until after their bodies had been left behind. By contrast, a very small number of devoted practitioners could manage to attain *gnōsis* already *during* embodiment – and this is what the rebirth was all about. As the "torments of matter" had already been expelled and they were enjoying a pure noetic body free from the cosmic constraints of time and space, there would be nothing left for them to surrender to the planetary daimons. As a result, they would not even need to "rise up" through the spheres in any literal or vertical sense, but could be up there in the Ogdoad from one moment to the next, as will be seen. Before we turn to that culminating experience, we need to look at the nature of the levels of life in the Hermetic universe: what exactly was meant by the Ogdoad and the Ennead, and how did they relate to the ultimate Source?

From the perspective of human beings moving upwards, the lower levels of life are rather unproblematic: from pure matter at the very bottom, the soul ascends through the seven planetary spheres that together constitute the cosmos, as delineated in CH I 25: the Moon, Mercury, Venus,

---

[51] CH XVI 11.
[52] CH I 22, 24–26; cf. XII 11 ("release from passibility").

the Sun, Mars, Jupiter, and Saturn. Much more difficult to understand are the three highest levels "above the cosmic framework": the Eighth or Ogdoad, the Ninth or Ennead, and finally that which I have referred to as the Source. The problem is that our dualistic consciousness leads us to imagine this triad in *spatial* terms, as three vertical levels stacked on top of the cosmos. Hence we think of the soul as leaving the cosmic domain, traveling upward through the Ogdoadic sphere, then leaving it again to enter the higher Enneadic sphere, and finally coming to rest there while gazing up to the highest level above it. In picturing the process this way, we forget that the very conditions of space and time pertained strictly to the seven-leveled cosmos, not to hypercosmic reality. From the nondualist perspective of the one and only Source, our spatial imagination is a mere concession to our limited understanding. We can also see this by being attentive to the tricks that language plays on our mind: we naturally call the Source "superior" to our own inferior point of view, but in doing so we misconstrue the relation in terms of vertical space. In fact the source cannot be superior, either spatially or even ontologically, because nothing else *is* – not even non-being.[53]

Thus it is not out of obscurity but because they wanted to be precise, that our authors are struggling so hard to convey some sense of perfect *gnōsis* through the imperfect medium of *logos* – an instrument that, unlike *nous*, simply cannot "get as far as the truth."[54] A particularly clear

---

[53] For this important notion reminiscent of Parmenides (below: Epilogue, p. 359 note 27), see also CH II 13 "he has left no room for non-being. All things that are, come into existence from things that are, not from things that are not"; and HD IX 1 "God is all things, and there is nothing external to God, not even that which is not [οὐδὲ τὸ μὴ ὄν]." See HT V, 262 note 149 for the specification in Armenian "for God is nothing, not even a single thing." Whereas Mahé finds no parallel for this assertion elsewhere in the Hermetica (see, however, CH V 11: "you are even what does not exist"), I read it as a radical implication of Hermetic nonduality, peculiarly reminiscent of Derridean deconstruction: if there is no such thing as *non-being*, that makes it impossible to think of *being* as its counterpart, so the binary breaks down and "what truly is" could as well be called "what truly is not." I read SH IIA 18 along similar lines: because only true reality (ἀλήθεια, see Chapter 7, p. 201 note 57) really *is* while what is not truly real (τὸ ψεῦδός) *is not* – not even as nothingness –, illusion is necessarily a manifestation of the real. Likewise the intentional paradoxes in HD I 1 (continued in I 2) imply radical nonduality: that the noetic God is immobile would seem contradictory from our perspective but is correct from the perspective of the Source (which "moves in sovereign stillness": Ascl. 31), and this immobile/noetic God in turn is ultimately one with the human "reasonable world" (for the Armenian term at the end of this fragment, see the debate between van den Broek and Mahé: HG 614 note 984 and HT V, 212 note 4, cf. HHE II 359 note 4 and WHDH, 118 note 4; here I suspect that van den Broek's "according to its ideal form" is probably closer to the intended meaning).

[54] CH IX 10.

example occurs in CH IV, where the Source is referred to by standard Hermetic terminology as the One and the Good:

[Y]ou cannot move through the Good – it has no boundary or ending, and for itself it has no beginning either, even though to us it seems to begin when we first get to know it [*gnōsin*]. That *gnōsis* therefore doesn't mean the beginning of the Good itself; but for us it is the beginning of what we will get to know. So let's seize that beginning and hurry to make our way through all things. For it is a very tortuous path, to abandon what is familiar and present so as to return to what is ancient and primordial.[55]

Far from being located at the top of a vertical hierarchy, the One is therefore beyond space and time altogether. Hence you cannot move through it, the way you can move through "many bodies ... many choirs of daimons ... many astral cycles and circuits,"[56] nor does a return to "what is ancient and primordial" have anything to do with going back in time. To "abandon what is familiar and present" means letting go of the entire apparatus, including language (*logos*), that allows us to navigate in time and space.

If we take this seriously, that which appears from our perspective as the ultimate "Source" or "Fountain" of Life and Light is actually beyond any description or imagination: this motionless source of motion is the invisible source of the visual and the silent source of *logos*, so it simply "cannot be captured, nor grasped, nor hunted down."[57] While CH I refers to it as the "sovereignty" or "sovereign power" (*authentia*), elsewhere throughout the Hermetica it is called the One and the Good.[58] Again, we easily miss the radicality of these terms. That it is the One does not mean that there is a second or third next to it as well, but rather that it is the one and only true reality[59]: "there is just one single soul, one single life, and one single matter, [i.e.] the one God."[60] Likewise, that it is the Good does not mean that something bad exists next to it, but that the Good is all that is; thus what appears to us as evil has no real

---

[55] CH IV 8–9.
[56] This spatio-temporal counterpart to the Good is described immediately before the passage just quoted: CH IV 8.
[57] *Ascl.* 31 (see larger quotation above, pp. 54–55).
[58] For these equivalences and their possible backgrounds in Egyptian religion and Iamblichean Neopythagoreanism, see notably Bull, *Tradition*, 131–146
[59] CH IV 1 (ἑνὸς μόνου; cf. HT I, 49 note 1), 5 (τὸ ἓν καὶ μόνον), 8 (idem); X 14 (ἑνὸς καὶ μόνου); XI 5 (μόνῳ καὶ ἑνί). I read SH XXI along the same lines: "pre-existent Being" is the Source, its counterpart is perceptible reality (οὐσία αἰσθητή), and in between are the "noetic and perceptive deities" (νοηματικοὶ καὶ αἰσθητοὶ θεοί).
[60] CH XI 11. For matter as participating in the One and the Good, cf. VI 1–2 and XII 21.

existence but must be understood as *privatio boni*.⁶¹ What this all means is that the Ennead and the Ogdoad should not be understood as "levels" or even as true realities "below" the One and the Good, but as different ways in which the latter manifests itself in the mirror of our dualistic and spatiotemporal consciousness.

The Hermetica talk about the supra-cosmic triad in terminologies that reflect Egyptian and Platonic-Neopythagorean backgrounds and can be highly confusing. In Table 9.1, I make a rough attempt at listing the main equivalences, based on the primary sources combined with interpretations provided by Mahé and Bull.⁶² The columns on the right refer to two parallel systems which according to Iamblichus were explained by Hermes in what he refers to as his "20.000" or even "36.525" books.⁶³

TABLE 9.1: *The supracosmic Triad*

NH VI⁶	NH VI⁶	CH I	CH XIII	Iamblichus 1	Iamblichus 2
Source	Unbegotten	Sovereignty	The Good	One/Source	Eiktōn
Ennead	Self-begotten	Nous/Poimandres	Light	Monas	Kmēph
Ogdoad	Begotten	[Logos?]	Life	[Soul?]	Amoun [etc.]

It is of course confusing that in the Neopythagorean system provided by Iamblichus, the Source (*pēgē*) that is called the One brings forth another unity, the Monas, which is therefore equivalent to the Ennead of NH VI⁶, the ninth. The latter is clearly the *nous*, and often described as both Life *and* Light:⁶⁴ in CH XIII we are told that since the two are

---

⁶¹ See also HD X 4: "Evil is the absence of Good, the Good is its own fullness." For the divine Source as the Good, see also *Ascl.* 1, 14; CH II 14-15-16; IV 5, 8-9; VI 3-5; X 1-2, 6; XII 21; XIV 4, 9; HD III 4.
⁶² Mahé, "Générations antédiluviennes"; Bull, *Tradition*, 131-146 (who calls attention to the relevance of the passage in Iamblichus, *Response to Porphyry* VIII 2-3). Like Bull (*Tradition*, 317 note 3), I am wholly unconvinced by Mahé's parallels with Jewish Adam-speculations (Mahé, "Mental Levels") and biblical antediluvian generations (Mahé, "Générations"). Note that I bracket entities which I consider questionable: I am unconvinced by Mahé's argument (ibid., 164, 167, 169) that the *Logos* in CH I is equivalent to the Ogdoad; and I am aware that the "soul" mentioned in Iamblichus' first system derives merely from Moderatus of Gades' identification of the demiurgic mind with the soul (Bull, *Tradition*, 136). For my separation between Life and Light in CH XIII, see text.
⁶³ Iamblichus, *Response to Porphyry* VIII 1.
⁶⁴ CH I 9, 12, 21 32; CH XIII 9, 18.

really a unity, the decad of healing forces turns into a henad (yet another unity!).[65] Moreover, in CH I we read that as the seven primal humans were born, "life became soul and light became *nous*."[66] Keeping in mind that Hermes perceived the *Nous* (Poimandres) as a boundless expanse of lovable light,[67] this makes it reasonable to assume that a human's *nous* is linked to the Ennead and his or her life-force to the Ogdoad (while in addition, Light and Life were probably gendered as the male and female aspect of the androgynous *nous*). If so, the Ogdoad becomes the realm of individual living souls, while the Ennead is the boundless noetic realm of Light beyond individuality.[68] They are united insofar as only noetic souls can reach the Ogdoad, but can be distinguished insofar as these souls are looking "up" from there to the Ennead: living entities gazing at the Light.

The community of living souls that constitute the Ogdoad are *gennētos* ("begotten"): generated by or born from the Ennead. The Ennead for its part is androgynous and therefore capable of ceaselessly generating or giving birth to itself: *autogennētos*, "self-begotten." We might think of this boundless world of divine luminosity as a powerhouse of creative energy that keeps itself going through its own internal dynamics, like a never-ending chain of nuclear explosions. But even this supreme spiritual Light of manifestation cannot have pulled itself up by its own bootstraps out of nowhere, so to speak. Where did it come from? It comes from a mysterious Source (*pēgē*) that remains utterly beyond manifestation and is alien to even the very process of birth and generation: *agennētos* ("unbegotten").[69] While comparisons with modern cosmology are obviously risky, it might perhaps be helpful to think of the Hermetic triad as a metaphysical (obviously not a physical) parallel to how we imagine the relation between our world of living conscious organisms, the sun on whose Light

---

[65] CH XIII 12. Could we be dealing with a scribal error and the author meant ennead instead of henad? This would make the argument much more logical: if Light and Life are a unity, the decad is reduced to an ennead, which again becomes a decad if one separates the two.
[66] CH I 17.
[67] CH I 4.
[68] Cf. CH X 16; but also I 26. We have seen that as the body dissolves, the *nous* leaves the soul to be judged: clearly it carries no responsibility for the soul's individual actions.
[69] For the triad unbegotten/self-begotten/begotten, cf. Mahé, "Le sens et la composition," 63–64; Mahé, "ΠΑΛΙΓΓΕΝΕΣΙΑ"; Mahé, "La Création"; Mahé, "Le rôle de l'élément astrologique," 162–163. I suggest that when SH IIA discusses the Demiurgic Sun subordinate only to the Primal One, the author may be alluding at least partly to the Enneadic reality of Light on which all Life depends as distinct from the singular and unique reality of the One (SH IIA 14–15, with very helpful footnote in Litwa, *Hermetica II*, 33 note 16). Note the divergent statement in HD X 5, where *nous* is called unbegotten.

all life in our solar system depends, and the strictly unimaginable concept of some ultimate "(non)reality" on the other side of the Big Bang.

BEYOND REBIRTH

Back to earth. Leaving the Fayyum area in Middle Egypt and moving further south up the Nile, one would reach Chēnoboskion, a place that was frequented by Christian desert ascetics. Somewhere around here, at some moment after the middle of the fourth century CE,[70] an unknown Egyptian sat down to copy some Coptic treatises attributed to Hermes Trismegistus. Having finished his work, he scribbled down a few lines for the person who had requested them. He tells him that he has "very many," indeed "numerous" Hermetic texts in his possession but did not copy them because his client might already have them.[71] Thus we learn that a great number of Hermetic treatises in Coptic must have been circulating in this area at the time. Of course, modern scholars read this scribal note with feelings of enormous frustration, imagining how much more we could have known about the Hermetica if only this collection had been preserved or the scribe had decided to copy a few more treatises! As it is, he left us just three texts, discovered as part of the Nag Hammadi Library in 1945. Two of them (NH VI[7] and VI[8]) are parallel to parts of the *Asclepius* and the Papyrus Mimaut, as we have seen; but the third one (NH VI[6]) was entirely new. Although its title is lost, it is usually referred to as the treatise on *The Ogdoad and the Ennead* and has revolutionized scholarly research about the Hermetica since the early 1970s.[72]

---

[70] On the chronological window for the production of the Nag Hammadi codices, see Lundhaug and Jenott, *Monastic Origins*, 9–11; on the exact location, see ibid., 11–21 (and cf. Quack, "Koptische Version," 309, who calls Nag Hammadi as the exact location "rather misleading").

[71] "Scribal Note," NH VI 65, 8–14 (HT V, 146–147). Discussion in HHE II, 460–468; Lundhaug and Jenott, *Monastic Origins*, 197–206. It is generally assumed that "his" must refer to Hermes Trismegistus (ibid., 199 note 77), so that those numerous uncopied texts must indeed have been Hermetic (e.g. HG, 445; HT V, 146; cf. Lundhaug and Jenott, *Monastic Origins*, 199 note 78).

[72] In chronological order, see notably KL (1971); Keizer (1973); Tröger (1973); Mahé, "Le sens et la composition" (1974); Mahé, "Le sens des symboles sexuels" (1975); HHE I (1978); Tröger, "On Investigating the Hermetic Documents" (1978); Dirkse, Brashler and Parrott, "Discourse on the Eighth and Ninth" (1979); HHE II (1982); Fowden, *Egyptian Hermes* (1986); Mahé, "ΠΑΛΙΓΓΕΝΕΣΙΑ" (1986); Mahé, "Création dans les *Hermetica*" (1986); Camplani, "Alcune note" (1986); Mahé, "Générations antédiluviennes" (1988); Mahé, "La voie d'immortalité" (1991); Mahé, "Le rôle de l'élément astrologique" (1993); Mahé, "Reading of the *Discourse of the Ogdoad and the Ennead*" (1998); van den Broek,

The Source 283

As specialists began studying the Nag Hammadi Hermetica, they believed to see strong similarities between CH XIII and NH VI⁶.[73] This was natural enough, as both treatises stand out for their focus on experiential practice rather than theoretical discussion. The authoritative voice of Jean-Pierre Mahé went an important step further, insisting already in his earliest publications that both texts do not just display similarities but describe *one and the same process*: that of Hermetic regeneration or rebirth.[74] However, note the many qualifications and reservations (here italicized by me) that Mahé made in the first volume of his groundbreaking *Hermès en Haute Égypte*:

We will insist with him [Keizer] on an essential point: the fusion of the theme of *anodos psuchēs* [the soul's ascent] with that of the *palingenesia* [rebirth]. *In principle these two themes are distinct*, and in fact it so happens that *other Hermetic writings present them separately*. But one of the features that are original in CH XIII and NH VI⁶ consists in posing that the soul's regeneration by the divine intellect is an anticipation of the ascent to the heavens; *let us go further and state that the two realities are equivalent. Certainly*, in the one and the other, *the idea is expressed in a very different style* ... [etc.]. *But*... "[75]

"Let us go further..." But why? Like Jens Holzhausen and Christian Bull, I must respectfully disagree with Mahé's thesis.[76] Much of his argument reflects the widespread but incorrect assumption that CH I describes a catastrophic Fall or *de*generation of the primal Human, which then needs to be repaired by *re*generation as in CH XIII.[77] This makes the rebirth

---

"Religious Practices in the Hermetic 'Lodge'" (2000); Krause, "Die hermetischen Nag Hammadi Texte" (2002); Mahé, "Mental Faculties and Cosmic Levels" (2002); NHD (2003); Mahé, "L'hymne hermétique" (2007); Van den Kerchove, *La voie* (2012); Bull, "Monkey Business" (2017); Bull, "Visionary Experience" (2017); Bull, "Hermes between Pagans and Christians" (2018); Bull, *Tradition* (2018); HT V (2019).

[73] HHE I, 41–42 (referring to Dirkse, Rudolph, Tröger and Keizer).
[74] As also noted by Bull, *Tradition*, 316–317 (with references to Mahé in note 2).
[75] HHE I, 42. For a further argument adduced by Mahé against his own thesis, see HT V, ccxv.
[76] CHD, 509; Hanegraaff, "Altered States of Knowledge"; Bull, *Tradition*, 316–371 (Mahé's response in HT V, ccxiv–ccxvi, contains no decisive counter-arguments). As for the three points of disagreement between Mahé and me, as helpfully listed by Bull (*Tradition*, 317–318), I respond as follows. (1) CH XIII 13 does not actually say that "seeing oneself" is what defines the rebirth, but rather specifies it as "to no longer picture reality in three bodily dimensions." (2) The rebirth has nothing to do with a primal "Fall" of man (see text). (3) Like Bull I see no evidence for Mahé's suggestion that the "ritual embrace" of NH VI⁶ signifies rebirth (see discussion below, p. 297 note 127).
[77] Mahé, "A Reading," 82; Mahé, "Générations antédiluviennes," 165 (referring explicitly to what he believes to be parallels in Genesis); HT V, cclv–cclvi ("chute ... dégénération ... cette funeste migration").

into a reversal of the famous "Fall of Man," whereas I have argued that in fact it corrects the effects of the *normal* process of individual human birth. Furthermore, Mahé provides no clear evidence for his belief that Tat's rebirth occurs in the Ogdoad and the Ennead;[78] on the contrary, it seems evident from CH XIII that it happens here on earth in an Egyptian desert. Far from being just a different version of the same rebirth experience, *The Ogdoad and the Ennead* describes something new and different: a direct experience of supra-cosmic realities that was possible only for those who had already become the *aiōn*.

To properly contextualize this treatise, I want to repeat once more that Hermetic spirituality is all about *life*. As death is a nonreality, the universal Source produces nothing else than spiritual light and an unceasing flow of life-giving energy. Becoming truly alive means letting go of anything that limits our ability to perceive and experience this reality, the only one that truly is. But while the rebirth results in an embodied state of *cosmic* consciousness, it does not give access automatically to *hyper*cosmic realities beyond the seven planetary spheres. In NH VI[6] we read how Hermes and an unnamed pupil – although we do not know for sure, I will follow Christian Bull's example and call him Tat[79] – take the next and final step of entering the Ogdoad and perceiving the Ennead as it flows forth from the Source.

NH VI[6] begins very much like CH XIII, with Tat reminding Hermes of an earlier promise: he would lead his *nous* up into the Ogdoad and take him to the Ennead, as this is the order of the tradition. Hermes confirms this, but makes a cautious reservation. Success will depend on Tat's human condition, his ability to perceive each of the required steps in his *nous*. This means that he must have woken up from the state of oblivion that comes with bodily incarnation and have "remembered" his true noetic essence.[80] That this is a reference to the *palingenesis* of

---

[78] Mahé, "ΠΑΛΙΓΓΕΝΕΣΙΑ," 143 (convincingly refuted by Bull, *Tradition*, 318 note 9); HT V, ccxiv.
[79] Bull, *Tradition*, 318 with note 13.
[80] NH VI[6] 52, 9–13. Van den Broek points out that while the Coptic p̄ ⲡⲙⲉⲉⲩⲉ means "remembering," the intention here is that Tat must "have insight" in the sense of *noēsis* (HG, 627–628 note 1076); cf. Rob, 322 ("if you hold in mind," i.e. in *nous*) and long discussion in Keizer, 88–89 note 2 (who prefers "consciousness"). Mahé notes that the "human condition" mentioned in NH VI[6] 52, 10 refers to the state of forgetfulness caused by coming under the dominion of the planetary powers at being born (HT V, 80); hence "remembering" depends on being reborn.

CH XIII is confirmed by the discussion that follows, which is all about noetic impregnation, generation, and giving birth. Hermes looks back at an earlier occurrence:

> When, through the Power [*dunamis*], I had received the Spirit [*pneuma*], I transmitted the energy [*energeia*] to you. While the understanding [*noēsis*] is in you, in me the Power has become as though pregnant; for as I conceived from the Source that flowed in me, I gave birth.[81]

The description is sexually explicit. The Power (*dunamis*) that resides in Hermes is grammatically feminine and described here as a womb. It got impregnated by the *pneuma* (masculine) that was flowing from the Source, so that Hermes could give birth to an *energy* (feminine) and transmit it to Tat.[82] We saw in CH XIII 2 how the womb of rebirth was described as "noetic wisdom in silence," impregnated by spiritual semen emitted by "the will of God." This resulted in the birth of a new body of divine Powers which, like everything noetic in the Hermetic universe, must have its own capacity of bringing forth new offspring. Tat here was the passive recipient of active life-giving Powers while Hermes seemed to play the role of a midwife, a facilitator of rebirth. Because the entire process is concerned with noetic energies that would be invisible to external observers, it must require some kind of intimate "energetic connection" or sympathetic *rapport* between the "father" and his spiritual "son."[83] The constellation is somewhat different in NH VI⁶, but again we will see Hermes in the active role of mediator or facilitator who guides Tat into a new level of visionary awareness. The former is channeling noetic energy while the latter is focusing on *noēsis*.

---

[81] NH VI⁶ 52, 14–20.

[82] For the gender aspects, see Keizer, 90–91 note 4. Cf. NH VI⁷ 64, 22–27 (quoted above, p. 235): "O Womb of all generation, we have known you! O Womb inseminated by the Father's nature, we have known you!"

[83] The concept of *rapport* was central to eighteenth-nineteenth century Mesmerism and Mesmeric somnambulism, a phenomenon that I see as remarkably similar in some crucial respects to the practical dimensions of Hermetic spirituality. See e.g. Ellenberger, *Discovery of the Unconscious*, 152–155; Baier, "Somnambulismus," 67–70. A full psychological elaboration was published by Pierre Janet, whose experimental research with thirty patients led him to conclude that *rapport* always involved a relation of "affection" or even "love" between the participants in which one had the active role of director while the other was being guided ("L'influence somnambulique," 125–129, 132–133, 141; see also e.g. Crabtree, *From Mesmer to Freud*, 89–105). Compare the descriptions of spiritual intimacy between teacher and pupil by Van den Kerchove in the second chapter of *La voie*, e.g. 86–87 (referring to CH X 17; cf. Kingsley, "An Introduction," 37).

Tat is impressed by Hermes' beautiful words,[84] but quite astonished by the implications. If it is true that Hermes has given birth,[85] and if Tat may count himself among his offspring, then does this mean that he has many brothers? Here an important step is taken beyond the scenario of CH XIII. As the active agent of Tat's regeneration, through whom the pneumatic seed was passed on, Hermes is perceived as more than just the facilitator or midwife of the rebirth – he is nothing less than Tat's spiritual father. This is obviously a point of great importance, as it establishes a unique personal relation between the individual Hermetic practitioner who has experienced rebirth and the spiritual master to whom he owes his new life. Tat seems to realize for the first time that Hermes must have given the rebirth to at least some and perhaps even many of the other pupils too. This makes them his spiritual brothers, not just metaphorically but in a quite literal sense.[86] Hermes confirms this: it is important that Tat recognizes them as his brothers and honors them properly, as fits the beauty of the rebirth.[87] As they were born again, Hermes has given each of them a new name.[88] They are pneumatics now, spiritual entities; they exist as immortal energies that have the power to nourish other souls and make them grow.[89]

---

[84] Most translators interpret καλως (καλῶς) as "good" ("well said"), but I attach importance to the Hermetic sensitivity to beauty. Only Krause and Labib make good use of the ability of the German language to say "schön gesagt" (KL, 171). The word recurs a few lines further on, when Hermes says "beautifully put, my child."

[85] The Coptic of NH VI⁶ 52, 26–27 says literally that Hermes has given birth to the Power, but this conflicts with the description as a womb that got pregnant. For the solution followed here, see HG, 628 note 1078 (based on an emendation by Camplani: SEC, 135 and 171 note 4).

[86] Although we have reason to assume that Hermetic practitioners could be both male and female (see above, Chapter 4, p. 82 with note 19, 92), NH VI⁶ makes no allusion to "sisters."

[87] NH VI⁶ 53, 9. Again (cf. note 78) I want to highlight the emphasis on beauty. Krause and Labib translate "es ist nötig für dich, daß du deine Brüder kennst und sie schön und geziemend ehrst" (KL, 171); all other translators give translations like "properly," "rightly" and so on.

[88] NH VI⁶ 53, 13; cf. HHE I, 92–93. No new name for Tat is mentioned in CH XIII, and we do not actually know the name of Hermes' pupil in NH VI⁶ (cf. note 73). Are we permitted to hypothesize that the very name "Hermes Trismegistus" could be such a rebirth name that was bestowed on an otherwise unknown individual who was believed to be reborn?

[89] NH VI⁶ 53, 14–20. On the Coptic ⲟⲩⲛ̅ⲧⲁⲩ ϩⲱⲟⲩ ⲙ̅ⲙⲁⲩ ("do they also possess?"), see Keizer, 95–96 note 10; Bull, *Tradition*, 322 with note 31. It has been assumed that we should fill in "names" (Keizer, l.c.), "mothers" (Turner in Keizer, l.c.; Tröger, 598–499; CHD, 518; NHD, 509; HH I, 67; Meyer, 413; HG, 449; HT V, 84), or "a (birth)day" (Rob, 323; cf. Meyer, 413 note 7), whereas Bull interprets ϩⲱⲟⲩ as "rain" (*Tradition*, 322–327). I would agree with Keizer that these possibilities remain a matter of speculation and are not necessary to interpret the passage.

As Tat is convinced by this explanation and wants to move on to the prayer that will initiate the Ogdoadic and Enneading revelation,[90] Hermes tells him "Child, let us pray to the Father of the All, together with your brothers who are my sons, that he may grant his *pneuma* so that I may speak."[91] The significance of this statement lies in the suggestion that those brothers are therefore physically present with them.[92] This makes NH VI[6] into something quite different from CH XIII: not the description of a rebirth experience that happens unexpectedly and involves just Hermes and Tat, but of a communal ceremony that must have been planned in advance. The most consistent scenario is that once a pupil had experienced the rebirth, he would be invited to a secret meeting reserved for those brethren who had already been reborn. I assume that the ceremony would not be open to all pupils, because the not-yet reborn who were merely living lives of *eusebeia* and remained on the level of the general discourses would not be able to understand what was happening or share in the experience. Tat's surprise at discovering that the other participants are his "brothers" would suggest that he was not informed in advance that all those in attendance had already been reborn.

Hermes' words confirm the difference between Tat's role and his own. They will pray to the Father to grant Hermes his *pneuma* so that he may speak. Since they are already having a conversation right now, this must obviously refer to more than normal speech. I remind the reader of my earlier discussion about the oral transmission of "sounds full of power" that are not conventional signifiers but carriers of divine energy.[93] We are about to see how that worked. But as Hermes is ready to begin the prayer, Tat interrupts him with a question. Having understood that the pupils around him are in fact his brethren, he now refers to them as the "offspring" or "generations."[94] It would seem that Tat feels a bit apprehensive and wants to make sure not to make mistakes. How exactly does one pray in unity with the

---

[90] I resist the common translation of ϣⲁϫⲉ as "discourse." Keizer (97 note 12) points out that it could just as well mean "word, matter, revelation" and Camplani (SEC, 137) suggests "prayer." What follows is indeed not a theoretical discourse but a prayer followed by an ecstatic vision.

[91] NH VI[6] 53, 27–31.

[92] HHE I, 91; Van den Kerchove, *La voie*, 91.

[93] Above, pp. 115–116; see also below, pp. 321–327.

[94] For the ambiguity of the word ϫⲱ(ⲱ)ⲙⲉ, which can mean either "generation" resp. "offspring" or "book," see discussion in Keizer, 91–94 note 6; HHE I, 42–43; Bull, *Tradition*, 321–322. I assume with Holzhausen that all instances in this first part of the treatise (NH VI[6] 52–54) are interpreted most plausibly in the former sense; by contrast, the instances in NH VI[6] 60–63 clearly refer to books.

brethren? Because of serious textual gaps at this point, any reconstruction of what follows must be uncertain; but Hermes seems to respond by reminding Tat about how, all along, these other rebirthers have been helping him to make progress in wisdom. When he was a baby, he used to raise questions that he would now consider foolish and ignorant (*anoēton*); therefore having been reborn recently, he must think of himself again as a spiritual infant who will have to rely on his older brethren to assist him along the path. Below, we will see what form that assistance takes. The explanation seems to restore Tat's confidence, as he understands how much progress he has made already thanks to their providential help. Hermes' response seems to confirm once more that those brethren are indeed present, ready to join in the prayer:

[Hermes] My child, when you understand [-*noein*] the truth of what you're saying, you will find your brothers (who are my children) praying with you.
[Tat] Father, I understand [-*noein*] nothing but the beauty that was given me by the generations [i.e., by the reborn brethren].
[Hermes] That is what you call the beauty of the soul – the step-by-step formation you have received. May the *noēsis* come to you and you will understand.
[Tat] I have understood [-*noein*], my Father....[95]

Note again the emphasis on beauty. As Tat is now ready to take the plunge, he restates what is about to happen. They will pray to God that he may grant his power [*dunamis*],[96] so that Hermes can transmit this noetic energy to Tat by means of his voice. This divine force is called "the gift of the Ogdoad,"[97] and Hermes repeats once more that each of them will have his own role to play: "Your job is to noeticize, mine is to be able to express the *logos* from the Source that wells up in me."[98]

THE SOUNDING COSMOS

To ask for the gift that will make this possible, Hermes and Tat (presumably together with the rest of the brethren) now begin to pray "with all their *nous* and all their heart and all their soul."[99]

---

[95] Many translators attribute part of Hermes' second statement to Tat (Keizer, 57; CHD, 519; KL, 173; HHE I, 69; SEC, 138; HG, 450; HT V, 86); but here I follow Tröger, 499; NHD, 510; Rob, 323; Meyer, 414. I find the second part of the final sentence too corrupt to allow speculation about its meaning. For the "beauty of the soul," cf. HD IX 4.
[96] NH VI⁶ 55, 6–7.
[97] NH VI⁶ 55, 15–16.
[98] NH VI⁶ 55, 19–22.
[99] NH VI⁶ 55, 11–13. For ⲙⲉⲉⲩⲉ as *nous*, see Bull, *Tradition*, 319 note 14.

> I call upon you who rules over the kingdom of power,
> whose *Logos* is an offspring of Light,
> whose words are immortal, eternal and immutable,
> whose will produces the life of images everywhere,
> whose nature [*phusis*] gives form [*morphē*] to essence [*ousia*],
> from whom souls ... and angels are put into motion
> ....
> to all who exist,
> whose providence extends to everyone ...
> who brings forth everyone,
> who has divided the *aiōn* among the spirits,
> who has fashioned everything,
> who has himself inside himself,
> carrying all things in his fullness.[100]

These first sentences are addressed to the supreme Hermetic triad.[101] The ultimate Source rules over the kingdom of power, which must be the Ennead, the domain of noetic powers. We have seen that the Ennead is Light and brings forth the *Logos*, the producer of superior "immortal, eternal and immutable" words – these I take to be the "sounds full of power" that Hermes will be uttering. The Source has also given birth to the life of images everywhere, which I assume must mean the *aiōn*, God's "incorporeal imagination" filled with *noēmata*. By giving form to essences, the Source has finally given birth to the living souls and angels that are moving in the Ogdoad. All these entities together constitute the unitary divine fullness of true reality, the God who is All in All.

Now that the divine triad has been properly invoked, the prayer moves on to its crucial middle part, culminating in an impressive series of vowels and *nomina barbara*:

> Invisible God, to whom one speaks in silence,
> whose image is moved as it expands and expands [as it moves],
> powerful beyond power,
> great beyond greatness,
> glorious beyond glory,

---

[100] NH VI⁶ 55, 24–56,2. In line four (55,30), the word for "logos" (λοгос) has that for "will" (ογωϣ) written above it.
[101] While Bull claims that the addressee is the Ennead (*Tradition*, 332–333), I rather agree here with Mahé (HT V, 89–90 note).

zōxathazō
a ō ō
e e ō ō
ē ē ē ō ō ō
i i i i ō ō ō ō
o o o o o ō ō ō ō ō
u u u u u u ō ō ō ō ō ō
ō ō ō ō ō ō ō [ō ō ō ō ō ō ō]
zōzazōth[102]

Clearly we are dealing here with those "sounds full of power" that, according to CH XVI 2, are superior to the "empty words" of the Greeks. While they are transmitted in a Coptic translation from a Greek original, what counts here is the contrast with philosophical discourse through *dianoia*. The first and final word, *zōxathazō* and *zōzazōth*, have no literal parallels elsewhere in Greek or Coptic literature but are reminiscent of well-known palindromes that occur in the Greek "magical" papyri and contemporary "magical" amulets, notably *zōthaxathōz* and *thōzaxazōth*.[103] That the versions in NH VI[6] are *not* palindromes is unlikely to be the result of transcription errors – most probably we are dealing with a deliberate attempt to make the formula ineffective for non-initiated readers.[104] After all, the authors were extremely serious in their belief that these sounds would unleash real and supremely sacred energetic power.

---

[102] NH VI[6] 56, 10–22. Line 2 I see as poetic rather than as a "meaningless tautology" (HG, 637 note 1115). Lines 3–5 seem parallel to CH I 31 (HG, 637 note 1116, referring to Tardieu). The succession "η η" in the manuscript should certainly be read as "ι ι ι" (see text). Like Camplani and van den Broek (SEC, 142; HG, 451 with note 1119) I add eight *omegas* at the end, as this follows with compelling logic from how the series is built up. Like Mahé (HHE I, 73) and most scholars after him, I assume that the number of omegas after the "ι ι ι" must be reduced from six to five. Bull however keeps the sixth omega and argues that the resulting number of thirty-six omegas is meant to represent the thirty-six decans (*Tradition*, 334 with note 80, 337–339). He argues that the invocation should have started with one omega before the alpha but the author or scribe smuggled in an extra omega in line 4 instead. But if so, why didn't he add that extra omega in the correct place? The argument that the omega series must run from 1 to 7 I find less than compelling: my reconstruction likewise begins with 1, but represented more logically by the first letter of the alphabet.

[103] The palindrome *zōthaxathōz* appears in PMG XIII, in the so-called *Leiden Kosmopoiia* (Papyrus Leiden J 395); *thōzaxazōth* appears on four so-called "magical amulets" (as pointed out by Bull, *Tradition*, 340–342 with images 1 and 2); see Bonner, *Studies in Magical Amulets*, and "The Campbell Bonner Magical Gems Database" classics.mfab.hu/talismans/cbd/539, 1437 and 1662, in one case (1437) written in the form of a "magical square."

[104] Keizer, 103 note 25, 163; HHE I, 106–107. I consider this option more likely because *neither* of the two versions is a palindrome, in spite of the fact that such words were likely to be copied with extra care precisely *because* they were not readily understandable. For changes in the vowel series, see above, note 102.

Mahé has drawn attention to an alchemical fragment titled "Organon of Hermes Trismegistus," where we read that the letter *zēta* (ζ, z) has the numerical value 7 and stands for *zōē* (ζωή, "life") while the letter *thēta* (θ, th) has the value 9 and stands for *thanatos* (θανατος, "death"). He further pointed out that the *thōzaxazōth* version in PGM XIII was linked explicitly to generativity.[105] Keeping in mind the Hermetic refusal to accept death as something real, this suggests that "life" was associated with the cosmic domain (7 planetary spheres) while so-called "death" was understood as true life in the Ennead (9), the ultimate noetic reality of eternal Light. This also helps explain a peculiar passage later on in our text, when Tat seems to falter for a moment and Hermes tells him to "return to the death-state."[106] Rather than slipping back into his habitual clouded state of consciousness "under the sway of death" that is conventionally referred to as "life," he must return to the superior state of Life and Light that we ignorantly call "death."

The manuscript of NH VI[6] presents the vowels in a continuous sequence, but the structure is clarified by dividing them over separate lines, as presented above. The first thing to note is the succession of the seven vowels of the Greek alphabet: this string "a e ē i o u ō" appears in many places elsewhere in the PGM as well, and was often understood as a divine name that could be turned into a formula.[107] The vowels appear to represent divine powers that reside in the seven planetary spheres, and as the number of vowels is successively expanded, we get 1+2+3+4+5+6+7=28 powers. Each vowel is followed by the same number of omegas (ω) plus one. Since the ceremony is initiated from down below, the intended sequence must be as follows: Moon (α), Mercury (ε), Venus (η), the Sun (ι), Mars (ο), Jupiter (υ), and Saturn (ω). As the number of these vowels expands progressively, the total number of powers that are being invoked at each step expands as well (1–3–6–10–15–21–28; or even 3–8–15–24–35–48–63 if one includes the omegas); hence each line of vocalizations takes considerably more time than the previous one; and furthermore, we may readily assume that the powers themselves were believed to get more potent the closer they were to the hypercosmic domain. Therefore we are watching an exponential build-up of numinous power, culminating in the long series of fifteen omegas sealed by the word *zōzazōth*.

---

[105] HHE I, 106–107; referring to CAA I, 23 (Greek), 24 (French); cf. SEC, 142–143 note 45.
[106] For the translation of ⲙⲟⲩ as "death-state," see below, p. 304 note 154.
[107] See already Reitzenstein, *Poimandres*, 266 (with reference to Dieterich, *Abraxas*, 185); discussion of many examples in Dornseiff, *Alphabet*, 35–68, 82–83; Dieleman, *Priests*, 64–80; see also Wellesz, "Music in the Treatises," 146–147; HHE I, 106; HG, 446–448.

292   *Hermetic Spirituality and the Historical Imagination*

We do not know exactly how these names were spoken or intoned, but the effect must certainly have been impressive, resulting in a solemn ceremonial atmosphere pregnant with expectation. While the first and final words are quite short, the vocalizations could obviously be modulated and drawn out. An important point that has not received enough attention is that next to being linked to the planetary spheres, the seven vowels could also be mapped on one of the musical scales or "modes." According to Neopythagorean theory as explained notably in Nicomachus of Gerasa's influential books on harmonics (later first/early second cent. CE), each planet rotating through the ether was continually producing a specific tonal pitch.[108] As a logical inference, the seven planets and vowels could be linked to the seven tones of the existing musical scales as well.[109] According to an oft-quoted passage of uncertain date, the Egyptian priests in fact used to sing successions of the seven vowels in their hymns of praise to the gods, "and the sound of these vowels has such euphony that men listen to it instead of the flute and the lyre."[110] Nicomachus' work makes it possible to see how the vowels could be linked to tonal pitches (see Table 9.2):[111]

---

[108] Nicomachus, *Manuale harmonices* 3 (Janus, *Musici scriptores graeci*, 241–242; Nicomachus, *Manuel d'harmonique*, 13–15; Nicomachus, *Manual of Harmonics*, 45–46). For Nicomachus' work, see the authoritative discussion in Mathiesen, *Apollo's Lyre*, 390–411; cf. short introduction by Levin in Nicomachus, *Manual*, 13–27.

[109] Nicomachus, *Manuale Harmonicum* 6 (Janus, *Musici*, 276–278; Nicomachus, *Manuel d'harmonique*, 50–51); Gersh, *From Iamblichus to Eriugena*, 295; Ruelle, "Chant des sept voyelles"; Ruelle, "Chant gnostico-magique"; Poirée, "Chant des sept voyelles"; Gastoué, *Origines du Chant Romain*, 24–31; Wellesz, "Music in the Treatises"; Godwin, *Mystery*, 19–33; Touliatos, "Nonsense Syllables"; Frankfurter, "Magic of Writing," 635–643.

[110] Demetrius, *Peri hermēneias* 71 (see Demetrius, *On Style* [Dorreen C. Innes, ed.], 394–395). The attribution to Aristotle's student Demetrius of Phaleron appears to be mistaken; as for the date of composition, opinions range from the second century BCE to the first century CE (ibid., 312–321).

[111] Mathiesen, *Apollo's Lyre*, 396–397, with Figure 57; cf. Wellesz, "Music," 148. The scale consists of relative proportions, not absolute pitches. A commentator on Nicomachus (*Manuale harmonicum* fr. 3) noted the puzzling reversal of Mercury and Venus (Mathiesen, *Apollo's Lyre*, 409; Levin in Nicomachus, *Manual*, 56) and turned Nicomachus' account upside down. The latter wrote that Saturn is spatially *hupatē* ("highest") but produces the lowest tone, whereas the Moon is *neatē* ("lowest") but produces the highest tone; the sun has the midway position (*mesē*), whereas the four other planets' locations are designated in relation to these three (*parhupatē* and *paraneatē* for Jupiter and Venus; *paramesē* and *hupermesē* for Mercury and Mars). The commentator reversed these technical terms in accordance with Plato's account in the *Republic* (617a-b; see Levin in Nicomachus, *Manual of Harmonics*, 52), making the Moon *hupatē* and Saturn *neatē*, a move that seems counter-intuitive in terms of their spatial locations but more logical in terms of their tonal pitches. Saturnus has the lowest sound in both scenarios.

TABLE 9.2: *Vowels, planets, and tonal pitches (Nicomachus of Gerasa)*

Greek	Transcription	Planet	Symbol	Tone
ω	ō	Saturn	♄	e
υ	u	Jupiter	♃	f
ο	o	Mars	♂	g
ι	i	Sun	☉	a
η	ē	Mercury	☿	b♭
ε	e	Venus	♀	c'
α	a	Moon	☾	d'

While this makes it possible in principle to write the vowel sequence of NH VI[6] down in musical notation, Nicomachus' choice is just one possibility among a much wider range of musical scales that were current in antiquity.[112] Since we do not know which one(s) would have been used by Hermetic practitioners, all we can say with confidence is that the scale would run from omega (Saturn) as the lowest tone to alpha (Moon) as the highest. In trying to reconstruct the invocation on this basis, I would call attention to a parallel scenario attributed to the second-century Valentinian teacher Marcus:

The first heaven utters the A, the one after it E, the third Ē, the fourth, which is in the middle of the seven, utters the power [*dunamin*] I, the fifth O, the sixth U, and the seventh, which is the fourth from the middle, expresses the Ō. ... All these powers, ... when lined up to one another, sound forth the praises of him by whom they were brought forth. The glory of this sound is sent up again to the Forefather. The echo [*ēchon*] of this utterance of praise is brought down to earth, ... and becomes the shaper and generator of the things on earth.[113]

I find it significant that the chant from down below receives an *echo* from up above. The most likely scenario for our invocation then is that Hermes and Tat are chanting the expanding series of seven successive vowels as their consciousness ascends ever more slowly *and* ever more powerfully from the

---

[112] Godwin presents a transcription of the second vowel sequence from NH VI[6] (to be discussed later); but in view of various previous attempts at musical transcription (see notably Poirée, "Chant des sept voyelles"), he points out that since the Greek musical system has seven different modes or octave-species and three different genera, there were in fact twenty-one possible combinations (*Mystery*, 44–47).

[113] Irenaeus, *Adv. Haer.* I.14.7 (Rousseau and Doutreleau ed., 228–229); Wilson, *Gnosis*, vol. 1, 207; cf. Frankfurter, "Magic of Writing," 641 (and cf. 642: when the soul that seeks purification is in need and distress, it can exclaim the letter Ω so that the soul up above may come to its aid).

sphere of the Moon towards the sphere of Saturn. At each step they receive a response, as their chant is echoed by a longer and progressively more powerful sound that is understood to be coming down to them from the seventh sphere. We may assume that in actual practice, the brethren around them would be giving voice to this echo by chanting the omegas at a low pitch, and the volume of singing would get louder as the invocation progressed. Having finally arrived at the level of Saturn, the voices coming "from below" would join those "above," as all participants would now be chanting the same vowel ō on the same pitch.[114] From a spatial point of view, this *upward* movement through the spheres can be pictured visually as in Table 9.3.

Meanwhile, from a musical point of view the seven-vowel sequence moves *downward*, beginning with the highest note (α) and slowly descending towards the lowest one (ω). For instance, if we were to choose the scale based on Nicomachus (see above), the invocation could be written down as in Figure 9.1: on the next page.

TABLE 9.3: *Vowel-singing and spiritual ascent through the seven spheres (NH VI6 56,17–22)*

	♄	ωω	ωωω	ωωωω	ωωωωω	ωωωωωω	ωωωωωωω	ωωωωωωωωωωωωωωωω
Planetary spheres →	♃						υυυυυυ	
	♂				οοοοο			
	☉			ιιιι				
	☿		ηηη					
	♀	εε						
	☾	α						
		1	2	3	4	5	6	7
	Succession of steps →							

It is important to emphasize that we are *not* witnessing a musical performance here[115] but a ceremonial invocation in which the human voice is used to achieve a strong "hypnotic" effect on the participants'

---

[114] While Mahé assumes that the omegas represent the Ogdoad, my interpretation confirms Bull's argument (Bull, *Tradition*, 334–353, reached by an entirely different route) that they refer to Saturn (to which Bull adds that they also represent the Decans: ibid., 337–339). Whether the fixed stars should be included or should rather be associated with the Ogdoad remains an open question for me.

[115] Wellesz dismisses Poirée's transcription efforts with the argument that the results do not resemble any music known from ancient Jewish, Syriac or Greek culture ("Music in the Treatises," 151). This critique misses the point, for the "melodies" should not be seen as attempts to make music but as a translation of cosmic powers into audible sounds, regardless of musical effect.

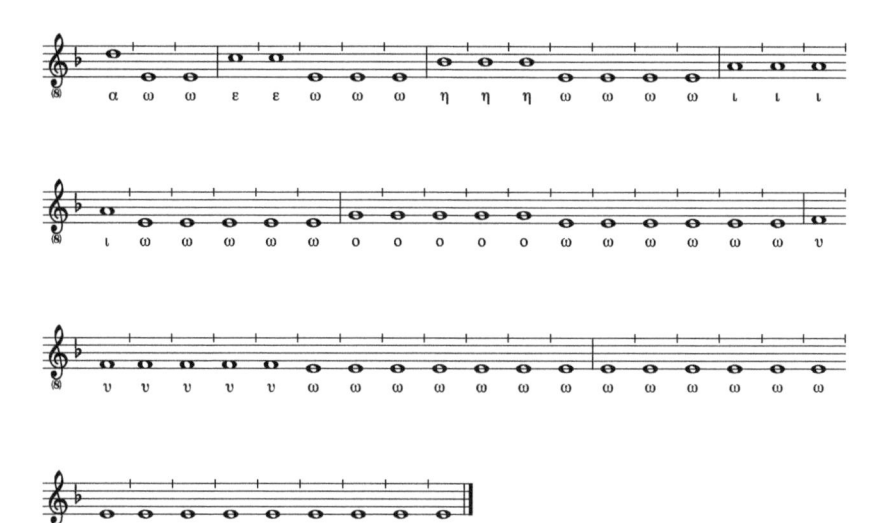

FIGURE 9.1: The invocation of spiritual ascent (NH VI⁶ 56,17-22)

consciousness.[116] Comparison with similar invocations from the papyri makes it likely that the altered state was further enhanced by inhalation of *kuphi* incense.[117] In the pregnant silence that follows the invocation, Hermes now prays directly to the ultimate unbegotten Source itself, asking it to send down its power (*dunamis*) that will grant wisdom (*sophia*), so that he and Tat will be able to share their experience of the Ogdoad and the Ennead.[118] Having walked the path of reverence (*eusebeia*), he says, they have now reached the *hebdomad*, the seventh sphere of Saturn.[119] Therefore their consciousness is still within the cosmic domain, but they are ready to move beyond it.

---

[116] On the relevance of hypnosis and hypnotic suggestion under conditions of *rapport*, see above, p. 285 with note 83.

[117] Vowel incantations appear in immediate connection with *kuphi* incense e.g. in the Mithras Liturgy (Betz, "Mithras Liturgy", 51 line 512; see remarks in Bull, *Tradition*, 417-418); PGM XIII 628-633 (also PGM XIII 343); see also Nicolas Myrepsus, *De suffimentis* 21:1 (Ruelle, "Chant gnostico-magique," 16; Touliatos, "Nonsense Syllables," 232).

[118] This prayer by Hermes extends from NH VI⁶ 56, 22-57,25. NH VI⁶ 57, 13 shows that the addressee is the Unbegotten. As the Coptic verb ϫⲱ in NH VI⁶ 56, 15 implies *verbal* communication (Keizer, 103 note 26), I assume that this refers to the sympathetic *rapport* that will enable Hermes and Tat to share the same experience while remaining in contact through their voice. While I sympathize with Bull's argument for translating ϫⲱ ⲚⲀⲚ as "sing" rather than "say" or "announce," it seems to me that we are not "in the midst of a hymn" anymore: Hermes' words refer not to the previous invocation through the singing of vowels but to the verbal exchange that is about to take place.

[119] Bull, *Tradition*, 351: the singing of the vowels has brought them "to the cusp of the Ogdoad."

By singing their hymn of praise, the Hermetic practitioners have been sending up "a reflection [or imprint, *tupos*] of the fullness [*plēroma*]."[120] I assume that this formulation refers to the vowel sequence which, as we have seen, represents the plenitude of the seven *cosmic* spheres.[121] The human voices from down below have the effect of carrying pneumatic energy from the cosmos upwards towards the hypercosmic levels. In order for Tat to actually perceive the vision (*theōria*) that will show him the image (*eikōn*) of the truth, the Source must respond to the invocation by sending down its own luminous spirit (*pneuma*). As this downward stream of divine pneumatic energy meets the upward stream of "eloquent *pneuma*," the latter will be ignited as by a spark of fire, thereby illuminating the practitioners' *nous* and give them divine *gnōsis*.[122] In other words, the noetic potential of the *pneuma* carried upward by chanting must be *activated* by the superior divine *pneuma*, the energetic power (*dunamis*) that responds from above. Exactly this is what Hermes must have meant at the outset, when he invited Tat to pray to "the Father of All ... that he may grant his *pneuma* so that I may speak."[123] The vowel song has brought spiritual father and son together in a hypnotic altered state of intimate energetic *rapport*. This condition enables Hermes to receive power "from the Source that wells up in [him]" so that he can pass it on to Tat, whose *nous* will thereby be opened to the vision of truth.[124]

As Hermes concludes his prayer, he makes sure to give all credit for what is about to happen to the Unbegotten Source from which all things have come. Ultimately, it is the one sovereign active force on which all else depends entirely, as it has brought forth both the Self-Begotten (the Ennead) and the Begotten (the Ogdoad), as well as everything else that has been generated and filled with soul.[125] This sovereign Source, also known as the One, is now asked to accept these "verbal offerings"

---

[120] NH VI⁶ 57, 8–9.
[121] As pointed out by Bull in an important remark, *plēroma* should not be understood in a "gnostic" sense as referring to the supernal or hypercosmic realms; on the contrary, in the Hermetica the term always refers to the plenitude of the *cosmos* (*Tradition*, 351–352).
[122] For the concept of "eloquent *pneuma*" (derived from PGM III 588) and its relevance to NH VI⁶, see Zago, "Pneuma éloquent." As she explains with reference to the PGM fragment, "the knowledge (*gnōsis*) ... is passed on through an illumination similar to that of fire that lightens a candle wick (ἐλλυχνιάζειν)" (ibid., 717).
[123] NH VI⁶ 53, 27–31.
[124] NH VI⁶ 55, 19–22.
[125] NH VI⁶ 57, 11–18.

(*logikē thusia*) that the practitioners have sent up with all their heart, all their soul, and all their power. In response, may he grant them immortal wisdom.[126]

BEYOND THE STARS

As Hermes has completed his prayer, he turns towards Tat with the words "my child, let us embrace in love!"[127] Again, our attention is drawn to the intimacy of filial *rapport* that has been established between the spiritual "father" and his reborn "son." From this moment on, we will be witnessing an extraordinary ecstatic experience: all of a sudden, Tat's consciousness is opened up to the hypercosmic realms, while Hermes is using his voice to give him feedback and guidance. The embrace is not only "an apt ritual gesture to conclude the hymn" but also, in some manner, sets the entire visionary process in motion.[128] I would consider the possibility that the embrace is not just short and transitory but is *maintained* as long as the vision lasts. Rather than Hermes and Tat just giving each other some kind of friendly bear hug for a couple of seconds, we may imagine them holding one another by the shoulders with outstretched arms and *remaining* in that position for the duration of the vision. While this interpretation must obviously remain speculative, it would fit what we know about physical procedures for inducing visionary trance, involving an active director and a passive recipient who establish a closed "energy circuit" while using their voices to communicate.[129]

---

[126] NH VI⁶ 57, 18–25. For the expression λογικὴ θυσία, see my remarks above, Chapter 8, p. 234 note 49. In this case, I assume that the reference is at least partly to the vowel sequence.

[127] NH VI⁶ 57, 26. Mahé's belief that *The Ogdoad and the Ennead* describes a ritual of rebirth relies for a very large part on his later translation of this single sentence as "let us embrace each other *with a kiss*" (HT V, 94; in contrast to his original translation in HHE I, 75), which then allows him to draw a parallel with the sacramental regenerative kiss of the Valentinian rite of the Bridal Chamber (Mahé, "Accolade ou baiser?"). Like Bull, I consider this far too slim a foundation to support such a heavy edifice, especially since the translation "in love" (or even "in truth") is at least as likely, if not more so (as conclusively argued by Bull, *Tradition*, 354–356).

[128] Bull, *Tradition*, 356.

[129] For a reliable introduction to Mesmeric standard practice see Gauld, *History of Hypnotism*, e.g. 99–110, based on the most useful original textbook by Kluge, *Versuch einer Darstellung* (1811). The condition of *rapport* was usually established by "holding the patient's shoulders, or lightly stroking his arms" (Gauld, *History*, 99; Kluge, *Versuch* § 271; see illustrations in Younger, *Magnetic and Botanic*, e.g. 14, 18, 22, 33, 37, 45, 69).

As "father and son" connect in this embrace, suddenly everything happens very fast, as shown by Hermes' words: "Rejoice in this! For the Power that is Light is already coming down from them to us!"[130] As a result of the vowel singing, Hermes' and Tat's consciousness has been lifted high up into the seventh cosmic sphere, and in this elevated condition they now feel the pneumatic stream of noetic Light energies from the Ennead coming down to them and igniting their own noetic capacity.[131] The effect on Tat is immediate: "I see, yes, I see unspeakable depths!"[132] But how does the vision develop after that exclamation? Because we do not know for certain which lines in the following section are supposed to be spoken by Hermes and which ones by Tat, any reconstruction must remain speculative to some extent.[133] In what follows I will provide a reading that I find most plausible, while explaining my choices in the footnotes.

It is clear at least that Hermes responds immediately to Tat's exclamation, because he addresses him as "my child"; but what follows next is impossible to reconstruct with certainty because of serious damage to the manuscript (see Figure 9.2 on the next page for an impression of what these papyri look like). Hermes seems to be confirming that the hypercosmic "depths" which have opened up to Tat's consciousness are indeed beyond verbal description.[134]

The few words that follow have been destroyed almost completely (see line 4 in figure 9.2), but most likely should read "I am *nous*" – a statement that gets repeated no fewer than three times in the short piece of text that follows and is clearly important.[135] If we read it as just a factual statement, we almost certainly miss the intention, as may be illustrated by a simple analogy. If a woman tells her daughter "I am your

---

[130] NH VI⁶ 57, 28–30.
[131] Contrary to Mahé (HHE I, 46, 75, 111–112; cf. Bull, *Tradition*, 355–356), I see no grave problem about the meaning of "from them" (ⲉⲃⲟⲗ ⲙ̄ⲙⲟⲟⲩ). Since the noetic world of the Ennead consists of "innumerable powers" (CH I 7), we are dealing not with just one single undivided power but with a stream of pneumatic energies.
[132] NH VI⁶ 57, 31.
[133] For a convenient summary of the choices made by other scholars, see Bull, *Tradition*, 357–358.
[134] NH VI⁶ 57, 33–58,4. That they have now "begun" to perceive these depths is based on Mahé's restoration ⲉⲧ[ⲁⲛⲡ̄ⲁⲣⲭⲉⲥ]ⲑⲁⲓ (HHE I, 76, probably following Tröger, 500; cf. CHD 523 with note 62). Mahé recently changed the translation to "c[ommen]ce dès main[tenant à tendre vers] les lieux!" (from now on, do begin reaching towards the places! HT V, 94), but this seems less convincing given the fact that Tat has already arrived there.
[135] NH VI⁶ 58, 4, 15, 21, 27. In the second instance Hermes says "I told you, my child, that I am *nous*," so it seems plausible that here he is referring back to the first instance in line 4.

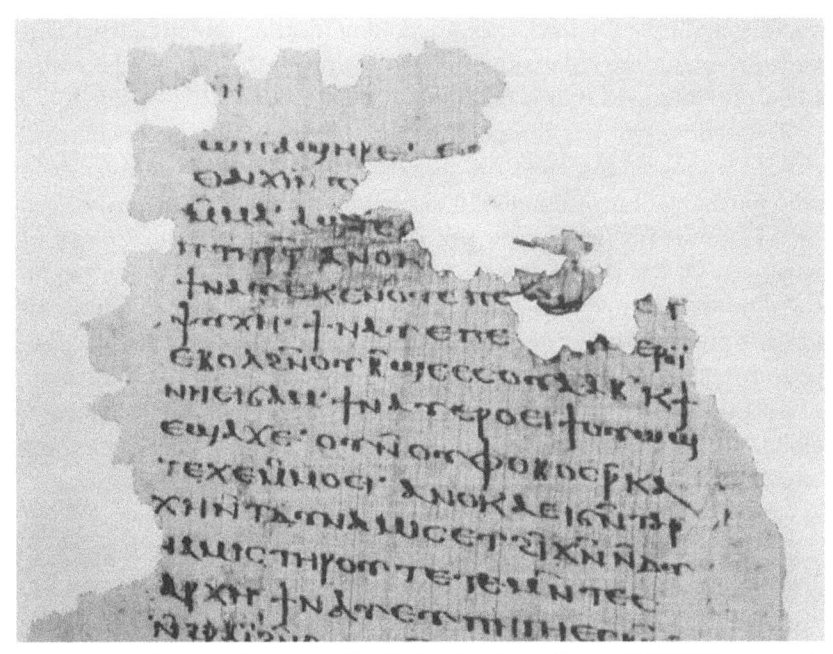

FIGURE 9.2: Papyrus fragment *The Ogdoad and the Ennead* (NH VI⁶ 58,1-13)

mother," she is making a statement of fact; but what she really means to say depends very much on the context. Imagine an orphan who has never known her parents, until one day an older woman who has been her friend for years tells her "I am your mother!"¹³⁶ In a similar manner, I want to suggest, Hermes is not just making a factual statement here – rather, he is revealing his true identity to his pupil, and this is obviously an event of considerable gravity. All of a sudden, Tat finds he is no longer facing the human person he knew, but is being addressed directly by Hermes' immortal noetic essence. The *nous* is speaking through his teacher's mouth. Having declared who he really is, Hermes tells his pupil what he himself is perceiving: he sees another *Nous*, the universal one that moves the soul.¹³⁷ As the consciousness of both participants is now

---

[136] I was inspired to draw this analogy by Robert Musil's short story "Der Amsel" (Musil, *Nachlaß zu Lebzeiten*, 131–154, here 153).

[137] NH VI⁶ 58, 5–6. The sentence reconstruction is not entirely certain. I assume that the addition ⲁⲩⲱ ("and") is correct, so that Hermes says "I am *nous* and I see another *nous* that moves the soul." Similar to KL, 177 ("Ich sehe auch einen Nus..."), van den Broek assigns the second part of the sentence to Tat and assumes that he does not see "another" *nous*

completely in the Ogdoad, they are communicating directly "from *nous* to *nous*" about their shared vision of the universal *Nous*, the boundless Light of the Ennead that is their own divine essence.

The next sentence is extremely ambiguous and could be attributed to either Hermes or Tat. Does the speaker say that he sees the *nous* ("him who moves me") *in* or because of his present altered state (described here by a Coptic term that ranges from "ecstasy" to "sleep" or "forgetfulness")?[138] Or has that power moved him *from* his prior state of "a pure forgetfulness" *to* one of true wakefulness?[139] Interestingly, all these readings are possible and amount to the same conclusion. Embodiment causes us to forget who we really are; but reversely, this ecstatic "death-state" of noetic illumination allows the speaker to forget his embodied state of clouded consciousness. As Tat is clearly at a loss for words to express what is happening to him, we now get a series of short exclamations:

> You give me power...
> I see myself!
> I want to speak – but fear holds me back.
> I have found the origin of the Power above all powers, who has no beginning.
> I see a fountain bubbling with life![140]

The pneumatic power or energy that sustains the vision comes from the *nous*, and is transmitted through Hermes to his pupil. It allows Tat to perceive his own noetic essence of universal Life and Light. The experience is obviously awe-inspiring, a true occasion of fear and trembling: not only does Tat gain true *gnōsis*, self-knowledge, by seeing in this instance who and what he really is – but moreover, he even glimpses the

---

but, like Hermes, "also" sees a *nous*. However, because ⲕⲉ- requires the definite article to mean "also," I stay with the more usual interpretation and its implication that Hermes is the speaker (with thanks to Korshi Dosoo, personal communication, 14 September 2020).

[138] NH VI⁶ 58, 6–7.
[139] For the first option see Keizer, 64 ("through a holy sleep"); Tröger, 500 ("durch heilige Vergessenheit"); CHD, 523 ("in heiliger Ekstase"); HHE I, 77 ("par une sainte extase"); HG, 451–452 ("in een heilige extase"); HT V, 96 ("en une sainte extase"); SEC, 145–146 ("attraverso un santo torpore"). For the second option see KL, 177 ("aus einem reinen Vergessen"); Rob, 324 ("from pure forgetfulness"); Meyer, 416 (idem). I have to disagree here with Bull, *Tradition*, 357: "I see the one that moves me from a holy sleep." Bull argues that Hermes' embrace has roused Tat from his contemplative sleep (ibid., 359–361), but this cannot be right: on the contrary, the true ecstatic vision or holy sleep clearly *begins* with the embrace.
[140] NH VI⁶ 58, 7–14. Theoretically these words plus the next sentence (58,15) could all be spoken by Hermes (in which case the "power" mentioned in the first sentence is that of the *nous*) but this assumption would weaken the clearly intended sense of bafflement and utter novelty.

mysterious origin (*archē*) of All That Is, the unbegotten One beyond the Ennead, the ultimate generative Source (*pēgē*) itself. Indeed he has found the origin of the Power above all powers.

Again Tat hears the words "I am *nous*" coming from the mouth of his teacher.[141] All he can say in response is that words truly fail him to describe the vision: "I have seen," he breathes in utter amazement, "it is impossible to express this in words...!"[142] It is at this point that the emphasis begins to move from noetic vision-beyond-vision to noetic sound-beyond-sound, for the *nous* that keeps speaking through Hermes now calls his attention to what he is *hearing* in the Ogdoad, silent hymns that are being sung all around them by the souls and by the angels up above: "[that's right] my child, for the entire Ogdoad and the souls that are in it and the angels are singing their hymns in silence. Yet I, *nous*, understand them [*noein*]."[143] All this makes perfect sense in terms of the basic Hermetic perspective on *nous* and *logos*, as explained in a particularly koan-like *Hermetic Definition*:

Nothing is incomprehensible for *nous*, nothing is inexpressible for *logos*. You understand while staying silent, and when you speak, you speak. Since *nous* conceives *logos* in silence, only speech that comes from silence and *nous* is salvation. But *logos* that comes [only] from *logos* is perdition. For the human being is mortal through his body but immortal through *logos*.[144]

So there is such a thing as powerful noetically inspired speech (*logos*), but it can only be *understood* in immediate noetic perception. It comes from the silent Source through mediation of the *nous*. Just as the noetic vision cannot be seen with bodily eyesight, noetic speech cannot be heard by

---

[141] NH VI⁶ 58, 14-15.
[142] NH VI⁶ 58, 16-17.
[143] NH VI⁶ 58, 17-22.
[144] HD V 2. Mahé and van den Broek assume that the second sentence is about empty talk (WHDH, 112 "when you talk, you [just] talk"; HG, 437 "als je praat, praat je [alleen maar]"); but this seems to conflict with the final sentence and would seem to rule out any noetically inspired speech whatsoever. I assume rather that whereas noetic understanding happens in silence, giving *expression* to what is understood requires speech – and the second part of the first sentence confirms that *logos* does in fact have that power. The point is that while salvational speech comes from the silence of the Source by mediation of *nous* (hence it is "a gift of God": HD V 3), speech that originates merely from *logos* is just a "human invention" that leads nowhere (HD V 3, "he who talks without *nous* says nothing"). CH I described how *logos* is involved in the creation of human beings as double entities that enjoy the unique combination of impermanent bodies and immortal noetic essence (again: HD V 3). This means that *logos* has noetic potential, and speech can be more than just empty talk; thus in NH VI⁶ 53, 31 we are told that the gift of divine *pneuma* makes it possible for Hermes to speak. On *logos* as powerful energy, see below, Chapter 10, pp. 321-327.

the bodily ears. Therefore noetic singing can surely not be heard by the bodily ears either. Noetic realities can only be perceived noetically and are beyond verbal expression by words alone.

For a moment Tat seems to slip back to his habitual state of a student asking the master for explanations: how is that done, singing in silence?[145] But again it is not clear who speaks the next sentence. Perhaps Tat realizes that this is no longer a time for didactic conversations and tells Hermes "[but I see that] speaking with you is not possible anymore. I keep my mouth shut, Father." Alternatively, it could be Hermes who says that he can no longer speak to his pupil, and Tat responds that he will shut up.[146] In any case, he expresses his wish to join in the silent hymn-singing. He tells Hermes "I want to hymn you in silence," and Hermes responds "yes, sing [to me] then, for I am *nous*."[147] Note the nuance: although it might seem as though Tat is singing a hymn to Hermes, in fact it will not be addressed to the human teacher anymore but to the universal *nous* who has been speaking through Hermes' mouth ever since he first appeared in NH VI⁶ 58, 4.

At this point we may assume a "silent" intermission of indefinite duration. Along with all the other souls in the Ogdoad, Tat's soul is singing a noetic hymn to the Ennead. He and Hermes are standing there surrounded by their brethren, while their souls are soaring high in a deep state of meditative ecstasy – as suggested above, we may assume that they are standing face to face while holding one another by the shoulders, eyes closed. We cannot tell how long this situation lasts, but finally there comes the moment when the spell is broken as Tat speaks again. After the extraordinary experience they have been going through, this is a moment of joyful satisfaction in which there is some room even for an element of subtle humor and relaxation:

I understand [noeticize] the *Nous*: Hermes, who is beyond Hermeneutics because he rests within himself!
I am glad to see you smile, Father... And the All rejoices too![148]

It is no surprise that Tat's words bring a smile to Hermes' face, for it is a good pun indeed, and very appropriate for the occasion. *Hermēneia*,

---

[145] NH VI⁶ 58, 22–23 might mean "how do they sing?" or "how does [or should] one sing?" For the interpretive addition "in silence," see Rob, 325 and Meyer, 416.
[146] NH VI⁶ 58, 23–24. Literally "I am closed-mouthed" (Keizer, 106 note 34). First option: CHD, 524; HG, 452 with 641 note 1138. Second option: KL, 177; Tröger, 500; HHE I, 77; Rob, 325; Meyer, 416; NHD, 513; Bull, *Tradition*, 361–362; HT V, 96. Robinson and Meyer turn Hermes' sentence into a question.
[147] NH VI⁶ 58, 25–27.
[148] NH VI⁶ 58, 28–59,1.

the art of interpretation, cannot reach as far as grasping Hermes' true essence, for the *nous* itself is beyond language and can only be experienced in direct noetic perception. As Tat was singing his silent hymn to the Ennead, his own *nous* was joined to the universal *Nous* and his soul was both enveloped by and filled with what Iamblichus would have called *emphutos gnōsis*.[149]

Having been granted this peak experience of ultimate reality, Tat now expresses his gratitude to the divine in a short prayer to the Source of Light and Life:

> No creature will be deprived of your Life,
> for you are the Lord of the inhabitants everywhere.
> Your providence keeps watch over us.
> I call [upon] you:
> Father
> Aiōn of Aiōns
> Great Divine Spirit
> who sends spiritual rain down on all.[150]

With this, we come to a slightly puzzling but fascinating episode. Tat asks Hermes for his opinion about what he just said, as though asking for confirmation or reassurance, but his master seems reluctant to respond: "About those things I say nothing, my child, for it is right before God that we keep silent about what is hidden."[151] As these words carry a subtle sense of reservation that falls short of the full support he has been receiving so far, Tat's confidence seems to waver for a moment. He suddenly fears losing the gift of enlightenment and asks for help: "O Trismegistus… do not let my soul be deprived of the vision, divine Being! Everything is possible for you as Master [or Scribe] of the whole universe."[152] This is the first time Tat addresses his master with the honorific title "thrice-greatest," and his formulation confirms what we already saw: Hermes the human teacher is still just a vessel for the ultimate Enneadic divinity,

---

[149] My formulation "enveloped by and filled with" refers deliberately to the passage about *emphutos gnōsis* in Iamblichus, *Response to Porphyry* I 3 (see above, pp. 112–113).

[150] NH VI⁶ 59, 1–9. For various translation dilemmas, see e.g. CHD, 524 note 70–71; SEC, 147 note 66; HG, 642–643 note 1143.

[151] NH VI⁶ 59, 11–14. Alternatively, the Coptic could be constructed so as to mean "the great divine vision" (e.g. Meyer, 417 note 28).

[152] NH VI⁶ 59, 15–19. As pointed out by Holzhausen (CHD, 525 note 73), ⲥⲁϩ can mean Writer/Scribe (Tröger, 501 "Schreiber"), Teacher (KL, 179 "Lehrer"), or Lord/Master (Keizer, 67, Rob, 325, and Meyer, 417 "Master"; HHE I, 79 and HT V, 98 "maître"; CHD, 525 "Herr"; NHD, 514 "Gebieter"; SEC, 147 "maestro"; HG, 452 "meester").

the master of the universe. Therefore it is also the *Nous* who responds to Tat's plea, speaking through Hermes' mouth: "Return to the death-state, my child, and do it all in silence. Ask for what you want in silence."[153] Tat is told to return to the Enneadic state of perfect noetic consciousness that allowed him to join in the silent hymns of angels and souls: the blessed condition in which souls that have attained salvation will find themselves after the dissolution of the body.[154]

At this point we must assume a second period of sustained silence. Without another word, Tat directs his consciousness back to the Ennead and joins again in the noetic singing of souls and angels. We cannot tell how long it lasts, but when he finally finishes his hymn, he cries out to his master to express his feelings. Again he uses the honorific title, and we see the emphasis moving back now from Tat's silent communion with the universal *Nous* to a more normal type of conversation with Hermes the human teacher:

Father Trismegistus, what shall I say? We have received this Light, and I myself see this same vision within you. I see the Ogdoad and the souls that are in it and the angels singing hymns to the Ennead and its powers. And I see the one who is endowed with all the powers and creates in the spirit [or: creates spirits].[155]

Tat's plea "not to be deprived of the vision" now seems to have been answered, for this exclamation and the conversation that follows suggest that both his noetic vision *and* his noetic hearing have somehow become permanent. Hermes urges his pupil to keep a reverent silence about the vision rather than rushing to speak about it to others, and tells him that henceforth it is fitting to never stop hymning the Father until the day he will leave his body. Tat agrees and says that internally he is singing a hymn right now. Having found the peace he had always been longing for, there is now plenty of room for praise. Interestingly, Tat inquires whether it is right for him to sing praises "when my heart is so full."[156] Presumably he wants to check whether it is acceptable not to stay with

---

[153] NH VI⁶ 59, 19–22.
[154] Keizer, 67 with 106 note 35 (cf. 105 note 31). Only in the early translations by Keizer and Krause/Labib do we find the Coptic пмоу rendered literally as "death" (Keizer, l.c. "death-state"; KL, 179 "Wende dich zum Tode"), initially confirmed by Mahé, "Le sens et la composition," 57–58 ("la mort"). Mahé later changed his mind (HHE I, 119) and emended the Coptic as п‹с›моу (HHE I, 79 "l'action de grâces" and HT V, 98 "la bénédiction"). In this he was followed by all later translators: see Tröger, 501; CHD, 525 with note 74 (both *Lobpreis*, "praise"); Rob, 325 ("praising"); Meyer, 417 ("praise"); SEC, 147 ("benedizione"); HG, 452 ("lofprijzing"). I propose we use the unamended text.
[155] NH VI⁶ 59, 25–60,1.
[156] NH VI⁶ 60, 12–13.

internal noetic hymning alone but burst out in physical and verbal praise as well. Hermes responds that it is right for him to do so, and his words may "get inscribed in this imperishable book."[157]

Which book? Most specialists see this as a reference to *The Ogdoad and the Ennead* itself, but that seems not entirely logical for what is presented as the transcript of an oral discussion. Keeping in mind that the Coptic term for "Master" could also mean "Scribe,"[158] I would suggest that Tat's words will be "engraved" or "imprinted" in his internal noetic world exactly as happens at the end of CH I and CH XIII.[159] In Chapter 10 I will return to these recurring references to the "engraving" or "imprinting" of prayers, hymns and visions so as to keep them from perishing. In any case, now that Hermes has given him permission, Tat does unburden his heart in a jubilant expression of praise and gratitude, a prayer addressed to the silent Generative Source of all that is:

Then I will offer up praise from the bottom of my heart – to the end of the universe and the beginning of all beginnings, the immortal treasure that all humans seek, the generative Source of Light and Truth, the sower of *Logos* and Source of Life eternal.[160] Not even a mystery discourse [*logos*] can ever speak of you, Lord. Therefore my *nous* wants to sing hymns to you every day. I am the instrument of your Spirit [*pneuma*], the *nous* is your plectrum, your Will uses me to make music.

I see myself. I have received power from you, for your love has made us alive.[161]

Hermes is impressed by Tat's prayer: "Beautiful, my child!"[162] The emphasis on music is particularly interesting here. Spoken language, *logos*, is insufficient even if it is "hidden," "secret," or "occult" (for as formulated

---

[157] NH VI⁶ 60, 16–17.
[158] See above, p. 303 with note 152.
[159] CH I 30; CH XIII 21, with discussion above, p. 262; and see HHE I, 122. For the dimension of a cosmic or noetic memory in this same context, see Bull, *Tradition*, 309–310.
[160] The Coptic ⲁⲅⲁⲡⲏ reflects the Greek ἀγάπη for "love" and is surprising here, partly because it is typical of the Christian New Testament but does not occur elsewhere in the Hermetica (in contrast to ἀγαπάω, see CH I 19 & 22, XVI 16, SH IIB 7; I thank Christian Bull for this specification in a private communication) and partly because the meaning is unclear: why would the generative Source of Life eternal be addressed as the *Love* of Life? Among various solutions discussed by Camplani in his very long footnote about these problems (SEC, 149–150 note 79; cf. HG, 648 note 1157) is the possibility that we are dealing with a scribal or translation error: if the original had πηγή instead of ἀγάπη, the text makes perfect sense. I provisorily accept this option here.
[161] NH VI⁶ 60, 17–61,2. In the final sentence, like van den Broek I follow Camplani's reconstruction of the Coptic ϯⲛⲁⲩ (SEC, 151 with note 82; HG, 453 and 645–646 note 1160).
[162] NH VI⁶ 61, 3. Again, almost all modern translation obscure the Hermetic concern with beauty (Keizer, 70 "well said"; Tröger, 501 and NHD, 515 "vortrefflich"; CHD, 526 "recht so"; HHE I, 83 and HT V, 102 "bien"; Rob, 326 and Meyer, 417 "right"; SEC, 151 "bene"; HG, 453 "goed zo"): only KL, 181 have "schön."

in CH IX 10, it cannot reach as far as the truth), but vocal music will rise higher than words. As the *Nous* itself touches the strings of Tat's heart, the sound will be heard in the silence of the unfathomable One.

As Tat is now capable of seeing the noetic Light by immediate perception, *emphutos gnōsis*, he knows that he is seeing his own immortal essence. The *nous* receives its power from the one and only Source, the *pēgē*, whose love has restored him to the true Life as it gave him the gift of wisdom.[163] Having finished his prayer, Tat now moves to the actual hymn, which again takes the shape of a string of vowels.

$$
\begin{array}{c}
a\ \bar{o} \\
e\ e\ \bar{o}\ \bar{o} \\
\bar{e}\ \bar{e}\ \bar{e}\ \bar{o}\ \bar{o}\ \bar{o} \\
i\ i\ i\ i\ \bar{o}\ \bar{o}\ \bar{o}\ \bar{o} \\
o\ o\ o\ o\ o\ \bar{o}\ \bar{o}\ \bar{o}\ \bar{o}\ \bar{o} \\
u\ u\ u\ u\ u\ u\ \bar{o}\ \bar{o}\ \bar{o}\ \bar{o}\ \bar{o}\ \bar{o} \\
\bar{o}\ \bar{o}\ \bar{o}\ \bar{o}\ \bar{o}\ \bar{o}\ \bar{o}\ \bar{o}\ \bar{o}\ \bar{o}\ \bar{o}\ \bar{o}\ \bar{o}\ \bar{o}^{164}
\end{array}
$$

Interestingly, this sequence is now said to be nothing less than the "mystery name" of the divinity itself.[165] It seems to me that more can be said about this second series of vowels than has been done in previous scholarship. First of all, it should *not* be confused with the purely noetic hymns "sung in silence" by the souls and angels in the Ogdoad and Ennead; on the contrary, we are dealing with actual vowels as in the first instance, linked to the seven cosmic spheres and intoned audibly by the human voice. Secondly, it should not be understood as a new invocation, presumably to reverse the ascent and make Tat's soul descend again from Saturn back to the Moon and finally to earth: if that were the case, we should expect the vowels to be sung in reverse order beginning with the fourteen omegas. Thirdly, this also explains the absence of *nomina barbara*. Because Tat's soul has been restored finally and irreversibly to the true noetic Life, no longer does his consciousness need to cross any fearsome

---

[163] Even if one does not follow Camplani's reading of NH VI⁶ 61, 2 (see above, p. 305 note 161), the point is repeated immediately in NH VI⁶ 61, 6. For the "gift" of wisdom, see NH VI⁶ 61, 3: "o grace!"

[164] NH VI⁶ 61, 10–15. Again we must assume intentional errors in the number of vowels (see above, p. 290 with note 102). Since the structural pattern seems perfectly clear, like Holzhausen (CHD, 526 with note 80) I add one omega in line 2 and one iota in line 4. Furthermore I delete two omegas from line 7; but note that Holzhausen follows a different logic, striking just one omega at the end so as to reach an expanding series of 6+7+8=21 omegas in lines 6–7.

[165] NH VI⁶ 61, 9. See HHE I, 124.

boundary between the cosmic conditions called "life" (actually under the sway of death) and "death" (the true life of the soul).[166] Fourthly, no longer do the vowels sung from down below receive a lengthier and more powerful echo from the superior noetic powers up above; I suggest that the series of omegas and vowels are of equal length because Tat's level of consciousness now equals that of the noetic powers. Finally, the same interior logic suggests a fifth point. As Tat is now one with the *Nous*, he has reached a state of perfect self-sufficiency, and this makes it unlikely that the omegas are sung by the brethren this second time. I assume that we are hearing nothing now but Tat's voice alone, singing the vowels at their proper pitches and probably drawing them out at length. Again, this closing hymn must therefore take some time to complete. Surrounded by his brethren, Tat finishes with a gesture of humility and gratitude as reflected in a final spoken sentence: "You exist with the *Pneuma*. I hymn you with reverence."[167] Therefore the ceremony ends as it should: in a spirit of *eusebeia*, the supreme Hermetic virtue.

---

[166] Mahé admitted in HHE I, 124 that he failed to understand the difference between the two vowel sequences and the absence of *nomina barbara*. Regarding the life/death boundary: as indicated above (p. 291), I accept Mahé's reference to the "Organon of Hermes Trismegistus" (HHE I, 106–107) as a key for understanding the latter.

[167] NH VI[6] 61, 15–17. Mahé originally rejected Tröger's translation in terms of "Frömmigkeit" (reverence, piety) and saw it as a reference to deification ("un état divin," HHE I 83 and 124; see criticism by van den Broek in HG, 646 note 1162), but he later changed his mind: see HT V, 104 ("pieusement").

10

The Conquest of Time

> *Au risque toujours et par essence de se perdre ainsi défini-*
> *tivement. Qui saura jamais telle disparition?*
> Jacques Derrida[1]

The ceremony is over. The hymns have fallen silent, the prayers are completed, the candles have been extinguished, the incense has wafted away. Hermes and Tat find themselves alone, talking about what must be done so that the experience will not be forgotten. "My child, write this book down in the temple of Diospolis in engraved letters of the writing of the House of Life," Hermes tells Tat, "and call it *The Ogdoad Reveals the Ennead*."[2] He must inscribe it on steles of turquoise, add a tablet of sapphire inscribed with the divine name, and support the whole of it on a pedestal of milk-stone.[3] This impressive memorial plaque must be placed in the sanctuary of Hermes at the right astrological moment, protected by eight guardian deities and an

---

[1] Derrida, *La dissemination* ("La pharmacie de Platon"), 79. "At the risk, always and essentially, of getting lost forever. Who will ever know of such disappearance?"

[2] NH VI⁶ 61, 18–21. The engraved letters are often translated simply as "hieroglyphs" (HHE I, 83; Rob, 326; Meyer, 418; CHD, 527; HG, 453; cf. KL, 181 "*Meisterbuchstaben*"), but Van den Kerchove insists on the literal translation with its explicit reference to the "House of Life," the temple scriptorium where sacred texts were composed and kept (*La voie*, 107, 110–115; cf. Keizer, 71; Tröger, 502; CHD, 527 note 82). Diospolis could mean Thebes (Diospolis Magna) or Hou (Diospolis Parva), south of Chēnoboskion that we know as Nag Hammadi (Van den Kerchove, *La voie*, 160 note 28).

[3] For these materials see Van den Kerchove, *La voie*, 166–170. Turquoise has a blue color that can shade into green; lapis lazuli is dark blue with patches of gold; milk-stone must be calcite, a white "sweating stone" whose liquid got naturally associated with milk.

apotropaic charm.[4] All of this to ensure that the knowledge will not get lost, the power of the name will not be misused, and the message will not be defiled by the ignorant and the profane. It is intended only for the pure of heart, those who sincerely turn to God in search of wisdom and *gnōsis*. Note, however, that neither such good intentions nor the virtue of *eusebeia* will ultimately be enough, for Hermes points out that even those who have done nothing to be ashamed of and have a perfectly clear conscience will still be unable to understand the mystery. In this life at least, perfect *gnōsis* is possible only for those who have gone through the rebirth.[5] As Tat has promised to follow the instructions, Hermes concludes that all is now perfect.

But is it, really? I just summarized what the author of NH VI[6] means to tell his readers at the end of the treatise; but his text tells us more than he intends, and something different as well. If we read again and pay attention to the details, we discover that something is out of joint. We are supposed to believe that these instructions are given by Tat's human teacher, the Hermes Trismegistus whom we know from the first part of this treatise and the rest of the Hermetic literature: the person who once met Poimandres face to face, who expelled the agents of darkness and guided Tat through the rebirth, who embraced his pupil and then led his consciousness to the Ogdoad and the Ennead, and who became a vessel of the *Nous* as it was speaking through his mouth. But in fact, the Hermes who is giving instructions here appears to be someone else – this is no longer Tat's thrice-greatest teacher but the ancient Egyptian deity Thoth, known as Hermes in Greek and identified as the planet Mercury under his Latin name. The text leaves no doubt about this point: place the steles "in *my* sanctuary," Tat is told, and do it "when *I am* in the sign of Virgo."[6] In other words, with a sudden jolt we find ourselves transported back from Roman Egypt to a time of mythical beginnings and into a "fictional narrative" about Egyptian gods and their dealings with humans. Hermes Trismegistus is gone. His place has been taken by Thoth.

---

[4] NH VI[6] 61, 26–62, 22 and 63, 15–32. On the "ogdoad" of guardian deities (four frog-headed males on the right, and four cat-headed females on the left), see Van den Kerchove, *La voie*, 171–178. The exact formulation of the charm is given in NH VI[6] 63, 16–31; but the text does not specify whether it should be engraved as well or ritually pronounced at the moment of consecration.

[5] NH VI[6] 62, 23–63, 14.

[6] NH VI[6] 62, 3–4 and 17–20. More precisely, Mercury must be in the constellation of Virgo, with the sun in Aries and "after fifteen degrees have passed me by" (for the astrological dimension, see discussions in Keizer, 111–118 notes 62–65; HHE I, 129–130; HG, 647–648 note 1169).

Content and composition of this final section therefore set it apart from what came before, and the attempt to make it all cohere is far from convincing.[7] But while the anonymous author could perhaps have done a better job, what he *tries* to do is perfectly consistent with the requirements of the genre. I have argued that its purpose must have been to show practitioners not just what they should think or do, but also what they could expect to experience if they got it all right. As suggested above, the genre of spiritual Hermetica is best defined in terms of inspirational narratives about the ideal teacher, the ideal student, the ideal discussion, the ideal message, the ideal proceedings, and the ideal rewards.[8] But what then must be done *after* the ideal devotee has finally reached the goal, having beheld the supreme vision of the Ogdoad and the Ennead, the ultimate experience of perfect *gnōsis*? We were just told the answer: he should write it all down.

But that is bizarre! What *is* there to be written down about a radically altered condition of rapt silence that is said to go far beyond anything words can express? We find ourselves face to face here with the ultimate paradox at the heart of the Hermetic mystery: Tat is told to write down what can never be written down. The authors are using language to tell us that language is powerless to convey the truth. They claim to send a message while pointing out that it is not to be found anywhere on the page.[9] What does this imply for our scholarly attempts to understand the content of these treatises? Can we in fact say anything about it at all? In particular, does Hermetic *gnōsis* mean anything that we can identify and recognize as "knowledge" in modern academic discourse? To gain some clarity about these dilemmas, I will take the final section of NH VI[6] as a subtle hint: let us go back to Thoth, the Egyptian Hermes, the mythical inventor of language.

---

[7] The lack of literary coherence is evident also from two other discrepancies. Firstly, if the conversation is supposed to come right after the Ogdoadic/Enneadic ascent, it is clear that Hermes and Tat have no "book" available to be copied or written down, just recollections of what just happened: the book still needs to be written, and cannot include this final part. Secondly, of course we are reading a Coptic text on papyrus translated from a Greek original, not a treatise engraved in Egyptian hieroglyphs on steles of turquoise.

[8] See Chapter 5, p. 122. Of course, in addition to the interpretive angle on which I focus in this chapter, the general idea of preserving a sacred book so as to save it for posterity is an extremely widespread and much-discussed literary commonplace; for many parallel cases see e.g. Burns, *Apocalypse*, 55–57.

[9] Hanegraaff, "Altered States of Knowledge," 130.

THE DRUG

One of the earliest references to Thoth in ancient Greek literature occurs in Plato's *Phaedrus*, where Socrates tells his friend a story he has heard. As we will see, it is significant that he did not *read* about it in some written account but presumably has it from an oral source. Plato seems to have known the ibis-headed Egyptian god under the name Theuth rather than Thoth, but it is evidently the same deity, so I will refer to him by his usual name.[10] Socrates has heard that Thoth one day appeared before the god Thamus, known as Ammon to the Egyptians, who was ruling as king over the whole of Egypt. Ammon is no one less here than the great Egyptian god Amun, known as "the hidden one," the chief of the Egyptian pantheon.[11] Thoth showed him all the useful arts he had just invented, asking Ammon to make them available to the Egyptians. But when they came to the art of writing [*grammasin*], a remarkable dialogue ensued:

Theuth said "O King, here is a knowledge that, once it is learned, will make the Egyptians wiser and will improve their memory; for it is a drug [*pharmakon*] of memory and wisdom that I have discovered."

But Thamus replied, "Most ingenious Theuth, to one it is given to create the elements of an art, but it is up to another to judge whether they will harm or profit those who will use them. Now you, the father of writing, have been led by your affection to describe its effects as the perfect opposite of what they really are! For it will actually introduce forgetfulness into the souls of those who learn it. They will cease to exercise their memory because they will rely on that which is written, calling things to remembrance by means of external signs [*hup'allotriōn tupōn*] and no longer from within themselves. What you have invented is a drug not of memory [*mnēmē*] but of reminding [*hupomnēsis*]. You provide your pupils with just the appearance of wisdom, not its true reality. You will enable them to hear of many things without proper instruction, and so they will seem to know many things, whereas in fact they will for the most part be ignorant – and unpleasant too, because they will not really be wise but will only appear so."[12]

Writing is described as a *pharmakon*. This term stands at the center of a famous analysis by Jacques Derrida, who called attention to its profound ambivalence.[13] A *pharmakon* could be a beneficial medicine

---

[10] On etymology and different spellings of the name, see Boylan, *Thoth the Hermes of Egypt*, 4; Kurth, "Thot," 498; Vos, "Thoth," 1621.
[11] Assmann, "Amun"; Otto, "Amun." For the identification of Ammon as Amun, see e.g. Cop, 200–201; van den Broek, "Hermes Trismegistus I," 478.
[12] Plato, *Phaedrus* 274e–275b.
[13] "La pharmacie de Platon" appears in Derrida, *La dissémination*, 77–213. Much of Derrida's notorious obscurity here is an effect of questionable translations, for the French original (while certainly difficult) is perfectly clear. Therefore I will avoid the standard English edition by Barbara Johnson (Derrida, *Dissemination*, 61–171) except for her helpful "Translator's Introduction" to the volume.

as well as a harmful poison, and in Plato's account it has been variously translated not just as "remedy" but also as "recipe," "potion," or "elixir."[14] This semantic range is best captured by the word "drug."[15] Thoth presents the art of writing as a beneficial drug for curing forgetfulness, a medicine or antidote against the effects of the passing of time.[16] Of course, that is exactly what the final section of *The Ogdoad and the Ennead* is all about: Thoth giving instructions about writing everything down, not just on papyrus but engraved on stone tablets that will stand the test of time and will be preserved in the innermost sanctuary of his own temple.

But in doing so, Thoth explicitly disregards the rebuke he had received from Ammon/Amun, the supreme "hidden god" who stands even above Thoth himself in the Egyptian pantheon. Amun objects that this new drug of writing is actually a harmful poison, and Socrates is telling Phaedrus the story because he agrees with that assessment. Writing is a surrogate that usurps the place of legitimate speech, *logos*, described as "the living and ensouled word of him who sees [*eidotos*]" which is "written in the soul of the learner"[17] *immediately* – by the agency of the living voice. It is of enormous importance to be precise about what this means. First of all, we have a person who "sees" truth in immediate noetic perception. That terminology is not just Hermetic but comes from Plato himself, who highlights *noēsis* as the supreme category of knowledge in a famous

---

[14] Plato, *Phèdre* (Vicaire), 83; Plato, *The Collected Dialogues* (Hamilton and Huntington Cairns ed.), 520 (Hackforth); Plato, *Complete Works* (Cooper), 551-552 (Nehamas and Woodruff); Plato, *Euthyphro / Apology / Crito / Phaedo / Phaedrus* (Loeb Classical Library, Plato vol. 1), 563 (Fowler). In fact, *pharmakon* had an even much wider range of meanings, including "pictorial color, painter's pigment, cosmetic application, perfume, magical talisman, and recreational intoxicant" (Rinella, *Pharmakon*, 237, 240).

[15] In this regard I follow Harvey Yunis in his commentary on *Phaedr.* 274e: *Plato Phaedrus*, 227, with reference to Artelt, *Studien zur Geschichte der Begriffe "Heilmittel" und "Gift."*

[16] Plato's concept of letters as "drugs for curing forgetfulness" (τὰ τῆς λήθης φάρμακ') may have come from Euripides (see Palamedes according to Fr. 578, in Euripides, *Fragments*, 52-53).

[17] Plato, *Phaedrus* 276a. Only this legitimate speech is said to go together with ἐπιστήμη (as well formulated by Hamilton and Huntington Cairns: Plato: *Collected Dialogues*, 521). Plato's εἰδότος is usually translated as "the one who knows," but it is of great importance that this knowledge is described by *visual* metaphors of immediate perception, as conveyed in English by our expression "I see!" when we want to say that we understand (see entry εἴδω in Liddell and Scott, *Greek-English Lexicon*, 483). Ψυχή poses problems too: occasionally it gets mistranslated as "mind" rather than "soul" (Fowler in Loeb Classical Library vol. I, 567), and ἔμψυχον is usually rendered as "breathing." "Animated" might be better, but is bound to be misunderstood as "lively" by modern readers, so I prefer "ensouled."

key passage of the *Republic*.[18] Secondly, this person decides to speak – but only to someone whom he trusts to be capable of understanding.[19] Thirdly, his spoken words leave an imprint in the soul of the listener. But while the speaker's *logos* is alive and flexible, its imprint is already an imitation or simulacrum, a secondary echo of the speaker's own *noēsis*: this is no longer direct knowledge but an indirect reflection of knowledge. Fourthly and finally, although the conversation may get recorded in writing, written letters and words can never be more than mere reminders. Since they are twice removed now from the original *noēsis*, they are strictly simulacra of simulacra, echoes of echoes, reflections of reflections. In sum, from immediate *noēsis* we go to living speech about an unspeakable knowledge, but what we finally end up with is a record of dead letters written in stone.

If this is the situation, then one has to take position. Thoth's perspective seems to be optimistic and pragmatic, as he emphasizes only the positive virtues of the *pharmakon*. Is it not a great thing that, thanks to this splendid invention, our spoken words can now be preserved for posterity? Is it not wonderful that later generations will be able to profit from what we have discovered, so that humanity can start building up an ever-accumulating store of written knowledge? But Ammon, by sharp contrast, gives voice to a profound linguistic pessimism. He knows that in the very act of translation, the essence of divine truth will get lost. Our word "translation" comes from the Latin *translatus*, the past participle of *transferre*, "to carry across." These very words reflect the insight that what happens in any act of translation is a *transfer* of meaning across a discontinuous gap or abyss.[20] When it comes to *noēsis* of absolute reality, however, something will have to be "carried over" not just from one language to another

---

[18] Plato's famous analogy of the "divided line" in *Republic* 509d–511e distinguishes between four "passions [παθήματα] of the psyche" on which we rely for all our knowledge: εἰκασία (perception of imaginal appearances), πίστις (belief or trust in a reliable core of perception), διάνοια (discursive thought), and νόησις (*noēsis*).

[19] See discussion in Chapter 4, p. 115. Specifically, Plato writes that the word that is "written in the soul of the learner" by means of oral conversation is thereby capable of "defending itself" (because the speaker will notice when the listener misunderstands, and can correct him immediately) and "knows to whom it should speak and to whom it should keep silent" (*Phaedrus* 276a).

[20] Even more explicit in the German *übersetzen* ("setting across," as for instance in lifting something up from a river's shore and putting it down on the other side) and the French *traduire* resp. *traduction* (viz. *transducere*, "leading across"). Interestingly, the Dutch *vertalen* follows an entirely different logic that is hard to convey in English, as it turns the word "language" (*taal*) into a verb.

but *across the very threshold of language itself.*[21] *Noēsis* of "that which cannot be spoken" is by definition immediate, "without mediation," and thus we have literally *no means* available to carry it across.[22]

All this leads to an inevitable conclusion: *noēsis* is not just difficult to convey, but a strict impossibility in the order of discourse.[23] Even the spoken *logos* – that which Socrates calls "the living and ensouled word of him who sees" – is already a surrogate or what Derrida refers to as a *supplément*.[24] Speech is a subtle enchantment of the soul that takes the place of *noēsis* while making the listener believe that it still carries truth.[25] But deceptive as it is, the bewitching effects of this *pharmakon* are held in check at least by the constraints of space and time, because (long before the invention of sound recordings) it required speakers and listeners to be *physically present* in a specific location during a limited period of time. Once the verbal exchange is over, nothing remains but fading memories in mortal brains. Precisely this is what changes dramatically under the impact of Thoth's invention, the *pharmakon* of writing. Not only is it a simulacrum of a simulacrum, twice removed from noetic truth and therefore doubly deceptive; but it carries a unique and unheard-of potential for enchantment, precisely because it is not transient but *permanent* and not living but *dead*. Human voices fall silent but written texts remain. Speech belongs to the living but what is dead may never die. Contrary to spoken words, writings can be disseminated among a potentially unlimited number of readers; it is impossible to control who will get access to them over long stretches of time; and as the author is no longer there to push back against misinterpretations, the text becomes autonomous while losing its protection – henceforth it is entirely at the mercy of its readers.

---

[21] See Chapter 1, p. 12.
[22] The idea of mediation is utterly central to the etymology of the English *mean* as both a noun and an adjective (see also the German *Mittel*, French *moyen*), and essential to understand *meaning* both as a noun and as a verb ("to mean"). Note that the argument affects the very meaning of "meaning": if the latter exists only in the very act of mediation, then that which it mediates must be strictly without meaning.
[23] Derrida, *La dissémination*, 208: "la dialectique supplée la *noēsis* impossible." Cf. Van den Kerchove, *La voie*, 115: "Thot's writings become the replacements [*remplaçants*] of the henceforth inaudible words of the god Rê."
[24] Johnson, "Translator's Introduction," xiii.
[25] Derrida, *La dissémination*, 145: "... if the *logos* is already a penetrating supplement, does this not mean that Socrates, 'he who does not write,' is a master of the *pharmakon* as well? And therefore isn't he the spitting image of a sophist? a *pharmakeus*? a magician, a sorcerer, even a poisoner?" What Plato really dreams about is "a memory without sign, that is to say, without supplement. *Mnēmē* without *hupomnēsis*, without *pharmakon*" (ibid., 135).

What is really at stake in the confrontation between Ammon and Thoth, then, is a fundamental conflict between two mutually incompatible orders of "knowledge." There is literally no place for *noēsis* in textual discourse. I want to emphasize the radicality of that conclusion, which means nothing less than that even the written sentence you just read is questionable at best, as the word *noēsis* suggests a presence where in fact there is an absence. The problem is not just that *nous* gets replaced, "supplemented," by more convenient terms such as "mind" or "intellect" while its activity gets obscured by conventional verbs such as "thinking" or "understanding," but that even the Hermetic treatises in their original language cannot claim to *say* anything at all about *nous* or *noēsis*. These written words are empty signifiers in the most radical sense. Even more than that: if we follow Ammon's perspective to its logical conclusion, there is no way to avoid the implication that the entire book you have been reading must be an act of delusion. Like all writers, including Plato himself and the authors of the Hermetica, I have been putting a spell on you and on myself as well. No reader can escape the influence of this potent *pharmakon*, this hallucinatory drug known as writing.

The textual universe that is conjured into existence by the *pharmakon* has no place for *noēsis* as "knowledge," but the reverse is true as well: the noetic has no place for written discourse as "knowledge" either. These two orders are mutually exclusive, not just in the sense that whenever one of them is present, the other is absent, but in a much more radical sense. If one of them is present, not even the *absence* of its counterpart can be said to be present, because even the very possibility of its appearance cannot possibly appear. This is in fact the conclusion drawn by Derrida in his references to Plato's Ammon, "the hidden one." He describes him as "the hidden source, which both illuminates and makes blind, of the *logos*,"[26] and as the origin of visibility which is itself

---

[26] Derrida, *La dissémination*, 102. This terminology of "the source" as a dazzling light is therefore original with Derrida himself: "In this play of representation, the point of origin becomes ungraspable. There are things, reflecting pools and images, an infinite reference from one to the other, but no longer a source" (*De la grammatologie*, 54–55; my translation corrects the standard one by Gayatri Chakravorty Spivak, *Of Grammatology*, 36). How central this universal Source is to Derrida's thinking about language is further confirmed by the opening quotation of *De la grammatologie* (p. 11), taken from a scholarly article about cuneiform script that finishes with the words of an anonymous Assyrian scribe: "He who will excel in the science of writing will shine like the sun" (*De la grammatologie*, 11; again mistranslated by Spivak, *Of Grammatology*, 3), to which the author comments that the sun for the Assyrians was "the symbol of eternity and universal knowledge" (Labat, "L'écriture cunéiforme," 87). Therefore it is no over-interpretation to conclude that "the Other of scripture" in Derrida's thought would be precisely *gnōsis* of the *pēgē*.

absolutely invisible[27] – in short, that which we have encountered as the Hermetic *pēgē*, the universal Source of noetic Life and Light.

Let us repeat. [Its disappearance] is therefore the precondition of discourse, taken this time as an aspect and not as the origin of *generalized* writing. This writing (is) *epekeina tēs ousias* ["beyond what is": Plato, *Rep.* 509b]. The disappearance of truth as presence, the withdrawal of the present origin of presence is the precondition of all (manifestation of) truth. The non-truth is truth. The non-presence is presence. The *différence* – the disappearance of the originary presence – conditions both the possibility and the impossibility of truth *at the same time*. At the same time. "At the same time" means that that which is present (*on*) in its truth, in the presence of its identity and the identity of its presence, *is doubled* as soon as it appears, as soon as it presents itself. *It appears, in its essence, as* the possibility of its own duplication. That is to say, in Platonic terms, of its non-truth in the most proper sense of the word, of its pseudo-truth reflected in the icon, the phantasm or the simulacrum.[28]

The crucial point to note about this extraordinary passage is that *epekeina tēs ousias* in Plato's *Republic* refers to the Good, equivalent to the Hermetic *pēgē*, but Derrida reverses the logic and tells us that *writing* is "beyond what is"! The point is that whatever *we* consider to be truth and a possible object of knowledge is its exact opposite from the perspective of the Source; but that likewise, the truth of the Source as an "object" of *noēsis* cannot be known or even be considered knowable in our scholarly order of "generalized writing." However, it is essential to see that even these very formulations serve both to illustrate *and* undermine that conclusion "at the same time." Language just forced me to describe the Source as an "object" of *noēsis*, although the point is precisely that *noēsis* of the Source is beyond object-subject distinctions. The very term *différence* leads us to imagine two different orders of truth and knowledge, as though these were two parallel worlds, thereby suggesting that the

---

[27] Derrida, *La dissémination*, 208.
[28] Derrida, *La dissémination*, 209–210. "Its disappearance" in square brackets here stands for Derrida's original formulation "bien-père-capital-soleil" ["good-father-capital-sun"] which would be incomprehensible without the preceding discussions. "Let us repeat" is programmatic and deeply ironic, since any repetition in the context of Derrida's discourse implies a *supplément* or surrogate. In French, "l'écriture *générale*" carries totalizing connotations that largely vanish in English translation; I assume that it means to suggest, in line with Derrida's general argument, that writing becomes the totality of discourse (here lies the significance of his statement that discourse is not the origin of writing but just an aspect or manifestation of it, *un moment* in French). Note that in the standard English translation, Johnson inexplicably deletes "de sa propre duplication. C'est-à-dire, en termes platoniciens de"; and that Derrida's spelling in this passage is *différence*, not his famous *différance* (on which, see Derrida, "La différance").

The Conquest of Time 317

soul could find salvation by the attainment of *gnōsis* in an "other world" of pure noetic consciousness; but the point is precisely that *there is no other world*. While *noēsis* leaves no place for textual discourse and textual discourse leaves no place for *noēsis*, yet we can never move from one order of knowledge to the other one.[29]

André-Jean Festugière was clearly sensitive to this radical alterity of *nous* and *noēsis*, and made it central to the fourth and final volume of his great study about the Hermetica. Our previous discussion will make it possible now to get a better view at what was actually going on in his argument. As indicated by the very title of the book, *Le Dieu inconnu et la Gnose* (The Unknown God and the Gnosis), Festugière could not conceive of his materials otherwise than in terms of a "gnostic dualism" that pictured God as radically opposed to the material world.[30] The central question that he sought to answer was formulated in his Preface: "can this God still be known, and if so, in what manner?"[31] Still, over a length of 267 erudite pages, the closest Festugière ever got to answering it was in the very final sentences, where he admitted his ultimate perplexity about what Hermetic *gnōsis* was all about.[32] In doing so, he alluded not to the Hermetica but to a passage by Porphyry, who claims that at the age of sixty-eight, spurred on by "a daimonic light" (*daimoniōi phōti*)

---

[29] Derrida himself does not escape from these dilemmas either. He identifies the Platonic opposition between *mnēmē* and *hupomnēsis* (memory and reminding) as "the great decision of philosophy, that through which it institutes itself" (*La dissémination*, 138, cf. 143, 156), by which he means the birth of metaphysics. But far from deconstructing metaphysics as such, his own argument is metaphysical through and through. It reduces all *logos* to writing, and *noēsis* becomes a strict impossibility because – in his own famous formulation – it is literally *hors-texte* (*La dissémination*, 119; cf. *De la grammatologie*, 227). Therefore *nous* is certainly not to be understood as a "metaphysical reality"; rather, it defines the limit of metaphysics. For very similar conclusions, see Loy, *Nonduality*, 262–275, esp. 270.

[30] Festugière's *Dieu inconnu* clearly echoed the "alien God" evoked in Adolf von Harnack's famous volume *Marcion: Das Evangelium vom fremden Gott* (1921): "He is *unknown* because in no way can he be understood from the perspective of the world and humanity; he is *alien* because there is absolutely no natural connection and no obligation that binds him to the world and humanity, *not even with his Geist*" (ibid., 4; I leave the German *Geist* untranslated here, as it would normally be translated as "spirit" but also serves as a common translation for *nous*). In his influential *The Gnostic Religion*, Hans Jonas admitted that the "vehicle of salvation" for Marcion was not *gnōsis* but *pistis*, a fact that would seem to put him "squarely outside the gnostic area"; nevertheless, he went on to argue that Marcion's anti-cosmic dualism, his idea of an unknown God, and his notion of salvation as liberation from an inferior and oppressive demiurge were all "so outstandingly gnostic that anyone who professes them in this historical context must be counted as one of the Gnostics" (ibid., 137). For this fatal confusion and its results, see above, pp. 85–86.

[31] RHT IV, ix.

[32] See Chapter 1, p. 19 note 32.

and following the way of ascent taught in Plato's *Symposium*, he himself was united (*henōthēnai*) with the divine reality "established above *nous* and the whole of the noetic (*huper de noun kai pan to noē*)."[33] Above the *nous*! In Hermetic terms, that would be the *pēgē*, the Source. Festugière was explicit in pointing out that *henōthēnai* here means unity in the strongest sense of the word, "since subject and object are no longer distinct, but identical."[34] That was exactly the right point to make, and with this conclusion he was actually holding the key that could have resolved the question to which his volume was devoted. Yet he ultimately failed to answer it because the preconceived frame of a "gnostic dualism" prevented him from doing so. What he could not see is that Hermetic metaphysics is grounded in an opposition *not* of spirit against matter, but of the nonduality of ultimate reality against the dualism of human consciousness.

The missing piece of the puzzle that could at least have pointed Festugière into the right direction had in fact been discovered about nine years earlier, at Nag Hammadi, in "a jar from Egypt" to which he reacted with enormous irritation – understandably perhaps, at least from a psychological point of view, as he must have intuited that its contents threatened the entire 1700-page edifice of *La Révélation d'Hermès Trismégiste*.[35] We have seen that *The Ogdoad and the Ennead* culminates in a silent noetic (comm)union with the Source – a perception that is no perception, an experience that is no experience, and a vision that is no vision either, because there is no subject to perceive or experience or see and no object to be perceived or experienced or seen.

THE INSCRIPTION

Precisely this collapse of the subject-object distinction led Iamblichus to point out that insofar as "knowledge" is "separated from its object by some degree of otherness,"*emphutos gnōsis* (innate *gnōsis*) cannot

---

[33] RHT IV, 267: ἐνωθῆναι here refers to Porphyry, *Life of Plotinus* 23: 17–18. Cf. Banner, *Philosophic Silence*, 45.
[34] RHT IV, 267.
[35] See his furious response to Jean Doresse's announcement in 1949 of the Nag Hammadi discovery (Doresse and Mina, "Nouveaux textes gnostiques coptes"), in the addenda to the second edition of Festugière's first volume (RHT I, 427–429). He must have been horrified: after fifteen years of diligent labor he finally believed to have demonstrated, once and for all, that "Hermetism is specifically Greek [and] had no profound connections with Egyptian thought or with the oriental gnosis," and there had never been a "Hermetic church" or "confraternity of mystics" either. And now the contents of "une jarre d'Égypte" (RHT I, 427) put a bombshell under the entire argument.

strictly be called knowledge at all.³⁶ It should now be clear why it made sense for him to say that. The phenomenon of "duplication" or *différance* as defined by Derrida – if indeed we can call it a phenomenon, since it is what makes things "appear" [*phainō*] in the first place – results *not* in a conventional dualism of matter versus mind (or equivalent terms such as body versus soul) but in *two mutually exclusive orders of knowledge*, those of the signifier and of the signified, in neither of which the other can even be conceived of, let alone referred to.³⁷ What "knowledge" means in the one is not what it means in the other; therefore *gnōsis* cannot be what we would describe as knowledge, and our concepts of knowledge cannot capture what *gnōsis* means. *Emphutos gnōsis* according to Iamblichus was not a matter of possible disagreement or discussion, something to which one may or may not concede, but "it is rather the case that we are enveloped by it, we are filled with it, and in fact it is only by virtue of knowing that the gods exist that we grasp what *we* are."³⁸ We have seen that in such statements, he was referring not to discourse (*dianoia*) but to an immediate non-verbal experience in the context of theurgical ritual, "the work of the gods."³⁹ Iamblichus' formulations carry two important implications. First of all, *gnōsis* of the gods meant "self-knowledge," in the radical nondual sense that had dawned on Hermes at the moment when he was gazing into Poimandres' eyes and understood that he himself was the Light gazing at him.⁴⁰ Secondly, it was defined not as learning something previously unknown, but as *re*-cognition or *anamnēsis* of innate *gnōsis*, not a new insight coming from outside but a reawakening of *mnēmē* "from within oneself."⁴¹

---

³⁶ Iamblichus, *Response to Porphyry* I 3; see discussion in Chapter 4, pp. 112–113.
³⁷ Derrida, *La dissémination*, 138–139, 158–159. Again, however, the paradox is that in the absence of a signified, there are no signifiers either; the very distinction on which the entire argument is built is itself a product of *différance*.
³⁸ Iamblichus, *Response to Porphyry* I 3; see Chapter 4, pp. 112–113.
³⁹ David Loy points out correctly that immediate experience is the blind spot in Derrida's argument, causing him to remain trapped in the framework of Western metaphysics that he claims to deconstruct: "The nondualist agrees that such dualities are ineluctably inscribed in language and thus are fundamental categories of thought; however, this means not that they are inescapable, but that their deconstruction points finally to an experience beyond language – or, more precisely, to a nondual way of experiencing language and thought" (*Nonduality*, 263).
⁴⁰ CH I 6–7; see Chapter 6, pp. 164–167.
⁴¹ Plato, *Phaedrus* 275a (see quotation above); *Theaetetus* 150d ("they discover within themselves a multitude of beautiful things, which they bring forth into the light").

Now what did that mean? So far, we have been concentrating on immediate *noēsis* as opposed to the double simulacrum of writing. In Plato's account and Derrida's analysis, the former is represented by Ammon and the latter by Thoth's *pharmakon*; in NH VI[6], the former refers to Tat's unitive experience and the latter to Thoth's command to write it all down in stone. No bridge can ever lead from text to *noēsis* (from our world of dualistic consciousness to the nondual reality of the Source, from the web of signifiers to the Signified, from our phenomenal world of manifestation to the "hidden one" or *Dieu inconnu*) because the very idea of such a bridge implies the presence of an abyss that can only exist in the former but never in the latter. If *nous* is in fact the exclusive universal reality of Life and Light emanating from the Source, then the only bridge that our *nous* needs to cross and leave behind consists in the dualistic illusion that there is a bridge. This verdict seems absolute and final. But what about the intermediary domain of the *spoken* word, *logos*, which is not twice but only one time removed from *noēsis*?

Hermes states in CH IX that "*logos* does not get to the truth," but adds that it is capable of guiding a person's *nous* up to a certain point from where it will then be able to reach the truth "by its own power."[42] This is consistent with what we have seen throughout this volume, and indeed with what *nous* and *noein* had always meant in Greek philosophy. As demonstrated in an extremely detailed analysis by Kurt von Fritz, these words were closely linked to the sense of vision and always had to do with penetrating "below the visible surface to the real essence of the contemplated object";[43] they did not have to do with reasoning but with direct perception[44]; however, while it was believed that *nous* "always sees the truth," this perception could be "stunned, dulled, or taken away" under the influence of passions such as greed or anger.[45] In sum, the main function of *nous* had always been "to discover the 'real' world or the 'real' character of the world as a whole, in contrast to the erroneous beliefs of most human beings," reflecting the philosophers'

---

[42] CH IX 10. A close parallel occurs in Philo, *Embassy to Gaius* 6: "For *logos* cannot attain to God, who is totally untouchable and unattainable, but it subsides and ebbs away, unable to find the proper words to use as a basis to reveal ... even his attendant powers" (transl. Dillon, *Middle Platonists*, 156; cf. [Philo], *Works of Philo*, 757).

[43] Von Fritz, "Νοῦς and νοεῖν," 89; "Νοῦς and νοεῖν, and their Derivates Pt. II," 31.

[44] Von Fritz, "Νοῦς and νοεῖν," 90; "Νοῦς and νοεῖν, and their Derivates Pt. I," 224–225; ibid. Pt. II, 19–21.

[45] Von Fritz, "Νοῦς and νοεῖν, and their Derivates Pt. I," 226.

new belief "that the world is altogether different from what people in general believe it to be."[46]

If so, then what exactly was the function of *logos*? How would it be able at least to guide a person's *nous* to the point from where it could take the final step "by its own power"? Much more is implied here than just the trivial notion that *nous* reaches further than words can tell. Rather, the vital function of *logos* in noetic understanding leads us back to the second key theme (next to nonduality) that has been neglected in previous scholarship but is in fact central to Hermetic spirituality: that of *embodiment*. Dualistic consciousness suggests the need for a movement of *dis*embodiment or *de*materialization that will lead from the darkness and ignorance of embodied existence to the pure transcendent light of spiritual *gnōsis*; and as we have seen at the example of Porphyry, this means that enlightenment and liberation become means of *escape* from "the tragicomedy of this mindless life,"[47] our world of division and suffering. However, we have also seen that for those in the lineage of Diotima and Iamblichus, that was a misconception in the most literal sense of the word. On the contrary, they insisted, the process of spiritual liberation and enlightenment was not about "leaving the cave" behind but about *giving birth in the cave*: the task for human beings was precisely to incarnate or embody divine beauty, goodness, and truth so as to make them manifest *in* our world. Now how was such a process supposed to happen? I want to suggest that asking the question means answering it: the way any pregnancy happens, of course! Not by talking about it but by actually *doing* it, in a generative act of insemination and conception driven by *erōs*. As will be seen, it is precisely at this point that the *logos* comes in.

The key can be found already in Plato's exact formulation: "the living and ensouled *logos* of him who sees" must be "written in the soul of the learner."[48] To understand what this means, we must come to terms with the fact that our common everyday understandings of *logos* ("word," "speech," "discourse," "reason") simply do *not* capture the meaning of this word in antiquity.[49] There is perhaps no stronger example of the

---

[46] Von Fritz, "Νοῦς and νοεῖν, and their Derivates Pt. II," 31.
[47] See above, Chapter 4, p. 104 (Porphyry fr. 275).
[48] Plato, *Phaedrus* 276a.
[49] Kelber, *Logoslehre*, 6. Short general overviews in e.g. Stead, "Logos"; Runia, "Logos." For detailed discussion see the two old but very thorough monographs by Heinze, *Lehre vom Logos*, and Aall, *Geschichte der Logosidee* (2 vols.). To get a good sense of the complexity and profound ambiguity of *logos* speculation in Middle Platonic metaphysics, there is no better resource than Dillon, *Middle Platonists*, esp. 155–161 (Philo) and 200–202 (Plutarch). For *logos* in Plotinus, see the short overview in Banner, *Philosophic Silence*, 264–265.

fundamental problem of translation to which I have been calling attention throughout this book.[50] *Logos* first became a topic of philosophical discussion in the fragments of Heraclitus, where it did *not* actually mean "word" or "speech" at all, but referred to the order or structure of the world of experience.[51] While Plato did not adopt that usage, he had Socrates discuss the spoken *logos* as an active living force that is capable of inscribing ideas directly in the listener's soul, as we have seen, very much the way images are imprinted in a piece of wax.[52] In Stoic thought, *logos* came to be understood as an active force operating in the universe, manifesting as multiple *logoi spermatikoi* that were capable of "impregnating" receptive entities; again, these were not "words" as we understand them, but rather something like spiritual spermatozoa, living seeds of vital generative power that permeated the whole of reality. These understandings of *logos* were continued and developed further in multiple variations by platonizing authors, notably Philo of Alexandria and the Middle Platonists. For instance Plutarch spoke of noetic forms or ideas flowing from the incomprehensible Source as images (*eikones*) and *logoi* that, again, could leave imprints like "figures stamped on wax."[53] In short: whenever the word *logos* was used in the sense of oral speech at least in these intellectual and religious contexts, it was *not* understood as we understand it today, as simply the spoken equivalent of written words. *Logoi* were much more than signifiers, if indeed they were signifiers at all. They were understood as active living forces or energies that could leave an imprint on reality, not just in a metaphorical sense but

---

[50] See above, pp. 5, 12–15, 43, 60, 114, 116, 135, 162, 166, 198, 201–202, 216–217, 245, 313. Instead of anachronistically projecting our modern understandings and translations onto *nous* and *logos* and thereby "identifying" them as relatively stable concepts that comfortably confirm our current discourse ("mind" or "intellect" in case of the former; "word," "speech," "discourse," or "reason" in case of the latter), I suggest we should proceed empirically, approaching them as empty signifiers that get filled with some specific meaning by whoever uses them in any specific instance throughout the history of discourse.

[51] Runia, "Logos," 984; Kirk and Raven, *Presocratic Philosophers*, 188–189. Already Heinze noted that Heraclitus simply did not connect his concept of *logos* with the meaning "word," and therefore wondered why he gave it that name at all (*Lehre vom Logos*, 56). Aall drew the same conclusion, but only to add that instead of "*word*," *logos* meant *Vernunft* ("reason," *Geschichte der Logosidee*, vol. 1, 31). He concluded quite lightheartedly that "we just shouldn't modernize and look among the philosophers of the fifth century BC for that which is the creation of a different philosophical era" (ibid., 31–32); in this he was correct, but of course it is precisely what was bound to happen anyway, and would keep happening throughout the history of philosophy.

[52] Plato, *Theaetetus* 191c–e. For this early dimension of *logos* as a means of influencing a person's πάθη, see notably Boeder, "Der frühgriechische Wortgebrauch," 101–102.

[53] Dillon, *Middle Platonists*, 46, 200, 208; cf. 159–160 for similar imagery in Philo.

quite literally, and could even *give birth* to new living entities by impregnating or fertilizing receptive souls. Again: quite literally.

If we now look at the Hermetic writings from this perspective, the relevance should become clear. First of all, consider the life-affirming pansexuality of Hermetic metaphysics and cosmology. The Hermetic *pēgē* is the Source of infinite fertility and self-fertilization, "a fountain bubbling with life."[54] Something gets "carried across" (transferred, translated) from this Source to the world of manifestation, *but it is not language*. It is spiritual seed: pure life-giving energy, the power of Light that illuminates the world by kindling everything it touches so that it comes alive. The abyss of radical discontinuity or mutual exclusion between two orders of knowledge, those of signifiers and signified, is no barrier at all for this unitary noetic life-force. The androgynous *nous* that flows from the Source keeps generating new entities out of itself, including *logos*.[55] After dark and moist nature has received this luminous *logos* in her womb, we have seen, she gives birth to a beautiful cosmos;[56] and human beings are born in this cosmos after a new act of insemination, when the grand Human enters that cosmos and makes love with his female counterpart of earth and water.[57] After splitting humanity into males and females, God orders them to procreate so that they may continue the process of life by embodying noetic essence in material receptacles.[58] This sacred duty is mirrored in the priestly process of drawing down noetic powers into material statues so as to make them alive as well.[59] Those who are really dedicated can pursue the Hermetic path of *re*birth, having their bodily vessels purified and inseminated by the spiritual powers so that a perfect noetic body can be born in it.[60] Finally, when Tat gets to experience the Ogdoad and the Ennead, this happens because a stream of pneumatic energy has come down to ignite his own *pneuma* and thereby illuminate his *nous* – yet another instance of spiritual fertilization.[61] In the most literal and explicit sense, then, Hermetic spirituality from beginning to end is all about "giving birth in beauty" by embodying noetic light and generating life.

---

[54] NH VI⁶ 58, 13–14. I hesitate to call the *pēgē* androgynous, as it seems to be beyond any male-female distinctions. It could technically be called "transgender" in the strict sense of transcending gender distinctions altogether.
[55] CH I 5.
[56] CH I 8.
[57] CH I 14.
[58] CH I 18.
[59] *Ascl.* 23–24, 37–38.
[60] CH XIII 8–10.
[61] NH VI⁶ 57, 28–30.

Logos as spoken language must be understood from this context. It is not only, and perhaps not even primarily, something discursive similar to writing – a transmission of information from speaker to listener by the indirect means of verbal signifiers that then need to be decoded and interpreted. Rather, it is a *direct* transmission of non-verbal fertilizing power that illuminates and makes alive. This explains why already Socrates described himself as a "midwife"[62] to the work of *logos*, and Hermes played a similar role in facilitating both Tat's rebirth and his ultimate noetic experience.[63] Speech of course has the unique capacity of carrying discursive content, as it guides a person's *nous* up to the point from where it can "reach the truth by its own power."[64] But in its most fundamental essence, according to the central Hermetic perspective, *logos* is a powerful and ultimately erotic energy[65] that must be channeled, built up, received, and maintained in the intimate connection between teacher and pupil. It can leave a strong *impression* on the pupil's soul (an imprint, like a seal stamped in wax); and it has the capacity to *inspire* – literally, to breathe life into the listener's psychophysical organism. We have seen that at least according to Iamblichus and some Hermetic treatises, it may even do its work without any discursive content at all, as "sounds full of power"[66] (*nomina barbara* or chanted vowels) that touch the soul immediately. Once more I want to emphasize the importance of intimacy and personal connection. In all these cases, the process requires a situation of *immediate close contact* at a specific location and a specific time. Whereas written words can be disseminated all over the world, *logos* may be immediately present but can never travel anywhere else.[67]

---

[62] Plato, *Theaetetus* 150b–e.
[63] See Chapter 8, pp. 244–253 with reference to CH XIII. In Chapter 9, pp. 285–286, we have seen an additional shift of Hermes' role from that of midwife or facilitator to that of generator or father, as it is he who actually transmitted the seed.
[64] CH IX 10.
[65] Obviously in the Platonic sense of *erōs* and erotics (*ta erōtika*) as expounded in the *Phaedrus* and Socrates' speech in the *Symposium*.
[66] CH XVI 2.
[67] Significantly (sic), Derrida refers to the limitless dispersal of textual signifiers in written discourse as *dissemination*, the spreading of seeds. This illustrates the programmatic reversal on which his entire argument is built. Like Plato's Theuth, the radical deconstructionist replaces living *logos* by its dead supplement in a violent act of usurpation (as emphasized explicitly in *La dissémination*, 110–113). He turns the Source *from* which signification wells up – the actual Signifier – into the transcendental Signified *to* which signs claim to refer; therefore the usurpation implies a reversal of the hierarchy, since the original source from which meaning flows now becomes the unattainable *telos* of the quest for meaning. And because signifiers cannot signify the Signified, all they are left with is referring to one another instead. *La dissémination* therefore means that *meaning* understood as a living process of direct "signification" initiated by the Source, which is literally *making signs*, is replaced by a limitless multiplication of dead seeds.

There are many kinds of *logos* in the Hermetica,[68] and they are full of references to fertilization, generation, and giving birth. The Greek original of the *Asclepius* was called *Logos teleios*, the "perfect," "complete," "final," or "initiatory" *logos*;[69] and we may now consider the possibility that it meant or at least partly implied something like the "perfect power" transmitted by Hermes' life-giving discourse. As we have seen, he calls for special attention before comparing his own *logos* to a "torrential river" flowing downward like a powerful waterfall, so fast that "a divine noetic concentration" (*divina sensus intentione*) is required in order to receive it at all.[70] Clearly this stream of *logos* comes flowing from the *nous* and has its ultimate origin in the *pēgē*. Thus if the expression *genikoi logoi* ("general discourses") referred to oral teachings, as seems likely,[71] these must have been conceived of as much more than just the passing on of information in some kind of school. In CH I we read how after Hermes' encounter with Poimandres, he "sowed" the words of wisdom in his listeners and found that his *logos* now "[gave] birth to good things."[72] In *The Ogdoad and the Ennead*, he must give expression in speech (*šače*, *logos*) to what comes out of the Source (*pēgē*) that wells up in him, so that Tat may receive its power and attain *noēsis*.[73] This *logos* itself is described as a luminous seed coming from the Father[74]; it carries salvational power because it consists not just of words referring to other words but has welled up directly from noetic silence.[75] As for the mysterious figure of Agathos Daimōn, Hermes' own teacher, it may well be significant that while he often uttered "divine *logoi*," he never wrote anything down.[76] All these references confirm that *logos* was understood as active divine energy, the fertile power of life itself that had to be transmitted through the human voice. This conclusion puts a final nail in the coffin of old-fashioned dismissals of the Hermetica as nothing

---

[68] See Chapter 8, p. 229 with note 34 (referring to Christian Wildberg).
[69] Wildberg confirms Peter Kingsley's remark that the semantic scope of *Logos teleios* is "much wider than any English translation" and allows for all these adjectives. The title as a whole could even be translated as *The teaching that is fulfilled*, *The final reckoning*, or *The last thing to be said* (Wildberg, "*General Discourses*," note 9; Kingsley, "An Introduction," 18).
[70] *Ascl.* 3, 19; see Chapter 3, p. 62 (with reference to other instances in the Hermetica).
[71] See Chapter 8, pp. 229–230.
[72] CH I 29–30.
[73] NH VI⁶ 55, 6–7 and 19–22 (ϣⲁϫⲉ, ⲡⲏⲅⲏ). Similar scenario in CH XIII 22.
[74] NH VI⁶ 55, 27.
[75] HD V 2; see Chapter 9, p. 301 with note 144.
[76] CH XII 8; see Chapter 9, pp. 266–267.

but "reading mysteries" or "narrative fictions." If the authors were at all serious about what they were writing, they would have to come together and actually *do* what they claimed had to be done. You could not initiate yourself or achieve rebirth just by reading about it; unless Poimandres himself chose to intervene in your solitude, you needed a human teacher who would not just tell you the right things but could transmit the noetic power of Light and Life.

Plato's Socrates says that this living and ensouled *logos* must be written (*graphetai*) in the pupil's soul, and this brings me to a final dimension of "embodiment" in Hermetic practice. In CH I, Hermes "engraves" (*anegraphamēn*) Poimandres' blessing in himself.[77] After Tat has been reborn according to CH XIII, he "records" (*tetheika*) Hermes' hymn in his inner world; and when he wants to sing a hymn himself, Hermes urges him to be cautious in wielding the power he has just received.[78] In *The Ogdoad and the Ennead*, a reflection or imprint (*tupos*) of the cosmic plenitude is sent up towards the noetic world;[79] and Hermes hopes that Tat's words of praise will "get inscribed" in his inner noetic universe, "this imperishable book."[80] These are all variations on the power of *logos* to leave an actual imprint or inscription, similar to how an image is stamped into wax. Again, this has nothing to do with a play of signifiers. *Logos* works as an active noetic power or energy that comes flowing from the hidden Source and impresses its fertilizing *sunthēmata* (signatures) on whatever is sufficiently receptive in the world of manifestation.[81]

By far the most important receptacle was the human soul, more specifically its *pathē*, its ability to be affected. A person could be touched by noetic energy transmitted through the living *logos* of a person who had "seen," for instance Socrates, Diotima, Agathos Daimōn, or Hermes. These impressions or imprints could be made permanent, as we just saw, by inscribing them deliberately and consciously in one's inner noetic world. Clearly this was not a matter of learning things at school or copying information from a book, but of receiving the impact of *logos* and integrating not just its discursive meanings but its energies in one's memory, the storage function of the imagination (*phantasia*). In modern terminology, such

---

[77] CH I 30.
[78] CH XIII 21; see discussion in Chapter 8, p. 262.
[79] NH VI⁶ 57, 8; see discussion in Chapter 9, p. 296.
[80] NH VI⁶ 60, 14–17; see discussion in Chapter 9, p. 305.
[81] On this function of *sunthēmata*, see Shaw, *Theurgy and the Soul*, 48–50 and 162–228; Struck, *Birth of the Symbol*, 219, 234, 259, and generally 204–253. See above, Chapter 3, p. 69 with note 95.

"soul scripture" did not consist of inherently empty signifiers that serve to construct and negotiate "meaning" in terms of their relations to other signifiers in a strictly horizontal economy of discourse. But neither did it consist of signifiers that would somehow be capable of doing the impossible, that is to say: of actually signifying the transcendental Signified, the *pēgē* beyond human understanding. *Sunthēmata* (signatures) inscribed in the soul through *logos* should simply not be confused at all with conventional signs that need to be sent, received and decoded in order to be interpreted and understood. It seems more adequate to think of them as activators of a presence that was believed to be always already there, but needed to be remembered or called back to conscious awareness: *nous*, the only ultimately true reality of universal Life and Light.[82]

DISSEMINATION

If this is what *logos* was all about, again the implication is that Hermetic spirituality could not possibly survive without a living community (small as it may have been) of devotees who were cultivating a practice of intimate personal contact requiring direct physical interaction. To receive spiritual power at all, you needed to participate, you needed to be involved, *you needed to be there*. This brings us back to the core of truth in Ammon's remarks to Thoth. Once Hermetic treatises would get "disseminated" beyond such personal networks of dedicated practitioners, nothing could be left of the *logos*: its place would be taken by a play of self-referential written signifiers, "a drug not of memory [*mnēmē*] but of reminding [*hupomnēsis*]."[83] As formulated with remarkable precision in one of the Armenian Definitions, *logos* could never be salvational for the followers of Hermes unless it had been conceived in silence by the *nous* and therefore came directly from silence; that is to say, from the Source.[84] If this living connection with the noetic Signified was broken, as happens necessarily in writing, signifiers would be left to fence for themselves and could only make sense now by referring to one another instead – a process qualified as "perdition" in the same Hermetic passage.[85] This would

---

[82] The most precise and philosophically sophisticated description of this perspective, which I see as absolutely central to Hermetic spirituality, remains Iamblichus, *Response to Porphyry* I 3 (see above, Chapter 4, pp. 112–113). In my understanding, his description of *emphutos gnōsis* catches the essence of the Platonic *mnēmē* and of Hermetic *gnōsis* as well.
[83] Plato, *Phaedrus* 275a.
[84] HD V 2; see Chapter 9, p. 301 note 144.
[85] HD V 2 (perdition: կորուստ).

seem to have become the fate of the Hermetic treatises. As practitioners died without successors and their fragile networks began to fall apart, posterity was left with nothing but written "reminders." In Ammon's formulation, these made it possible now for uncommitted outsiders "to hear of many things without proper instruction." As an inevitable result, such readers would "seem to know many things" about the Hermetica "whereas in fact they will for the most part be ignorant – and unpleasant too, because they will not really be wise but will only appear so."[86]

The overwhelming majority of readers whose statements have survived were Christians.[87] If they occasionally quoted or referred to fragments from the Hermetica, the truth is that this did not reflect any great desire on their part to understand Hermetic spirituality on its own terms, to recover what it had really been all about. Their intention was not to learn but to teach. Regardless of whether these Christian authors sympathized with Hermes or rejected him as a peddler of pagan delusions, their central motivation was always to bolster their own theological discourse and promote their own apologetic agendas.[88] As a result, isolated Hermetic statements got caught in a discursive net of signifiers that served goals and objectives very different from what the original authors had in mind. Most of these scattered references therefore teach us much more about the Christian beliefs of their authors than about the nature and purposes of Hermetic spirituality. A rare exception was discussed in Chapter 9, where we saw that a fragment preserved in (ps.-)Didymus the Blind and Cyril of Alexandria contains a precious quotation about the Hermetic *pēgē* attributed most probably to Agathos Daimōn.[89] The other chief example comes from the same work by Cyril, his polemics against Julian, and gives strong support to some of my chief conclusions about the Hermetica. Cyril first quoted a passage preserved by Stobaeus,

---

[86] Plato, *Phaedrus* 275a–b.
[87] For these fragments or testimonies I rely on Scott IV, HT IV, HG, 396–431, and Litwa, *Hermetica II*, 175–339. Some of these editions are more complete than others, and the numbering system is not uniform (discussion in HG, 396; Litwa, *Hermetica II*, 175–176, 257–258). By far the most important testimonies by non-Christians are those of Zosimos and Iamblichus, discussed in Chapter 4. Practically all other non-Christian testimonies are concerned specifically with received ideas and speculations about the identity of Hermes Trismegistus (presented separately as TH 1–38 in Litwa, *Hermetica II*, 257–339), a topic that is of considerable interest in itself but of marginal importance to my concerns in this book. For a general overview of the Christian reception in late antiquity, see Moreschini, *Hermes Christianus*, 27–89.
[88] Same conclusion in van Bladel, *Arabic Hermes*, 12–13.
[89] See Chapter 9, pp. 267–269.

where Hermes writes that it is difficult to noeticize God and impossible to put such *noēsis* into words. What is corporeal cannot signify (*sēmēnai*) what is incorporeal and what is imperfect cannot comprehend (*katalambanesthai*) what is perfect: for whereas only the perfect divinity is true (*alēthes*), our human perception is "shrouded by appearances (*phantasias*)."[90] To this passage Cyril added a reference to the vision of the *pēgē* and its noetic emanations as described in *The Ogdoad and the Ennead*:

> So if there is an incorporeal eye, let it go out from the body to the vision of the Beautiful, fly up and soar on high, seeking to behold not a shape nor a body, nor forms [*ideas*], but rather that which made these things, that which is at rest, calm, stable, unchanging, the All and Alone [*to auto panta kai monon*], the One, the Being from itself, the Being in itself, the Being like itself which is like no other nor unlike itself.[91]

Originally, the author of this passage meant to say that one should seek to behold the supreme beauty of the *pēgē* through the eye of the *nous* in a state of *ekstasis*. But Cyril's audience would read it essentially as a theological statement: for them, this would be a commendable description of the utterly transcendent Christian deity, suggesting that even pagan authorities like Hermes had sometimes glimpsed the truth.[92] This apologetic agenda of finding "'Pagan' Witnesses to the Truth of Christianity"[93] entirely dominates the surviving record of indirect Hermetic references: they were quoted to support polemics against reincarnation (Tertullian), praise for the supreme majesty of the unspeakable and incorporeal God (Ps.-Cyprian, Lactantius, Marcellus of Ancyra), discussions of fate and divine providence (Lactantius, Didymus), the virtue of *eusebeia* and warnings against demons (Lactantius), biblical accounts of creation (Lactantius, Cyril), and the idea that Christ was the divine *Logos* (Lactantius, Marcellus of Ancyra, Cyril). It is of course no surprise that most of these authors came from northern Africa, where the Hermetica must have been known best. Tertullian, Ps.-Cyprian, and Quodvultdeus were from Carthago; Lactantius from the Roman province of Africa

---

[90] SH I 1. Cyril, *Against Julian* 1.43 (see Kyrill, *Werke I*, 73); Litwa, *Hermetica II*, 27–28 (SH I) and 207–208 (HF 25). Most of the other fragments from Cyril are about the *logos*.

[91] Cyril, *Against Julian* 1.43 (see Kyrill, *Werke I*, 73; transl. Litwa, *Hermetica II*, 208 with minimal changes; cf. HT IV, 129–130; HG, 420).

[92] For the basic agreement between Christians and contemporary pagans about divine transcendence, see Digeser, *Making of a Christian Empire*, 6–7, 65 (cf. 68 for the expression *summus deus*, avoided by most Christians except for Arnobius and Lactantius).

[93] Van den Broek, "Hermes and Christ."

nowadays known as Tunisia; Didymus and Cyril from Alexandria in Egypt; and Augustine from Thagaste in Numidia, nowadays Algeria.[94]

The most important of these authors next to Cyril are Lactantius and Augustine. To understand Lactantius' many references to Hermes, it is important to see that he wrote his *Divine Institutes* right between the end of Diocletian's reign in 305 CE and Galerius' Edict of Toleration of 311 CE, which would be followed one year later by the conversion to Christianity of Constantine I. At the emperor's court in Nicomedia during the winter of 302–303 CE, Lactantius was in the audience as two major intellectuals argued in favor of persecuting the Christians.[95] One of them was the governor of Bithynia, Sossianus Hierocles; the other was no one else than Porphyry of Tyre, the pupil of Plotinus and conversation partner of Iamblichus. Porphyry argued that while Christians must be pitied for their delusions and needed instruction, they should be punished for sedition if they kept worshiping a mere human like Jesus. This was the opening shot in what would become known as the Diocletian persecution, 303–305 CE. As Lactantius could think of no existing treatise that might serve as an efficient response to Porphyry's arguments, he decided to write one himself. The result has been described as "the most comprehensive and sophisticated Christian treatise in Latin before Augustine's *City of God*."[96] Since the persecution was in very recent memory and Constantine I had not yet emerged as Christian emperor, the stakes for Christians like Lactantius were high; after all, they could not possibly foresee whether the recent policy of toleration would last – for all they knew, a pagan restoration and new persecutions might be just around the corner. Under such conditions, Lactantius' strategy was to mitigate hostile sentiments by trying to convince pagan readers that their very own spiritual authorities – notably Plato and Hermes Trismegistus – expressed perspectives quite close to those of the Christians.[97] It helped a

---

[94] The chief exceptions, together responsible for just a few isolated fragments, all came from the area that is now Turkey: Marcellus (Ancyra, now Ankara), Ephrem the Syrian (Nisibis, now Nusaybin), and Gregory of Nazianz (Arianzum in Cappadocia, now near Sivrihisar).

[95] For these winter lectures and their importance to the Diocletian persecution, as for the general context and background to Lactantius' *Divine Institutes*, I rely on Digeser, *Making of a Christian Empire*, 17; Digeser, "Lactantius, Porphyry, and the Debate."

[96] Digeser, *Making*, 11.

[97] Detailed discussion in Digeser, *Making*, 64–90; cf. van den Broek, "Hermes and Christ," 130–136. As pointed out by Digeser, we can trust the accuracy of Lactantius' account because "the usefulness of Hermetist theology would have disappeared had he wantonly and obviously misrepresented its key ideas" (Digeser, *Making*, 72).

lot that he personally agreed – in the sharpest possible contrast with his successor Augustine a century later – that human error resulted not from sin but from "ignorance of oneself" (*ignoratio sui*). Lactantius thought of Jesus Christ as "a teacher who saves through *gnōsis* and the example of a virtuous life."[98] This seems to have been his sincere conviction, not just a strategy to attract converts.[99]

About a century later, the atmosphere had hardened. After a failed attempt at restoring traditional worship by the emperor Julian (361–363 CE), Christianity had become firmly established as the state religion of the Roman Empire during the reign of Theodosius I from 379 to 395 CE. As a result, the full machinery of suppression now got turned against pagan religion.[100] In Book Eight of *The City of God* (completed in 426 CE), Aurelius Augustine polemicized at length against the Latin *Asclepius*, and his remarks were to have a decisive impact on the fate of the Hermetica.[101] He believed that the Egyptian Hermes had lived after Moses but earlier than Plato, and dismissed him as an advocate of pagan idolatry. Of course he was referring to the passages about statue animation in *Asclepius* 23–24 and 37–38.[102] As for Hermes' lament over the future decline of Egypt, Augustine interpreted it as prophesying the victory of Christianity over paganism.[103] We have no evidence that he knew the original *Logos teleios* or any other treatises in Greek that would eventually be included in the *Corpus Hermeticum*. During the later reception history of the

---

[98] Digeser, *Making*, 9, 78, 83; cf. Lactantius, *Divine Institutes* I 1.25.
[99] Digeser, *Making*, 84, 90.
[100] Concerning the contested "paganism" terminology, I am convinced by the careful argumentation in Cameron, *Last Pagans of Rome*, 14–32. Whether or not pagans "saw themselves fighting a battle against Christianity" (a traditional scholarly assumption that Cameron qualifies as a "romantic myth," ibid., 3), there is no doubt that for their part at least, "late antique Christians certainly saw themselves as engaged in a battle with paganism" (ibid., 10, cf. 7). For the complicated history of the Christian suppression of paganism, leading e.g. to death penalties by the time of Justinian's reign, see e.g. Lane Fox, *Pagans and Christians*; MacMullen, *Christianizing the Roman Empire*; Chuvin, *Chronicle*.
[101] Augustine, *De Civ. Dei* VIII 23–26. Detailed analysis in Hanegraaff, "Hermetism" (with attention also to Hermetic allusions in Augustine's *Contra Faustum*, *De baptismo*, and perhaps the *Confessiones*: ibid., 1135–1136). For Augustine's impact on the medieval and early modern reception of the Hermetica, especially after the revival of his condemnation by William of Auvergne in the thirteenth century, see Hanegraaff, "Hermes Trismegistus and Hermetism."
[102] See discussion in Chapter 3, pp. 61–72 (for Augustine's interpretation, see especially note 91, with reference to Hanegraaff, "Hermetism," 1136).
[103] *Ascl.* 24–25; NH VI[8] 70–73. Discussion in Chapter 3, pp. 72–76.

Hermetica, the effect of Augustine's condemnation was mitigated by Lactantius' far more positive perspective – in fact, it so happened that the Lactantian view was adopted in an anti-Arian tract by Quodvultdeus that got miscategorized as a work of Augustine.[104] Only as late as the thirteenth century did Augustine's true position begin to make a strong comeback in the work of William of Auvergne, who saw the *Asclepius* as a horrible defense of idolatry that must be exterminated "with sword and fire."[105]

Next to such references in the works of Cyril, Lactantius, Augustine and a few other early Christian authors, Hermetic treatises began entering what I have referred to as the narrow bottleneck of textual transmission in the Byzantine world. As discussed in Chapter 5, they were now entirely at the mercy of scribes. We have seen that by the eleventh century, just one single damaged manuscript of the Greek treatises had survived apart from the fragments in Johannes Stobaeus' collection. Only the *Asclepius* was known to Western intellectuals during the Latin Middle Ages.[106] We have to wait until the fourteenth century to see signs of a growing interest in copying the collection known today as the *Corpus Hermeticum*. As for the Hermetic Definitions translated into Armenian, they were resting undisturbed among countless other manuscripts in a library in Yerevan,[107] while the Coptic Hermetic papyri lay hidden in a cave near Nag Hammadi. Only in the twentieth century did all these scattered seeds return to the light of day.

As for the dissemination of spiritual Hermetica through manuscripts in Arabic, a process that seems to have begun in the eighth century CE, much remains unknown because most of the manuscripts have never been printed.[108] On the following pages I rely on Kevin

---

[104] Quodvultdeus, *Adversus quinque Haereses*; see Gilly, "Überlieferung des *Asclepius*," 338–339, cf. Hanegraaff, "Hermetism," 1137.
[105] Porreca, "Hermes Trismegistus"; Gilly, "Überlieferung," 345–347.
[106] Generally on the medieval reception of the *Asclepius*, see many contributions in Lucentini, Parri and Perrone Compagni, *Hermetism*; Lucentini and Perrone Compagni, "Hermetic Literature II"; Moreschini, *Hermes Christianus*, 91–131.
[107] With the specification that a number of them also survive in Greek in the thirteenth-fourteenth century codex Clarkianus gr. 11 at the Oxford Bodleian Library (see Litwa, *Hermetica II*, 161–162).
[108] Van Bladel, *Arabic Hermes*, 3, 10: "There are probably more works attributed to Hermes surviving in Arabic than in any other language, and the majority of them are still unknown and unpublished." Walbridge, *Wisdom*, 17: "The problem of Hermes Trismegistus is a scholarly swamp of substantial acreage, muddiness, and gloom, and its Arabic bayous are far less explored than the Greek."

van Bladel's indispensable study *The Arabic Hermes,* which, among many other things, makes clear that modern scholarship has been riddled by vague and inconsistent terminology combined with sweeping claims built on flimsy evidence.[109] If we focus on the dissemination specifically of *spiritual* Hermetica in Syriac and Arabic sources,[110] the evidence seems to come down to the following. The opening lines of CH XIII found their way into a late sixth/early seventh-century Syriac text intended for converting "the unbaptized Ḥarrānians" to Christianity.[111] During the ninth century, the important Islamic philosopher al-Kindī apparently read an Arabic translation that circulated among these same Ḥarrānians, in which Hermes taught his son about the unity of God.[112] Starting around the same time, the early Ismāʿīlī movement regarded Hermes as a prophet who taught a doctrine of heavenly ascent, but it is far from clear whether they were using sources similar to our spiritual Hermetica.[113] SH I 1 was quoted by the tenth-century philologist Ibn Durayd.[114] In Egypt itself during the next century, al-Mubaššir ibn Fātik mentioned Agathodaimōn (Ġūṭādīmūn), Hermes (Idrīs), his son Tat (Ṣāb), Asclepius, and King Ammon in a collection of wisdom sayings (*ḥikam*) that must owe something to the original Greek Hermetica available to him in libraries sponsored by the Fāṭimids.[115] This extremely influential collection was translated into Spanish, Latin, French, Provençal and English,

---

[109] On the vague use of terms such as "hermetic" or "hermetism" and their negative effects, see van Bladel, *Arabic Hermes,* 19–21; as for sweeping claims, see van Bladel's extremely detailed analysis and deconstruction of scholarly myth-making focused on Ḥarrān as the supposed center of a "Hermetic Tradition," ibid., 64–114.

[110] Van Bladel emphasizes correctly that before Ficino's translation of the *Corpus Hermeticum* (1471), Hermes Trismegistus' fame rested essentially on talismanic, astrological, and alchemical texts attributed to him (*Arabic Hermes,* 114).

[111] *Nbîyawwātâ d-pillôsôpê ḥanpê,* published with English translation in Brock, "Syriac Collection" (van Bladel, *Arabic Hermes,* 83–85).

[112] An-Nadīm, *Fihrist* 385.1-2; transl. van Bladel, *Arabic Hermes,* 89 (with discussion, ibid., 86–90).

[113] Van Bladel, *Arabic Hermes,* 168–172, and 180–182 about the "Brethren of Purity."

[114] Rosenthal, "Sayings of the Ancients," 54, 183; van Bladel, *Arabic Hermes,* 196.

[115] Al-Mubaššir, *Kitāb Muḫtār al-ḥikam.* See van Bladel, *Arabic Hermes,* 94–95, 184–196. Translation of the relevant passages in ibid., 185–188. See al-Mubaššir's reliance notably on an unidentified scholar from the tenth century, supposedly a Ḥarrānian Ṣabian employed at the court of Baghdad, who saw Hermes as the founder of the universal primordial religion that had been spread all over the world (ibid., 188 with note 99, 235–236).

and probably played some role in the Renaissance reception of the Hermetica.[116] In the thirteenth century, Ibn al-Qifṭī wrote that some portions of dialogue between Hermes and his pupil Ṭāṭi had been translated into Arabic, but unfortunately were quite disorganized and incomplete because the original had been decayed and fragmented.[117] To this, Ibn al-ʿIbrī added a tantalizing remark: "The manuscript is extant with us in Syriac."[118] Finally, the only substantial Hermetic text in Arabic that could be construed as "spiritual" is the thirteenth-century *Kitāb fī Zaǧr an-nafs* (The Rebuke of the Soul), but its message is evidently Christian and its dependence on any original Hermetic sources is debatable at the very best.[119]

These data demonstrate that at least some parts of the spiritual Hermetica got disseminated through Persian, Syriac, and Arabic translations, but the evidence is fragmentary and hard to interpret. Similar to what happened in the Greek and Latin contexts, Hermetic statements fell under the sway of the dominant discursive power of new textual universes that shared very little in common with their original context. None of the above provides evidence for a Hermetic *tradition* in the Arabic context, only for the continuing presence of "Hermes" in Christian and Muslim *discourse*. People were still talking about Hermes, but his prophecy seemed to have come true: "every divine *logos* will be forced to fall silent."[120]

---

[116] Rosenthal, "Al-Mubashshir ibn Fâtik"; van Bladel, *Arabic Hermes*, 185, 195–196, 236. The "Testament to Ammon" contained in the Spanish and Latin translations (translated in ibid., 212–213) is full of references to Quranic terminology and shows clearly how far the mythology around Hermes had drifted apart from the original spiritual Hermetica discussed here.

[117] Ibn al-Qifṭī, *Taʾrīḫ al-ḥukamā* 349.23–350.2 (van Bladel, *Arabic Hermes*, 91 with note 118).

[118] Ibn al-ʿIbrī, *Taʾrīḫ muḫtaṣar ad-duwal* 12.1–3 (van Bladel, *Arabic Hermes*, 91 with note 120).

[119] Overview of editions in van Bladel, *Arabic Hermes*, 226 with note 248. The English translation in Scott IV, 281–352 is based on Bardenhewer's Latin translation (*Hermes Trismegisti ... De castigatione animae libellum*). Fleischer's old edition of the Arabic with German translation (*Hermes Trismegistus an die menschliche Seele*; cf. Fleischer, "Hermes Trismegistus: An die menschliche Seele") contains some elements that could perhaps have an ultimate origin in Greek Hermetic originals (e.g. the emphasis on images and visions reflecting the eternal noetic ideas, repeated references to noetic Life and Light, the importance of waking up to knowledge of one's self) but many non-Hermetic ideas as well (e.g. rejection of polytheism, emphasis on sin, physical death as salvation, dire warnings against women and intoxicating drinks).

[120] *Ascl.* 25; NH VI⁸ 73, 16–18 (λογος).

TRANSMISSION

Or perhaps not entirely. "On a strange day" during the 1170s or early 1180s, a young man from Persia had a life-changing experience. His name was Shihāb al-Dīn Abū al-Futūḥ Yaḥyā ibn Ḥabash ibn Amīrak al-Suhrawardī and he had been born around 1154 CE (549 AH) near Zanjān in northwestern Iran.[121] Having studied Peripatetic philosophy and theology in the tradition of Ibn Sīnā (Avicenna), he was wandering through northern Syria and Anatolia when Aristotle himself appeared to his inner gaze in a luminous vision. The revelation left Suhrawardī convinced that true knowledge could not be gained indirectly through cogitation and rational demonstration but only by an immediate experience of illumination in the most literal sense, referred to by him as *knowledge by presence*. In his subsequent writings, he claimed that this path had been taught by all the ancient sages ever since the time of Hermes, "the father of philosophers."[122] What makes this case unique is Suhrawardī's insistence that written words and logical demonstrations are powerless to convey true knowledge or *gnōsis* (*ma'rifa*),[123] because the latter can only be experienced *immediately* in a context of spiritual practice:

That there are dominating lights, that the Creator of all is a light, that the archetypes are among the dominating lights – the pure souls have often beheld this to be so when they have detached themselves from their bodily temples. Then they seek proof of it for others. All those possessing insight and detachment bear witness to this. Most of the allusions of the prophets and the great philosophers point to this. Plato, Socrates before him, and those before Socrates – like Hermes, Agathodaimon, and Empedocles – all held this view. Most said plainly that they had beheld it in the world of light. ... The author of these lines was once zealous in defense of the Peripatetic path in denying these things. He was indeed nearly resolved upon that view, "until he saw his Lord's demonstration" [Qur'an 12:24]. Whoso questions the truth of this – whoever is unconvinced by the proof – let him engage in mystical disciplines and service to those visionaries, that perchance he will, as one dazzled by the thunderbolt,

---

[121] For Suhrawardī's biography see Razavi, *Suhrawardi and the School of Illumination*, 1–4 (the "strange day": ibid. 58); Walbridge, "Suhrawardī and Illuminationism," 201–203; Walbridge and Ziai, "Translators' Introduction," xv–xvii. For Suhrawardī in his wider social, political, and discursive contexts, see Ohlander, *Sufism in an Age of Transition*.

[122] Suhrawardī, *Ḥikmat al-ishrāq*, Introduction 4 (Suhrawardī, *Philosophy of Illumination*, 2).

[123] Razavi, *Suhrawardi*, 8, 65, 75, 113, 124. Specifically on Suhrawardī's deconstruction of conventional types of knowledge (by definition, sense perception, and *a priori* concepts or innate ideas), see ibid., 92–100.

see the light blazing in the Kingdom of Power and will witness the heavenly essences that Hermes and Plato beheld.[124]

Suhrawardī was emphatic that spiritual essence could be *known* only through immediate experience, direct acquaintance.[125] One had to silence the five external senses so that the "inner senses" could open up to the perception of luminous realities, for that was "the purpose of the path of knowledge."[126] Doing so required diligent spiritual practice, including the cultivation of moral virtues (truthfulness, humility, compassion, absence of jealousy), fasting, reduction of sleep, and invocation of divine names (*dhikr*) – all of it under the direction of a spiritual master, for "without a master one does not get anywhere."[127] The category of "being" in Suhrawardī's ontology gave way to that of "light," and the unique source of true reality was referred to as the light of lights (*nūr al-anwār*).[128] Self-knowledge therefore had to consist in recognizing the identity of one's own essence with that very same universal light,[129] in a radically nondual experience that annulled the subject-object distinction.[130] As summarized by Mehdi Amin Razavi in a splendid analysis on which I am relying here,

---

[124] Suhrawardī, *Ḥikmat al-ishrāq* II 2.12 (165–166); transl. Walbridge and Ziai (Suhrawardī, *Philosophy of Illumination*), 107–108. On the specific tradition of meditative practices referred to by Suhrawardī as the "sciences of the folk" (*'ulūm al-qawm*), see Ohlander, *Sufism*, 146–148: they sought to gain control over "the subtle desires and hidden passions of the soul, its voracity, evil intention, and destructive inclinations," involved a practice of "scrupulous examination and self-observation" in order to cultivate inner and outer stability, led towards practices of renunciation, and culminated in the "sciences of direct witnessing" (*'ulūm al-mushāhadāt*).

[125] Walbridge and Ziai, "Translators' Introduction," xx–xxi; Razavi, *Suhrawardi*, 33–35, 100–113. Suhrawardī is explicit that the insights of his *Ḥikmat al-ishrāq* "first did not come to me through thinking or discourse but its attainment was of a different nature," i.e. it came from his direct vision and only afterwards did he seek to formulate their rational basis (*Ḥikmat al-ishrāq*, Introduction, 3; different translations in Razavi, *Suhrawardi*, 32–33, 52–53, 58; on "vision" as direct noetic perception, see ibid., 90). On the importance of immediacy, see also Ohlander, *Sufism*, 145: "what differentiates these sciences ... is that they are experiential sciences (*'ulūm dhawqiyya*) which like the sweetness of sugar cannot be described discursively, but must be tasted; they cannot be learned anywhere but in the '*madrasa* of *taqwā*' and cannot be accessed save through the practice of renunciation."

[126] Suhrawardi, *Opera*, 182 (Razavi, *Suhrawardi*, 61). On light and its varieties, see Razavi, *Suhrawardi*, 60–61, 78–81; on opening the inner senses, see ibid., 65–68.

[127] Razavi, *Suhrawardi*, 71–72.

[128] Razavi, *Suhrawardi*, 31–32, 37. For Suhrawardī's rejection of mind-body dualism as just "a superficial distinction," resulting in a position of strict spiritual monism, see ibid., 40–41.

[129] Specifically on self-knowledge, see the fascinating dialogue with "Aristotle" translated in Razavi, *Suhrawardi*, 59–60; and analysis in ibid., 90–92.

[130] Razavi, *Suhrawardi*, 102–117.

Since all things are ultimately made up of light, and because it is absurd to say that one needs light to find another light, in order for an epistemic relation to occur the veil that is separating the subject and the object has to be removed. In this case, self or light, which are equivalent in Suhrawardī's philosophy, is knowledge as well. "To know is to exist and to exist is to know" therefore constitutes a major epistemological theme and one of the important contributions of Suhrawardī to Islamic philosophy.[131]

After what we have seen in the previous chapters, the remarkable similarities with Hermetic spirituality hardly need further emphasis. The question is how to account for them. Suhrawardī stands out in the history of reception by the fact that his entire worldview is grounded explicitly not in theorizing but in immediate experiential practice, based on a regime of "spiritual exercises" for which he claimed the authority of Hermes, Agathodaimon, Pythagoras, Empedocles, Socrates, and Plato. All of this seems far too specific to be explained from what we presently know about the scattered textual fragments attributed to Hermes that were available in the Islamic world. Is it possible then that Hermetic spirituality somehow managed to survive after all, not just through textual dissemination but as the transmission of a living experiential practice?

Kevin van Bladel has called attention to a previously neglected dimension of Hermetic reception history that may well be crucial in this regard. It is very likely that as early as the third century CE, when Hermetic practice was still alive in Egypt, works attributed to Hermes Trismegistus were translated from Greek to Middle Persian.[132] None of these translations survives today, but it is entirely possible that some of them were available to Suhrawardī at the time, either directly in his native language or otherwise in Arabic translations. Furthermore, of course, we simply do not know how many spiritual Hermetica in Arabic might still have been floating around at the time, whether in Ḥarrān or anywhere else.[133] Since absence of evidence is no evidence of absence, we can only speculate about the possibility of lost Hermetic treatises in Persian, Syriac, or Arabic, and wonder how explicit some of them might have been about experiential practice and spiritual techniques of the kind that we

---

[131] Razavi, *Suhrawardi*, 113. The impossibility of separating ontology from epistemology seems perfectly similar to what I concluded about the noetic Light in Plotinus and the Hermetica (see above, pp. 60–61).
[132] Van Bladel, *Arabic Hermes*, 23–63.
[133] Van Bladel's convincing deconstruction of Ḥarrān as the center of a "Hermetic school" with a "Hermetic theology" (see above, note 109) does not affect the evidence for Ḥarrān as a "pagan city" where Hermetic writings were held in esteem (*Arabic Hermes*, 113).

find in *The Ogdoad and the Ennead*. All of this is unknown. However, in this particular case there is another possibility of direct transmission as well. It has to do with a Hermetic culture that seems to have persisted in Panopolis (Akhmīm or Ikhmīm), and rests upon some passages where Suhrawardī outlines the historical genealogy of his own tradition. He claims that it began with Hermes among the Egyptians and included Asclepius as well, from where the path of transmission led on to Empedocles and Pythagoras. The specifically Pythagorean branch continued with Socrates, Plato, Aristotle, and Ibn Sīnā; but an independent offshoot "passed to the brother of Ikhmīm," from there to "the wayfarer of Tustar and his followers," through whom it finally reached Suhrawardī himself.[134] Who were those people?

The Egyptian Ḏū l-Nūn al-Miṣrī from Akhmīm, the former Panopolis (d. probably 859–860 CE/ 245 AH), was one of the most influential teachers in the formative period of Sufism and one of the first to discuss the concept of *maʿrifa*, usually translated as *gnōsis*.[135] He traveled widely, and met his later pupil Abū Muḥammad Sahl b. ʿAbd Allāh al-Tustarī (d. 896 CE/283 AH) during a pilgrimage to Mecca.[136] Ḏū l-Nūn spoke of a communion of "subtle lights" flowing down from the divine Source, and Tustarī would go on to teach a doctrine of God as light.[137] A recurring theme in the sayings attributed to Ḏū l-Nūn is the "invisible community" of *awliyāʾ* (God's friends or pious servants), who live anonymous lives in this world while their hearts and spirits "travel in the upper, spiritual worlds, reaching and even penetrating the highest veils that separate God from creation."[138] They were believed to function as "ultimate mediators," whose devotion guaranteed the world's spiritual wellbeing and even its physical existence.[139]

Of particular importance for our concerns is that Ḏū l-Nūn would appear to have participated in a Hermetic tradition that had continued to exist in

---

[134] Suhrawardī, *al-Mashāriʿ waʾl-Muṭāraḥāt*, para. 223; transl. Walbridge, *Leaven of the Ancients*, 1. For parallels elsewhere in Suhrawardī's oeuvre, see Ebstein, "Ḏū l-Nūn al-Miṣrī," 604 with note 186; see two examples in Razavi, *Suhrawardi*, 10 (Aristotle himself tells Suhrawardī that not the Peripatetics but "the Sufis Basṭāmi and Tustari are the real philosophers"), 52 ("The light of the path which stretches into the past is the substance of Pythagoras ... and was sent down upon Tustari and his followers"). For the structure of these genealogies, see Walbridge, *Leaven*, 29–31.

[135] For all factual data I rely on Ebstein, "Ḏū l-Nūn al-Miṣrī," here 561–563, 581–583.

[136] Böwering, *Mystical Vision*, 50–58; Walbridge, *Wisdom of the Mystic East*, 44–46.

[137] Ebstein, "Ḏū l-Nūn al-Miṣrī," 583 with note 97; Böwering, *Mystical Vision*, 145–184.

[138] Ebstein, "Ḏū l-Nūn al-Miṣrī," 584–585 (I have left out the Arabic terminology).

[139] Ebstein, "Ḏū l-Nūn al-Miṣrī," 586.

his city since the time of Zosimos.[140] Because this point is somewhat controversial among specialists, I will here briefly summarize the documentary evidence on which it rests. A contemporary alchemist, Buṭrus al-Ḥakīm al-Iḫmīmī, mentioned Ḏū l-Nūn next to Hermes and Zosimos[141]; and Ḏū l-Nūn was himself described as an alchemist at least from the tenth century on, as far as we can tell, first by ʿAbd Allāh Muḥammad b. Umayl al-Tamīmī[142] and then by Muḥammad b. Isḥāq b. al-Nadīm in his well-known *Kitāb al-Fihrist*.[143] He was credited with several alchemical works that are no longer extant but seem to have been criticized as "fanciful presumptions" in the work (lost as well) of a rival alchemist from Akhmīm. The latter's name was Abū Ḥarrī ʿUṯmān b. Suwayd al-Iḫmīmī, and he may well have been the author of the Arabic origin of a famous alchemical text in Latin, the *Turba Philosophorum*.[144] According to Ṣāʿid al-Andalusī (eleventh-century), Ḏū l-Nūn belonged to an alchemical Sufi tradition that was concerned with the "science of the hidden realm" and included the famous alchemical authority Ǧābir b. Ḥayyān, al-Ḥāriṯ al-Muḥāsibī, and Ḏū l-Nūn's pupil al-Tustarī.[145] ʿAlī b. al-Ḥusayn al-Masʿūdī (tenth century) had claimed that Ḏū l-Nūn used to visit the ancient Egyptian temples (*barābī*) in Akhmīm to study the hieroglyphic scripture and imagery;[146] and an Andalusī contemporary of Ṣāʿid, Abū ʿUbayd al-Bakrī, wrote more specifically that Ḏū l-Nūn in his youth had been in the service of a priest (*rāhib*) at the temple of Akhmīm, who had taught him the hieroglyphic writings on its walls "and showed him the sacrifice, the incense and the name of the spiritual power,

---

[140] Walbridge, *Wisdom*, 44–45; Sezgin, *Geschichte des arabischen Schrifttums*, vol. 1, 643–644; vol. 4, 273. On this continuation of alchemy in Akhmīm from the third to the ninth century, see Kingsley, *Ancient Philosophy, Mystery, and Magic*, 59, 221 with notes 12–13, 389.

[141] Sezgin, *Geschichte des arabischen Schrifttums*, vol. 4, 274; Walbridge, *Wisdom*, 45.

[142] Ibn Umayl, *al-Māʾ al-waraqī* (The Book of the Silvery Water); see Ebstein, "Ḏū l-Nūn al-Miṣrī," 600 with note 165.

[143] Ebstein, "Ḏū l-Nūn al-Miṣrī," 600.

[144] All titles in Ebstein, "Ḏū l-Nūn al-Miṣrī," 600–601 with notes 167–169; also in Ullmann, *Natur- und Geheimwissenschaften*, 196–197. For Uṯmān b. Suwayd as the original author of the *Turba*, see Plessner, "Place of the *Turba Philosophorum*," 333–334; Kingsley, *Ancient Philosophy, Mystery and Magic*, 58–59 (with references in note 28), 389–390; Kingsley, "From Pythagoras to the *Turba Philosophorum*."

[145] Ṣāʿid b. Aḥmad al-Andalusī, *Kitāb Ṭabaqāt al-umam*; see Ebstein, "Ḏū l-Nūn al-Miṣrī," 601 with note 171. Ebstein seems to have an agenda of minimizing or dismissing references to "alchemy and the occult" wherever possible, stating that "clearly" neither al-Muḥāsibī nor al-Tustarī had anything to do with it (ibid.); but he does not explain why al-Andalusī's claim to the contrary should be dismissed.

[146] Al-Masʿūdi, *Kitāb Murūǧ al-ḏahab wa-maʿādin al-ǧawhar* (see Ebstein, "Ḏū l-Nūn al-Miṣrī," 597 with note 158).

ordering him to conceal this."[147] Ṣāʿid's report was also quoted a century later by the Egyptian Ibn al-Qifṭī, who confirmed the tradition of Ḏū l-Nūn's connection to the "temple of ancient wisdom" with its "wonderful images and strange patterns."[148] At least from the fourteenth century onwards, these same claims are found in several non-Sufi sources from North Africa and Egypt.[149] Finally, poems and treatises on alchemy were attributed to Ḏū l-Nūn, whether rightly or wrongly, by a whole series of North African and Egyptian authors from the twelfth through the fourteenth century.[150]

Ḏū l-Nūn's involvement in alchemy was bound to be controversial among Sufis and has remained so among scholars of Sufism,[151] largely because the practice was often associated with theurgy and magic. This may help explain the guarded "yes – but" response by one of his pupils, Abū ʿAbd Allāh b. al-Ǧalā, to the question of whether his master had indeed been an alchemist: "yes, but he was an alchemist [who practiced] the alchemy of Ṣubayḥ al-Aswad." The identity of that person remains unknown, but the remainder of Ibn al-Ǧalā's response shows that the kind of alchemy he had in mind implied miraculous powers of a kind that were commonly attributed to the *awliyāʾ*.[152] The important fact about al-Ǧalā's response is that, in spite of the suspicions it might evoke among Sufis, he

---

[147] Al-Bakrī, *al-Masālik wa-l-mamālik*; see Ebstein, "Ḏū l-Nūn al-Miṣrī," 602 with note 173.
[148] ʿAlī b. Yūsuf b. al-Qifṭī, *Taʾrīḫ al-ḥukamā*; see Ebstein, "Ḏū l-Nūn al-Miṣrī," 601–602 with note 172.
[149] Ebstein, "Ḏū l-Nūn al-Miṣrī," 602–603, with references in notes 174–175.
[150] Ebstein, "Ḏū l-Nūn al-Miṣrī," 603–604. Brockelmann, Massignon, Ullmann and Van Ess all expressed doubts concerning the authenticity of these poems and alchemical works, but without giving arguments; the precise philological analysis required to clarify this issue has not yet been done (ibid., 604 note 185).
[151] Kingsley, *Ancient Philosophy, Mystery, and Magic*, 389: these connections have been "a source of embarrassment for those interested in maintaining the purely Islamic nature of Sufism and denying its links with previous, non-Arab traditions."
[152] Ibn al-ʿArabī, *al-Kawkab al-durrī*; Ebstein, "Ḏū l-Nūn al-Miṣrī," 607–608. Ebstein concludes from al-Ǧalā's response that Ḏū l-Nūn "was not an alchemist *per se*, but rather enjoyed miraculous powers" (ibid.), ignoring the fact that actually the answer was "yes." As far as I can tell, Ebstein's scepticism about "Ḏū l-Nūn the Occultist" (ibid., 597–612) is built on the widespread assumption that Hermetism and alchemy imply somewhat distasteful "occult tendencies" typical of "magicians and theurgists" whose practice is all about "boldly manipulating God's creation," in sharp contrast with the passive, humble, devotional stance of the ideal Sufi mystic as exemplified by Ḏū l-Nūn (ibid. 607). My previous discussions of Zosimos, Iamblichus, and indeed of Hermetic spirituality as a whole shows that these are polemical stereotypes which fail to account for the evidence; notably, we have seen that Zosimos' alchemical-Hermetic spirituality had nothing to do with "magic and manipulation" (practices that he would attribute rather to his opponents, priests such as Neilos) but exemplifies precisely the ideal of humble devotion presumably shared by Ḏū l-Nūn.

confirmed his master's identity as an alchemist. Summing up, all this information about Ḏū l-Nūn, his pupils, and his wider context, lends plausibility to Suhrawardī's claim about an illuminative tradition with Hermetic origins transmitted to him through Sufi alchemists linked to Panopolis.[153]

Of course, it is in the very nature of private experiential practices passed on by oral transmission that they are bound to get lost in any process of textual transmission. Written references can never give more than indirect evidence at best. Since Suhrawardī defined true illumination in terms of *knowledge by presence*, the unavoidable implication is that for him, what passes as written "knowledge" must refer ultimately to an *absence* of true knowledge. Again, what he called the "light of lights" cannot be understood in modern linguistic terms as a transcendental Signified (the essentially passive object of signification). On the contrary, it would have to be conceived of as the only *active* Signifier *immanent* in reality.[154] On such a foundation, the essence of oral transmission could not consist just in the passing on, by word of mouth, of carefully guarded "secrets" reserved for an elite. Rather, we are led back to the understanding of *logos* as an active energy. It was believed to bring practitioners in immediate contact with what, for lack of a better word, we might think of as a stream of luminous fertile power that came from the "light of lights" and had been carried and kept alive by practitioners from one generation to the next. Whatever we may think of such a claim from our sceptical modern perspectives, by all accounts this is what spiritual "transmission" meant to them. The Light from the Source was *present*. Therefore the sense of it being "absent" from human consciousness had to be the very definition of "ignorance." The cure of that condition, of course, was *gnōsis*.

---

[153] This conclusion finds support in Walbridge, *Wisdom*, 44–46; Kingsley, *Ancient Philosophy, Mystery, and Magic*, 371–391 (I leave it to others to evaluate Kingsley's larger claims about the Hermetica as rooted in a tradition going all the way back to Empedocles, Parmenides and Pythagoreanism; for Suhrawardī's views of Empedocles and Pythagoras, see Walbridge, *Leaven*, 39–82). For the sceptical perspective, see van Bladel, *Arabic Hermes*, 223–226; Ebstein, "Ḏū l-Nūn al-Miṣrī."

[154] See above, note 67. It all depends on whether the so-called transcendental Signified is framed as the passive object or the active subject of signification. Modern linguistic theory in the lineage of de Saussure, including poststructuralist developments such as Derridean deconstruction, take the former perspective for granted because there is no other possibility in the order of secular discourse. As a result, pre- or non-secular perspectives are excluded by fiat and cannot even become a topic of discussion. From a perspective of consistent methodological agnosticism (Hanegraaff, "Empirical Method"; above, Prologue, pp. 4–5), the challenge rather is to take the "emic" perspective seriously and evaluate it from a nonreductive "etic" point of view.

THOTH'S SECRET

Having come close now to the end of this chapter and this book, we will return one more time from the domain of history to our point of mythical beginnings: the Egyptian god Thoth, the inventor of writing, in his conversations with the supreme deity known as "the hidden one" (Plato's *Phaedrus* 274e–275b) and with Tat the Hermetic pupil (NH VI⁶ 61,18–63,32). In this triple constellation based on two different texts, Ammon stands for the ultimate Source of meaning beyond human comprehension, Tat is the representative of humanity, and Thoth is positioned halfway between the two. On these final pages I want to widen the scope of discussion and try to show why Plato's story is not just relevant to the Hermetica, but has paradigmatic implications for the broader question of what research in the humanities is or should be all about. How do we interpret this foundational myth about the nature of writing? And how do we approach the study of human culture? I would suggest that the answer to either of these two questions determines our answer to the other one as well, and is decisive for how we approach the study of textual sources.

First I need to quickly summarize my argument in this chapter. I have argued that Hermetic spirituality as experiential practice depended in crucial ways on the spoken word exchanged between teachers and pupils.[155] But *logos* functioned not just as a conventional means of communication in which units of information are transmitted between senders and receivers,[156] for it was understood as an active force or energy with the capacity to *inscribe* knowledge directly in the pupil's soul. As such, it depended on physical and temporal immediacy and could be transmitted only by a living tradition. The implication is that without a community

---

[155] For the didactic "chain of transmission" between teachers and pupils, the standard discussion remains Van den Kerchove, *La voie*, 23–184.

[156] The linguistic and semiotic paradigm that treats signifiers as units of information is exemplified not only by Ferdinand de Saussure's *Premier cours de linguistique générale* but also by the father of information technology Claude Shannon in his equally groundbreaking "Mathematical Theory of Communication" (1948). In this technical sense, which was new and confusing at the time, information came to denote "whatever can be coded for transmission through a channel that connects a source with a receiver, regardless of semantic content" (Roszak, *Cult of Information*, 13). The fusion between information technology and Saussurian linguistics and its cultural effects are famously analyzed in the first chapter of Lyotard, *The Postmodern Condition*. By contrast, Hermeneutics is concerned explicitly not with *information* and linguistic coding but with *knowledge* (e.g. Gadamer, "Text und Interpretation," 341; Gadamer, "Destruktion und Dekonstruktion," 370–371). While information can be either true or false, knowledge is true by definition (if untrue, it is not knowledge but error or falsehood).

of practitioners in which the Hermetic *logos* was kept alive, one would have nothing else to rely on than Thoth's *pharmakon*, the art of writing. Now if we follow Derrida, this could only lead to a limitless dissemination of dead seeds, empty signifiers cut off from the Source of meaning. His argument takes its cue from Ammon's linguistic pessimism and has enormous implications for the study of textual sources, the *sine qua non* of the humanities. Ammon states that writing can never be more than a mere "drug of reminding." If that is the final word about how immediate human experience relates to written language, one is forced to conclude that Thoth's instructions to Tat – "write it all down, so that the knowledge may not get lost!" – are not just futile and empty but may even be deceptive. It would seem as though the mythical inventor of writing is actively deluding Tat about the nature of his *pharmakon* and its powers, as he seeks to instill confidence in what he secretly knows to be a drug of delusion that will take the place of true knowledge. This general line of argument has the further implication that any attempt to recover the meaning of the Hermetica – including the entire project to which this book is devoted – must be rather pointless as well. The scriptural traces that authors have left for us to decipher are like footsteps in the snow, ephemeral traces of an absence. Nothing meaningful is present there.

Such conclusions follow with inexorable logic from the basic premises of Deconstruction and allied perspectives known as Theory or Critique, all of them marked by a (post)structural emphasis on discontinuity, rupture, gaps, hiatuses, and lacunae.[157] As reflected most clearly in Derrida's central notion of *différance*, their keynote is the inevitable failure of communication and understanding. If meaningful content is absent by definition, textual Hermeneutics as a process of *unveiling* becomes strictly impossible. Its place is then taken by a procedure of *unmasking* that can have no other objective than exposing mechanisms of power, manipulation, and attempts at domination.[158] This basic perspective has been referred to since the 1960s as "the hermeneutics of suspicion,"[159] and it would be hard to think of a clearer example (or, for that matter,

---

[157] E.g. Meredith, *Experiencing the Postmetaphysical Self*, 1–4; Coole, *Negativity*, 41, 75–84, and *passim*; Dallmayr, "Prelude," 84; Bernstein, "Conversation That Never Happened," 588; idem, "Constellation," 277.

[158] Felski, *Limits of Critique*, 32; Felski, "Suspicious Minds," 216.

[159] The standard reference is Ricoeur, *De l'interprétation* ch. II.3 (Ricoeur, *Freud and Philosophy*, 32–36), but note that he did not use the exact term himself until 1971; see Scott-Baumann, *Ricoeur and the Hermeneutics of Suspicion*, 63. For an impressive analysis of *critique* as an intellectual "mood and method" grounded in the hermeneutics of suspicion and a general ethos of "againstness," see Felski, *Limits of Critique*.

a more brilliant one) than Derrida's narrative in "Plato's Pharmacy." It is important to see that his basic storyline frames Thoth explicitly as a political opportunist and revolutionary engaged in "complots, perfidious operations, and maneuvers of usurpation directed against the king"[160] (Ammon). Thoth's true objective is to break the structure of meaningful communication through *logos*, and his vote of confidence in the beneficial powers of written discourse is exposed by Derrida as nothing but a mask for hiding the usurper's patricidal strategy: to erase the very Source of Life and Light from living memory and replace it by the totalizing regime of *l'écriture générale*.[161] Evidently this makes Thoth the radical inversion of his Greek counterpart: the place of Hermes the mediator, the communicator *par excellence* and messenger of the gods, is taken over by a deity who *erases* mediation! Derrida's deconstruction of the Greek "metaphysics of presence" is operated by Thoth's *pharmakon*, the infinite web of mutually self-referential signifiers that keep self-disseminating in perpetuity. This violent revolution, this *Umwertung aller Werte*, is presented as a liberation of humanity from the despotic power of the transcendental Signifier – the entire drama belongs evidently in the intellectual lineage of Nietzsche and the death of God.

As Deconstruction was making its career in the humanities during the final decades of the twentieth century, its chief rival was Hermeneutics, developed in its classical form by Hans-Georg Gadamer.[162] With deep backgrounds in liberal humanism and German post-classical culture, this philosophical perspective was named after Hermes[163] because its most basic sympathies lie not with rupture and revolution but with mediation and communication. Interpretation (*hermēneia*) is understood quite literally in terms of translation across boundaries, the transfer of significant meaning in the service of dialogue and understanding.[164] But *hermēneia* is

---

[160] Derrida, *La dissémination*, 111.
[161] Derrida, *La dissémination*, 104–118. Derrida insists on the revolutionary violence of the takeover: "One would have understood nothing about this 'linguistic''immanence' if one saw in it just the peaceful element of a fictitious war, an inoffensive play of words, in contrast with some *polemos* raging in 'reality'" (ibid.). For the pervasive theme of patricide, see ibid., 93–118 ("The Father of the *Logos*" followed by "The Inscription of the Sons") and 178–194 ("The Family Scene").
[162] Frank, "Limits of the Human Control of Language," 150 and passim; Madison, "Gadamer/Derrida," 192–193 and passim; Botz-Bornstein, "Speech, Writing, and Play in Gadamer and Derrida," 249.
[163] Whether the etymological connection is correct is interesting but of secondary importance here; see Gadamer, "Klassische und philosophische Hermeneutik," 92; Gadamer, "Logik oder Rhetorik," 294–295.
[164] On understanding as translation, see Gadamer, *Hermeneutik I*, 387–393, 406.

extraordinarily difficult, even to such an extent that it is hard to explain how it can be possible at all.[165] Paradoxically, we do not begin to understand unless we understand that we do *not* understand; misunderstanding is always easy while understanding is always hard, and it can never be taken for granted or treated as final.

Why is this so? The basic instrument of interpretation is our own human consciousness, that is to say, everything that falls within the *horizon* of the person who seeks to understand. This means that the critical tools of Hermeneutics must first be directed not at our textual or personal others but at ourselves, and therefore our understanding of otherness rests ultimately on our capacity of self-understanding.[166] Against the background of previous discussions in this book, it is essential to not confuse "self-knowledge" in this Gadamerian-hermeneutical sense with theological notions similar to *gnōsis* as self-knowledge or, for that matter, with a Platonic understanding of *anamnēsis* as self-remembering. The difference lies in the fact that our human consciousness (the instrument of interpretation) is defined precisely by its *historicity*, its horizon of temporality conditioned by our mortality and finitude.[167] Hermetic *gnōsis* could be defined as gaining access to the universal "spiritual" horizon of *nous*, a horizon that is in fact no horizon because, by definition, it has no temporal or spatial limits. By the sharpest possible contrast, Hermeneutic understanding requires a horizon of human consciousness to remain intact, so that it can get expanded in the process of merging with the equally limited horizon of the (personal or textual) other that is being understood. We have seen that textual understanding requires such a merging of horizons (*Horizontverschmelzung*), and the same is true for our attempts at understanding other human beings in situations of dialogue and conversation. In order for such exchanges to have a chance at success, participants must be on the same page at least about essentials. Notably they must agree about the very possibility of understanding, its fundamental desirability, the nature and purpose of critique, and its dialectical interdependence with self-critique.

These boundary conditions turned out to be absent during the most paradigmatic encounter between Deconstruction and Hermeneutics, a famous

---

[165] Hermeneutics is born from the basic experience of strangeness and the universal possibility of misunderstanding (Gadamer, *Hermeneutik I*, 182–183), to such an extent that its actual occurrence may be qualified not as natural but as a miracle (ibid., 297, 316, 347); cf. Di Cesare, *Gadamer*, 71.
[166] Gadamer, *Hermeneutik I*, 265; Gadamer, "Wahrheit in den Geisteswissenschaften," 40–41; Di Cesare, *Gadamer*, 86–88.
[167] Gadamer, "Hermeneutik und Historismus," 406–408.

or notorious "conversation that never took place" in 1981 between its two leading representatives at the Goethe Institute in Paris.[168] Gadamer, who was fluent in French, had been studying Derrida since the early 1960s and was eager to discuss their perspectives on text and interpretation (the title of his paper). However, he discovered with dismay that all his attempts to reach out to his colleague in search for common ground, all his professions of genuine interest in finding a basis for mutual understanding (*Verständigung*) and engage in an actual discussion, were interpreted by default as attempts at appropriation, manipulation, and domination.[169] Derrida's response made perfectly clear that, for him, "good will" could only be a mask of the will to power.[170] With hindsight, as pointed out by Gadamer's biographer, this spectacular failure of communication was all but unavoidable: "Hermeneutics holds that mutual understanding [*Verständigung*] is always possible in principle, while Deconstruction by contrast considers it impossible by definition."[171] Expressions of openness, trust and the search for understanding are therefore dismissed by default, as pious humanistic delusions or manifestations of false consciousness that must be met with eternal suspicion.[172] To borrow a formulation from Roland Barthes, the assumption was that "[t]o speak, and even more so to discourse, is not to communicate ... it is to subjugate."[173]

[168] All relevant materials, with excellent commentaries, in Michelfelder and Palmer, *Dialogue and Deconstruction*. Short overviews in Michelfelder and Palmer, "Introduction"; Grondin, *Hans-Georg Gadamer*, 366–273; Simms, *Hans-Georg Gadamer*, 126–134.

[169] Discussion in Madison, "Gadamer/Derrida," 194, 197; Simon, "Good Will to Understand and the Will to Power"; Bernstein, "Conversation," 594; Swartz and Cilliers, "Dialogue Disrupted," 4–6, 9, 15; Gadamer, "Hermeneutics and Logocentrism," 119; Grondin, *Hans-Georg Gadamer*, 371; Simms, *Hans-Georg Gadamer*, 126–134.

[170] Derrida's "Three Questions to Hans-Georg Gadamer" were originally titled "Good Will to Power" ("Bonnes volontés de puissance") and attacked Gadamer's prior assumption of "good will" (ibid., 52; referring to Gadamer, "Text und Interpretation," 343). For Gadamer's utter puzzlement by this response and his professed inability to "understand" such an attitude, see his "Reply to Jacques Derrida," originally titled "And Yet: The Power of Good Will" ("Und dennoch: Macht des Guten Willens").

[171] Grondin, *Hans-Georg Gadamer*, 369.

[172] The virulent antihumanism of Deconstruction and critical theories is well known (e.g. Ferry and Renaut, *La pensée 68*; Baring, *Young Derrida*, 4–5, 21–47, 259–294; Cusset, *French Theory*, e.g. 7–8, 32, 62, 123, 316) and does stand in utter contrast to the deep humanistic commitments of Hermeneutics; see e.g. Gadamer, *Hermeneutik I*, 9–47; Di Cesare, *Gadamer*, 38–41.

[173] Barthes, *Leçon*, 12; Compagnon, *Literature, Theory, and Common Sense*, 91. For Gadamer's response to such a perspective, see Gadamer, "Hermeneutics of Suspicion"; see also Gadamer, *Hermeneutik I*, 316 ("forms not of domination but of service"), 334, 384. As hermeneutics is based on radical openness and human finitude, it precisely "prevents totalization, blocks perfection, forbids the completion of becoming, and denies both the absolute and absolutism" (Di Cesare, *Gadamer*, 101).

What really happened in this (non)encounter, and was indeed bound to happen, can be inferred from the mythical constellation outlined in "Plato's Pharmacy." Gadamer as an avatar of Hermes, the promotor of Hermeneutics, could not appear otherwise than as the Thoth of Derrida's imagination. Mediation was ruled out in advance, because even the metaphorical gesture of reaching out a hand could only be an act of concealed aggression. Moreover, as the advocate of meaning and dialogue, the older man was bound to be perceived as what Derrida calls "the father of the *logos*," and so he found himself confronted by the mythical son who sets out to break his power and take his place.[174] In sum, Gadamer assumed the double role of mediator (Hermes) *and* Source of meaning (Ammon). Derrida, for his part, assumed the position of Thoth as both the breaker of mediation and the usurper of meaning. It seems to me that this catches the essence of the non/relation between Deconstruction and Hermeneutics that has been evident ever since. The revolutionary takeover described in "Plato's Pharmacy" can be seen as a mythical blueprint for the spectacular career of radical Deconstruction, Critical Theories, and the hermeneutics of suspicion as it would unfold in the humanities.[175]

But if this was the underlying script, how much basis did it have in reality? The predictable response will be another question – "whose reality"? The truth is that how we read the encounter depends ultimately on our personal assumptions and prior opinions (*Vormeinungen*), the patterns of prejudice (*Vorurteil*) that define our horizon of interpretation, our very possibilities of understanding as well as our limitations in that regard. Whether we throw our lot with Deconstruction or Hermeneutics is ultimately not a question of arguments or logic but of personal preferences, prior intuitions, pre-argumentative positions, political ideologies, and ethical choices.[176] As we are reading our texts, we choose again and again to either believe or not believe that they say what they mean and mean what they say. We either decide to trust our discursive others or to be suspicious of them on principle. If our axiom is that claims of knowledge are always attempts at gaining power, no amount of evidence will convince us otherwise.

---

[174] Derrida, *La dissémination*, 93–104 ("Le père du *logos*").
[175] For historical overviews, see e.g. Cusset, *French Theory*; Hunter, "History of Theory"; Hunter, "Time of Theory"; Hunter, "Spirituality and Philosophy"; Hunter, "Mythos, Ethos, and Pathos of the Humanities."
[176] The so-called social-intuitionist principle in moral psychology shows that ethical disagreements about "right" or "wrong" cannot be resolved by rational debate because they rely on pre-rational intuitions; see Haidt, *Righteous Mind*, 3–108.

It will by now be obvious that this is not the direction I have taken in this book. On the contrary, if we dare to lower our guard and risk applying a hermeneutics of trust,[177] we are bound to make discoveries that should perhaps have been obvious all along. To stick with our paradigmatic key reference in this chapter: the plain fact is that nothing in Plato's *Phaedrus* suggests, even remotely or indirectly, that Thoth appears before Ammon with sinister intentions. The enemy behind the mask is just a spectral absence or ghost, a delusionary effect of hermeneutic paranoia.[178] What gets mistaken as a mask is simply a face. Plato's Thoth appears before Ammon as a friend of humanity, a promotor of mediation very similar to his Greek counterpart. In short, he is Hermes. As far as we can tell from his words – and why should we not believe them? – he is sincerely convinced that the gift of writing will enable human beings to communicate better across boundaries of time and space. And it is in a very similar role that, at the end of *The Ogdoad and the Ennead*, he tells Tat to use the gift of writing to pass the message of spiritual liberation on to future generations.

But the question still remains: how? None of these good intentions imply that Thoth-Hermes is right. To be sure, we might still consider him naïve or overconfident; and in fact, Gadamerian Hermeneutics lends ample support to Ammon's reservations about the *pharmakon* of writing. *Perfect* interpretation is forever beyond our reach, not for any contingent lack of time or resources but because Hermeneutics deals in *human* meaning. The point is that Ammon responds to Thoth's announcement

---

[177] Trust in Gadamerian Hermeneutics is a basic human attitude, not "belief" in the sense of blind acceptance without arguments or proof. In this regard, the hermeneutics of trust has been misperceived in Anglo-American debate from the very beginning, due to the fact that Ricoeur was apparently still unaware of Gadamer when he wrote *De l'interprétation* (1965), translated in 1970 as *Freud and Philosophy* (*Wahrheit und Methode* became famous only after its second edition, 1965). As a result, he pitted the "hermeneutics of suspicion" against a "hermeneutics of faith" (*la foi*) represented by Gerardus van der Leeuw, Mircea Eliade and Maurice Leenhardt (*Freud and Philosophy*, 28–32), leading to an unfortunate polarization in which critical theory stands opposed to "religionist" phenomenology of religion, while Gadamerian Hermeneutics gets eclipsed or wrongly associated with "faith" and its theological implications. For the enormous impact of Gadamer's Hermeneutics on Ricoeur's later work, see e.g. Simms, *Hans-Georg Gadamer*, 120–126.

[178] The terminology of paranoia is current in circles of *critique* itself: see notably Kosofsky Sedgwick, "Paranoid Reading"; Felski, *Limits of critique*, 34–35. For paranoia and overinterpretation, see Eco, *Interpretation and Overinterpretation*, 48, 94 (and the fictional parallel about semiotic overinterpretation and conspiratorial paranoia, *Il pendolo di Foucault*).

neither with a hermeneutics of suspicion nor with a hermeneutics of trust but with *no hermeneutics at all*. Because understanding requires a horizon of temporality (that is, of human mortality), it can only ever exist in historical consciousness. This is why textual Hermeneutics will never allow us to hear the silent hymns of the Ennead or see the "fountain bubbling with life" – significantly, the first thing Tat says after perceiving the *pēgē* is that "it is impossible to express this in words." However, contrary to what is suggested by Deconstruction and its backgrounds in Saussurean linguistics, I hold that the meaning of written texts does *not* depend on signification alone.[179] This is the final point I want to make about Plato's story and its implications. I consider it essential not just for reading the Hermetica, but for reading texts of profound quality in the humanities as a whole.[180]

Thoth had in fact discovered a *pharmakon* with mysterious powers that were wholly beyond Ammon's comprehension. He *did* have a powerful trick up his sleeve – very much like Hermes the trickster, the master of liminality who effortlessly crosses boundaries that we think can never be crossed.[181] The beneficial secret he knew is that texts can be profoundly meaningful *as texts*. We overlook something essential if we see nothing in them but intermediaries that can be dismissed after the message has been received.[182] Thoth's secret is that texts, in addition to their function as media for communication, can also be potent *signifiers in their own right*. They do not just speak on behalf of an other but possess agency of their own. This should perhaps not come as a big revelation, since it has

---

[179] For the fundamental argument, see Gadamer, *Hermeneutik I*, 418–422, 432–437.
[180] It is not possible here to unpack the notion of "quality" (and its relation to the category of *qualia*, important in modern philosophies of consciousness), but I see it as arguably the most important and certainly the most neglected key term in the humanities. If Robert Pirsig is right that all attempts at defining "quality" fail, as argued in his maverick classic *Zen and the Art of Motorcycle Maintenance*, we need to investigate the reasons for its indefinability and their philosophical implications.
[181] For the many faces of Hermes, see Miller and Strauss Clay, *Tracking Hermes, Pursuing Mercury*; for a delightful evocation of mythological Hermes imagery, see Faivre, *Eternal Hermes*; on the relevance of Hermes to Hermeneutics, see Nixon, *Hans-Georg Gadamer*, 28–30.
[182] "When you get the message, hang up the phone" (Watts, *Joyous Cosmology*, rev. first ed., 26). The flip side of that assumption is that in the absence of a message (the signified), texts become mediators with nothing to mediate. However, the crucial difference between Deconstruction and Hermeneutics is that while the former interprets that situation in terms of empty linguistic signifiers left to their own devices – *langue* in Saussurean terms – the latter insists on the primacy of *parole* (e.g. Gadamer, "Hermeneutics of Suspicion," 81; Gadamer, "Destruktion und Dekonstruktion," 370–371).

always been known to readers of great literature. I would suggest that what defines the intrinsic quality of profound texts ("Plato's Pharmacy" being as good an example as any) is their ability to enter our minds and engage us in fruitful dialogue, provided that for our part we know how to listen and respond.[183] We can obviously ask them critical questions, they may hold depths of hidden meaning that were not apparent to their authors, and we certainly do not need to agree with what they say. But as a rule, I further suggest, there is no need for us to apply hermeneutic violence to our texts so as to make them confess their crimes.[184] Quite like the victims of heresy trials, they are much more likely to reveal their *true* secrets freely and of their own accord, if we choose to approach them in a positive spirit: critically but with respect, out of profound and genuine interest in what they have to tell us and what we might learn from engaging them in dialogue. Such at least has been my attitude and method in reading the Hermetica. In such a hermeneutic encounter, the textual medium *is* the message that only mortal human readers have the capacity to understand.[185] Even the Source does not have a clue in that regard – if it did, it would not be the Source!

This final dimension of the Hermetica makes them into more than just a record or memorial of past opinions and events, a mere "drug of reminding."[186] Rather, their meaning unfolds in the very process of reading, the hermeneutical circle of interpretation:

We are thrown back on connections of meaning and sound that articulate the structure of the whole, and this happens not just once, but always again and again. We leaf backwards, as it were, then start over again, read anew, discover new connections of meaning; and all of this does not end the way it normally

---

[183] On hermeneutic dialogue and the agency of texts, see Chapter 5, pp. 132–138.

[184] The apt comparison between "suspicious hermeneutics" in literary Critique and heresy trials or inquisitorial procedures in early modernity comes from Felski, "Suspicious Minds," 219. Unfortunately she did not follow up on her announcement of a longer discussion in her book, originally titled "The Demon of Interpretation" (*Limits of Critique*, 10).

[185] The famous slogan "the medium is the message" has a different meaning in Marshall McLuhan's *Understanding Media* (ch. 1) than in the present context, where it means that form and content cannot be analytically separated in high-quality texts, such as literature, as well as in music or visual art.

[186] About texts as no more than "middle products" in the process of communication, see Gadamer, "Text und Interpretation," 341; about the difference in that regard with "literary" texts, defined by their ability to produce meaning out of themselves in the very act of interpretation, ibid., 351–352; and for the role of the reader, see ibid., 356 (*Dazwischenreden* versus *Mitreden*); cf. the excellent analysis of what I here describe as "Thoth's Secret" in Di Cesare, *Gadamer*, 55–58.

happens when we leave a text behind us – with the conscious certainty that the thing has finally been understood. It is the other way around. As more connections of meaning and sound enter our consciousness, we only get ever more deeply involved. We do not leave the text behind, but let ourselves enter into it. And then we find ourselves in it, the way every speaker finds himself in the words that he utters, the way he is in them and does not keep them at a distance (as in the case of somebody who uses tools, takes them up, and then puts them away).[187]

Such has certainly been my experience while reading and endlessly rereading the spiritual Hermetica in quest of their meaning. That meaning has not been exhausted, and never will be. I have absolutely no doubt that next time I enter this textual world, I will discover new dimensions that escaped me so far. This will lead me to ask new questions and draw new connections, which may well make it necessary for me to revise my prior opinions and allow my interpretive horizon to drift beyond what has been written down in this book. This is because, far from being just a collection of philosophical banalities (as believed by an older generation of scholars), far from being reducible to a play of empty signifiers (as critical theorists would have it), and in spite of all the damage and corruptions that were inflicted on them during centuries of transmission, somehow these texts still possess a dimension of depth that is the mark of literary classics. Thoth did invent a drug, not just of reminding but "of memory and wisdom."[188] His *pharmakon* made it possible for human beings to concoct Hermetic remedies of their own for curing forgetfulness. And so they did.

> To be conscious is not to be in time
> but only in time can the moment in the rose-garden,
> the moment in the arbour where the rain beat,
> the moment in the draughty church at smokefall
> be remembered; involved with past and future.
> Only through time time is conquered.[189]

---

[187] Gadamer, "Text und Interpretation," 358. Note the specific point that is being made here: readers find themselves "in" the text, the way they find themselves in their own speech at the moment of speaking. The immediacy of reading is therefore like the immediacy of speech, as opposed to spoken or written language understood as a medium for communication.
[188] Plato, *Phaedr.* 274e.
[189] T.S. Eliot, "Burnt Norton" (*Four Quartets*).

Epilogue

> Die Geisterwelt ist nicht verschlossen;
> Dein Sinn ist zu, dein Herz ist todt!
> Johann Wolfgang von Goethe[1]

All good writers put a spell on their audience. Whenever you are reading a book, you find yourself listening to an authorial voice that tries to expose you to mental imagery and draw you into a story.[2] Powerful texts appeal to your emotions so as to capture your attention and keep you engaged. Academic writing is no exception. The real-life influence of scholarly narratives relies not just on factual evidence and reasonable arguments but at least as much, if not more, on their ability to use words for the purpose of enchantment. Still, no spell will take hold unless it finds a receptive target. The imagery must speak to the readers' lived experience, and historical narratives must resonate with what they feel is happening in their own world. In case of a successful match, scholarly writings "make sense" of what readers experience as relevant, so that their imagination is captured and their attention is held. The mental imagery must be powerful and the story must seem plausible – but here's

---

[1] Goethe, *Faust I* ("the world of spirits is not closed; it's your sense that is shut, it's your heart that is dead!"); Trunz ed., 22.
[2] In cognitive studies, the strange phenomenon of mental text-image interaction is studied in terms of Allan Paivio's influential dual coding theory (e.g. Paivio, *Mental Representations*; Sadoski and Paivio, *Imagery and Text*). My discussion on the following pages owes something to a famous chapter on the manipulation of *phantasmata* in Couliano, *Eros and Magic*, 87–106, and its impressive literary development in John Crowley's Hermetic "Aegypt" tetralogy (*The Solitudes*; *Love and Sleep*; *Daemonomania*; *Endless Things*).

the thing: the information does not need to be correct. None of these *phantasmata* needs to be real.[3]

I can think of no better example than the story of "gnosticism" told by scholars during the twentieth century. In 1934, one year after Hitler took power, the German Jewish philosopher Hans Jonas (1903–1993) published the first part of his monograph *Gnosis und spätantiker Geist* (Gnosis and the Spirit of Late Antiquity). By then, Jonas himself had already fled the country. Readers at the time complained about the difficult language inspired by Jonas' teacher, Martin Heidegger, but the book made an impact. It planted a powerful image in the minds of its readers: that of the gnostic as a *stranger*, a homeless wanderer lost in a hostile world. After the war, Jonas published a book in English that became a bestseller: *The Gnostic Religion: The Message of the Alien God and the Beginnings of Christianity*. It came out in 1958, in the shadow of the holocaust and the atomic bomb, and resonated powerfully with the dark existentialist mood of the time.[4] *Alienation* was the key to its enormous appeal. Human beings found themselves "thrown" into an alien world from which salvation seemed impossible because it would depend on contact with an alien God – a remote spiritual reality so utterly "other" that its very essence had to be far beyond what human minds could even grasp. This imagery reflected a sense of catastrophe and spiritual abandonment that was shared across the political spectrum during the first decades of the Cold War.[5] Seduced by the spell of consumer society, the masses seemed now so alienated from reality that they had lost even the sense of their own alienation – "the society of the spectacle" had become their only reality.[6] In such a situation, what was believed to define the "gnostic" was the fact that he had woken up to his true condition. Yes, he was lost – but at least he knew it. From the

---

[3] For the basic argument, see Hanegraaff, "Religion and the Historical Imagination."
[4] Jonas, *Gnosis und spätantiker Geist I*, esp. 94–140; and Jonas, *The Gnostic Religion*, 48–99, with its series of section titles: "the 'Alien,' 'Beyond,' 'Without,' 'This World' and 'The Other World,' Worlds and Aeons, The Cosmic Habitation (*das Weltgehäuse*) and the Stranger's Sojourn, 'Light' and 'Darkness,' 'Life' and 'Death,' 'Mixture,' 'Dispersal,' the 'One,' and the 'Many,' 'Fall,' 'Sinking,' 'Capture,' Forlornness (*das Geworfensein*), Dread, Homesickness, Numbness, Sleep, Intoxication, The Noise of the World, The 'Call from Without,' The 'Alien Man'." For a particularly incisive analysis, see Waldstein, "Hans Jonas' Construct 'Gnosticism'." See also Lazier, *God Interrupted*, 27–72; Wolin, *Heidegger's Children*, 101–133; King, *What is Gnosticism?*, 115–137.
[5] See e.g. Safranski, *Ein Meister aus Deutschland*, 451 (about Gehlen, Adorno and Heidegger).
[6] Debord, *Society of the Spectacle*.

iron cage of modernity after the death of God, salvation had become impossible. As famously formulated by Heidegger in a 1966 interview, "only a god can save us now."[7]

Whatever we may think of this existentialist analysis of modernity and the human condition, Jonas' narrative of the gnostic "principle" or "syndrome" as the core phenomenon of late antiquity was certainly not correct. When he began his researches during the 1920s, Heidegger's existentialism was the key with which Jonas believed to unlock not just the gnostic sources but even "the whole epoch" of the first centuries CE, including the Hermetica.[8] But eventually, the directional logic got reversed: for many scholars and philosophers in the wake of Jonas' work, this concept of "gnosticism" now became the key to unlock modernity![9] That very concept, however, was a modern phantasm. Among specialized scholars of late antiquity, Jonas' story of "the gnostic religion" has not survived the progress of textual and historical research. The image of existential alienation at the core of his work found its way into popular culture and remains a potent theme to the present day,[10] but academic specialists have thoroughly dismantled it by now, as a "dubious category" that may create an illusion of deep insight but in fact cannot account for the textual sources that it claims to interpret.[11]

A very different spell of *phantasmata* was set loose in the scholarly community by the publications of André-Jean Festugière. Like Jonas' work on "gnosticism," his large study of the Hermetica was conceived in the unstable period of the interbellum and reflects a somewhat similar mood of existential crisis and fear of cultural decline. Having lost two of his brothers at an early age, Father Festugière was obsessed with the problem of evil and tormented by doubts about whether God loved humanity. He deeply longed for an earthly paradise unspoiled by the

---

[7] Anonymus, "'Nur noch ein Gott kann uns retten'," 209. Heidegger gave this interview on the binding condition that it would be published only after his death, which occurred in 1976.
[8] Jonas, "The Gnostic Syndrome"; Jonas, *The Gnostic Religion*, 26–27.
[9] Jonas, "Epilogue: Gnosticism, Nihilism and Existentialism," 320–321; Waldstein, "Hans Jonas' Construct 'Gnosticism'," 344–345. See for instance the cases of Eric Voegelin and Carl Raschke as analyzed in Hanegraaff, "On the Construction," 29–40.
[10] See e.g. Trompf, *Gnostic World*, 619–697; DeConick and Roig Lanzillotta, *Gnostic Countercultures*.
[11] E.g. Williams, *Rethinking "Gnosticism"*; Williams, "On Ancient 'Gnosticism' as a Problematic Category"; King, *What is Gnosticism?* (about Jonas, see pp. 115–137); and see above, Chapter 4, pp. 85–86.

Fall of Man.[12] "God fills everything with his great silent shadow," he wrote late in life, "and all places seem desolate that do not speak of Him."[13] In the second volume of *La révélation d'Hermès Trismégiste*, by far the longest of the four, he evoked a lost world in which the divine was not yet absent but, on the contrary, was felt to be present everywhere. Festugière referred to this spiritual perspective as *La religion du monde* (The Religion of the World). The descent from such positive world-affirmation into "gnostic" pessimism and world-denial, one manifestation of which he saw in the Hermetica, was depicted as all of a piece with the "decline of rationalism" and the rise of "oriental cults."[14] Again, my argument is that this particular vision of late antiquity enchanted the minds of scholars *not* because it emerged so clearly from the primary sources, but rather because it resonated with what those scholars feared might be happening all around them in their own time as well. If it all made so much sense to them, that is because these ancient texts appeared to their consciousness where they had to appear: within the confines of their own contemporary horizon.

After the end of World War II, it took some decades for the mood to change. In a well-known lecture about cultural fashions and history of religions, Mircea Eliade describes how for large parts of the population, the atmosphere of French existentialism had given way during the 1960s to something entirely different:

[W]hat was new and exhilarating for the French reader was the optimistic and holistic outlook which coupled science with esoterism and presented a living, fascinating, and mysterious cosmos, in which human life again became meaningful and promised an endless perfectibility. Man was no longer condemned to a rather dreary *condition humaine*; instead he was called both to conquer his physical universe and to unravel the other, enigmatic universes revealed by the occultists and gnostics. ... Man was no longer estranged and useless in an absurd world, into which he had come by accident and to no purpose.[15]

---

[12] Saffrey, "Le père André-Jean Festugière," 297: "... all his life, Father Festugière was possessed by the problem of evil. Not that he doubted God's existence, but his question was: 'Does God love human beings?'." His older brother was killed in World War I in 1916, and a younger brother died of tuberculosis in 1921 (ibid., 299). Saffrey describes Festugière's struggle with loneliness and despair, and translates a beautiful passage about a few days of paradisical peace in the garden of a convent in 1949 (304–305).
[13] Saffrey, "Le père André-Jean Festugière," 304.
[14] RHT I, 1–66.
[15] Eliade, "Cultural Fashions," 10–11; on the continuation of "gnostic" existentialist patterns in esoteric contexts after the sixties, see Hanegraaff, "Fiction in the Desert of the Real."

Eliade's immediate reference here was to the "fantastic realism" associated with the French journal *Planète* and its many international offshoots, which has made a big career in popular culture up to the present; but he might just as well have been writing these lines about the Hermetic Tradition as described by Frances A. Yates, whose work he discussed in a closely related setting.[16] In her bestselling *Giordano Bruno and the Hermetic Tradition* (1964), Yates relied on Festugière for all her information about the original Hermetic literature; but she entirely sidelined the pessimistic-existentialist "gnostic" outlook while enthusiastically embracing the "religion of the world" that had actually played a very minor role in Festugière's view of the Hermetica.[17] Her thoroughly world-affirming vision of Hermeticism came to dominate a large new wave of academic research in history of science and intellectual history;[18] and so this is what countless scholars, not to mention the wider public, would henceforth imagine the Hermetica had been all about. The contrast with Jonas' perspective could not have been more extreme. As scholars were focusing most of their attention now on "the Hermetic Tradition" in the Renaissance and early modern science, they mostly took it for granted that the Hermetica must have been all about an optimistic pagan worldview of Egyptian "natural magic" – even though in actual fact, magic plays no role of any significance in the *Corpus Hermeticum*.[19] Taking

---

[16] Eliade discussed Yates in another lecture from the same period, "The Occult and the Modern World," published together with the Cultural Fashions essay in *Occultism, Witchcraft, and Cultural Fashions* (1976). The enormous direct and indirect international impact of *Planète* (and its offshoots in many different languages), closely linked to Pauwels and Bergier's runaway bestseller *Le matin des magiciens* (The Morning of the Magicians, 1960), remains a seriously neglected topic in the modern study of Western esotericism. See Renard, "Le mouvement *Planète*" and the unpublished Ph.D. dissertation by Karbovnik, "L'ésotérisme grand public."

[17] Yates quotes this formulation no less than sixteen times at strategic points throughout her book: see *Giordano Bruno*, 2, 6, 11, 41, 59, 82, 118, 128, 153, 176, 180, 250, 260, 302, 355, 417. As we have seen above (p. 126 with note 27), and has been noted by many critics, Festugière's second volume devotes just 71 pages to the Hermetica, while the remainder of his 610-page volume deals with "parallels" such as Xenophon, Plato, the Stoa, and Philo.

[18] For discussion and further references, see e.g. Cohen, *Scientific Revolution*, 169–183; Hanegraaff, *Esotericism and the Academy*, 322–334.

[19] See Hanegraaff, *Esotericism and the Academy*, 333 note 285: Yates' interpretation of hermeticism in terms of astral magic reflects an extreme focus on *Ascl.* 23–24/37–38 at the expense of the CH. Her narrative is fatally undermined by the fact that "what was new in the Renaissance (the *Corpus Hermeticum*) was not magical, and what could be construed as 'magical' (the *Picatrix* and *Asclepius* 23–24/37–38) was not new" (Hanegraaff, "How Hermetic was Renaissance Hermetism?," 181).

Frances Yates at her word, they were bound to see Hermeticism as celebrating the Dignity of Man, the "great miracle" interpreted as a supreme magical operator, placed in the midst of a beautiful enchanted cosmos in which everything was alive and teeming with mysterious incalculable forces.[20]

What Hans Jonas did for "gnosticism," then, Frances Yates did for "the Hermetic Tradition." She brought it to the attention of a mass audience, by telling stories about the past that were really stories about the present with implications for the future. Jonas conjured up the frightening modern vision of an inhuman universe, a mute world of spiritual desolation that responds with nothing but blank indifference (or rather, does not respond at all) to any of our feelings or hopes or desires.[21] Yates, in the greatest possible contrast, placed "man the great miracle" in the midst of an utterly enchanted participatory universe, "where every thing, every being, every force is like a voice yet to be understood ... where every word that is pronounced has innumerable echoes and resonances; where the stars are looking, listening, and exchanging signs among themselves the way we do ourselves. A universe, finally, that is an immense dialogue ..."[22] Thus general readers of the Hermetica are offered a choice between two dominant hermeneutical frames that reflect radically opposed attitudes or ways of being in the world. One vision tells us that Hermetic practitioners found themselves living in an alien, disenchanted, indifferent, or hostile world to which they could respond only

---

[20] I deliberately refer to the famous formulations by Weber, *Wissenschaft als Beruf*, 488. On widespread misinterpretations of Giovanni Pico della Mirandola's "Oratio," culminating in Kristeller's presentation in an iconic volume on Renaissance philosophy (Cassirer, Kristeller and Randall, *Renaissance Philosophy of Man*, 213–254), see Copenhaver, *Magic and the Dignity of Man*.

[21] See the quotations from Pascal's *Pensées* III 205 (that "infinite immensity of spaces which I do not know and which do not know me"; slightly different translation in Jonas, *Gnostic Religion*, 322) and Nietzsche's poem *Vereinsamt* ("The world – a gate / to a thousand deserts mute and chill! / Who once has lost / what you have lost stands nowhere still," ibid., 324). For a brilliant analysis see Houellebecq, *H.P. Lovecraft: Contre le monde, contre la vie*; and commentary in Hanegraaff, "Fiction in the Desert of the Real," 86–90. Houellebecq's famous novels, notably *Les particules élémentaires* (1998) and *Plateforme* (2001), evoke this world of utter spiritual alienation as the default condition of (post)modernity under conditions of neoliberal economics.

[22] Garin, *Medioevo e rinascimento*, 154. For Yates' fundamental debt to Garin's cosmological vision as expressed in such passages, and their common reliance on Festugière's work, see Hanegraaff, *Esotericism and the Academy*, 330. Actually, Garin's and Yates' view of "hermeticism" was remarkably close to earlier understandings of "gnosticism" prior to Jonas or Festugière, as seen in the case of Jacques Matter's pioneering *Histoire critique du gnosticisme* (1828): see Hanegraaff, *Esotericism and the Academy*, 336.

with negative feelings such as loneliness, distance, suspicion, and fear. The other vision saw them as living in a thoroughly enchanted universe of correspondences and sympathies, a world of open communication and generous hospitality in which humans are welcome, a cosmos that inspired positive feelings such as confidence, trust, enthusiasm, and love.

Both perspectives have powerful appeal for the modern and postmodern imagination, but my argument is that neither of them is adequate to make sense of Hermetic spirituality. The first one is commonly associated with "dualism" and the second with "monism," but those categories are inflexible and misleading. It is certainly true that many Hermetic materials concerned with magic or astrology reflect a "holistic" (rather than monistic) worldview of correspondences and occult causalities;[23] but the dynamics of cosmic sympathy and antipathy were of little theoretical or practical importance to Hermetic spirituality per se. As far as we can tell from our treatises, practitioners were not concerned with "operating on the world" by manipulating its powers along Yatesian lines but were trying to achieve spiritual liberation on an individual level. Such liberation, however, did not imply an escape from the body and materiality, in terms of the soul's return from a hostile cosmos to its true spiritual home as imagined by Porphyry or depicted by Hans Jonas. It was not really about where the soul was, or where it would go, but about the state it was in.

Therefore the sense of alienation that we do encounter in the Hermetica is best understood *psychologically*, as a "state of mind" or modification of consciousness that was explained in terms of enslavement or addiction to delusionary mental imagery. The soul had lost its original ability to perceive reality as it really is.[24] It is true that this problematic condition was seen as resulting from the soul's descent into the "seething cauldron" of the body, but it does not follow that embodiment was therefore considered a mistake or catastrophe that must be corrected by returning to a disembodied state. Rather, if the soul suffered risks and discomforts, that was the price for leaving home and venturing out into wholly new realities. The *positive* challenge of incarnation consisted precisely in the opportunity it provided for the soul to achieve spiritual liberation *in a fully embodied state*. This required healing the soul from negative passions, so that it could open itself

---

[23] On correspondences and occult causality as opposed to instrumental causality, see Hanegraaff, *Western Esotericism*, 124–128; for worldviews of metaphysical radicalism and of mediation as an alternative to simple dualism/monism, ibid., 69–85. On "holism" (a term invented by the South-African statesman J.C. Smuts), see Hanegraaff, *New Age Religion*, 119–158.

[24] See the quotation from Goethe's *Faust* above this Epilogue.

to the beauty of existence while still living in this world. Being human was a unique gift, defined precisely by this wondrous ability to participate simultaneously in *both* dimensions of reality, the physical and the spiritual.

Two dimensions, one reality. The core metaphysics of Hermetic spirituality, or so I have argued, should be understood in terms of radical *nonduality*. This means that the experiential world of multiple phenomena in which we find ourselves is not ultimately real, in the sense that how things *appear* to our dualistic consciousness is not how things really *are*.[25] The human quest for enlightenment or *gnōsis* could be described as the individual soul's *hypnerotomachia*, a dreamlike quest or strife for felicity driven by the power of *erōs*.[26] And yet it was precisely by pursuing their passionate desires all the way through this worldly labyrinth of merely phenomenal experiences that souls could finally discover the ultimate oneness of true being – the secret that *nothing unreal exists*.[27] It follows that *embodiment* cannot be understood in dualistic terms (as the descent of something purely spiritual into its purely material opposite) but should rather be imagined as a unitary spiritual event that is *experienced* in terms of materiality. As formulated by John Sallis in his analysis of the *chōra*,

> What there is, then, in a dream is an image that goes unrecognized as an image, an image that in the dream is simply taken as the original. And in contrast to the

---

[25] As suggested in my analysis of the *aiōn* and the *chōra* in Chapter 7 (and supported by modern philosophers such as John Sallis), the philosophical/psychological perspective seems very close to Kant's distinction between *phenomena* and *noumena*, with the transcendental imagination as mediator between the two. See also the cognitive science built on evolutionary biology developed by Hoffman, *Case Against Reality*, 1–21.

[26] I borrow this term from the famous fifteenth-century *Hypnerotomachia Poliphili* attributed to Francesco Colonna; see Godwin, *Pagan Dream of the Renaissance*, 21–37.

[27] The paradox is deliberate and inevitable, because the distinctions of dualism versus nondualism and unreality versus reality are themselves dualistic (cf. Loy, *Nonduality*, 5; Dyczkowski, *Doctrine of Vibration*, 34–57). I see Hermetic nonduality as extremely similar to the famous perspective of Parmenides and its dazzling implications (see Mansfeld and Primavesi, *Vorsokratiker*, 322): *nothing is but what is*, and therefore *what is not is not and cannot be considered to be*. As formulated by Aristotle, this means that "no existing thing either comes into being or perishes, because what comes into being must originate either from what exists or from what does not, and both are impossible: what is does not become (for it already is) and nothing can come to be from what is not" (*Physica* 191 A27; cf. *De Caelo* 298 B14). I am inclined to interpret the much-discussed sentence τὸ γὰρ αὐτὸ νοεῖν τε καὶ εἶναι as "for what is there for noeticizing and for being is one and the same" (discussion in Kingsley, *Reality*, 69–72; Geldard, *Parmenides*, 23, 44–46), implying that even the delusions of noetic consciousness *are* and cannot *not* be (remarkably similar to the argument of Kashmiri Śaivism against Advaita Vedānta: Dyczkowski, *Doctrine of Vibration*, 36–38). I see the same nondual logic at work in the Hermetic view that there is no death but only life (above, pp. 271–273).

dreamer there is the one who can distinguish between the image and its original, the one who is *wakeful to the difference* and who *even in a vision of an image* will set its original apart from it.[28]

In this Platonic analogy of life as a dream, Hermetic *gnōsis* could be defined with great precision as being "wakeful to the difference" *not* just after having actually woken up but even while still being in the embodied state of imaginal consciousness. The profound alteration of noetic consciousness caused by (or known as) embodiment resulted in a world of intense experiential phenomena that were quite chaotic and difficult to control, but could be cultivated and perfected by the soul's deliberate and persistent efforts. The guiding virtue in this supreme enterprise was *eusebeia*, an attitude of profound reverence for the Source of universal Light and Life, and the ultimate goal was to be fully alive and conscious in a permanent state of *gnōsis*.[29] The task of human souls was to help give birth in beauty to divine goodness and truth, so that the world of appearances might become a perfect mirror of its ideal noetic origin and ground.

Nonduality and embodiment must therefore take the place of monism and dualism in our interpretations of Hermetic texts. But those traditional frameworks inspired by modernist visions of the human condition are not the only ones that have been dominant in the historical imagination. On the level of cultural and political ideologies, I have highlighted the grand narrative of *philhellenism* and its far-reaching influence on how scholars imagined Egypt as part of "the Orient."[30] In the second volume of his foundational monograph *Hermès en Haute-Égypte*, published in 1982, Jean-Pierre Mahé identified this key factor very clearly. He wrote that his great predecessor, Father Festugière, had made an excellent start with his highly innovative and illuminating analysis of *L'astrologie et les sciences occultes* (1942). But unfortunately the three remaining volumes of his *magnum opus*, about the so-called "philosophical" Hermetica, were "not at the same level of eminence and homogeneity" because "the author's judgment [got] distorted by the very principles of his method"

---

[28] Sallis, *Chorology*, 121 (emphasis added).
[29] On the ideal of spiritual enlightenment or illumination as a permanent state, see Jacobs, "Getting off the Wheel."
[30] Marchand, "From Liberalism to Neoromanticism"; Hanegraaff, "Out of Egypt." Philhellenism and Orientalism are best understood as two sides of the same coin, as can be seen from the detailed analyses in Marchand's two large companion monographs *Down from Olympus* and *German Orientalism*. Among other things, this means that much of Edward Said's well-known critique of Orientalism should better be directed at Philhellenism.

and reflected a "grave error of perspective."[31] Mahé was of course referring to the extreme philhellenist agenda of minimizing any Egyptian or "Oriental" influence in the interest of Greek or Hellenic superiority.

The most general trend of research as it developed after Mahé might be described as a gradual but thorough correction of philhellenist bias and a recovery of what Fowden referred to as *The Egyptian Hermes* (1986). Rejecting philhellenism means accepting Egypt, along with other parts of what used to be called "the Orient" (the world of the "barbarians" from a Greek perspective), as integrated *completely* and on terms of *full equality* in the complex fabric of Hellenistic culture in the Roman period. As old habits die slowly, even today this principle is by no means so self-evident as one might perhaps expect.[32] One important implication, in my opinion, is that there should really be no room for disparaging terminologies (such as "magic" understood as the Romans did, not to mention references to "murky" practices or "sub-philosophical" thinking, and the like) that send a normative message of superiority/inferiority in discussing religious practices or forms of intellectual speculation.[33] My insistence on this point is part of a larger reconstructionist agenda of moving beyond traditional grand narratives of "Western culture" towards new, entirely different, and far more complex ones that must fully *include* and integrate what used to be marginalized or excluded as "rejected knowledge." In my earlier work I focused on the deep discursive patterns of rejection and exclusion directed against Platonic Orientalism and its intellectual legacy, culminating in Protestant and Enlightenment ideologies that even today still largely dominate our collective imagination.[34] I insisted in very strong terms that the full scope of what used to be rejected and discredited as "nonsense" must henceforth be *included* again by historians:

[W]e need to discard our ingrained habits of historiographical eclecticism (simply put: our tendency to privilege what we like, and ignore what we don't) and try to cultivate an *anti-eclectic historiography*, "one that does not select only what it believes to be 'true' or 'serious,' but questions the established canon of modern

---

[31] HHE II, 20–25.
[32] For the highly representative case of Iamblichus, see for instance the discussion of recent and current perspectives in Quack, "(H)abamons Stimme?," 150–156. For a very recent example focused on the *Corpus Hermeticum*, see Law, *Das Corpus Hermeticum*, 49–57 (Hanegraaff, Review of Law, 180).
[33] See Chapter 2, pp. 42–44 and Chapter 4, p. 101 with note 93, 109. Regarding "magic," I consider Otto's *Magie* as the decisive analysis (see Hanegraaff, Review of Otto; Hanegraaff, "Magic").
[34] Hanegraaff, *Esotericism and the Academy*.

intellectual and academic culture (its collective 'memory bank') and recognizes that our common heritage is of much greater richness and complexity than one would infer from standard academic textbooks." Such a program of anti-eclectic historiography is incompatible not just with normative programs of any kind, but also, more generally, with any procedure that pre-selects the sources, and/or reads them selectively, to fit the preferences and criteria defined *a priori* by some theoretical program (which, thereby, almost inevitably comes to function as a hidden ideology).[35]

In the history of Hermetic scholarship, philhellenism is the ultimate example of such a "theoretical program" and "hidden ideology." Precisely because philhellenists were so passionately committed to nineteenth-century idealizations of "Greek rationality," as the superior and exclusive foundation of all true and reliable knowledge, they were singularly ill-equipped to understand what Hermetic authors actually meant by *noēsis* and *gnōsis*.

Philhellenism as a historical phenomenon is defined not just by a Greek-Hellenic bias, but by a "Judeo-Christian" one as well.[36] This means that Western civilization used to be imagined as resting on two pillars: not just Greek rationality and science, but also a tradition of religious morality grounded in Jewish and Christian scripture. What underpins this deeply Eurocentric vision is an evolutionist and quasi-providentialist grand narrative that makes post-Reformation Christianity the triumphant pinnacle or culmination of religious and civilizational progress worldwide. A major implication is that Islamic civilizations get marginalized or wholly erased from what "Western culture" is supposedly all about, along with northern Africa and the Byzantine world. Moving beyond philhellenism means rejecting this logic entirely, in favor of a comprehensive historiographical vision that must include and integrate all those domains – again *completely* and on terms of *full equality* – as parts of the complex fabric and dynamic development of Western culture over the entire period from

---

[35] Hanegraaff, "Power of Ideas," 20–21 (with self-quotation referring to Hanegraaff, *Esotericism and the Academy*, 377; emphasis added).

[36] On this popular but extremely problematic nineteenth-century neologism, which explicitly sets Islam apart from the two other great Abrahamic religions and became a major ideological component of American Cold War discourse, see Gaston, *Imagining Judeo-Christian America*. How many philhellenist scholars actually used the exact coinage "Judeo-Christian" in their own work is less important for our concerns than the fact that they undoubtedly accepted its premise that the foundations of Western civilization are Jewish and Christian but not Islamic. For the enormous sensitivity of these issues in the context of contemporary debates about "European identity," see for instance Hirschkind, *Feeling of History*, 1–34.

Epilogue 363

antiquity to the present.[37] In studying the Hermetica, this means resisting the sometimes barely conscious habit of projecting Christian-theological notions on to non-Christian texts. Notable examples discussed in previous chapters are the biblical notion of a "Fall of Man"; a disproportionate search for Jewish or biblical influences and parallels to early Christianity at the expense of "pagan" hellenistic dimensions; an almost instinctive tendency to interpret formulations such as "son of God" or "the third god" against a background of Christian *Logos*-theology; and, of course, such dominant heresiological frames as "gnostic dualism" or an "arrogant spiritual elitism" combined with modern-existentialist notions of alienation.

Finally, no factor has dominated the historical imagination more powerfully than the very language of Western metaphysics.[38] Throughout this book, I have questioned and deconstructed default interpretations of *nous* and *logos* as well as *noēsis* and *gnōsis*, insisting that this Hermetic key vocabulary can simply *not* be understood in terms of our standard conceptual repertoire. The sober fact is that we have no equivalents for these words in our modern languages. The usual dictionary translations function very much as what Derrida calls *suppléments*: they add themselves to the original words, only to usurp their very meaning and put themselves in their place.[39] As a result, casual readers of the Hermetica in modern translations are drawn into a web of significations entirely different from the original one, and this leads them to believe that the authors were deeply invested in such comfortably familiar topics as "the intellect," "reason," "thinking," "knowledge," or "the mind." However, the meanings and resonances that occur to *us* when we use that language

---

[37] For the basic argument regarding Islam, see Bulliet, *The Case for Islamo-Christian Civilization*, 1–45. See also e.g. Fowden, *Empire to Commonwealth* and *Before and After Muḥammad*; Melvin-Koushki, "*Taḥqīq* vs. *Taqlīd*" ("Helleno-Islamo-Judeo-Christian" culture resp. "the Hellenic-Abrahamic synthesis," which I would think of rather in terms of a continuous evolving Hellenic-Abrahamic *dialectics*: a stable synthesis is never achieved).

[38] A close competitor in this regard would be the traditional language of "religion." For the modern de/construction of this concept, its problems and limitations, and possible ways towards positive *re*construction, see Hanegraaff, "Reconstructing 'Religion'"; Hanegraaff, "Imagining the Future Study." This dimension is relevant to the Hermetica wherever we encounter topics that are in some way sensitive or controversial within the normative theologies of exclusive monotheism, such as e.g. "magic," "idolatry," or "spirituality."

[39] On the French *supplément* as both "addition" and "substitute," see Johnson, "Translator's Introduction," xiii; see also, of course, the central deconstructionist notion of "representation."

are very different from those that informed the discourse of the authors. This is perhaps the most central point that my book is trying to make, and the most central issue that it seeks to address. What *were* they talking about? And how can *we* talk about it in our language? Can we talk about it at all?

Those questions lead us back to the mystery of *translation* that, in my firm opinion, goes to the heart of what the humanities are or should be all about. From my references to George Steiner in Chapter 1 to the confrontation between Jacques Derrida and Hans-Georg Gadamer in Chapter 10, I have been suggesting that our ability to translate (in the sense of *transferre* or *übersetzen*, the transfer of some meaning across a liminal space of discontinuity)[40] is a profoundly baffling phenomenon that cannot be separated from the greater mysteries of *communication, interpretation,* and *understanding* on which all human culture ultimately depends.[41] But a key factor that tends to be neglected or misunderstood in this context is – once again – the poorly understood faculty that we refer to as *imagination*. The central tradition of Aristotle and Kant insists (and I concur) that its activity is not limited to the production of merely "imaginary" or "imaginative" deceptions or delusions, but pertains without restriction to *all* operations of human cognition – including, of course, everything that is involved in historical research and textual hermeneutics.[42]

Most modern readers experience some difficulties grasping this point, because it seems to conflict with our default post-Enlightenment assumptions about fantasy and imagination as *contrary* to rational knowledge and the reality principle. But in fact, this difficulty of understanding once again illustrates the very problem of translation that is at issue here, for it so happens that – exactly like *nous*, *logos*, *noēsis* and *gnōsis* – the Greek word *phantasia* has no good equivalent in our modern languages. As explained in a meticulous analysis by Chiara Bottici,

> The contrast [of *phantasia*] with the modern view of imagination as purely imaginary could not be greater. The proportions of this rupture are evident in the embarrassment of modern translators who cannot render the Greek term *phantasia* with the literal translation "*fantasy*" because this would mean the opposite

---

[40] Chapter 1, pp. 13–15; Chapter 10, pp. 313–314 with note 20.
[41] See the very titles of Steiner's opening chapters, "Understanding as Translation" and "Language and Gnosis" (*After Babel*, 1–114).
[42] The decisive analysis is Castoriadis, "Discovery of the Imagination," who distinguishes between Aristotle's "second imagination" understood as a "superfluous doublet" dependent on sensation (ibid., 223–225) and the "first imagination" that is basic to *any* kind of thinking or noetic activity whatsoever (ibid., 227–245).

of what Aristotle had in mind when writing those passages. Alternative modern terms are needed to capture the meaning of Aristotle's *phantasia*: "actual vision" or "true appearance," that is, expressions that mean exactly the opposite of what literal translations such as "imagination" and "fantasy" would convey to modern readers.[43]

The term *phantasia* did not refer to mental delusions or creative inventions divorced from reality, but meant simply "appearance" or "presentation" (from *phainesthai*, to appear).[44] As such, it covered absolutely everything that appears to be present in consciousness. In his fundamental formulation that "the soul never noeticizes without a phantasm" (*oudepote noei aneu phantasmatos hē psuchē*),[45] Aristotle therefore referred to the imagination as nothing less than "the condition for thought insofar as it alone can present to thought the object as sensible without matter."[46] In other words, no mental or intellectual activity of *any* kind is possible without the faculty of imagination: "there is *always* phantasm; we are *always* imagining."[47] It is a truly remarkable fact of intellectual history that this crucial Aristotelian insight was ignored and misunderstood for about twenty-two centuries, until its rediscovery by Kant and Fichte – after which it got covered up once again, first by Kant himself and then by Hegel, who re-established the well-known but reductive view of imagination as merely reproductive, recombinatory, deficient, illusory, deceptive, or suspect.[48]

---

[43] Bottici, *Imaginal Politics*, 20–21.
[44] Bottici, *Imaginal Politics*, 20. On φαντᾰσία as derived from φαίνεσθαι, see Camassa, "*Phantasia* da Platone ai neoplatonici," 23–25; Bottici, *Imaginal Politics*, 20 with 206 note 18: our understanding of the imagination as a creative faculty appears "only very late and very rarely." For a longer discussion, see Nussbaum, *Aristotle's De Motu Animalium*, 221–273 (with reservations: Bottici, *Imaginal Politics*, 20–21 with 207 note 20).
[45] Aristotle, *De anima* III 7.431a (cf. parallel statements in III 7 and 8, and in *De memoria* quoted in Castoriadis, "Discovery," 233); see discussion in Chapter 7, pp. 204–207. The proposition was intended to be "universal, absolute, without restriction" (ibid., 239).
[46] Castoriadis, "Discovery," 231 (note that "sensible" potentially refers to all the senses, not just visuality). The question of whether "noeticizing" must be understood here just in our restricted sense of "thinking" or should include the broader range of meaning explored throughout this book is fascinating and important, but not essential to my present argument.
[47] Castoriadis, "Discovery," 228, 235–236; and see references to Aristotle on p. 233. Modern cognitive reseach confirms that "imaginative operations of meaning construction ... work at lightning speed, below the horizon of consciousness" (Fauconnier and Turner, *The Way We Think*, 8; Hanegraaff, "Religion and the Historical Imagination," 133–135).
[48] Castoriadis, "Discovery," 215; Schulte–Sasse, "Einbildungskraft/Imagination," 89–93. For Kant's cover-up between the first and second edition of *Kritik der reinen Vernunft*, see sources quoted above, Chapter 7, pp. 211–212 with note 95. For Fichte and Hegel, see Castoriadis, "Discovery," 214–215; Castoriadis, *Imaginary Institution of Society*, 391–392 note 53.

It is in terms of these intellectual traditions that my book as a whole, and this Epilogue more in particular, insists so strongly on the historical imagination.[49] All forms of scholarly practice in the humanities (notably translation, interpretation, and understanding) depend on the unique capacity of our imagination to re-present reality so as to make it appear to our consciousness and, in the very act of doing so, "to see in a thing what it is not, to see it other than it is."[50] The practice of history, too, is therefore "impossible and inconceivable outside of the *productive* or *creative imagination*" that manifests itself inevitably in the constitution of "a universe of *significations*."[51] Without this reflective mirror in which we perceive all things that reach our consciousness, yet always perceive them differently from how they really are, we would simply be unable to understand anything at all.[52] If so, then *what does it mean to understand* – in general and in principle? I suggest that the core process can be defined in remarkably simple terms as an act of communication: something meaningful gets transferred across a liminal space, by a tricky mediator who cannot fully be trusted.[53] A message is sent, and a message is received.

But is it still the same message? To be perfectly honest, we have every reason to doubt it. I find it significant that after his 1,700-page attempt to interpret the Hermetic literature, Festugière's final words were about the limits of communication and understanding: "the historian knows only what he is being told. He does not penetrate the secret of the heart."

---

[49] In different formulations, this focus is actually basic to all my work since the 1990s. My 1996 study *New Age Religion and Western Culture* focused on what happens when traditional forms of Western esotericism get reflected "in the mirror of secular thought," that is, when they get re-interpreted in the secular imagination. My 2012 monograph *Esotericism and the Academy* explored how, in the imagination of Protestant and Enlightenment thinkers, these traditions appeared as the radical counterpart of their own ideal identity. History of reception could be defined as history of creative (re)imagination.

[50] Castoriadis, *Imaginary Institution of Society*, 127, and the extraordinary concluding passage on p. 142. The concept of "radical imagination" implies that its ultimate root (*radix*) is beyond definition and discursive analysis ("Discovery," 238). That the collective imagination is key to the very possibility of human culture is central to the entire argument of Yuval Noah Harari's bestselling *Sapiens*, esp. 30–36, 122–133, 200–201, 406.

[51] Castoriadis, "Discovery," 146. As for the "universe of significations," see his critique of "extremist tendencies of structuralism" (undoubtedly including Derridean Deconstruction) in Castoriadis, *Imaginary Institution of Society*, 137–142.

[52] E.g. Warnock, *Imagination*, 30; Bottici, *Imaginal Politics*, 4.

[53] The mythical and linguistic allusions in this sentence are deliberate, and I am aware that the formulation has considerable implications in terms of philosophical hermeneutics, notably with respect to "meaning" and "signification." While my basic position can be inferred from the discussion of Gadamer and Derrida in Chapter 10, pp. 342–351, I hope to develop the notion of "radical understanding" at greater length in a separate publication.

On a very similar note of resignation, Fowden finished his monograph by admitting that the spiritual way of Hermetic *gnōsis* remains "immune from the scrutiny of philologist, philosopher, and historian alike."[54] Therefore having reached the end of my own book about Hermetic spirituality, will I have to draw a similar conclusion? The answer is "yes and no." Scholarly writing is indeed a *pharmakon* of enchantment, as I have been arguing throughout this Epilogue: it induces altered states of knowledge that cause the imagination to be filled with *phantasmata*. They never give us the naked truth, only appearances and re-presentations of what could possibly be meant. And yet this very act of imaginal[55] *deception* is always, and necessarily, an act of *revelation* – in the sense that it (and it alone) allows us to actually see things that would otherwise be invisible, to understand what without their presence would remain forever beyond our comprehension. In a radical formulation by Elliot R. Wolfson, "language is decidedly inadequate to mark the middle ground wherein concealing and revealing are identical in virtue of being different and different in virtue of being identical."[56]

This paradoxical phenomenon of imaginal perception is not just central to Hermetic spirituality – it lies at the heart of the hermeneutic enterprise that I believe the humanities are all about. The *pharmakon* to which you have been exposed, dear reader, was designed to change your consciousness, stimulate your imagination, broaden your horizon, even open doors to noetic insight.[57] I have deliberately tried to draw your mind

---

[54] RHT IV, 267; Fowden, *Egyptian Hermes*, 215. See above, Chapter 1, p. 19 with note 32.

[55] In using the term "imaginal," I take my cue from the excellent discussion by Bottici: "in contrast to the unreal and fictitious, which is associated with the imaginary, the imaginal has no embedded ontological status; it makes no assumption as to the reality of the images that fall within its conceptual domain" (*Imaginal Politics*, 57). Contrary to the perspectives of Henry Corbin (who introduced the term to current philosophical debate; ibid., 55; cf. Hanegraaff, *Esotericism and the Academy*, 299–302) and James Hillman (who developed it further and whose ontological assumptions are noted by Bottici, *Imaginal Politics*, 58–59), this reflects the radical agnosticism basic to my own work (see above, Prologue, pp. 4–5).

[56] Wolfson, *Language, Eros, Being*, 229 (see above, Chapter 1, p. 14 note 10). For the paradoxical dialectics of veiling and unveiling and its relation to the "middle ground" of imagination, see ibid., 224–242; see also Wolfson, *Through a Speculum That Shines*, esp. 58–73.

[57] In terms of Plato, *Rep.* 509d–511e (see above, Chapter 10, pp. 312–313 with note 18), scholarly understanding can include a noetic dimension in sofar as we depend for all our knowledge on the four passions (*pathēmata*) of the psyche: *eikasia*, *pistis*, *dianoia*, and *noēsis*. My term "horizon" obviously refers to Gadamer's hermeneutics as discussed in Chapters 5 and 10.

into profoundly ambiguous realms of human experience and practice, for although their very existence has seldom been recognized in academic research, I see them as essential to human psychology and deserving of very serious attention. These final lines are therefore not a conclusion. I close this particular book in the hope that it may serve to open others.

Bibliography

Aall, Anathon, *Der Logos: Geschichte seiner Entwicklung in der griechischen Philosophie und der christlichen Litteratur*, 2 vols., O.R. Reisland: Leipzig 1896/1899.
Adler, William and Paul Tuffin, *The Chronography of George Synkellos: A Byzantine Chronicle of Universal History from the Creation*, Oxford University Press 2002.
Alden, Robert L., "Ecstasy and the Prophets," *Bulletin of the Evangelical Theological Society* 9:3 (1996), 148–156.
Alföldy, Géza, "The Crisis of the Third Century as Seen by Contemporaries," *Greek, Roman and Byzantine Studies* 15:1 (1974), 89–111.
Allegro, John M., *The Sacred Mushroom and the Cross: A Study of the Nature and Origins of Christianity within the Fertility Cults of the Ancient Near East*, Hodder & Stoughton: London 1970.
Alpers, Svetlana, "The Museum as a Way of Seeing," in: Ivan Karp and Steven D. Lavine (eds.), *Exhibiting Cultures: The Poetics and Politics of Museum Display*, Smithsonian Institute Press: Washington and London 1991, 25–32.
André, Marie-Sophie and Christophe Beaufils, *Papus biographie: La Belle Époque de l'occultisme*, Berg International: Paris 1995.
Anonymus, "'Nur noch ein Gott kann uns retten': SPIEGEL-Gespräch mit Martin Heidegger am 23. September 1966," *Der Spiegel* 23 (1976), 193–219.
Aquili, Eugene d' and Andrew B. Newberg, *The Mystical Mind: Probing the Biology of Religious Experience*, Fortress Press: Minneapolis 1999.
Aristotle, *Generation of Animals* (A.L. Peck, transl. & introd.) (Loeb Classical Library), William Heinemann/Harvard University Press: London/Cambridge MA 1943.
Arlandson, James Malcolm, *Women, Class, and Society in Early Christianity: Models from Luke-Acts*, Hendrickson: Peabody 1997.
Armstrong, A. Hilary, "Iamblichus and Egypt," *Les études philosophiques* 2/3 (1987), 179–188.
Arnim, Ioannes ab, *Stoicorum veterum fragmenta*, vol. 3, B.G. Teubner: Stuttgart 1964.

Artelt, Walter, *Studien zur Geschichte der Begriffe "Heilmittel" und "Gift": Urzeit – Homer – Corpus Hippocraticum*, Wissenschaftliche Buchgesellschaft: Darmstadt 1937.

Asad, Talil, "Toward a Genealogy of the Concept of Ritual," in: Talil Asad, *Genealogies of Religion: Discipline and Reasons of Power in Christianity and Islam*, The Johns Hopkins University Press: Baltimore MD/London 1993, 55–79

Ashton, E.B., "Translating Philosophie," *Delos: A Journal On & Of Translation* 6 (1971), 16–29.

Asprem, Egil, *The Problem of Disenchantment: Scientific Naturalism and Esoteric Discourse 1900–1939*, Brill: Leiden/Boston 2014 (State University of New York Press: Albany 2018).

Assmann, Jan, "Amun," in: van der Toorn, Becking and van der Horst, *Dictionary of Deities and Demons*, 47–54.

Moses the Egyptian: The Memory of Egypt in Western Monotheism, Harvard University Press: Cambridge MA/London 1997.

The Search for God in Ancient Egypt, Cornell University Press: Ithaca/London 2001.

Death and Salvation in Ancient Egypt, Cornell University Press: Ithaca/London 2005.

Die Mosaische Unterscheidung, oder der Preis des Monotheismus, Carl Hanser: Munich/Vienna 2003.

Assmann, Jan and David Frankfurter, "Egypt," in: Johnston, *Religions of the Ancient World*, 155–172.

Athanassiadi, Polymnia, "Dreams, Theurgy and Freelance Divination: The Testimony of Iamblichus," *Journal of Roman Studies* 83 (1993), 115–130.

"The Oecumenism of Iamblichus: Latent Knowledge and Its Awakening" (review article of H.J. Blumenthal and E.G. Clark, eds., *The Divine Iamblichus: Philosopher and Man of Gods*), *Journal of Roman Studies* 85 (1995), 244–250.

"The Creation of Orthodoxy in Neoplatonism," in: Gillian Clark and Tessa Rajak (eds.), *Philosophy and Power in the Graeco-Roman World: Essays in Honour of Miriam Griffin*, Oxford University Press 2002, 271–291.

La lutte pour l'orthodoxie dans le Platonisme tardif: De Numénius à Damascius, Les Belles Lettres: Paris 2006.

Aufrère, Sydney H., "Parfums et onguents liturgiques du laboratoire d'Edfou: Composition, codes végétaux et minéraux dans l'Égypte ancienne," in: Ryka Gyselen (ed.), *Parfums d'Orient* (Res Orientales XI), Groupe pour l'Étude de la Civilisation du Moyen-Orient: Bures-sur-Yvette 1998, 29–64.

Bagnall, Roger S., *Egypt in Late Antiquity*, Princeton University Press 1993.

Baier, Karl, "Somnambulismus als medium der Vergesellschaftung: Mesmerisch beeinflusste Auffassungen des Sozialen vom 18. zum späten 19. Jahrhundert," in: Nacim Ghanbari and Marcus Hahn (eds.), *Reinigungsarbeit = Zeitschrift für Kulturwissenschaften* 1 (2013), 65–80.

Bailey, Donald M., "Classical Architecture," in: Riggs, *Oxford Handbook of Roman Egypt*, 189–204.

Banner, Nicholas, *Philosophic Silence and the "One" in Plotinus*, Cambridge University Press 2018.
Bardenhewer, Otto, *Hermetis Trismegisti qui apud Arabes fertur De Castigatione Animae libellum*, Ad. Marcus: Bonn 1873.
Baring, Edward, *The Young Derrida and French Philosophy 1945–1968*, Cambridge University Press 2011.
Barthes, Roland, *Leçon*, Éditions du Seuil: Paris 1978.
Barušs, Imants, *Alterations of Consciousness: An Empirical Analysis for Social Scientists*, American Psychological Association: Washington 2003.
Baumann, Gerd, "Grammars of Identity/Alterity: A Structural Approach," in: Gerd Baumann and Andre Gingrich (eds.), *Grammars of Identity/Alterity: A Structural Approach*, Berghahn: New York/Oxford 2004, 18–50.
Becchi, Francesco, "The Doctrine of the Passions: Plutarch, Posidonius and Galen," in: Lautaro Roig Lanzillotta and Israel Muñoz Gallarte (eds.), *Plutarch in the Religious and Philosophical Discourse of Late Antiquity*, Brill: Leiden/Boston 2012, 43–53.
Beinlich-Seeber, Christine, "Renenutet," in: Wolfgang Helck and Wolfhart Westendorf (eds.), *Lexikon der Ägyptologie,* vol. 5, Otto Harrassowitz: Wiesbaden 1984, 232–236.
Bell, Catherine, "Performance," in: Mark C. Taylor (ed.), *Critical Terms for Religious Studies*, The University of Chicago Press 1998, 205–224.
Bentall, Richard P., "Hallucinatory Experiences," in: Etzel Cardeña, Steven J. Lynn and Stanley Krippner (eds.), *Varieties of Anomalous Experience: Examining the Scientific Evidence*, American Psychological Association: Washington 2000, 85–120.
Bergemann, Lutz, "Inkubation, Photagogie und Seelengefährt bei Iamblich: Zum Zusammenhang von Mystik, Ritual and Metaphysik in Iamblichs *De Mysteriis* und in den *Chaldaeischen Orakeln*," in: Helmut Seng and Michel Tardieu (eds.), *Die Chaldaeischen Orakel: Kontext, Interpretation, Rezeption*, Universitätsverlag Winter: Heidelberg 2010, 79–92.
Bernstein, Richard J., "The Constellation of Hermeneutics, Critical Theory, and Deconstruction," in: Robert J. Dostal, *The Cambridge Companion to Gadamer*, Cambridge University Press 2002, 267–282.
"The Conversation That Never Happened (Gadamer/Derrida)," *The Review of Metaphysics* 61:3 (2008), 577–603.
Berthelot, M. (ed.), *La chimie au moyen âge*, vol. 2, Imprimerie Nationale: Paris 1893 [CMA II]
Berthelot, M., "Sur les voyages de Galien et de Zosime dans l'Archipel et en Asie, et sur la matière médicale dans l'antiquité," *Journal des Savants* (1895), 382–387.
Berthelot, M. and Charles-Emmanuel Ruelle (eds.), *Collection des anciens alchimistes grecs*, 2 vols., Georges Steinheil: Paris 1888 [CAA I, CAA II].
Bertol, Elisabetta, Vittorio Fineschi, Steven B. Karch, Francesco Mari and Irene Riezzo, "*Nymphaea* Cults in Ancient Egypt and the New World: A Lesson in Empirical Pharmacology," *Journal of the Royal Society of Medicine* 97:2 (2004), 84–85.

Betz, Hans Dieter, "Schöpfung und Erlösung im hermetischen Fragment 'Kore Kosmou'," *Zeitschrift für Theologie und Kirche* 63:2 (1966), 160–187.
———, *The "Mithras Liturgy": Text, Translation, and Commentary*, Mohr Siebeck: Tübingen 2003.
——— (ed.), *The Greek Magical Papyri in Translation, Including the Demotic Spells*, The University of Chicago Press 1986.
Bickerman, Elias J., Review of Nock and Festugière, *American Journal of Philology* 69:4 (1948), 457–458.
Bladel, Kevin van, *The Arabic Hermes: From Pagan Sage to Prophet of Science*, Oxford University Press 2009.
Bod, Rens, *A New History of the Humanities: The Search for Principles and Patterns from Antiquity to the Present*, Oxford University Press 2013.
Boeder, Heribert, "Der frühgriechische Wortgebrauch von *Logos* und *Aletheia*," *Archiv für Begriffsgeschichte* 4 (1959), 82–112.
Bogdan, Henrik, *Western Esotericism and Rituals of Initiation*, State University of New York Press: Albany 2007.
Böhme, Hartmut and Gernot Böhme, *Das Andere der Vernunft: Zur Entwicklung von Rationalitätsstrukturen am Beispiel Kants*, Suhrkamp: Frankfurt a.M. 1983.
Bonner, Campbell, *Studies in Magical Amulets, Chiefly Graeco-Egyptian*, The University of Michigan Press: Ann Arbor 1950.
Borghesi, Francesco, Michael Papio and Massimo Riva (eds.), *Pico della Mirandola: Oration on the Dignity of Man. A New Translation and Commentary*, Cambridge University Press 2012.
Bos, A.P., "A 'Dreaming Kronos' in a Lost Work by Aristotle," *L'antiquité classique* 58 (1989), 88–111.
Bottici, Chiara, *Imaginal Politics: Images Beyond Imagination and the Imaginary*, Columbia University Press: New York 2019.
Botz-Bornstein, Thorsten, "Speech, Writing, and Play in Gadamer and Derrida," *Cosmos and History: The Journal of Natural and Social Philosophy* 9:1 (2013), 249–264.
Boudewijnse, Barbara, "The Conceptualization of Ritual," *Jaarboek voor Liturgie-onderzoek* 11 (1995), 31–56.
Bouillet, M.-N., *Les Ennéades de Plotin, chef de l'école néoplatonicienne*, vol. 2, Librairie de L. Hachette: Paris 1859.
Bousset, Wilhelm, *Kyrios Christos: Geschichte des Christusglaubens von den Anfängen des Christentums bis Irenaeus*, Vandenhoeck & Ruprecht: Göttingen 1913.
———, Review of Joseph Kroll, *Göttingische gelehrte Anzeigen* 176 (1914), 697–755.
Bouyer, Louis, "Mysticism: An Essay on the History of the Word," in: R. Woods (ed.), *Understanding Mysticism*, Image Books: Garden City NY 1980, 42–55.
Böwering, Gerhard, *The Mystical Vision of Existence in Classical Islam: The Qur'ānic Hermeneutics of the Ṣūfī Sahl At-Tustarī (d. 283/896)*, Walter de Gruyter: Berlin/New York 1980.
Boyancé, Pierre, "Théurgie et télestique néoplatoniciennes," *Revue de l'histoire des religions* 47 (1955), 189–209.

Boylan, Patrick, *Thoth the Hermes of Egypt: A Study of Some Aspects of Theological Thought in Ancient Egypt*, Humphrey Milford/Oxford University Press: London etc. 1922.
Brabec de Mori, Bernd, "From the Native's Point of View: How Shipibo-Konibo Experience and Interpret Ayahuasca Drinking with 'Gringos'," in: Beatriz Caiuby Labate and Clancy Cavnar (eds.), *Ayahuasca Shamanism in the Amazon and Beyond*, Oxford University Press 2014, 206–230.
Brakke, David, *The Gnostics: Myth, Ritual, and Diversity in Early Christianity*, Harvard University Press: Cambridge MA/London 2010.
Brann, Eva T.H., *The World of the Imagination: Sum and Substance*, Rowman & Littlefield: Maryland 1991.
Brashear, William M., "The Greek Magical Papyri: An Introduction and Survey; Annotated Bibliography (1928–1994)," in: Wolfgang Haase (ed.), *Aufstieg und Niedergang der Römischen Welt II*, Bd. 18: Religion, 5. Teilband, Walter de Gruyter: Berlin/New York 1995, 3380–3684.
Bräuninger, Friedrich, *Untersuchungen zu den Schriften des Hermes Trismegistos*, C. Schulze & Co: Gräfenhainichen 1926.
Brierre de Boismont, A., *Des hallucinations, ou histoire raisonnée des apparitions, des visions, des songes, de l'extase, des rêves, du magnétisme et du somnambulisme*, 3rd ed., Germer Baillière: Paris 1862.
Brisson, Luc, "Amélius: Sa vie, son oeuvre, sa doctrine, son style," in: Wolfgang Haase (ed.), *Aufstieg und Niedergang der römischen Welt: Geschichte und Kultur Roms im Spiegel der neueren Forschung*, Tl. II: Principat, Bd. 36, Walter de Gruyter: Berlin/New York 1987, 793–860.
Brock, Sebastian, "A Syriac Collection of Prophecies of the Pagan Philosophers," *Orientalia Lovaniensia Periodica* 14 (1983), 203–246.
—— "Some Syriac Excerpts from Greek Collections of Pagan Prophecies," *Vigiliae Christianae* 38 (1984), 77–90.
Broek, Roelof van den, "Religious Practices in the Hermetic 'Lodge': New Light from Nag Hammadi," in: van den Broek and van Heertum, *From Poimandres to Jacob Böhme*, 77–95.
—— "Hermes and Christ: 'Pagan' Witnesses to the Truth of Christianity," in: van den Broek and van Heertum, *From Poimandres to Jacob Böhme*, 115–144.
—— "Hermes Trismegistus I," in: Hanegraaff, *Dictionary*, 474–478.
—— "Hermetic Literature I," in: Hanegraaff, *Dictionary*, 487-499.
—— "Hermetism," in: Hanegraaff, *Dictionary*, 558-570.
—— *Hermes Trismegistus: Inleiding, Teksten, Commentaren*, In de Pelikaan: Amsterdam 2006.
—— "Spiritual Transformation in Ancient Hermetism and Gnosticism," in: R.A. Gilbert (ed.), *Knowledge of the Heart: Gnostic Movements and Secret Traditions* (Canonbury Papers 5), Ian Allan: London 2008, 30–43.
Broek, Roelof van den and M.J. Vermaseren (eds.), *Studies in Gnosticism and Hellenistic Religions presented to Gilles Quispel on the Occasion of his 65th Birthday*, E.J. Brill: Leiden 1981.
Broek, Roelof van den and Gilles Quispel (introd., transl. & comm.), *Corpus Hermeticum*, In de Pelikaan: Amsterdam 1991.

Broek, Roelof van den and Wouter J. Hanegraaff (eds.), *Gnosis and Hermeticism from Antiquity to Modern Times*, State University of New York Press: Albany 1998.
Broek, Roelof van den and Cis van Heertum (eds.), *From Poimandres to Jacob Böhme: Gnosis, Hermetism and the Christian Tradition*, In de Pelikaan: Amsterdam 2000.
Broek, Roelof van den and Gilles Quispel (eds.), *Hermetische Geschriften*, In de Pelikaan: Amsterdam 2016 [HG].
Browne, C.A., "Rhetorical and Religious Aspects of Greek Alchemy," *Ambix* 3:1/2 (1948), 15–25.
Broze, Michèle and Carine Van Liefferinge, "L'Hermès commun du prophète Abamon: Philosophie grecque et théologie égyptienne dans le prologue du De Mysteriis de Jamblique," in: Françoise Labrique (ed.), *Religions méditerranéennes et orientales de l'antiquité*, Institut Français d'Archéologie Orientale: Cairo 2002, 35–44.
Büchli, Jörg, *Der Poimandres, ein paganisiertes Evangelium: Sprachliche und Begriffliche Untersuchungen zum 1. Traktat des Corpus Hermeticum*, J.C.B. Mohr (Paul Siebeck): Tübingen 1987.
Bucke, Richard Maurice, *Man's Moral Nature: An Essay*, G.P. Putnam: New York 1879.
  Cosmic Consciousness: A Study in the Evolution of the Human Mind (1901), Innes & Sons: Philadelphia 1905.
Bull, Christian H., "The Notion of Mysteries in the Formation of Hermetic Tradition," in: Bull, Lied & Turner, *Mystery and Secrecy*, 399–425.
  "Ancient Hermetism and Esotericism," *Aries* 15 (2015), 109–135.
  "No End to Sacrifice in Hermetism," in: Peter Jackson and Anna-Pya Sjödin (eds.), *Philosophy and the End of Sacrifice: Disengaging Ritual in Ancient India, Greece and Beyond*, Equinox: Sheffield 2016, 143–166.
  "Visionary Experience and Ritual Realism in the Ascent of the Discourse on the Eighth and the Ninth (NHC VI,6)," *Gnosis: Journal of Gnostic Studies* 2 (2017), 169–193.
  "Monkey Business: Magical Vowels and Cosmic Levels in the *Discourse on the Eighth and the Ninth* (NCH VI,6), *Studi e materiali di storia delle religioni* 83 (2017), 75–94.
  "Hermes between Pagans and Christians: The Nag Hammadi Hermetica in Context," in: Hugo Lundhaug and Lance Jenott (eds.), *The Nag Hammadi Codices and Late Antique Egypt*, Mohr Siebeck: Tübingen 2018, 207–260.
  "Wicked Angels and the Good Demon: The Origins of Alchemy according to the *Physica* of Hermes," *Gnosis: Journal of Gnostic Studies* 3 (2018), 3–33.
  "The Great Demon of the Air and the Punishment of Souls: The *Perfect Discourse* (NHC VI,8) and Hermetic and Monastic Demonologies," in: Eric Crégheur, Louis Painchaud and Tuomas Rasimus (eds.), *Nag Hammadi à 70 ans: Qu'avons-nous appris? / Nag Hammadi at 70: What Have We Learned?*, Peeters: Louvain 2018, 105–120.
  The Tradition of Hermes Trismegistus: The Egyptian Priestly Figure as a Teacher of Hellenized Wisdom, Brill: Leiden/Boston 2018.

Bull, Christian H., Liv Ingeborg Lied and John D. Turner (eds.), *Mystery and Secrecy in the Nag Hammadi Collection and Other Ancient Literature: Ideas and Practices. Studies for Einar Thomassen at Sixty*, Brill: Leiden/Boston 2012.

Bulliet, Richard W., *The Case for Islamo-Christian Civilization*, Columbia University Press: New York 2004.

Burkert, Walter, "Platon oder Pythagoras? Zum Ursprung des Wortes 'Philosophie'," *Hermes* 88: 2 (1960), 159–177.

— *Ancient Mystery Cults*, Harvard University Press: Cambridge Mass./London 1987

— *The Orientalizing Revolution: Near Eastern Influence on Greek Culture in the Early Archaic Age*, Harvard University Press: Cambridge Mass./London 1992.

Burns, Dylan M., *Apocalypse of the Alien God: Platonism and the Exile of Sethian Gnosticism*, University of Pennsylvania Press: Philadelphia 2014.

— "μίξεώς τινι τέχνη κρείττονι: Alchemical Metaphor in the *Paraphrase of Shem* (*NHC* VII,1)," *Aries* 15:1 (2015), 81–108.

— "Gnosticism, Gnostics, and Gnosis," in: Trompf, *Gnostic World*, 9–25.

Camassa, Giorgio, "*Phantasia* di Platone ai neoplatonici," in: Fattori and Bianchi, *Phantasia – Imaginatio*, 23–55.

Cameron, Alan, *The Last Pagans of Rome*, Oxford University Press 2011.

Camplani, Alberto, "Alcune note sul testo dei VI codice di Nag Hammadi: La Predizione di Hermes ad Asclepius," *Augustinianum* 26 (1986), 349–368.

— *Scritti ermetici in copto*, Paideia: Brescia 2000 [SEC].

Cancik, Hubert and Hildegard Cancik-Lindemaier, "'Tempel der ganzen Welt': Ägypten und Rom," in: Sibylle Meyer (ed.), *Egypt: Temple of the Whole World: Studies in Honour of Jan Assmann*, Brill: Leiden/Boston 2003, 41–57.

Carozzi, Pier Angelo, "Gnose et sotériologie dans la 'Korè Kosmou' hermétique," in: Julien Ries (ed.), *Gnosticisme et monde hellénistique: Actes du Colloque de Louvain-la-Neuve (11–14 mars 1980)*, Institut Orientaliste: Louvain-la-Neuve 1982, 61–78.

Carpenter, Edward, *From Adam's Peak to Elephanta: Sketches in Ceylon and India*, Swan Sonnenschein/Macmillan: London/New York 1892.

Casevitz, Michel, "*Mantis*: Le vrai sens," *Revue des études grecques* 105: 500–501(1992), 1–18.

Cassirer, Ernst, Paul Oskar Kristeller and John Herman Randall, Jr., *The Renaissance Philosophy of Man*, The University of Chicago Press: Chicago/London 1948.

Castoriadis, Cornelius, *The Imaginary Institution of Society*, Polity Press: Cambridge/Malden 1987.

— "The Discovery of the Imagination," in: *World in Fragments: Writings on Politics, Society, Psychoanalysis and the Imagination*, Stanford University Press 1997, 213–245.

Castrucci, Greta, "The Cither of Mantinea and the Mysteries of the Wise Woman (Platonic Suggestions)," *Athenaeum* 106:2 (2018), 405–473.

Champier, Symphorien, "Commentarium in Diffinitiones Asclepij cum textu eiusdem," in: E. Garin et alii, *Umanesimo e esoterismo*, Cedam – Casa Editrice Dott. Antonio Milani: Padova 1960, 248–259.

Chantraine, Pierre, *Dictionnaire étymologique de la langue grecque: Histoire des mots*, Klincksieck: Paris 1999.
Charron, Régine, "The *Apocryphon of John* (NHC II, 1) and Graeco-Egyptian Alchemical Literature," *Vigiliae Christianae* 59 (2005), 438–456.
Chauveau, Michel, *Egypt in the Age of Cleopatra: History and Society under the Ptolemies*, Cornell University Press: Ithaca/London 2000.
Cherniss, Harold, Review of Festugière (*La révélation d'Hermès Trismégiste*, vol. 2), *Gnomon* 22:5/6 (1950), 204–216.
Chlup, Radek, "The Ritualization of Language in the *Hermetica*," *Aries* 7 (2007), 133–159.
Chopra, Deepak, *Quantum Healing: Exploring the Frontiers of Mind/Body Medicine*, Bantam: New York 1989.
Churton, Tobias, *Occult Paris: The Lost Magic of the Belle Époque*, Inner Traditions: Rochester/Toronto 2016.
Chuvin, Pierre, *A Chronicle of the Last Pagans*, Harvard University Press: Cambridge Mass./London 1990.
Cicero, Marcus Tullius, *De re publica / De legibus / Cato Maior de senectute / Laelius de amicitia* (J.G.F. Powell, ed.), Oxford University Press 2006.
Ciraolo, Leda J., "The Warmth and Breath of Life: Animating Physical Object πάρεδροι in the Greek Magical Papyri," *Society of Biblical Literature Seminar Papers* 128:31 (1992), 240–254.
Clarke, Emma C., *Iamblichus' De Mysteriis: A Manifesto of the Miraculous*, Ashgate: Farnham 2001.
Cohen, H. Floris, *The Scientific Revolution: A Historiographical Inquiry*, The University of Chicago Press: Chicago/London 1994.
Collins, Adela Yarbro, "Apocalypse Now: The State of Apocalyptic Studies Near the End of the First Decade of the Twentieth Century," *Harvard Theological Review* 104:4 (2011), 447–457.
Collins, John J., "Introduction: Towards the Morphology of a Genre," *Semeia* 14 (1979), 1–19.
—— *The Apocalyptic Imagination: An Introduction to Jewish Apocalyptic Literature*, 2nd ed., William B. Eerdmans/Dove: Grand Rapids/Livonia 1998.
Colonna, Francesco, *Hypnerotomachia Poliphili: The Strife of Love in a Dream* (Joscelyn Godwin, transl. & introd.), Thames & Hudson: London 1999.
Colpe, Carsten and Jens Holzhausen (eds.), *Das Corpus Hermeticum Deutsch*, 2 vols., fromman-holzboog: Stuttgart/Bad Cannstatt 1997 [CHD].
Combarieu, Jules (ed.), *Congrès international d'histoire de la musique tenu à Paris à la Bibliothèque de l'Opéra du 23 au 29 juillet 1900: Documents, mémoires et voeux*, Saint-Pierre: Solesmes 1901.
Compagnon, Antoine, *Literature, Theory, and Common Sense*, Princeton University Press: Princeton/Oxford 1998.
Conrad, Joseph, *Heart of Darkness, with The Congo Diary* (Robert Hampson, ed.), Penguin 2000.
Coole, Diana, *Negativity and Politics: Dionysus and Dialectics from Kant to Poststructuralism*, Routledge: London/New York 2000.
Copenhaver, Brian P., *Hermetica: The Greek Corpus Hermeticum and the Latin Asclepius in a New English Translation, with Notes and Introduction*, Cambridge University Press 1992 [Cop].

Magic and the Dignity of Man: Pico della Mirandola and his Oration in Modern Memory, Harvard University Press: Boston 2019.

Coppens, J., Review of Scott, *Hermetica* vols. 1–2, *Revue d'histoire ecclésiastique* 22:2 (1926), 348–352.

Corrigan, Kevin, "'Solitary' Mysticism in Plotinus, Proclus, Gregory of Nyssa, and Pseudo-Dionysius," *The Journal of Religion* 76:1 (1996), 28–42.

Couliano, Ioan P., *Eros and Magic in the Renaissance*, The University of Chicago Press: Chicago/London 1987.

Cowan, Thomas Patrick, "Sidelined to the Ghetto: William Burroughs in the Time of the Archons," Research Master Thesis, University of Amsterdam 2019.

Cox Miller, Patricia, "In Praise of Nonsense," in: Arthur H. Armstrong (ed.), *Classical Mediterranean Spirituality: Egyptian, Greek, Roman*, Crossroad: New York 1986, 481–505.

Crabtree, Adam, *From Mesmer to Freud: Magnetic Sleep and the Roots of Psychological Healing*, Yale University Press: New Haven/London 1993.

Crawford, Matthew R., "Reconsidering the Relationship between (Pseudo-)Didymus's *De Trinitate* and Cyril of Alexandria's *Contra Julianum*," *The Journal of Theological Studies* (NS) 71:1 (2020), 236–257.

Crowley, John, *The Solitudes / Love and Sleep / Daemonomania / Endless Things*, The Overlook Press: Woodstock/New York 1987, 1994, 2000, 2007.

Cumont, Franz, "Écrits Hermétiques II: Le médecin Thessalus et les plantes astrales d'Hermès Trismégiste," *Revue de philologie, de littérature et d'histoire anciennes* 42: 2 (1918), 85–108.

———, Review of Scott, *Hermetica* vol. 1, *The Journal of Roman Studies* 15 (1925), 272–274.

Cusset, François, *French Theory: How Foucault, Derrida, Deleuze, & Co. Transformed the Intellectual Life of the United States*, University of Minnesota Press: Minneapolis/London 2008.

Dainton, Barry, *Stream of Consciousness: Unity and Continuity in Conscious Experience*, Routledge: Abingdon/New York 2000.

Dallmayr, Fred R., "Prelude: Hermeneutics and Deconstruction. Gadamer and Derrida in Dialogue," in: Michelfelder and Palmer, *Dialogue and Deconstruction*, 75–92.

Daumas, François, "Le fonds Égyptien de l'Hermétisme," in: Julien Ries (ed.), in collaboration with Yvonne Janssens and Jean-Marie Sevrin, *Gnosticisme et monde hellénistique: Actes du Colloque de Louvain-la-Neuve (11–14 mars 1980)*, Institut Orientaliste: Louvain-la-Neuve 1982, 3–25.

Davis, Erik, *High Weirdness: Drugs, Esoterica, and Visionary Experience in the Seventies*, Strange Attractor Press/The MIT Press: London/Cambridge Mass. 2019.

Davis, Richard H., *Lives of Indian Images*, Princeton University Press 1997.

Debord, Guy, *The Society of the Spectacle* (1967), Bureau of Public Secrets: Berkeley 2014.

DeConick, April D. and Lautaro Roig Lanzillotta (eds.), *Gnostic Countercultures: Terror and Intrigue*, Brill: Leiden/Boston 2020.

Delia, Diana, "The Population of Roman Alexandria," *Transactions of the American Philological Association* 118 (1988), 275–292.

Demetrius, *On Style* (Doreen C. Innes, ed. & transl.)(Loeb Classical Library 199), Harvard University Press: Cambridge Mass./London 1995.
Denier van der Gon, W.H., "De driewerf-grootste Hermes over de wedergeboorte," *Tijdschrift voor Wijsbegeerte* 12 (1918), 142–179.
Derchain, Philippe, "L'authenticité de l'inspiration égyptienne dans le 'Corpus Hermeticum'," *Revue de l'histoire des religions* 161:2 (1962), 175–198.
"Pseudo-Jamblique ou Abammôn?," *Chronique d'Égypte* 38 (1963), 220–226.
"Noch einmal Hermes Trismegistos," *Göttinger Miszellen* 15 (1975), 7–10.
"La recette du kyphi," *Revue d'Égyptologie* 28 (1976), 61–65.
"L'*Atelier des Orfèvres* à Dendara et les origines de l'alchimie," *Chronique d'Égypte* 65, fasc. 130 (1990), 219–242.
Derrida, Jacques, *De la grammatologie*, Les Éditions de Minuit: Paris 1967.
Of Grammatology: Corrected Edition, The Johns Hopkins University Press: Baltimore/London 1974.
"La différance," in: Michel Foucault, Roland Barthes and Jacques Derrida, *Théorie d'ensemble*, Éditions du Seuil: Paris 1968, 41–66.
La dissémination, Éditions du Seuil: Paris 1972.
Dissemination (translated, with an Introduction and Additional Notes, by Barbara Johnson), The Athlone Press: London 1981.
"Three Questions to Hans-Georg Gadamer," in: Michelfelder and Palmer, *Dialogue and Deconstruction*, 52–54.
On the Name, Stanford University Press 1995.
Dey, Joseph, ΠΑΛΙΓΓΕΝΕΣΙΑ: *Ein Beitrag zur Klärung der religionsgeschichtlichen Bedeutung von Tit 3,5*, Verlag der Aschendorffschen Verlagsbuchhandlung: Münster 1937.
Di Cesare, Donatella Ester, *Gadamer: A Philosophical Portrait*, Indiana University Press: Bloomington/Indianapolis 2007.
Utopia of Understanding: Between Babel and Auschwitz, State University of New York Press: Albany 2012.
Dickey, Eleanor, "Classical Scholarship: The Byzantine Contribution," in: Kaldellis and Siniossoglou, *Cambridge Intellectual History of Byzantium*, 63–78.
Dickie, Matthew W., *Magic and Magicians in the Greco-Roman World*, Routledge: London/New York 2003.
Dieleman, Jacco, *Priests, Tongues, and Rites: The London-Leiden Magical Manuscripts and Translation in Egyptian Ritual (100–300 CE)*, Brill: Leiden/Boston 2005.
"Coping with a Difficult Life: Magic, Healing, and Sacred Knowledge," in: Riggs, *Oxford Handbook of Roman Egypt*, 337–361.
Diels, Hermannus, *Doxographi Graeci*, G. Reimer: Berlin 1879.
Dieterich, Albrecht, *Abraxas: Studien zur Religionsgeschichte des spätern Altertums*, B.G. Teubner: Leipzig 1891.
Eine Mithrasliturgie, B.G. Teubner: Leipzig 1903.
Digeser, Elizabeth DePalma, "Lactantius, Porphyry, and the Debate over Religious Toleration," *The Journal of Roman Studies* 88 (1998), 129–146.
The Making of a Christian Empire: Lactantius and Rome, Cornell University Press: Ithaca/London 2000.

Dijkstra, Bram, *Idols of Perversity: Fantasies of Feminine Evil in Fin-de-Siècle Culture*, Oxford University Press 1986.
Dillon, John, *The Middle Platonists: A Study of Platonism 80 B.C. to A.D. 220*, Duckworth: London 1977.
"Iamblichus of Chalcis (c. 240–325 A.D.)," in: Wolfgang Haase (ed.), *Aufstieg und Niedergang der römischen Welt: Geschichte und Kultur Roms im Spiegel der neueren Forschung*, Tl. II: Principat, Bd. 36, Walter de Gruyter: Berlin/New York 1987, 862–909.
Dillon, John (ed.), *Iamblichi Chalcidensis in Platonis dialogos commentariorum fragmenta*, E.J. Brill: Leiden 1973.
Dirkse, Peter A., James Brashler and Douglas M. Parrott, "The Discourse on the Eighth and Ninth, NH VI,6: 52,1–63,32," in: Parrott, *Nag Hammadi Codices*, 341–345.
Dittenberger, Wilhelmus (ed.), *Orientis Graeci Inscriptiones Selectae: Supplementum Sylloges Inscriptionum Graecarum*, vol. 2, S. Hirzel: Leipzig 1905.
[Diverse authors], "State-Specific Sciences," *Science* 180: 4090 (1973), 1005–1008.
Dodd, C.H., *The Bible and the Greeks*, 2nd ed., Hodder & Stoughton: London 1954.
Review of Nock/Festugière I–IV and van Moorsel, *Journal of Theological Studies* 7 (1956), 299–308.
Dodds, E.R., *The Greeks and the Irrational*, University of California Press: Berkeley/Los Angeles/London 1951.
"Appendix II: The Astral Body in Neoplatonism," in: Proclus, *The Elements of Theology*, Clarendon: Oxford 1963, 313–321.
Pagan and Christian in an Age of Anxiety, Cambridge University Press 1965.
Doniger, Wendy and Gregory Spinner, "Misconceptions: Female Imaginations and Male Fantasies in Parental Imprinting," *Daedalus* 127:1 (1998), 97–129.
Doresse, Jean and Togo Mina, "Nouveaux textes gnostiques coptes découverts en Haute-Égypte: La bibliothèque de Chenoboskion," *Vigiliae Christianae* 3 (1949), 129–141.
Dornseiff, Franz, *Das Alphabet in Mystik und Magie* (orig. 1925), Reprint-Verlag: Leipzig n.d.
Dörrie, Heinrich, Review of *Banber Matenadarani* vol. 3, *Gnomon* 29:6 (1957), 445–450.
Dosoo, Korshi, "Rituals of Apparition in the Theban Magical Library," Ph.D. Dissertation, Macquarie University: Sydney 2014.
"A History of the Theban Magical Library," *Bulletin of the American Society of Papyrologists* 53 (2016), 251–274.
Dover, K.J. (ed.), *Plato: Symposium*, Cambridge University Press 1980.
Dubois, Jean-Daniel, "Préface," in: Van den Kerchove, *La voie d'Hermès*, xvii–xix.
Durand, M.-G. de, "Un traité hermétique conservé en arménien," *Revue de l'histoire des religions* 190:1 (1976), 55–72.
Dyczkowski, Mark S.G., *The Doctrine of Vibration: An Analysis of the Doctrines and Practices of Kashmir Shaivism*, Motilal Banarsidass: Delhi 1989.

Ebstein, Michael, "Ḏū l-Nūn al-Miṣrī and Early Islamic Mysticism," *Arabica* 61 (2014), 559–612.
Eco, Umberto, *Il pendolo di Foucault*, Bompiani: Milan 1988.
Eco, Umberto (with Richard Rorty, Jonathan Culler, and Christine Brooke-Rose), *Interpretation and Overinterpretation*, Cambridge University Press 1992.
Edmonds, Radcliffe, "Did the Mithraists Inhale? A Technique for Theurgic Ascent in the Mithras Liturgy, the Chaldaean Oracles, and some Mithraic Frescoes," *The Ancient World* 32:1 (2001), 10–24.
Eliade, Mircea, *Occultism, Witchcraft, and Cultural Fashions: Essays in Comparative Religions*, The University of Chicago Press: Chicago/London 1976.
— "Cultural Fashions and History of Religions," in: *Occultism, Witchcraft, and Cultural Fashions*, 1–17.
— "The Occult and the Modern World," in: *Occultism, Witchcraft, and Cultural Fashions*, 47–68.
Ellenberger, Henri F., *The Discovery of the Unconscious: The History and Evolution of Dynamic Psychiatry*, Basic Books: n.p. 1970.
Emboden, William A., "Transcultural Use of Narcotic Water Lilies in Ancient Egyptian and Maya Drug Ritual," *Journal of Ethnopharmacology* 3 (1981), 39–83.
— "The Sacred Journey in Dynastic Egypt: Shamanistic Trance in the Context of the Narcotic Water Lily and the Mandrake," *Journal of Psychoactive Drugs* 21:1 (1989), 61–75.
Euripides, *Fragments* (Christopher Collard and Martin Cropp, ed. & transl.) (Loeb Classical Library), Harvard University Press 2009.
Evans, Nancy, "Diotima and Demeter as Mystagogues in Plato's *Symposium*," *Hypatia* 21:2 (2006), 1–27.
Faivre, Antoine, *The Eternal Hermes: From Greek God to Alchemical Magus*, Phanes Press: Grand Rapids 1995.
Fattori, M. and M. Bianchi (eds.), *Phantasia – Imaginatio: V° Colloquio Internazionale Roma 9–11 gennaio 1986*, Edizioni dell'Ateneo: Rome 1988.
Fauconnier, Gilles and Mark Turner, *The Way We Think: Conceptual Blending and the Mind's Hidden Complexities*, Basic Books: n.p. 2003.
Faxneld, Per, *Satanic Feminism: Lucifer as the Liberator of Woman in Nineteenth-Century Culture*, Oxford University Press 2017.
Felski, Rita, "Suspicious Minds," *Poetics Today* 32:2 (2011), 215–234.
— *The Limits of Critique*, The University of Chicago Press: Chicago/London 2015.
Ferry, Luc and Alain Renaut, *La pensée 68: Essai sur l'anti-humanisme contemporain*, Gallimard: Paris 1988.
Festugière, André-Jean, "Hermetica," *Harvard Theological Review* 31:1 (1938), 1–20.
— "La création des âmes dans la Korè Kosmou," in: *Pisculi: Studien zur Religion und Kultur des Altertums, Franz Joseph Dölger zum sechzigsten Geburtstage dargeboten von Freunden, Verehrern und Schülern*, Aschendorff: Münster in Westfalen 1939, 102–116.
— "L'expérience religieuse du médecin Thessalos," *Revue biblique* 48:1 (1939), 45–77.
— *La révélation d'Hermès Trismégiste*, 4 vols., Les Belles Lettres: Paris 1942, 1949, 1953, 1954 (repr. in one volume 2006) [RHT I, RHT II, RHT III, RHT IV].

"*Corpus Hermeticum* 13.12," *Classical Philology* 48:4 (1953), 237–238.
Personal Religion among the Greeks, University of California Press: Berkeley 1954.
Hermétisme et mystique païenne, Aubier-Montaigne: Paris 1967.
Ficino, Marsilio, *Platonic Theology*, vol. 4: *Books XII–XIV*, The I Tatti Renaissance Library/Harvard University Press: Cambridge Mass./London 2004.
Finamore, John F., *Iamblichus and the Theory of the Vehicle of the Soul*, Scholars Press: Chico 1985.
Fleischer, Heinrich Leberecht, "Hermes Trismegistus: An die menschliche Seele," *Zeitschrift für die historische Theologie* 10:4 (1840), 87–117.
Hermes Trismegistus: An die menschliche Seele, F.A. Brockhaus: Leipzig 1870.
Flower, Michael Attyah, *The Seer in Ancient Greece*, University of California Press: Berkeley/Los Angeles/London 2008.
Foucault, Michel, "Technologies of the Self," in: Luther H. Martin, Huck Gutman and Patrick H. Hutton (eds.), *Technologies of the Self: A Seminar with Michel Foucault*, Tavistock: London 1988, 16–49.
Fougères, Gustave, "Bas-reliefs de Mantinée: Apollon, Marsyas et les muses," *Bulletin de correspondance hellénique* 12 (1888), 105–128.
"Stèle de Mantinée," *Bulletin de correspondance hellénique* 12 (1888), 376–380.
Mantinée et l'Arcadie orientale, Albert Fontemoing: Paris 1898.
Fowden, Garth, "Late Antique Paganism Reasoned and Revealed," *The Journal of Roman Studies* 71 (1981), 178–182.
"The Pagan Holy Man in Late Antique Society," *The Journal of Hellenic Studies* 102 (1982), 33–59.
The Egyptian Hermes: A Historical Approach to the Late Pagan Mind, Princeton University Press 1986.
Empire to Commonwealth: Consequences of Monotheism in Late Antiquity, Princeton University Press 1993.
Before and After Muḥammad: The First Millennium Refocused, Princeton University Press: Princeton/Oxford 2014.
Frank, Manfred, "Limits of the Human Control of Language: Dialogue as the Place of Difference between Neostructuralism and Hermeneutics," in: Michelfelder and Palmer, *Dialogue and Deconstruction*, 150–161.
Frankfurter, David, *Religion in Roman Egypt: Assimilation and Resistance*, Princeton University Press 1998.
"Voices, Books, and Dreams: The Diversification of Divination Media in Late Antique Egypt," in: Sarah Iles Johnston and Peter T. Struck (eds.), *Mantikê: Studies in Ancient Divination*, Brill: Leiden/Boston 2005, 233–254.
"Religious Practice and Piety," in: Riggs, *Oxford Handbook of Roman Egypt*, 319–336.
"The Magic of Writing in Mediterranean Antiquity," in: Frankfurter, *Guide to the Study of Ancient Magic*, Brill: Leiden/Boston 2019, 626–658.
Fraser, Kyle A., "Zosimos of Panopolis and the Book of Enoch: Alchemy as Forbidden Knowledge," *Aries* 4:2 (2004), 125–147.
"Baptised in *Gnôsis*: The Spiritual Alchemy of Zosimos of Panopolis," *Dionysius* 25 (2007), 33–54.

Frede, Dorothea, "The Cognitive Role of *Phantasia* in Aristotle," in: Rorty and Nussbaum, *Essays on Aristotle's* De Anima, 280–296.
Frede, Michael, "Numenius," in: Wolfgang Haase (ed.), *Aufstieg und Niedergang der römischen Welt: Geschichte und Kultur Roms im Spiegel der neueren Forschung*, Tl. II: Principat, Bd. 36, Walter de Gruyter: Berlin/New York 1987, 1034–1075.
Freedberg, David, *The Power of Images: Studies in the History and Theory of Response*, The University of Chicago Press: Chicago/London 1989.
Friedrich, Hans-Veit (ed.), *Thessalos von Tralles: Griechisch und lateinisch*, Anton Hain: Meisenheim am Glan 1968.
Fritz, Kurt von, "Νοῦς and νοεῖν in the Homeric Poems," *Classical Philology* 38:2 (1943), 79–93.
"Νοῦς and νοεῖν and their Derivatives in Pre-Socratic Philosophy (excluding Anaxagoras), Part I: From the Beginnings to Parmenides," *Classical Philology* 40:4 (1945), 223–242.
"Νοῦς and νοεῖν and their Derivatives in Pre-Socratic Philosophy (excluding Anaxagoras), Part II: The Post-Parmenidean Period," *Classical Philology* 41:1 (1946), 12–34.
Frolov, Andrey V., Lilia A. Akhmetova and Clarke H. Scholtz, "Revision of the Obligate Mushroom-Feeding African 'Dung Beetle' Genus *Coptorhina* Hope (Coleoptera: Scarabaeidae: Scarabaeinae)," *Journal of Natural History* 42:21-24 (2008), 1477–1508.
Gadamer, Hans-Georg, *Hermeneutik I: Wahrheit und Methode. Grundzüge einer philosophischen Hermeneutik*, J.C.B. Mohr (Paul Siebeck): München 1986.
Hermeneutik II: Wahrheit und Methode. Ergänzungen / Register, J.C.B. Mohr (Paul Siebeck): München 1986.
"Wahrheit in den Geisteswissenschaften," (1953) in: Gadamer, *Hermeneutik II*, 37–43.
"Vom Zirkel des Verstehens," (1959) in: Gadamer, *Hermeneutik II*, 57–65.
"Klassische und philosophische Hermeneutik," (1968) in: Gadamer, *Hermeneutik II*, 92–117.
"Die Idee der Hegelschen Logik," (1971) in: Gadamer, *Neuere Philosophie I: Hegel, Husserl, Heidegger*, J.C.B. Mohr (Paul Siebeck): Tübingen 1987, 65–86.
"Logik oder Rhetorik? Nochmals zur Frühgeschichte der Hermeneutik," (1976) in: Gadamer, *Hermeneutik II*, 292–300.
"Text und Interpretation," (1983) in: Gadamer, *Hermeneutik II*, 330–360.
"Destruktion und Dekonstruktion," (1985) in: Gadamer, *Hermeneutik II*, 361–272.
"Hermeneutik und Historismus," (1965) in: Gadamer, *Hermeneutik II*, 387–424.
"Reply to Jacques Derrida," in: Michelfelder and Palmer, *Dialogue and Deconstruction*, 55–57.
"The Hermeneutics of Suspicion," (1984) in: J.N. Mohanty (ed.), *Phenomenology and the Human Sciences*, Martinus Nijhoff: Dordrecht/Boston/Lancaster 1985, 73–83.
"Hermeneutics and Logocentrism," (1987) in: Michelfelder and Palmer, *Dialogue and Deconstruction*, 114–125.

"Dialogischer Rückblick auf das Gesammelte Werk und dessen Wirkungsgeschichte," in: Jean Grondin, *Gadamer: Lesebuch*, Mohr: Tübingen 1996, 280–295.
Gall, Dorothee (ed.), *Die göttliche Weisheit des Hermes Trismegistos: Pseudo-Apuleius, Asclepius*, Mohr Siebeck: Tübingen 2021 [GWHT].
Ganschinietz, R., "Agathodaimon," in: August Pauly and Georg Wissowa (eds.), *Real-Encyclopädie der classischen Altertumswissenschaft*, Supplementband 3, J.B Metzler: Stuttgart 1918, 37–60.
Garin, Eugenio, *Medioevo e rinascimento: Studi e ricerche*, Gius. Laterza & Figli: Bari 1954.
Gaston, K. Healan, *Imagining Judeo-Christian America: Religion, Secularism, and the Redefinition of Democracy*, The University of Chicago Press: Chicago/London 2019.
Gastoué, Amédée, *Les origines du Chant Romain: L'antiphone Grégorien*, Alphonse Picard & Fils: Paris 1907.
Gauld, Alan, *A History of Hypnotism*, Cambridge University Press 1992.
Geens, Karolien, "Panopolis, a Nome Capital in Egypt in the Roman and Byzantine Period (ca. AD 200–600)," Ph.D. Dissertation, Catholic University Leuven: Leuven 2007; repr. Trismegistos Online Publications: Special Series I (2014).
Geldard, Richard G., *Parmenides and the Way of Truth*, Monkfish: Rhinebeck NY 2007.
George, Leonard, "Mental Imagery Enhancement Training in Behavior Therapy: Current Status and Future Prospects," *Psychotherapy* 23:1 (1986), 81–92.
Gersh, Stephen, *From Iamblichus to Eriugena*, Brill: Leiden 1978.
Gibson, Sophie, *Aristoxenus of Tarentum and the Birth of Musicology*, Routledge: Oxfordshire 2005.
Gilly, Carlos, "Die Überlieferung des *Asclepius* im Mittelalter," in: van den Broek and van Heertum, *From Poimandres to Jacob Böhme*, 335–367.
Giversen, Søren, Tage Petersen and Jørgen Podemann Sørensen (eds.), *The Nag Hammadi Texts in the History of Religions: Proceedings of the International Conference at the Royal Academy of Sciences and Letters in Copenhagen, September 19–24, 1995* (Historisk-filosofiske Skrifter 26), C.A. Reitzel: Copenhagen 2002.
Godderis, Jan, *Bestaan de dingen alleen als men ze ziet? Historische, fenomenologisch-psychiatrische en metapsychologische reflecties inzake de waarneming, de verbeelding en het hallucineren*, Garant: Leuven/Apeldoorn 2001.
Godel, R., "Socrate et Diotime," *Bulletin de l'Association Budé: Lettres d'humanité* 13 (1954), 3–30.
Godwin, Joscelyn, *The Mystery of the Seven Vowels, in Theory and Practice*, Phanes Press: Grand Rapids 1991.
The Pagan Dream of the Renaissance, Thames & Hudson: London 2002.
Goethe, Johann Wolfgang von, *Faust: Der Tragödie erster und zweiter Teil. Urfaust* (Erich Trunz, ed. & comm.), C.H. Beck: München 1986.
Goulet, R., "Anatolius," in: R. Goulet (ed.), *Dictionnaire des philosophes antiques*, vol. 1, CNRS éditions: Paris 2016, 179–183.
Graf, Fritz, *Gottesnähe und Schadenzauber: Die Magie in der griechisch-römischen Antike*, C.H. Beck: München 1996.

Granger, Frank, "The Poemander of Hermes Trismegistus," *The Journal of Theological Studies* 5 (1904), 395–412.
Grant, Robert M., Review of Nock and Festugière, *Journal of Near Eastern Studies* 8:1 (1949), 56–58.
Grese, William C., *Corpus Hermeticum XIII and Early Christian Literature*, Brill: Leiden 1979.
— "The Hermetica and New Testament Research," *Biblical Research* 28 (1983), 37–54.
Grimes, Shannon, *Becoming Gold: Zosimos of Panopolis and the Alchemical Arts in Roman Egypt*, Rubedo Press: Auckland 2018.
Griswold, Charles, "Plato's Metaphilosophy: Why Plato Wrote Dialogues," in: *Platonic Writings, Platonic Reading*, Routledge: New York 1988, 143–167.
Grof, Stanislav, *Beyond the Brain: Birth, Death, and Transcendence in Psychotherapy*, State University of New York Press: Albany 1985.
Grondin, Jean, *Hans-Georg Gadamer: Eine Biographie*, 2nd ed., Mohr Siebeck: Tübingen 2013.
Guzmán, Gastón, *The Genus* Psilocybe: *A Systematic Revision of the Known Species including the History, Distribution, and Chemistry of the Hallucinogenic Species* (Beihefte zur Nova Hedwigia 74), J. Cramer: Vaduz 1983.
— "Supplement to the Monograph of the Genus *Psilocybe*," *Bibliotheca Mycologica* 159 (1995), 91–141.
Hadot, Pierre, "Exercices spirituels," in: *Exercices spirituels et philosophie antique*, Albin Michel: Paris 1993, 19–74.
— *What is Ancient Philosophy?*, The Belknap Press of Harvard University Press: Cambridge Mass./London 2002.
Haenchen, Ernst, "Aufbau und Theologie des 'Poimandres'," *Zeitschrift für Theologie und Kirche* 53 (1956), 149–191.
Haidt, Jonathan, *The Righteous Mind: Why Good People are Divided by Politics and Religion*, Penguin: London 2012.
Halbertal, Moshe and Avishai Margalit, *Idolatry*, Harvard University Press: Cambridge Mass./London 1992.
Hallum, Bink, "Zosimus Arabus: The Reception of Zosimos of Panopolis in the Arabic/Islamic World," Ph.D. Dissertation, The Warburg Institute: London 2008.
— "Neilos," in: Keyser and Irby-Massie, *Encyclopedia*, 570.
— "Theosebeia," in: Keyser and Irby-Massie, *Encyclopedia*, 802–803.
— "Zōsimos of Panōpolis," in: Keyser and Irby-Massie, *Encyclopedia*, 852–853.
Hammer, Olav, *Claiming Knowledge: Strategies of Epistemology from Theosophy to the New Age*, Brill: Leiden/Boston/Köln 2001.
Hanegraaff, Wouter J., "Empirical Method in the Study of Esotericism," *Method & Theory in the Study of Religion* 7:2 (1995), 99–129.
— *New Age Religion and Western Culture: Esotericism in the Mirror of Secular Thought*, Brill: Leiden/Boston 1996 (State University of New York Press: Albany 1998).
— "On the Construction of 'Esoteric Traditions'," in: Antoine Faivre and Wouter J. Hanegraaff (eds.), *Western Esotericism and the Science of*

Religion: Selected Papers presented at the 17th Congress of the International Association for the History of Religions, Mexico City 1995, Peeters: Louvain 1998, 11–61.
"Defining Religion in Spite of History," in: Jan G. Platvoet and Arie L. Molendijk (eds.), *The Pragmatics of Defining Religion: Contexts, Concepts and Contests*, Brill: Leiden/Boston/Köln 1999, 337–378.
Het einde van de hermetische traditie (inauguration speech), Vossiuspers AUP: Amsterdam 1999.
"The Trouble with Images: Anti-Image Polemics and Western Esotericism," in: Olav Hammer and Kocku von Stuckrad (eds.), *Polemical Encounters: Esoteric Discourse and Its Others*, Brill: Leiden/Boston 2007, 107–136.
"Fiction in the Desert of the Real: Lovecraft's Cthulhu Mythos," *Aries* 7 (2007), 85–109.
Review of Lucentini, Parri and Perrone Compagni, *Aries* 7:2 (2007), 227–229.
"Altered States of Knowledge: The Attainment of *Gnōsis* in the Hermetica," *The International Journal of the Platonic Tradition* 2 (2008), 128–163.
"Reason, Faith, and Gnosis: Potentials and Problematics of a Typological Construct," in: Peter Meusburger, Michael Welker and Edgar Wunder (eds.), *Clashes of Knowledge: Orthodoxies and Heterodoxies in Science and Religion*, Springer: New York 2008, 133–144.
"Better than Magic: Cornelius Agrippa and Lazzarellian Hermetism," *Magic, Ritual & Witchcraft* 4:1 (2009), 1–25.
"Will-Erich Peuckert and the Light of Nature," in: Arthur Versluis, Claire Fanger, Lee Irwin and Melinda Phillips (eds.), *Esotericism, Religion, and Nature*, North American Academic Press: Michigan 2009, 281–305.
"The Platonic Frenzies in Marsilio Ficino," in: Jitse Dijkstra, Justin Kroesen and Yme Kuiper (eds.), *Myths, Martyrs, and Modernity: Studies in the History of Religions in Honour of Jan N. Bremmer*, Brill: Leiden/Boston 2010, 553–567.
"Magnetic Gnosis: Somnambulism and the Quest for Absolute Knowledge," in: Andreas B. Kilcher and Philipp Theisohn (eds.), *Die Enzyklopädie der Esoterik: Allwissenheitsmythen und universalwissenschaftliche Modelle in der Esoterik der Neuzeit*, Wilhelm Fink: München 2010, 259–275.
"Teaching Experiential Dimensions of Western Esotericism," in: William B. Parsons (ed.), *Teaching Mysticism*, Oxford University Press 2011, 154–169.
Esotericism and the Academy: Rejected Knowledge in Western Culture, Cambridge University Press 2012.
"Academic Suicide," *Creative Reading*, 1 September 2012, wouterjhanegraaff.blogspot.com
Western Esotericism: A Guide for the Perplexed, Bloomsbury: London 2013.
"The Power of Ideas: Esotericism, Historicism, and the Limits of Discourse," *Religion* 43:2 (2013), 252–273.
"Entheogenic Esotericism," in: Egil Asprem and Kennet Granholm (eds.), *Contemporary Esotericism*, Equinox: Sheffield/Bristol 2013, 392–409.
"Hermetism," in: Karla Pollmann *et alii* (eds.), *The Oxford Guide to the Historical Reception of Augustine*, Oxford University Press 2013, 1135–1139.

Review of Bernd-Christian Otto, *Aries* 14 (2014), 114–120.
"How Hermetic was Renaissance Hermetism?," *Aries* 15:2 (2015), 179–209.
"Trance," in: Robert A. Segal and Kocku von Stuckrad (eds.), *Vocabulary for the Study of Religion*, vol. 3, Brill: Leiden/Boston 2015, 511–513.
"Gnosis," in: Magee, *Cambridge Handbook*, 381–392.
"Magic," in: Magee, *Cambridge Handbook*, 393–404.
"Reconstructing 'Religion' from the Bottom Up," *Numen* 63 (2016), 576–605.
"Religion and the Historical Imagination: Esoteric Tradition as Poetic Invention," in: Christoph Bochinger and Jörg Rüpke (eds.), in cooperation with Elisabeth Begemann, *Dynamics of Religion : Past and Present*, De Gruyter: Berlin 2017, 131–153.
"The Theosophical Imagination," *Correspondences* 5 (2017), 3–39.
"Hermes Trismegistus & Hermetism," in: Marco Sgarbi (ed.), *The Encyclopedia of Renaissance Philosophy*, Springer: New York 2018.
"Imagining the Future Study of Religion and Spirituality," *Religion* 50:1 (2020), 72–82.
"The Third Kind: Gilles Quispel and Gnosis," *Creative Reading*, 11 July 2020, wouterjhanegraaff.blogspot.com.
"Psychedelica in de Westerse cultuur: Onnodige psychiatrisering van visionaire ervaringen," *Tijdschrift voor Psychiatrie* 62 (2020), 713–720.
Review of Esteban Law, *Isis* 112:1 (2021), 179–180.
"Out of Egypt: Hermetic Theosophy between Reitzenstein and Mead," in: Charles M. Stang and Jason Ānanda Josephson Storm (eds.), *Theosophy and the Study of Religion*, Brill: Leiden/Boston [forthcoming].
Hanegraaff, Wouter J. and Ruud M. Bouthoorn, *Lodovico Lazzarelli (1447-1500): The Hermetic Writings and Related Documents*, Arizona Center for Medieval and Renaissance Studies: Tempe, Arizona 2005.
Harari, Yuval Noah, *Sapiens: A Brief History of Humankind*, Vintage Books: London 2011.
Harker, Andrew, "The Jews in Roman Egypt: Trials and Rebellions," in: Riggs, *Oxford Handbook of Roman Egypt*, 277–287.
Harland, Philip A., "Journeys in Pursuit of Divine Wisdom: Thessalos and Other Seekers," in: Philip A. Harland (ed.), *Travel and Religion in Antiquity*, Wilfrid Laurier University Press: Waterloo 2011, 123–140.
Harnack, Adolf von, *Marcion: Das Evangelium vom fremden Gott: Eine Monographie zur Geschichte der Grundlegung der Katholischen Kirche*, J.C. Hinrichs: Leipzig 1921.
Hartogsohn, Ido, "Constructing Drug Effects: A History of Set and Setting," *Drug Science, Policy and Law* 4 (2017), 1–17.
Heidegger, Martin, *Was heisst Denken?*, Vittorio Klostermann: Frankfurt a.M. 2002.
What Is Called Thinking?, Harper & Row: New York/Evanston/London 1968.
Kant und das Problem der Metaphysik (Gesamtausgabe I.3), Vittorio Klostermann: Frankfurt a.M. 1991.

Heilen, Stephan, "Some Metrical Fragments from Nechepsos and Petosiris," in: Isabelle Boehm and Wolfgang Hübner (eds.), *La poésie astrologique dans l'antiquité*, Collection du CEROR 38 (Paris 2011), 23–93.

Heinze, Max, *Die Lehre vom Logos in der griechischen Philosophie*, Ferdinand Schmidt: Oldenburg 1872.

Herklotz, Friederike, "*Aegypta Capta*: Augustus and the Annexation of Egypt," in: Riggs, *Oxford Handbook of Roman Egypt*, 11–21.

Higgins, R.A. and R.P. Winnington-Ingram, "Lute-Players in Greek Art," *The Journal of Hellenic Studies* 85 (1965), 62–71.

Hirschkind, Charles, *The Feeling of History: Islam, Romanticism, and Andalusia*, The University of Chicago Press: Chicago/London 2021.

Hodkinson, Stephen and Hilary Hodkinson, "Mantineia and the Mantinike: Settlement and Society in a Greek Polis," *The Annual of the British School at Athens* 76 (1981), 239–296.

Hoffman, Donald, *The Case against Reality: How Evolution Hid the Truth from Our Eyes*, Allen Lane: London 2019.

Holt, Robert R., "Imagery: The Return of the Ostracized," *American Psychologist* 19:4 (1964), 254–264.

Holzhausen, Jens, *Der "Mythos vom Menschen" im hellenistischen Ägypten: Eine Studie zum "Poimandres" (= CH), zu Valentin und dem gnostischen Mythos*, Athenäeum: Hain Hanstein 1994.

Hopfner, Theodor, *Griechisch-Ägyptischer Offenbarungszauber, mit einer eingehenden Darstellung des griechisch-synkretistischen Daemonen-glaubens und der Voraussetzungen und Mittel des Zaubers überhaupt und der magischen Divination im besonderen*, H. Haessel-Verlag: Leipzig 1921.

Horst, Pieter Willem van der, *Chaeremon: Egyptian Priest and Stoic Philosopher. The Fragments Collected and Translated with Explanatory Notes*, E.J. Brill: Leiden/New York/Copenhagen/Köln 1987.

Houellebecq, Michel, *H.P. Lovecraft: Contre le monde, contra la vie*, Éditions du Rocher: Paris 1991.

Les particules élémentaires, Flammarion: Paris 1998.

Plateforme, Flammarion: Paris 2001.

Huet, Marie-Hélène, *Monstrous Imagination*, Harvard University Press: Cambridge Mass. 1993.

Hughes, Aaron W., *The Texture of the Divine: Imagination in Medieval Islamic and Jewish Thought*, Indiana University Press: Bloomington/Indianapolis 2004.

Hunter, Erica C.D., "Beautiful Black Bronzes: Zosimos' Treatises in Cam. Mm. 6.29," in: Alessandra Giumlia-Mair (ed.), *I bronzi antichi: Produzione e tecnologia: Atti del XV Congresso Internazionale sui Bronzi Antichi*, Monique Mergoil: Montagnac 2002, 655–660.

Hunter, Ian, "The History of Theory," *Critial Inquiry* 33:1 (2006), 78–112.

"The Time of Theory," *Postcolonial Studies* 10:1 (2007), 5–22.

"Spirituality and Philosophy in Post-Structural Theory," *History of European Ideas* 35 (2009), 265–275.

"The Mythos, Ethos, and Pathos of the Humanities," *History of European Ideas* 40:1 (2013), 1–26.

Huss, Boaz, *Mystifying Kabbalah: Academic Scholarship, National Theology, and New Age Spirituality*, Oxford University Press 2020.
Hyland, Drew A., *Finitude and Transcendence in the Platonic Dialogues*, State University of New York Press: Albany 1995.
— *Questioning Platonism: Continental Interpretations of Plato*, State University of New York Press: Albany 2004.
— *Plato and the Question of Beauty*, Indiana University Press: Bloomington/Indianapolis 2008.
Iamblichus, *Iamblichus:* De mysteriis (Emma C. Clarke, John M. Dillon and Jackson P. Hershbell, ed. & transl.), Brill: Leiden/Boston 2004.
— *Réponse à Porphyre (*De Mysteriis*)* (Henri Dominique Saffrey and Alain-Philippe Segonds, ed. & transl.), Les Belles Lettres: Paris 2018.
Ideler, Iulius Ludovicus, *Physici et medici graeci*, vol. 2, Reimer: Berlin 1842.
Inglisian, Vahan, "Chalkedon und die armenische Kirche," in: Aloys Grillmeier and Heinrich Bacht (eds.), *Das Konzil von Chalkedon: Geschichte und Gegenwart*, Bd. II: *Entscheidung um Chalkedon*, Echter-Verlag: Würzburg 1953, 361–417.
Introvigne, Massimo, "Martinism: Second Period," in: Hanegraaff, *Dictionary*, 780–783.
Inwood, Brad (ed. & translation), *The Poem of Empedocles*, University of Toronto Press: Toronto/Buffalo/London 2001.
Irenaeus of Lyon, *Contre les hérésies: Livre I* (Adelin Rousseau and Louis Doutreleau, eds.), vol. II (Texte et Traduction), Les Éditions du Cerf: Paris 1979.
Iversen, Erik, *Egyptian and Hermetic Doctrine*, Museum Tusculanum Press: Copenhagen 1984.
Jackson, Howard M., "Κόρη Κόσμου: Isis, Pupil of the Eye of the World," *Chronique d'Égypte* 61: 121 (1986), 116–135.
— "The Seer Nikotheos and his Lost Apocalypse in the Light of Sethian Apocalypses from Nag Hammadi and the Apocalypse of Elchasai," *Novum Testamentum* 32:3 (1990), 250–277.
— "A New Proposal for the Origin of the Hermetic God Poimandres," *Zeitschrift für Papyrologie und Epigraphik* 128 (1999), 95–106.
Jackson, Howard M. (ed. & transl.), *Zosimos of Panopolis: On the Letter Omega*, Scholars Press: Missoula 1978.
Jackson, Stanley W., "The Imagination and Psychological Healing," *Journal of the History of the Behavioral Sciences* 26 (1990), 345–358.
Jacobs, Bas J.H., "Getting off the Wheel: A Conceptual History of the New Age Concept of Enlightenment," *Numen* 67 (2020), 373–401.
Jacobsen, Johanna Micaela, "Boundary Breaking and Compliance: Will-Erich Peuckert and 20th Century German *Volkskunde*," Ph.D. Dissertation, University of Pennsylvania 2007.
James, William, *The Varieties of Religious Experience: A Study in Human Nature* (1902), Collins: Glasgow 1960.
Janet, Pierre, "L'influence somnambulique et le besoin de direction," *Revue philosophique de la France et de l'étranger* 43 (1897), 113–143.
Janowitz, Naomi, *Icons of Power: Ritual Practices in Late Antiquity*, The Pennsylvania State University Press: University Park 2002.

Jansen, H. Ludin, "Die Frage nach Tendenz und Verfasserschaft im Poimandres," in: G. Widengren and D. Hellholm (eds.), *Proceedings of the International Colloquium on Gnosticism*, Stockholm 1977, 157–163.

Janus, Carolus (ed.), *Musici Scriptores Graeci*, B.G. Teubner: Leipzig 1895.

Johnson, Barbara, "Translator's Introduction," in: Derrida, *Dissemination*, vii–xxxiii.

Johnston, Sarah Iles, "Rising to the Occasion: Theurgic Ascent in its Cultural Milieu," in: Peter Schäfer and Hans G. Kippenberg (eds.), *Envisioning Magic: A Princeton Seminar and Symposium*, Brill: Leiden/New York/Köln 1997, 165–194.

"*Fiat Lux, Fiat Ritus*: Divine Light and the Late Antique Defense of Ritual," in: Matthew T. Kapstein (ed.), *The Presence of Light: Divine Radiance and Religious Experience*, The University of Chicago Press 2004, 5–24.

"Animating Statues: A Case Study in Ritual," *Arethusa* 41:3 (2008), 445–477.

"The Authority of Greek Mythic Narratives in the Magical Papyri," *Archiv für Religionsgeschichte* 16:1 (2015), 51–65.

Johnston, Sarah Iles (ed.), *Religions of the Ancient World*, The Belknap Press of Harvard University Press: Cambridge Mass./London 2004.

Jonas, Hans, *The Gnostic Religion: The Message of the Alien God and the Beginnings of Christianity*, Beacon Press: Boston 1958.

"Epilogue: Gnosticism, Nihilism and Existentialism," in: Jonas, *The Gnostic Religion*, 320–340.

Gnosis und spätantiker Geist, 2 vols. (orig. 1934 / 1954), Vandenhoeck & Ruprecht: Göttingen 1964 / 1966.

"The Gnostic Syndrome: Typology of its Thought, Imagination, and Mood," in: *Philosophical Essays: From Ancient Creed to Technological Man*, The University of Chicago Press: Chicago/London 1974, 263–276.

Jones, Alexander, "Precision of Time Observation in Greco-Roman Astrology and Astronomy," in: M. Morfouli and E. Nicolaidis (eds.), *Time Accuracy in Physics and Astronomy* [forthcoming].

Jong, Albert F. de, "Zosimus of Panopolis," in: Hanegraaff, *Dictionary*, 1183–1186.

Jördens, Andreas, "Status and Citizenship," in: Riggs, *Oxford Handbook of Roman Egypt*, 247–259.

Kaiser, Ursula Ulrike and Hans-Gebhard Bethge (eds.), *Nag Hammadi Deutsch: Studienausgabe*, 3rd revised ed., Walter de Gruyter: Berlin/Boston 2013 [NHDS].

Kaldellis, Anthony, *Hellenism in Byzantium: The Transformations of Greek Identity and the Reception of the Classical Tradition*, Cambridge University Press 2007.

Kaldellis, Anthony and Niketas Siniossoglou (eds.), *The Cambridge Intellectual History of Byzantium*, Cambridge University Press 2017.

Kaldellis, Anthony and Niketas Siniossoglou, "Introduction," in: Kaldellis and Siniossoglou, *Cambridge Intellectual History of Byzantium*, 1–24.

Karbovnik, Damien, "L'ésotérisme grand public: Le réalisme fantastique et sa réception. Contribution à une sociohistoire de l'occulture," Ph.D. Thesis, L'Université Paul-Valéry Montpellier 3, 2017.

Karnes, Michelle, *Imagination, Meditation & Cognition in the Middle Ages*, The University of Chicago Press: Chicago/London 2011.
Keizer, Lewis S., "The Eighth Reveals the Ninth: Tractate 6 of Nag Hammadi Codex VI," Ph.D. Dissertation, Graduate Theological Union: Berkeley 1973 [Keizer].
Kelber, Wilhelm, *Die Logoslehre: Von Heraklit bis Origenes*, Urachhaus: Stuttgart 1958.
Kerkeslager, Allen, "The Jews in Egypt and Cyrenaica, 66–c. 235 CE," in: Steven T. Katz (ed.), *The Cambridge History of Judaism*, vol. 4: *The Late Roman-Rabbinic Period*, Cambridge University Press, 53–68.
Keyser, Paul and Georgia Irby-Massie (eds.), *Encyclopedia of Ancient Natural Scientists: The Greek Tradition and Its Many Heirs*, Routledge: London/New York 2008.
Kilcher, Andreas B. (ed.), *Constructing Tradition: Means and Myths of Transmission in Western Esotericism*, Brill: Leiden & Boston 2010.
King, Karen L., *What is Gnosticism?*, The Belknap Press of Harvard University Press: Cambridge Mass./London 2003.
Kingsley, Peter, "From Pythagoras to the *Turba Philosophorum*: Egypt and Pythagorean Tradition," *Journal of the Warburg and Courtauld Institutes* 57 (1994), 1–13.
— *Ancient Philosophy, Mystery, and Magic: Empedocles and Pythagorean Tradition*, Clarendon Press: Oxford 1995.
— "An Introduction to the Hermetica: Approaching Ancient Esoteric Tradition," in: van den Broek and van Heertum, *From Poimandres to Jacob Böhme*, 17–40.
— "Poimandres: The Etymology of the Name and the Origins of the Hermetica," in: van den Broek & van Heertum, *From Poimandres to Jacob Böhme*, 41–76 (orig. *Journal of the Warburg and Courtauld Institutes* 56 [1993], 1–24).
— *Reality*, The Golden Sufi Center: Point Reyes 2003.
Kirk, Geoffrey S., John E. Raven, *The Presocratic Philosophers: A Critical History with a Selection of Texts*, Cambridge University Press 1971.
Kissling, Robert C., "The ΟΧΗΜΑ-ΠΝΕΥΜΑ of the Neoplatonists and the *De Insomniis* of Synesius of Cyrene," *The American Journal of Philology* 43:4 (1922), 318–330.
Klotz, David, *Caesar in the City of Amun: Egyptian Temple Construction and Theology in Roman Thebes*, Brepols: Turnhout 2012.
Kluge, Carl Alexander Ferdinand, *Versuch einer Darstellung des animalischen Magnetismus als Heilmittel*, Realschulbuchhandlung: Berlin 1815.
Kneller, Jane, *Kant and the Power of Imagination*, Cambridge University Press 2007.
Kodera, Sergius, "The Stuff Dreams are Made Of: Ficino's Magic Mirrors," *Accademia* 1 (1999), 85–100.
Köhlenberg, Leo, *Gnosis als wereldreligie: Leven en werk van Gilles Quispel*, Synthese: Rotterdam 2013.
Kosofsky Sedgwick, Eve, "Paranoid Reading and Reparative Reading, or, You're So Paranoid, You Probably Think This Essay Is About You," in: Kosofsky Sedgwick, *Touching Feeling: Affect, Pedagogy, Performativity*, Duke University Press: Durham/London 2003, 123–151.

Kosslyn, Stephen M., "Mental Images and the Brain," *Cognitive Neuropsychology* 22:3/4 (2005), 333-347.
Kosslyn, Stephen M., William L. Thompson and Giorgio Ganis, *The Case of Mental Imagery*, Oxford University Press 2006.
Kurth, D., "Thot," in: Wolfgang Helck and Wolfhart Westendorf (eds.), *Lexikon der Ägyptologie*, vol. 6, Otto Harrassowitz: Wiesbaden 1986, 497-523.
Krause, Martin and Pahor Labib, *Gnostische und Hermetische Schriften aus Codex II und Codex VI*, J.J. Augustin: Glückstadt 1971 [KL].
Krause, Martin, "Die hermetischen Nag Hammadi Texte," in: Giversen, Petersen and Podemann Sørensen, *Nag Hammadi Texts*, 61-71.
Kripal, Jeffrey J., *Authors of the Impossible: The Paranormal and the Sacred*, The University of Chicago Press: Chicago/London 2010.
Kurzke, Hermann, "Immer auf dem Balkon? Thomas Manns Selbstinszenierung in den *Betrachtungen eines Unpolitischen*," in: Michael Ansel, Hans-Edwin Friedrich and Gerhard Lauer (eds.), *Die Erfindung des Schriftstellers Thomas Mann*, Walter de Gruyter: Berlin/New York 2009, 411-420.
Kyrill von Alexandrien, *Werke I: Gegen Julian*, 2 vols. (Christoph Riedweg, Wolfram Kinzig and Thomas Brüggemann, eds.), De Gruyter: Berlin/Boston 2016/2017.
Labat, René, "L'écriture cunéiforme et la civilisation mésopotamienne," in: *L'écriture et la psychologie des peuples*, Armand Colin: Paris 1963, 73-87.
Lactantius, *Divine Institutes* (Anthony Bowen and Peter Garnsey, transl. & introd.), Liverpool University Press 2003.
Łajtar, Adam, "The Theban Region under the Roman Empire," in: Riggs, *Oxford Handbook of Roman Egypt*, 171-188.
Lamb, W.R.M., "Introduction to the *Symposium*," in: Plato, *Lysis – Symposium – Gorgias* (Loeb Classical Library), Harvard University Press: Cambridge Mass./London 1925, 74-79.
Lamberth, David C., *William James and the Metaphysics of Experience*, Cambridge University Press 1999.
Lampe, G.W.H., *A Patristic Greek Lexikon*, At the Clarendon Press: Oxford 1961.
Lane Fox, Robin, *Pagans and Christians*, Penguin: Harmondsworth 1986.
Law, Esteban, *Das Corpus Hermeticum – Wirkungsgeschichte: Transzendenz, Immanenz, Ethik. Das Corpus Hermeticum im Rahmen der abendländischen Tradition*. Vol. 1: *Characteristik des Corpus Hermeticum*, frommann-holzboog: Stuttgart/Bad Canstatt 2018.
Law, John, *After Method: Mess in Social Science Research*, Routledge: London/New York 2004.
Layton, Bentley, "Prolegomena to the Study of Ancient Gnosticism," in: L. Michael White and O. Larry Yarbrough (eds.), *The Social World of the First Christians: Essays in Honor of Wayne A. Meeks*, Fortress: Minneapolis 1995, 334-350.
Layton, Bentley (ed.), *The Gnostic Scriptures: A New Translation with Annotations and Introductions*, Doubleday: New York etc. 1987.
Lazier, Benjamin, *God Interrupted: Heresy and the European Imagination between the World Wars*, Princeton University Press 2008.

Lévy, I., "Statues divines et animaux sacrés dans l'apologétique gréco-égyptienne," *Annuaire de l'Institut de Philologie et d'Histoire Orientales* 3 (1935), 295–301.

Lewis, James R. and Olav Hammer (eds.), *The Invention of Sacred Tradition*, Cambridge University Press 2007.

Lewis, Nicola Denzey, *Cosmology and Fate in Gnosticism and Graeco-Roman Antiquity*, Brill: Leiden/Boston 2013.

Lewy, Hans, *Chaldaean Oracles and Theurgy* (3rd édition par Michel Tardieu, avec un supplément "Les Oracles Chaldaïques 1891–2011"), Institut d'Études Augustiniennes: Paris 2011.

Leyden, W. von, "Time, Number, and Eternity in Plato and Aristotle," *The Philosophical Quarterly* 14:54 (1964), 35–52.

Liddell, Henry George and Robert Scott, *A Greek-English Lexicon, with a Revised Supplement*, Clarendon Press: Oxford 1996.

LiDonnici, Lynn R., "Single-Stemmed Wormwood, Pinecones and Myrrh: Expense and Availability of Recipe Ingredients in the *Greek Magical Papyri*," *Kernos* 14 (2001), 61–91.

——— "Beans, Fleawort, and the Blood of a Hamadryas Baboon: Recipe Ingredients in Greco-Roman Magical Materials," in: Paul Mirecki and Marvin Meyer (eds.), *Magic and Ritual in the Ancient World*, Brill: Leiden/Boston/Köln 2002, 359–377.

Lindsay, Jack, *The Origins of Alchemy in Roman Egypt*, Frederick Muller: London 1970.

Litwa, M. David, "'Immortalized In This Very Hour': Deification in the 'Mithras Liturgy'," in: *Becoming Divine: An Introduction to Deification in Western Culture*, Cascade: Eugene 2013, 69–85.

——— *Hermetica II: The Excerpts of Stobaeus, Papyrus Fragments, and Ancient Testimonies in an English Translation with Notes and Introductions*, Cambridge University Press 2018.

Loret, Victor, "Le kyphi, parfum sacré des anciens égyptiens," *Journal asiatique*, 8e série, vol. 10 (1887), 76–132.

Lorton, David, "The Theology of Cult Statues in Ancient Egypt," in: Michael B. Dick (ed.), *Born in Heaven, Made on Earth: The Making of the Cult Image in the Ancient Near East*, Eisenbrauns: Winona Lake, Indiana 1999, 123–210.

Louth, Andrew, "Pagan Theurgy and Christian Sacramentalism in Denys the Areopagite," *Journal of Theological Studies* 37 (1986), 432–438.

Lovejoy, Arthur O., *The Great Chain of Being: A Study of the History of an Idea* (1936), Harvard University Press: Cambridge Mass./London 1964.

Loy, David R., *Nonduality: In Buddhism and Beyond*, Wisdom Publications: Somerville 1988.

Lucentini, Paolo, Ilaria Parri and Vittoria Perrone Compagni (eds.), *Hermetism from Late Antiquity to Humanism / La tradizione ermetica dal mondo tardo-antico all'umanesimo*, Brepols: Turnhout 2003.

Lucentini, Paolo and Vittoria Perrone Compagni, "Hermetic Literature II," in: Hanegraaff, *Dictionary*, 499–529.

Luck, Georg, *Arcana Mundi: Magic and the Occult in the Greek and Roman World. A Collection of Ancient Texts*, The Johns Hopkins University Press: Baltimore/London 1985; 2nd ed. 2006.

"The Doctrine of Salvation in the Hermetic Writings," *The Second Century* 8 (1991), 31–41.

"Theurgy and Forms of Worship in Neoplatonism," in: *Ancient Pathways and Hidden Pursuits: Religion, Morals, and Magic in the Ancient World*, The University of Michigan Press: Ann Arbor 2000, 110–152.

Review of Wasson, Hofmann and Ruck, *The American Journal of Philology* 122:1 (2001), 135–138.

"Psychoactive Substances in Religion and Magic," in: *Arcana Mundi* (2nd ed.), 479–492.

Ludwig, Arnold M., "Altered States of Consciousness," in: Charles T. Tart (eds.), *Altered States of Consciousness*, Anchor Books/Doubleday & Co.: Garden City/New York 1969, 11–24.

Luhrmann, Tanya M., *Persuasions of the Witch's Craft: Ritual Magic in Contemporary England*, Harvard University Press: Cambridge Mass. 1989.

"Hallucinations and Sensory Overrides, *Annual Review of Anthropology* 40 (2011), 71–85.

Lundhaug, Hugo and Lance Jenott, *The Monastic Origins of the Nag Hammadi Codices*, Mohr Siebeck: Tübingen 2017.

Luther, Martin, *Tischreden*, Bd. 5, Martin Luthers Werke: *Kritische Gesamtausgabe*, Hermann Böhlaus Nachfolger: Weimar 1919.

Lyotard, François, *The Postmodern Condition: A Report on Knowledge*, Manchester University Press 1984.

MacCoull, L.S.B., "Plotinus the Egyptian?," *Mnemosyne* (4th ser.) 52:3 (1999), 330–333.

MacDonald, Paul S., *History of the Concept of Mind: Speculations about Soul, Mind and Spirit from Homer to Hume*, Ashgate: Aldershot/Burlington 2003.

MacMullen, Ramsay, "Nationalism in Roman Egypt," *Aegyptus* 44: 3/4 (1964), 179–199.

Christianizing the Roman Empire A.D. 100–400, Yale University Press: New Haven/London 1984.

MacPhail, John A., *Porphyry's Homeric Questions on the Iliad: Text, Translation, Commentary*, De Gruyter: Berlin/New York 2011.

Macrobius, Ambrosius Theodosius, *Commentary on the Dream of Scipio* (William Harris Stahl, ed.), Columbia University Press: New York 1990.

Commentarii in Somnium Scipionis (Jacob Willis, ed.), Teubner: Stuttgart/Leipzig 1994.

Madison, G.B., "Gadamer/Derrida: The Hermeneutics of Irony and Power," in: Michelfelder and Palmer, *Dialogue and Deconstruction*, 192–198.

Magee, Glenn Alexander (ed.), *The Cambridge Handbook of Western Mysticism and Esotericism*, Cambridge University Press 2016.

Mahé, Jean-Pierre, "La prière d'actions de grâces du codex VI de Nag-Hamadi et le discours parfait," *Zeitschrift für Papyrologie und Epigraphik* 13 (1974), 40–60.

"Le sens et la composition du traité hermétique 'l'Ogdoade et l'Ennéade,' conservé dans le codex VI de Nag Hamadi," *Revue des sciences religieuses* 48:1 (1974), 54–65.

"Le sens des symboles sexuels dans quelques textes hermétiques et gnostiques," in: Jacques-É. Ménard (ed.), *Les Textes de Nag Hammadi: Colloque du Centre d'Histoire des Religions (Strasbourg, 23–25 Octobre 1974)*, E.J. Brill: Leiden 1975, 123–145.

"'Les définitions d'Hermès Trismégiste à Asclépius' (Traduction de l'arménien)," *Revue des sciences religieuses* 50:3 (1976), 193–214.

Hermès en Haute-Égypte, vol. 1: *Les textes Hermétiques de Nag Hammadi et leurs parallèles grecs et latins*, Les Presses de l'Université Laval: Québec 1978 [HHE I].

"Le fragment du *Discours parfait* dans la Bibliothèque de Nag Hammadi," in: Bernard Barc (ed.), *Colloque international sur les textes de Nag Hammadi (Québec, 22–25 août 1978)*, Les Presses de l'Université Laval & Éditions Peeters: Québec & Louvain 1981, 304–327.

Hermès en Haute-Égypte, vol. 2: *Le fragment du* Discours Parfait *et les* Définitions Hermétiques Arméniennes, Les Presses de l'Université Laval: Québec 1982 [HHE II].

"ΠΑΛΙΓΓΕΝΕΣΙΑ et structure du monde supérieur dans les *Hermetica* et le traité d'*Eugnoste* de Nag Hammadi," in: *Deuxième journée d'Études Coptes, Strasbourg 25 Mai 1984*, Peeters: Louvain 1986, 137–149.

"La Création dans les *Hermetica*," *Recherches Augustiniennes* 21 (1986), 3–53.

"Générations antédiluviennes et chute des éons dans l'hermétisme et dans la gnose," in: R. van den Broek, T. Baarda and J. Mansfeld (eds.), *Knowledge of God in the Graeco-Roman World*, Brill: Leiden/New York/København/Köln 1988, 160–177.

"La voie d'immortalité à la lumière des *Hermetica* de Nag Hammadi et de découvertes plus récentes," *Vigiliae Christianae* 45 (1991), 347–374.

"Le rôle de l'élément astrologique dans les écrits philosophiques d'Hermès Trismégiste," in: J.-H. Abry (ed.), *Les tablettes astrologiques de Grand (Vosges) et l'astrologie en Gaule romaine*, De Boccard: Paris 1993, 161–167.

"A Reading of the *Discourse on the Ogdoad and the Ennead* (Nag Hammadi Codex VI.6)," in: van den Broek and Hanegraaff, *Gnosis and Hermeticism*, 79–85.

"Théorie et pratique dans *l'Asclepius*," in: Lucentini, Parri and Perrone Compagni, *Hermetism*, 5–23.

"Introduction," in: Salaman, van Oyen and Wharton, *The Way of Hermes*, 101–108.

"Mental Faculties and Cosmic Levels in *The Eighth and the Ninth* (NH VI,6) and Related Hermetic Writings," in: Giversen, Petersen and Podemann Sørensen, *Nag Hammadi Texts*, 73–83.

"Hermes Trismegistos," in: Lindsay Jones (ed.), *Encyclopedia of Religion* (2nd ed.), vol. 6, Thomson Gale: Farmington Hills 2005, 3938–3944.

"Accolade ou baiser? Sur un rite hermétique de régénération: ἀσπάζεσθαι en NH VI, 57,26 et 65,4," in: L. Painchaud and P.-H. Poirier (eds.), *Coptica, Gnostica, Manichaica: Mélanges offerts à Wolf-Peter Funk*, Les Presses de l'Université Laval/Peeters: Québec/Louvain & Paris 2006, 557–564.

"Le hymne hermétique: Une propédeutique du silence," in: Yves Lehmann (ed.), *L'hymne antique et son public*, Brepols: Turnhout 2007, 275–289.

Hermès Trismégiste, Tome 5: *Paralipomènes grec, copte, arménien – Codex VI de Nag Hammadi – Codex Clarkianus 11 Oxoniensis – Définitions Hermétiques, Divers*, Les Belles Lettres: Paris 2019 [HT V].
Majercik, Ruth, *The Chaldean Oracles: Text, Translation, and Commentary*, E.J. Brill: Leiden/New York/Copenhagen/Köln 1989.
Manandyan, H., "Ermeay Eṙameci aṙ Asklepios Sahmankʻ," *Banber Matenadarani* 3 (1956), 287–314.
Mann, Thomas, *Joseph und seine Brüder*, vol. 2 (Grosse Kommentierte Frankfurter Ausgabe 8.2), S. Fischer: Frankfurt a.M. 2018.
Betrachtungen eines Unpolitischen: Kommentar (Hermann Kurzke, ed.; Grosse Kommentierte Frankfurter Ausgabe 13.2), S. Fischer: Frankfurt a.M. 2009.
Mansfeld, Jaap and Oliver Primavesi, *Die Vorsokratiker*, Philipp Reclam: Stuttgart 2012.
Marchand, Suzanne, *Down From Olympus: Archaeology and Philhellenism in Germany, 1750–1970*, Princeton University Press 1996.
"From Liberalism to Neoromanticism: Albrecht Dieterich, Richard Reitzenstein, and the Religious Turn in *Fin-de-Siècle* German Classical Studies," in: I. Gildenhard and Martin Rühl (eds.), *Out of Arcadia: Classics and Politics in Germany in the Age of Burckhardt, Nietzsche and Wilamowitz*, Bulletin of the Institute of Classical Studies (Suppl. 79): London 2003, 129–160.
German Orientalism in the Age of Empire: Religion, Race, and Scholarship, Cambridge University Press 2009.
Marcus, Ralph, "The Name Poimandrēs," *Journal of Near Eastern Studies* 8:1 (1949), 40–43.
Martelli, Matteo, "'Divine Water' in the Alchemical Writings of Pseudo-Democritus," *Ambix* 56:1 (2009), 5–22.
"Greek Alchemists at Work: 'Alchemical Laboratory' in the Greco-Roman World," *Nuncius* 26 (2011), 271–311.
"The Alchemical Art of Dyeing: The Fourfold Division of Alchemy and the Enochian Tradition," in: S. Dupré (ed.), "Laboratories of Art," *Archimedes* 37 (2014), 1–22.
"Alchemy, Medicine and Religion: Zosimus of Panopolis and the Egyptian Priests," in: Reinhard Feldmeier *et alii* (eds.), *Religion in the Roman Empire* 3:2 (2017), 202–220.
"Zosime gréco-syriaque, Plutarque et la teinture noire des statues égyptiennes," [unpublished ms.]
Martelli, Matteo and Maddalena Rumor, "Near Eastern Origins of Graeco-Egyptian Alchemy," in: Klaus Geus and Mark Geller (eds.), *Esoteric Knowledge in Antiquity* (Preprint 454), Max-Planck-Institut für Wissenschaftsgeschichte: Berlin 2014, 37–62.
Mathiesen, Thomas J., *Apollo's Lyre: Greek Music and Music Theory in Antiquity and the Middle Ages*, University of Nebraska Press: Lincoln/London 1999.
Matter, Jacques, *Histoire critique du gnosticisme et de son influence sur les sectes religieuses et philosophiques des six premiers siècles de l'ère chrétienne*, 2 vols., F.G. Levrault: Paris 1828
Matthews, John, *The Journey of Theophanes: Travel, Business, and Daily Life in the Roman East*, Yale University Press: New Haven/London 2006.

Maurizio, L., "Anthropology and Spirit Possession: A Reconsideration of the Pythia's Role at Delphi," *The Journal of Hellenic Studies* 115 (1995), 69–86.

McLuhan, Marshall, *Understanding Media: The Extensions of Man*, McGraw-Hill: New York 1964.

Mead, G.R.S., *Thrice-Greatest Hermes: Studies in Hellenistic Theosophy and Gnosis*, 3 vols., The Theosophical Publishing Society: London/Benares 1906.

Melvin-Koushki, Matthew, "*Taḥqīq* vs. *Taqlīd* in the Renaissances of Western Early Modernity," *Philological Encounters* 3 (2018), 193–249.

Meredith, Fionola, *Experiencing the Postmetaphysical Self: Between Hermeneutics and Deconstruction*, Palgrave: New York 2005.

Mertens, Michèle, *Un traité gréco-égyptien d'alchimie: La lettre d'Isis à Horus. Texte établi et traduit avec introduction et notes*, Université de Liège 1983–1984.

――― "Une scène initiatique alchimique: La 'Lettre d'Isis à Horus'," *Revue de l'histoire des religions* 205:1 (1988), 3–23.

――― "Sur la trace des anges rebelles dans les traditions ésotériques du début de notre ère jusqu'au XVIIe siècle," in: Julien Ries (ed.), *Anges et démons: Actes du colloque de Liège et de Louvain-la-Neuve 25-26 novembre 1987*, Centre d'Histoire des Religions: Louvain-la-Neuve 1989, 383–398.

――― *Zosime de Panopolis: Mémoires authentiques*, Les Belles Lettres: Paris 1995.

――― "Alchemy, Hermetism and Gnosticism at Panopolis c. 300 A.D.: The Evidence of Zosimus," in: A. Egberts, B.P. Muhs and J. van der Vliet (eds.), *Perspectives on Panopolis: An Egyptian Town from Alexander the Great to the Arab Conquest*, Brill: Leiden/Boston/Köln 2002, 165–175.

――― "Graeco-Egyptian Alchemy in Byzantium," in: Paul Magdalino and Maria Mavroudi (eds.), *The Occult Sciences in Byzantium*, La Pomme d'Or: Geneva 2006, 205–230.

Meslin, Michel, "Réalités psychiques et valeurs religieuses dans les cultes orientaux (Ie–IVe siècles)," *Revue Historique* 252: 2 (1974), 289–314.

Meyer, Marvin (ed.), *The Nag Hammadi Scriptures: The Revised and Updated Translation of Sacred Gnostic Texts*, Harper: New York 2007 [Meyer].

Michelfelder, Diane and Richard E. Palmer, "Introduction," in: Michelfelder and Palmer, *Dialogue and Deconstruction*, 1–18.

Michelfelder, Diane P. and Richard E. Palmer (eds.), *Dialogue and Deconstruction: The Gadamer-Derrida Encounter*, State University of New York Press: Albany 1989.

Migne, J.-P., *Patrologiae cursus completus ...: Series Graeca*, vol. 122, Imprimerie Catholique: Paris 1889.

Miller, John F. and Jenny Strauss Clay (eds.), *Tracking Hermes, Pursuing Mercury*, Oxford University Press 2019.

Miller, Dana R., *The Third Kind in Plato's Timaeus*, Vandenhoeck & Ruprecht: Göttingen 2003.

Minnen, Peter van, "Urban Craftsmen in Roman Egypt," *Münstersche Beiträge zur Antiken Handelsgeschichte* 6:1 (1987), 31–88.

――― "Did Ancient Women Learn a Trade outside the Home? A Note on SB XVIII 13305," *Zeitschrift für Papyrologie und Epigraphik* 123 (1998), 201–203.

Modrak, Deborah, "Φαντασία Reconsidered," *Archiv für Geschichte der Philosophie* 68 (1986), 47–69.

Moorsel, G. van, *The Mysteries of Hermes Trismegistus: A Phenomenological Study in the Process of Spiritualisation in the Corpus Hermeticum and Latin Asclepius*, Kemink & Zoon: Utrecht 1955.

Morenz, S., *La religion égyptienne*, Payot: Paris 1962.

Moreschini, Claudio, *Dall'Asclepius al Crater hermetis: Studi sull'ermetismo latino tardo-antico e rinascimentale*, Giardini: Pisa 1985.

——— *Hermes Christianus: The Intermingling of Hermetic Piety and Christian Thought*, Brepols: Turnhout 2011.

——— "Die Rezeption des *Asclepius* in der Renaissance," in: Gall, *Göttliche Weisheit*, 283–306.

Moreschini, Claudio (ed.), *Apulei Platonici Madaurensis opera quae supersunt*, vol. 3: *De philosophia libri*, Teubner: Stuttgart & Leipzig 1991.

Moret, Alexandre, *Le rituel du culte divin journalier en Égypte, d'après les Papyrus de Berlin et les textes du temple de Séti I*er*, a Abydos* (Annales du Musée Guimet 14), Ernest Leroux: Paris 1902.

Moullou, Dorina, Lambros T. Doulos and Frangiskos V. Topalis, "Artificial Light Sources in Roman, Byzantine, and Post-Byzantine Eras: An Evaluation of their Performance," *Chronos* 32 (2015), 119–132.

Moyer, Ian, "Thessalos of Tralles and Cultural Exchange," in: Scott Noegel, Joel Walker and Brandon Wheeler (eds.), *Prayer, Magic, and the Stars in the Ancient and Late Antique World*, The Pennsylvania State University Press: University Park 2003, 39–56.

——— *Egypt and the Limits of Hellenism*, Cambridge University Press 2011.

——— "Isidorus at the Gates of the Temple," in: Ian Rutherford (ed.), *Greco-Egyptian Interactions: Literature, Translation, and Culture, 500 BCE-300 CE*, Oxford University Press 2016, 209–244.

Moyer, Ian S. and Jacco Dieleman, "Miniaturization and the Opening of the Mouth in a Greek Magical Text (*PGM* XII.270-350)," *Journal of Ancient Near Eastern Religions* 3 (2003), 47–72.

Musil, Robert, *Nachlaß zu Lebzeiten*, Rowohlt: Reinbek bei Hamburg 1962.

Mussies, Gerard, "Catalogues of Sins and Virtues Personified (NHC II, 5)," in: van den Broek & Vermaseren, *Studies*, 315–335.

Nagel, Jennifer, *Knowledge: A Very Short Introduction*, Oxford University Press 2014.

Nagy, Gregory, "Ancient Greek Poetry, Prophecy, and Concept of Theory," in: J.L. Kugel (ed.), *Poetry and Prophecy: The Beginning of a Literary Tradition*, Cornell University Press: Ithaca 1990, 56–64.

Nickelsburg, George W.E. and James C. VanderKam, *1 Enoch: The Hermeneia Translation*, Fortress Press: Minneapolis 2012.

Nicomachus of Gerasa, *Manuel d'harmonique et autres textes relatifs à la musique* (Ch.-Ém. Ruelle, ed. & transl.), Baur: Paris 1881.

——— *The Manual of Harmonics of Nicomachus the Pythagorean* (Flora R. Levin, ed. & transl.), Phanes Press: Grand Rapids 1994.

Nilsson, Martin P., "Krater," *The Harvard Theological Review* 51:2 (1958), 53–58.

Nixon, Jon, *Hans-Georg Gadamer: The Hermeneutical Imagination*, Springer: Cham 2017.
Nock, A.D., "A New Edition of the Hermetic Writings," *The Journal of Egyptian Archaeology* 11:3-4 (1925), 126-137.
― Review of Scott, *Hermetica* vol. 2, *The Journal of Egyptian Archaeology* 13: 3-4 (1927), 268.
Nock, A.D. and A.-J. Festugière, *Hermès Trismégiste*, 4 vols. (1946, 1954), Les Belles Lettres: Paris 1991, 1992, 2002, 2019 [HT I, HT II, HT III, HT IV].
Noll, Richard, "Mental Imagery Cultivation as a Cultural Phenomenon: The Role of Visions in Shamanism," *Current Anthropology* 26:4 (1985), 443-461.
Numenius, *Fragments* (Édouard des Places, ed. & transl.), Les Belles Lettres: Paris 2003.
Nussbaum, Martha Craven, *Aristotle's* De motu animalium*: Text with Translation, Commentary, and Interpretive Essay*, Princeton University Press 1978.
Obeyesekere, Gananath, *Medusa's Hair: An Essay on Personal Symbols and Religious Experience*, The University of Chicago Press: Chicago/London 1981.
Oesterreich, T.K., *Possession: Demoniacal and Other among Primitive Races, in Antiquity, the Middle Ages, and Modern Times*, University Books: New York 1966.
Ohlander, Erik S., *Sufism in an Age of Transition: 'Umar al-Suhrawardī and the Rise of the Islamic Mystical Brotherhoods*, Brill: Leiden/Boston 2008.
Onians, R.B., *The Origins of European Thought: About the Body, the Mind, the Soul, the World, Time, and Fate*, Cambridge University Press 1951.
Otto, Bernd-Christian, *Magie: Rezeptions- und diskursgeschichtliche Analysen von der Antike bis zur Neuzeit*, De Gruyter: Berlin/New York 2011.
Otto, Eberhard, "Amun," in: Wolfgang Helck and Eberhard Otto (eds.), *Lexikon der Ägyptologie*, vol. 1, Otto Harassowitz: Wiesbaden 1975, 237-248.
Page, D.L., *Select Papyri in Four Volumes*, vol. 4, William Heinemann/Harvard University Press: London/Cambridge Mass. 1970.
Pagels, Elaine, *The Origin of Satan*, Vintage Books: New York 1996.
Paivio, Allan, *Mental Representations: A Dual Coding Approach*, Oxford University Press/Clarendon Press: New York/Oxford 1990.
Papadopoulos, Costas & Holley Moyes (eds.), *The Oxford Handbook of Light in Archaeology*, Oxford University Press [forthcoming].
Paramelle, Joseph and Jean-Pierre Mahé, "Extraits hermétiques inédits dans un manuscrit d'Oxford," *Revue des études grecques* 104 (1991), 109-139.
Parássoglou, George M., "A Prefectural Edict Regulating Temple Activities," *Zeitschrift für Papyrologie und Epigraphik* 13 (1974), 21-37.
Parlebas, Jacques, "L'origine égyptienne de l'appellation 'Hermès Trismégiste'," *Göttinger Miszellen* 13 (1974), 25-28.
Parri, Ilaria, "Tempo et eternità nell'*Asclepius*," in: Lucentini, Parri and Perrone Compagni, *Hermetism*, 45-62.
― *La via filosofica di Ermete: Studio sull'*Asclepius, Polistampa: Florence 2005.
Parrott, Douglas M. (ed.), *Nag Hammadi Codices V, 2-5 and VI, with Papyrus Berolensis 8502, 1 and 4*, E.J. Brill: Leiden 1979.
Pasi, Marco, "Arthur Machen's Panic Fears: Western Esotericism and the Irruption of Negative Epistemology," *Aries* 7 (2007), 63-83.

Pauwels, Louis and Jacques Bergier, *Le matin des magiciens*, Gallimard: Paris 1960.
Pearson, Birger A., "Jewish Elements in *Corpus Hermeticum* I," in: van den Broek and Vermaseren, *Studies*, 336–348.
Peters, F.E., *Greek Philosophical Terms: A Historical Lexicon*, New York University Press/University of London Press: New York/London 1967.
Petersen, Tage, "Hermetic Dualism? CH.VI against the Background of Nag Hammadi Dualistic Gnosticism," in: Giversen, Petersen and Sørensen, *Nag Hammadi Texts*, 95–102.
Peterson, Erik, "Herkunft und Bedeutung der ΜΟΝΟΣ ΠΡΟΣ ΜΟΝΟΝ-Formel bei Plotin," *Philologos: Zeitschrift für das klassische Altertum* 88 (N.F. 42), 30–41.
Pfister, Friedrich, "Ekstase," in: *Reallexikon für Antike und Christentum*, vol. 4, Hiersemann: Stuttgart 1959, 944–987.
"Rauchopfer," in: August Pauly and Georg Wissowa (eds.), *Real-Encyclopädie der classischen Altertumswissenschaft*, 2. Reihe, I A.1, J.B Metzler: Stuttgart 1914, 267–286.
[Philo of Alexandria], *The Works of Philo: Complete and Unabridged* (C.D. Yonge, transl.), Hendrickson 1993.
Philonenko, M., "O vitae vera vita (*Asclepius* 41)," *Revue de l'histoire et de philosophie religieuses* 68 (1988), 429–433.
"L'hymnodie secrète du *Corpus Hermeticum* (13, 17) et le cantique de Moïse (*Deutéronome* 33)," in: Yves Lehmann (ed.), *L'hymne antique et son public*, Brepols: Turnhout 2007, 291–299.
Pingree, David, "Hellenophilia versus the History of Science," *Isis* 83: 4 (1992), 554–563.
Pirsig, Robert, *Zen and the Art of Motorcycle Maintenance*, William Morrow and Co.: New York 1974.
Plato, *Euthyphro – Apology – Crito – Phaedo – Phaedrus* (Loeb Classical Library; Harold North Fowler, transl.), Harvard University Press: Cambridge Mass./London 1914.
Republic (Loeb Classical Library; Chris Emlyn-Jones and William Preddy, eds. & transl.), Harvard University Press: Cambridge Mass./London 2013.
The Collected Dialogues (Edith Hamilton and Huntington Cairns, eds.), Bollingen/Princeton University Press 1989.
Complete Works (John M. Cooper, ed.), Hackett Publishing Company: Indianapolis/Cambridge 1997.
Phaedrus (Harvey Yunis, ed. & commentary), Cambridge University Press 2011.
Phèdre (Oeuvres complètes IV.3; Léon Robin, Claudio Moreschini and Paul Vicaire), Les Belles Lettres: Paris 2019.
Pleše, Zlatko, "Dualism in the Hermetic Writings," *Χώρα: Revue d'études anciennes et médiévales*, Special issue "Dualismes: Doctrines religieuses et traditions philosophiques" (2015), 261–278.
Plessner, M., "The Place of the *Turba Philosophorum* in the Development of Alchemy," *Isis* 45:4 (1954), 331–338.
Plotinus, *Ennead IV* (Loeb Classical Library; A.H. Armstrong, transl.), Harvard University Press: Cambridge Mass./London 1984, repr. 1995.

Les Ennéades (Marie-Nicolas Bouillet, transl.), vol. 2, L. Hachette & Cie: Paris 1859.
[Plutarch], *Plutarch's Lives* (Loeb Classical Library), vol. 1 & 6, Harvard University Press/William Heinemann: Cambridge Mass./London 1967, 1954.
Plutarch, *Moralia* (Loeb Classical Library), vols. 5–7, Harvard University Press: Cambridge Mass. 1957, 1959, 1962.
Podemann Sørensen, Jørgen, "Ancient Egyptian Religious Thought and the XVIth Hermetic Tractate," in: Gertie Englund (ed.), *The Religion of the Ancient Egyptians: Cognitive Structures and Popular Expressions*, n.p.: Uppsala 1987.
"The Secret Hymn in Hermetic Texts," in: Bull, Lied and Turner, *Mystery and Secrecy*, 465–486.
Poirée, Élie, "Chant des sept voyelles," in: Combarieu, *Congrès International*, 28–38.
[Porphyry], *Porphyry the Philosopher to his Wife Marcella* (Alice Zimmern, transl. and introduction), George Redway: London 1896.
Porphyre: Lettre à Anébon l'Égyptien (Henri Dominique Saffrey and Alain-Philippe Segonds, ed. & transl.), Les Belles Lettres: Paris 2012.
Porphyry, *Vie de Pythagore / Lettre à Marcella* (Édouard des Places, ed.), Les Belles Lettres: Paris 2010.
Porreca, David, "Hermes Trismegistus: William of Auvergne's Mythical Authority," *Archives d'Histoire Doctrinale et Littéraire du Moyen Âge* 67 (2000), 143–158.
Port, Matthijs van de, *Ecstatic Encounters: Bahian Candomblé and the Quest for the Really Real*, Amsterdam University Press 2011.
Principe, Walter, "Toward Defining Spirituality," *Studies in Religion / Sciences Religieuses* 12:2 (1983), 127–141.
Principe, Lawrence M., *The Secrets of Alchemy*, The University of Chicago Press 2013.
Puech, H.-C., Review of Scott, *Hermetica* vol. 1, *Revue des études anciennes* 27 (1925), 166–168.
Puech, H.-C. and J. Doresse, "Nouveaux écrits gnostiques découverts en Égypte," *Comptes rendus des séances de l'Académie des Inscriptions et Belles-Lettres* 92:1 (1948), 87–95.
Quack, Joachim Friedrich, "Religious Personnel," in: Johnston, *Religions of the Ancient World*, 288–293.
"(H)abamons Stimme? Zum ägyptischen Hintergrund der Jamblich zugeschriebenen Schrift *De mysteriis*," in: Michael Erler and Martin Andreas Stadler (eds.), *Platonismus und spätägyptische Religion: Plutarch und die Ägyptenrezeption in der römischen Kaiserzeit*, De Gruyter: Berlin/Boston 2017, 149–174.
"Der *Asclepius* im Kontext der apokalyptischen Literatur," in: Gall, *Göttliche Weisheit*, 265–282.
Quispel, Gilles, "The *Asclepius*: From the Hermetic Lodge in Alexandria to the Greek Eucharist and the Roman Mass," in: van den Broek and Hanegraaff, *Gnosis and Hermeticism*, 69–77.

"Hermes Trismegistus and the Origins of Gnosticism," in: van den Broek and van Heertum, *From Poimandres to Jacob Böhme*, 145–165.
"Reincarnation and Magic in the *Asclepius*," in: van den Broek and van Heertum, *From Poimandres to Jacob Böhme*, 167–231.
Quispel, Gilles (ed.), *Gnosis: De derde component van de Europese cultuurtraditie*, Hes: Utrecht 1988.
Quispel, Gilles (transl. & comm.), *Asclepius: De volkomen openbaring van Hermes Trismegistus*, In de Pelikaan: Amsterdam 1996.
Rabbow, Paul, *Seelenführung: Methodik der Exerzitien in der Antike*, Kösel Verlag: Munich 1954.
Raffel, Burton, "The Forked Tongue: On the Translation Process," *Delos: A Journal On & Of Translation* 5 (1970), 49–61, 121–134.
Razavi, Mehdi Amin, *Suhrawardi and the School of Illumination*, Curzon: Surrey 1997.
Rea, John, "A New Version of P. Yale Inv. 299," *Zeitschrift für Papyrologie und Epigraphik* 27 (1977), 151–156.
Rees, D.A., "Aristotle's Treatment of *Phantasia*," *The Society for Ancient Greek Philosophy Newsletter* (1962), 1–16.
Reitzenstein, Richard, *Poimandres: Studien zur griechisch-ägyptischen und frühchristlichen Literatur*, B.G. Teubner: Leipzig 1904.
"Zum *Asclepius* des Pseudo-Apuleius," *Archiv für Religionswissenschaft* 7 (1904), 393–411.
"Zur Geschichte der Alchemie und des Mystizismus," *Nachrichten der königliche Gesellschaft der Wissenschaften zu Göttingen, Phil.-Hist. Klasse* 2 (1919), 1–37.
Review of Scott, *Hermetica* vol. 1, *Gnomon* 1:5 (1925), 249–253.
Review of Scott, *Hermetica* vol. 2, *Gnomon* 3:5 (1927), 266–283.
Die hellenistischen Mysterienreligionen nach ihren Grundgedanken und Wirkungen, Wissenschaftliche Buchgesellschaft: Darmstadt 1956.
Renard, Jean-Bruno, "Le mouvement *Planète*: Un épisode important de l'histoire culturelle française," *Politica Hermetica* 10 (1996), 152–167.
Reynolds, L.D. and N.G. Wilson, *Scribes and Scholars: A Guide to the Transmission of Greek and Latin Literature*, Oxford University Press 2013.
Ricoeur, Paul, *De l'interprétation: Essai sur Freud*, Éditions du Seuil: Paris 1965.
Freud and Philosophy: An Essay on Interpretation, Yale University Press: New Haven/London 1970.
Riess, Ernestus, *Nechepsonis et Petosiridis fragmenta magica* (Bonn 1890), repr. *Philologus*, Suppl. VI:1 (1891-1893), 325–394.
Review of Scott, *Hermetica* vols. 1-2, *The American Journal of Philology* 47:2 (1926), 191–197.
Review of Scott, *Hermetica* vol. 3, *The American Journal of Philology* 48:2 (1927), 191–195.
Riggs, Christina (ed.), *The Oxford Handbook of Roman Egypt*, Oxford University Press 2012.
Rinella, Michael A., *Pharmakon: Plato, Drug Culture, and Identity in Ancient Athens*, Lexington: Plymouth 2012.

Ritner, Robert K., *The Mechanics of Ancient Egyptian Magical Practice*, The Oriental Institute of the University of Chicago: Chicago, Ill. 1993.
"Egyptian Magical Practice under the Roman Empire: The Demotic Spells and their Religious Context," in: Wolfgang Haase (ed.), *Aufstieg und Niedergang der Römischen Welt* II, Bd. 18: Religion, 5. Teilband, Walter de Gruyter: Berlin/New York 1995, 3333–3379.
"Egypt under Roman Rule: The Legacy of Ancient Egypt," in: Carl F. Petry (ed.), *The Cambridge History of Egypt*, vol. 1: *Islamic Egypt, 640-1517*, Cambridge University Press 1998, 1–33.
Roberts, Alexander, James Donaldson and Arthur Cleveland Coxe (eds.), *The Ante-Nicene Fathers*, vol. 5: *Fathers of the Third Century*, Cosimo: New York 2007.
Robertson, David G., "A Gnostic History of Religions," *Method & Theory in the Study of Religion* 32:1 (2020), 75–88.
Robins, Gay, "Cult Statues in Ancient Egypt," in: Neal H. Wallis (ed.), *Cult Image and Divine Representation in the Ancient Near East*, American Schools of Oriental Research: Boston 2005, 1–12.
Robinson, James M. (ed.), *The Nag Hammadi Library in English*, E.J. Brill: Leiden/New York/København/Köln 1988 [Rob].
Rorty, Amélie Oksenberg and Martha C. Nussbaum (eds.), *Essays on Aristotle's De Anima*, Oxford University Press 1995.
Rose, H.J., "Thrice-Great Hermes," *The Classical Review* 39: 5–6 (1925), 133–135.
"Scott on the Hermetica," *The Classical Review* 40:6 (1926), 204–205.
"ΣΥΝ ΔΕ ΔΥ' ΕΡΧΟΜΕΝΩ...," *The Classical Review* 50:6 (1936), 222–223.
Rosen, Stanley, "Is Metaphysics Possible?," *Review of Metaphysics* 45:2 (1991), 235–257.
Rosenthal, F., "Sayings of the Ancients from Ibn Durayd's *Kitâb al-Majtanâ*," *Orientaliana* 27 (1958), 29–54, 150–183.
"Al-Mubashshir ibn Fâtik: Prolegomena to an Abortive Edition," *Oriens* 13/14 (1960/1961), 132–158.
Roszak, Theodore, *The Cult of Information: A Neo-Luddite Treatise on High-Tech, Artificial Intelligence, and the True Art of Thinking*, University of California Press 1994.
Rouget, Gilbert, *Music and Trance: A Theory of the Relations between Music and Possession*, The University of Chicago Press: Chicago/London 1985.
Rowland, Christopher, *The Open Heaven: A Study of Apocalyptic in Judaism and Early Christianity*, SPCK: London 1982.
Ruelle, Charles-Émile, "Le chant des sept voyelles grecques, d'après Démétrius & le Papyrus de Leyde," *Revue des études grecques* 2:5 (1889), 38–44.
"Le chant gnostico-magique des sept voyelles grecques," in: Combarieu, *Congrès International*, 15–27.
Runia, D.T., "Logos," in: van der Toorn, Becking and van der Horst, *Dictionary of Deities and Demons*, 983–994.
Ryan, Mark B., *A Different Dimension: Reflections on the History of Transpersonal Thought*, Westphalia Press: Washington DC 2018.
Ryholt, Kim, "New Light on the Legendary King Nechepsos of Egypt," *The Journal of Egyptian Archaeology* 97 (2011), 61–72.

Sacks, Oliver, *Hallucinations*, Picador: London 2012.
Sadoski, Mark and Allan Paivio, *Imagery and Text: A Dual Coding Theory of Reading and Writing*, Lawrence Erlbaum Associates Publishers: Mahwah NJ/London 2001.
Saffrey, Henri Dominique, "Le Père André-Jean Festugière, O.P. (1898–1982): Portrait," in: E. Lucchesi and H.D. Saffrey (eds.), *Mémorial André-Jean Festugière: Antiquité Païenne et Chrétienne. Vingt-cinq études*, Patrick Cramer: Genève 1984, vii–xv.
Safranski, Rüdiger, *Ein Meister aus Deutschland: Heidegger und seine Zeit*, Fischer: Frankfurt a.M. 1997.
Salaman, Clement, Dorine van Oyen and William D. Wharton (eds.), *The Way of Hermes: The* Corpus Hermeticum / *The* Definitions of Hermes Trismegistus to Asclepius, Duckworth: London 1999 [WHCH].
Salaman, Clement, Asclepius: *The Perfect Discourse of Hermes Trismegistus*, Duckworth: London 2007 [SA].
Sallis, John, *Being and Logos: Reading the Platonic Dialogues*, Indiana University Press: Bloomington/Indianapolis 1996.
Chorology: On Beginning in Plato's Timaeus, Indiana University Press: Bloomington/Indianapolis 1999.
Sándor, András, "Poeticity," *Poetics* 18 (1989), 299–316.
Sarbin, Theodore R. and Joseph B. Juhasz, "The Historical Background of the Concept of Hallucination," *Journal of the History of the Behavioral Sciences* 3:4 (1967), 339–358.
Sauneron, Serge, *The Priests of Ancient Egypt*, Grove Press/Evergreen Books: New York/London 1960.
Saussure, Ferdinand de, *Premier cours de linguistique générale (1907) d'après les cahiers d'Albert Riedlinger / Saussure's First Course of Lectures on General Linguistics (1907) from the Notebooks of Albert Riedlinger*, Pergamon: Oxford/New York/Seoul/Tokyo 1996.
Scarborough, John, "The Pharmacology of Sacred Plants, Herbs, and Roots," in: Christopher A. Faraone and Dirk Obbink (eds.), *Magika Hiera: Ancient Greek Magic and Religion*, Oxford University Press: New York/Oxford 1991, 138–174.
Schenke, Hans-Martin, Hans-Gebhard Bethge and Ursula Ulrike Kaiser, *Nag Hammadi Deutsch*, vol. 2: *NHC V,2-XIII,1, BG 1 und 4*, Walter de Gruyter: Berlin/New York 2003 [NHD].
Schmidt, Leigh Eric, "The Making of Modern 'Mysticism'," *Journal of the American Academy of Religion* 71:2 (2003), 273–302.
Restless Souls: The Making of American Spirituality, 2nd ed., University of California Press: Berkeley/Los Angeles/London 2012.
Schofield, Malcolm, "Aristotle on the Imagination," in: Rorty and Nussbaum, *Essays on Aristotle's De Anima*, 250–279.
Schulte-Sasse, Jochen, "Einbildungskraft / Imagination," in: Karlheinz Barck, Martin Fontius, Dieter Schlenstedt, Burkhart Steinwachs and Friedrich Wolfzettel (eds.), *Ästhetische Grundbegriffe: Studienausgabe*, vol. 2, J.B. Metzler: Stuttgart/Weimar 2010, 88–120.

Scott, Walter, *Hermetica: The Ancient Greek and Latin Writings which contain Religious or Philosophic Teachings ascribed to Hermes Trismegistus*, 4 vols. (orig. 1924, 1925, 1926, 1936), repr. Shambhala: Boston 1985/1993 [Scott I, Scott II, Scott III, Scott IV].

Scott-Baumann, Alison, *Ricoeur and the Hermeneutics of Suspicion*, Continuum: New York 2009.

Sedley, David, "Thrice-greatest Hermes," *The Times Literary Supplement*, 31 December 1993, 8.

Sezgin, Fuat, *Geschichte des arabischen Schrifttums*, vol. 1, E.J. Brill: Leiden 1967. *Geschichte des arabischen Schrifttums*, vol. 4, E.J. Brill: Leiden 1971.

Shannon, Claude E., "A Mathematical Theory of Communication," *The Bell System Technical Journal* 27 (1948), 378–423, 623–656.

Shanon, Benny, *The Antipodes of the Mind: Charting the Phenomenology of the Ayahuasca Experience*, Oxford University Press 2002.

Shantz, Colleen, *Paul in Ecstasy: The Neurobiology of the Apostle's Life and Thought*, Cambridge University Press 2009.

Shaw, Gregory, "Theurgy: Rituals of Unification in the Neoplatonism of Iamblichus," *Traditio* 41 (1985), 1–28.

"A Pythagorean Approach to Theurgy," *Incognita* 2 (1991), 48–78.

Theurgy and the Soul: The Neoplatonism of Iamblichus, The Pennsylvania State University Press: University Park 1995.

Review of Emma C. Clarke, *Iamblichus' De Mysteriis*, *Ancient Philosophy* 23:2 (2009), 488–494.

"The *Chôra* of the *Timaeus* and Iamblichean Theurgy," *Horizons* 3:2 (2012), 103–129.

"Theurgy and the Platonist's Luminous Body," in: April D. DeConick, Gregory Shaw and John D. Turner (eds.), *Practicing Gnosis: Ritual, Magic, Theurgy and Liturgy in Nag Hammadi, Manichaean and Other Ancient Literature. Essays in Honor of Birger A. Pearson*, Brill: Leiden/Boston 2013, 537–557.

"Taking the Shape of the Gods: A Theurgic Reading of Hermetic Rebirth," *Aries* 15 (2015), 136–169.

Sherwood Taylor, F., "The Visions of Zosimos," *Ambix* 1:1 (1937), 88–92.

Shields, Christopher, *Aristotle: De Anima* (transl., introd., comm.), Clarendon Press: Oxford 2016.

Sicherl, Martin, *Die Handschriften, Ausgaben und Übersetzungen von Iamblichos De Mysteriis: Eine kritisch-historische Studie*, Akademie-Verlag: Berlin 1957.

Simms, Karl, *Hans-Georg Gadamer*, Routledge: London/New York 2015.

Simon, Josef, "Good Will to Understand and the Will to Power: Remarks on an 'Improbable Debate'," in: Michelfelder and Palmer, *Dialogue and Deconstruction*, 162–175.

Simplicius, *In libros Aristotelis De Anima commentaria* (Michael Hayduck, ed.), G. Reimer: Berlin 1882.

Smith, Andrew, *Porphyry's Place in the Neoplatonic Tradition: A Study in Post-Plotinian Neoplatonism*, Martinus Nijhoff: The Hague 1974.

Smith, Jonathan Z., *Map is not Territory: Studies in the History of Religions*, The University of Chicago Press: Chicago/London 1978, 172–189.

"Towards Interpreting Demonic Powers in Hellenistic and Roman Antiquity," in: Wolfgang Haase (ed.), *Aufstieg und Niedergang der römischen Welt: Religion (Heidentum, Römische Religion, Allgemeines)*, vol. 16.1, De Gruyter: Berlin/Boston 1978, 425–439.
"The Temple and the Magician," in: *Map is not Territory*, 172–189.
"In Comparison a Magic Dwells," in: *Imagining Religion: From Babylon to Jonestown*, The University of Chicago Press: Chicago & London 1982, 19–35.
To Take Place: Toward Theory in Ritual, The University of Chicago Press: Chicago & London 1987.
Drudgery Divine: On the Comparison of Early Christianities and the Religions of Late Antiquity, The University of Chicago Press 1990.
"Here, There, and Anywhere," in: Noegel, Walker and Wheeler, *Prayer, Magic, and the Stars*, 21–36; repr. in Smith, *Relating Religion: Essays in the Study of Religion*, The University of Chicago Press 2004, 323–339.
Song, Euree, "Ashamed of Being in the Body? Plotinus versus Porphyry," in: Filip Karfík and Euree Song (eds.), *Plato Revived: Essays on Ancient Platonism in Honour of Dominic J. O'Meara*, De Gruyter: Berlin/New York 2013, 96–116.
Sørensen, Jørgen Podemann, "cooyn̄: The Late Egyptian Background of *Gnosis*," in: Giversen, Petersen and Sørensen, *Nag Hammadi Texts*, 137–145.
Spengler, Oswald, *Der Untergang des Abendlandes: Umrisse einer Morphologie der Weltgeschichte* (1923), Marix Verlag: Wiesbaden 2007.
Stadter, Philip A., "General Introduction," in: Plutarch, *Greek Lives*, Oxford University Press 1998, viii–xxvi; *Roman Lives*, Oxford University Press 1999, ix–xxviii.
Stang, Charles M., *Our Divine Double*, Harvard University Press: Cambridge Mass./London 2016.
Stead, G. Christopher, "Logos," in: *Theologische Realenzyklopädie*, vol. 21, Walter de Gruyter: Berlin/New York 1991, 432–444.
Steel, Carlos G., *The Changing Self: A Study on the soul in Later Neoplatonism. Iamblichus, Damascius and Priscianus*, Paleis der Academien: Brussels 1978.
Steiner, George, *After Babel: Aspects of Language and Translation* (orig. 1975), Oxford University Press 1998.
Sternberg-al Hotabi, Heike, "Ägyptische Religion und Hermetismus am Beispiel des *Asclepius*," in: Gall, *Göttliche Weisheit*, 223–263.
Stolzenberg, Daniel, "Unpropitious Tinctures: Alchemy, Astrology & Gnosis according to Zosimos of Panopolis," *Archives internationales d'histoire des sciences* 49: 142 (1999), 3–31.
Stone, Michael E., "A Reconsideration of Apocalyptic Visions," *Harvard Theological Review* 96:2 (2003), 167–180.
Ancient Judaism: New Visions and Views, William B. Eerdmans: Grand Rapids, Mich./Cambridge 2011.
Streib, Heinz and Raph W. Hood, "'Spirituality' as Privatized Experience-Oriented Religion: Empirical and Conceptual Perspectives," *Implicit Religion* 14:4 (2011), 433–453.
Streib, Heinz and Ralph W. Hood (eds.), *Semantics and Psychology of Spirituality: A Cross-Cultural Analysis*, Springer: Berlin/Heidelberg 2016.

Struck, Peter R., *Birth of the Symbol: Ancient Readers at the Limits of their Texts*, Princeton University Press 2004.
Stuckrad, Kocku von, *Das Ringen um die Astrologie: Jüdische und christliche Beiträge zum antiken Zeitverständnis*, De Gruyter: Berlin/New York 2000.
Swartz, Chantélle and Paul Cilliers, "Dialogue Disrupted: Derrida, Gadamer and the Ethics of Discussion," *South African Journal of Philosophy* 22:1 (2003), 1–18.
Tacoma, Laurens E., "Settlement and Population," in: Riggs, *Oxford Handbook of Roman Egypt*, 122–135.
Tallet, Gaëlle, "Oracles," in: Riggs, *Oxford Handbook of Roman Egypt*, 398–418.
Tanaseanu-Döbler, Ilinca, *Theurgy in Late Antiquity: The Invention of a Ritual Tradition*, Vandenhoeck & Ruprecht: Göttingen 2013.
Tardieu, Michel, *Écrits gnostiques: Codex de Berlin*, Les éditions du Cerf: Paris 1984.
Tart, Charles T., "States of Consciousness and State-Specific Sciences," *Science* 176: 4040 (1972), 1203–1210.
— "Investigating Altered States of Consciousness on their Own Terms: A Proposal for the Creation of State-Specific Sciences," *Ciência e Cultura* 50:2/3 (1998), 103–116.
— *States of Consciousness*, Authors Guild Backinprint: Lincoln 2000.
— "Preface: Extending our Knowledge of Consciousness," in: Etzel Cardeña and Michael Winkelman (eds.), *Altering Consciousness: Multidisciplinary Perspectives*, vol. 1, Praeger: Santa Barbara 2011, ix–xx.
Tirian, Abraham, "The Hellenizing School: Its Time, Place, and Scope of Activities Reconsidered," in: Nina G. Garsoïan, Thomas F. Mathews and Robert W. Thomson (eds.), *East of Byzantium: Syria and Armenia in the Formative Period*, Dumbarton Oaks Center for Byzantine Studies/Trustees for Harvard University: Washington 1982, 175–186.
Toorn, Karel van der, Bob Becking and Pieter W. van der Horst (eds.), *Dictionary of Deities and Demons in the Bible (DDD)*, Brill: Leiden/New York/Köln 1995.
Touliatos, Diane, "Nonsense Syllables in the Music of the Ancient Greek and Byzantine Traditions," *The Journal of Musicology* 7:2 (1989), 231–243.
Traherne, Thomas, *Selected Poems and Prose* (Alan Bradford, ed.), Penguin: Harmondsworth 1991.
Tröger, Karl-Wolfgang, *Mysterienglaube und Gnosis in* Corpus Hermeticum XIII, Akademie-Verlag: Berlin 1971.
— "Die sechste und siebte Schrift aus Nag-Hammadi-Codex VI," *Theologische Literaturzeitung* 98:7 (1973), 495–503 [Tröger].
— "On Investigating the Hermetic Documents contained in Nag Hammadi Codex VI: The Present State of Research," in: R. McL. Wilson (ed.), *Nag Hammadi and Gnosis: Papers read at the First International Congress of Coptology (Cairo, December 1976)*, E.J. Brill: Leiden 1978, 117–121.
Trompf, Garry W. (ed.), *The Gnostic World*, Routledge: London/New York 2019.
Ullmann, Manfred, *Die Natur- und Geheimwissenschaften im Islam*, E.J. Brill: Leiden 1972.

Ustinova, Yulia, *Caves and the Ancient Greek Mind: Descending Underground in the Search for Ultimate Truth*, Oxford University Press 2009.
Divine Mania: Alterations of Consciousness in Ancient Greece, Routledge: London/New York 2017.
Van den Kerchove, Anna, "Redécouverte de fragments hermétiques oubliés: le P.Berol. 17 027," *Archiv für Papyrusforschung* 52 (2006), 162–180.
"La voie d'Hermès, la question des sacrifices et les 'cultes orientaux'," *Meditteranea* 4 (2007), 191–204.
"L'image de Dieu, l'aimant et le fer: La représentation du divin dans le traité hermétique CH IV," *Mythos* 2 (2008), 77–86.
La voie d'Hermès: Pratiques rituelles et traités hermétiques, Brill: Leiden/Boston 2012.
"Poimandrès, figure d'autorité dans la tradition hermétique," *Revue de l'histoire des religions* 231, fasc. 1 (2014), 27–46.
Hermès Trismégiste, Éditions Entrelacs: Paris 2017.
"Visions et légitimation: Voie hermétique de la connaissance et du salut dans *Corpus Hermeticum* I," in: Anna Van den Kerchove and Luciana Gabriela Soares Santoprete (eds), *Gnose et Manichéisme: Entre les Oasis d'Égypte et la Route de la Soie. Hommage à Jean-Daniel Dubois*, Brepols: Turnhout 2017, 793–811
"The Notion of Truth in Some Hermetic Texts and Chaldaean Oracles," *Gnosis: Journal of Gnostic Studies* 3 (2018), 34–53.
Vanderlip, Vera Frederika, *The Four Greek Hymns of Isidorus and the Cult of Isis*, A.M. Hakkert: Toronto 1972.
Vandorpe, Katelijn, "Identity," in: Riggs, *Oxford Handbook of Roman Egypt*, 260–276.
Van Liefferinge, Carine, *La Théurgie: Des Oracles Chaldaïques à Proclus* (Kernos Suppl. 9), Centre International d'Étude de la Religion Grecque Antique: Liège 1999.
Venit, Marjorie S., "Alexandria," in: Riggs, *Oxford Handbook of Roman Egypt*, 103–121.
Venticinque, Philip F., "Family Affairs: Guild Relationships and Family Relationships in Roman Egypt," *Greek, Roman, and Byzantine Studies* 50 (2010), 273–294.
Visconti, A., *Aristosseno di Taranto: Biografia e formazione spirituale*, Centre Jean Bérard: Naples 1999.
Vogel, C.J. de, "The *Sōma-Sēma* Formula: Its Function in Plato and Plotinus compared to Christian Writers," in: H.J. Blumenthal and R.A. Markus (eds.), *Neoplatonism and Early Christian Thought: Essays in Honour of A.H. Armstrong*, Variorum: London 1981, 79–95.
Vos, R.L., "Thoth," in: van der Toorn, Becking and van der Horst, *Dictionary of Deities and Demons*, 1621–1628.
Vugt, Marieke K. van, "Cognitive Benefits of Mindfulness Meditation," in: Kirk Warren Brown, J. David Creswell and Richard M. Ryan (eds.), *Handbook of Mindfulness: Theory, Research, and Practice*, The Guilford Press: New York/London 2015, 190–207.

Waghorne, Joanne Punzo and Norman Cutler (eds.), *Gods of Flesh, Gods of Stone: The Embodiment of Divinity in India*, Columbia University Press: New York 1985.

Walbridge, John, *The Leaven of the Ancients: Suhrawardī and the Heritage of the Greeks*, State University of New York Press: Albany 2000.

The Wisdom of the Mystic East: Suhrawardī and Platonic Orientalism, State University of New York Press: Albany 2001.

"Suhrawardī and Illuminationism," in: Peter Adamson and Richard C. Taylor (eds.), *The Cambridge Companion to Arabic Philosophy*, Cambridge University Press 2005, 201–223.

Walbridge, John and Hossein Ziai (ed. & transl.), *Suhrawardī: The Philosophy of Illumination*, Brigham Young University Press: Provo 1999.

Walbridge, John and Hossein Ziai, "Translators' Introduction," in: Walbridge and Ziai, *Suhrawardī*, xv–xxxvii.

Waldstein, Michael, "Hans Jonas' Construct 'Gnosticism': Analysis and Critique," *Journal of Early Christian Studies* 8:3 (2000), 341–372.

Waltzing, J.-P., *Étude historique sur les corporations professionnelles chez les Romains, depuis les origines jusqu'à la chute de l'Empire d'Occident*, vol. 1, Peeters: Louvain 1895.

Wardman, Alan, *Plutarch's Lives*, Paul Elek: London 1974.

Warnock, Mary, *Imagination*, University of California Press: Berkeley/Los Angeles 1976.

Wasson, R. Gordon, Albert Hofmann and Carl A.P. Ruck, *The Road to Eleusis: Unveiling the Secret of the Mysteries*, Twentieth Anniversary Edition, William Dailey Rare Books Ltd: Los Angeles 1998.

Waszink, J.H., "The Dreaming Kronos in the *Corpus Hermeticum*," in: *Mélanges H. Grégoire*, vol. 2 (Annuaire de l'Institut de philologie et d'histoire orientales et slaves 10), Brussels 1950, 639–651.

Watson, Gerard, *Phantasia in Classical Thought*, Galway University Press: 1988.

Watts, Alan, *The Joyous Cosmology: Adventures in the Chemistry of Consciousness*, Vintage: New York 1965.

Watts, Edward J., *Hypatia: The Life and Legend of an Ancient Philosopher*, Oxford University Press 2017.

Webb, James, *The Occult Underground*, Open Court: La Salle Ill. 1974.

Weber, Max, *Wissenschaft als Beruf 1917/1919, Politik als Beruf 1919* (Studienausgabe der Max Weber-Gesamtausgabe Band 1/17; Wolfgang J. Mommsen and Wolfgang Schluchter, eds.), J.C.B. Mohr (Paul Siebeck): Tübingen 1994.

Wedin, Michael V., *Mind and Imagination in Aristotle*, Yale University Press: New Haven/London 1988.

Wellesz, Egon, "Music in the Treatises of Greek Gnostics and Alchemists," *Ambix* 4:3–4 (1951), 145–158.

Whitehouse, David J.M., "The Hymns of the *Corpus Hermeticum*: Forms with a Diverse Functional History," Ph.D. Dissertation, Harvard University 1985.

Whittaker, John, "Harpocration and Serenus in a Paris Manuscript," *Scriptorium* 33:1 (1979), 59–62.

Wigtil, David N., "Incorrect Apocalyptic: The Hermetic 'Asclepius' as an Improvement on the Greek Original," in: Hildegard Temporini and Wolfgang Haase (eds.), *Aufstieg und Niedergang der Römischen Welt*, vol. 2, Walter de Gruyter: Berlin/New York 1984, 2282-2297.

Wildberg, Christian, "*Corpus Hermeticum*, Tractate III: The Genesis of a Genesis," in: Lance Jenott and Sarit K. Gribetz (eds.), *Jewish and Christian Cosmogony in Late Antiquity*, Mohr Siebeck: Tübingen 2013, 124-149.

"The *General Discourses* of Hermes Trismegistus," in: Christian Brockmann, Daniel Deckers, Lutz Koch and Stefano Valente (eds.), *Handschriften- und Textforschung heute: Zur Überlieferung der griechischen Literatur. Festschrift für Dieter Harlfinger aus Anlass seines 70. Geburtstages*, Dr. Ludwig Reichert Verlag: Wiesbaden 2014, 137-146.

"Astral Discourse in the *Corpus Hermeticum*," in: Alan C. Bowen and Francesca Rochberg (eds.), *Hellenistic Astronomy: The Science in Its Contexts*, Brill: Leiden/Boston 2020, 580-604.

Wilkins, Eliza Gregory, *"Know Thyself" in Greek and Latin Literature*, The University of Chicago Libraries: Chicago 1917.

Williams, Michael Allen, *Rethinking "Gnosticism": An Argument for Dismantling a Dubious Category*, Princeton University Press 1996.

"On Ancient 'Gnosticism' as a Problematic Category," in: Trompf, *Gnostic World*, 100-117.

Wilson, R.McL. (ed.), *Gnosis: A Selection of Gnostic Texts*, vol. 1, Clarendon Press: Oxford 1972.

Wilson, Robert R., "Prophecy and Ecstasy: A Reexamination," *Journal of Biblical Literature* 98:3 (1979), 321-337.

Windisch, Hans, "Urchristentum und Hermesmystik," *Theologisch Tijdschrift* 52 (1918), 186-214.

Wolfson, Elliot R., *Through a Speculum that Shines: Vision and Imagination in Medieval Jewish Mysticism*, Princeton University Press 1994.

Language, Eros, Being: Kabbalistic Hermeneutics and Poetic Imagination, Fordham University Press: New York 2005.

Wolin, Richard, *Heidegger's Children: Hannah Arendt, Karl Löwith, Hans Jonas, and Herbert Marcuse*, Princeton University Press: Princeton/Oxford 2001.

[Wordsworth, William], *The Collected Poems of William Wordsworth*, Wordsworth Editions: Hertfordshire 1994.

Wright, Wilmer Cave, *Philostratus and Eunapius: The Lives of the Sophists*, William Heinemann/G.P. Putman: London/New York 1922.

Wulff, David M., *Psychology of Religion: Classic & Contemporary*, John Wiley & Sons: New York etc. 1997.

Yates, Frances A., *Giordano Bruno and the Hermetic Tradition*, Routledge and Kegan Paul/The University of Chicago Press: London/Chicago 1964.

Yébenes, Sabino Perea, "El *kyphi*, un perfume ritual, mágico y medicinal en el universo egipcio grecorromano," *Espacio, Tiempo y Forma*, Serie II, *Historia Antigua* 24 (2011), 349-362.

Younger, D., *The Magnetic and Botanic Family Physician, and Domestic Practice of Natural Medicine, with Illustrations showing Various Phases of Mesmeric Treatment*, E.W. Allen: London n.d.

Yurdin, Joel, "Aristotelian Imagination and the Explanation of Behavior," in: Gerd van Riel and Pierre Destrée (eds.), *Ancient Perspectives on Aristotle's De Anima*, Leuven University Press 2009, 71–87.

Zago, Michela, "Le pneuma éloquent: Un parallèle entre le *Papyrus Mimaut* et NHC VI,6," in: Mohammad Ali Amir-Moezzi, Jean-Daniel Dubois, Christelle Jullien and Florence Jullien (eds.), *Pensée grecque et sagesse d'orient: Hommage à Michel Tardieu*, Brepols: Turnhout 2009, 715–734.

Zandee, Jan, "Het Hermetisme en het Oude Egypte," in: Gilles Quispel (ed.), *De Hermetische Gnosis in de loop der eeuwen*, Tirion: Baarn 1992, 96–174.

Zenk, Benjamin John, "*Verständigung*: Gadamer on Understanding as Agreement," in: Andrzej Wiercinski (ed.), *Hermeneutics – Ethics – Education*, Lit Verlag: Vienna 2015, 29–38.

Zielinski, Tadeusz, "Hermes und die Hermetik I/II," *Archiv für Religionswissenschaft* 8 (1905), 321–372 & 9 (1906), 25–60.

Zosimos of Panopolis, *Mémoires authentiques* (Les Alchimistes Grecs IV.1; Michèle Mertens, ed. & transl.), Les Belles Lettres: Paris 1995 [ZMA].

Zuntz, G., "On the Hymns in *Corpus Hermeticum* XIII," *Hermes* (1955), 69–92. "Notes on the *Corpus Hermeticum*," *The Harvard Theological Review* 49:1 (1956), 73–78.

Index of Texts

Hermetica

Asclepius
1	57, 229, 280
3	62, 176, 325
5	58, 195
5–6	108
6	59, 176, 195
7	61, 157, 206
8	54, 59, 195
9	195
9–11	54
10	54, 58
11	194–195
12	73, 182, 195, 276
13	194–195
14	73, 238, 280
16	238
17	218
18	60–61
19	58, 325
20	55–56, 269
20–21	56, 169
21	57, 177, 238
21–29	51
22	58, 61, 64, 195
22–23	59
23	58, 62, 65, 67, 195
23–24	323, 356
24	53, 62, 195, 224
24–25	74, 274, 331
25	334
26	76, 195
27	58, 238, 272
28	276
29	195, 271
31	55, 269, 278–279
32	60–61, 262
34	194
37	195
37–38	69, 72, 323, 331, 356
41	51, 204, 232–235, 238
42	263

Corpus Hermeticum
CH I	8–9, 21, 47, 98, 138, 140, 143, 156, 172, 209, 212, 227–228, 231, 235, 242, 251, 277, 279–280, 283, 301, 305
1	27, 156
1–3	160
2	163, 166
3	163, 175
4	27, 281
4–5	164
4–11	160
4–26	160
5	169, 323
6	125, 127, 164, 166, 201, 203
6–7	319
7	232, 298
8	167–169, 194, 323
8–26	162, 167
9	280
10	169
11	167, 169

12	194, 280	9	157
12–23	160	9–11	206
13–14	174	10	209
14	171, 173, 175, 194, 261, 323	10–11	238
15	170–171, 175	11	157, 200, 219, 241, 250
16	175, 195, 257	CH V	142, 144, 209, 231
17	281	1	215, 231, 238
18	124, 176–177, 180, 323	2	157, 200
19	151, 157, 177, 274, 305	6	194
20	178, 272	7	194
21	179, 280	8	55
22	179–180, 195, 197, 206, 272, 277, 305	10	55, 232
		10–11	186, 231, 233–234, 261
22–23	151, 157, 196	11	232, 278
23	181, 276	CH VI	142, 201, 209
24	272–273	1	194
24–26	160, 277	1–2	238
25	171, 277	2	149
26	184, 281	2–4	151
27	151, 185, 195	3	149
27–28	185	3–5	280
27–29	160	4	154, 157, 206
28	185	4–5	199
28–29	274	5	195
29	186	6	149, 151, 195
29–30	325	CH VII	143, 209
30	157, 184, 305, 326	1	153, 185
30–31	160	1–2	151, 200
31	55, 186, 290	1–3	157
32	186, 280	2	150, 185, 274
CH II	128, 130, 141, 144	2–3	152, 244
13	278	3	194–195
14–16	280	CH VIII	142, 209
16	232	1	271–272
17	177, 276	2	58, 238
CH III	130, 140, 209, 229	3–4	272
1	164	4	176
2	164	5	58
3	169	CH IX	142, 201, 203, 209, 241
CH IV	98, 128, 130, 142, 176, 179, 209	1–2	201, 251
		3–4	151
1	204, 279	4	194–195, 224, 226
2	195	5	196
2–4	204	8	201
3	150, 180, 276	9	224
4	61, 149–150, 197, 208	10	195, 204, 234, 241, 278, 306, 320, 324
4–5	91		
5	151, 195, 279–280	CH X	128, 130, 142–143, 201, 209, 212, 250, 276
6	151		
7	91, 151, 195	1	229
8	197, 276, 279	1–2	280
8–9	279, 280	3	207, 238

3–4	207	2	149–150, 197
4	197, 208	2–4	151
4–5	157	3	150, 152, 157, 196
4–6	194	5–9	197
5	200, 208	7	258
5–6	208	8	267, 325
6	250, 280	11	277
7	229, 275	12	204
7–8	276	13	204
8	152, 179	14	204
8–9	151	15	271
9	157, 195, 226	16	176
9–10	201	16–18	272
10	194, 200–201	18	274
12	149	21	194, 280
13	204, 273	CH XIII	10, 19, 21, 47, 98, 138, 143, 209, 215, 225, 227–228, 231, 234–236, 250, 255, 280, 283–287, 305, 324, 333
14	58, 279		
15	149, 194, 198, 274		
16	273–274, 281		
17	273, 285		
18	196, 273	1	157, 229, 236–237, 239
19	195, 275	1–2	242
19–22	276	2	239, 242, 246, 251, 285
20	276	3	157, 240–241, 250
20–21	151, 196	4	237, 241–242, 250
21	196–197	5	242–243
22	58, 197	6	243
23	197	7	95, 157, 244–245
24	197, 274	8	204, 250
25	27, 195	8–9	247
CH XI	10, 59, 143, 209, 212, 214–215, 217–219, 231, 252–253, 255	8–10	323
		9	280
		10	252
1	201	11	157, 252, 256
2	213, 272	12	250, 253, 280–281
3	194, 213	13	252, 263, 283
5	279	14	157, 256, 272, 274
6	157, 214	15	156, 253, 257
6–7	194	16	232, 258
7–8	214	17	157, 259–260
11	214, 279	18	204, 261, 280
12	275	19–20	261
13	194–195, 214	21	204, 238, 262, 305, 326
14	177, 238, 271	22	263, 325
14–15	176, 214, 272	CH XIV	141, 209
15	195	4	195, 198, 280
17	195, 218, 238	8	224
18	214, 231, 253	9	280
18–20	216	CH XV	123
20	214, 231, 256	CH XVI	117, 142, 209, 223
21	194, 219	2	116, 185, 207, 290, 324
CH XII	142, 209	7	238

9	272	6	59
11	196, 275, 277	HD X	
13–14	223, 244	1	56, 206
14–15	90	3	197
15	223	4	280
16	204, 305	5	281
CH XVII	66, 142	6	150, 272
CH XVIII	140		

Hermetic Fragments (HT IV)

Hermetic Definitions

HD I		HF 3a	55
1	58, 278	HF 25	329
2	278	HF 29	268
4	55, 273	HF 31	268
5	272	HF 32a–b	268

Hermetica Oxoniensa

HD II		HO III	
1	273	1–3	151
3	272	HO IV	
6	214, 273	1	151
HD III		2–4	184
1	232	HO V	
4	280	1–9	198
HD IV		2–4	56
1	197		

Hermetica Vindobonensia

HD V		HV 1 (A)	59
1	204, 216	HV 2 (B)	55
2	301, 325, 327		
3	301		

Nag Hammadi Hermetica

HD VI		NH VI[6]	21, 47, 138, 143, 226,
1	59, 217, 273–274		228, 231, 257, 280,
2	274		282–307, 309–310
3	256, 272	52–54	287
HD VII		52,9–13	284
1	256	52,10	284
1–2	59	52,14–20	285
1–3	256	52,26–27	286
2	256	53,9	286
3	256, 274	53,13	286
4	197, 223	53,14–20	286
5	58, 152	53,27–31	287, 296
HD VIII		53,31	301
3	63, 271	55,6–7	288, 325
4	197	55,11–13	288
5	200	55,15–16	288
6	59, 148, 217, 276	55,19–22	288, 296, 325
7	244, 272	55,23–57,25	229
HD IX		55,24–56,2	289
1	278	55,27	325
2	157, 166, 217	55,30	289
3	195, 226	56,10–22	290
4	149, 180		
5	152, 197, 273–274		

Index of Texts

56,15	295	NH VI⁷	51, 282
56,22–57,25	295	64,8	204
57,8	326	64,9–14	234
57,8–9	296	64,18–19	234
57,11–18	296	64,22–27	235, 285
57,13	295	65,3–7	235
57,18–25	297	NH VI 65, 8–14	282
57,26	297	NH VI⁸	51, 282
57,28–30	298, 323	65	56–57, 169
57,31	298	66	61
57,33–58,4	298	68	58, 64
58,1–11	298	69	62, 65
58,4	298, 302	69,8–9	195
58,5–6	299	69,3	195
58,6–7	300	70–73	74, 331
58,7–14	300	73,5–12	96
58,13–14	323	73,16–18	334
58,14–15	301	74	76
58,15	298, 300	76,10–19	272
58,16–17	301	76,22–77,37	276
58,17–22	301		
58, 21	298	*Stobaei Hermetica*	
58,22–23	302	SH I	329
58,23–24	302	1	55, 206, 329, 333
58,25–27	302	2	55, 199
58,27	298	SH I-XXII	143
58,28–59,1	302	SH IIA	201, 281
59,1–9	303	3–12	206
59,11–14	303	3–4	218
59,15–19	303	13	252
59,19–22	304	14–15	281
59,25–60,1	304	16	272
60,12–13	304	17	206
60,14–17	326	18	278
60,16–17	305	SH IIB	275
60,17–61,2	305	2	257
60–63	287	3	252
61,2	306	4	257
61,3	305–306	6–7	182
61,6	306	7	305
61,9	306	SH III	182
61,10–15	306	1	229
61,15–17	307	3	272
61,18–21	308	6	272
61,18–63,32	342	7	149, 223
61,26–62,22	309	SH IV	223
62,3–4	309	6–16	223
62,17–20	309	8	90, 223
62,23–63,14	309	10–11	272
63,1–4	229	16	223
63,15–32	309	21–22	149
63,16–31	309	SH V	223

Index of Texts

SH VI
  7–11   223
  10   223
  18   55, 199, 227, 250
SH VII
  1–2   276
  3   223
SH VIII   222
SH X   217
SH XI 2
  1   55
  4–5   272
  5   149
  6   58
  9   271
  10   271
  11   55
  13   149
  15   149
  16   206
  17   274
  18   199
  18–20   149
  26   151
  29   149
  31–35   272
  35   272
  37   273
  48   149
SH XII   56
SH XII–XIV   222
SH XVII
  2   182
  4–6   203
SH XVIII   197
SH XIX
  5–6   273
SH XX
  4   197
SH XXI   279
SH XXIII   141
  39–42   276
SH XXIII–XXVII   49, 141, 195
SH XXIV
  13   54
  15   54
SH XXV
  8   149–150
SH XXV–XXVI   276
SH XXVI   275
  13   273
SH XXVIII–XXIX   143

SH XXIX   222

"Magical" Papyri

Demotic Papyri
PDM XIV
  295–308   38
  805–840   38
  875–885   38
  93–114   38

Greek Papyri
PGM I
  1–42   39
  232–247   39
PGM II
  1–64   39
PGM III   234
  165–186   39
  588   296
  591–610   50–51, 234
  596–598   234
  599–600   234
  601–605   235
PGM IV
  475–829   36
  479–491   38
  512   38
  539   36, 40
  558–560   41
  574   41
  735–736   36
  752–772   38
  773–775   39
  791–792   39
  850–929   39
  930–1114   39
  3209–3254   39
PGM V
  304–369   39
PGM VII
  467–477   39
  505–528   39
PGM VIII
  64–110   39
PGM XII   31
  179–181   39
  270–350   67
  401–444   39
PGM XIII
  124–136   39
  343   295

Index of Texts

628–633	295		245a	191
824–841	233		247c-d	190
PGM XIV	31		248e	66
PGM XIXb			249d	15, 190
1–3	39		265b	66
			274e	312, 351

Frequently Quoted Philosophers

			274e–275b	311, 342
			275a	327
Iamblichus, *Response to Porphyry*			275a-b	328
			275d–276a	115
I 1	103, 117		276a	313

Plato, *Republic*

I 1–2	117		398ff	188
I 12	109, 111		509b	316
I 14	109		509d–511e	367
I 3	112, 303, 319, 327		507d–508d	193
I 4	110		509d–511e	313
I 5	107			

Plato, *Symposium*

I 6	108		176e	188
I 8	108–109, 216		201–212	189
I 9	67, 108, 110		201c–212b	187
II 10	110		206b	192
II 11	109		206c	192
II 8	110		206c-d	107
III 5	110		206c-e	107
III 6	110		206d	107
III 9	110		206e	106
III 12	108		209d	192
III 14	34–35, 43, 72, 110		210a-d	192
III 17–19	109		210d	192, 218
III 20	107		210d–211c	107
IV 1	109		210e	190
V 16	111		210e–211b	15
V 23	68–69		211a-b	190
V 25	109		211d–212a	193
V 26	111		296e	190

Plato, *Theaetus*

VII	118		150b-e	324
VII 4	114–115		155d	191, 194

Plato, *Timaeus*

VII 5	116		22b	117
VIII 1	280		27d5–28a4	210
VIII 4	100, 117		43a–44b	107
VIII 4–5	100		52a-b	211
X 1	109		71e–72b	188

Plotinus, *Enneads*

X 4	109		III.6.7	212
X 6	109		IV.3.11	66
X 7	100		IV.8.1	105

Plato, *Apology*

30a-b	157		IV.8.4	104
21b-e	15		IV.8.8	104

Plato, *Phaedrus*

230d-e	2		VI.9.11	106
244–245c	242			

Index of Persons

Aall, Anathon, 321–322
Adler, William, 89
Adorno, Theodor Wiesengrund, 353
Akhmetova, Lilia A., 38
Alexander the Great, 26, 28, 75
Alföldy, Géza, 48
Allegro, John M., 44
Alpers, Svetlana, 70
Alypius, 102
Ambrosios, 25
Amelius, 118
Amenemhet III, 24, 156, 265–266
Anatolios, 25
Anatolius, 101–102
André, Marie-Sophie, 81
Anebo, 103, 117
Apuleius, 51–52
Aquili, Eugene d', 157
Aristotle, 66, 90, 168, 204–205, 207, 211, 292, 335–336, 338, 359, 364–365
Arlandson, James Malcolm, 78
Armstrong, A. Hilary, 101, 105
Arnim, Ioannes ab, 147
Arnobius, 92, 329
Artelt, Walter, 312
Asad, Talil, 227
Ashton, E.B., 20
Asprem, Egil, 4
Assmann, Jan, 29, 53, 63–65, 70, 72–73, 75, 127, 134, 200, 266, 274, 311
al-Aswad, Ṣubayḥ, 340
Athanassiadi, Polymnia, 67, 97, 101–102, 106, 114, 117–118

Aufrère, Sydney H., 38, 71
Augustine, Aurelius, 51, 68, 100, 127, 330–332
Augustus, 28–29
Aurelian, 48
Austin, J.L., 248
Avicenna. See Ibn Sīnā
Axiothea, 188

Bagnall, Roger S., 25, 29
Baier, Karl, 285
Bailey, Donald M., 25
al-Bakrī, Abū 'Ubayd, 339–340
Banner, Nicholas, xi, 60, 162–163, 270, 318, 321
Bardenhewer, Otto, 334
Baring, Edward, 346
Barthes, Roland, 346
Barušs, Imants, 3
Basṭāmī, 338
Basten, Rosalie, x–xi
Baumann, Gerd, 134
Beaufils, Christophe, 81
Becchi, Francesco, 147
Beinlich-Seeber, Christine, 264
Bell, Catherine, 227
Bentall, Richard P., 158
Bergemann, Lutz, 37
Bergier, Jacques, 356
Bernstein, Richard J., 343, 346
Berthelot, Marcellin, 78, 83, 87
Bertol, Elisabetta, 38
Betz, Hans Dieter, 36, 38–42, 141, 295

Index of Persons

Bianchi, M., 205
Bickerman, Elias J., 16, 126
Bladel, Kevin van, 9, 233, 267, 328, 332–334, 337, 341
Blavatsky, Helena P., 254
Bod, Rens, 188
Boeder, Heribert, 322
Bogdan, Henrik, 227
Böhme, Gernot, 212
Böhme, Hartmut, 212
Bonner, Campbell, 290
Borghesi, Francesco, 59
Bos, A.P., 208
Bottici, Chiara, 205, 364–367
Botz-Bornstein, Thorsten, 344
Boudewijnse, Barbara, 227
Bouillet, M.–N., 104
Bousset, Wilhelm, 19, 49, 79, 209, 237
Bouthoorn, Ruud M., 6, 123
Bouyer, Louis, 13
Böwering, Gerhard, 338
Boyancé, Pierre, 65
Boylan, Patrick, 311
Brabec de Mori, Bernd, 46
Brakke, David, 85–86
Brann, Eva T.H., 205
Brashear, William M., 43
Brashler, James, 282
Bräuninger, Friedrich, 209
Brierre de Boismont, A., 158
Brisson, Luc, 118
Brock, Sebastian, 242, 333
Brockelmann, C., 340
Broek, Roelof van den, ix–x, 24, 53, 73, 76, 123, 159, 168, 174, 178–179, 181, 183, 217, 230–231, 235, 266–268, 272, 274, 278, 282, 284, 290, 299, 301, 305, 307, 311, 329–330
Browne, C.A., 83
Broze, Michèle, 13
Buchanan, Josef Rodes, 254
Büchli, Jörg, 156
Bucke, Richard Maurice, 254–255
Bull, Christian, xi, 15–16, 18–19, 24–27, 29–30, 32, 37–38, 49, 54, 64, 66–67, 75, 79, 81, 89–90, 94, 96, 98, 122, 141, 150, 156, 163, 171, 203, 208, 210, 226–227, 233–234, 236, 239–242, 244–246, 248, 250–251, 257–258, 261–262, 265–268, 276, 279–280, 283–284, 286, 288–290, 294–298, 300, 302, 305
Bulliet, Richard W., 363

Burkert, Walter, 15, 17, 44
Burns, Dylan M., xi, 63, 85–87, 93, 106, 245, 310
Burroughs, William, 93

Cairns, Huntington, 312
Camassa, Giorgio, 365
Cameron, Alan, 220, 331
Camplani, Alberto, 282, 286–287, 290, 305–306
Cancik, Hubert, 53
Cancik-Lindemaier, Hildegard, 53
Carozzi, Pier Angelo, 141
Carpenter, Edward, 254
Casevitz, Michel, 188
Cassirer, Ernst, 357
Castoriadis, Cornelius, 205, 207, 217, 364–366
Castrucci, Greta, 187–189
Chaeremon, 29
Champier, Symphorien, 123
Chantraine, Pierre, 188
Charron, Régine, 83, 87–88
Chauveau, Michel, 28
Cherniss, Harold, 125
Chlup, Radek, 49, 210, 231
Chopra, Deepak, 7
Chrysippus, 147
Churton, Tobias, 81
Chuvin, Pierre, 331
Cicero, 147, 220, 224
Cilliers, Paul, 346
Ciraolo, Leda J., 67
Clarke, Emma C., 34, 44, 72, 100–102, 108–110, 112–113
Clement of Alexandria, 27, 218
Cleopatra VII, 28
Cohen, H. Floris, 356
Collins, Adela Yarbro, 159
Collins, John J., 159
Colonna, Francesco, 359
Compagnon, Antoine, 346
Conrad, Joseph, 23
Constantine the Great, 50, 76, 330
Coole, Diana, 343
Cooper, John M., 312
Copenhaver, Brian P., 53, 56, 59, 179, 241, 261, 357
Coppens, J., 52
Corbin, Henry, 367
Corrigan, Kevin, 106
Cosmas of Jerusalem, 93

Couliano, Ioan P., 352
Cowan, Thomas Patrick, 93
Cox Miller, Patricia, 233
Coxe, Arthur Cleveland, 48
Crabtree, Adam, 285
Crawford, Matthew R., 267–268
Crowley, John, 352
Cumont, Franz, 26, 52
Cusset, François, 346–347
Cutler, Norman, 70
Cyprian, 48
Cyprian, Pseudo-, 329
Cyril of Alexandria, 27, 50, 267–268, 328–330, 332

Dainton, Barry, 3
Dallmayr, Fred R., 343
Daumas, François, 267
Davis, Erik, 4, 139
Davis, Richard H., 70
Debord, Guy, 353
DeConick, April D., 86, 354
Delia, Diana, 23
Demetrius of Phaleron, 292
Democritus, 217
Denier van der Gon, W.H., 236
Denton, Elizabeth, 254
Denton, William, 254
Derchain, Philippe, 33, 63, 65–66, 233, 267
Derrida, Jacques, 2, 211, 308, 311, 314–317, 319–320, 324, 343–344, 346–347, 363–364, 366
Des Places, Édouard, 104, 117, 270
Descartes, René, 202
Dey, Joseph, 236–238
Di Cesare, Donatella Ester, 1, 133, 345–346, 350
Dickey, Eleanor, 124, 128
Dickie, Matthew W., 43
Didymus the Blind, 267–268, 328–330
Dieleman, Jacco, 16, 26, 29–34, 39, 67, 291
Diels, Hermannus, 168
Dieterich, Albrecht, 36, 39, 291
Digeser, Elisabeth DePalma, 329–331
Dijkstra, Bram, 174
Dillon, John, 42, 72, 101–102, 223, 320–322
Diocletian, 330
Diotima, 16, 106–107, 187–193, 258, 321, 326
Dirkse, Peter A., 282–283
Dittenberger, Wilhelmus, 25

Dodd, C.H. 8, 126, 141, 156, 160, 164–165, 174
Dodds, E.R., 34–35, 65, 153
Donaldson, James, 48
Doniger, Wendy, 168
Doresse, Jean, 26, 318
Dornseiff, Franz, 291
Dörrie, Heinrich, 130
Dosoo, Korshi, xi, 29–34, 300
Doulos, Lambros T., 34
Doutreleau, Louis, 293
Dover, K.J., 107
Ḏū l-Nūn al-Miṣrī, 338–341
Dubois, Jean-Daniel, 148
Durand, Gilbert, 130
Durkheim, Emile, 46
Dyczkowski, Mark S.G., 359

Ebstein, Michael, 338–341
Eco, Umberto, 348
Edmonds, Radcliffe, 37, 40, 42
Eliade, Mircea, 348, 355–356
Eliot, T.S., 351
Ellenberger, Henri F., 285
Emboden, William A., 38
Empedocles, 168, 335, 337–338, 341
Ephrem the Syrian, 330
Epicurus, 217
Epigone, 188
Epiphanius, 29
Eunapius, 101–102
Euripides, 312
Eusebius of Caesarea, 127
Evans, Nancy, 107, 188–189, 192–193, 238

Faivre, Antoine, 349
Fattori, M., 205
Fauconnier, Gilles, 365
Faxneld, Per, 174
Felski, Rita, 136, 343, 348, 350
Ferguson, A.S., 153, 208
Ferry, Luc, 346
Festugière, André-Jean, 12–13, 15, 18–20, 26, 36, 49, 52–53, 67, 80–82, 87, 103, 120–121, 123–126, 130, 134, 137, 141, 160, 166, 168, 172–174, 179–180, 193, 204, 207–208, 210, 213, 215, 218, 236–237, 240–241, 246, 248–249, 252, 257, 259, 261, 263, 270–271, 317–318, 354–357, 360, 366
Feuerbach, Ludwig, 68
Fichte, Johann Gottlieb, 365

Ficino, Marsilio, 103, 123–124, 220, 333
Finamore, John F., 35, 107
Firmicus Maternus, 27
Fleischer, Heinrich Leberecht, 334
Flower, Michael Attyah, 188
Foucault, Michel, 47
Fougères, Gustave, 188
Fowden, Garth, 15–16, 18–20, 24–27, 31, 49–50, 53, 76–78, 82, 84–85, 91, 98, 100–101, 117, 122, 124, 141, 195, 210, 223, 225–226, 230, 234, 236, 282, 361, 363, 367
Fowler, Harold North, 312
Frank, Manfred, 344
Frankfurter, David, 24, 26, 29, 32–33, 45–46, 75, 292–293
Fraser, Kyle A., 19, 49, 78–79, 83, 85, 87–89, 93, 96–98, 150
Frede, Dorothea, 205
Frede, Michael, 117
Freedberg, David, 70
Friedrich, Hans-Veit, 26–27, 29–30
Fritz, Kurt von, 202, 216, 320
Frolov, Andrey V., 38

Ǧābir b. Ḥayyān, 339
Gadamer, Hans-Georg 1, 6, 14, 80, 114, 132–133, 135, 138, 342, 344–351, 364, 366–367
al-Ǧalā, Abū 'Abd Allāh b., 340
Galen, 71, 78
Galerius, 330
Ganis, Giorgio, 254
Ganschinietz, R., 266
Garin, Eugenio, 357
Gaston, K. Healan, 362
Gastoué, Amédée, 292
Gauld, Alan, 297
Geens, Karolien, 93
Gehlen, Arnold, 353
Geldard, Richard G., 359
Gennep, Arnold van, 227
George, Leonard, 254
Gersh, Stephen, 292
Gibson, Sophie, 188
Gilly, Carlos, 332
Godderis, Jan, 158
Godel, R., 15, 188
Godwin, Joscelyn, xi, 292–293, 359
Goethe, Johann Wolfgang von, 352, 358
Goulet, R., 102
Graf, Fritz, 43

Granger, Frank, 162
Grant, Robert M., 19
Gregory of Nazianz, 330
Grese, William C., 8, 13, 174, 236–237, 239–240, 242–244, 246–250, 252, 257–258, 261, 263
Griffith, F. Ll., 162
Grimes, Shannon, 77–78, 84, 88, 94–95
Griswold, Charles, 189
Grof, Stanislav, 40
Grondin, Jean, 346
Guzmán, Gastón, 38

Hackforth, R., 312
Hadot, Pierre, 15, 19–20, 146–148, 227
Hadrian, 28
Haenchen, Ernst, 153, 156, 160, 163–164, 166, 171–175, 183
Haidt, Jonathan, 347
Halbertal, Moshe, 63, 134
Hallum, Bink, 77–78, 88
Hamilton, Edith, 312
Hammer, Olav, 9
Hammill, Peter, 77
Hanegraaff, Wouter J., 2, 4–6, 8–9, 13, 16, 20, 43, 44, 46, 51, 57–59, 63, 68–70, 72, 80–81, 84, 86, 117, 123, 127, 130, 133–136, 139, 148, 157, 195, 228, 254, 259, 272, 283, 310, 331–332, 341, 353–358, 360–363, 365, 367
Hanegraaff-Lissenberg, Leonie, xii
Harari, Yuval Noah, 366
Harker, Andrew, 23
Harland, Philip A., 26, 29
Harnack, Adolf von, 19, 317
Hartogsohn, Ido, xi, 40, 45
Hegel, G.W.F., 20, 365
Heidegger, Martin, 202–203, 212, 234, 237, 353–354
Heilen, Stephan, 27
Heinze, Max, 321–322
Hense, Otto, 129
Heraclides, 153
Heraclitus, 322
Herklotz, Friederike, 28
Herodian, 48
Hershbell, Jackson P., 72, 101–102
Hierocles, 111
Higgins, R.A., 188
Hillman, James, 367
Hirschkind, Charles, 362
Hodkinson, Hilary, 188

Hodkinson, Stephen, 188
Hofmann, Albert, 44
Holt, Robert R., 254
Holzhausen, Jens, 53, 156, 174–175, 204, 218, 231–232, 239–241, 246, 256–257, 261, 269, 272–273, 283, 287, 303, 306
Homer, 13, 216–217
Hood, Ralph W., 20
Hopfner, Theodor, 33, 39, 67, 71
Horst, Pieter W. van der, 29
Houellebecq, Michel, 357
Huet, Marie-Hélène, 168
Hughes, Aaron W., 205
Hunter, Erica C.D., 95
Hunter, Ian, 347
Huss, Boaz, 191
Hyland, Drew A., 189–190, 192–193, 211

Iamblichus, xi, 4, 9, 15, 22, 34–35, 43, 49, 57, 67–72, 78–79, 100–119, 138–139, 148–149, 155, 164, 166, 216, 232, 244, 258, 280, 303, 318–319, 321, 324, 327–328, 330, 340, 361
Ibn al-'Arabī, Ibn, 340
Ibn al-'Ibrī, 334
Ibn Durayd, 333
Ibn Sīnā, 335, 338
Ibn Umayl, 339
Ideler, Iulius Ludovicus, 83
al-Iḫmīmī, Abū Ḥarrī 'Uṯmān b. Suwayd, 339
al-Iḫmīmī, Buṯrus al-Ḥakīm, 339
Inglisian, Vahan, 131
Innes, Doreen C., 292
Introvigne, Massimo, 81
Inwood, Brad, 168
Irenaeus, 293
Isidorus, 264–266

Jackson, Howard M., 24, 78, 87–88, 91–93, 99–100, 141, 156, 163, 265–266
Jackson, Stanley W., 254
Jacobs, Bas, xii, 360
Jacobsen, Johanna Micaela, 44
James, William, 255
Janet, Pierre, 285
Janowitz, Naomi, 88
Jansen, H. Ludin, 156
Janus, Carolus, 292
Jenott, Lance, 25, 282
Jesus, 127, 331
Johnson, Barbara, 311, 314, 316, 363

Johnston, Sarah Iles, 35, 37, 39, 65–67, 69, 71–72, 109
Jonas, Hans, 85, 173, 236–237, 239, 317, 353–354, 356–358
Jones, Alexander, 222
Jong, Albert F. de, xii, 78
Jördens, Andreas, 23
Josephus, 127
Juhasz, Joseph B., 158, 254
Julia Eudia, 188
Julian (Emperor), 50, 267, 328, 331
Julian the Chaldaean, 117
Julian the Theurgist, 117
Jung, Carl Gustav, 84
Jurasek, Norberto, xii
Justinian, 331

Kaldellis, Anthony, 127–128
Kant, Immanuel, 20, 212, 359, 364–365
Karbovnik, Damien, 356
Karnes, Michelle, 205
Keizer, Lewis S., 282–288, 290, 295, 300, 302–305, 308–309
Kelber, Wilhelm, 321
Kerkeslager, Allen, 63
Kilcher, Andreas B., 9
al-Kindī, Abū Yūsuf Ya'qūb ibn isḥāq, 333
King, Karen L., 85, 353–354
Kingsley, Peter, 12–13, 19, 25, 62, 120, 137, 162, 200, 236, 285, 325, 339–341, 359
Kirk, Geoffrey S., 322
Kissling, Robert C., 35
Klotz, David, 30
Kluge, Carl Alexander Ferdinand, 297
Kneller, Jane, 212
Kodera, Sergius, 66
Köhlenberg, Leo, 81
Kosofsky Sedgwick, Eve, 348
Kosslyn, Stephen M., 254
Krause, Martin, 283, 286, 304
Kripal, Jeffrey J., xii, 139, 254, 274
Kristeller, Paul Oskar, 357
Kurth, D., 311
Kurzke, Hermann, 264

Labat, René, 315
Labib, Pahor, 286, 304
Lactantius, 50, 127, 276, 329–332
Łajtar, Adam, 26
Lamb, W.R.M., 187

Index of Persons

Lamberth, David C., 4
Lampe, G.W.H., 245
Lane Fox, Robin, 75, 331
Lasthenia, 188
Law, Esteban, 57, 121, 139, 361
Law, John, 45
Layton, Bentley, 86, 113
Lazier, Benjamin, 85, 237, 353
Lazzarelli, Lodovico, 123
Leenhardt, Maurice, 348
Leeuw, Gerardus van der, 348
Levin, Flora R., 292
Lévy, I., 66
Lewis, James R., 9
Lewis, Nicola Denzey, 222-223
Lewy, Hans, 35, 38, 65-67, 149
Leyden, W. von, 217
Liddell, Henry George, 245, 312
LiDonnici, Lynn R., 33, 38-39
Lindsay, Jack, 49, 75, 83, 87, 94
Litwa, M. David, 37, 55, 129, 141, 150, 201, 217, 223, 266-268, 271, 281, 328-329, 332
Loret, Victor, 33
Lorton, David, 63
Louth, Andrew, 35
Lovejoy, Arthur O., 55, 106, 270
Loy, David R., 317, 319, 359
Lucentini, Paolo, 332
Luck, Georg, 33, 37, 44, 71, 83, 197, 258
Ludwig, Arnold M., 157
Luhrmann, Tanya M., 158, 254
Lundhaug, Hugo, 25, 282
Luther, Martin, 11
Lyotard, Jean-François, 342

MacCoull, L.S.B., 60, 66
MacDonald, Paul S., 14
MacMullen, Ramsay, 23-24, 331
MacPhail, John A., 102
Macrobius Ambrosius Theodosius, 220-222, 224
Macrobius Plotinus Eusthatius, 220
Madison, G.B., 344, 346
Mahé, Jean-Pierre, 15-16, 18-19, 49-51, 53, 56, 62, 67, 74, 79, 121, 123-126, 128, 130-131, 156, 162, 164, 175, 200, 209-210, 217-218, 222-223, 226, 230, 234, 238, 246, 250, 258, 260, 278, 280-284, 289-291, 294, 297-298, 301, 304, 307, 360-361

Majercik, Ruth, 35, 37-38, 42, 65, 117
Manandyan, H., 130-131
Mann, Thomas, 119, 264
Mansfeld, Jaap, 202, 359
Marcella, 104
Marcellus of Ancyra, 329-330
Marchand, Suzanne, 17, 19, 133, 360
Marcion, 317
Marcus (Valentinian teacher), 293
Marcus, Ralph, 162
Marcus Aurelius, 146
Margalit, Avishai, 63, 134
Martelli, Matteo, xi, 77, 82, 87-90, 94-95, 98
Mary the Jewess, 82
Massignon, Louis, 340
al-Masʿūdi, ʿAli b. al-Ḥusayn, 233, 339
Mathiesen, Thomas J., 292
Matter, Jacques, 357
Matthews, John, 25, 29
Maurizio, L., 188
Mauss, Marcel, 46
Maximus of Tyrus, 66
McLuhan, Marshall, 350
Mead, G.R.S., 43, 67-68, 130, 181, 244
Melvin-Koushki, Matthew, xi, 363
Memmia, 188
Meredith, Fionola, 343
Mertens, Michèle, 25, 77-78, 84-85, 87, 89-90, 92, 99-100
Meslin, Michel, 33
Metochites, Theodoros, 127
Meyer, Marvin, 53, 286, 300, 302-305, 308
Michelfelder, Diane, 346
Migne, J.-P., 38
Miller, Dana R., 210-211
Miller, John F., 349
Mina, Togo, 26, 318
Minnen, Peter van, 77
Moderatus of Gades, 280
Modrak, Deborah, 205
Moorsel, G. van, 19, 81, 236, 242
Morenz, S., 200, 218
Moreschini, Claudio, 16, 50, 52-53, 57-60, 62, 67, 123-124, 328, 332
Moret, Alexandre, 63
Moullou, Dorina, 34
Moyer, Ian, 26-27, 29-32, 46, 67, 75, 264-267
Moyes, Holley, 34
al-Mubaššir ibn Fātik, 267, 333

al-Muḥāsibī, al-Ḥariṯ, 339
Musil, Robert, 299
Mussies, Gerard, 249
Myrepsus, Nicolas, 295

al-Nadīm, Muḥammad b. Isḥāq, 339
An-Nadīm, 333
Nagel, Jennifer, 1
Nagy, Gregory, 188
Nehamas, Alexander, 312
Neilos, 82, 88, 95–96, 98, 340
Newberg, Andrew B., 157
Nickelsburg, George W.E., 89
Nicomachus of Gerasa, 292–294
Nietzsche, Friedrich, 344, 357
Nikippa, 188
Nikotheos, 93
Nilsson, Martin P., 150
Nixon, Jon, 349
Nock, Arthur Darby, 18, 52–53, 67, 123–125, 130, 160, 168, 179–180, 204, 208, 213, 236, 257, 261
Noll, Richard, 254
Numenius, 117–118, 270
Nussbaum, Martha Craven, 365

Obeyesekere, Gananath, 110
Oesterreich, T.K., 110
Ohlander, Erik S., 335–336
Onians, R.B., 13
Oréal, Elsa, 103
Origen, 147
Otto, Bernd-Christian, 29, 43, 361
Otto, Eberhard, 311

Page, D.L., 25
Pagels, Elaine, 113
Paivio, Allan, 352
Palamedes, 312
Palmer, Richard E., 346
Papadopoulos, Costas, 34
Papio, Michael, 59
Papus, 81
Paramelle, Joseph, 123
Parássoglou, George M., 75
Parlebas, Jacques, 267
Parmenides, 202, 217, 278, 341, 359
Parri, Ilaria, 53, 57–58, 332
Parrott, Douglas M., 282
Pascal, Blaise, 357
Pasi, Marco, xi, 93
Paul, 184

Pauwels, Louis, 356
Pearson, Birger A., 156, 159, 174
Peck, A.L., 168
Perrone Compagni, Vittoria, 332
Peters, F.E., 147
Petersen, Tage, 210
Peterson, Erik, 30
Peuckert, Will-Erich, 44
Pfister, Friedrich, 71, 157
Phaënna, 188
Philo of Alexandria, 126–127, 320–322, 356
Philonenko, M., 234, 258
Photios, 129
Pico della Mirandola, Giovanni, 59, 357
Pingree, David, 17
Pirsig, Robert, 349
Plato, 2, 15, 66, 100, 104, 106–107, 114–115, 117, 129, 187–194, 207, 210–211, 213, 217–218, 221, 224, 242, 292, 311–316, 318–322, 324, 326–328, 330–331, 335, 337–338, 342, 348–349, 351, 356, 367
Pleše, Zlatko, 210
Plessner, M., 339
Plotinus, 60, 66, 78, 101–102, 104–107, 109, 111, 115, 117–118, 163, 212, 321, 330, 337
Plutarch, 33–34, 110, 145–147, 223, 321–322
Podemann Sørensen, Jørgen, 19, 200, 258
Poirée, Élie, 292–294
Polycrateia, 188
Porphyry of Tyrus, 78, 100–109, 111–112, 114–117, 149, 317–318, 321, 330, 358
Porramanres. See Amenemhet III
Porreca, David, 332
Port, Matthijs van de, 137, 139
Powell, J.G.F., 220, 224
Preisendanz, Karl, 42–43
Primavesi, Oliver, 202, 359
Principe, Lawrence M., 78, 84, 88
Principe, Walter, 20
Proclus, 37, 66–67, 93, 107
Psellos, 37, 38, 124
Pseudo-Clement, 33
Ptolemy I Soter, 28
Puech, H.-C., 26, 52
Pythagoras, 117, 129, 221, 337–338, 341

Index of Persons

al-Qifṭī, ʿAlī b. Yūsuf b., 334, 340
Quack, Joachim Friedrich, 72, 76, 94, 103, 282, 361
Quispel, Gilles, 51–53, 81, 86, 197, 218, 226, 242, 244, 252, 257, 261
Quodvultdeus, 329, 332

Rabbow, Paul, 146
Randall, John Herman, 357
Raschke, Carl, 354
Raven, John E., 322
Razavi, Mehdi Amin, 335–336, 338
Rea, John, 75
Rees, D.A., 205
Reitzenstein, Richard, 16–17, 19, 52, 79–80, 83, 123–124, 133, 156, 164, 167, 171, 173, 175, 218, 225, 234, 236, 239, 257, 291
Renard, Jean-Bruno, 356
Renaut, Alain, 346
Reynolds, L.D., 123
Ricoeur, Paul, 343, 348
Riess, Ernestus, 27, 52, 125
Rinella, Michael A., 312
Ritner, Robert K., 26, 28–31, 42–43, 46, 75
Riva, Massimo, 59
Roberts, Alexander, 48
Robertson, David G., 86
Robins, Gay, 65
Robinson, James M., 302
Roig Lanzillotta, Lautaro, 354
Rose, H.J., 52
Rosen, Stanley, 189
Rosenthal, F., 333–334
Roszak, Theodore, 342
Rouget, Gilbert, 157
Rousseau, Adelin, 293
Rowland, Christopher, 159
Ruck, Carl A.P., 44
Rudolph, Kurt, 283
Ruelle, Charles-Émile, 292, 295
Rumor, Maddalena, 89
Runia, D.T., 321–322
Ryan, Mark B., 254
Ryholt, Kim, 27

Sacks, Oliver, 158
Sadoski, Mark, 352
Saffrey, Henri Dominique, 72, 101, 103–104, 109, 355
Safranski, Rüdiger, 353
Ṣāʿid b. Aḥmad al-Andalusī, 339–340
Said, Edward, 117, 360
Saif, Liana, xi
Salaman, Clement, 53, 68, 173–174, 181, 232, 242, 257, 261
Sallis, John, 189, 211–212, 359–360
Sándor, András, 59
Sarbin, Theodore R., 158, 254
Saturninus, Q. Aemilius, 75
Sauneron, Serge, 30
Saussure, Ferdinand de, 341–342
Scarborough, John, 33, 39
Schmidt, Leigh Eric, 13, 20, 191
Schofield, Malcolm, 205
Scholtz, Clarke H., 38
Schulte-Sasse, Jochen, 365
Scipio Aemilianus, 220, 224
Scipio Africanus, 220
Scott, Robert, 245, 312
Scott, Walter, 17, 51–53, 78, 124–126, 129–130, 163–166, 171, 173, 213, 232, 239–240, 245, 248, 262, 328, 334
Scott-Baumann, Alison, 343
Searle, John R., 248
Sedley, David, 13
Segonds, Alain-Philippe, 72, 101, 103–104, 109
Seneca, 146
Septimia Zenobia, 48, 75
Severus Alexander, 48
Sezgin, Fuat, 339
Shannon, Claude E., 342
Shanon, Benny, 72
Shantz, Colleen, 157
Shaw, Gregory, xi, 35, 49, 66, 68–69, 102, 106–109, 111, 113–115, 210–211, 258, 326
Sherwood Taylor, F., 83
Shields, Christopher, 205
Sicherl, Martin, 103
Simms, Karl, 8, 346, 348
Simon, Josef, 346
Simplicius, 35, 217
Siniossoglou, Niketas, 128
Smith, Andrew, 101, 104
Smith, Jonathan Z., 8, 26–27, 29–30, 45–46, 97, 223
Socrates, 2, 15–16, 106–107, 115, 187–193, 311–312, 314, 322, 324, 326, 335, 337–338
Song, Euree, 104
Sossianus Hierocles, 330

Spengler, Oswald, 134
Spinner, Gregory, 168
Spivak, Gayatri Chakravorty, 315
Stadter, Philip A., 145–146
Stahl, William Harris, 221
Stang, Charles M., 274
Stead, G. Christopher, 321
Steel, Carlos G., 104–105, 107, 110
Steiner, George, 8, 14, 20, 364
Sternberg-el Hotabi, Heike, 49
Stobaeus, Johannes, 54, 123, 128–130, 142, 328, 332
Stobaeus, Septimius, 128
Stolzenberg, Daniel, 85, 87–88, 91–93
Stone, Michael E., 159
Strabo, 29
Strauss Clay, Jenny, 349
Streib, Heinz, 20
Struck, Peter R., 41, 69, 326
Stuckrad, Kocku von, 222
Suhrawardī, Shihāb al-Dīn Abū al-Futūḥ Yaḥyā ibn Ḥabash ibn Amīrak, xi, 335–341
Swartz, Chantélle, 346
Syncellus, 89

Tacoma, Laurens E., 24
Tallet, Gaëlle, 32, 46
al-Tamīmī, 'Abd Allāh Muḥammad b. Umayl, 339
Tanaseanu-Döbler, Ilinca, 35, 37, 40, 44
Taphnoutiē, 82, 98
Tardieu, Michel, 13, 290
Tart, Charles T., 3
Tertullian, 329
Thales of Miletus, 223
Theodora, 188
Theodosius I, 331
Theosebeia, 9, 25, 77–79, 82, 87–88, 91, 93–94, 97–100, 119, 155
Thessalos, 26–35
Thomas, Paul, 67
Thompson, William L., 254
Tiedemann, Dietrich, 169
Tirian, Abraham, 131
Topalis, Frangiskos V., 34
Touliatos, Diane, 292, 295
Traherne, Thomas, 145
Tröger, Karl-Wolfgang, 236–237, 240, 242, 244, 248, 282–283, 286, 288, 298, 300, 302–305, 307–308

Trompf, Garry W., 85, 354
Tuffin, Paul, 89
Turbo, Q. Marcius, 63
Turnèbe, Adrien, 123
Turner, Mark, 365
Turner, Victor, 227, 286
al-Tustarī, Abū Muḥammad Sahl b. 'Abd Allāh, 338–339

Ullmann, Manfred, 339–340
Ustinova, Yulia, 15, 148, 157–158, 191, 242
Uṯmān b. Suwayd, 339

Van den Kerchove, Anna, 12, 15, 18–20, 60, 62–64, 66–69, 72–73, 96, 115–116, 119–121, 123–124, 131, 140, 149–151, 156, 159, 162–163, 173, 181, 184, 194–195, 198, 200, 207, 225–227, 229–231, 234–236, 239–240, 243, 246–248, 263, 266, 275, 283, 285, 287, 308–309, 314, 342
VanderKam, James C., 89
Vanderlip, Vera Frederika, 264–265
Van Liefferinge, Carine, 13, 65–66
Venit, Marjorie S., 23
Venticinque, Philip F., 77
Vettius Valens, 27, 183
Visconti, A., 188
Voegelin, Eric, 354
Vogel, C.J. de, 107, 222
Vos, R.L., 311
Vugt, Marieke K. van, 146

Wachsmuth, Curth, 129
Waghorne, Joanne Punzo, 70
Walbridge, John, 117, 332, 335–336, 338–339, 341
Waldstein, Michael, 353–354
Waltzing, J.-P., 78
Wardman, Alan, 146
Warnock, Mary 212, 366
Wasson, R. Gordon, 44
Waszink, J.H., 208
Watson, Gerard, 205
Watts, Alan, 349
Watts, Edward J., 23
Webb, James, 81
Weber, Max, 357
Wedin, Michael V., 205
Wellesz, Egon, 291–292, 294
Wellmann, M., 39
Whitehouse, David J.M., 258

Index of Persons

Whittaker, John, 100
Wigtil, David N., 14, 50, 74
Wildberg, Christian, xi, 124–125, 129–130, 164, 169, 229–230, 325
Wilkins, Eliza Gregory, 104
William of Auvergne, 331–332
Williams, Michael, 85, 354
Williamson, Timothy, xi
Willis, Jacob, 221
Wilson, N.G., 123
Wilson, R. McL., 293
Wilson, Robert R., 159
Windisch, Hans, 16
Winnington-Ingram, R.P., 188
Wolfson, Elliot R., 14, 209, 367
Wolin, Richard, 353
Woodruff, Paul, 312
Wordsworth, William, 187
Wright, Wilmer Cave, 101
Wulff, David M., 157

Xenophon, 356

Yates, Frances A., 9, 356–357
Yeats, William Butler, 48
Yébenes, Sabino Perea, 33
Younger, D., 297
Yunis, Harvey, 312
Yurdin, Joel, 205

Zago, Michela, 234, 296
Zandee, Jan, 65
Zenk, Benjamin John, 136
Ziai, Hossein, 335–336
Zielinski, Tadeusz, 17, 49, 153, 172, 204
Zimmern, Alice, 104
Zosimos, 9, 22, 25, 49, 77–100, 104, 119, 150, 155, 223, 267, 328, 339–340
Zuntz, G., 231, 236, 258, 260, 262

Index of Subjects

Addiction, 151, 154–155, 182–184
Admiration, 62, 95, 151, 194–195, 198, 200
Advaita Vedānta, 359
Afterlife, 182, 266, 275
Agathē Tuchē, 266
Agathos Daimōn, 89, 265–269, 271, 325–326, 328, 333, 335, 337
Agnosticism, 4–5, 269, 341, 367
Aiōn, 10, 100, 143, 213–215, 217–219, 231, 241, 252–253, 255, 261–262, 267, 270–271, 275, 284, 289, 303, 359
Akhmīm. See Panopolis
Alchemy, 17–18, 21, 78, 83–84, 88, 333, 339–341
Alētheia, 201
Alexandria, 23–24, 26–28, 31, 60, 75, 78, 81–82, 102–103, 127, 226
Alexandrian Judaism, 126–127, 238
Alienation, 353–354, 357–358, 363
Alterations (Altered States) of Consciousness. See Consciousness, Alterations of
Alterations (Altered States) of Knowledge. See Knowledge, Altered States of
Alterity, 134, 136–138, 232, 345
Amenhotep son of Hapu, 27, 29–30
Ammon
  God (Amun), 26, 311–313, 315, 320, 327–328, 342–343, 347–349
  Hermetic pupil, 49, 232–233
  King, 100, 116–117, 333, 344

Amulets, 41, 290
Anamnēsis, 240, 319, 345
Anchoēs, 265
Androgyny, 56, 169–170, 175–176, 238, 281, 323
Angels, 69, 89, 92, 269, 289, 301, 304, 306
  wicked or fallen, 74, 76, 88–91, 96
Anger, 245, 249
Anoēton, 13, 162, 166, 239
Anti-eclectic historiography, 361–362
Antihumanism, 346
Apamea, 101–102, 118
Apocalypse (revelation), 156, 162
Apocalyptic, 156, 159
Apocryphon of John, 93
Arabic transmission of Hermetica, 332–334
Archontism, 93
Arithmology, 221, 250
Armenian Hermetica. See *Definitions of Hermes Trismegistus to Asclepius*
Asael, 89
Ascent, 36, 182–183, 266, 277–278, 283, 333
Asclepius
  God, 27, 29–30, 33, 90, 338
  Hermetic pupil, 49, 61–66, 74, 95–96, 116–117, 120–121, 195, 198–199, 232–233, 268, 333
Asclepius, 47, 50–53, 81, 170, 175, 269, 282, 325, 331–332, 356
Asebeia. See Irreverence

428

Index of Subjects

Astonishment, 191, 194–195, 198–199, 212, 219, 271
Astrology, 17–18, 21, 222, 248, 333
Attention (prosochē), 110, 146, 157, 180
Auditions, 159–160, 166–167
Avenging daimōn, 181, 276
Awe, 208
Awliyā', 338, 340

Badness (see also Corruption), 149, 152, 197, 199, 271
Bafflement, 139, 300
Baptism, 87, 97–98, 149–150, 155, 235
Beauty, 10–11, 54–55, 57, 106–108, 167, 190–194, 196–201, 207–209, 214, 218–219, 257–258, 260, 270, 273, 275, 286, 288, 305, 319, 329, 359
and Goodness and Truth. See Goodness-Beauty-Truth
See also Birth in Beauty, Giving
Becoming, 211–213, 217
Begotten, 280–281, 296
Being, 211, 213, 216–217
Belief, 194
Biblical influences/models, 9, 156, 171–172, 174, 176, 363
Bibliotheca Philosophica Hermetica, ix
Birth, 90, 107, 190, 192–193, 222, 224–225, 237–238, 272–274, 281, 284–286, 323, 325
Birth in beauty, Giving, 106, 192–193, 219, 224, 321, 323, 360
Bitus, 100, 117
Bodhisattvas, 258
Body, 92, 98–99, 104, 111, 143, 148, 153–155, 186, 204, 210, 218–219, 225, 241, 250–252, 256, 258, 272, 274, 358
as garment, 152–154, 183, 185
as vessel, 149–154, 182
hatred of, 151, 153
of rebirth, 241, 250, 253, 256, 277, 285
Book of Chemeu, 89–90
Book of Imouth, 90
Breathing, 40, 247, 312
Brethren, 287–288, 294, 302, 307
Bridal Chamber, 297
Byzantium, 127–128, 131, 332

Candomblé, 137, 139
Causality (instrumental vs. occult), 69, 358
Chalcedon, Council of, 131

Chaldaean Oracles, 37, 103, 117–119
Chēmeia, 89, 90
Chemeu, 89–91, 267
Chēnoboskion, 25, 282, 308
Chōra, 211–213, 217, 359
Christianity/Christians, 50, 63–64, 68, 76, 328–332
Clairvoyance, 254
Code-names, 39
Cognition, 364
Communal practice, 229, 232, 287, 291, 327
Communication, 15, 116, 204–205, 342–344, 346, 350–351, 364, 366
Communities, Hermetic, 79–82, 119–122, 230, 327–328, 342–343
Comparison, 7–9
Conception, 107, 321
Consciousness, 3–5, 56, 60, 345, 349, 365–366
Alterations of, 3–4, 6, 33, 39–40, 42, 47, 71, 99, 104–105, 107, 110, 112, 120, 148, 154–155, 157–160, 163, 175, 179, 184–186, 190–191, 208–209, 221–222, 225, 227–229, 236, 238, 241–244, 253–255, 291, 297–300, 358, 360
Conspiracy thinking, 93, 96, 348
Corpus Hermeticum, 123–125, 128–129, 131, 331–333, 356
scribal transmission of, 123–128
Correspondences, 358
Corruption, 148–149, 151–152, 157, 183, 198–199, 224, 245, 249, 274
Cosmic consciousness, 254–256, 270–271, 284
Cosmopolitanism, 46, 64, 96
Cosmos, 168–170, 200, 203, 213–214, 216, 224
Crisis of the third century, 48, 75, 94
Critical Theories, 346–348
Critique, 343, 345, 348, 350

Daimons, 59, 69, 88–91, 93–94, 96–99, 107, 142, 154–155, 223, 244–245, 269–270
Death, 177–178, 221, 223–224, 256, 266, 271–277, 291, 307, 334
and bodily dissolution, 176, 178, 180, 272–273, 281
and erōs, 176–177
as diminished life, 274, 291, 307

Index of Subjects

Death (cont.)
  as a state of consciousness, 74, 83, 152, 177–179, 185–186, 265
  as non-existent, 142, 214, 220, 271, 284, 291, 359
  as transformation, 271–272
  See also Afterlife
Death-state, 291, 300, 304
Decadence, 134, 171, 174
Deceit, 245, 247, 249
Decline, 134, 266, 354–355
Deconstruction, 278, 319, 324, 341, 343–347, 349, 363, 366
Defamiliarization, 9
Definitions of Hermes Trismegistus to Asclepius, 130–131
Deification, 143, 184, 228, 250, 253, 256, 277
Deisidaimonia, 195, 208, 272
Delusion(s), 61, 154, 156, 168, 200, 206, 212, 237, 278, 315, 320, 358–359
Delusionary images. See Phantasms
Demeter, 192
Demiurge, 86, 143, 169–172, 186, 317
Demons, 76, 329
Demotic Magical Papyri, 38
Desert, 120, 236, 284
Desire(s), 92, 97, 151, 181, 183–184, 204–206, 215
Dialogue, 345, 347, 350
Dialogue of the Philosophers and Cleopatra, 83–84, 88, 111, 150
Dianoia, 110, 162, 189, 211, 290, 313, 319
Différance/Différence, 316, 319, 343
Diocletian persecution, 330
Diospolis, 308
Diospolis Magna. See Thebes
Discourse, 314–317, 319, 321, 327, 344
Disenchantment, 4, 357
Dissemination, 324, 327, 332, 343
Dream of Scipio, 220–224
Dreams/Dreaming, 159, 242, 359–360
Drugs. See Psychoactive agents
Dualism, 85–86, 96, 106, 169, 179, 186, 199, 209–213, 215, 224, 232, 237, 248, 266, 317–320, 336, 358–360, 363
  dualistic consciousness, 250, 269–270, 278, 280, 320–321, 359
  pedagogical, 210
Dvin, Second Council of, 131

Echo, 307
Ecstasy, 36, 71, 157, 160, 219, 242, 297, 300, 302, 329
Egypt, 27–28, 32, 46, 48, 53, 63, 76, 134–135, 233, 260, 265, 274, 337, 360–361
  anti-Egyptianism, 17, 43, 45, 103, 134
  as Temple, 53, 65, 76, 224, 271
  decline of, 72–76, 331
Eiktōn, 280
Eilithuia, 107
Eleusinian mysteries, 44, 189, 192
Elitism, 61, 182, 197, 275, 277, 363
Embodiment, 4, 64–66, 75, 79, 85, 99, 104–108, 111, 155, 174–175, 177, 181–182, 198, 200, 208, 221, 223–225, 234, 237–238, 251–252, 271, 273–274, 277, 284, 300, 321, 323, 326, 358–360
Embrace, 283, 297, 300
Emic/etic, 135, 341
Emphutos gnōsis. See Gnōsis, Emphutos
Empiricism, 4–5
Enchantment, 2, 179, 314, 352, 357–358, 367
Energy/Energies, 73, 90–91, 105, 107, 111–112, 115–116, 143, 154–155, 223, 225, 243–246, 249–251, 253, 261, 270, 285–288, 296, 298, 301, 322–323, 325–326
Engraving. See Imprinting
Enlightenment, 61, 120, 122, 148, 155–167, 179, 184, 186, 196–197, 200, 225, 255, 262, 296, 300, 303, 321, 323, 335, 341, 359–360
Ennead, 10, 57, 163, 182, 184, 263, 271, 277–278, 280–281, 284, 289, 291, 296, 298, 300–302, 304, 306, 309, 323, 349
Enochian *Book of the Watchers*, 89
Enslavement, 93, 148, 151, 154, 184, 200, 206, 216, 219, 358
Enthusiasm, 71, 110
Envy, 65, 95, 150, 197, 245, 247, 249, 276, 336
Epicureanism, 146, 148
Epistēmē, 189–190, 201
Epithumia, 192–193
Eranos, 86
Erōs, 57, 176, 321, 324, 359
Erotics, 252, 324
Essenians, 235

Index of Subjects

Eternity, 15, 55, 57, 111, 113, 165, 176–178, 211, 215, 217, 235, 252–253, 255, 265, 268–269, 271, 289, 291, 305, 315, 334
Etic. See Emic/etic
Eurocentrism, 362
Eusebeia. See Reverence
Evil, 171–172, 176, 178, 181, 186, 197, 199, 354–355
Existentialism, 237, 353–356, 363
Exorcism, 122, 244–245, 247

Fall (of Man), 9, 64, 156, 171–177, 179, 186, 266, 283–284, 353, 355, 363
Fantastic realism, 356
Fantasy, 364–365
Fate. See Heimarmenē
Fayyum, 24, 266–267, 282
Fear, 195, 205, 208, 226, 272
Felix culpa, 172
Femininity, 171, 173–174, 237, 246, 285
Fertility/Fertilization, 56, 225, 265–266, 323–326
Fictional narratives, 31, 36, 80, 82, 84, 103, 159–160, 255, 309, 326
Fire, 40, 164–165, 175, 196, 214, 255, 260
Forgetfulness, 198, 274, 284, 300, 311, 351
Forms, Theory of. See Ideas, Theory of
Fumigations, 38, 71, 98

Gender, 56–58, 107, 168, 170, 238, 246, 281, 285, 323
Genera, 57–58
General discourses, 229–230, 237, 287, 325
Generosity, 150, 179, 214, 225, 228, 261
Generous sharing, 247–249
Genesis, 139, 156, 283
Gnōsis, 1, 3–5, 14, 19, 86, 104, 112–113, 115, 137–138, 142, 148, 150, 154, 160, 162–163, 166–167, 177, 179, 184–186, 189, 195, 198–201, 204, 208–209, 218–219, 226, 234–235, 246–249, 256, 260, 263, 275, 277–279, 296, 300, 309–310, 315, 317, 319, 321, 327, 331, 335, 338, 341, 345, 359–360, 362–364, 367
  as Re-cognition, 113, 179, 319
  emphutos gnōsis, 112–114, 138–139, 166, 303, 306, 318–319, 327
Gnostic confirmation bias, 93, 98, 199

Gnosticism, 85–87, 91, 93, 96, 98, 106, 172–173, 179, 186, 199, 209, 224, 237, 270, 317–318, 353–357, 363
God. See Source, The
Goodness/The Good, 112, 143, 149, 152–153, 181, 183, 189–192, 195–196, 199, 201, 207–209, 214, 218–219, 224, 247, 249, 261, 270, 275, 279–280, 316
Goodness-Beauty-Truth, 54, 108, 154, 177, 182, 190, 195–196, 224, 271, 321, 360
Gratitude, 54–56, 184, 228, 231, 233–234, 262, 271
Greece (against Egypt/the Orient), 134–135
Greed, 245, 247–249
Greek language, 12–14, 17, 23, 52, 100, 114, 116–117
Greek "Magical" Papyri, 17, 33, 39, 42–43, 217, 234, 290–291
Grief, 245–246, 248–249

Hallucination, 39, 71, 155, 157–158, 221, 315
Hallucinogens, 33, 38, 40
Ḥarrān, 333, 235, 337
Healing, 84, 97, 108, 111, 147, 179, 186, 244–245, 247–248, 250
  of the body, 111–112
  of the soul, 9, 78, 112, 148–150, 155, 358
Hearing, 301
  internal, 256–259
Heart, 13–14, 54, 150, 200, 233, 306
  eyes of the heart, 11, 13, 153, 200, 206–207, 214
  knowledge of the heart, 13, 185, 206
  opening the heart, 10, 197, 200, 271
Hegelianism, 133–134
Heimarmenē, 84–85, 91–93, 99–100, 107, 143, 167, 169, 175, 196–197, 222–223, 252–253, 258, 329
Helios Mithras, 36, 42
Hellenic-Abrahamic dialectics, 363
Herbs, 38–40, 69, 71
Hermēneia, 5, 10, 302, 344
Hermeneutic circle, 6, 133, 350
Hermeneutics, 5, 8, 14, 80, 132–138, 302, 342–349, 364, 366–367
  of faith, 348
  of suspicion, 343, 347–350
  of trust, 348–349

Index of Subjects

Hermes, 10, 25, 27, 344, 347, 348, 349
Hermes Muriomegas, 100
Hermes Trismegistus, 9–11, 24–25, 73, 92–96, 100, 117–118, 120–121, 124, 129, 156, 212, 267–268, 271, 309, 324–326, 328, 331, 333, 335–337
  honorific name, 286, 303
Hermetic "philosophy," 12, 15–16
Hermetic spirituality, 11–22, 342
Hermetic tradition, 6, 9, 334, 338, 356–357
Hermetica
  "philosophical," 16–18, 21
  "technical," 18, 21
Hermopolis Magna, 24–25
Hermouthis, 264–265
Hieroglyphs, 308
Hinterland, 45
Historical consciousness/Historicity, 135, 345, 349
Historiography, Anti-eclectic. See Anti-eclectic historiography
Horizon, Hermeneutic, 8, 132, 345, 347, 351, 355, 367
Horoscope, 222
Horus, 49, 73, 141
House of Life, 308
Hubris, 97, 172
Human, Grand, 170–177, 180, 242, 250–251, 261
Human beings as double, 58–59, 64, 68, 79, 274, 301
Humanism, 344, 346
Humanities, 5, 342–343, 344, 347, 349, 364, 366–367
Hymns, 122, 180, 186, 229, 231, 234, 258–260, 262–263, 295–296, 301–306, 308, 326, 349
Hypernoetic, 269
Hypnerotomachia, 359
Hypnosis, 294–297

Ideas, Theory of, 189
Idolatry, 51, 63, 65, 68, 70, 76, 134, 331–332, 363
Idrīs, 333
Ignorance, 148–155, 157, 185–186, 196, 245–246, 248–249, 341
Illumination. See Enlightenment
Image of Divinity, 206–207, 212, 215, 219

Imagery, Mental, 2, 200, 209, 219, 253–254, 352–353, 358
Imaginal, 5, 367
Imagination, 44, 55, 59, 72, 110, 122, 138, 146, 154, 180, 185, 205, 207, 212, 215–216, 218, 225, 231, 251, 262, 326, 352, 358, 360–361, 364, 367
  anachronistic, 80, 322
  and ochēma, 35, 37–38
  aristotelian theory of, 205, 207, 211
  as deception and revelation, 367
  as faculty of perception, 35, 216, 257
  as key to luminous epiphanies, 35
  collective, 366
  empowered by kuphi, 33–34
  generative, 231
  historical/scholarly, 2, 5, 17, 134, 173, 352–368
  incorporeal, 214–215, 217, 231, 253–254, 256, 262–263, 267, 289
  influence on offspring, 168
  mnemohistorical, 127
  radical, 366
  secular, 366
  transcendental, 212, 217, 359
Imhotep/Imouthes, 27, 29, 90
Immediacy, 115, 139, 230, 324, 335–336, 342, 351
Immortality, 51, 177, 220, 272
Impregnation, 107, 170, 285, 322–323
Imprinting (also: engraving, recording, inscribing), 168, 184, 262, 296, 305, 313, 322, 324, 326, 342
Incarnation. See Embodiment
Incense, 31, 33, 37–38, 70–71, 96, 98, 233, 295, 308, 339
Incomprehensibility, 41, 54–55, 208, 269, 322
Ineffability, 55, 92, 99, 203, 212, 251
Information, 342
Inhaling, 36–38, 40–41, 71
Initiation, 225–228, 235
Injustice, 245, 247, 249
Inscribing. See Imprinting
Insemination, 167–169, 174, 235, 246–247, 256, 321, 323
Inspiration (divine, spiritual), 75, 189, 192, 229, 301, 324

Index of Subjects

Intemperance, 245, 247–249
Interpretation, 8, 10, 135–136, 345, 348, 350, 364, 366
Intoxication, 221, 225, 353
Invocation, 36, 40, 246, 248, 259, 261, 293–296
Irreverence, 194, 196, 275–277
Isis, 49, 82, 141, 225, 264–265
Islam, 362–363
Ismāʿīlī movement, 333

Jealousy. See Envy
Jews/Judaism, 23, 62–63, 127–128, 134, 156, 363
See also Alexandrian Judaism
Joy, 228, 246–249, 252, 255, 260
Judgment, 275, 277, 281
Justice, 247, 248–249, 261

Kentritis, 39
Khemenu. See Hermopolis Magna
Kiss. See Embrace
Kitāb fī Zaǧr an-nafs, 334
Kmēph, 89, 267, 280
Knowledge, 1–4, 9–10, 15, 112–113, 138, 189–190, 194, 198, 201–204, 310, 312–313, 315–319, 337, 341–343, 347, 367
altered states of, 3, 9, 155, 209, 367
by acquaintance, 1, 113, 115, 235, 336
by presence, 335, 341
deep knowledge, 137, 139, 367
innate. See Gnōsis, emphutos gnōsis
propositional, 1, 113, 235
see also Self-Knowledge
Korē Kosmou, 94, 141
Kratēr. See Mixing-bowl
Kronos, 208
Kuphi, 33–34, 37–39, 110, 233, 295

Language (see also Names, Orality, Signifiers, Writing), 1–2, 5, 10, 12, 14–15, 18, 44, 54–56, 190, 203, 210, 279, 310, 315–316, 319, 323–324, 343, 351
Lecanomancy, 34
Lesemysterien. See Reading Mysteries
Letter from Isis to Horus, 89
Liberation, 11, 90–91, 93, 95–96, 148, 185, 200, 219, 271, 317, 321, 348, 358

Life, 11, 57, 65, 126, 143, 168, 175–176, 178–179, 182, 186, 202, 214, 225, 233, 235, 238, 244, 246–247, 249, 253, 260–262, 265–266, 268–270, 272, 277, 279–281, 284, 291, 300, 303, 305–307, 316, 320, 326–327, 334, 344, 360
Light, 11, 40, 61, 65, 67, 71, 73, 83, 92, 109–111, 125–126, 163–169, 175–179, 182, 185–186, 193, 202, 207–208, 214, 225, 233, 235, 238, 244, 246–247, 249, 253, 260–262, 265, 268–270, 274, 277, 279–281, 284, 289, 291, 298, 300, 303–306, 315–316, 319–320, 323, 326–327, 334–337, 341, 344, 360
artificial, 34
identical with Poimandres, 164–167, 212
in possession trance, 42, 110–111, 155
light of lights, 336, 341
light-world, 168
luminous ephiphanies, 109
voice of, 164, 165
see also Phōtagōgia
Liminality, 349, 364, 366
Linguistics, 342, 349
Literary fictions. See Fictional narratives
Locative/Non-locative, 45, 64, 96
Logoi spermatikoi, 246, 322
Logos, 61, 126, 142–143, 162, 164–166, 190, 201–205, 207, 210, 234, 245, 253, 261, 263, 273, 278, 280, 288–289, 301, 305, 312–315, 317, 320–327, 343–344, 363–364
as body of rebirth, 250
as emanation of nous, 125–126, 164, 166–167, 169, 174, 178, 246, 251
as energetic power, 114–116, 186, 322, 325–326, 341–342
as mediator, 203–204, 251
as Poimandres, 184
as that which makes sense, 203
as that which sees and hears, 126, 164–165, 167, 175, 184, 201, 203, 209, 251
in Christian theology, 125–126, 329, 363
Stoic, 160, 322

Logos teleios, 9, 47–76, 95–96, 128, 231, 259, 325, 331
Love (see also Erōs), 55, 57, 107, 163, 171, 175, 180, 187–188, 192, 195, 214, 244, 251, 305–306
Lust, 245, 247–249
LXX, 160

Ma'rifa, 335, 338
Magic, 16–18, 21, 29, 42–46, 228, 340, 356, 361, 363
Magnetism, 206–207, 209
Mania, 15, 188, 190, 242, 244
Manichaeism, 274
Mantes, 188, 190, 193
Mantineia, 187–188
Martinism, 81
Matter, 91, 97–99, 143, 168, 174, 200, 203, 212, 214, 221, 223, 225, 245, 251, 279, 318, 359
Meaning, 7, 8, 14–15, 191, 314, 324, 327, 343–344, 347–351, 366
Mediation, 314, 344, 347–349, 351, 358
Meditation, 97, 146–148, 157, 180, 229, 239, 244, 246, 336
Membres, 98
Memory, 205, 251, 262, 305, 311, 314, 317, 319, 326–327, 344
Memphis, 24
Mendesian wine, 38
Mesmerism, 285, 297
Metaphysics, 317–319, 344, 359, 363
Middle Platonism, 321–322
Mindfulness, 146
Mirroring, 33–34, 66, 173–174, 200, 366
Mithras Liturgy, 36–44, 66, 295
Mixing-bowl, 97–98, 142, 149–151, 155, 208
Mnemohistory, 85, 106, 127
Moira, 107
Monas, 206–207, 209, 215, 219, 221, 280
Monism, 209–210, 358, 360
Monotheism, Exclusive, 63, 65, 363
Moses, 124, 331
Museum effect, 70
Music, 188, 191–193, 292–294, 305–306
Myrrh, 38–39
Mystery, 189
Mysticism, 3, 12–13, 191, 209, 237

Nag Hammadi, 25, 51, 234, 252, 282–283, 308, 318
Names/Naming, 54, 56, 114–116, 186, 269, 286, 291–292, 306, 308–309, 336
Narcissism, 173
Narcotics, 33, 38
Narmouthis, 264
Narrative fictions. See Fictional narratives
Narratives. See Story-telling
Nature, 167–171, 173–178, 180, 183, 203, 242, 251, 261
Nechepso, 27, 30–31
Negative epistemology, 93
New Age, 7, 12, 58
Noein, 178, 202, 243, 257, 288, 301, 320
Noēsis, 5, 60–61, 92, 142, 162–163, 189, 200–209, 219, 243, 251, 284–285, 288, 312–317, 320, 325, 336, 362–364, 367
Noeticizing, 55, 166, 178, 198, 205–206, 210, 216, 234, 365
Nomina barbara, 41, 114–115, 185, 289, 306–307, 324
Nonduality, 165–166, 168, 210, 212, 214, 232, 248, 269, 278, 318–321, 336, 359–360
Noumena, 168, 217, 231, 269, 359
Nous, 8, 12–15, 20, 56, 58, 60–62, 64–65, 74, 92, 98, 105, 120, 125–126, 137, 141–143, 149–151, 155–156, 162–170, 174, 176–182, 184–185, 190, 192–193, 196–197, 199–205, 207–208, 212–214, 216, 218–219, 223, 234, 239–241, 248, 250–252, 256–258, 260–262, 268–275, 278, 280–281, 284, 288, 196, 298–307, 309, 315, 317–318, 320–325, 327, 329, 345, 363–364
  absence of, 181–182, 197
  as gift, 180–181, 197, 276
  as natural endowment, 179–180, 197
  as tormentor, 196–197
  both ontological and epistemological, 163
  identical with Poimandres, 164, 166

Ochēma, 35, 37–38, 107, 111, 273, 275
Offerings, 234, 263
  Verbal, 296–297

Index of Subjects

Ogdoad, 10, 57, 182, 184, 257–259, 263, 277–278, 280–281, 284, 289, 294, 296, 300–301, 304, 306, 309, 323
　of eight guardian deities, 309
Ogdoad and the Ennead, The, 138, 271, 282, 284, 312, 318, 325–326, 329, 338, 348
One, The, 60, 185, 206–207, 209, 271, 279–281, 296, 301, 306, 329
Optimism/Pessimism, 49, 55, 80, 96, 209, 270
Orality, 114–116, 230, 305, 313, 322, 325, 341
Organon of Hermes Trismegistus, 291, 307
Orient, 19, 49, 134, 209, 318, 355, 360–361
Orientalism, 360
Osiris, 268
Otherness. See Alterity
Ouranos, 208
Out-of-body experiences, 111, 208, 212, 215, 219, 250
Overinterpretation, 348
Oxyrhynchus, 24

Paganism, 17, 50, 63, 76, 126–128, 133–134, 139, 156, 233, 235, 328–331, 356, 363
　concept of, 331
　suppression of, 331
Pain, 148–150
Paintings, 217–218
Palindromes, 290
Palingenesis. See Rebirth
Panopolis (see also Akhmīm), 25, 77–79, 81–82, 93, 338–339, 341
Papyrus Mimaut, 50–51, 282
Paranoia, 348
Passions, 10, 84, 91, 95–97, 141, 143, 147–155, 157, 179–186, 192–193, 196, 198, 200, 206, 219, 223, 225, 229, 239, 248, 250–251, 256, 263, 270, 273–274, 277, 313, 320, 326, 336, 358–359, 367
Patricide, 344, 347
Payment for ritual services, 32–33, 46
Pēgē. See Source, The
Perception, Theory of, 201–205
Perfection, 97
Perseverance, 247, 249, 261

Pessimism. See Optimism/Pessimism
Petosiris, 27
Phallus, 235
Phantasia, 364, 365
Phantasms, 2, 61, 147, 154, 180, 199, 204–207, 209, 212, 215–217, 219, 221, 225, 236, 238, 273, 313, 316, 329, 352–354, 358, 365, 367
Pharmakon, 2, 83–84, 87, 150, 311–315, 320, 327, 343–344, 348–351, 367
Phenomena, 158, 168, 206, 217, 231, 269, 359
Philhellenism, 16, 18, 133–134, 360–362
Philosophy, 15–17, 21, 188, 193
Phōtagōgia, 34
Physika of Hermes, 88–89, 94
Picatrix, 356
Pistis, 317
Place, 45, 57, 93, 96–97
Planète (journal), 356
Planets/Planetary spheres, 170, 175, 183
Platonic Orientalism, 117–118, 361
Pleasure, 148–150
Plēroma, 271, 296
Pneuma, 13, 20, 37–38, 40–41, 62, 64–65, 88, 99, 143, 164, 175, 204, 261, 268–269, 273, 285, 287, 296, 301, 305, 307, 323
Poetics, 59
Poetry, 191–193
Poimandres, 97–98, 125–126, 155–156, 158–160, 162–170, 175, 177–184, 197, 206, 257, 266, 277, 280–281, 309, 319, 326
　etymology of the name, 162
Possession, 42, 110–111, 152, 159
Poststructuralism, 341, 343
Power, Addiction to, 183–184, 193
Power (Dunamis), 285–286, 288, 295–296, 298
Praise, 54, 184, 186, 231–232, 304–305
Prayer, 229, 231–235, 263, 287–288, 295, 305, 308
Pregnancy, 56, 107, 321
Prejudice, 80, 103, 132, 134–136, 347
Presence, Metaphysics of, 315–316, 344
Priests, 28–30, 32–34, 39, 43, 45–46, 70, 73, 75, 79, 91, 93–96, 117, 122, 271, 292

Procreation, 56, 143, 176–177, 181–182, 238, 251, 323
Projection, Hermeneutic, 132–133
Prototype theory, 80
Psilocybin, 38
Psychoactive agents (see also Hallucinogens, Herbs), 38–40, 44, 47, 71–72, 98, 110
Psychology, Hermetic, 200–209
Psychometry, 254
Punishment, 141, 143, 150, 178, 181, 196, 245, 276
Pythagoreanism, xi, 102, 115, 150, 188, 221, 235, 279–280, 292, 338, 341

Quality, 349

Rapport (Mesmeric), 285, 295–297
Reading mysteries, 118, 225, 326
Rebirth, 10–11, 41, 92, 99, 143–144, 182, 228, 235–237, 239–241, 243–246, 250–253, 255–256, 258–259, 262–263, 267, 270–271, 274–275, 277, 283–287, 297, 309, 323–324
Recklessness, 245, 249
Recording. See Imprinting
Reified imaginal formations, 2, 5
Reincarnation, 143, 182, 218, 276, 329
Rejected knowledge, 5, 16, 361
Religion (concept), 363
Religion of the world, 106, 210, 270, 355–356
Religionism, 5, 86, 348
Renenutet, 264
Response (primary/secondary), 70
Revelation(s), 160, 162, 202, 235
Reverence, 10, 143, 194–197, 199–200, 219, 233, 262, 265, 271–272, 275–277, 287, 295, 304, 307, 309, 329, 360
Ritual, 227–228, 232–233, 240–242, 247–248
Rituals of apparition, 30–31, 33

Sacrifice (see also Offerings), 69, 71–72, 83, 93–94, 96–98, 233–234
Śaivism, Kashmiri, 359
Scarab, 38
Schools, Hermetic, 121–122, 326
Scribal note (Nag Hammadi), 282
Scribes, 123, 125–128, 131, 136, 138, 332
Secrecy/Secrets, 98, 115, 143, 236, 341, 349–350

Seduction, 171, 173
Self-begotten, 280–281, 296
Self-control, 246, 247, 249, 260
Self-improvement, 145–146
Self-knowledge, 92, 95, 99, 104, 177, 179, 319, 334, 336, 345
Semen, 56, 168, 239, 246, 285–286, 323–325, 343
Semiotics, 114, 342
Sense perception, 201–202, 204–205, 210–211, 243, 251, 273
Senses, 54–55, 70, 104, 107, 156–157, 178–181, 183, 201, 203–204, 208, 211, 216–217, 238, 270, 273–274
  interior, 61, 120, 152, 157, 236
Service, Ethics of, 54, 271
Set/Setting, 40
Sethianism, 93
Sexuality, 50, 56–57, 168, 171, 173–174, 176–177, 181, 184, 192–193, 235, 238, 323
Shamanism, 148
Shedet, 24
Signifiers/Signification, 116, 311, 314, 319–320, 322–324, 326–328, 341–342, 344, 349, 366
  empty signifiers, 5, 315, 322, 343, 349, 351
Silence, 36, 40, 157, 184–186, 208, 239, 246, 258–260, 263, 285, 289, 295, 301–304, 306, 310, 327
Simulacra, 313–314, 316, 320
Sin, 149, 171–173, 175–178, 186, 334
Singing, 292–298, 301–307
Skēnos, 250, 253, 257
Sleep, 38, 104, 151, 156, 175, 184–185, 208–209, 219–220, 223, 242, 300, 336, 353
Sobek, 264–265
Social-intuitionist principle, 347
Sokonōpis, 264–265
Solitude, 236, 270
Solomon, 98
Solon, 116–117
Somnambulism, 254, 285
Son of God, 92, 125–126, 239, 363
Souchos, 264, 265
Soul, 14, 60, 74, 78, 90–91, 97–99, 111, 143, 149–152, 154, 192, 204, 214, 220–225, 227, 238, 273, 276, 280–281, 326
  care of the, 96, 157
  fully descended, 105, 149

Index of Subjects

partly descended, 104
sickness of the, 152, 155
Souls, 79, 167, 281, 289, 301, 304
Sounds, 116, 185, 287, 289–290, 324
Source, The, 10–11, 54–58, 61, 65, 97, 106, 120, 122, 150, 163, 167, 177, 179, 180, 196, 213–214, 225, 232–234, 238, 259–260, 262, 268–272, 276–281, 284–285, 288–289, 295–296, 301, 303, 305–306, 315–316, 318, 320, 322–325, 327–329, 341–344, 347, 349–350, 360
Space, 57, 59, 96, 278–279
Speech, 287, 301, 312–314, 320–321, 324, 342
Spirit, 13–14, 79, 84, 98–99, 106, 261, 304, 318
  Universal Spirit, 268, 303
  See also *Pneuma*
Spirits, 83–84, 268, 289, 304
Spiritual exercises, 19, 146, 226–227, 239, 244, 337
Spirituality, Concept of, 19–22
Statues, 61–72, 75, 78–79, 94–97, 142, 233
  animation of, 61–72, 74, 95–96, 233, 323, 331
  illumination of, 66–67, 69–70, 72
Stereotype appropriation, 32, 46
Stillness, 269–270, 278
Stoa, 57, 140, 146, 148, 160, 322
Stobaean Hermetica, 128–131, 218, 332
Story-telling, 2, 5–6, 352
Stranger, 237–238, 240, 353
Strasbourg Cosmogony, 25
Suffering, 108, 186, 258
Sufism, 338–341
Suicide, 224
Sun, 40–41, 142, 233, 315
Sunthēmata, 67, 69, 109, 326–327
Superstition, 36, 45, 75, 135
Supplément, 314–316, 363

Talismans, 333
Tat, 49, 121, 197–198, 206–208, 232–233, 236–263, 284–310, 320, 323–326, 333, 342–343, 348–349
Technologies of the self, 47
Telestic art, 65–67, 70
Temple(s), 45, 65–67, 73, 75, 94–97, 120, 122, 142, 233, 270
Terrestrial gods, 62, 64, 69

Testimonia, Hermetic, 130, 328
Thamus, 311
Theban Magical Library, 30–31, 34, 36, 42–43
Thebes, 26–27, 29, 31–32
Theosophy, Hermetic, 16, 35
Theosophy, Modern, 130, 254
Therapeutae, 235
Theurgy, xi, 30, 35–40, 44, 66, 68–69, 71, 79, 100–118, 155, 224, 244, 319, 340
Thinking, 202–203
Thiouis, 264
Third Kind, 209–219, 231
Thoth, 25, 309–315, 320, 327, 342–344, 347–349, 351
Time, 57, 113, 143, 213, 278–279
Tinctures, 87–99
  natural, 88, 91, 93, 97–98
  propitious, 88, 90–91, 93–94, 96
Torment(or)s, 98, 245, 247–250, 253, 256, 277
Training, Spiritual, 227–228
Trance. See Consciousness, Alterations of
Translation, 5, 12, 14–15, 43, 53, 56, 116, 135, 234, 313, 322, 344, 364, 366
Transmission
  Oral, 114–115, 146, 287
  Spiritual, 89, 121, 133, 139, 324, 335–341–342
  Textual, 9, 51–53, 58, 123, 129, 131–133, 137–139, 332
Treachery, 245, 249
Triad, Hermetic, 92, 99, 249–250, 260, 268, 278–282, 289
Truth, 15, 190–192, 201, 203–204, 224, 247–249, 261, 305, 316, 320
  and Beauty and Goodness. See Goodness-Beauty-Truth
Truthfulness, 183–184, 196, 336
Tübingen Theosophy, 268
Turba Philosophorum, 339

Unbegotten, 280–281, 295–296
Understanding, 4–5, 7–10, 12, 15, 37, 132–133, 135–137, 343, 345, 347, 349, 364, 366
Unknown God, 210, 270, 317

Vegetarianism, 229, 235
Vehicle of the Soul. See Ochēma
Verständigung, 136, 346
Vice(s), 145, 150, 181–183, 249
Virtue(s), 145, 181–183, 193, 249, 250

Vision(s), 25, 27, 29, 31, 35–36, 38, 45–47, 111, 122, 156–160, 162–163, 166–167, 178, 184–185, 207–208, 212, 254–255, 287, 296–297, 304–305, 310, 320, 336
Visualization, 111, 254
Vowels, 289–298, 306–307, 324

Waset. See Thebes
Water-lilies, 38
Way of Hermes, 11, 15, 21, 50, 80, 100, 118, 120, 122, 148, 150, 155, 171, 210, 225–228
Weirdness, 139, 345
Western culture/civilization, 361–362
Western esotericism, 5, 356, 366
Witches' ointment, 44
Womb, 235, 239, 246, 250, 252, 259, 285–286, 323
Women, 82, 88, 92, 286, 334
Wonder, 54, 62, 194–195, 198, 200, 214, 271
World-affirmation, 209–210, 266, 270, 356
World-denial, 209, 355
Writing, 114–116, 310–320, 326–327, 341–344, 348, 351

Zodiac, 248, 250, 252
Zoroaster, 92

Milton Keynes UK
Ingram Content Group UK Ltd.
UKHW042308140924
448363UK00003B/4